MAKING THE SWITCH

FROM PAPER TO DIGITAL?

Let the American Medical Association's many resources help you move from paper-based to electronic health records.

Practical EHR: Electronic Record Solutions for Compliance and Quality Care

Filled with practical information, this new resource is designed to help physicians and medical practices get the most from their current Electronic Health Record (EHR) system. In addition to delivering compliance and quality of care solutions, this book offers valuable insight on topics such as:

- EHR review at the point of care
- Medical records and E/M compliance
- Evaluation and design of the electronic history and physical
- Practice transition and health information transformation
- Samples of practical EHR forms

Available June 2008—reserve your copy today!

"If you don't have EHR Implementation: A Step by Step Guide for the Medical Practice, *you have no business going into electronic health records. This is your guide. Follow it. I did."*
—Stephen Z. Fadem, MD

Guides physicians and administrators through the evaluation, selection, negotiation and culture management transition [that often accompanies the move] to an electronic environment.

A must-have working guidebook that addresses security preparedness, measuring your EHR "ROI," remittance implementation, work flow analyses and more!

Order today! Visit *www.amabookstore.com* or call (800) 621-8335.

AMA
AMERICAN MEDICAL ASSOCIATION

Healthcare Common Procedure Coding System

HCPCS 2009

Medicare's National Level II Codes

Color-coded

Complete drug index

AMA
AMERICAN MEDICAL ASSOCIATION

First printing November 2008

OP095109
ISBN: 978-1-60359-065-5

2009 Product Updates and Errata
Special reports, code changes, and regulatory information can be found by visiting *www.ama-assn.org/go/cpt*. Click on HCPCS 2009 Product Updates and Errata. Please bookmark this page and use it as a resource for the latest information.

To stay current on important HCPCS developments go to *www.cms.hhs.gov/MedHCPCSGenInfo/*.

Additional copies of this publication may be ordered by telephoning (800) 621-8335, or visit us at *www.amabookstore.com*.

Introduction

ORGANIZATION OF HCPCS

The American Medical Association's (AMA) 2009 *HCPCS Level II* code book contains mandated changes and new codes for use as of January 1, 2009. Deleted codes have also been indicated and cross-referenced to active codes when possible. New codes have been added to the appropriate sections, eliminating the time-consuming step of looking in two places for a code. However, keep in mind that the information in this codebook is a reproduction of the 2009 HCPCS; additional information on coverage issues may have been provided to Medicare contractors after publication. All contractors periodically update their systems and records throughout the year. If this book does not agree with your contractor, it is either because of a mid-year update or correction or a specific local or regional coverage policy.

We have included codes noted in addendum B of the 2009 Outpatient Prospective Payment System (OPPS) update as published in the *Federal Register* and from transmittals through 2008 that include codes not discussed in other Centers for Medicare and Medicaid Services (CMS) documents. The sources for these codes are often noted in blue beneath the description.

HOW TO USE THE AMA HCPCS LEVEL II CODE BOOK

Index

Because HCPCS is organized by code number rather than by service or supply name, the index enables the coder to locate any code without looking through individual ranges of codes. Just look up the medical or surgical supply, service, orthotic, prosthetic, or generic or brand name drug in question to find the appropriate codes. This index also refers to many of the brand names by which these items are known.

Table of Drugs

The brand names of drugs listed are examples only and may not include all products available for that type of drug. Our table of drugs lists HCPCS codes from any available sections including A codes, C codes, J codes, S codes, and Q codes under brand and generic drug names with amount, route of administration, and code numbers. While we try to make the table comprehensive, it is not all-inclusive.

Color-coded Coverage Instructions

The AMA *HCPCS Level II* book provides colored symbols for each coverage and reimbursement instruction. A legend to these symbols is provided on the bottom of each two-page spread.

Blue Color Bar—Special Coverage Instructions
A blue bar for "special coverage instructions" over a code means that special coverage instructions apply to that code. These special instructions are also typically given in the form of Medicare Pub.100 reference numbers. The appendixes provide the full text of the cited Medicare Pub.100 references.

A4211 **Supplies for self-administered injections**

Yellow Color Bar—Contractor Discretion
Issues that are left to "contractor discretion" are covered with a yellow bar. Contact the contractor for specific coverage information on those codes.

A4248 **Chlorhexidine containing antiseptic, 1 ml**

Red Color Bar—Not Covered by or Invalid for Medicare
Codes that are not covered by or are invalid for Medicare are covered by a red bar. The pertinent Medicare internet-only manuals (Pub. 100) reference numbers are also given explaining why a particular code is not covered. These numbers refer to the appendixes, where we have listed the Medicare references.

A4232 **Syringe with needle for external insulin pump, sterile, 3cc**

Codes in the AMA *HCPCS Level II* follow the AMA CPT® codebook conventions to indicate new, revised, and deleted codes.

- A black circle (●) precedes a new code.
- A black triangle (▲) precedes a code with revised terminology or rules.
- A circle (○) precedes a reissued code.
- Codes deleted from the 2009 active codes appear with a strike-out.

●	J0641	**Injection, levoleucovorin calcium, 0.5 mg**
▲	A6010	**Collagen based wound filler, dry form, sterile, per gram of collagen**
○	J7611	**Albuterol, inhalation solution, FDA-approved final product, noncompounded, administered through DME, concentrated form, 1 mg**
	~~C9003~~	~~**Palivizumab-RSV-IgM, per 50 mg**~~

☑ Quantity Alert
Many codes in HCPCS report quantities that may not coincide with quantities available in the marketplace. For instance, a HCPCS code for an ostomy pouch with skin barrier reports each pouch, but the product is generally sold in a package of 10; "10" must be indicated in the quantity box on the CMS claim form to ensure proper reimbursement. This symbol indicates that care should be taken to verify quantities in this code.

☑ **A4207** **Syringe with needle, sterile 2 cc, each**

♀ Female Only
This icon identifies procedures that should only be reported for female patients.

A4280 **Adhesive skin support attachment for use with external breast prosthesis, each** ♀

♂ Male Only
This icon identifies procedures that should only be reported for male patients.

A4326 **Male external catheter specialty type with integral collection chamber, any type, each** ♂

A Age Edit
This icon denotes codes intended for use with a specific age group, such as neonate, newborn, pediatric, and adult. Carefully review the code description to ensure that the code you report most appropriately reflects the patient's age.

D6985 **Pediatric partial denture, fixed primary** A

M Maternity
This icon identifies procedures that by definition should only be used for maternity patients generally between 12 and 55 years of age.

H1001 **Prenatal care, at-risk enhanced service; antepartum management** M

A2-Z3 ASC Payment Indicators
Codes designated as being paid by ASC groupings that were effective at the time of printing are denoted by the group number.

G0105 **Colorectal cancer screening; colonoscopy on individual at high risk** A2

♿ DMEPOS
Use this icon to identify when to consult the CMS durable medical equipment, prosthetics, orthotics, and supplies (DMEPOS) for payment of this durable medical item.

A4600 **Sleeve for intermittent limb compression device, replacement only, each** ♿

⊘ Skilled Nursing Facility (SNF)
Use this icon to identify certain items and services excluded from SNF consolidated billing. These items may be billed directly to the Medicare contractor by the provider or supplier of the service or item.

A4653 **Peritoneal dialysis catheter anchoring device, belt, each** ⊘

Drugs commonly reported with a code are listed underneath by brand or generic name.

J7310 **Ganciclovir, 4.5 mg, long-acting implant**
Use this code for Vitasert.

CMS does not use consistent terminology when a code for a specific procedure is not listed. The code description may include any of the following terms: unlisted, not otherwise classified (NOC), unspecified, unclassified, other, and miscellaneous. If you are sure there is no code for the service or supply provided or used, be sure to provide adequate documentation to the payer. Check with the payer for more information.

A0999 **Unlisted ambulance service**

OPPS Status Indicators

[A]-[Y] OPPS status indicators

Status indicators identify how individual HCPCS Level II codes are paid or not paid under the OPPS. The same status indicator is assigned to all the codes within an ambulatory payment classification (APC). Consult the payer or resource to learn which CPT codes fall within various APCs. Status indicators for HCPCS and their definitions follow:

[A] Services furnished to a hospital outpatient that are paid under a fee schedule or payment system other than OPPS, for example:

- Ambulance Services
- Clinical Diagnostic Laboratory Services
- Non-Implantable Prosthetic and Orthotic Devices
- EPO for ESRD Patients
- Physical, Occupational, and Speech Therapy
- Routine Dialysis Services for ESRD Patients Provided in a Certified Dialysis Unit of a Hospital
- Diagnostic Mammography
- Screening Mammography

[B] Codes that are not recognized by OPPS when submitted on an outpatient hospital Part B bill type (12x and 13x)

[C] Inpatient Procedures

[E] Items, Codes, and Services:

- That are not covered by any Medicare outpatient benefit based on statutory exclusion.
- That are not covered by any Medicare outpatient benefit for reasons other than statutory exclusion
- That are not recognized by Medicare for outpatient claims but for which an alternate code for the same item or service may be available
- For which separate payment is not provided on outpatient claims

[F] Corneal Tissue Acquisition; Certain CRNA Services and Hepatitis B Vaccines

[G] Pass-Through Drugs and Biologicals

[H] Pass-Through Device Categories and Therapeutic Radiopharmaceuticals

[K] Nonpass-Through Drugs and Biologicals

[L] Influenza Vaccine; Pneumococcal Pneumonia Vaccine

[M] Items and Services Not Billable to the Fiscal Intermediary/MAC

[N] Items and Services Packaged into APC Rates

[P] Partial Hospitalization

[Q1] STVX-Packaged Codes

[Q2] T-Packaged Codes

[Q3] Codes That May Be Paid Through a Composite APC

[R] Blood and Blood Products

[S] Significant Procedure, Not Discounted when Multiple

[T] Significant Procedure, Multiple Reduction Applies

[U] Brachytherapy Sources

[V] Clinic or Emergency Department Visit

[X] Ancillary Services

[Y] Non-Implantable Durable Medical Equipment

[A]	**A4321**	**Therapeutic agent for urinary catheter irrigation**
[B]	**Q4005**	**Cast supplies, long arm cast, adult (11 years +), plaster**
[C]	**G0341**	**Percutaneous islet cell transplant, includes portal vein catheterization and infusion**
[E]	**A0021**	**Ambulance service, outside state per mile, transport (Medicaid only)**
[F]	**V2785**	**Processing, preserving and transporting corneal tissue**
[G]	**J1300**	**Injection, eculizumab, 10 mg**
[H]	**C1821**	**Interspinous process distraction device (implantable)**
[K]	**J7501**	**Azathioprine, parenteral, 100 mg**
[M]	**G0333**	**Dispense fee initial 30 day**
[N]	**A4220**	**Refill kit for implantable infusion pump**
[P]	**G0129**	**Occupational therapy requiring the skills of a qualified occupational therapist, furnished as a component of a partial hospitalization treatment program, per day**
[Q3]	**G0379**	**Direct admission of patient for hospital observation care**
[S]	**G0251**	**Linear accelerator based stereotactic radiosurgery, delivery including collimator changes and custom plugging, fractionated treatment, all lesions, per session, maximum five sessions per course of treatment**
[T]	**C9724**	**Endoscopic full-thickness plication in the gastric cardia using endoscopic plication system (EPS); includes endoscopy**
[V]	**G0101**	**Cervical or vaginal cancer screening; pelvic and clinical breast examination**
[X]	**Q0035**	**Cardiokymography**
[Y]	**A4222**	**Infusion supplies for external drug infusion pump, per cassette or bag (list drugs separately)**

ASC Payment Indicators

A2-Z3 **ASC Payment Indicators**

This icon identifies the new ASC status payment indicators, effective January 1, 2009. They indicate how the ASC payment rate was derived and/or how the procedure, item, or service is treated under the revised ASC payment system. For more information about these new indicators and how they affect billing, consult Ingenix's *Outpatient Billing Editor.*

- A2 Surgical procedure on ASC list in CY 2007; payment based on OPPS relative payment weight
- F4 Corneal tissue acquisition, hepatitis B vaccine; paid at reasonable cost
- G2 Nonoffice-based surgical procedure added in CY 2008 or later; payment based on OPPS relative payment weight
- H2 Brachytherapy source paid separately when provided integral to a surgical procedure on ASC list; payment contractor-priced
- H8 Device-intensive procedure on ASC list in CY 2007; paid at adjusted rate
- J7 OPPS pass-through device paid separately when provided integral to a surgical procedure on ASC list; payment contractor-priced
- J8 Device-intensive procedure added to ASC list in CY 2008 or later; paid at adjusted rate
- K2 Drugs and biologicals paid separately when provided integral to a surgical procedure on ASC list; payment based on OPPS rate
- K7 Unclassified drugs and biologicals; payment contractor-priced
- L1 Influenza vaccine; pneumococcal vaccine; packaged item/service; no separate payment made
- L6 New Technology Intraocular Lens (NTIOL); special payment
- N1 Packaged service/item; no separate payment made
- P2 Office-based surgical procedure added to ASC list in CY 2008 or later with MPFS nonfacility PE RVUs; payment based on OPPS relative payment weight
- P3 Office-based surgical procedure added to ASC list in CY 2008 or later with MPFS nonfacility PE RVUs; payment based on MPFS nonfacility PE RVUs
- R2 Office-based surgical procedure added to ASC list in CY 2008 or later without MPFS nonfacility PE RVUs; payment based on OPPS relative payment weight
- Z2 Radiology service paid separately when provided integral to a surgical procedure on ASC list; payment based on OPPS relative payment weight
- Z3 Radiology service paid separately when provided integral to a surgical procedure on ASC list; payment based on MPFS nonfacility PE RVUs

A2	G0105	**Coloerectal cancer screening; colonoscopy on individual at high risk**	A2 ⃠
F4	V2785	**Processing, preserving and transporting corneal tissue**	F4
G2	C9716	**Creations of thermal anal lesions by radiofrequency energy**	G2
H2	A9527	**Iodine I-125, sodium iodide solution, therapeutic per millicurie**	H2
N1	L8690	**Auditory osseointegrated device, includes all internal and external components**	N1
K2	J0128	**Injection, abarelix, 10 mg**	K2
K7	C9399	**Unclassified drugs or biologicals**	K7

MED: This notation precedes an instruction pertaining to this code in the CMS Publication 100 (Pub 100) electronic manual or in a National Coverage Determination (NCD). These CMS sources, formerly called the Medicare Carriers Manual (MCM) and Coverage Issues Manual (CIM), present the rules for submitting these services to the federal government or its contractors and are included in the appendix of this book.

A4300 **Implantable access catheter, (e.g., venous, arterial, epidural subarachnoid, or peritoneal, etc.) external access**

MED: 100-2, 15, 120

AHA: American Hospital Association Coding Clinic for HCPCS citations help you find expanded information about specific codes and their usage.

A4290 **Sacral nerve stimulation test lead, each**

AHA: 1Q, '02, 9

Special reports, code changes, and regulatory information can be found at www.ama-assn.org/go/cpt. Click on HCPCS 2009 Product Updates and Errata.

ABOUT HCPCS CODES

AMA does not develop or maintain HCPCS Level II codes. The federal government does.

Any supplier or manufacturer can submit a request for coding modification to the HCPCS Level II national codes. A document explaining the HCPCS modification process, as well as a detailed format for submitting a recommendation for a modification to HCPCS Level II codes, is available on the HCPCS web site at http://www.cms.hhs.gov/MedHCPCSGenInfo/Downloads/2008_ALPHA.pdf. Besides the information requested in this format, a requestor should also submit any additional descriptive material, including the manufacturer's product literature and information that is believed would be helpful in furthering CMS's understanding of the medical features of the item for which a coding modification is being recommended. The HCPCS coding review process is an ongoing, continuous process.

Requests for coding modifications should be sent to the following address:

Felicia Eggleston, CMS HCPCS Workgroup Coordinator
Center for Medicare Management
Centers for Medicare and Medicaid Services
C5-08-27
7500 Security Boulevard
Baltimore, MD 21244-1850

HOW TO USE HCPCS LEVEL II

Coders should keep in mind, however, that the insurance companies and government do not base payment solely on what was done for the patient. They need to know why the services were performed. In addition to using the HCPCS coding system for procedures and supplies, coders must also use the ICD-9-CM coding system to denote the diagnosis. This code book will not discuss ICD-9-CM codes, which can be found in a current ICD-9-CM code book for diagnosis codes. To locate a HCPCS Level II code, follow these steps:

1. Identify the services or procedures that the patient received.

   Example:

   Patient administered PSA exam.

2. Look up the appropriate term in the index.

   Example:

   Screening

   prostate

   Coding Tip: Coders who are unable to find the procedure or service in the index can look in the table of contents for the type of procedure or device to narrow the code choices. Also, coders should remember to check the unlisted procedure guidelines for additional choices.

3. Assign a tentative code.

   Example:

   Code G0103

   Coding Tip: To the right of the terminology, there may be a single code or multiple codes, a cross-reference, or an indication that the code has been deleted. Tentatively assign all codes listed.

4. Locate the code or codes in the appropriate section. When multiple codes are listed in the index, be sure to read the narrative of all codes listed to find the appropriate code based on the service performed.

   Example:

   G0103 Prostate cancer screening; prostate specific antigen test (PSA)

5. Check for color bars, symbols, notes, and references.

   Example:

   A **G0103 Prostate cancer screening; prostate specific antigen test (PSA)** ♂

   MED: 100-3, 210.1; 100-4, 18, 50

6. Review the appendixes for the reference definitions and other guidelines for coverage issues that apply.

7. Determine whether any modifiers should be used.

8. Assign the code.

   Example:

   The code assigned is G0103.

CODING STANDARDS

Levels of Use

Coders may find that the same procedure is coded at two or even three levels. Which code is correct? There are certain rules to follow if this should occur.

When both a CPT and a HCPCS Level II code have virtually identical narratives for a procedure or service, the CPT code should be used. If, however, the narratives are not identical (eg, the CPT code narrative is generic, whereas the HCPCS Level II code is specific), the Level II code should be used.

Be sure to check for a national code when a CPT code description contains an instruction to include additional information, such as describing a specific medication. For example, when billing Medicare or Medicaid for supplies, avoid using CPT code *99070, Supplies and materials (except spectacles), provided by the physician over and above those usually included with the office visit or other services rendered (list drugs, trays, supplies, or materials provided).* There are many HCPCS Level II codes that specify supplies in more detail.

Special Reports

Submit a special report with the claim when a new, unusual, or variable procedure is provided or a modifier is used. Include the following information:

- A copy of the appropriate report (eg, operative, X ray), explaining the nature, extent, and need for the procedure
- Documentation of the medical necessity of the procedure
- Documentation of the time and effort necessary to perform the procedure

10% LMD, J7100
5% dextrose/normal saline, J7042
5% dextrose/water, J7060

A

Abarelix, J0128
Abatacept, J0129
Abbokinase, J3364, J3365
Abciximab, J0130
Abdomen/abdominal
dressing holder/binder, A4461, A4463
pad, low profile, L1270
Abduction
control, each, L2624
pillow, E1399
rotation bar, foot, L3140-L3170
Abortion, S2260-S2267
Abscess, incision and drainage, D7510-D7520
Absorption dressing, A6251-A6256
Abutments
for implants, D6056-D6057
retainers for resin bonded "Maryland bridge", D6545
Accession of brush biopsy sample, D0486
Accession of tissue, dental, D0472-D0474
Accessories
ambulation devices, E0153-E0159
artifcial kidney and machine (*see also* ESRD), E1510-E1699
beds, E0271-E0280, E0305-E0326
oxygen, E1354-E1358
wheelchairs, E0950-E1010, E1050-E1298, E2201-E2231, E2295, E2300-E2367, K0001-K0108
Access system, A4301
AccuChek
blood glucose meter, E0607
test strips, box of 50, A4253
Accurate
prosthetic sock, L8420-L8435
stump sock, L8470-L8485
Acetate concentrate for hemodialysis, A4708
Acetazolamide sodium, J1120
Acetylcysteine
inhalation solution, J7608
injection, J0132
Achromycin, J0120
Acid concentrate for hemodialysis, A4709
ACTH, J0800
Acthar, J0800
Actimmune, J9216
Action neoprene supports, L1825
Action Patriot manual wheelchair, K0004
Action Xtra, Action MVP, Action Pro-T, manual wheelchair, K0005
Active Life
convex one-piece urostomy pouch, A4421
flush away, A5051
one-piece
drainable custom pouch, A5061
pre-cut closed-end pouch, A5051
stoma cap, A5055
Activity therapy, G0176
Acyclovir, J0133
Adalimumab, J0135
Adaptor
neurostimulator, C1883
pacing lead, C1883
Addition
cushion AK, L5648
cushion BK, L5646
harness upper extremity, L6675-L6676
to lower extremity orthotic, K0672
to lower extremity prosthesis, L5970-L5990
wrist, flexion, extension, L6620
Adenocard, J0150
Adenosine, J0150-J0152
Adhesive
barrier, C1765
catheter, A4364
disc or foam pad, A5126
medical, A4364
Nu-Hope
1 oz bottle with applicator, A4364
3 oz bottle with applicator, A4364
ostomy, A4364
pads, A6203-A6205, A6212-A6214, A6219-A6221, A6237-A6239, A6245-A6247, A6254-A6256
remover, A4365, A4455
support, breast prosthesis, A4280
tape, A4450, A4452
tissue, G0168
Adjunctive services, dental, D9220-D9310
Adjustabrace 3, L2999
Adjustment, bariatric band, S2083
Administration
hepatitis B vaccine, G0010
influenza virus vaccine, G0008
medication, T1502-T1503
direct observation, H0033
pneumococcal vaccine, G0009
Adoptive immunotherapy, S2107
Adrenalin, J0170
Adrenal transplant, S2103
Adriamycin, J9000
Adrucil, J9190
AdvantaJet, A4210
AFO, E1815, E1830, L1900-L1990, L4392, L4396
Agalsidase beta, J0180
Aimsco Ultra Thin syringe, 1 cc or 1/2 cc, each, A4206
Air ambulance — *see also* Ambulance
Air bubble detector, dialysis, E1530
Aircast, L4350-L4380
Aircast air stirrup ankle brace, L1906
Air fluidized bed, E0194
Airlife Brand Misty-Neb nebulizer, E0580
Air pressure pad/mattress, E0186, E0197
AirSep, E0601
Air travel and nonemergency transportation, A0140
Airway device, E0485-E0486
Akineton, J0190
Alarm
enuresis, S8270
pressure, dialysis, E1540
Alatrofloxacin mesylate, J0200
Albumarc, P9041
Albumin, human, P9041, P9045-P9047
Albuterol, J7611, J7613
Alcohol
abuse service, G0396, G0397, H0047
pint, A4244
testing, H0048
wipes, A4245
Aldesleukin, J9015
Aldomet, J0210
Aldurazyme, J1931
Alefacept, J0215
Alemtuzumab, J9010
injection, S0088
Alferon N, J9215
Algiderm, alginate dressing, A6196-A6199
Alginate dressing, A6196-A6199
Alglucerase, J0205
Algosteril, alginate dressing, A6196-A6199
Alimta, J9305
Alkaban-AQ, J9360
Alkaline battery for blood glucose monitor, A4233-A4236
Alkeran, J8600
Allogenic cord blood harvest, S2140
Allograft
Cymetra, Q4112
GRAFTJACKET, Q4113
Allograft — *continued*
small intestine and liver, S2053
soft dental tissue, D4275
Alpha 1-proteinase inhibitor, human, J0256
Alteplase recombinant, J2997
Alternating pressure mattress/pad, E0181, E0277
pump, E0182
Alternative communication device, i.e., communication board, E1902
Alveoloplasty
with extraction(s), D7310-D7311
without extractions, D7320-D7321
Alveolus, fracture, D7770
Amalgam, restoration, dental, D2140-D2161
Amantadine hydrochloride, G9017, G9033
Ambulance, A0021-A0999
air, A0436
disposable supplies, A0382-A0398
oxygen, A0422
response, treatment, no transport, A0998
Ambulation device, E0100-E0159
Ambulation stimulator
spinal cord injured, E0762
Amcort, J3302
A-methaPred, J2920, J2930
Amevive, J0215
Amifostine, J0207
Amikacin sulfate, J0278
Aminaid, enteral nutrition, B4154
Aminolevulinic acid, topical, J7308
Aminophylline, J0280
Amiodarone hydrochloride, J0282
Amirosyn-RF, parenteral nutrition, B5000
Amitriptyline HCl, J1320
Ammonia N-13
diagnostic imaging agent, A9526
Ammonia test paper, A4774
Amobarbital, J0300
Amphocin, J0285
Amphotericin B, J0285
cholesterol sulfate, J0288
lipid complex, J0287
liposome, J0289
Ampicillin sodium, J0290
sodium/sulbactam sodium, J0295
Amputee
adapter, wheelchair, E0959
prosthesis, L5000-L7510, L7520, L7900, L8400-L8465
stump sock, L8470
wheelchair, E1170-E1190, E1200
Amygdalin, J3570
Amytal, J0300
Anabolin LA 100, J2320-J2322
Analgesia, dental, D9230, D9241, D9242
nonintravenous conscious sedation, D9248
Analysis
saliva sample, D0418
Anastrozole, S0170
Ancef, J0690
Anchor, screw, C1713
Andrest 90-4, J0900
Andro-Cyp, J1070-J1080
Andro-Estro 90-4, J0900
Androgyn L.A., J0900
Andro L.A. 200, J3130
Androlone
-D 100, J2321
Andronaq
-LA, J1070
Andronate
-100, J1070
-200, J1080
Andropository 100, J3120
Andryl 200, J3130
Anectine, J0330
Anergan (25, 50), J2550
Anesthesia
dental, D9210-D9221
dialysis, A4736-A4737
Angiography
iliac artery, G0278
magnetic resonance, C8901-C8914, C8918-C8920
reconstruction, G0288
renal artery, G0275
Angioplasty
percutaneous, G0392-G0393
Anidulafungin, J0348
Anistreplase, J0350
Ankle-foot orthotic AFO, L1900-L1990, L2106-L2116
Dorsiwedge Night Splint, L4398 or A4570 or, L2999
Specialist
Ankle Foot Orthotic, L1930
Tibial Pre-formed Fracture Brace, L2116
Surround Ankle Stirrup Braces with Floam, L1906
Antagon, S0132
Anterior-posterior orthotic
lateral orthotic, L0700, L0710
Antibiotic home infusion therapy, S9494-S9504
Antibody testing, HIV-1, S3645
Anticeptic
chlorhexidine, A4248
Anticoagulation clinic, S9401
Antiemetic drug, prescription
oral, Q0163-Q0181
Antifungal home infusion therapy, S9494-S9504
Anti-hemophilic factor (Factor VIII), J7190-J7192
Anti-hemophilic factor (Factor VIIa) recombinant, J7189
Anti-inhibitors, J7198
Anti-neoplastic drug, NOC, J9999
Antispas, J0500
Antithrombin III, J7197
Antiviral home infusion therapy, S9494-S9504
Anzemet, J1260
Apexifcation, dental, D3351-D3353
Apicoectomy, dental, D3410-D3426
A.P.L., J0725
Apligraf, Q4101
Apnea monitor, E0618-E0619
with recording feature, E0619
electrodes, A4556
lead wires, A4557
Apomorphine hydrochloride, J0364
Appliance
cleaner, A5131
orthodontic
fixed, D8220
removable, D8210
removal, D7997
pneumatic, E0655-E0673
Application
fluoride, D1203-D1206
Aprepitant, J8501
Apresoline, J0360
Aprotinin, J0365
AquaMEPHYTON, J3430
AquaPedic sectional gel flotation, E0196
Aqueous
shunt, L8612
Ara-C, J9100
Aralen, J0390
Aramine, J0380
Aranesp
ESRD, J0882
non-ESRD, J0881
Arbutamine HCl, J0395
Arch support, L3040-L3100
Aredia, J2430
Argatroban, C9121
Argyle Sentinel Seal chest drainage unit, E0460

Aristocort
forte, J3302
intralesional, J3302
Aristospan
Intra-articular, J3303
Intralesional, J3303
Arm
sling
deluxe, A4565
mesh cradle, A4565
universal
arm, A4565
elevator, A4565
wheelchair, E0973
Arrestin, J3250
Arrow, power wheelchair, K0014
Arsenic trioxide, J9017
Arthrocentesis, dental, D7870
Arthroereisis
subtalar, S2117
Arthroplasty, dental, D7865
Arthroscopy
dental, D7872-D7877
knee
harvest of cartilage, S2112
removal loose body, FB, G0289
shoulder
with capsulorrhaphy, S2300
Arthrotomy, dental, D7860
Artifcial
kidney machines and accessories (*see also* Dialysis), E1510-E1699
larynx, L8500
saliva, A9155
Asparaginase, J9020
Aspart insulin, S5551
Aspiration, bone marrow, G0364
Assertive community treatment, H0039-H0040
Assessment
alcohol and/or substance, G0396-G0397
audiologic, V5008-V5020
family, H1011
geriatric, S0250
mental health, H0031
speech, V5362-V5364
Assisted living, T2030-T2031
Assistive listening device, V5268-V5274
alerting device, V5269
cochlear implant assistive device, V5273
TDD, V5272
telephone amplifier, V5268
television caption decoder, V5271
Asthma
education, S9441
Astramorph, J2275
Atgam, J7504
Ativan, J2060
Atropine
inhalation solution
concentrated, J7635
unit dose, J7636
sulfate, J0460
Attends, adult diapers, A4335
Audiologic assessment, V5008-V5020
Audiometry, S0618
Auditory osseointegrated device, L8690
replacement external processor, L8691
Augmentation
sinus, D7951
Auricular prosthesis, D5914, D5927
Aurothioglucose, J2910
Autoclix lancet device, A4258
Auto-Glide folding walker, E0143
Autolance lancet device, A4258
Autolet lancet device, A4258
Autolet Lite lancet device, A4258
Autolet Mark II lancet device, A4258
Autoplex T, J7198
Avastin, J9035
Avonex, J1825
Azacitidine, J9025
Azathioprine, J7500
parenteral, J7501
Azithromycin
injection, J0456
oral, Q0144
Aztreonam, S0073

B

Babysitter, child of parents in treatment, T1009
Back supports, L0430-L0710
Baclofen, J0475, J0476
intrathecal, J0475-J0476
Bacterial sensitivity study, P7001
Bactocill, J2700
Bag
drainage, A4357
irrigation supply, A4398
spacer, for metered dose inhaler, A4627
urinary, A4358, A5112
BAL in oil, J0470
Balken, fracture frame, E0946
Bandage
adhesive, A6413
compression
high, A6452
light, A6448-A6450
medium, A6451
conforming, A6442-A6447
Orthoflex elastic plastic bandages, A4580
padding, A6441
self-adherent, A6413, A6453-A6455
Specialist Plaster bandages, A4580
Banflex, J2360
Bariatric
bed, E0302-E0304
brief/diaper, T4543
surgery, S2083
Barium enema, G0106
cancer screening, G0120
Barrier
with flange, A4373
4 x 4, A4372
adhesion, C1765
Baseball finger splint, A4570
Basiliximab, J0480
Bath chair, E0240
Bathtub
chair, E0240
heat unit, E0249
stool or bench, E0245
transfer bench, E0247, E0248
transfer rail, E0246
wall rail, E0241, E0242
Battery, L7360, L7364
blood glucose monitor, A4233-A4236
charger, L7362, L7366, L8695, L8699, Q0495
cochlear implant device
alkaline, L8622
lithium, L8623-L8624
zinc, L8621
hearing device, V5266
lithium, A4601, L7367
charger, L7368
replacement
ear pulse generator, A4638
external defibrillator, K0607
external infusion pump, K0601-K0605
six volt battery, L7360
TENS, A4630
twelve volt bettery, L7364
ventilator, A4611-A4613
ventricular assist device, Q0496, Q0503
wheelchair, E2397, K0733
Bayer chemical reagent strips, box of 100 glucose/ketone urine test strips, A4250
BCG live, intravesical, J9031
BCW 600, manual wheelchair, K0007
BCW Power, power wheelchair, K0014
BCW recliner, manual wheelchair, K0007
B-D alcohol swabs, box, A4245
B-D disposable insulin syringes, up to 1 cc, per syringe, A4206
B-D lancets, per box of 100, A4258
Bebax, foot orthotic, L3160
Becaplermin gel, S0157
Bed
accessory, E0315
air fluidized, E0194
cradle, any type, E0280
drainage bag, bottle, A4357, A5102
extra size for bariatric patients, E0302-E0304
hospital, E0250-E0270
full electric, home care, without mattress, E0297
manual, without mattress, E0293
pediatric, E0328-E0329
safety enclosure frame/canopy, E0316
semi-electric, without mattress, E0295
pan, E0275, E0276
Moore, E0275
rail, E0305, E0310
safety enclosure frame/canopy, hospital bed, E0316
Behavioral health, H0002-H0030
day treatment, H2013
per hour, H2012
Behavior management, dental care, D9920
Bell-Horn
prosthetic shrinker, L8440-L8465
Belt
adapter, A4421
extremity, E0945
Little Ones Sur-Fit pediatric, A4367
ostomy, A4367
pelvic, E0944
ventricular assist device, Q0499
wheelchair, E0978, K0098
Bena-D (10, 50), J1200
Benadryl, J1200
Benahist (10, 50), J1200
Ben-Allergin-50, J1200
Bench, bathtub (*see also* Bathtub), E0245
Benesch boot, L3212-L3214
Benoject (-10, -50), J1200
Bentyl, J0500
Benztropine, J0515
Berkeley shell, foot orthotic, L3000
Berubigen, J3420
Betadine, A4246
swabs/wipes, A4247
Betalin 12, J3420
Betameth, J0704
Betamethasone, J7622-J7624
acetate and betamethasone sodium phosphate, J0702
sodium phosphate, J0704
Betaseron, J1830
Bethanechol chloride, J0520
Bevacizumab, J9035
Bicarbonate concentration for hemodialysis, A4706-A4707
Bicillin, Bicillin C-R, Bicillin C-R 900/300, and Bicillin L-A, J0530-J0580
BiCNU, J9050
Bifocal, glass or plastic, V2200-V2299
Bilirubin (phototherapy) light, E0202
Binder
extremity, nonelastic, A4465
Biofeedback device, E0746
Bio Flote alternating air pressure pump, pad system, E0181, E0182
Biologic materials, dental, D4265
Biologics, unclassified, J3590
Biopsy
bone marrow with aspiration, G0364
Biopsy — *continued*
hard tissue, dental, D7285
soft tissue, dental, D7286
transepithelial brush, D7288
concentrated, J7628
unit dose, J7629
Biperiden lactate, J0190
Birth control pills, S4993
Birthing classes, S9436-S9439, S9442
Bite disposable jaw locks, E0700
Bitewing radiographs, D0270-D0277
Bitewings, D0272-D0274, D0277
Bivalirudin, J0583
Bleaching, dental
external, per arch, D9972
external, per tooth, D9973
internal, per tooth, D9974
Blenoxane, J9040
Bleomycin sulfate, J9040
Blood
Congo red, P2029
glucose monitor, A4258, E0607
with integrated lancing system, E2101
with voice synthesizer, E2100
disposable, A9275
glucose test strips, A4253
ketone test strips, A4252
leak detector, dialysis, E1560
leukocyte poor, P9016
mucoprotein, P2038
pressure equipment, A4660, A4663, A4670
pump, dialysis, E1620
split unit, P9011
strips
blood glucose test or reagent strips, A4253
blood ketone test or reagent strip, A4252
supply, P9010-P9022
testing supplies, A4770
transfusion, home, S9538
tubing, A4750, A4755
leukocytes reduced, P9051-P9056
CMV-negative, P9051, P9053, P9055
Bock Dynamic, foot prosthesis, L5972
Bock, Otto — *see* Otto Bock
Body jacket
scoliosis, L1300, L1310
Body sock, L0984
Body wrap
foam positioners, E0191
therapeutic overlay, E0199
Bond or cement, ostomy, skin, A4364
Bone replacement graft, dental, D7953
Bone tissue excision, dental, D7471-D7490
Boot
pelvic, E0944
surgical, ambulatory, L3260
walking
nonpneumatic, L4386
pneumatic, L4360
Bortezomib, J9041
Boston type spinal orthotic, L1200
Botulinum toxin
type A, J0585
type B, J0587
Brachytherapy
cesium 131, C2642-C2643
gold 198, C1716
iodine 125, A9527
iridium 192
high dose, C1717
nonhigh dose, C1719
needle, C1715
nonhigh dose rate iridium 192, C1719
nonstranded
NOS, C2699
cesium-131, C2643
gold-198, C1716
iodine-125, C2634, C2639
iridium-192, C1717, C1719

Brachytherapy — *continued*
nonstranded — *continued*
palladium-103, C2635-C2636, C2641
ytterbium-169, C2637
yttrium-90, C2616
placement of endorectal intracavitary applicator, C9725
radioelements, Q3001
stranded
NOS, C2698
cesium-131, C2642
iodine-125, C2638
palladium-103, C2640
Brake attachment, wheeled walker, E0159
Breast
exam (with pelvic exam), G0101
exam (without pelvic exam), S0613
mammography, G0202-G0206
milk processing, T2101
placement/removal applicator, C9726
prosthesis, L8000-L8035, L8600
adhesive skin support, A4280
pump, E0602-E0604
supplies, A4281-A4286
reconstruction, S2066-S2067
Breathing circuit, A4618
Brethine, J3105
Bricanyl subcutaneous, J3105
Bridge
recement, D6930
repair, by report, D6980
Brief
adult, T4521-T4524
bariatric, T4543
pediatric, T4529-T4530
Brompheniramine maleate, J0945
Broncho-Cath endobronchial tubes, with CPAP system, E0601
Bruxism appliance, D9940
Buck's, traction
frame, E0870
stand, E0880
Budesonide, J7626-J7627, J7633-J7634
Bulb for therapeutic light box, A4634
Bumetanide, S0171
Bupivicaine, S0020
Buprenorphine hydrochloride, J0592
Bupropion HCl, S0106
Burn
garment, A6501, A6512-A6513
matrix, Q4103
Bus, nonemergency, A0110
Busulfan, injection, J0594
Butorphanol tartrate, J0595
nasal spray, S0012

C

Cabergoline, J8515
Caffeine citrate, J0706
Calcimar, J0630
Calcitonin-salmon, J0630
Calcitrol, J0636, S0161
Calcium
disodium edetate, J0600
disodium versenate, J0600
EDTA, J0600
gluconate, J0610
glycerophosphate and calcium lactate, J0620
lactate and calcium glycerophosphate, J0620
leucovorin, J0640
Calibrator solution, A4256
Calphosan, J0620
Camisole, post mastectomy, S8460
Camping therapy, T2036-T2037
Camptosar, J9206
Canavan disease, genetic test, S3851
Cancer screening
barium enema, G0122
breast exam, G0101
cervical exam, G0101
Cancer screening — *continued*
colorectal, G0104-G0106, G0120-G0122, G0328
prostate, G0102-G0103
Cane, E0100, E0105
accessory, A4636, A4637
Easy-Care quad, E0105
quad canes, E0105
Quadri-Poise, E0105
wooden, E0100
Canister
disposable, used with suction pump, A7000
non-disposable, used with suction pump, A7001
Cannula
fistula, set (for dialysis), A4730
nasal, A4615
tracheostomy, A4623
Capecitabine, oral, J8520, J8521
Carbocaine with Neo-Cobefrin, J0670
Carbon filter, A4680
Carboplatin, J9045
Cardiac event, recorder implantable, C1764, E0616
Cardiokymography, Q0035
Cardiovascular services, M0300-M0301
Cardioverter-defibrillator, C1721, C1722, C1882
Carelet safety lancet, A4258
Carex
adjustable bath/shower stool, E0245
aluminum crutches, E0114
cane, E0100
folding walker, E0135
shower bench, E0245
Carmus bischl nitro, J9050
Carmustine, J9050
Carnitor, J1955
Casec, enteral nutrition, B4155
Case management, G9012, T1016-T1017
per month, T2022
Caspofungin acetate, J0637
Cast
dental diagnostic study models, D0470
diagnostic, dental, D0470
gauntlet, Q4013-Q4016
hand restoration, L6900-L6915
hip spica, Q4025-Q4028
long arm, Q4005-Q4008
materials, special, A4590
plaster, A4580
post and core, dental, D2952
each additional, D2953
short arm, Q4009-Q4012
shoulder, Q4003-Q4004
supplies, A4580, A4590, Q4050
Delta-Cast Elite Casting Material, A4590
Delta-Lite Conformable Casting Tape, A4590
Delta-Lite C-Splint Fibreglass Immobilizer, A4590
Delta-Lite "S" Fibreglass Casting Tape, A4590
Flashcast Elite Casting Material, A4590
Orthoflex Elastic Plaster Bandages, A4580
Orthoplast Splints (and Orthoplast II Splints), A4590
Specialist Plaster Bandages, A4580
Specialist Plaster Roll Immobilizer, A4580
Specialist Plaster Splints, A4580
thermoplastic, L2106, L2126
Caster, wheelchair, E2214, E2219, E2395-E2396
Catheter, A4300-A4365
anchoring device, A4333, A4334
percutaneous, A5200
balloon, C1727
brachytherapy, C1728
Catheter — *continued*
cap, disposable (dialysis), A4860
diagnostic, C1730, C1731
ablation, C1732, C1733
drainage, C1729
electrophysiology, C2630
external collection device, A4326-A4330
guiding, C1887
hemodialysis, C1750, C1752
implantable access, A4301
implantable intraspinal, E0785
indwelling, A4338-A4346
infusion, C1752
insertion
midline venous, home health, S5523
tray, A4354
intermittent, with insertion supplies, A4353
intracardiac echocardiography, C1759
intradiscal, C1754
intraspinal, C1755
intravascular ultrasound, C1753
irrigation supplies, A4355
lubricant, A4332
male, A4326, A4349
nonvascular balloon dilatation, C1726
occlusion, C2628
oropharyngeal suction, A4628
pacing, transesophageal, C1756
pleural, A7042
suprapubic, cystoscopic, C2627
thrombectomy, emobolectomy, C1757
tracheal suction, A4605, A4624
transluminal
angioplasty
laser, C1885
nonlaser, C1725
atherectomy
directional, C1714
rotational, C1724
ureteral, C1758
CBC, G0306-G0307
Cefadyl, J0710
Cefazolin sodium, J0690
Cefepime HCl, J0692
Cefizox, J0715
Cefotaxime sodium, J0698
Cefotetan disodium, S0074
Cefoxitin, J0694
Ceftazidime, J0713
Ceftizoxime sodium, J0715
Ceftoperazone, S0021
Ceftriaxone sodium, J0696
Cefuroxime sodium, J0697
Celestone phosphate, J0704
Cellular therapy, M0075
Cel-U-Jec, J0704
Cement, ostomy, A4364
Cenacort
A-40, J3301
Forte, J3302
Centrifuge, for dialysis, E1500
Cephalin flocculation, blood, P2028
Cephalothin sodium, J1890
Cephapirin sodium, J0710
Ceredase, J0205
Cerezyme, J1785
Certified nurse assistant, S9122
Cerubidine, J9150
Cerumen removal, G0268
Cervical
collar, L0120, L0130, L0140, L0150
halo, L0810-L0830
head harness/halter, E0942
helmet, A8000-A8004
orthotic, L0180-L0200
traction equipment, not requiring frame, E0855
Cervical cap contraceptive, A4261
Cervical-thoracic-lumbar-sacral orthotic (CTLSO), L0700, L0710, L1000, L1001
Cesium-131, C2642-C2643
Cetuximab, J9055
Chair
adjustable, dialysis, E1570
bathtub, E0240
commode, E0163-E0165
lift, E0627
rollabout, E1031
shower or bath, E0240
sitz bath, E0160-E0162
Challenger manual wheelchair, K0009
Champion 1000 manual wheelchair, K0004
Champion 30000, manual wheelchair, K0005
Chealamide, J3520
CheckMate Plus blood glucose monitor, E0607
Chelation therapy, M0300
home infusion, administration, S9355
Chemical endarterectomy, M0300
Chemistry and toxicology tests, P2028-P3001
Chemodenervation, vocal cord, S2341
Chemotherapy
dental, D4381
drug, oral, not otherwise classified, J8999
drugs
Actimmune, J9216
Adriamycin, J9000
Adrucil, J9190
aldesleukin, J9015
alemtuzumab, J9010
Alferon N, J9215
Alimta, J9305
Alkeran, J9245
Ara-C, J9100
Arranon, J9261
arsenic trioxide, J9017
asparaginase, J9020
Avasin, J9035
BCG live, J9031
bendamustine, J9033
bevacizumab, J9035
BiCNU, J9050
Blenoxane, J9040
bleomycin sulfate, J9040
bortezomib, J9041
Campath, J9010
Camptosar, J9206
carboplatin, J9045
Carmustine, J9050
Cerubidine, J9150
cetuximab, J9055
chyclophosphamide, J9070, J9080, J9091-J9097
cisplatin, J9060, J9062
cladribine, J9065
Cosmegen, J9120
cytarabine, J9098, J9100, J9110
Cytosar-U, J9100, J9110
Cytoxan, J9070, J9080, J9090-J9097
dacarbazine, J9130, J9140
Dactinomycin, J9120
daunorubicin, J9140, J9150-J9151
Daunoxome, J9151
denileukin diftitox, J9160
diethyistilbestrol diphosphate, J9165
docetaxel, J9170
Doxil, J9001
doxorubicin HCl, J9000-J9001
DTIC-Dome, J9130, J9140
Ellence, J9178
Eloxatin, J9263
Elspar, J9020
epirubicin, J9178
Erbitux, J9055
etoposide, J9181

Chemotherapy — *continued*
drugs — *continued*
Fastodex, J9395
floxuridine, J9200
Fludara, J9185
fludarabine phosphate, J9185
fluorouracil, J9190
Folex, J9250, J9260
FUDR, J9200
fulvestrant, J9395
gemcitabine HCl, J9201
gemtuzumab ozogamicin, J9300
Gemzar, J9201
goserelin acetate implant, J9202
Herceptin, J9355
Hycamtin, J9350
Idamycin, J9211
idarubicin HCl, J9211
IFEX, J9208
ifosfamide, J9208
Il-2, J9015
Imuron, J9035
Infergen, J9212
interferon alfacon-1, recombinant, J9212
interferon alfa–2a, recombinant, J9213
Interferon alfa–2b, recombinant, J9214
interferon alfa–N3, J9215
interferon gamma–1b, J9216
Interleukin, J9015
Intron A, J9214
irinotecan, J9206
ixabepilone, J9207
IXEMPRA, J9207
leuprolide acetate, J9217-J9219
Leustatin, J9065
L-phenylalanine mustard, J9245
Lupron, J9218
Lupron Depot, J9217
Lupron Implant, J9219
mechlorethamine HCl, J9230
melphalan HCl, J9245
mesna, J9209
Mesnex, J9209
methotrexate sodium, J9250, J9260
Mithacin, J9270
mitomycin, J9280, J9290-J9291
Mitoxane, J9208
mitoxantrone HCl, J9293
Mustrgen, J9230
Mutamycin, J9280, J9290-J9291
Mylotarg, J9300
nabilone, oral, J8650
nalarabine, J9261
Navantrone, J9293
Navelbine, J9390
nelarabine, J9261
Neosar, J9070, J9080, J9090, J9091, J9092
Nipent, J9268
Oncaspar, J9266
Ontak, J9160
oxaliplatin, J9263
paclitaxel, J9265
Paraplatin, J9045
pegaspargase, J9266
pentostatin, J9268
Photofrin, J9600
Plantinol, J9060, J9062
plicamycin, J9270
porfimer sodium, J9600
premetrexed, J9305
Proleukin, J9015
RituXan, J9310
rituximab, J9310
Roferon-A, J9213
Rubex, J9000
Stilphostrol, J9165
streptozocin, J9320
Taxol, J9265
Taxotere, J9170
temsirolimus, J9330
TheraCys, J9031

Chemotherapy — *continued*
drugs — *continued*
Thioplex, J9340
thiotepa, J9340
Tice BCG, J9031
Toposar, J9181
topotecan, J9350
TORISEL, J9330
trastuzumab, J9355
TREANDA, J9033
Trisenox, J9017
valrubicin, J9357
Valstar, J9357
Velban, J9360
Velcade, J9041
VePesid, J9181
vinblastine sulfate, J9360
vincristine sulfate, J9370, J9375, J9380
vinorelbine tartrate, J9390
Zanosar, J9320
Zoladex, J9202
home infusion, continous, S9325-S9379, S9494-S9497
Chemstrip bG, box of 50 blood glucose test strips, A4253
Chemstrip K, box of 100 ketone urine test strips, A4250
Chemstrip UGK, box of 100 glucose/ketone urine test strips, A4250
Chest shell (cuirass), E0457
Chest wrap, E0459
Childbirth, S9442
cesarean birth, S9438
class, S9442
Lamaze, S9436
preparation, S9436
refresher, S9437
VBAC (vaginal birth after cesarean), S9439
Childcare, T2026-T2027
parents in treatment, T1009
Chin
cup, cervical, L0150
strap (for CPAP device), A7036
Chlorambucil, S0172
Chloramphenicol sodium succinate, J0720
Chlordiazepoxide HCl, J1990
Chlorhexidine, A4248
Chloromycetin sodium succinate, J0720
Chloroprocaine HCl, J2400
Chloroquine HCl, J0390
Chlorothiazide sodium, J1205
Chlorpromazine HCl, J3230, Q0171-Q0172
Chondrocyte cell harvest, arthroscopic, S2112
Chopart prosthetic
ankle, L5050, L5060
below knee, L5100
Chorex (-5, -10), J0725
Chorignon, J0725
Chorionic gonadotropin, J0725
Choron 10, J0725
Chromic phosphate, A9564
Chronimed Comfort insulin infusion set
23", A4230
43", A4230
Chux's, A4554
Cida
exostatic cervical collar, L0140, L0150
form fit collar, L0120
Cidofovir, J0740
Cilastatin sodium, imipenem, J0743
Cimetidine hydrochloride, S0023
Ciprofloxacin, J0744
Circulating tumor test, S3711
Cisplatin, J9060, J9062
Cladribine, J9065
Claforan, J0698
Clamp
external urethral, A4356

Classes, S9441-S9446
asthma, S9441
birthing, S9442
exercise, S9451
infant safety, S9447
lactation, S9443
nutrition, S9452
parenting, S9444
smoking cessation, S9453
stress management, S9454
weight management, S9449
Clavicle
splint, L3650, L3660
support
2-buckle closure, L3660
4-buckle closure, L3660
Cleaning solvent, Nu-Hope
4 oz bottle, A4455
16 oz bottle, A4455
Cleanser, wound, A6260
Cleft palate, feeder, S8265
Clevis, hip orthotic, L2570, L2600, L2610
Clindamycin phosphate, S0077
Clinical trials
lodging costs, S9994
meals, S9996
phase II, S9990
phase III, S9991
service, S9988
transportation costs, S9992
Clinic visit/encounter, T1015
multidisciplinary, child services, T1025
Clonidine, J0735
Closure device, vascular, C1760
Clotting time tube, A4771
Clozapine, S0136
Clubfoot wedge, L3380
Cobex, J3420
Cochlear implant, L8614
battery
alkaline, L8622
lithium, L8623-L8624
zinc, L8621
headset, L8615
microphone, L8616
replacement, L8619
transmitter cable, L8618
transmitting coil, L8617
zinc, L8621
Codeine phosphate, J0745
Codimal-A, J0945
Cogentin, J0515
Coil, imaging, C1770
Colchicine, J0760
Colistimethate sodium
inhalation solution, S0142
injection, J0770
Collagen
implant, urinary tract, L8603
microporous nonhuman origin, C9352-C9353
skintest, Q3031
wound dressing, A6021-A6024
Collar, cervical
contour (low, standard), L0120
multiple, post, L0180-L0200
nonadjust (foam), L0120
Philly One-piece extrication collar, L0150
tracheotomy, L0172
Philadelphia tracheotomy cervical collar, L0172
traction, E0856
Turtle Neck safety collars, E0942
Collection
microorganisms for culture and sensitivity, D0415
saliva samples, D0417
Colonoscopy, cancer screening
patient at high risk, G0105
patient not at high risk, G0121
Coloplast
closed pouch, A5051
drainable pouch, A5061

Coloplast — *continued*
drainable pouch — *continued*
closed, A5054
small, A5063
skin barrier
4 x 4, A4362
6 x 6, A5121
8 x 8, A5122
stoma cap, A5055
Coly-Mycin M, J0770
Coma stimulation, S9056
Combined connective tissue and double pedicle graft, dental, D4276
Combo-Seat universal raised toilet seat, E0244
Commode, E0160-E0171
chair, E0163-E0165, E0170-E0171
lift, E0172, E0625
pail, E0167
seat, wheelchair, E0968
Communication board, E1902
Compa-Z, J0780
Compazine, J0780
Composite dressing, A6203-A6205
Compressed gas system, E0424-E0480
Compression
bandage
high, A6452
light, A6448
medium, A6451
burn garment, A6501-A6512
burn mask, A6513
stockings, A6530-A6549
wrap, A6545
Compressogrip prosthetic shrinker, L8440-L8465
Compressor, E0565, E0570, E0650-E0652, K0738
Concentrator
oxygen, E1390-E1392
rental, E1392
Condom
female, A4268
male, A4267
Conductive
garment (for TENS), E0731
paste or gel, A4558
Conductivity meter (for dialysis), E1550
Condylectomy, D7840
Cone Beam
CT craniofacial, D0360
three dimensional reconstruction, D0363
two dimensional reconstruction, D0362
Conforming bandage, A6442-A6447
Congenital torticollis orthotic, L0112
Congo red, blood, P2029
Connector bar, dental, D6920
dental implant, supported, D6055
Conscious sedation, dental, D9241-D9242
Consultation
dental, D9210, D9310
biopsy, D0485
slides, D0484
telehealth, G0406-G0408
Contact layer, A6206-A6208
Contact lens, S0500, S0512-S0514, V2500-V2599
Continent device, A5081, A5082
Continuous passive motion exercise device, E0936
Continuous positive airway pressure (CPAP) device, E0601
chin strap, A7036
face mask, A7030-A7031
filter, A7038-A7039
headgear, A7035
nasal application accessories, A7032-A7034
oral interface, A7044
tubing, A7037

Contraceptive
cervical cap, A4261
condom
female, A4268
male, A4267
diaphragm, A4266
foam, A4269
gel, A4269
hormone patch, J7304
implant, J7306
intrauterine, copper, J7300
Levonorgestrel, implants and supplies, J7302, J7306
pills, S4993
spermacide, A4269
vaginal ring, J7303
Contracts, maintenance, ESRD, A4890
Contrast material
high osmolar, Q9958-Q9964
injection during MRI, A9576-A9579, Q9953
low osmolar, Q9951, Q9965-Q9967
nonradioactive NOC, A9698
oral MRI, Q9954
Controlyte, enteral nutrition, B4155
Coordinated care fee, G9009-G9012
Cophene-B, J0945
Coping, D2975
metal, D6975
Copying fee, medical records, S9981-S9982
Core buildup, dental, D2950, D6973
Corgonject-5, J0725
Corneal tissue processing, V2785
Corn, trim or remove, S0390
Coronary artery bypass surgery, direct
with coronary arterial and venous grafts
single, each, S2208
two arterial and single venous, S2209
with coronary arterial grafts, only
single, S2205
two grafts, S2206
with coronary venous grafts, only
single, S2207
Coronoidectomy, dental, D7991
Corset, spinal orthotic, L0970-L0976
Corticorelin ovine triflutate, J0795
Corticotropin, J0800
Cortrosyn, J0835
Corvert, J1742
Cosmegen, J9120
Cosyntropin, J0835
Cotranzine, J0780
Cough stimulation device, E0482
Counseling
end of life, S0257
for control of dental disease, D1310, D1320
genetic, S0265
Coupling gel/paste, A4559
Cover, shower
ventricular assist device, Q0501
Cover, wound
alginate dressing, A6196-A6198
foam dressing, A6209-A6214
hydrocolloid dressing, A6234-A6239
hydrogel dressing, A6242-A6248
specialty absorptive dressing, A6251-A6256
CPAP (continuous positive airway pressure) device, E0601
chin strap, A7036
exhalation port, A7045
face mask, A7030-A7031
headgear, A7035
humidifier, E0561-E0562
nasal application accessories, A7032-A7034
oral interface, A7044
supplies, E0470-E0472, E0561-E0562
tubing, A7037
Cradle, bed, E0280
Creation
anal lesions by radiofrequency, C9716
Crisis intervention, H2011, T2034
Criticare HN, enteral nutrition, B4153
Cromolyn sodium, inhalation solution, unit dose, J7631
Crown
abutment supported, D6094, D6194
additional construction, D2971
as retainer for FPD, D6720-D6792
composite resin, D2390
implant/abutment supported, D6058-D6067
implant/abutment supported retainer for FPD, D6720-D6792
indirect resin based composite, D6710
individual restoration, D2710-D2799
lengthening, D4249
prefabricated, D2930-D2933
provisional, D2799
recementation, D2920
repair, D2980
resin-based composite, D2710, D2712
stainless steel, D2934
titanium, D2794, D6794
Crutch
substitute
lower leg platform, E0118
Crutches, E0110-E0116
accessories, A4635-A4637, E2207
aluminum, E0114
articulating, spring assisted, E0117
forearm, E0111
Ortho-Ease, E0111
underarm, other than wood, pair, E0114
Quikfit Custom Pack, E0114
Red Dot, E0114
underarm, wood, single, E0113
Ready-for-use, E0113
wooden, E0112
Cryoprecipitate, each unit, P9012
Crysticillin (300 A.S., 600 A.S.), J2510
CTLSO, L0700, L0710, L1000-L1120
Cubicin, J0878
Cuirass, E0457
Culture sensitivity study, P7001
Curasorb, alginate dressing, A6196-A6199
Curettage, apical, perpendicular, D3410-D3426
Cushion
decubitus care, E0190
Oral/Nasal, A7029
positioning, E0190
wheelchair
AK addition, L5648
BK addition, L5646
skin protection, K0734-K0737
skin protection, K0734-K0737
Customized item (in addition to code for basic item), S1002
Custom Masterhinge Hip Hinge 3, L2999
Cyanocobalamin cobalt, A9546, A9559
Cycler
disposable set, A4671
Cycler dialysis machine, E1594
Cyclophosphamide, J9070-J9092
lyophilized, J9093-J9097
oral, J8530
Cyclosporine, J7502, J7515, J7516
Cylinder tank carrier, E2208
Cymetra, Q4112
Cystourethroscopy
for uthereral calculi, S2070
Cytarabine, J9100, J9110
liposome, J9098
CytoGam, J0850
Cytologic
sample collection, dental, D7287
smears, dental, D0480
Cytomegalovirus immune globulin (human), J0850
Cytopathology, screening, G0123, G0124, G0141, G0143-G0148
Cytosar-U, J9100
Cytovene, J1570
Cytoxan, J8530, J9070-J9097

D

D-5-W, J7070
Dacarbazine, J9130, J9140
Daclizumab, J7513
Dactinomycin, J9120
Dalalone, J1100
Dalfopristin, J2270
Dalteparin sodium, J1645
Daptomycin, J0878
Darbepoetin alfa
ESRD, J0882
non-ESRD, J0881
Daunorubicin
citrate, J9151
HCl, J9150
DaunoXome, J9151
DDAVP, J2597
Debridement
endodontic, D3221
periodontal, D4355
Decadron, J1100
-LA, J8540
oral, J8540
phosphate, J1100
Deca-Durabolin, J2320-J2322
Decaject, J1100
Decaject-LA, J1094
Decalcification procedure, D0475
Decitabine , J0894
Decolone
-100, J2321
-50, J2320
De-Comberol, J1060
Decompression
disc, S2348
hip core, S2325
vertebral axial, S9090
Decubitus care equipment, E0181
cushion or pillow, E0190
mattress
AquaPedic Sectional Gel Flotation, E0196
Iris Pressure Reduction/Relief, dry, E0184
PressureGuard II, air, E0186
TenderFlo II, E0187
TenderGel II, E0196
pressure pads, overlays, E0197-E0199
Body Wrap, E0199
Geo-Matt, E0199
Iris, E0199
PressureKair, E0197
Richfoam Convoluted and Flat, E0199
pressure pads, with pumps, E0181
Bio Flote, E0181
KoalaKair, E0181
protectors
heel or elbow, E0191
Body Wrap Foam Positioners, E0191
Pre-Vent, E0191
pump, E0182
Bio Flote, E0182
Pillo, E0182
TenderCloud, E0182
Deferoxamine mesylate, J0895
Dehist, J0945
Dehydroergotamine mesylate, J1110
Deionizer, water purification system, E1615
Deladumone (OB), J0900
Delatest, J3120
Delatestadiol, J0900
Delatestryl, J3120, J3130
Delestrogen, J0970
Delivery/set-up/dispensing, A9901
Delivery to high risk area requiring escort, S9381
Delta-Cast Elite Casting Material, A4590
Delta-Cortef, J7510
Delta-Lite Conformable Casting Tape, A4590
Delta-Lite C-Splint Fibreglass Immobilizer, A4590
Delta-Lite "S" Fibreglass Casting Tape, A4590
Deltasone, J7506
Deluxe item, S1001
Demadex, J3265
Demerol HCl, J2175
Demonstration project
clinic, G9140
low vision therapist, G9043
occupational therapist, G9041
orientation and mobility specialist, G9042
rehabilitation teacher, G9044
Dennis Browne, foot orthotic, L3140, L3150
Dentures (removable)
adjustments, D5410-D5422
complete, D5110-D5140
overdenture, D5860-D5861
partial, D5211-D5281
mandibular, D5226
maxillary, D5225
precision attachment, D5862
rebase, D5710-D5721
reline, D5730-D5761
repairs, D5510, D5520, D5610-D5650
temporary, D5810-D5821
DepAndro
100, J1070
200, J1080
Dep-Androgyn, J1060
DepMedalone
40, J1030
80, J1040
Depo
-Medrol, J1020, J1030, J1040
-Provera, J1051, J1055
-Testadiol, J1060
-Testosterone, J1070, J1080
Depo-estradiol cypionate, J1000
Depogen, J1000
Depoject, J1030, J1040
Depopred
-40, J1030
-80, J1040
Depotest, J1070, J1080
Depotestogen, J1060
Derata injection device, A4210
Dermagraft, Q4106
Dermal tissue
native, nondenatured collagen, C9358
regeneration template (DRT), Q4105
Desensitizing medicament, dental, D9910
Desensitizing resin, dental, D9911
Desferal mesylate, J0895
Desmopressin acetate, J2597
Detector, blood leak, dialysis, E1560
Device
auditory osseointegrated, L8691, L8695
continuous passive motion, E0936
intermittent limb compression, E0676
joint, C1776
ocular, C1784
reaching/grabbing, A9281
retrieval, C1773
tissue localization and excision, C1819
urinary incontinence repair, C1771, C2631
DeVilbiss
9000D, E0601
9001D, E0601

Dexacen-4, J1100
Dexamethasone
acetate, J1094
inhalation solution
concentrated, J7637
unit dose, J7638
oral, J8540
sodium phosphate, J1100
Dexasone, J1100
Dexone, J1100
Dexrazoxane HCl, J1190
Dextran, J7100, J7110
Dextroamphetamine sulfate, S0160
Dextrose, S5010-S5014
saline (normal), J7042
water, J7060, J7070
Dextrostick, A4772
D.H.E. 45, J1110
Diabetes
alcohol swabs, per box, A4245
battery for blood glucose monitor, A4233-A4236
bent needle set for insulin pump infusion, A4231
blood glucose monitor, E0607
with integrated lancer, E2101
with voice synthesizer, E2100
blood glucose test strips, box of 50, A4253
drugs
Humalin, J1815, J1817
Humalog, J1817, S5551
insulin, J1815, J1817, S5551
Novolin, J1815, J1817
evaluation and management LOPS, G0245
injection device, needle-free, A4210
insulin pump, external, E0784
infusion set, A4231
syringe with needle, A4232
lancet device, A4258
lancets, box of 100, A4259
non-needle cannula for insulin infusion, A4232
retinal exam, S3000
self management training
group, G0109
individual, G0108
shoe
fitting, A5500
inlay, A5508
insert, A5512-A5513
modification, A5503-A5507
syringe, disposable
box of 100, S8490
each, A4206
urine glucose/ketone test strips, box of 100, A4250
Diabetic management program
E/M of sensory neuropathy, G0246-G0247
follow-up visit to MD provider, S9141
follow-up visit to non-MD provider, S9140
foot care, G0247
group session, S9455
insulin pump initiation, S9145
nurse visit, S9460
Diagnostic
dental services, D0120-D0999
radiology services, D0210-D0340
Dialet lancet device, A4258
Dialysate
concentrate additives, A4765
peritoneal dialysis solution, A4720-A4726, A4766
solution, A4728
testing solution, A4760
Dialysis
access system, C1881
air bubble detector, E1530
anesthetic, A4736-A4737
bath conductivity, meter, E1550
blood leak detector, E1560
centrifuge, E1500
cleaning solution, A4674
Dialysis — *continued*
concentrate
acetate, A4708
acid, A4709
bicarbonate, A4706-A4707
drain bag/bottle, A4911
emergency treatment, G0257
equipment, E1510-E1702
extension line, A4672-A4673
filter, A4680
fluid barrier, E1575
heating pad, E0210
hemostats, E1637
home equipment repair, A4890
infusion pump, E1520
mask, surgical, A4928
peritoneal
clamps, E1634
pressure alarm, E1540
scale, E1639
shunt, A4740
supplies, A4671-A4918
surgical mask, A4928
syringe, A4657
tourniquet, A4929
unipuncture control system, E1580
Dialyzer, artificial kidney, A4690
Diamox, J1120
Diaper service, T4538
Diaphragm, contraceptive, A4266
Diazepam, J3360
Diazoxide, J1730
Dibent, J0500
Didanosine, S0137
Didronel, J1436
Dietary education, S9449, S9452
Dietary planning, dental nutrition, D1310
Diethylstilbestrol
diphosphate, J9165
Diflucan injection, J1450
Digoxin, J1160
Digoxin immune fab, J1265
Dihydrex, J1200
Dihydroergotamine mesylate, J1110
Dilantin, J1165
Dilaudid, J1170
Dilomine, J0500
Dilor, J1180
Dimenhydrinate, J1240
Dimercaprol, J0470
Dimethyl sulfoxide (DMSO), J1212
Dinate, J1240
Dioval (XX, 40), J0970, J1380, J1390
Diphenacen-50, J1200
Diphenhydramine HCl, J1200
oral, Q0163
Dipyridamole, J1245
Disarticulation
lower extremities, prosthesis, L5000-L5999
upper extremities, prosthesis, L6000-L6692
Discoloration, dental, removal, D9970
Disease management program, S0317
Disetronic
glass cartridge syringe for insulin pump, each, A4232
H-Tron insulin pump, E0784
insulin infusion set with bent needle, with or without wings, each, A4231
Diskard head halter, E0940
Disk decompression, lumbar, S2348
Diskectomy, lumbar, S2350, S2351
single interspace, S2350
Disotate, J3520
Di-Spaz, J0500
Dispensing fee
BICROS, V5240
binaural, V5160
CROS, V5200
monaural hearing aid, V5241
new spectacle lenses, S0595
Dispensing fee — *continued*
pharmacy
inhalation drugs, G0333, Q0513-Q0514
Disposable
diapers, A4335
glucose monitor, A9275
supplies, ambulance, A0382-A0398
underpads, A4554
Ditate-DS, J0900
Diuril sodium, J1205
D-med 80, J1040
DMSO, J1212
DNA analysis, S3840
fecal, S3890
Dobutamine HCl, J1250
Dobutrex, J1250
Docetaxel, J9170
Dolasetron mesylate, J1260, Q0180
oral, S0174
Dolophine HCl, J1230
Dome, J9130
and mouthpiece (for nebulizer), A7016
Dommanate, J1240
Don-Joy
cervical support collar, L0150
deluxe knee immobilizer, L1830
rib belt, L0210
wrist forearm splint, L3984
Donor cadaver
harvesting multivisceral organs, with allografts, S2055
Dopamine HCl, J1265
Dornase alpha, inhalation solution, unit dose, J7639
Dornix Plus, E0601
Dorsiwedge Night Splint, A4570, L2999, L4398
Dosimeter, implantable radiation, ea, A4650
Double bar
AK, knee-ankle-foot orthotic, L2020, L2030
BK, ankle-foot orthotic, L1990
Doxercalciferol, J1270
Doxil, J9001
Doxorubicin HCl, J9000
Drainage
bag, A4357, A4358, A4911
board, postural, E0606
bottle, A4911, A5102
Dramamine, J1240
Dramanate, J1240
Dramilin, J1240
Dramocen, J1240
Dramoject, J1240
Dressing — *see also* Bandage, A6021-A6404
alginate, A6196-A6199
composite, A6200-A6205
contact layer, A6206-A6208
film, A6257-A6259
foam, A6209-A6215
gauze, A6216-A6230, A6402-A6404
holder/binder, A4461, A4463
hydrocolloid, A6234-A6241
hydrogel, A6242-A6248
specialty absorptive, A6251-A6256
tape, A4450, A4452
transparent film, A6257-A6259
tubular, A6457
Dronabinol, Q0167-Q0168
Droperidol, J1790
and fentanyl citrate, J1810
Dropper, A4649
Drug delivery system
controlled dose delivery system, K0730
disposable, A4306
Drugs — *see also* Table of Drugs
administered through a metered dose inhaler, J3535
chemotherapy, J8999-J9999
dental
injection, D9610
Drugs — *see also* Table of Drugs — *continued*
dental — *continued*
other, D9910
disposable delivery system, 50 ml or greater per hour, A4305
disposable delivery system, 5 ml or less per hour, A4306
immunosuppressive, J7500-J7599
infusion supplies, A4221, A4222, A4230-A4232
injections (*see also* drug name), J0120-J8999
not otherwise classifed, J3490, J7599, J7699, J7799, J8499, J8999, J9999
prescription, oral, J8499, J8999
Dry pressure pad/mattress, E0184, E0199
Dry socket, localized osteitis, D9930
DTIC-Dome, J9130
Dunlap
heating pad, E0210
hot water bottle, E0220
Duo-Gen L.A., J0900
Duolock curved tail closures, A4421
Durable medical equipment (DME), E0100-E8002
Duracillin A.S., J2510
Duraclon, J0735
Duragen (-10, -20, -40), J0970, J1380, J1390
Duralone
-40, J1030
-80, J1040
Duramorph, J2275
Duratest
-100, J1070
-200, J1080
Duratestrin, J1060
Durathate-200, J3130
Durr-Fillauer
cervical collar, L0140
Pavlik harness, L1620
Dymenate, J1240
Dyphylline, J1180

E

Ear wax removal, G0268
Easy Care
folding walker, E0143
quad cane, E0105
ECG
initial Medicare ECG, G0403-G0405
monitor, S0345-S0347
Echocardiogram
transesophageal, C8925-C8928
transthoracic, C8921-C8924, C8929-C8930
Echosclerotherapy, S2202
Economy knee splint, L1830
Edetate
calcium disodium, J0600
edetate disodium, J3520
Education
asthma, S9441
birthing, S9436-S9439, S9442
diabetes, S9145
exercise, S9451
family planning, individualized programs, school based, T1018
infant safety, S9447
lactation, S9443
Lamaze, S9436
parenting, S9444
smoking cessation, S9453
stress management, S9454
weight management, S9449
Efalizumab, S0162
Eggcrate dry pressure pad/mattress, E0184, E0199
Elastic support, A6530-A6549
Elavil, J1320
Elbow
brace, universal rehabilitation, L3720
disarticulation, endoskeletal, L6450

Elbow — *continued*
Masterhinge Elbow Brace 3, L3999
orthotic (EO), E1800, L3700-L3740
protector, E0191
Electrical work, dialysis equipment, A4870
Electric hand
adult, L7007
pediatric, L7008
Electric heat pad for peritoneal dialysis, E0210
Electric hook, L7009
Electric stimulator supplies, A4595
Electrocardiographic monitoring, S0345-S0347
Electrodes, per pair, A4556
Electrodiagnostic Testing, S3905
Electromagnetic therapy, G0295, G0329
Electron beam computed tomography, S8092
Electron microscopy - diagnostic, D0481
Elevating leg rest, K0195
Elevator, air pressure, heel, E0370
Ellence, J9178
Elliotts B solution, J9175
Eloxatin, J9263
Elspar, J9020
Embolization, protection system, C1884
for tumor destruction, S2095
Embryo
cryopreserved transferred, S4037
monitor/store cryopreserved, S4040
Emergency
dental treatment, D9430
facility visit, G0380-G0384
EMG, E0746
Eminase, J0350
Enameloplasty, D9971
Enbrel, J1438
Encounter, clinic, T1015
Endarterectomy, chemical, M0300
Endodontic procedures, D3110-D3999
End of life care planning, S0257
Endoscope sheath, A4270
Endoscopy
full thickness plication gastric cardia, C9724
nasal, S2344
Endoskeletal system, addition, L5925, L5984
Enema
bag, reusable, A4458
barium, G0106
cancer screening, G0120
Enfuvirtide, J1324
Enovil, J1320
Enoxaparin sodium, J1650
Enrich, enteral nutrition, B4150
Ensure, enteral nutrition, B4150
HN, B4150
Plus, B4152
Plus HN, B4152
powder, B4150
Enteral
administration services, feeding, S9340-S9343
feeding supply kit (syringe) (pump) (gravity), B4034-B4036
fiber or additive, B4104
formulae, B4150-B4162
electrolytes, B4102, B4103
for metabolic disease, B4157
intact nutrients, B4149, B4150, B4152
pediatric, B4158-B4162
gastronomy tube, B4087-B4088
nutrition infusion pump (with alarm) (without), B9000, B9002
supplies, not otherwise classified, B9998
Epinephrine, J0170
Epiribicin HCl, J9178
Epoetin alfa
ESRD, J0886, Q4081
non-ESRD, J0885
Epoprostenol, J1325
dilutant, sterile, S0155
infusion pump, K0455
Equestrian/hippotherapy, S8940
Equilibration, dental, D9951-D9952
Erbitux, J9055
Ergonovine maleate, J1330
Ertapenem sodium, J1335
Erythromycin lactobionate, J1364
ESRD End Stage Renal Disease — *see also* Dialysis
bundle demo/basic, G9013
expanded, G9014
machines and accessories, E1510-E1699
plumbing, A4870
services, E1510-E1699
supplies, A4651-A4913
Estra-D, J1000
Estradiol, J1000, J1060
cypionate and testosterone cypionate, J1060
L.A., J0970, J1380, J1390
L.A. 20, J0970, J1380, J1390
L.A. 40, J0970, J1380, J1390
valerate and testosterone enanthate, J0900
Estra-L (20, 40), J0970, J1380, J1390
Estra-Testrin, J0900
Estro-Cyp, J1000
Estrogen conjugated, J1410
Estroject L.A., J1000
Estrone (5, Aqueous), J1435
Estronol, J1435
-L.A., J1000
Ethanolamine oleate, J1430
Ethyol, J0207
Etidronate disodium, J1436
Evaluation
comprehensive, multi-discipline, H2000
dental, D0120-D0180
for power mobility device, G0372
self assessment, depression, S3005
team for handicapped, T1024
Everone, J3120, J3130
Exactech lancet device, A4258
Examination
breast, S0613
breast and pelvic, G0101
brush biopsy sample, D0486
diabetic for LOPS, G0245-G0246
for college, S0622
initial Medicare, G0402
oral, D0120-D0160
related to surgical procedure, S0260
Excision, tissue localization, C1819
Exercise
class, S9451
continuous passive motion device, E0936
equipment, A9300
Exo-Static overdoor traction unit, E0860
Exostosis (tuberosity) removal
lateral, D7471
osseous tuberosity, D7485
reduction of fibrous tuberosity, D7972
Exposure
anatomical crown, D4230-D4231
External
ambulatory infusion pump, E0781, E0784
counterpulsation, G0166
power, battery components, L7360-L7499
power, elbow, L7191
External defibrillator
battery replacement, K0607
electrode replacement, K0609
garment replacement, K0608
Extractions, D7111-D7140
Extractions — *continued*
surgical, D7210-D7250
Extraoral films, D0250, D0260
Extremity belt/harness, E0945
Eye
lens (contact) (spectacle), S0500-S0514, V2100-V2615
pad, A6410-A6411
patch, A6410-A6411
prosthetic, V2623-V2629
service (miscellaneous), V2700-V2799
E-ZJect disposable insulin syringes, up to 1 cc, per syringe, A4206
E-ZJect Lite Angle lancets, box of 100, A4259
E-Z-lets lancet device, A4258
E-Z Lite wheelchair, E1250

F

Fabrazyme, J0180
Face tent, oxygen, A4619
Factor IX, anti-hemophilic factor, J7193-J7195
Factor VIIa, anti-hemophilic factor, J7189
Factor VIII, anti-hemophilic factor, J7190-J7192
Factrel, J1620
Family stabilization, S9482
Famotidine, S0028
Fastodex, J9395
FDG, A9552
Fee, coordinated care, G9009-G9012
Fentanyl citrate, J3010
and droperidol, J1810
Fern test, Q0114
Fertility services
donor service (sperm or embryo), S4025
in vitro fertilization, S4013-S4022
ovulation induction, S4042
sperm procurement, S4026, S4030-S4031
Fetal surgery, repair teratoma, S2405
Fiberotomy, dental, transeptal, D7291
Filgrastim (G-CSF), J1440, J1441
Filler
bone, C9359
wound
alginate, A6199
foam, A6215
hydrocolloid, A6240-A6241
hydrogel, A6248
not elsewhere classified, A6261-A6262
Film
dressing, A6257-A6259
radiographic, dental, D0210-D0340
Filter
carbon, A4680
CPAP device, A7038-A7039
dialysis carbon, A4680
ostomy, A4368
tracheostoma, A4481
vena cava, C1880
ventricular assist device, Q0500
Finasteride, S0138
Finger
splint
baseball, A4570
fold-over, A4570
four-pronged, A4570
static, Q4049
Fisher&Paykel HC220, E0601
Fistula
cannulation set, A4730
oroantral, D7260
salivary, D7983
Fitness club membership, S9970
Fixed partial dentures (bridges), retainers
crowns, D6720-D6792
implant/abutment support, D6068-D6077
inlay/onlay, D6545-D6615
Fixed partial dentures (bridges), retainers — *continued*
pontics, D6205-D6252
recementation, D6930
repair, D6980
resin bonded, D6545
Flap, gingival, D4240, D4241
Flashcast Elite casting material, A4590
Flexoject, J2360
Flexon, J2360
Flipper, dental prosthesis, D5820-D5821
Flolan, J1325
Flowable Wound Matrix, Q4114
Flowmeter, E0440, E0555, E0580
Flow rate meter, peak, A4614
Floxuridine, J9200
Fluconazole, injection, J1450
Fludara, J9185
Fludarabine phosphate, J9185
Fluid barrier, dialysis, E1575
Flunisolide, J7641
Fluocinolone acetonide, J7311
Fluoride
custom tray/gel carrier, D5986
dispensing for home use, D9630
topical, D1206
Fluorine-18 fluorodeoxyglucose
contrast material, A9552
imaging using dual-head coincidence detection system, S8085
Fluorouracil, J9190
Fluphenazine decanoate, J2680
Flutamide, S0175
Flutter device, S8185
Fluvestrant, J9395
Foam
dressing, A6209-A6215
pad adhesive, A5126
Folding walker, E0135, E0143
Fold-over finger splint, A4570
Folex, J9260
PFS, J9260
Foley catheter, A4312-A4316, A4338-A4346
Follitropin
beta, S0128
Follutein, J0725
Fomepizole, J1451
Fomivirsen sodium, intraocular, J1452
Fondaparinux sodium, J1652
Food supplement, S9434
Food thickener, B4100
Foot care, routine, G0247, S0390
Foot, cast boot
Specialist Closed-Back Cast Boot, L3260
Specialist Gaitkeeper Boot, L3260
Specialist Open-Back Cast Boot, L3260
Specialist Toe Insert for Specialist Closed-Back Cast Boot and Specialist Health/Post Operative Shoe, A9270
Footdrop splint, L4398
Foot, insoles/heel cups
Specialist Heel Cups, L3485
Specialist Insoles, L3510
Footplate, E0175, E0970
Foot, soles
Masterfoot Walking Cast Sole, L3649
Solo Cast Sole, L3540
Footwear, orthopedic, L3201-L3265
Forearm crutches, E0110, E0111
Fortaz, J0713
Forteo, J3110
Fortex, alginate dressing, A6196-A6199
Foscarnet sodium, J1455
Foscavir, J1455
Fosphenytoin, Q2009, S0078
Foster care, H0041-H0042
Four Poster, fracture frame, E0946
Four-pronged finger splint, A4570

Fracture
bedpan, E0276
frame, E0920, E0930, E0946-E0948
orthotic, L2106-L2136
orthotic additions, L3995
pelvic bone, G0412-G0415
Specialist Pre-Formed Humeral Fracture Brace, L3980
Fractures, dental, treatment
alveolus, D7670, D7770
malar/zygomatic arch
incision, D7650-D7660
surgical incision, D7750-D7760
mandible
compound closed reduction, D7740
compound open reduction, D7730
simple closed reduction, D7640
simple open reduction, D7630
maxilla
compound closed reduction, D7720
compound open reduction, D7710
simple closed reduction, D7620
simple open reduction, D7610
Fragmin, J1645
Frame
meaning spectacles, V2020, V2025
sales tax, S9999
safety, for hospital bed, E0316
standing system, E0638, E0641, E0642
FreAmine HBC, parenteral nutrition, B5100
Frejka, hip orthotic, L1600
replacement cover, L1610
Frenectomy/frenotomy (frenulectomy), D7960
Frenuloplasty, D7963
FUDR, J9200
Fulvestrant, J9395
Fungizone, J0285
Furomide MD, J1940
Furosemide, J1940

G

Gadobenate dimeglumine, A9577-A9578
Gadolinium, A9579
Gadoteridol, A9576
Gait trainer
pediatric
anterior, E8002
posterior, E8000
upright, E8001
Gallium Ga-67, A9556
Gallium nitrate, J1457
Galsulfase, J1458
Gamastan, J1460
Gamma globulin, J1460
GammaGraft, Q4111
Gamulin RH, J2790
Ganciclovir
implant, J7310
sodium, J1570
Ganirelix acetate, S0132
Garamycin, J1580
Gas system
compressed, E0424, E0425
gaseous, E0430, E0431, E0441, E0443
liquid, E0434-E0440, E0442, E0444
Gastric
band adjustment, S2083
Gastric suction pump, E2000
Gastrostomy tube, B4087-B4088
Gatifloxacin, J1590
Gaucher disease, genetic test, S3848
Gauze, A6216-A6230, A6266
impregnated, A6222-A6230, A6266
nonimpregnated, A6216, A6221, A6402
pads, A6216-A6230, A6402-A6404
Johnson&Johnson, A6402
Kendall, A6402
Moore, A6402
Gefitinib, J8565
Gel
conductive, A4558
coupling for ultrasound, A4559
pressure pad, E0185, E0196
sheet, dermal or epidermal, A6025
Gemcitabine HCl, J9201
Gemtuzumab ozogamicin, J9300
GemZar, J9201
Gene expression profiling panel, S3854
Generator
neurostimulator, C1767, C1820
Genetic
counseling, S0265
testing, S3800, S3818-S3853, S3855, S3860-S3862
Genmould Creamy Plaster, A4580
Gentamicin (sulfate), J1580
Gentran, J7100, J7110
Geo-Matt
therapeutic overlay, E0199
Geronimo PR, power wheelchair, K0011
Gerval Protein, enteral nutrition, B4155
Gestational home visit
for diabetes, S9214
for hypertension, S9211
for preeclampsia, S9213
GIFT, S4013
Gingival flap, D4240, D4241
Gingiva, pericoronal, removal, D7971
Gingivectomy/gingivoplasty, D4210-D4211
Glasses
air conduction, V5070
binaural, V5120-V5150
bone conduction, V5080
frames, V2020, V2025
hearing aid, V5150, V5190, V5230
lens, V2100-V2499, V2610, V2718, V2730, V2755, V2770, V2780
Glass ionomer (resin restoration), D2330-D2394
Glatiramer acetate, J1595
Glaucoma screening, G0117-G0118
Global fee, urgent care center, S9083
Gloves
dialysis, A4927
non-sterile, A4927
sterile, A4930
Glucagon HCl, J1610
Glucometer
3 blood glucose meter, E0607
3 blood glucose test strips, box of 50, A4253
II blood glucose meter, E0607
II blood glucose test strips, box of 50, A4253
Glucose
monitor device, continuous, noninvasive, S1030-S1031
receiver, A9278
sensor, A9276
test strips, A4253, A4772
transmitter, A9277
Glukor, J0725
Gluteal pad, L2650
Glycopyrrolate, inhalation solution
concentrated, J7642
unit dose, J7643
Gold
foil dental, D2410-D2430
sodium thiomalate, J1600
Gomco
aspirators, E0600
Gonadorelin HCl, J1620
Gonic, J0725
Goserelin acetate implant (*see also* Implant), J9202
Grab bar, trapeze, E0910, E0940
Grade-aid, wheelchair, E0974
Gradient pressure aids, S8421-S8429
Graft
dental
bone replacement, D4263-D4264
maxillofacial soft/hard tissue, D7955
osseous, osteoperiostal or cartilage
mandible or maxilla, D7950
soft tissue, D4270-D4273
soft tissue and pedicle, D4276
vascular, C1768
GRAFTJACKET, Q4107
injectable, Q4113
Granisetron HCl, J1626, Q0166, S0091
Gravity traction device, E0941
Gravlee jet washer, A4470
Greissing, foot prosthesis, L5978
Guided tissue regeneration, dental, D4266-D4267
Guide wire, C1769
Guilford multiple-post collar, cervical orthotic, L0190
Gynogen, J1380, J1390
L.A. (10, 20, 40), J0970, J1380, J1390

H

Haberman Feeder, S8265
Habilitation, T2012-T2021
Hair analysis (excluding arsenic), P2031
Haldol, J1630
decanoate (-50, -100), J1631
Hallus-valgus dynamic splint, L3100
Hallux prosthetic implant, L8642
Haloperidol, J1630
decanoate, J1631
Halo procedures, L0810-L0859
Halter, cervical head, E0942
Hand
electric, L7007-L7008
mechanical, L6708-L6709
orthotic (WHFO), E1805, E1825, L3808, L3900-L3923
partial prosthesis, L6000-L6020
restoration, L6900-L6915
rims, wheelchair, E0967
Handgrip (cane, crutch, walker), A4636
Harness, E0942, E0944, E0945
Harvest
multivisceral organs, cadaver donor, S2055
peripheral stem cell, S2150
Harvey arm abduction orthotic, L3960
Health club membership, S9970
Hearing devices, L8614, V5008-V5299
accessories/supplies, V5267
analog, V5242-V5251
battery, V5266
BICROS, V5210-V5230
CROS, V5170-V5190
digital, V5250-V5261
dispensing fee, V5241
BICROS, V5240
bilateral, V5110
CROS, V5200
monaural, V5241
unspecified, V5090
ear impression, V5275
ear mold/insert, V5264-V5265
programmable analog
binaural, V5252-V5253
monaural, V5244-V5247
CIC, V5244
Heat
application, E0200-E0239
lamp, E0200, E0205
pad, E0210, E0215, E0217, E0218, E0238, E0249
units, E0239
Hydroacollator, mobile, E0239
Thermalator T-12-M, E0239
Heater (nebulizer), E1372
Heating pad, Dunlap, E0210
for peritoneal dialysis, E0210
Heel
elevator, air, E0370
loop/holder, E0951
pad, L3480, L3485
protector, E0191
shoe, L3430-L3485
stabilizer, L3170
Helicopter, ambulance — *see also* Ambulance, A0431
Helmet
cervical, A8000-A8004
custom, A8002-A8003
hard, A8001, A8003
interface replacement, A8004
prefabricated, A8000-A8001
soft, A8000, A8002
Hemalet lancet device, A4258
Hematopoietic hormone administration, S9537
Hemin, J1640
Hemipelvectomy prosthesis, L5280
Hemisection, dental, D3920
Hemi-wheelchair, E1083-E1086
Hemodialysis
acetate concentrate, A4708
acid solution, A4709
bicarbonate concentrate, A4706-A4707
catheter, C1750, C1752
drain bag/bottle, A4911
machine, E1590
mask, surgical, A4928
protamine sulfate, A4802
surgical mask, A4928
tourniquet, A4929
Hemodialyzer, portable, E1635
Hemofil M, J7190
Hemophilia clotting factor, J7190-J7199
Hemostats, for dialysis, E1637
Hemostix, A4773
Heparin
infusion pump (for dialysis), E1520
lock flush, J1642
sodium, J1644
HepatAmine, parenteral nutrition, B5100
Hepatic-aid, enteral nutrition, B4154
Hep-Lock (U/P), J1642
Herceptin, J9355
Hexadrol phosphate, J1100
Hexalite, A4590
Hexior power wheelchair, K0014
High Frequency chest wall oscillation equipment, A7025-A7026, E0483
High osmolar contrast
up to 149 mgs iodine, Q9958
150-199 mgs iodine, Q9959
200-249 mgs iodine, Q9960
250-299 mgs iodine, Q9961
300-349 mgs iodine, Q9962
350-399 mgs iodine, Q9963
400 or greater mgs iodine, Q9964
Hip
Custom Masterhinge Hip Hinge 3, L2999
disarticulation prosthesis, L5250, L5270
Masterhinge Hip Hinge 3, L2999
orthotic (HO), L1600-L1686
Hip-knee-ankle-foot orthotic (HKAFO), L2040-L2090
Histaject, J0945
Histerone (-50, -100), J3140
History and physical
related to surgical procedure, S0260
Histrelin
acetate injection, J1675
implant, J9225
HIV-1 antibody testing, S3645
HKAFO, L2040-L2090
HN2, J9230
Holder
heel, E0951
surgical dressing, A4461, A4463
toe, E0952

Hole cutter tool, A4421
Hollister
belt adapter, A4421
closed pouch, A5051, A5052
colostomy/ileostomy kit, A5061
drainable pouches, A5061
with flange, A5063
medical adhesive, A4364
pediatric ostomy belt, A4367
remover, adhesive, A4455
skin barrier, A4362, A5122
skin cleanser, A4335
skin conditioning creme, A4335
skin gel protective dressing wipes, A5120
stoma cap, A5055
two-piece pediatric ostomy system, A5054, A5063, A5073
urostomy pouch, A5071, A5072
Home health
aide, S9122, T1030-T1031
home health setting, G0156
care
certified nurse assistant, S9122, T1021
home health aide, S9122, T1021
management
episodic, S0272
hospice, S0271
standard, S0270
nursing care, S9122-S9124, T1030-T1031
outside capitation arrangement, S0273-S0274
re-certification, G0179-G0180
gestational
assessment, T1028
delivery suppies, S8415
diabetes, S9214
hypertension, S9211
pre-eclampsia, S9213
preterm labor, S9208-S9209
hydration therapy, S9373-S9379
infusion therapy, S9325-S9379, S9494-S9497, S9537-S9810
insertion midline venous catheter, S5523
nursing services, S0274, S9212-S9213
physician services, S0270-S0273
postpartum hypertension, S9212
services of
clinical social worker, G0155
occupational therapist, G0152
physical therapist, G0151
skilled nurse, G0154
speech/language pathologist, G0153
transfusion, blood products, S9538
wound care, S9097
Home uterine monitor, S9001
Hook
electric, L7009
mechanical, L6706-L6707
Hospice
care, Q5001-Q5008, S9126, T2041-T2046
evaluation and counseling services, G0337
referral visit, S0255
Hospital
call
dental, D9420
observation
direct admit, G0379
per hour, G0378
Hot water bottle, E0220
Houdini security suit, E0700
House call, dental, D9410
Housing, supported, H0043-H0044
Hoyer patient lifts, E0621, E0625, E0630
H-Tron insulin pump, E0784
H-Tron Plus insulin pump, E0784
Hudson
adult multi-vent venturi style mask, A4620
nasal cannula, A4615
oxygen supply tubing, A4616
UC-BL type shoe insert, L3000
Humalog, J1815, J1817, S5550
Human insulin, J1815, J1817
Humidifer, E0550-E0560
water chamber, A7046
Humira, J0135
Humulin insulin, J1815, J1817
Hyaluronidase
bovine, J3470
ovine, up to 150 units, J3471
ovine,up to 999 units, J3472
recombinant, J3473
Hyate, J7191
Hybolin
decanoate, J2321
Hycamtin, J9350
Hydralazine HCl, J0360
Hydrate, J1240
Hydration therapy, S9373-S9379
Hydraulic patient lift, E0630
Hydrocollator, E0225, E0239
Hydrocolloid dressing, A6234-A6241
Hydrocortisone
acetate, J1700
sodium phosphate, J1710
sodium succinate, J1720
Hydrocortone
acetate, J1700
phosphate, J1710
Hydrogel dressing, A6242-A6248
Hydromorphone, J1170, S0092
Hydroxyurea, S0176
Hydroxyzine HCl, J3410
pamoate, Q0177-Q0178
Hyoscyamine sulfate, J1980
Hyperbaric oxygen chamber, topical, A4575
Hyperstat IV, J1730
Hypertonic saline solution, J7130
Hypo-Let lancet device, A4258
Hypothermia
intragastric, M0100
HypRho-D, J2790
Hyrexin-50, J1200
Hyzine-;50, J3410

I

I-125 sodium iothalamate, A9554
I-131
sodium iodide, A9531
capsule, A9517, A9528
solution, A9529-A9530
tositumomab, A9544-A9545
I&D
Intraoral, D7511, D7521
Ibandronate sodium injection, J1740
Ibutilide fumarate, J1742
Ice cap or collar, E0230
Idamycin, J9211
Idarubicin HCl, J9211
Ifex, J9208
Ifosfamide, J9208
IL-2, J9015
Iletin insulin, J1815, J1817, S5552
Ilfeld, hip orthotic, L1650
Images, oral/facial, D0350
Imaging, C1770
coil, MRI, C1770
Imatinib, S0088
Imiglucerase, J1785
Imitrex, J3030
Immunoassay
alpha microglobulin-1, S3628
Immunofluorescence
direct, D0482
indirect, D0483
Immunosuppressive drug, not otherwise classified, J7599
Impacted tooth, removal, D7220-D7241
Impaction
tooth, treatment, D7283
Implant
access system, A4301
aqueous shunt, L8612
auditory device
brainstem, S2235
middle ear, S2230
breast, L8600
cochlear, L8614, L8619
collagen, urinary tract, L8603
contraceptive, J7306
dental
chin, D7995
endodontic, D3460
endosteal/endosseous, D6010
eposteal/subperiosteal, D6040
facial, D7995
maintenance, D6080
other implant service, D6053-D6079
supported prosthetics, D6053-D6079
removal, D6100
repair, D6090, D6095
transosteal/tensosseous, D6050
dextranomer/hyaluronic acid copolymer, urinary tract, L8604
ganciclovir, J7310
goserelin acetate, J9202
hallux, L8642
infusion pump, E0782, E0783
injectable bulking agent, urinary tract, L8606
interspinous process distraction device, C1821
joint, L8630, L8641, L8658
lacrimal duct, A4262, A4263
levonorgestral, J7306
maintenance procedures, D6080, D6100
maxillofacial, D5913-D5937
metacarpophalangeal joint, L8630
metatarsal joint, L8641
neurostimulator, pulse generator or receiver, E0755, L8685-L8688
Norplant, J7306
not otherwise specified, L8699
ocular, L8610
ossicular, L8613
osteogenesis stimulator, E0749
percutaneous access system, A4301
prosthetic device, C9899
removal, dental, D6100
repair, dental, D6090
urinary tract, L8603-L8604
vascular access portal, A4300
vascular graft, L8670
yttrium 90, S2095
Zoladex, J9202
Implantable radiation dosimeter, ea, A4650
Implantation/reimplantation, tooth, D7270
intentional reimplantation, D3470
Impregnated gauze dressing, A6222-A6230
Imuran, J7500, J7501
Inapsine, J1790
Incontinence
appliances and supplies, A4310, A5051-A5093, A5102-A5114, A5120-A5200
brief or diaper, T4521-T4524, T4543
disposable/liner, T4535
garment, A4520
pediatric
brief or diaper, T4529-T4530
pull-on protection, T4531-T4532
reusable
diaper or brief, T4539
pull-on protection, T4536
treatment system, E0740
underpad
disposable, T4541, T4542
Incontinence — *continued*
underpad — *continued*
reusable, T4537, T4540
youth
brief or diaper, T4533
pull-on protection, T4534
Inderal, J1800
Indium 111
capromab pendetide, A9507
ibritumomab tiuxetan, A9542
labeled
platelets, A9571
white blood cells, A9570
oxyguinoline, A9547
pentetate, A9548, A9572
pentetreotide, A9572
satumomab pendetide, A4642
Infant safety, CPR, training, S9447
Infergen, J9212
Infliximab injection, J1745
Infusion
catheter, C1752
IV, OPPS, C8957
pump, C1772, C2626
ambulatory, with administrative equipment, E0781
epoprostenol, K0455
heparin, dialysis, E1520
implantable, E0782, E0783
implantable, refill kit, A4220
insulin, E0784
mechanical, reusable, E0779, E0780
nonprogrammable, C1891
supplies, A4221, A4222, A4230-A4232
Versa-Pole IV, E0776
supplies, A4222, A4223
therapy, home, S9347, S9351, S9497-S9504
Inhalation drugs
acetylcysteine, J7608
albuterol, J7609, J7610, J7611, J7613
Alupent, J7668-J7669
atropine, J7635-J7636
Atrovent, J7644
Azmacort, J7684
beclomethasone, J7622
betamethasone, J7624
bitolterol mesylate, J7628-J7629
Brcanyl, J7680-J7681
Brethine, J7680-J7681
budesonide, J7626-J7627, J7633-J7634
colistimethate sodium, S0142
cromolyn sodium, J7631
dexamethasone, J7637-J7638
dornase alpha, J7639
flunisolide, J7641
formoterol, J7606, J7640
Gastrocrom, J7631
glycopyrolate, J7642-J7643
iloprost, Q4080
Intal, J7631
ipratropium bromide, J7644-J7645
isoetharine HCl, J7647-J7650
isoproterenol HCl, J7657-J7660
levalbuterol, J7607, J7612, J7614, J7615
metaproterenol sulfate, J7667-J7670
methacholine chloride, J7674
Mucomyst, J7608
Mucosil, J7608
Nasalcrom, J7631
NOC, J7699
pentamidine isethionate, J7676
Pulmicort Respules, J7627
terbutaline sulfate, J7680-J7681
Tobi, J7682
tobramycin, J7682, J7685
Tornalate, J7628-J7629
triamcinolone, J7683-J7684
Initial
ECG, Medicare, G0403-G0405
physical exam, Medicare, G0402

Injectable
allograft, Q4112-Q4113
bulking agent, urinary tract, L8606
flowable wound matrix, Q4114
Injection — *see also* Table of Drugs
contrast material, during MRI, A9576-A9579, Q9953
dental service, D9610, D9630
sacroiliac joint, G0259-G0260
supplies for self-administered, A4211
Injection adjustment, bariatric band, S2083
Inlay, dental
fixed partial denture retainers
metallic, D6545-D6615
porcelain/ceramic, D6548-D6609
metallic, D2510-D2530
porcelain/ceramic, D2610-D2630
recement inlay, D2910
intentional replantation, D3470, D7270
resin-based composite, D2650-D2652
titanium, D6624
Innovar, J1810
Insert
convex, for ostomy, A5093
diabetic, for shoe, A5512-A5513
implant
soft palate, C9727
vaginal cylinder for brachytherapy, S2270
Insertion
tray, A4310-A4316
vaginal cylinder, S2270
In-situ tissue hybridization, D0479
Insulin, J1815, J1817
delivery device, A9274, E0784, S5565-S5571
home infusion administration, S9353
intermediate acting, S5552
long acting, S5553
NPH, J1815, S5552
rapid onset, S5550-S5551
Intal, J7631
Integra
bilayer matrix wound dressing, Q4104
dermal regeneration template, Q4105
flowable wound matrix, Q4114
matrix, Q4108
Interferon
Alfa, J9212-J9215
Alfacon-1, J9212
Beta-1a, J1825, Q3025-Q3026
Beta-1b, J1830
Gamma, J9216
home injection, S9559
Intergrilin injection, J1327
Intermittent
limb compression device, E0676
peritoneal dialysis system, E1592
positive pressure breathing (IPPB) machine, E0500
Interphalangeal joint, prosthetic implant, L8658
Interscapular thoracic prosthesis
endoskeletal, L6570
upper limb, L6350-L6370
Interspinous process distraction device, C1821
Intervention
alcohol and/or drug, H0050
Intrafallopian transfer
complete cycle, gamete, S4013
complete cycle, zygote, S4014
donor egg cycle, S4023
incomplete cycle, S4017
Intraocular lenses, C1780, Q1003-Q1005, V2630-V2632
new technology
category 3, Q1003
category 4, Q1004
category 5, Q1005
presbyopia correcting function, V2788
Intraoral radiographs, D0210-D0240
Intrauterine device
copper contraceptive, J7300
other, S4989
Progestacert, S4989
Intravenous sedation/analgesia, dental, D9241-D9242
Introducer sheath
guiding, C1766, C1892, C1893
other than guiding, C1894, C2629, C2629
Intron A, J9214
Iodine 125, A9527, A9532, C2638-C2639
Iodine I-123, A9509, A9516
Iodine I-131
albumin, A9524
iobenguane sulfate, A9508
sodium iodide, A9517
Iodine swabs/wipes, A4247
IPD
system, E1592
IPPB machine, E0500
Ipratropium bromide
administered through DME, J7644-J7645
Iressa, J8565
Irinotecan, J9206
Iris Preventix pressure relief/reduction mattress, E0184
Iris therapeutic overlays, E0199
IRM ankle-foot orthotic, L1950
Iron
sucrose, J1756
Irrigation/evacuation system, bowel
control unit, E0350
disposable supplies for, E0352
Irrigation supplies, A4320, A4322, A4355, A4397-A4400
Surfit
irrigation sleeve, A4397
night drainage container set, A5102
Visi-flow irrigator, A4398, A4399
Islet cell transplant
laparoscopy, G0342
laparotomy, G0343
percutaneous, G0341
Isocaine HCl, J0670
Isocal, enteral nutrition, B4150
HCN, B4152
Isoetharine
inhalation solution
concentrated, J7647
unit dose, J7649-J7650
Isolates, B4150, B4152
Isoproterenol HCl
administered through DME, J7657-J7660
Isotein, enteral nutrition, B4153
Isuprel, J7658-J7659
Itraconazole, J1835
IUD, J7300
IV
infusion, OPPS, C8957
pole, E0776, K0105
solution
5% dextrose/normal saline, J7042
10% LMD, J7100
D-5-W, J7070
dextran, J7100, J7110
Gentran, J7100, J7110
normal saline, A4217, J7030-J7040, J7050
Rheomacrodex, J7100
Ringer's lactate, J7120

J

Jace tribrace, L1832
Jacket
scoliosis, L1300, L1310
J-cell battery, replacement for blood glucose monitor, A4234
Jejunostomy tube, B4087-B4088
Jenamicin, J1580
Joint device, C1776
transcutaneous electrical stimulation, E0762

K

Kabikinase, J2995
Kaleinate, J0610
Kaltostat, alginate dressing, A6196-A6199
Kanamycin sulfate, J1840, J1850
Kantrex, J1840, J1850
Kartop Patient Lift, toilet or bathroom (*see also* Lift), E0625
Keflin, J1890
Kefurox, J0697
Kefzol, J0690
Kenaject -40, J3301
Kenalog (-10, -40), J3301
Keratectomy photorefractive, S0810
Keratoprosthesis, C1818
Kestrone-5, J1435
Keto-Diastix, box of 100 glucose/ketone urine test strips, A4250
Ketorolac thomethamine, J1885
Key-Pred
-25,-50, J2650
K-Flex, J2360
Kidney
ESRD supply, A4651-A4913
system, E1510
wearable artifcial, E1632
Kingsley gloves, above hands, L6890
Kits
enteral feeding supply (syringe) (pump) (gravity), B4034-B4036
fistula cannulation (set), A4730
parenteral nutrition, B4220-B4224
surgical dressing (tray), A4550
tracheostomy, A4625
Klebcil, J1840, J1850
Knee
Adjustabrace 3, L2999
disarticulation, prosthesis, L5150-L5160
extension/fexion device, E1812
immobilizer, L1830
joint, miniature, L5826
Knee-O-Prene Hinged Knee Sleeve, L1810
Knee-O-Prene Hinged Wraparound Knee Support, L1810
locks, L2405-L2425
Masterbrace 3, L2999
Masterhinge Adjustabrace 3, L2999
orthotic (KO), E1810, L1800-L1846
Performance Wrap (KO), L1825
Knee-ankle-foot orthotic (KAFO), L2000-L2038, L2126-L2136
Knee-O-Prene Hinged Knee Sleeve, L1810
Knee-O-Prene Hinged Wraparound Knee Support, L1810
KnitRite
prosthetic
sheath, L8400-L8415
sock, L8420-L8435
stump sock, L8470-L8485
Kodel clavicle splint, L3660
Kogenate, J7192
Konakion, J3430
Konyne-HT, J7194
K-Y Lubricating Jelly, A4332, A4402
Kyphosis pad, L1020, L1025
Kytril, J1626

L

Laboratory tests
chemistry, P2028-P2038
microbiology, P7001
miscellaneous, P9010-P9615, Q0111-Q0115
toxicology, P3000-P3001, Q0091
Labor care (not resulting in delivery), S4005
Lacrimal duct implant
permanent, A4263
temporary, A4262
Lactated Ringer's infusion, J7120
LAE 20, J0970, J1380, J1390
Laetrile, J3570
Lancet, A4258, A4259
Lanoxin, J1160
Laparoscopy, surgical
esophagomyotomy, S2079
repair
Laronidase, J1931
Laryngectomy
tube, A7520-A7522
Larynx, artifcial, L8500
Laser
application, S8948
assisted uvulopalatoplasty (LAUP), S2080
in situ keratomileusis, S0800
myringotomy, S2225
Laser skin piercing device, for blood collection, E0620
replacement lens, A4257
Lasix, J1940
LAUP, S2080
Lead
adaptor
neurostimulator, C1883
pacing, C1883
cardioverter, defibrillator, C1777, C1895, C1896
environmental, home evaluation, T1029
neurostimulator, C1778
neurostimulator/test kit, C1897
pacemaker, C1779, C1898, C1899
Lederle, J8610
LeFort
I osteotomy, D7946-D7947
II osteotomy, D7948-D7949
III osteotomy, D7948-D7949
Leg
bag, A4358, A5112
extensions for walker, E0158
Nextep Contour Lower Leg Walker, L2999
Nextep Low Silhouette Lower Leg Walkers, L2999
rest, elevating, K0195
rest, wheelchair, E0990
strap, A5113, A5114, K0038, K0039
Legg Perthes orthotic, A4565, L1700-L1755
Lens
aniseikonic, V2118, V2318
contact, V2500-V2599
deluxe feature, V2702
eye, S0504-S0508, S0580-S0590, V2100-V2615, V2700-V2799
intraocular, C1780, V2630-V2632
low vision, V2600-V2615
mirror coating, V2761
occupational multifocal, V2786
polarization, V2762
polycarbonate, V2784
progressive, V2781
skin piercing device, replacement, A4257
tint, V2744
addition, V2745
Lente insulin, J1815, S5552
Lenticular lens
bifocal, V2221
single vision, V2121
trifocal, V2321
Lepirudin, J1945
Lerman Minerva spinal orthotic, L0174
Lesions, surgical excision, dental, D7410-D7465
Leucovorin calcium, J0640
Leukocyte
poor blood, each unit, P9016
Leuprolide acetate, J1950, J9217, J9218

Leuprolide acetate implant, J9219
Leustat, J9065
Leustatin, J9065
Levamisole HCl, S0177
Levaquin I.U., J1956
Levine, stomach tube, B4087-B4088
Levocarnitine, J1955
Levo-Dromoran, J1960
Levofloxacin, J1956
Levonorgestrel, contraceptive implants and supplies, J7302, J7306
Levorphanol tartrate, J1960
Librium, J1990
Lice infestation treatment, A9180
Lidocaine HCl for intravenous infusion, J2001
Lifescan lancets, box of 100, A4259
Lifestand manual wheelchair, K0009
Lifestyle modification program, coronary heart disease, S0340-S0342
Lift
combination, E0637
patient, and seat, E0621-E0635
Hoyer
Home Care, E0621
Partner All-Purpose, hydraulic, E0630
Partner Power Multifunction, E0625
shoe, L3300-L3334
standing frame system, E0638
Lift-Aid patient lifts, E0621
Light box, E0203
Lincocin, J2010
Lincomycin HCl, J2010
Lioresal, J0475
Liquaemin sodium, J1644
Lispro insulin, S5551
Lithium battery for blood glucose monitor, A4233-A4236
Lithrotripsy, gallstones, S9034
Little Ones
drainable pouch, A5063
mini-pouch, A5054
one-piece custom drainable pouch, A5061
one-piece custom urostomy pouch, A5071
pediatric belt, A4367
pediatric urine collector, A4335
urostomy pouch, transparent, A5073
Lively, knee-ankle-foot orthotic, L2038
LMD, 10%, J7100
Lobectomy, lung, donor, S2061
Localized osteitis, dry socket, D9110, D9930
Lodging
NOS, S9976
recipient, escort nonemergency transport, A0180, A0200
transplant-related, S9975
Lomustine, S0178
Lonalac powder, enteral nutrition, B4150
Lorazepam, J2060
Lovenox, J1650
Lower limb, prosthesis, addition, L5968
Low osmolar contrast
100-199 mgs iodine, Q9965
200-299 mgs iodine, Q9966
300-399 mgs iodine, Q9967
400 or greater mgs iodine, Q9951
Low vision
rehabilitation service, G9041-G9044
LPN services, T1003
Lubricant, A4332, A4402
Lufyllin, J1180
Lumbar
orthotic, L0625-L0627
pad, L1030, L1040
sacral orthotic (LSO), L0628-L0640
Luminal sodium, J2560
Lunelle, J1056
Lung volume reduction surgery services, G0302-G0305
Lupron, J9218
depot, J1950
Lutrepulse, J1620
LVRS services, G0302-G0305
Lymphedema therapy, S8950
Lymphocyte immune globulin, J7504, J7511

M

Madamist II medication compressor/nebulizer, E0570
Magnacal, enteral nutrition, B4152
Magnesium sulphate, J3475
Magnetic
resonance angiography, C8901-C8914, C8918-C8920
resonance imaging, low field, S8042
source imaging, S8035
Maintenance contract, ESRD, A4890
Malar bone, fracture repair, D7650, D7750, D7760
Malibu cervical turtleneck safety collar, L0150
Malocclusion correction, D8010-D8999
Mammography, G0202-G0206
Management
disease, S0316-S0317
Mandible, fracture, D7630-D7640, D7730-D7740
Mannitol, J2150
Mapping
topographic brain, S8040
vessels, G0365
Marker
tissue, A4648, C1879
Marmine, J1240
Maryland bridge (resin-bonded fixed prosthesis)
pontic, D6210-D6252
retainer/abutment, D6545
Mask
burn compression, A6513
CPAP, A7027
oxygen, A4620
surgical, for dialysis, A4928
Mastectomy
bra, L8002
camisole, S8460
form, L8020
prosthesis, L8000-L8039, L8600
sleeve, L8010
Masterbrace 3, L2999
Masterfoot Walking Cast Sole, L3649
Masterhinge Adjustabrace 3, L2999
Masterhinge Elbow Brace 3, L3999
Masterhinge Hip Hinge 3, L2999
Masterhinge Shoulder Brace 3, L3999
Mattress
air pressure, E0186, E0197
alternating pressure, E0277
pad, Bio Flote, E0181
pad, KoalaKair, E0181
AquaPedic Sectional, E0196
decubitus care, E0196
dry pressure, E0184
flotation, E0184
gel pressure, E0196
hospital bed, E0271, E0272
non-powered, pressure reducing, E0373
Iris Preventix pressure relief/reduction, E0184
Overlay, E0371-E0372
pressure reducing, E0181
TenderFlor II, E0187
TenderGel II, E0196
water pressure, E0187, E0198
powered, pressure reducing, E0277
Maxilla, fracture, D7610-D7620, D7710-D7720
Maxillofacial dental procedures, D5911-D5999
MCP, multi-axial rotation unit, L5986
MCT Oil, enteral nutrition, B4155
Meals
adults in treatment, T1010
per diem NOS, S9977
Mecasermin, J2170
Mechanical
hand, L6708-L6709
hook, L6706-L6707
Mechlorethamine HCl, J9230
Medialization material for vocal cord, C1878
Medical and surgical supplies, A4206-A6404
Medical conference, S0220-S0221
Medical food, S9435
Medical records copying fee, S9981-S9982
Medicare "welcome"
ECG, G0403-G0405
physical, G0402
Medi-Jector injection device, A4210
MediSense 2 Pen blood glucose monitor, E0607
Medralone
40, J1030
80, J1040
Medrol, J7509
Medroxyprogesterone acetate, J1055
with estradiol cypionate, J1056
Mefoxin, J0694
Megestrol acetate, S0179
Melphalan HCl, J9245
oral, J8600
Menotropins, S0122
Mental health
assessment, H0031
hospitalization, H0035
peer services, H0038
self-help, H0038
service plan, H0032
services, NOS, H0046
supportive treatment, H0026-H0037
Mepergan, J2180
Meperidine, J2175
and promethazine, J2180
Mepivacaine HCl, J0670
Mercaptopurine, S0108
Meritene, enteral nutrition, B4150
powder, B4150
Meropenem, J2185
Mesh, C1781
Mesna, J9209
Mesnex, J9209
Metabolism error, food supplement, S9434
Metacarpophalangeal joint prosthesis, L8630
Metaraminol bitartrate, J0380
Metatarsal joint, prosthetic implant, L8641
Meter, bath conductivity, dialysis, E1550
Methacholine chloride, J7674
Methadone, J1230
oral, S0109
Methergine, J2210
Methocarbamol, J2800
Methotrexate, oral, J8610
sodium, J9250, J9260
Methyldopate HCl, J0210
Methylene blue injection, A9535
Methylergonovine maleate, J2210
Methylprednisolone
acetate, J1020-J1040
oral, J7509
sodium succinate, J2920, J2930
Metoclopramide HCl, J2765
Metronidazole, S0030
Meunster Suspension, socket prosthesis, L6110
Miacalcin, J0630
Micafungin sodium, J2248
Microabrasion, enamel, D9970
Microbiology test, P7001
Microcapillary tube, A4651
Microcapillary tube — *continued*
sealant, A4652
Micro-Fine
disposable insulin syringes, up to 1 cc, per syringe, A4206
lancets, box of 100, A4259
Microlipids, enteral nutrition, B4155
Microspirometer, S8190
Midazolam HCl, J2250
Mileage, ambulance, A0380, A0390
Milk, breast
processing, T2101
Milrinone lactate, J2260
Milwaukee spinal orthotic, L1000
Minerva, spinal orthotic, L0700, L0710
Mini-bus, nonemergency transportation, A0120
Minimed
3 cc syringe, A4232
506 insulin pump, E0784
insulin infusion set with bent needle wings, each, A4231
Sof-Set 24" insulin infusion set, each, A4230
Minoxidil, S0139
Mitomycin, J9280-J9291
Mitoxantrone HCl, J9293
Mobilite hospital beds, E0293, E0295, E0297
Moducal, enteral nutrition, B4155
Moisture exchanger for use with invasive mechanical ventilation, A4483
Moisturizer, skin, A6250
Monarc-M, J7190
Monitor
apnea, E0618
blood glucose, E0607
Accu-Check, E0607
Tracer II, E0607
blood pressure, A4670
device, A9279
ECG, S0345-S0347
pacemaker, E0610, E0615
ventilator, E0450
Monitoring
electrocardiographic, S0345-S0347
Monoclonal antibodies, J7505
Monoject disposable insulin syringes, up to 1 cc, per syringe, A4206
Monojector lancet device, A4258
Morcellator, C1782
Morphine sulfate, J2270, J2271, S0093
sterile, preservative-free, J2275
Moulage, facial, D5911-D5912
Mouth exam, athletic, D9941
Mouthpiece (for respiratory equipment), A4617
Moxifloxacin, J2280
M-Prednisol-40, J1030
-80, J1040
MRI
contrast material, A9576-A9579, Q9954
low field, S8042
Mucoprotein, blood, P2038
Multifetal pregnancy reduction, ultrasound guidance, S8055
Multiple post collar, cervical, L0180-L0200
Multipositional patient support system, E0636
Muscular dystrophy, genetic test, S3853
Muse, J0275
Mutamycin, J9280
Mycophenolate mofetil, J7517
Mycophenolic acid, J7518
Mylotarg, J9300
Myochrysine, J1600
Myolin, J2360
Myotonic muscular dystrophy, genetic test, S3853
Myringotomy, S2225

N

Nabilone, oral, J8650
Nafcillin sodium, S0032
Nail trim, G0127, S0390
Nalbuphine HCl, J2300
Naloxone HCl, J2310
Naltrexone depot injection, J2315
Nandrobolic L.A., J2321
Nandrolone
  decanoate, J2320-J2322
Narcan, J2310
Narrowing device, wheelchair, E0969
Nasahist B, J0945
Nasal
  application device (for CPAP device), A7032-A7034
  vaccine inhalation, J3530
Nasogastric tubing, B4081, B4082
Navelbine, J9390
ND Stat, J0945
Nebcin, J3260
Nebulizer, E0570-E0585
  aerosol compressor, E0571
  aerosol mask, A7015
  aerosols, E0580
    Airlife Brand Misty-Neb, E0580
    Power-Mist, E0580
    Up-Draft Neb-U-Mist, E0580
    Up-Mist hand-held nebulizer, E0580
  compressor, with, E0570
    Madamist II medication compressor/nebulizer, E0570
    Pulmo-Aide compressor/nebulizer, E0570
    Schuco Mist nebulizer system, E0570
  corrugated tubing
    disposable, A7010, A7018
    non-disposable, A7011
  distilled water, A7018
  filter
    disposable, A7013
    non-disposable, A7014
  heater, E1372
  large volume
    disposable, prefilled, A7008
    disposable, unfilled, A7007
  not used with oxygen
    durable glass, A7017
  pneumatic, administration set, A7003, A7005, A7006
  pneumatic, nonfiltered, A7004
  portable, E0570
  small volume, E0574
  spacer or nebulizer, S8100
    with mask, S8101
  ultrasonic, dome and mouthpiece, A7016
  ultrasonic, reservoir bottle nondisposable, A7009
  water, A7018
  water collection device large volume nebulizer, A7012
    distilled water, A7018
NebuPent, J2545
Needle, A4215
  with syringe, A4206-A4209
  brachytherapy, C1715
  non-coring, A4212
Negative pressure wound therapy
  dressing set, A6550
  pump, E2402
Nelarabine, J9261
Nembutal sodium solution, J2515
Neocyten, J2360
Neo-Durabolic, J2320-J2322
Neomax knee support, L1800
Neoplasms, dental, D7410-D7465
Neoquess, J0500
Neosar, J9070-J9092
Neostigmine methylsulfate, J2710
Neo-Synephrine, J2370
NephrAmine, parenteral nutrition, B5000
Nesacaine MPF, J2400
Nesiritide, J2325
Neulasta, J2505
Neumega, J2355
Neuromuscular stimulator, E0745
  ambulation of spinal cord injured, E0762
Neuro-Pulse, E0720
Neurostimulator
  functional transcutaneous, E0764
  generator, C1767, C1820
  implantable
    electrode, L8680
    pulse generator, L8685-L8688
    receiver, L8682
  lead, C1778
  patient programmer, L8681
  receiver and/or transmitter, C1816
  transmitter
    external, L8683-L8684
Neutrexin, J3305
Newington
  Legg Perthes orthotic, L1710
  mobility frame, L1500
Newport Lite hip orthotic, L1685
Nextep Contour Lower Leg Walker, L2999
Nextep Low Silhouette Lower Leg Walkers, L2999
Nicotine
  gum, S4995
  patches, S4990-S4991
Niemann-Pick disease, genetic test, S3849
Nightguard, D9940
Nipent, J9268
Nitrogen mustard, J9230
Nitrous oxide, dental analgesia, D9230
Nonchemotherapy drug, oral, J8499
Noncovered services, A9270, G0293-G0294
Nonemergency transportation, A0080-A0210
Nonimpregnated gauze dressing, A6216, A6221, A6402, A6404
Nonintravenous conscious sedation, dental, D9248
Nonprescription drug, A9150
Nonthermal pulsed high frequency radiowaves treatment device, E0761
Nordryl, J1200
Norflex, J2360
Normal saline, A4216-A4217, J7030, J7040, J7042, J7050, J7130
Norplant System contraceptive, J7306
Northwestern Suspension, socket prosthesis, L6110
Not otherwise classifed drug, J3490, J7599, J7699, J7799, J8499, J8999, J9999, Q0181
Novantrone, J9293
Novo Nordisk insulin, J1815, J1817
Novo Seven, J7189
NPH insulin, J1815, S5552
Nubain, J2300
NuHope
  adhesive, 1 oz bottle with applicator, A4364
  adhesive, 3 oz bottle with applicator, A4364
  cleaning solvent, 16 oz bottle, A4455
  cleaning solvent, 4 oz bottle, A4455
  hole cutter tool, A4421
Numorphan H.P., J2410
Nursing care, in home
  licensed practical nurse, S9124
  registered nurse, S9123
Nursing home visit, dental, D9410
Nursing services, S9211-S9212, T1000-T1004
Nutri-Source, enteral nutrition, B4155
Nutrition
  counseling
    dental, D1310, D1320
    dietary, S9452
  enteral formulae, B4150-B4162
Nutrition — *continued*
  enteral infusion pump, B9000, B9002
  medical food, S9433
  parenteral infusion pump, B9004, B9006
  parenteral solution, B4164-B5200
Nutritional counseling, dietition visit, S9470

O

O&P Express
  above knee, L5210
  ankle-foot orthotic with bilateral uprights, L1990
  anterior floor reaction orthotic, L1945
  below knee, L5105
  elbow disarticulation, L6200
  hip disarticulation, L5250
  hip-knee-ankle-foot orthotic, L2080
  interscapular thoracic, L6370
  knee-ankle-foot orthotic, L2000, L2010, L2020, L2036
  knee disarticulation, L5150, L5160
  Legg Perthes orthotic, Patten bottom type, L1755
  Legg Perthes orthotic, Scottish Rite, L1730
  partial foot, L5000, L5020
  plastic foot drop brace, L1960
  supply/accessory/service, L9900
Oasis
  burn matrix, Q4103
  wound matrix, Q4102
Observation service
  direct admission, G0379
  per hour, G0378
Obturator prosthesis
  definitive, D5932
  dental
    postsurgical, D5932
    refitting, D5933
    surgical, D5931
  interim, D5936
  surgical, D5931
Occipital/mandibular support, cervical, L0160
Occlusal
  adjustment, dental, D9951-D9952
  guard, dental, D9940
  orthotic device, D7877
Occlusion/analysis, D9950
Occupational multifocal lens, V2786
Occupational therapist
  home health setting, G0152
Occupational therapy, S9129
Octafluoropropae microspheres, Q9956
Octreotide
  intramuscular form, J2353
  subcutaneous or intravenous form, J2354
Ocular device, C1784
Ocular prosthetic implant, L8610
Oculinum, J0585
Odansetron HCl, J2405, Q0179
Odontoplasty (enameloplasty), D9971
Office service, M0064
Offobock cosmetic gloves, L6895
O-Flex, J2360
Ofloxacin, S0034
Ohio Willow
  prosthetic sheath
    above knee, L8410
    below knee, L8400
    upper limb, L8415
  prosthetic sock, L8420-L8435
  stump sock, L8470-L8485
Olanzapine, S0166
Omalizumab, J2357
Omnipen-N, J0290
Oncaspar, J9266
Oncology
  breast cancer, G9071-G9073, G9131
Oncology — *continued*
  chronic myelogenous leukemia, G9139
  colon cancer, G9083-G9089
  coordination of care, G9054
  demonstration project, G9056
  esophageal cancer, G9096-G9099
  evaluation, G9050
  expectant management, G9053
  gastric cancer, G9100-G9104
  head and neck, G9110-G9112
  management
    adheres to guidelines, G9056
    differs from guidelines, G9057-G9060, G9062
    not addressed by guidelines, G9061
  management of care, G9054
  multiple myeloma, G9128, G9130
  no directed therapy, G9053
  non-Hodgkin's lymphoma, G9123-G9125, G9134-G9138
  nonsmall cell lung cancer, G9063-G9070
  ovarian cancer, G9113-G9117, G9126
  pancreatic cancer, G9105-G9108
  prostate cancer, G9077-G9083, G9132-G9133
  rectal cancer, G9090-G9095
  staging, G9050
  supervising care, G9054
  surveillance for recurrence, G9052
  treatment decision making, G9051
  unspecified service, G9055
  work up, G9050
Oncoscint, A4642
Oncovin, J9370
Ondanestron HCl, S0181
One-Button foldaway walker, E0143
One Touch
  Basic blood glucose meter, E0607
  Basic test strips, box of 50, A4253
  Profile blood glucose meter, E0607
Onlay, dental
  fixed partial denture retainer, metallic, D6602, D6615
  metallic, D2542-D2544
  porcelain/ceramic, D2642-D2644
  resin-based composite, D2662, D2664
  titanium, D6634
Operculectomy, D7971
Oprelvekin, J2355
Oral
  airway device, E0485-E0486
  disease
    test for detection, D0431
    test for susceptibility, D0421
  examination, D0120-D0160
  hygiene instruction, D1330
  interpreter or sign language services, T1013
  pathology
    accession of tissue, D0472-D0474
    bacteriologic studies, D0415
    cytology, D0480
    other oral pathology procedures, D0502
Oral and maxillofacial surgery, D7111-D7999
Oraminic II, J0945
Organ donor procurement, S2152
Ormazine, J3230
Oropharyngeal suction catheter, A4628
Orphenadrine, J2360
Orphenate, J2360
Orthodontics, D8010-D8999
Ortho-Ease forearm crutches, E0111
Orthoflex Elastic Plaster Bandages, A4580
Orthoguard hip orthotic, L1685
Orthomedics
  ankle-foot orthotic, L1900
  pediatric hip abduction splint, L1640

Orthomedics — *continued*
plastic foot drop brace, L1960
single axis shoe insert, L2180
ultralight airplane arm abduction splint, L3960
upper extremity fracture orthotic combination, L3763
humeral, L3980
radius/ulnar, L3982
Orthomerica
below knee test socket, L5620
pediatric hip abduction splint, L1640
plastic foot drop brace, L1960
single axis shoe insert, L2180
upper extremity fracture orthotic
humeral, L3980
radius/ulnar, L3982
Orthopedic devices, E0910-E0948
cervical
Diskard head halters, E0942
Turtle Neck safety collars, E0942
Orthopedic shoes
arch support, L3040-L3100
footwear, L3201-L3265
insert, L3000-L3030
lift, L3300-L3334
miscellaneous additions, L3500-L3595
positioning device, L3140-L3170
transfer, L3600-L3649
wedge, L3340-L3420
Orthoplast Splints (and Orthoplast II Splints), A4590
Orthotic additions
carbon graphite lamination, L2755
cervical congenital torticollis, L0112
electric lock, L6638
electronic elbow with microprocessor, L7181
endoskeletal knee-shin system, L5848
with microprocessor, L5856, L5857
fracture, L2180-L2192, L3995
halo, L0859
lock mechanism for elbow, L6698
lower extremity, K0672, L2200-L2999, L5646-L5648, L5781-L5782, L5984
ratchet lock, L2430
removable soft interface, K0672
replacement strap, L4002
rocker bottom for ankle, L2232
scoliosis, L1010-L1120, L1210-L1290
shoe, L3300-L3595, L3649
shoulder lock, L6646-L6648
socket insert for elbow, L6694-L6697
spinal, L0970-L0999
suspension sleeve for knee, L5685
upper extremity joint, L3956
upper limb, L3956, L3970-L3974, L3995
vacuum pump, L5781-L5782
Orthotic appliance, D7880
Orthotic devices
additions, L5988-L5990, L6611, L6624, L6639
ankle-foot (*see also* Orthopedic shoes), E1815, E1830, L1900-L1990, L2108-L2116, L3160
anterior-posterior-lateral, L0700, L0710
cervical, L0112, L0180-L0200
cervical-thoracic-lumbar-sacral, L0700, L0710
cervical thoracic lumbar sacral, L1001
congenital trorticollis, L0112
cranial-cervical, L0113
cranial remolding, S1040
elbow, E1800, L3700-L3740
finger, L3925, L3927
fracture, L3980-L3984
halo, L0810-L0830
hand, E1805, E1825, L3900-L3929

Orthotic devices — *continued*
hip, L1600-L1686
hip-knee-ankle-foot, L2040-L2090
interface material, E1820
knee, E1810, L1800-L1860
knee-ankle-foot, L2000-L2038, L2126-L2136
Legg Perthes, A4565, L1700-L1755
lumbar, L0625-L0627
lumbar-sacral, L0628-L0640
lumbar-sacral, hip, femur, L1690
multiple post collar, L0180-L0200
not otherwise specified, L0999, L1499, L2999, L3999, L5999, L7499, L8039
pneumatic splint, L4350-L4380
repair or replacement, L4000-L4210
replace soft interface material, L4392-L4394
sacroiliac, L0621-L0624
scoliosis, L1000, L1200, L1300-L1499
shoe, *see* Orthopedic shoes
shoulder, L3650-L3675
shoulder-elbow-wrist-hand, L3960-L3969
spinal, cervical, L0112, L0180-L0200
thoracic, L0210
thoracic-hip-knee-ankle, L1500-L1520
toe, E1830
transfer (shoe orthotic), L3600-L3640
walking splint, nonpneumatic, L4386
wrist hand, L3150
wrist hand finger, L3806-L3808, L3931
Or-Tyl, J0500
Oseltamivir phosphate, G9019, G9035
Osmolite, enteral nutrition, B4150
HN, B4150
Osseous dental surgery, graft, D4260-D4264
Ossicula prosthetic implant, L8613
Osteitis, localized, dry socket, D9930
Osteogenic stimulator, E0747-E0749, E0760
Osteoplasty, D7940
Osteotomy, D7944
Osteotomy
dental, D7941-D7945
segmented/subapical, D7944
Osteotomy, periacetabular, S2115
Ostomy
absorbant material, A4422
accessories, A5093
adhesive remover wipes, A4365
appliance belt, A4367
clamp, A4363
filter, A4368
irrigation supply, A4398, A4399
pediatric one-piece system, A5061, A5062
pediatric two-piece drainable pouch, A5063
pouch, A4416-A4420, A4423-A4434
drainable, A4412, A4413
pediatric, A5061-A5062
skin barrier, A4411, A4414-A4415
extended wear, A4407-A4410
paste, A4405-A4406
wipes or swabs, A5120
vent, A4366
Otto Bock prosthesis
battery charger, six volt, L7362
battery, six volt, L7360
hook adapter, L6628
lamination collar, L6629
pincher tool, L6810
wrist, L6629, L7260
Overdenture, D5860-D5861
Overlay, mattress, E0371-E0373
Ovulation induction, S4042
Owens & Minor
cervical collar, L0140
cervical helmet, L0120
Oxacillin sodium, J2700

Oxaliplatin, J9263
Oximeter, E0445
probe, A4606
Oxi-Uni-Pak, E0430
Oxygen
ambulance, A0422
battery
charger, E1357
pack, E1356
chamber, hyperbaric, topical, A4575
concentrator, E1390, E1391
portable, rental, E1392
gaseous, K0738, S8120
liquid, S8121
mask, A4620
medication supplies, A4611-A4627
portable, E0443-E0444, K0738
power adapter, E1358
rack/stand, E1355
regulator, E1353
respiratory equipment/supplies, A4611-A4627, E0424-E0480
Argyle Sentinel seal chest drainage unit, E0460
Oxi-Uni-Pak, E0430
supplies and equipment, E0425-E0444, E0455, E1353-E1406
tent, E0455
tubing, A4616
water vapor enriching system, E1405, E1406
wheeled cart, E1354
Oxymorphone HCl, J2410
Oxytetracycline HCl, J2460
Oxytocin, J2590
removable soft interface, K0672

P

Pacemaker
dual chamber
non-rate responsive, C2619
rate responsive, C1785
lead, C1779, C1898, C1899
monitor, E0610, E0615
other than single or dual chamber, C2621
single chamber
non-rate responsive, C2620
rate responsive, C1786
Pacer manual wheelchair, K0003
Packing strips, A6407
Paclitaxel, J9265
protein bound particles, J9264
Pad
abdominal, L1270
adhesive, A6203-A6205, A6212-A6214, A6219-A6221, A6237-A6239, A6245-A6247, A6254-A6256
alginate, A6196-A6199
alternating pressure, E0181
arm, K0019
asis, L1250
condylar, L2810
crutch, A4635
gel pressure, E0185, E0196
gluteal, L2650
gradient pressure pads, S8421-S8429
heating, E0210, E0215, E0217, E0238, E0249
heel, L3480, L3485
kyphosis, L1020, L1025
lumbar, L1030, L1040, L1240
nonadhesive (dressing), A6209-A6211, A6216-A6218, A6222-A6224, A6228-A6230, A6234-A6236, A6242-A6244
orthotic device interface, E1820
pressure, E0181-E0182
replacement, infrared heat system, A4639
rib gusset, L1280
sheepskin, E0188, E0189
shoe, L3430-L3485
stabilizer, L3170

Pad — *continued*
sternal, L1050
thoracic, L1060, L1260
triceps, L6100
trocanteric, L1290
truss, L8320, L8330
water circulating, cold, with pump, E0218
water circulating, heat, unit, E0249
water circulating, heat, with pump, E0217
water pressure, E0198
Padden Shoulder Immobilizer, L3670
Pail, for use with commode chair, E0167
Palladium, C2640-C2641
Palonosetron HCl, J2469
Pamidronate disodium, J2430
Panel
gene
for management of breast cancer, S3854
Pan, for use with commode chair, E0167
Pantoprazole sodium, C9113, S0164
Papanicolaou (Pap) screening smear, P3000, P3001, Q0091
Papaverine HCl, J2440
Paraffin, A4265
bath unit, E0235
Paragard T 380-A, IUD, J7300
Paramedic intercept, S0208
Paranasal sinus ultrasound, S9024
Paraplatin, J9045
Parapodium, mobility frame, L1500
Parenteral nutrition
administration kit, B4224
home infusion therapy, S9364-S9368
pump, B9004, B9006
solution, B4164-B5200
supplies, not otherwise classified, B9999
supply kit, B4220, B4222
Parenting class, S9444
infant safety, S9447
Paricalcitol, J2501
Parking fee, nonemergency transport, A0170
Partial dentures
fixed
implant/adjustment-supported retainers, D6068-D6077
pontic, D6210-D6252
retainers, D6545-D6792
removable, D5211-D5281
PASRR, T2010-T2011
Passive motion
continuous exercise device, E0936
Paste, conductive, A4558
conductive, A4558
coupling for ultrasound, A4559
Pathology and laboratory tests, P9010-P9615
surgical
prostate, G0416-G0419
Patient lift, E0625, E0637, E0639, E0640
Patten Bottom, Legg Perthes orthotic, L1755
Pavlik harness, hip orthotic, L1650
Peak flow meter, S8110
portable, S8096
Pediatric hip abduction splint
Orthomedics, L1640
Orthomerica, L1640
Pediculosis treatment, A9180
PEFR, peak expiratory flow rate meter, A4614
Pegademase bovine, J2504
Pegaspargase, J9266
Pegasys, S0145
Pegfilgastrim, J2505
Peg-L-asparaginase, J9266
Pelvic and breast exam, G0101
Pelvic belt/harness/boot, E0944
Pemetrexed, J9305

Penicillin G
benzathine and penicillin G procaine, J0530-J0580
potassium, J2540
procaine, aqueous, J2510
Penlet II lancet device, A4258
Penlet lancet device, A4258
Pentamidine isethionate, J2545, S0080
Pentastarch, J2513
Pentazocine HCl, J3070
Pentobarbital sodium, J2515
Pentostatin, J9268
Percussor, E0480
Percutaneous
access system, A4301
Perflexane lipid microspheres, Q9955
Perflutren lipid microsphere, Q9957
Performance Wrap (KO), L1825
Periapical service, D3410-D3470
Periodontal procedures, D4210-D4999
Periradicular/apicoectomy, D3410-D3426
Perlstein, ankle-foot orthotic, L1920
Permapen, J0560-J0580
Peroneal strap, L0980
Peroxide, A4244
Perphenazine, J3310, Q0175-Q0176
Persantine, J1245
Personal care services, T1019-T1020
Pessary, A4561-A4562
PET imaging
any site, NOS, G0235
breast, G0252
whole body, G0219
Pfzerpen, J2540
A.S., J2510
PGE1, J0270
Phamacologicals, dental, D9610, D9630
Pharmacy
compounding and dispensing, S9430
dispensing fee
inhalation drugs
per 30 days, Q0513
per 90 days, Q0514
supply fee
imitial immunosuppressive drugs, Q0510
oral anticancer antiemetic or immunosuppressive drug, Q0511-Q0512
Pharmaplast disposable insulin syringes, per syringe, A4206
Phelps, ankle-foot orthotic, L1920
Phenazine (25, 50), J2550
Phenergan, J2550
Phenobarbital sodium, J2560
Phentolamine mesylate, J2760
Phenylephrine HCl, J2370
Phenytoin sodium, J1165
Philadelphia tracheotomy cervical collar, L0172
Philly One-piece Extrication collar, L0150
pHisoHex solution, A4246
Photofrin, J9600
Photographs, dental, diagnostic, D0350
Phototherapy
home visit service (Bili-Lite), S9098
keratectomy (PKT), S0812
light (bilirubin), E0202
Physical exam
for college, S0622
related to surgical procedure, S0260
Physical therapy, S8990
shoulder stretch device, E1841
Physical therapy/therapist
home health setting, G0151, S9131
Physician management
home care
episodic, S0272
hospice monthly, S0271
standard monthly, S0270
Physician quality reporting indicators (PQRI)
ABI, G8407-G8409, G8513-G8515
ACE or ARB therapy, G8472-G8475, G8479-G8481, G8506
alarm symptoms, G8248, G8274
antibiotic prophylaxis, G8152-G8196, G8527-G8529
anticoagulant, G8226
antidepressant medication, G8126-G8131
antiplatelet therapy, G8226, G8521-G8523
antivirals, G8458-G8463
asthma, G8370, G8391
atrial fibrillation, G8183-G8184
AV fistula, G8530-G8532
back pain, G8493, G8502
beta-blocker, G8450-G8452
blood pressure, G8476-G8478
BMI, G8417-G8422
breast cancer, G8376, G8380-G8381
cancer stage
lung and esophageal, G8518-G8520
CEA, G8523-G8526
chemotherapy, G8371-G8374
cognitive impairment, G8434-G8436
colon cancer, G8371-G8372, G8377
chemotherapy, G8373
COPD, G8093-G8094
coronary artery bypass graft (CABG), G8159-G8167, G8497, G8544
coronary artery disease (CAD), G8036-G8041, G8182, G8489, G8498
CT or MRI, G8243
deep vein thrombosis prophylactic, G8217
depression, G8431-G8433, G8466-G8467, G8510-G8511
DEXA, G8399-G8400
diabetes, G8016-G8026, G8385-G8386, G8390, G8485, G8494
dysphagia screening, G8234
elder maltreatment, G8534-G8538
EMR/CCHIT, G8447-G8449
endoscopy
end stage renal disease measure reporting, G8488
ESRD, G8075-G8082, G8085, G8387-G8388
fall risk, G8516-G8517
footwear evaluation, G8410, G8415-G8416
functional outcome, G8539-G8543
glaucoma, G8305-G8308
hearing assessment, G8057-G8059
heart failure patient, G8027-G8032, G8183-G8184
HIV/AIDS, G8491, G8500
influenza vaccination, G8108-G8110, G8423-G8426, G8482-G8484
intraocular pressure, G8302-G8304
kidney disease, G8487, G8495
left ventricular ejection fraction (LVEF), G8395-G8396, G8450-G8452, G8468-G8472
leukemia, G8375, G8384
mammogram, G8111-G8114
medication list/review, G8427-G8430
mole assessment, G8246
multiple myeloma, G8382
mycardial infarction, G8006-G8011, G8033-G8035
myelodysplastic syndrome (MDS), G8384, G8389
neurological exam, G8404-G8406
osteoporosis, G8051-G8053, G8099-G8100, G8103-G8104, G8106-G8107, G8185-G8186, G8401
pain, G8440-G8442, G8508-G8509, G8512
perioperative care, G8492, G8501
Physician quality reporting indicators (PQRI) — *continued*
pneumococcal vaccination, G8115-G8117
pneumonia, G8012-G8014
prescriptiona, G8443-G8446
preventive care, G8486, G8496
prophylactic antibiotic, G8503-G8505
prostate cancer, G8464-G8465
radiation therapy, G8378-G8379, G8383
rehabilitation, G8238
retinopathy, G8397-G8398
rheumatoid arthritis, G8490, G8499
systemic clinical database registry, G8533
thromboembolism prophylaxis, G8155-G8157
tobacco use, G8402-G8403, G8453-G8457
TPA, G8231
treatment plan, G8437-G8439
urinary incontinence assessment, G8060-G8062
verification of medication, G8507
warfarin therapy, G8183-G8184
Phytonadione, J3430
Pillo pump, E0182
Pillow
abduction, E1399
decubitus care, E0190
nasal, A7029
positioning, E0190
Pin retention, per tooth, D2951
Pinworm examination, Q0113
Piperacillin sodium, S0081
Pit and fissure sealant, D1351
Pitocin, J2590
Placement
applicator, breast, C9726
fixation device, D7998
interim implant body, D6012
interstitial device radiotherapy, other than prostate, C9728
temporary anchorage device, D7292-D7294
Planing, dental root, D0350
Plasma
frozen, P9058-P9060
multiple donor, pooled, frozen, P9023
protein fraction, P9048
single donor, fresh frozen, P9017
Plastazote, L3002, L3252, L3253, L3265, L5654-L5658
Plaster
bandages
Orthoflex Elastic Plaster Bandages, A4580
Specialist Plaster Bandages, A4580
Genmould Creamy Plaster, A4580
Specialist J-Splint Plaster Roll Immobilizer, A4580
Specialist Plaster Roll Immobilizer, A4580
Specialist Plaster Splints, A4580
Platelet
concentrate, each unit, P9019
rich plasma, each unit, P9020
Platelets, P9032-P9040, P9052-P9053
Platform attachment
forearm crutch, E0153
walker, E0154
Platform, for home blood glucose monitor, A4255
Platinol, J9060, J9062
Plenaxis, J0128
Pleural catheter, A7042
drainage bottle, A7043
Plicamycin, J9270
Plumbing, for home ESRD equipment, A4870
PMD
See power mobility device
Pneumatic
appliance, E0655-E0673, L4350-L4380
compressor, E0650-E0652, E0675
splint, L4350-L4380
tire, wheelchair, E2211, E2214
insert, E2213
tube, E2212, E2215
Pneumatic nebulizer
administration set
small volume
filtered, A7006
non-filtered, A7003
non-disposable, A7005
small volume, disposable, A7004
Pneumococcal conjugate vaccine, S0195
Polaris, E0601
Polaris Lt, E0601
Polocaine, J0670
Polycillin-N, J0290
Polycose, enteral nutrition
liquid, B4155
powder, B4155
Poly-l-lactic acid, S0196
Pontic
indirect resin based composite, D6205
titanium, D6214
Poor blood, each unit, P9016
Porfimer, J9600
Pork insulin, J1815, J1817
Port
indwelling, C1788
Portable
equipment transfer, R0070-R0076
hemodialyzer system, E1635
nebulizer, E0570
x-ray equipment, Q0092
Portagen Powder, enteral nutrition, B4150
Posey restraints, E0700
Positive airway pressure device supply, A7046
Post and core, dental, D2952-D2954, D2957, D6970-D6972, D6976-D6977
Post-coital examination, Q0115
Postdischarge services
LVRS surgery, G0305
Post removal, dental, D2955
Postural drainage board, E0606
Potassium
chloride, J3480
hydroxide (KOH) preparation, Q0112
Pouch
Active Life convex one-piece urostomy, A4421
closed, A4387, A5052
drainable, A4388-A4389, A5061
fecal collection, A4330
Little Ones Sur-fit mini, A5054
ostomy, A4375-A4378, A4387-A4391, A4416-A4420, A4423-A4434, A5051-A5054, A5061-A5063
pediatric, drainable, A5061
Pouchkins pediatric ostomy system, A5061, A5062, A5073
Sur-Fit, drainable, A5063
urinary, A4379-A4383, A4391, A5071-A5073
urosotomy, A5073
Power
mist nebulizer, E0580
mobility device, K0800-K0812, K0899
wheelchair, K0813-K0898
pediatric, E1239
Power mobility device
does not meet criteria, K0899
group 1, K0800-K0802, K0813-K0816
group 2, K0806-K0808, K0820-K0843
group 3, K0849-K0864

Power mobility device — *continued*
group 4, K0868-K0886
group 5, K0890-K0891
not coded by SADMERC, K0899
not otherwise classified (NOC), K0812, K0898
Power operated vehicle
group 1, K0800-K0802
group 2, K0806-K0808
not otherwise classified (NOC), K0812
Pralidoxime chloride, J2730
Precision attachment, dental, D5862, D6950
Precision, enteral nutrition
HN, B4153
Isotonic, B4153
Predalone-50, J2650
Predcor (-25, -50), J2650
Predicort-50, J2650
Prednisolone
acetate, J2650
oral, J7506, J7510
Prednisone, J7506
Predoject-50, J2650
Prefabricated crown, D2930-D2933
Prefabricated post and core, dental, D2954, D6972
each additional (same tooth), D2957, D6977
Pregnancy care, H1000-H1005
Pregnyl, J0725
Premarin IV, J1410
Premium knee sleeve, L1830
Prenatal care, H1000-H1005
Preoperative Services
LVRS surgery, G0302-G0304
Preparation
saliva samples, D0417
Preparatory prosthesis, L5510-L5595
Prescription drug, — *see also* Table of Drugs, J3490, J8499
chemotherapy, J8999, J9999
nonchemotherapy, J8499
Pressure
alarm, dialysis, E1540
pad, E0181-E0182
PressureGuard II, E0186
PressureKair mattress overlay, E0197
Prestige blood glucose monitor, E0607
Pre-Vent heel & elbow protector, E0191
Prevention, developmental delay, H2037
Preventive
dental procedures, D1110-D1550
foot care, S0390
health Medicare
ECG, G0403-G0405
exam, G0402
Primacor, J2260
PriMatrix, Q4110
Primaxin, J0743
Priscoline HCl, J2670
Probe
cryoablation, C2618
oximeter, A4606
percutaneous lumbar discectomy, C2614
Procainamide HCl, J2690
Procarbazine HCl, S0182
Processing
breast milk, T2101
Prochlorperazine, J0780, Q0164-Q0165
oral, S0183
Procrit, J0885-J0886
Procurement, organ donor, S2152
Procuren, S9055
Profasi HP, J0725
Proflnine Heat-Treated, J7194
Progesterone, J2675
Prograf, J7507
Prolastin, J0256
Proleukin, J9015
Prolixin decanoate, J2680
Prolotherapy, M0076
Promazine HCl, J2950
Promethazine and meperdine, J2180
Promethazine HCl, J2550, Q0169-Q0170
Promix, enteral nutrition, B4155
Pronation/supination device, forearm, E1802
Pronestyl, J2690
Propac, enteral nutrition, B4155
Prophylaxis, dental, D1110, D1120
Proplex (-T and SX-T), J7194
Propranolol HCl, J1800
Prorex (-25, -50), J2550
Prostaglandin E1, J0270
Prostaphlin, J2700
Prostate
specific antigen test (PSA), G0103
surgical pathology, G0416-G0419
Prosthesis
addition
lower extremity prosthesis, L5858
adhesive, used for facial
remover, A4365
auricular, D5914
breast, C1789, L8000-L8035, L8600
cranial, D5924
dental, fixed, D6210-D6999
dental, removable, D5110-D5899
eye, L8610, V2623-V2629
finger joint, L8659
ftting, L5400-L5460, L6380-L6388
grasper, L6881
hand, L6000-L6020, L6708-L6709, L7007-L7008
hemifacial, L8044
hook, L6703-L6707, L7009
implants, L8600-L8699
larynx, L8500, L8505
lower extremity, L5700-L5999, L8642
mandibular resection, D5934-D5935
maxiofacial, provided by a nonphysician, L8040-L8048
metacarpal, L8631
midfacial, L8041
miscellaneous service, L8499
nasal septal, L8047
obturator, D5931-D5933, D5936
ocular, D5916
orbital, D5915
palatal, D5954-D5959
partial facial, L8046
penile
inflatable, C1813
non-inflatable, C2622
repair, L7520
repair or modification, maxillofacial, L8048-L8049
socks (shrinker, sheath, stump sock), L8400-L8480
tracheoesophageal, L8511-L8514
tracheoesophageal gelatin capsule, L8515
tracheostomy speaking, L8501
unspecified maxillofacial, L8048
upper extremity, L6000-L6915
urinary sphincter, C1815
vacuum erection system, L7900
Prosthetic
additions
lower extremity, L5610
upper extremity, L6600-L7274
device, implanted, C9899
hand, L6708-L6709, L6713-L6714, L6722
hook, L6706-L6707, L6711-L6712, L6721, L6722, L7009
shrinker, L8440-L8465
Prosthetic shrinker, L8440-L8465
Prosthodontic procedures
fixed, D6210-D6999
implant-supported, D6055-D6079
maxillofacial, D5911-D5999
pediatric partial denture, D6985
removable, D5110-D5999
Prostigmin, J2710
Prostin VR Pediatric, J0270
Protamine sulfate, A4802, J2720
Protectant, skin, A6250
Protector, heel or elbow, E0191
Protirelin, J2725
Protonix, S0164
Protopam chloride, J2730
Provisional, dental
retainer crown (FPD), D6793
single crown, D2799
Prozine-50, J2950
Psychiatric care, H0036-H0037, H2013-H2014
Psychological services
CORF, G0409
psychotherapy
group, G0410-G0411
PTK, S0812
Pulmo-Aide compressor
nebulizer, E0570
Pulpal debridement, D3221
Pulpal therapy, on primary teeth, D3230, D3240
Pulp cap, D3110, D3120
Pulp capping, D3110, D3120
Pulpotomy, D3220, D3222
vitality test, D0460
Pulp sedation, D2940
Pulp vitality test, D0460
Pulse generator
ear, E2120
battery, A4638
Pump
alternating pressure pad, E0182
ambulatory infusion, E0781
ambulatory insulin, E0784
Bio Flote alternating pressure pad, E0182
blood, dialysis, E1620
breast, E0602-E0604
supplies, A4281-A4286
Broncho-Cath endobronchial tubes, with CPAP, E0601
enteral infusion, B9000, B9002
supply, K0552
gastric suction, E2000
Gomco lightweight mobile aspirator, E0600
Gomco portable aspirator, E0600
heparin infusion, E1520
implantable infusion, E0782, E0783
implantable infusion, refill kit, A4220
infusion
nonprogrammable, C1891, C2626
supplies, A4230-A4232
insulin, external, E0784
instruction, S9145
negative pressure wound therapy, E2402
parenteral infusion, B9004, B9006, K0455
Pillo alternating pressure pad, E0182
speech aid, D5952-D5953, D5960
suction
CPAP, E0601
gastric, E2000
portable, E0600
TenderCloud alternating pressure pad, E0182
water circulating pad, E0217, E0218, E0236
Purification system, E1610, E1615
Purified pork insulin, J1815, J1817
Pyeloscopy
for ureteral calculi, S2070
Pyridoxine HCl, J3415

Q

Quad cane, E0105
Quadri-Poise canes, E0105
Quelicin, J0330
Quick Check blood glucose test strips, box of 50, A4253
Quick release restraints, E0700
Quikfit crutch, E0114
Quik-Fold Walkers, E0141, E0143
Quinoprestin, J2770

R

Rack/stand, oxygen, E1355
Radiation, dental
carrier, D5983
cone locator, D5985
shield, D5984
Radiation dosimeter, implantable, ea, A4650
Radiation therapy, intraoperative, S8049
Radioelements for brachytherapy, Q3001
Radiofrequency transmitter, sacral root neurostimulator, replacement, L8684
Radiograph, dental, D0210-D0340
Radioimmunoscintigraphy, S8080
Radiolabeled product provided during inpatient stay, C9898
Radiology service, R0070-R0076
Radiopharmaceutical
ammonia N-13, A9526
chromic phosphate P32, A9564
cyanocobalamin cobalt Co 57, A9559
diagnostic imaging agent, A4641, A4642, A9544, A9605
gallium Ga 67, A9556
I-131 tositumomab, A9544
indium I-111
ibitumomab tiuxetan, A9542
pentreotide, A9572
satumomab pendetide, A4642
inpatient, C9898
rubidium RB-82, A9555
sodium
fluoride F-18, diagnostic, A9580
iodide I-131, A9528-A9531
phosphate, A9563
technetium Tc 99m
arcitumomab, A9568
bicisate, A9557
depreotide, A9536
disofenin, A9510
exametazime, A9521, A9569
fanolesomab, A9566
glucepatate, A9550
labeled red blood cells, A9560
macroaggregated albumin, A9540
mebrofenin, A9537
medronate, A9503
mertiatide, A9562
oxidronate, A9561
pentetate, A9539, A9567
pertechnetate, A9512
sestamibi, A9500
sulfur colloid, A9541
teboroxime, A9501
tetrofosmin, A9502
therapeutic, A9517, A9543, A9545, A9600, A9605
xenon Xe 133, A9558
yttrium 90 ibritumomab tiuxetan, A9543
Rail
bathtub, E0241, E0242, E0246
bed, E0305, E0310
toilet, E0243
Rancho hip action, hip orthotic, L1680
Range of motion device
shoulder, E1841
Raptiva, S0162
Rasburicase, J2783
Rascal, power wheelchair, K0010
Ready-For-Use wooden crutches, E0113
Reassessment, nutrition therapy, G0270-G0271
Receiver
interstitial glucose monitor, A9278
Recement
cast or prefabricated post and core, D2915
crown, D2920, D6092
denture, D6093
inlay, D2910

Recement — *continued*
retainers, D8693
Recombinant
ankle splints, L4392-L4398
DNA insulin, J1815, J1817
Recombinate, J7192
Reconstruction
breast, S2066-S2067
Red blood cells, P9038-P9040
Red blood cells, each unit, P9021, P9022
Red Dot
crutches, E0114
folding walkers, E0135, E0143
Redisol, J3420
Regitine, J2760
Reglan, J2765
Regular insulin, J1815
Regulator, oxygen, E1353
Rehabilitation
program, H2001
service
juveniles, H2033
mental health clubhouse, H2030-H2031
psychosocial, H2017-H2018
social work and psychological, G0409
substance abuse, H2034-H2036
supported employment, H2023-H2024
vestibular, S9476
Reimplantation, dental
accidentally evulsed, D7270
intentional, D3470
Relefact TRH, J2725
Relenza, G9018
Remicade, J1745
Removal
applicator, breast, C9726
fixed space maintainer, D1555
RemRes, E0601
REMStar, E0601
Renacidin, Q2004
RenAmin, parenteral nutrition, B5000
Renu, enteral nutrition, B4150
ReoPro, TRH, J0130
Repair
contract, ERSD, A4890
dental, D2980, D3351-D3353, D5510-D5630, D6090, D6980, D7852, D7955
durable medical equipment, E1340
hearing aid, V5014, V5336
hernia
diphragmatic
fetus, S2400
laparoscopy
home dialysis equipment, A4890
occlusal guard, dental, D9942
orthotic, L4000-L4130
prosthetic, L7500, L7510, L7520
skilled technical, E1340
Replacement
battery, A4233-A4236, A4630
ear pulse generator, A4638
external infusion pump, K0601-K0605
handgrip for cane, crutch, walker, A4636
implant/abutment prosthesis, D6091
ostomy filters, A4421
sleeve, intermittent limb compression device, A4600
tip for cane, crutch, walker, A4637
underarm pad for crutch, A4635
Repositioning device, mandibular, S8262
Rep-Pred
40, J1030
80, J1040
ResCap headgear, A7035
Reservoir
metered dose inhaler, A4627
Residential care, T2032-T2033
Resin dental restoration, D2330-D2394
Resipiradyne II Plus pulmonary function/ventilation monitor, E0450
ResMed Sb Elite, E0601
RespiGam, J1565
Respiratory syncytial virus immune globulin, J1565
Respiratory therapy, G0237-G0238
Respite care, T1005
in home, S9125
not in home, H0045
Restorations, dental
amalgam, D2140-D2161
gold foil, D2410-D2430
inlay/onlay, D2510-D2664, D6600-D6615
resin-based composite, D2330-D2394
Restorative
dental work, D2330-D2999
injection
face, S0196
Restorative injection, face, S0196
Restraint
any type, E0710
belts
Posey, E0700
Secure-All, E0700
Bite disposable jaw locks, E0700
body holders
Houdini security suit, E0700
Quick Release, one piece, E0700
Secure-All, one piece, E0700
System2 zippered, E0700
UltraCare vest-style
with sleeves, E0700
hand
Secure-All finger control mit, E0700
limb holders
Posey, E0700
Quick Release, E0700
Secure-All, E0700
pelvic
Secure-All, E0700
Resurfacing
total hip, S2118
Retail therapy item, miscellaneous, T1999
Retainers, dental
fixed partial denture, D6545-D6792
implant/abutment supported, D6068-D6077
orthodontic, D8680
Retinal
device, intraoperative, C1784
exam for diabetes, S3000
tamponade, C1814
telescreening, S0625
Retinoblastoma, genetic test, S3841
Retrieval device, insertable, C1773
Retrograde dental filling, D3430
Rhesonativ, J2790
Rheumatrex, J8610
RhoGAM, J2790
Rho(D) immune globulin, human, J2790, J2792
minidose, J2788
Rib belt
thoracic, L0210, L0220
Don-Joy, L0210
Rice ankle splint, L1904
Richfoam convoluted&flat overlays, E0199
Ride Lite 200, Ride Lite 9000, manual wheelchair, K0004
Ridge augmentation/sinus lift, dental, D7950
Rimantadine HCl, G9020, G9036
Rimso, J1212
Ringer's lactate infusion, J7120
Ring, ostomy, A4404
Risperidone, long acting, J2794
Rituxan, J9310
Rituximab, J9310
Riveton, foot orthotic, L3140, L3150
RN services, T1002
Road Savage power wheelchair, K0011
Road Warrior power wheelchair, K0011
Robaxin, J2800
Robin-Aids, prosthesis
partial hand, L6000-L6020
Robotic surgical system, S2900
Rocephin, J0696
Rocking bed, E0462
Rollabout chair, E1031
Root canal therapy, D3310-D3353
Root planning and scaling, dental, D4341
Root removal, dental, D7140, D7250
Root resection/amputation, dental, D3450
Ropivacaine hydrochloride, J2795
RSV immune globulin, J1565
Rubex, J9000
Rubidium RB-82, A9555
Rubramin PSC, J3420

S

Sabre power wheelchair, K0011
Sacral nerve stimulation test
lead, each, A4290
Sacroiliac
injection, G0259-G0260
orthotic, L0621-L0624
Safe, hand prosthesis, L5972
Safety
enclosure frame/canopy, for hospital bed, E0316
equipment, E0700
eyeglass frames, S0516
vest, wheelchair, E0980
Saline, A4216-A4217
hypertonic, J7130
solution, J7030-J7050
Saliva
analysis, D0418
artificial, A9155
collection and preparation, D0417
Salivary gland excision, D7983
Saliva test, hormone level
during menopause, S3650
preterm labor risk, S3652
Samarium Sm-153 lexidronamm, A9605
Sam Brown, Legg Perthes orthotic, A4565
Sansibar Plus, E0601
Saquinavir, S0140
Sargramostim (GM-CSF), J2820
Satumomab pendetide, A4642
Scale, for dialysis, E1639
Schuco
mist nebulizer system, E0570
vac aspirator, E0600
Scintimammography, S8080
Scleral lens bandage, S0515
Scoliosis, L1000, L1200, L1300-L1499
additions, L1010-L1120, L1210-L1290
Scott ankle splint, canvas, L1904
Scott-Craig, stirrup orthotic, L2260
Scottish-Rite, Legg Perthes orthotic, L1730
Screening
abdominal aortic aneurysm, G0389
alcohol and/or drug, H0049
cervical or vaginal, G0101
colorectal cancer, G0104-G0106, G0120-G0122
cytopathology, G0123-G0124, G0141, G0143-G0148
digital rectal, annual, S0605
early periodic screening diagnosis and treatment (EPSDT), S0302
glaucoma, G0117-G0118
gynecological
established patient, S0612
new patient, S0610
maternal serum quad marker, S3626
newborn metabolic, S3620
Screening — *continued*
ophthalmological, including refraction
established patient, S0621
new patient, S0620
preadmission, T2010-T2011
proctoscopy, S0601
program participation, T1023
prostate
digital, rectal, G0102
prostate specific antigen test (PSA), G0103
retinal telescreening, S0625
Sealant
dental, D1351
pulmonary, liquid, C2615
skin, A6250
tooth, D1351
Seat
attachment, walker, E0156
insert, wheelchair, E0992
lift (patient), E0621, E0627-E0629
positiioning, T5001
Seattle Carbon Copy II, foot prosthesis, L5976
Sectioning
denture, D9120
Secure-All
restraints, E0700
universal pelvic traction belt, E0890
Sedation, dental
deep, D9220-D9221
intravenous, conscious, D9241-D9242
non-intravenous, D9248
Sedative filling, dental, D2940
Selestoject, J0704
Semilente insulin, J1815
Sensitivity study, P7001
sensor
invasive blood glucose monitor, A9276
Septal defect implant system, C1817
Sequestrectomy, dental, D7550
Sermorelin acetate, Q0515
Serum clotting time tube, A4771
SEWHO, L3960-L3974
Sexa, G0130
Sheath
introducer
guiding, C1766, C1892, C1893
other than guiding, C1894, C2629, C2629
Sheepskin pad, E0188, E0189
Shoes
arch support, L3040-L3100
for diabetics, A5500-A5508
insert, L3000-L3030
for diabetics, A5512-A5513
lift, L3300-L3334
miscellaneous additions, L3500-L3595
orthopedic (*see* Orthopedic shoes), L3201-L3265
positioning device, L3140-L3170
post-operative
Specialist Health/Post Operative Shoe, A9270
transfer, L3600-L3649
wedge, L3340-L3485
Shoulder
abduction positioner, L3999
braces, L3999
Masterhinge Shoulder Brace 3, L3999
disarticulation, prosthetic, L6300-L6320, L6550
orthotic (SO), L3650-L3675
elastic shoulder immobilizer, L3670
Padden Shoulder Immobilizer, L3670
Sling and Swathe, L3670
Velpeau Sling Immobilizer, L3670
spinal, cervical, L0112

Shoulder-elbow-wrist-hand orthotic (SEWHO), L3960-L3969
Shower chair, E0240
Shunt accessory for dialysis, A4740
aqueous, L8612
Sialodochoplasty, D7982
Sialography, D0310
Sialolithotomy, D7980
Sickle cell anemia, genetic test, S3850
Sierra wrist flexion unit, L6805
Sigmoidoscopy, cancer screening, G0104, G0106
Sign language or oral interpreter services, T1013
Sildenafil citrate, S0090
Silenzio Elite, E0601
Single bar "AK," ankle-foot orthotic, L2000, L2010
Single bar "BK," ankle-foot orthotic, L1980
Sinus lift, dental, D7950
Sinusol-B, J0945
Sinusotomy, in dentistry, D7560
Sirolimus, J7520
Sitz bath, E0160-E0162
Skilled nurse, G0128
home health setting, G0154
Skin
barrier, ostomy, A4362, A4369, A4385
bond or cement, ostomy, A4364
gel protective dressing wipes, A5120
sealant, protectant, moisturizer, A6250
Skin substitute
Apligraf, Q4101
Cymetra, Q4112
Dermagraft, Q4106
GammaGraft, Q4111
GRAFTJACKET, Q4107, Q4113
Integra, Q4104-Q4105, Q4108, Q4114
not otherwise specified, Q4100
Oasis, Q4102-Q4103
PriMatrix, Q4110
TissueMend, Q4109
Sleep study
home, G0398-G0400
Sleeve
intermittent limb compression device, A4600
mastectomy, L8010
Sling, A4565
axilla, L1010
Legg Perthes, A4565
lumbar, L1090
patient lift, E0621, E0630, E0635
pelvic, L2580
Sam Brown, A4565
SEWHO, L3969
trapezius, L1070
Sling and Swathe, orthotic, L3670
Smoking cessation
classes, S9453
treatment, S9075
Social worker
CORF, G0409
home health setting, G0155
nonemergency transport, A0160
visit in home, S9127
Sock
body sock, L0984
prosthetic sock, L8420-L8435, L8480, L8485
stump sock, L8470-L8485
Sodium
chromate Cr-51, A9553
ferric gluconate in sucrose, J2916
iothalamate I-125, A9554
sodium iodide I-131
diagnostic imaging agent, A9528, A9531
therapeutic agent, A9530
succinate, J1720
Softclix lancet device, A4258
Soft Touch II lancet device, A4258
Soft Touch lancets, box of 100, A4259
Solganal, J2910
Solo Cast Sole, L3540
Solo LX, E0601
Solu-Cortef, J1720
Solu-Medrol, J2920, J2930
Solurex, J1100
Solurex LA, J1100
Solution
calibrator, A4256
dialysate, A4728, A4760
enteral formulae, B4150-B4155
parenteral nutrition, B4164-B5200
Somatrem, J2940
Somatropin, J2941
S.O.M.I. brace, L0190, L0200
S.O.M.I. multiple-post collar, cervical orthotic, L0190
Sorbent cartridge, ESRD, E1636
Sorbsan, alginate dressing, A6196-A6198
Source
brachytherapy
gold 198, C1716
iodine 125, C2638-C2639
non-high dose rate iridium 192, C1719
palladium 103, C2640-C2641
yttrium 90, C2616
SO, vest type abduction retrainer, L3675
Space maintainer, dental, D1510-D1550
Spacer
interphalangeal joint, L8658
Sparine, J2950
Spasmoject, J0500
Specialist Ankle Foot Orthotic, L1930
Specialist Closed-Back Cast Boot, L3260
Specialist Gaitkeeper Boot, L3260
Specialist Health/Post Operative Shoe, A9270
Specialist Heel Cups, L3485
Specialist Insoles, L3510
Specialist J-Splint Plaster Roll Immobilizer, A4580
Specialist Open-Back Cast Boot, L3260
Specialist Plaster Bandages, A4580
Specialist Plaster Roll Immobilizer, A4580
Specialist Plaster Splints, A4580
Specialist Pre-Formed Humeral Fracture Brace, L3980
Specialist Pre-Formed Ulnar Fracture Brace, L3982
Specialist Tibial Pre-formed Fracture Brace, L2116
Specialist Toe Insert for Specialist Closed-Back Cast Boot and Specialist Health/Post Operative Shoe, A9270
Specialty absorptive dressing, A6251-A6256
Spectacles, S0504-S0510, S0516-S0518
dispensing, S0595
Spectinomycin HCl, J3320
Speech aid
adult, D5953
pediatric, D5952
Speech and language pathologist
home health setting, G0153
Speech assessment, V5362-V5364
speech generating device
software, E2511
supplies, E2500-E2599
Speech therapy, S9128, S9152
Spenco shoe insert, foot orthotic, L3001
Sperm procurement, S4026, S4030-S4031
donor service, S4025
Sphygmomanometer/blood pressure, A4660
Spinal orthotic
Boston type, L1200
cervical, L0112, L0180-L0200
cervical-thoracic-lumbar-sacral orthotic (CTLSO), L0700, L0710, L1000
halo, L0810-L0830
Milwaukee, L1000
multiple post collar, L0180-L0200
scoliosis, L1000, L1200, L1300-L1499
torso supports, L0970-L0999
Spirometer
electronic, E0487, S8190
nonelectronic, A9284
Splint, A4570, L3100, L4350-L4380
ankle, L4392-L4398, S8451
digit, prefabricated, S8450
dynamic, E1800, E1805, E1810, E1815
elbow, S8452
finger, static, Q4049
footdrop, L4398
long arm, Q4017-Q4020
long leg, Q4041-Q4044
Orthoplast Splints (and Orthoplast II Splints), A4590
pneumatic, L4350
short arm, Q4021-Q4024
short leg, Q4045-Q4046
Specialist Plaster Splints, A4580
supplies, Q4051
Thumb-O-Prene Splint, L3999
toad finger, A4570
wrist, S8451
Splinting, dental
commissure, D5987
provisional, D4320-D4321
surgical, D5988
Spoke protectors, each, K0065
Sports supports hinged knee support, L1832
Stainless steel crown, D2930-D2931, D2933
Stains
immunohistochemical, D0478
microorganisms, D0476
not for microorganisms, D0477
Standing frame system, E0638, E0641-E0642
Star Lumen tubing, A4616
Sten, foot prosthesis, L5972
Stent
coated
with delivery system, C1874
without delivery system, C1875
with delivery system, C1876
without delivery system, C1877
in dentistry, D5982
noncoronary
temporary, C2617, C2625
Stent placement, transcatheter
intracoronary, G0290-G0291
Stereotactic radiosurgery, G0251
therapy, G0339, G0340
Sterile cefuroxime sodium, J0697
Sterile water, A4216-A4218
Stilphostrol, J9165
Stimulated intrauterine insemination, S4035
Stimulation
electrical, G0281-G0283
electromagnetic, G0295
Stimulators
cough, device, E0482
electric, supplies, A4595
joint, E0762
neuromuscular, E0744, E0745, E0764
osteogenesis, electrical, E0747-E0749
salivary reflex, E0755
transcutaneous, E0770
ultrasound, E0760
Stocking
gradient compression, A6530-A6549
Stoma
cap, A5055
catheter, A5082
cone, A4399
plug, A5081
Stomach tube, B4083
Stomahesive
skin barrier, A4362, A5122
sterile wafer, A4362
strips, A4362
Storm Arrow power wheelchair, K0014
Storm Torque power wheelchair, K0011
Streptase, J2995
Streptokinase, J2995
Streptomycin sulfate, J3000
Streptozocin, J9320
Stress breaker, in dentistry, D6940
Stress management class, S9454
Stretch device, E1086, E1801, E1811, E1816, E1818, E1841
Strip(s)
blood, A4253
glucose test, A4253, A4772
Nu-Hope
adhesive, 1 oz bottle with applicator, A4364
adhesive, 3 oz bottle with applicator, A4364
urine reagent, A4250
Strontium 89 chloride, A9600
Study
gastrointestinal fat absorption, S3708
sleep, G0398-G0400
Stump sock, L8470-L8485
Stylet, A4212
Sublimaze, J3010
Substance abuse treatment, T1006-T1012
childcare during, T1009
couples counseling, T1006
family counseling, T1006
meals during, T1010
other than tobacco, G0396, G0397
skills development, T1012
treatment plan, T1007
Succinylcholine chloride, J0330
Sucostrin, J0330
Suction pump
portable, E0600
Sulfamethoxazole and trimethoprim, S0039
Sullivan
CPAP, E0601
Sumacal, enteral nutrition, B4155
Sumatriptan succinate, J3030
Sunbeam moist/dry heat pad, E0215
Sunglass frames, S0518
Supplies
infection control NOS, S8301
Supply/accessory/service, A9900
Supply fee
pharmacy
anticancer oral antiemetic or immunosuppressive drug, Q0511-Q0512
immunosuppresive drugs, Q0510
Support
arch, L3040-L3090
cervical, L0120
elastic, A6530-A6549
spinal, L0970-L0999
vaginal, A4561-A4562
Supported housing, H0043-H0044
Supra crestal fibrotomy, D7291
Supreme bG Meter, E0607
Sure-Gait folding walker, E0141, E0143
Sure-Safe raised toilet seat, E0244
SureStep blood glucose monitor, E0607
Sur-Fit
closed-end pouch, A5054

Sur-Fit — *continued*
disposable convex inserts, A5093
drainable pouch, A5063
flange cap, A5055
irrigation sleeve, A4397
urostomy pouch, A5073
Sur-Fit/Active Life tail closures, A4421
Surgery
oral, D7111-D7999
stereotactic, G0251
Surgical
ambulatory center, in dentistry, D9420
arthroscopy
knee, G0289, S2112
shoulder, S2300
boot, L3208-L3211
mask, for dialysis, A4928
stocking, A4490-A4510
supplies, miscellaneous, A4649
tray, A4550
SurgiMend Collagen Matrix, C9358
Sus-Phrine, J0170
Sustacal, enteral nutrition, B4150
HC, B4152
Sustagen Powder, enteral nutrition, B4150
Suturing, complicated, in dentistry, D7911-D7912
Swabs, betadine or iodine, A4247
Swede, ACT, Cross, or Elite manual wheelchair, K0005
Swede Basic F# manual wheelchair, K0004
Swedish knee orthotic, L1850
Swivel adaptor, S8186
Synkayvite, J3430
Synovectomy, D7854
Syntocinon, J2590
Syringe, A4213
with needle, A4206-A4209
dialysis, A4657
insulin, box of 100, S8490
System2 zippered body holder, E0700
Sytobex, J3420

T

Tables, bed, E0274, E0315
Tachdijan, Legg Perthes orthotic, L1720
Tacrine hydrochloride, S0014
Tacrolimus, oral, J7507
Talwin, J3070
Tamoxifen citrate, S0187
Tamponade
retinal, C1814
Tape
nonwaterproof, A4450
waterproof, A4452
Taxi, nonemergency transportation, A0100
Taxol, J9265
Taxotere, J9170
Tay-Sachs, genetic test, S3847
Tazidime, J0713
multiple-post collar, cervical orthotic, L0190
TechneScan, A9512
Technetium Tc 99
arcitumomab, A9568
biscate, A9557
depreotide, A9536
disofenin, A9510
exametazime, A9521, A9569
fanolesomab, A9566
glucepatate, A9550
labeled red blood cells, A9560
macroaggregated albumin, A9540
mebrofenin, A9537
medronate, A9503
mertiatide, A9562
oxidronate, A9561
pentetate, A9539, A9567
pertechretate, A9512
pyrophosphate, A9538
Technetium Tc 99 — *continued*
sestamibi, A9500
succimer, A9551
sulfur colloid, A9541
teboroxime, A9501
tetrofosmin, A9502
Technol
Colles splint, L3763
wrist and forearm splint, L3906
TEEV, J0900
Telehealth
consultation, G0406-G0408
transmission, T1014
Telemonitoring, for CHF, equipment rental, S9109
Television
amplifier, V5270
caption decoder, V5271
Temozolomide, J8700
Temporomandibular joint (TMJ)
radiographs, D0320-D0321
treatment, D7810-D7899
TenderCloud electric air pump, E0182
TenderFlo II, E0187
TenderGel II, E0196
Tenderlet lancet device, A4258
Teniposide, Q2017
TenoGlide Tendon Protector Sheet, C9356
TENS, A4595, E0720-E0749
Neuro-Pulse, E0720
Tent, oxygen, E0455
Teriparatide, J3110
Terminal devices, L6703-L6714, L6721-L6722
Terramycin IM, J2460
Terumo disposable insulin syringes, up to 1 cc, per syringe, A4206
Testa-C, J1080
Testadiate-Depo, J1080
Testaqua, J3140
Test-Estra-C, J1060
Test-Estro Cypionates, J1060
Testex, J3150
Testing
electrodiagnostic, S3905
genetic, S3800, S3818-S3853, S3855, S3860-S3862
Test materials, home monitoring, G0249
Testoject
-50, J3140
-LA, J1070, J1080
Testone
LA 100, J3120
LA 200, J3130
Testosterone
aqueous, J3140
cypionate, J1070, J1080
cypionate and estradiol cypionate, J1060
enanthate and estradiol valerate, J0900, J3120, J3130
pellet, S0189
propionate, J3150
suspension, J3140
Testradiate, J0900
Testradiol 90/4, J0900
Testrin PA, J3120, J3130
Tetanus immune globulin, human, J1670
Tetracycline, J0120
Thalassemia, genetic test
alpha, S3845
hemoglobin E beta, S3846
Thallous chloride Tl 201, A9505
Theelin aqueous, J1435
Theophylline, J2810
TheraCys, J9031
Therapeutic
agent, A4321
procedures, respiratory, G0239
Therapeutic radiopharmaceutical
I-131 tositumomab, A9545
sodium iodide I-131, A9530
Therapy
activity, G0176
lymphedema, S8950
nutrition, reassessment, G0270-G0271
respiratory, G0237-G0239
Thermalator T-12-M, E0239
Thermometer
oral, A4931
rectal, A4932
Thiamine HCl, J3411
Thickener, food, B4100
Thiethylperazine maleate, Q0174
Thinning solvent, NuHope, 2 oz bottle, A4455
Thiotepa, J9340
Thomas
heel wedge, foot orthotic, L3465, L3470
Thoracic-hip-knee-ankle (THKO), L1500-L1520
Big Hug, L1510
Chameleon, L1510
Easy Stand, L1500
Little Hug, L1510
Tristander, L1510
Thoracic-lumbar-sacral orthotic (TLSO)
scoliosis, L1200-L1290
Thoracic orthotic, L0210
Thorazine, J3230
Thumb
Thumb-O-Prene Splint, L3999
Thymoglobulin, J7511
Thymol turbidity, blood, P2033
Thypinone, J2725
Thyrotropin
alpha, J3240
Thytropar, J3240
Tibia
Specialist Tibial Pre-formed Fracture Brace, L2116
Toad finger splint, A4570
Ticarcillin disodium and clavulanate potassium, S0040
Tice BCG, J9031
Ticon, J3250
Tigan, J3250
Tigecycline injection, J3243
Tiject-20, J3250
Tinzaparin sodium, J1655
Tip (cane, crutch, walker) replacement, A4637
Tire, wheelchair, E2214, E2220
Tirofiban HCl, J3246
Tissue
conditioning, dental, D5850-D5851
connective
human, C1762
non-human, C1763
dermal
excision of hyperplastic, dental, D7970
localization and excision device, C1819
marker, A4648
Tissue marker, implantable, A4648, C1879
TissueMend, Q4109
TLSO, L0450-L0492, L1200-L1290
Tobacco counseling, D1320
Tobramycin
inhalation solution, J7682, J7685
sulfate, J3260
unit dose, J7682
Toe
holder, E0952
Specialist Toe Insert for Specialist Closed-Back Cast Boot and Specialist Health/Post Operative Shoe, A9270
Toilet accessories, E0167-E0175, E0243, E0244, E0625
raised toilet seat, E0244
Combo-Seat Universal, E0244
Moore, E0244
Toilet accessories — *continued*
raised toilet seat — *continued*
Sure-Safe, E0244
seat lift, E0172
transfer bench, E0247, E0248
Tolazoline HCl, J2670
Toll, non-emergency transport, A0170
Tomographic radiograph, dental, D0322
Tooth, natural
caries susceptibility test, D0425
impacted, removal, D7220-D7241
intentional reimplantation, D3470
pulp vitality test, D0460
reimplantation, evulsed tooth, D7270
surgical exposure, D7280
surgical repositioning, D7290
transplantation, D7272
Topical hyperbaric oxygen chamber, A4575
Topical medicament carrier, D5991
Topographic brain mapping, S8040
Topotecan, J9350
Toronto, Legg Perthes orthotic, L1700
Torsemide, J3265
Torus, removal of
mandibularis, D7473
palatinus, D7472
Totacillin-N, J0290
Total hip resurfacing, S2118
Total Universal Buck's Boot, E0870
Tourniquet, for dialysis, A4929
TPN, home infusion therapy, S9364-S9368
Tracer blood glucose
meter, E0607
strips, box of 50, A4253
Tracer II Diabetes Care System, E0607
Tracer Wheelchairs, E1240, E1250, E1260, E1270, E1280, E1285, E1290, E1295
Tracheal suction catheter, A4624
Tracheoesophageal prosthesis supplies, L8511-L8514
Tracheostoma
adhesive disc, A7506
filter, A7504
filter holder, A7503, A7507, A7509
housing, A7505, A7508
replacement diaphragm, faceplate, A7502
valve, A7501
Tracheostomy
care kit, A4629
filter, A4481
mask, A7525
speaking valve, L8501
supplies, A4623-A4626, A4628, A4629, A7523-A7526, S8189
tube, A7520-A7522
Tracheotomy, in dentistry, D7990
Traction equipment, E0840-E0948
cervical equipment
not requiring frame, E0855
stand or frame, E0849
device
cervical, E0856
extremity, E0870, E0880
Total Universal Buck's Boot, E0870
head harness/halter, cervical, E0942
occipital-pull head halter, E0942
overdoor, cervical, E0860
Exo-Static, E0860
pelvic, E0890, E0900
Secure-All universal, belt, E0890
Training
child development, T1027
diabetes, G0108, G0109
home care, S5108-S5109
INR monitoring device, G0248
medication, H0034
skills, H2014
Tramacal, enteral nutrition, B4154
Transcutaneous electrical nerve stimulator (TENS), E0720-E0749

- **Transducer protector, dialysis**, E1575
- **Transfer (shoe orthoses)**, L3600-L3640
- **Transfer board or device**, E0705
- **Transfusion, blood products, at home**, S9538
- **Transmitter**
  - interstitial glucose monitor, A9277
- **Transparent film (for dressing)**, A6257-A6259
- **Transplant**
  - autologous chondrocyte, J7330
  - bone marrow, allogeneic, S2150
  - islet cell, G0341-G0343
  - islet cell tissue, allogeneic, S2102
  - multivisceral organs, S2054
  - pancreas/kidney, S2065
  - small intestine and liver allografts, S2053
  - tooth, D7272
- **Transportation**
  - ambulance, A0021-A0999
  - corneal tissue, V2785
  - EKG (portable), R0076
  - extra attendent, A0424
  - handicapped, A0130
  - nonemergency, A0080-A0210, T2001-T2005, T2049
    - mileage, S0215
  - parking fees, A0170
  - service, including ambulance, A0021-A0999
  - taxi, nonemergency, A0100
  - toll, nonemergency, A0170
  - volunteer, nonemergency, A0080, A0090
  - waiting time, T2007
  - x-ray (portable), R0070, R0075
- **Transport chair**, E1037-E1038
  - heavy weight, E1039
- **Trapeze bar**, E0910-E0912, E0940
- **Traum-aid, enteral nutrition**, B4154
- **Trauma response team**, G0390
- **Travasorb, enteral nutrition**, B4150
  - Hepatic, B4154
  - HN, B4153
  - MCT, B4154
  - Renal, B4154
- **Traveler manual wheelchair**, K0001
- **Tray**
  - insertion, A4310-A4316, A4354
  - irrigation, A4320
  - surgical (*see also* kits), A4550
  - wheelchair, E0950
- **Treatment**
  - fracture
    - pelvic bone, G0412-G0415
- **Treprostinil**, J3285
- **Triam-A**, J3301
- **Trifocal, glass or plastic**, V2300-V2399
- **Trifupromazine HCl**, J3400
- **Trigeminal division block anesthesia**, D9212
- **Tri-Kort**, J3301
- **Trilafon**, J3310
- **Trilog**, J3301
- **Trilone**, J3302
- **Trimethobenzamide HCl**, J3250, Q0173
- **Trimetrexate glucoronate**, J3305
- **Trim nails**, G0127
- **Triptorelin pamoate**, J3315
- **Trismus appliance**, D5937
- **Trobicin**, J3320
- **Trovan**, J0200
- **Truform prosthetic shrinker**, L8440-L8465
- **Truss**, L8300-L8330
- **Tub**
  - transfer bench, E0247-E0248
- **Tube/Tubing**
  - with integrated heating element, A4604
  - anchoring device, A5200
  - blood, A4750, A4755
  - chest
    - drainage container, A7041

Tube/Tubing — *continued*
  - chest — *continued*
    - drain valve, A7040
  - CPAP device, A7037
  - gastrostomy/jejunostomy, B4087-B4088
  - irrigation, A4355
  - microcapillary, calibrated, A4651
    - sealant, A4652
  - nasogastric, B4081, B4082
  - oxygen, A4616
  - serum clotting time, A4771
  - stomach, B4083
  - suction pump, each, A7002
  - tire, E2212-E2213, E2215
  - tracheostomy or larygotomy plug, A7527
  - urinary drainage, A4331
- **Tumor**
  - infiltrating lymphocyte therapy, S2107
  - oral, removal, dentistry, D7440-D7465
- **Tumor destruction**
  - embolization, S2095
- **Turtle Neck safety collars**, E0942

U

- **Ulcers**
  - electromagnetic therapy, G0329
- **Ultra Blood Glucose**
  - monitor, E0607
  - test strips, box of 50, A4253
- **UltraCare vest-style body holder**, E0700
- **Ultrafast computed tomography**, S8092
- **Ultrafine disposable insulin syringes, per syringe**, A4206
- **Ultralente insulin**, J1815
- **Ultrasound**
  - abdominal aortic aneurysm screen, G0389
  - aerosol generator, E0574
  - guidance for multifetal pregnancy reduction, S8055
  - paranasal sinus, S9024
- **Ultraviolet light-therapy**
  - bulb, A4633
  - cabinet, E0691-E0694
  - system panel, E0691-E0693
- **Ultrazine-10**, J0780
- **Unasyn**, J0295
- **Unclassified drug**, J3490
- **Underpads, disposable**, A4554
- **Unilet lancet device**, A4258
- **Unipuncture control system, dialysis**, E1580
- **Unistik lancet device**, A4258
- **Universal**
  - remover for adhesives, A4455
  - socket insert
    - above knee, L5694
    - below knee, L5690
  - telescoping versarail bed rail, E0310
- **Up-Draft Neb-U-Mist**, E0580
- **Upper extremity addition, locking elbow**, L6693
- **Upper extremity fracture orthotic**, L3980-L3999
- **Upper limb prosthesis**, L6000-L7499
- **Urea**, J3350
- **Ureaphil**, J3350
- **Urecholine**, J0520
- **Ureteroscopy**
  - for ureteral calculi, S2070
- **Urethral suppository, Alprostadil**, J0275
- **Urgent care**, S9088
  - global fee, S9083
- **Urinal**, E0325, E0326
- **Urinary**
  - catheter, A4338-A4346, A4351-A4353
  - catheter irrigation, A4321

Urinary — *continued*
  - collection and retention (supplies), A4310-A4358
  - incontinence repair device, C1771, C2631
  - incontinence supplies, A4310-A4421, A4423-A4434, A5051-A5093, A5102-A5114, A5120-A5200
  - leg bag, A5105, A5112
  - tract implant, collagen, L8603
- **Urine**
  - collector, A4335
  - sensitivity study, P7001
  - tests, A4250
- **Urofollitropin**, J3355
- **Urokinase**, J3364, J3365
- **Urostomy pouch**, A5073
- **USMC**
  - hinged Swedish knee cage, L1850
  - universal knee immobilizer, L1830
- **U-V lens**, V2755
- **Uvulopalatoplasty, laser assisted**, S2080

V

- **Vabra aspirator**, A4480
- **Vaccination, administration**
  - hepatitis B, G0010
  - influenza virus, G0008
  - pneumococcal, G0009
- **Vacuum erection system**, L7900
- **Vaginal**
  - contraceptive ring, J7303
- **Valergen (10, 20, 40)**, J0970, J1380, J1390
- **Valertest No. 1, 2**, J0900
- **Valium**, J3360
- **Valrubicin**, J9357
- **Valstar**, J9357
- **Vancocin**, J3370
- **Vancoled**, J3370
- **Vancomycin HCl**, J3370
- **Vaporizer**, E0605
- **Vascular**
  - catheter (appliances and supplies), A4300-A4306
  - closure device, C1760
  - synthetic, L8670
- **Velban**, J9360
- **Velcade**, J9041
- **V Elite**, E0601
- **Velosulin**, J1815
- **Velpeau Sling Immobilizer**, L3670
- **Veneers, dental**, D2960-D2962
- **Vent**
  - ostomy, A4366
- **Ventilator**
  - battery, A4611-A4613
  - moisture exchanger, disposable, A4483
  - negative pressure, E0460
  - pressure support, E0463, E0464
  - volume control, E0450, E0461
  - volume, stationary or portable, E0450, E0483
- **Ventilator tray**
  - wheelchair, E1029-E1030
- **Ventricular assist device**
  - battery, Q0496, Q0503
    - charger, Q0495
    - clips, Q0497
  - belt, Q0499
  - driver, Q0480
  - emergency
    - hand pump, Q0494
    - power cable, Q0492-Q0493
    - power source, Q0490-Q0491
  - filter, Q0500
  - holster, Q0498
  - leads, Q0487-Q0488
  - microprocessor control unit, Q0481-Q0482
  - miscellaneous supply, Q0505
  - mobility cart, Q0502
  - monitor
    - control cable, Q0485-Q0486

Ventricular assist device — *continued*
  - monitor — *continued*
    - display module, Q0483-Q0484
  - power
    - back base, Q0489
      - adapter, Q0504
    - emergency
      - power source, Q0490-Q0491
      - power supply cable, Q0492-Q0493
  - shower cover, Q0501
  - vest, Q0499
- **VePesid**, J8560, J9181
- **Versa-Pole IV pole**, E0776
- **Versed**, J2250
- **Vertebral axial decompression**, S9090
- **Verteporfin**, J3396
- **Vesprin**, J3400
- **Vest**, E0980
  - safety, wheelchair, E0980
  - ventricular assist device, Q0499
- **Vestibular rehabilitation**, S9476
- **Vestibuloplasty**, D7340-D7350
- **V-Gan (25, 50)**, J2550
- **Vidaza**, J9025
- **Vinblastine sulfate**, J9360
- **Vincasar PFS**, J9370
- **Vincristine sulfate**, J9370-J9380
- **Vinorelbine tartrate**, J9390
- **Viral culture**, D0416
- **Visi-flow**
  - irrigation, A4367, A4397, A4398, A4399, A4402, A4421
  - stoma cone, A4399
- **Vision Record wheelchair**, K0005
- **Vision service**, S0500-S0592, V2020-V2799
- **Visit**
  - emergency department
    - type B, G0380-G0384
  - home by nurse practitioner, S0274
  - home by physician, S0273
  - nurse home, T1031
- **Visi wheelchair tray**, E0950
- **Vistaject**, J3410
- **Vistaril**, J3410
- **Vistide**, J0740
- **Vitajet**, A4210
- **Vital HN, enteral nutrition**, B4153
- **Vitamin**
  - multiple, A9153
  - prenatal 30-day supply, S0197
  - single, A9152
  - supplement in ESRD, S0194
- **Vitamin B12 cyanocobalamin**, J3420
- **Vitamin B17**, J3570
- **Vitamin K**, J3430
- **Vitrasert**, J7310
- **Vivonex, enteral nutrition**
  - HN, B4153
  - T.E.N., B4153
- **Vocal cord**
  - chemodenervation, S2341
  - medialization material, implantable, C1878
- **Von Hippel-Lindau disease, genetic test**, S3842
- **Von Rosen, hip orthotic**, L1630
- **Voriconazole**, J3465
- **Vortex power wheelchair**, K0014
- **VPlus**, E0601

W

- **Walker**, E0130-E0144
  - accessories, A4636, A4637
  - attachments, E0153-E0159
  - enclosed with wheels, E0144
  - folding
    - Auto-Glide, E0143
    - Easy Care, E0143
    - framed with wheels, E0144
    - heavy duty
      - with wheels, E0148
      - without wheels, E0149

Walker — *continued*
folding — *continued*
heavy duty, multiple braking system, E0141
One-Button, E0143
Quik-Fold, E0141, E0143
Red Dot, E0135, E0143
Sure-Gait, E0141, E0143
Water
ambulance, A0429
distilled (for nebulizer), A7018
for nebulizer, A7018
pressure pad/mattress, E0187, E0198
purification system (ESRD), E1610, E1615
softening system (ESRD), E1625
treated, A4714
Water chamber
humidifier, A7046
Wedge, positioning, E0190
Wedges, shoe, L3340-L3420
Wehamine, J1240
Wehdryl, J1200
Weight management class, S9449
Wellcovorin, J0640
Wet mount, Q0111
Wheel attachment, rigid pickup walker, E0155
Wheelchair, E0950-E1298, K0001-K0108
accessories, E0950-E2399
elevating leg rest, E0990
wheel lock, E2206
tray, E0950
Visi, E0950
amputee, E1170-E1200
battery, E2397, K0733
bearings, any type, E2210
braking system and lock, E2228
component or accessory, NOS, K0108
control hand or chin, E2373-E2374
controller, E2375-E2377
crutch and cane holder, E2207
cushion
back, E2291, E2293, E2605, E2606, E2608-E2617, E2620, E2621
custom, E2609
seat, E2610
general, E2601, E2602
positioning, E2605, E2606, E2607
Wheelchair — *continued*
cushion — *continued*
seat — *continued*
replacement cover, E2619
skin protection, E2603, E2604, E2607, K0734-K0737
skin protection, K0734-K0737
cylinder tank carrier, E2208
hand rim, E0967, E2205
heavy-duty
shock absorber, E1015-E1016
Tracer, E1280, E1285, E1290, E1295
lightweight, E1240-E1270
EZ Lite, E1250
Tracer, E1240, E1250, E1260, E1270
manual, adult, E1161
accessories, E2201-E2204, E2300-E2399
motorized, E1239, K0010-K0898
narrowing device, E0969
pediatric, E1229, E1231-E1238
back
contoured, E2293
planar, E2291
modification, E1011
power, E1239
power, NOS, E1239
seat
contoured, E2294
planar, E2292
power, accessories, E2300-E2399
gear box, E2369
motor, E2368
motor and gear box, E2370
reclining back, E1014
residual limb support, E1020
seat or back cushion, K0669
specially sized, E1220-E1230
support, E1020
tire, E2211, E2214, E2220-E2222, E2381-E2392
valve, E2393
transfer board or device, E0705
transport chair, E1037-E1038
van, nonemergency, A0130, S0209
wheel, E2227, E2394-E2395
WHFO, with inflatable air chamber, L3807
Whirlpool equipment, E1300-E1310
Wig, A9282
Win RhoSD, J2792
Wipes, A4245, A4247
Allkare protective barrier, A5120
Wire, guide, C1769
WIZZ-ard manual wheelchair, K0006
Wooden canes, E0100
Wound
cleanser, A6260
cover
alginate dressing, A6196-A6198
collagen dressing, A6021-A6024
foam dressing, A6209-A6214
hydrocolloid dressing, A6234-A6239
hydrogel dressing, A6242-A6248
packing strips, A6407
specialty absorptive dressing, A6251-A6256
warming card, E0232
warming device, E0231
non-contact warming cover, A6000
dental, D7910-D7912
electrical stimulation, E0769
filler
alginate, A6199
foam, A6215
hydrocolloid, A6240-A6241
hydrogel, A6242-A6248
not elsewhere classified, A6261-A6262
healing
other growth factor preparation, S9055
Procuren, S9055
matrix, Q4102, Q4114
dressing, Q4104
packing strips, A6407
pouch, A6154
warming device, E0231
cover, A6000
warming card, E0232
therapy
negative pressure
supplies, A6550
Wrap
abdominal aneurysm, M0301
compression, A6545
Wrist
brace, cock-up, L3908
disarticulation prosthesis, L6050, L6055
Wrist — *continued*
hand/finger orthotic (WHFO), E1805, E1825, L3806-L3808
Specialist Pre-Formed Ulnar Fracture Brace, L3982
Wycillin, J2510
Wydase, J3470

X

Xcaliber power wheelchair, K0014
Xenon Xe-133, A9558
Xolair, J2357
X-ray
dental, D0210-D0340
implant, D6190
equipment
portable, Q0092, R0070, R0075

Y

Y set tubing for peritoneal dialysis, A4719
Yttrium 90
ibritumomab tiuxeton, A9543
microsphere
brachytherapy, C2616
procedure, S2095

Z

Zanamivir, G9018, G9034
Zantac, J2780
Zenapax, J7513
Zetran, J3360
Zidovudine, J3485
ZIFT, S4014
Zinacef, J0697
Zinecard, J1190
Ziprasidone mesylate, J3486
Zithromax
I.V., J0456
oral, Q0144
Zofran, J2405
oral, S0181
Zoladex, J9202
Zoledronic acid, J3487
Zolicef, J0690
Zosyn, J2543
Zygomatic arch, fracture treatment, D7650, D7660, D7750, D7760
Zyprexa, S0166
Zyvok, J2020

TRANSPORTATION SERVICES INCLUDING AMBULANCE A0000-A0999

This code range includes ground and air ambulance, nonemergency transportation (taxi, bus, automobile, wheelchair van), and ancillary transportation-related fees.

HCPCS Level II codes for ambulance services must be reported with modifiers that indicate pick-up origins and destinations. The modifier describing the arrangement (QM, QN) is listed first. The modifiers describing the origin and destination are listed second. Origin and destination modifiers are created by combining two alpha characters from the following list. Each alpha character, with the exception of X, represents either an origin or a destination. Each pair of alpha characters creates one modifier. The first position represents the origin and the second the destination. The modifiers most commonly used are:

D	Diagnostic or therapeutic site other than "P" or "H" when these are used as origin codes
E	Residential, domiciliary, custodial facility (other than 1819 facility)
G	Hospital-based ESRD facility
H	Hospital
I	Site of transfer (e.g., airport or helicopter pad) between modes of ambulance transport
J	Free standing ESRD facility
N	Skilled nursing facility (SNF)
P	Physician's office
R	Residence
S	Scene of accident or acute event
X	Intermediate stop at physician's office on way to hospital (destination code only)

Note: Modifier X can only be used as a designation code in the second position of a modifier.

See S0215. For Medicaid, see T codes and T modifiers.

E **A0021** **Ambulance service, outside state per mile, transport (Medicaid only)**

E **A0080** **Nonemergency transportation, per mile — vehicle provided by volunteer (individual or organization), with no vested interest**

E **A0090** **Nonemergency transportation, per mile — vehicle provided by individual (family member, self, neighbor) with vested interest**

E **A0100** **Nonemergency transportation; taxi**

E **A0110** **Nonemergency transportation and bus, intra- or interstate carrier**

E **A0120** **Nonemergency transportation: mini-bus, mountain area transports, or other transportation systems**

E **A0130** **Nonemergency transportation: wheelchair van**

E **A0140** **Nonemergency transportation and air travel (private or commercial) intra- or interstate**

E **A0160** **Nonemergency transportation: per mile — caseworker or social worker**

E **A0170** **Transportation ancillary: parking fees, tolls, other**

E **A0180** **Nonemergency transportation: ancillary: lodging, recipient**

E **A0190** **Nonemergency transportation: ancillary: meals, recipient**

E **A0200** **Nonemergency transportation: ancillary: lodging, escort**

E **A0210** **Nonemergency transportation: ancillary: meals, escort**

E **A0225** **Ambulance service, neonatal transport, base rate, emergency transport, one way**
MED: 100-4,1,10.1.4.1

E ☑ **A0380** **BLS mileage (per mile)**
See code(s): A0425
MED: 100-2,6,10; 100-4,1,10.1.4.1

A **A0382** **BLS routine disposable supplies**

A **A0384** **BLS specialized service disposable supplies; defibrillation (used by ALS ambulances and BLS ambulances in jurisdictions where defibrillation is permitted in BLS ambulances)**

E ☑ **A0390** **ALS mileage (per mile)**
See code(s): A0425
MED: 100-4,1,10.1.4.1

A **A0392** **ALS specialized service disposable supplies; defibrillation (to be used only in jurisdictions where defibrillation cannot be performed in BLS ambulances)**

A **A0394** **ALS specialized service disposable supplies; IV drug therapy**

A **A0396** **ALS specialized service disposable supplies; esophageal intubation**

A **A0398** **ALS routine disposable supplies**

WAITING TIME TABLE

Units	Time
1	1/2 to 1 hr.
2	1 to 1-1/2 hrs.
3	1-1/2 to 2 hrs.
4	2 to 2-1/2 hrs.
5	2-1/2 to 3 hrs.
6	3 to 3-1/2 hrs.
7	3-1/2 to 4 hrs.
8	4 to 4-1/2 hrs.
9	4-1/2 to 5 hrs.
10	5 to 5-1/2 hrs.

A **A0420** **Ambulance waiting time (ALS or BLS), one-half (1/2) hour increments** ⦸

A **A0422** **Ambulance (ALS or BLS) oxygen and oxygen supplies, life sustaining situation** ⦸

A **A0424** **Extra ambulance attendant, ground (ALS or BLS) or air (fixed or rotary winged); (requires medical review)** ⦸
Pertinent documentation to evaluate medical appropriateness should be included when this code is reported.

A **A0425** **Ground mileage, per statute mile**
MED: 100-2,6,10; 100-2,10,20; 100-4,1,10.1.4.1

A **A0426** **Ambulance service, advanced life support, nonemergency transport, level 1 (ALS 1)**
MED: 100-2,6,10; 100-2,10,20; 100-4,1,10.1.4.1

A **A0427** **Ambulance service, advanced life support, emergency transport, level 1 (ALS 1 — emergency)**
MED: 100-2,6,10; 100-2,10,20; 100-4,1,10.1.4.1

A **A0428** **Ambulance service, basic life support, nonemergency transport, (BLS)**
MED: 100-2,6,10; 100-2,10,20; 100-4,1,10.1.4.1

A **A0429** **Ambulance service, basic life support, emergency transport (BLS, emergency)**
MED: 100-2,6,10; 100-2,10,20; 100-4,1,10.1.4.1

A A0430 Ambulance service, conventional air services, transport, one way (fixed wing)
MED: 100-2,6,10; 100-2,10,20; 100-4,1,10.1.4.1

A A0431 Ambulance service, conventional air services, transport, one way (rotary wing)
MED: 100-2,6,10; 100-2,10,20; 100-4,1,10.1.4.1

A A0432 Paramedic intercept (PI), rural area, transport furnished by a volunteer ambulance company which is prohibited by state law from billing third-party payers
MED: 100-2,10,20

A A0433 Advanced life support, level 2 (ALS 2)
MED: 100-2,10,20

A A0434 Specialty care transport (SCT)
MED: 100-2,10,20

A A0435 Fixed wing air mileage, per statute mile
MED: 100-2,10,20

A A0436 Rotary wing air mileage, per statute mile
MED: 100-2,10,20

E A0888 Noncovered ambulance mileage, per mile (e.g., for miles traveled beyond closest appropriate facility)
MED: 100-2,10,20

E A0998 Ambulance response and treatment, no transport

A A0999 Unlisted ambulance service ⃠
Determine if an alternative HCPCS Level II or a CPT code better describes the service being reported. This code should be used only if a more specific code is unavailable.
MED: 100-2,10,20; 100-4,1,10.1.4.1

MEDICAL AND SURGICAL SUPPLIES A4000-A8999

This section covers a wide variety of medical, surgical, and some durable medical equipment (DME) related supplies and accessories. DME-related supplies, accessories, maintenance, and repair required to ensure the proper functioning of this equipment is generally covered by Medicare under the prosthetic devices provision.

MISCELLANEOUS SUPPLIES

These codes are to be filed with the Medicare local contractor, unless otherwise noted (if incident to a physicians' services, not separately billable) unless they represent incidental services or supplies which are referred to the DME Medicare Administrative Contractor (DME MAC).

E ☑ A4206 Syringe with needle, sterile, 1 cc or less, each

E ☑ A4207 Syringe with needle, sterile 2 cc, each

E ☑ A4208 Syringe with needle, sterile 3 cc, each

E ☑ A4209 Syringe with needle, sterile 5 cc or greater, each

E ☑ A4210 Needle-free injection device, each
Sometimes covered by commercial payers with preauthorization and physician letter stating need (e.g., for insulin injection in young children).
MED: 100-3,280.1

E A4211 Supplies for self-administered injections
When a drug that is usually injected by the patient (e.g., insulin or calcitonin) is injected by the physician, it is excluded from Medicare coverage unless administered in an emergency situation (e.g., diabetic coma).
MED: 100-2,15,50

B A4212 Noncoring needle or stylet with or without catheter

E A4213 Syringe, sterile, 20 cc or greater, each

E A4215 Needle, sterile, any size, each

A ☑ A4216 Sterile water, saline and/or dextrose, diluent/flush, 10 ml ♿
MED: 100-2,15,50

A ☑ A4217 Sterile water/saline, 500 ml ♿
MED: 100-2,15,50

N A4218 Sterile saline or water, metered dose dispenser, 10 ml N1

N A4220 Refill kit for implantable infusion pump N1
Implantable infusion pumps are covered by Medicare for 5-FUdR therapy for unresected liver or colorectal cancer and for opioid drug therapy for intractable pain. They are not covered by Medicare for heparin therapy for thromboembolic disease. Report drugs separately.
MED: 100-3,280.14

Y A4221 Supplies for maintenance of drug infusion catheter, per week (list drug separately) ♿

Y A4222 Infusion supplies for external drug infusion pump, per cassette or bag (list drugs separately) ♿

E ☑ A4223 Infusion supplies not used with external infusion pump, per cassette or bag (list drugs separately)

N ☑ A4230 Infusion set for external insulin pump, nonneedle cannula type
Covered by some commercial payers as ongoing supply to preauthorized pump.
MED: 100-3,280.14

N ☑ A4231 Infusion set for external insulin pump, needle type
Covered by some commercial payers as ongoing supply to preauthorized pump.
MED: 100-3,280.14

E ☑ A4232 Syringe with needle for external insulin pump, sterile, 3 cc
Covered by some commercial payers as ongoing supply to preauthorized pump.
MED: 100-3,280.14

Y ☑ A4233 Replacement battery, alkaline (other than J cell), for use with medically necessary home blood glucose monitor owned by patient, each

Y ☑ A4234 Replacement battery, alkaline, J cell, for use with medically necessary home blood glucose monitor owned by patient, each

Y ☑ A4235 Replacement battery, lithium, for use with medically necessary home blood glucose monitor owned by patient, each

Y ☑ A4236 Replacement battery, silver oxide, for use with medically necessary home blood glucose monitor owned by patient, each

E ☑ A4244 Alcohol or peroxide, per pint

E ☑ A4245 Alcohol wipes, per box

E ☑ A4246 Betadine or pHisoHex solution, per pint

E ☑ A4247 Betadine or iodine swabs/wipes, per box

N ☑ A4248 Chlorhexidine containing antiseptic, 1 ml N1

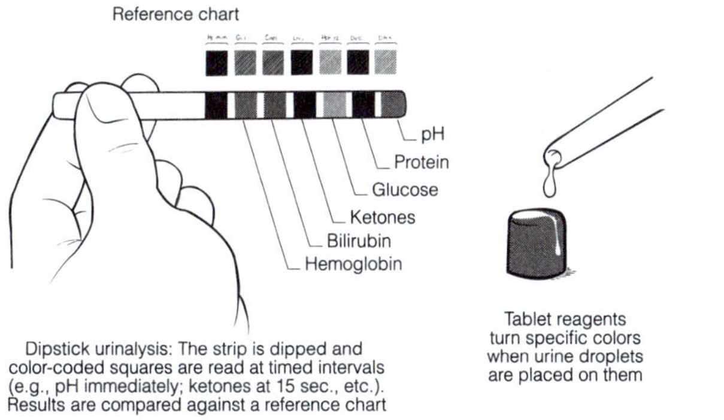

E ☑ **A4250** **Urine test or reagent strips or tablets (100 tablets or strips)**
MED: 100-2,15,110

E ☑ **A4252** **Blood ketone test or reagent strip, each**

Y ☑ **A4253** **Blood glucose test or reagent strips for home blood glucose monitor, per 50 strips** ♿
Medicare covers glucose strips for diabetic patients using home glucose monitoring devices prescribed by their physicians.
MED: 100-3,40.2

Y ☑ **A4255** **Platforms for home blood glucose monitor, 50 per box** ♿
Some Medicare contractors cover monitor platforms for diabetic patients using home glucose monitoring devices prescribed by their physicians. Some commercial payers also provide this coverage to noninsulin dependent diabetics.
MED: 100-3,40.2

Y **A4256** **Normal, low, and high calibrator solution/chips** ♿
Some Medicare contractors cover calibration solutions or chips for diabetic patients using home glucose monitoring devices prescribed by their physicians. Some commercial payers also provide this coverage to noninsulin dependent diabetics.
MED: 100-3,40.2

Y ☑ **A4257** **Replacement lens shield cartridge for use with laser skin piercing device, each** ♿

Y ☑ **A4258** **Spring-powered device for lancet, each** ♿
Some Medicare contractors cover lancing devices for diabetic patients using home glucose monitoring devices prescribed by their physicians. Medicare jurisdiction: DME regional contractor. Some commercial payers also provide this coverage to noninsulin dependent diabetics.
MED: 100-3,40.2

Y ☑ **A4259** **Lancets, per box of 100** ♿
Medicare covers lancets for diabetic patients using home glucose monitoring devices prescribed by their physicians. Medicare jurisdiction: DME regional contractor. Some commercial payers also provide this coverage to noninsulin dependent diabetics.
MED: 100-3,40.2

E **A4261** **Cervical cap for contraceptive use** ♀

N ☑ **A4262** **Temporary, absorbable lacrimal duct implant, each** N1
Always report concurrent to the implant procedure.

N ☑ **A4263** **Permanent, long-term, nondissolvable lacrimal duct implant, each** N1
Always report concurrent to the implant procedure.

Y ☑ **A4265** **Paraffin, per pound** ♿
MED: 100-3,280.1

E **A4266** **Diaphragm for contraceptive use** ♀

E ☑ **A4267** **Contraceptive supply, condom, male, each** ♂

E ☑ **A4268** **Contraceptive supply, condom, female, each** ♀

E ☑ **A4269** **Contraceptive supply, spermicide (e.g., foam, gel), each** ♀

N ☑ **A4270** **Disposable endoscope sheath, each** N1

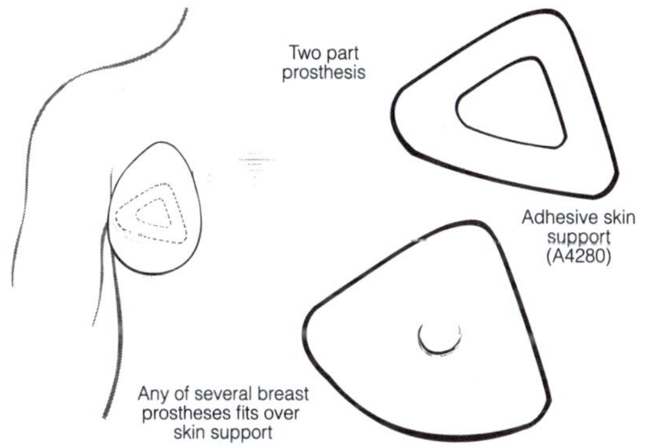

A ☑ **A4280** **Adhesive skin support attachment for use with external breast prosthesis, each** A ♀ ♿

E **A4281** **Tubing for breast pump, replacement** M ♀

E **A4282** **Adapter for breast pump, replacement** M ♀

E **A4283** **Cap for breast pump bottle, replacement** M ♀

E **A4284** **Breast shield and splash protector for use with breast pump, replacement** M ♀

E **A4285** **Polycarbonate bottle for use with breast pump, replacement** M ♀

E **A4286** **Locking ring for breast pump, replacement** M ♀

B ☑ **A4290** **Sacral nerve stimulation test lead, each**
AHA: 1Q,'02,9

VASCULAR CATHETERS

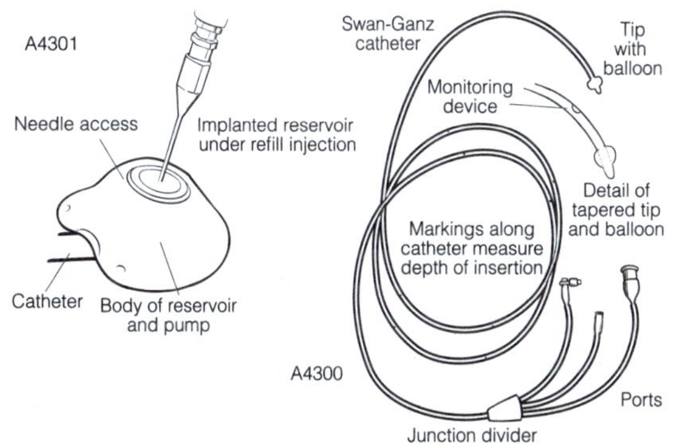

N **A4300** **Implantable access catheter, (e.g., venous, arterial, epidural subarachnoid, or peritoneal, etc.) external access** N1
MED: 100-2,15,120

N **A4301** **Implantable access total catheter, port/reservoir (e.g., venous, arterial, epidural, subarachnoid, peritoneal, etc.)** N1

N ☑ **A4305** **Disposable drug delivery system, flow rate of 50 ml or greater per hour** N1

N **A4306** **Disposable drug delivery system, flow rate of less than 50 ml per hour** N1

INCONTINENCE APPLIANCES AND CARE SUPPLIES

Covered by Medicare when the medical record indicates incontinence is permanent, or of long and indefinite duration.

A **A4310** Insertion tray without drainage bag and without catheter (accessories only) ♿
MED: 100-2,15,120

A **A4311** Insertion tray without drainage bag with indwelling catheter, Foley type, 2-way latex with coating (Teflon, silicone, silicone elastomer or hydrophilic, etc.) ♿
MED: 100-2,15,120

A **A4312** Insertion tray without drainage bag with indwelling catheter, Foley type, 2-way, all silicone ♿
MED: 100-2,15,120

A **A4313** Insertion tray without drainage bag with indwelling catheter, Foley type, 3-way, for continuous irrigation ♿
MED: 100-2,15,120

A **A4314** Insertion tray with drainage bag with indwelling catheter, Foley type, 2-way latex with coating (Teflon, silicone, silicone elastomer or hydrophilic, etc.) ♿
MED: 100-2,15,120

A **A4315** Insertion tray with drainage bag with indwelling catheter, Foley type, 2-way, all silicone ♿
MED: 100-2,15,120

A **A4316** Insertion tray with drainage bag with indwelling catheter, Foley type, 3-way, for continuous irrigation ♿
MED: 100-2,15,120

A **A4320** Irrigation tray with bulb or piston syringe, any purpose ♿
MED: 100-2,15,120

A **A4321** Therapeutic agent for urinary catheter irrigation ♿
MED: 100-2,15,120

A ☑ **A4322** Irrigation syringe, bulb or piston, each ♿
MED: 100-2,15,120

A ☑ **A4326** Male external catheter with integral collection chamber, any type, each ♂ ♿
MED: 100-2,15,120

A ☑ **A4327** Female external urinary collection device; meatal cup, each ♀ ♿
MED: 100-2,15,120

A ☑ **A4328** Female external urinary collection device; pouch, each ♀ ♿
MED: 100-2,15,120

A ☑ **A4330** Perianal fecal collection pouch with adhesive, each ♿
MED: 100-2,15,120

A ☑ **A4331** Extension drainage tubing, any type, any length, with connector/adaptor, for use with urinary leg bag or urostomy pouch, each ♿
MED: 100-2,15,120

A ☑ **A4332** Lubricant, individual sterile packet, each ♿
MED: 100-2,15,120

A ☑ **A4333** Urinary catheter anchoring device, adhesive skin attachment, each ♿
MED: 100-2,15,120

A ☑ **A4334** Urinary catheter anchoring device, leg strap, each ♿
MED: 100-2,15,120

A **A4335** Incontinence supply; miscellaneous
MED: 100-2,15,120

A ☑ **A4338** Indwelling catheter; Foley type, 2-way latex with coating (Teflon, silicone, silicone elastomer, or hydrophilic, etc.), each ♿
MED: 100-2,15,120

A ☑ **A4340** Indwelling catheter; specialty type, (e.g., Coude, mushroom, wing, etc.), each ♿
MED: 100-2,15,120

A ☑ **A4344** Indwelling catheter, Foley type, 2-way, all silicone, each ♿
MED: 100-2,15,120

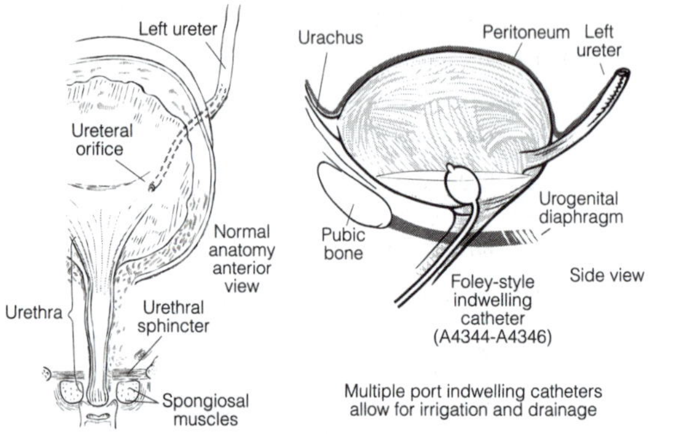

Multiple port indwelling catheters allow for irrigation and drainage

A ☑ **A4346** Indwelling catheter; Foley type, 3-way for continuous irrigation, each ♿
MED: 100-2,15,120

A ☑ **A4349** Male external catheter, with or without adhesive, disposable, each ♂
MED: 100-2,15,120

A ☑ **A4351** Intermittent urinary catheter; straight tip, with or without coating (Teflon, silicone, silicone elastomer, or hydrophilic, etc.), each ♿
MED: 100-2,15,120

A ☑ **A4352** Intermittent urinary catheter; Coude (curved) tip, with or without coating (Teflon, silicone, silicone elastomeric, or hydrophilic, etc.), each ♿
MED: 100-2,15,120

A **A4353** Intermittent urinary catheter, with insertion supplies ♿
MED: 100-2,15,120

A **A4354** Insertion tray with drainage bag but without catheter ♿
MED: 100-2,15,120

A ☑ **A4355** Irrigation tubing set for continuous bladder irrigation through a 3-way indwelling Foley catheter, each ♿
MED: 100-2,15,120

EXTERNAL URINARY SUPPLIES

A ☑ **A4356** External urethral clamp or compression device (not to be used for catheter clamp), each ♿
MED: 100-2,15,120

A ☑ **A4357** Bedside drainage bag, day or night, with or without antireflux device, with or without tube, each ♿
MED: 100-2,15,120

A ☑ **A4358** Urinary drainage bag, leg or abdomen, vinyl, with or without tube, with straps, each ♿
MED: 100-2,15,120

OSTOMY SUPPLIES

A ☑ **A4361** Ostomy faceplate, each ♿
MED: 100-2,15,120

A ☑ **A4362** Skin barrier; solid, 4 x 4 or equivalent; each ♿
See code(s) A4461 or A4463

A **A4363** Ostomy clamp, any type, replacement only, each ♿

A ☑ **A4364** Adhesive, liquid or equal, any type, per oz ♿
MED: 100-2,15,120

A ☑ **A4365** Adhesive remover wipes, any type, per 50 ♿
MED: 100-2,15,120

A ☑ **A4366** Ostomy vent, any type, each ♿

A ☑ **A4367** Ostomy belt, each ♿
MED: 100-2,15,120

A ☑ **A4368** Ostomy filter, any type, each ♿

A ☑ **A4369** Ostomy skin barrier, liquid (spray, brush, etc.), per oz ♿
MED: 100-2,15,120

A ☑ **A4371** Ostomy skin barrier, powder, per oz ♿
MED: 100-2,15,120

A ☑ **A4372** Ostomy skin barrier, solid 4 x 4 or equivalent, standard wear, with built-in convexity, each ♿
MED: 100-2,15,120

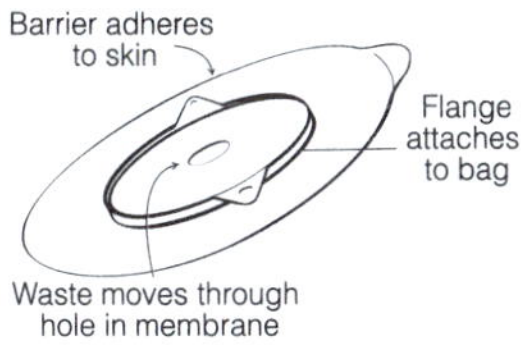

Faceplate flange and skin barrier combination (A4373)

A ☑ **A4373** Ostomy skin barrier, with flange (solid, flexible or accordian), with built-in convexity, any size, each ♿
MED: 100-2,15,120

A ☑ **A4375** Ostomy pouch, drainable, with faceplate attached, plastic, each ♿
MED: 100-2,15,120

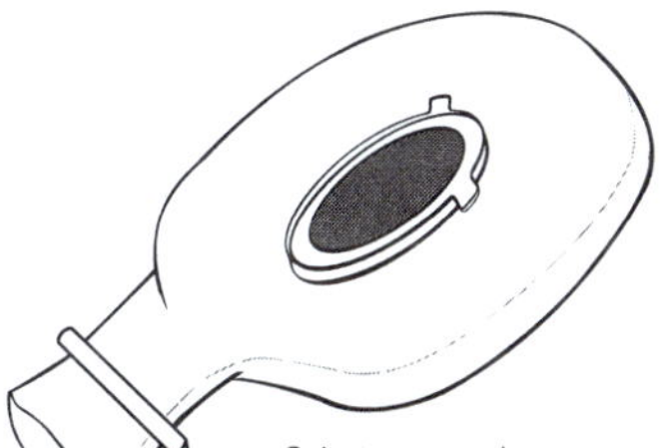

Colostomy pouch with faceplate and drain (A4376)

A ☑ **A4376** Ostomy pouch, drainable, with faceplate attached, rubber, each ♿
MED: 100-2,15,120

A ☑ **A4377** Ostomy pouch, drainable, for use on faceplate, plastic, each ♿
MED: 100-2,15,120

A ☑ **A4378** Ostomy pouch, drainable, for use on faceplate, rubber, each ♿
MED: 100-2,15,120

A ☑ **A4379** Ostomy pouch, urinary, with faceplate attached, plastic, each ♿
MED: 100-2,15,120

A ☑ **A4380** Ostomy pouch, urinary, with faceplate attached, rubber, each ♿
MED: 100-2,15,120

A ☑ **A4381** Ostomy pouch, urinary, for use on faceplate, plastic, each ♿
MED: 100-2,15,120

A ☑ **A4382** Ostomy pouch, urinary, for use on faceplate, heavy plastic, each ♿
MED: 100-2,15,120

A ☑ **A4383** Ostomy pouch, urinary, for use on faceplate, rubber, each ♿
MED: 100-2,15,120

A ☑ **A4384** Ostomy faceplate equivalent, silicone ring, each ♿
MED: 100-2,15,120

A ☑ **A4385** Ostomy skin barrier, solid 4 x 4 or equivalent, extended wear, without built-in convexity, each ♿
MED: 100-2,15,120

A ☑ **A4387** Ostomy pouch, closed, with barrier attached, with built-in convexity (1 piece), each ♿
MED: 100-2,15,120

A ☑ **A4388** Ostomy pouch, drainable, with extended wear barrier attached, (1 piece), each ♿
MED: 100-2,15,120

A ☑ **A4389** Ostomy pouch, drainable, with barrier attached, with built-in convexity (1 piece), each ♿
MED: 100-2,15,120

A ☑ **A4390** Ostomy pouch, drainable, with extended wear barrier attached, with built-in convexity (1 piece), each ♿
MED: 100-2,15,120

A ☑ **A4391** Ostomy pouch, urinary, with extended wear barrier attached (1 piece), each ♿
MED: 100-2,15,120

A ☑ **A4392** Ostomy pouch, urinary, with standard wear barrier attached, with built-in convexity (1 piece), each ♿
MED: 100-2,15,120

A ☑ **A4393** Ostomy pouch, urinary, with extended wear barrier attached, with built-in convexity (1 piece), each ♿
MED: 100-2,15,120

A ☑ **A4394** Ostomy deodorant, with or without lubricant, for use in ostomy pouch, per fl oz ♿
MED: 100-2,15,120

A ☑ **A4395** Ostomy deodorant for use in ostomy pouch, solid, per tablet ♿
MED: 100-2,15,120

A **A4396** Ostomy belt with peristomal hernia support ♿
MED: 100-2,15,120

A ☑ **A4397** Irrigation supply; sleeve, each ♿
MED: 100-2,15,120

A ☑ **A4398** Ostomy irrigation supply; bag, each ♿
MED: 100-2,15,120

A **A4399** Ostomy irrigation supply; cone/catheter, including brush ♿
MED: 100-2,15,120

A **A4400** Ostomy irrigation set ♿
MED: 100-2,15,120

A ☑ **A4402** Lubricant, per oz ♿
MED: 100-2,15,120

A ☑ **A4404** Ostomy ring, each ♿
MED: 100-2,15,120

A ☑ **A4405** Ostomy skin barrier, nonpectin-based, paste, per oz ♿
MED: 100-2,15,120

A ☑ **A4406** Ostomy skin barrier, pectin-based, paste, per oz ♿
MED: 100-2,15,120

A ☑ **A4407** Ostomy skin barrier, with flange (solid, flexible, or accordion), extended wear, with built-in convexity, 4 x 4 in or smaller, each

MED: 100-2,15,120

A ☑ **A4408** Ostomy skin barrier, with flange (solid, flexible or accordion), extended wear, with built-in convexity, larger than 4 x 4 in, each

MED: 100-2,15,120

A ☑ **A4409** Ostomy skin barrier, with flange (solid, flexible or accordion), extended wear, without built-in convexity, 4 x 4 in or smaller, each

MED: 100-2,15,120

A ☑ **A4410** Ostomy skin barrier, with flange (solid, flexible or accordion), extended wear, without built-in convexity, larger than 4 x 4 in, each

MED: 100-2,15,120

A ☑ **A4411** Ostomy skin barrier, solid 4 x 4 or equivalent, extended wear, with built-in convexity, each

A ☑ **A4412** Ostomy pouch, drainable, high output, for use on a barrier with flange (2 piece system), without filter, each

MED: 100-2,15,120

A ☑ **A4413** Ostomy pouch, drainable, high output, for use on a barrier with flange (2-piece system), with filter, each

MED: 100-2,15,120

A ☑ **A4414** Ostomy skin barrier, with flange (solid, flexible or accordion), without built-in convexity, 4 x 4 in or smaller, each

MED: 100-2,15,120

A ☑ **A4415** Ostomy skin barrier, with flange (solid, flexible or accordion), without built-in convexity, larger than 4 x 4 in, each

MED: 100-2,15,120

A ☑ **A4416** Ostomy pouch, closed, with barrier attached, with filter (1 piece), each

A ☑ **A4417** Ostomy pouch, closed, with barrier attached, with built-in convexity, with filter (1 piece), each

A ☑ **A4418** Ostomy pouch, closed; without barrier attached, with filter (1 piece), each

A ☑ **A4419** Ostomy pouch, closed; for use on barrier with nonlocking flange, with filter (2 piece), each

A ☑ **A4420** Ostomy pouch, closed; for use on barrier with locking flange (2 piece), each

E **A4421** Ostomy supply; miscellaneous

Determine if an alternative HCPCS Level II or a CPT code better describes the service being reported. This code should be used only if a more specific code is unavailable.

MED: 100-2,15,120

A ☑ **A4422** Ostomy absorbent material (sheet/pad/crystal packet) for use in ostomy pouch to thicken liquid stomal output, each

MED: 100-2,15,120

A ☑ **A4423** Ostomy pouch, closed; for use on barrier with locking flange, with filter (2 piece), each

A ☑ **A4424** Ostomy pouch, drainable, with barrier attached, with filter (1 piece), each

A ☑ **A4425** Ostomy pouch, drainable; for use on barrier with nonlocking flange, with filter (2-piece system), each

A ☑ **A4426** Ostomy pouch, drainable; for use on barrier with locking flange (2-piece system), each

A ☑ **A4427** Ostomy pouch, drainable; for use on barrier with locking flange, with filter (2-piece system), each

A ☑ **A4428** Ostomy pouch, urinary, with extended wear barrier attached, with faucet-type tap with valve (1 piece), each

A ☑ **A4429** Ostomy pouch, urinary, with barrier attached, with built-in convexity, with faucet-type tap with valve (1 piece), each

A ☑ **A4430** Ostomy pouch, urinary, with extended wear barrier attached, with built-in convexity, with faucet-type tap with valve (1 piece), each

A ☑ **A4431** Ostomy pouch, urinary; with barrier attached, with faucet-type tap with valve (1 piece), each

A ☑ **A4432** Ostomy pouch, urinary; for use on barrier with nonlocking flange, with faucet-type tap with valve (2 piece), each

A ☑ **A4433** Ostomy pouch, urinary; for use on barrier with locking flange (2 piece), each

A ☑ **A4434** Ostomy pouch, urinary; for use on barrier with locking flange, with faucet-type tap with valve (2 piece), each

ADDITIONAL MISCELLANEOUS SUPPLIES

A ☑ **A4450** Tape, nonwaterproof, per 18 sq in

See also code A4452.

MED: 100-2,15,120

A ☑ **A4452** Tape, waterproof, per 18 sq in

See also code A4450.

MED: 100-2,15,120

A ☑ **A4455** Adhesive remover or solvent (for tape, cement or other adhesive), per oz

MED: 100-2,15,120

E **A4458** Enema bag with tubing, reusable

A ☑ **A4461** Surgical dressing holder, nonreusable, each

A ☑ **A4463** Surgical dressing holder, reusable, each

N **A4465** Nonelastic binder for extremity

N **A4470** Gravlee jet washer

MED: 100-2,16,90; 100-3,230.5

N **A4480** VABRA aspirator ♀

MED: 100-2,16,90; 100-3,230.6

A ☑ **A4481** Tracheostoma filter, any type, any size, each

MED: 100-2,15,120

A **A4483** Moisture exchanger, disposable, for use with invasive mechanical ventilation

MED: 100-2,15,120

E ☑ **A4490** Surgical stockings above knee length, each

MED: 100-2,15,100; 100-2,15,110; 100-3,280.1

E ☑ **A4495** Surgical stockings thigh length, each

MED: 100-2,15,100; 100-2,15,110; 100-3,280.1

E ☑ **A4500** Surgical stockings below knee length, each

MED: 100-2,15,100; 100-2,15,110; 100-3,280.1

E ☑ **A4510** Surgical stockings full-length, each

MED: 100-2,15,100; 100-2,15,110; 100-3,280.1

E ☑ **A4520** Incontinence garment, any type, (e.g., brief, diaper), each

MED: 100-3,280.1

B **A4550** Surgical trays

E ☑ **A4554** Disposable underpads, all sizes
MED: 100-2,15,120; 100-3,280.1

Y ☑ **A4556** Electrodes (e.g., apnea monitor), per pair

Y ☑ **A4557** Lead wires (e.g., apnea monitor), per pair

Y ☑ **A4558** Conductive gel or paste, for use with electrical device (e.g., TENS, NMES), per oz

Y ☑ **A4559** Coupling gel or paste, for use with ultrasound device, per oz

N **A4561** Pessary, rubber, any type

N **A4562** Pessary, nonrubber, any type
Medicare jurisdiction: DME regional contractor.

N **A4565** Slings
Dressings applied by a physician are included as part of the professional service. Surgical dressings obtained by the patient to perform homecare as prescribed by the physician are covered.

E **A4570** Splint
Dressings applied by a physician are included as part of the professional service.
MED: 100-2,6,10; 100-2,15,100; 100-4,4,240

E **A4575** Topical hyperbaric oxygen chamber, disposable
MED: 100-3,20.29

E **A4580** Cast supplies (e.g., plaster)
See Q4001-Q4048.
MED: 100-2,6,10; 100-2,15,100; 100-4,4,240

E **A4590** Special casting material (e.g., fiberglass)
See Q4001-Q4048.
MED: 100-2,6,10; 100-2,15,100; 100-4,4,240

Y **A4595** Electrical stimulator supplies, 2 lead, per month, (e.g., TENS, NMES)
MED: 100-3,160.13

Y ☑ **A4600** Sleeve for intermittent limb compression device, replacement only, each

Y **A4601** Lithium ion battery for nonprosthetic use, replacement

Y **A4604** Tubing with integrated heating element for use with positive airway pressure device

Y ☑ **A4605** Tracheal suction catheter, closed system, each

A **A4606** Oxygen probe for use with oximeter device, replacement

Y ☑ **A4608** Transtracheal oxygen catheter, each

SUPPLIES FOR OXYGEN AND RELATED RESPIRATORY EQUIPMENT

Y **A4611** Battery, heavy-duty; replacement for patient-owned ventilator

Y **A4612** Battery cables; replacement for patient-owned ventilator

Y ☑ **A4613** Battery charger; replacement for patient-owned ventilator

Y **A4614** Peak expiratory flow rate meter, hand held

Y **A4615** Cannula, nasal
MED: 100-3,160.6; 100-4,20,100.2

Y ☑ **A4616** Tubing (oxygen), per foot
MED: 100-3,160.6; 100-4,20,100.2

Y **A4617** Mouthpiece
MED: 100-3,160.6; 100-4,20,100.2

Y **A4618** Breathing circuits
MED: 100-3,160.6; 100-4,20,100.2

Y **A4619** Face tent
MED: 100-3,160.6; 100-4,20,100.2

Y **A4620** Variable concentration mask
MED: 100-3,160.6; 100-4,20,100.2

A **A4623** Tracheostomy, inner cannula
MED: 100-2,15,120; 100-3,20.9

Y ☑ **A4624** Tracheal suction catheter, any type other than closed system, each

A **A4625** Tracheostomy care kit for new tracheostomy
MED: 100-2,15,120

A ☑ **A4626** Tracheostomy cleaning brush, each
MED: 100-2,15,120

E **A4627** Spacer, bag or reservoir, with or without mask, for use with metered dose inhaler
MED: 100-2,15,110

Y ☑ **A4628** Oropharyngeal suction catheter, each

A **A4629** Tracheostomy care kit for established tracheostomy
MED: 100-2,15,120

SUPPLIES FOR OTHER DURABLE MEDICAL EQUIPMENT

Y ☑ **A4630** Replacement batteries, medically necessary, transcutaneous electrical stimulator, owned by patient
MED: 100-3,160.7

Y ☑ **A4633** Replacement bulb/lamp for ultraviolet light therapy system, each

A **A4634** Replacement bulb for therapeutic light box, tabletop model

Y ☑ **A4635** Underarm pad, crutch, replacement, each
MED: 100-3,280.1

Y ☑ **A4636** Replacement, handgrip, cane, crutch, or walker, each
MED: 100-3,280.1

Y ☑ **A4637** Replacement, tip, cane, crutch, walker, each
MED: 100-3,280.1

Y ☑ **A4638** Replacement battery for patient-owned ear pulse generator, each

Y ☑ **A4639** Replacement pad for infrared heating pad system, each

Y **A4640** Replacement pad for use with medically necessary alternating pressure pad owned by patient
MED: 100-3,280.1; 100-8,5,5.2.3

SUPPLIES FOR RADIOLOGIC PROCEDURES

N **A4641** Radiopharmaceutical, diagnostic, not otherwise classified N1
MED: 100-4,13,60.3.1

N ☑ **A4642** Indium In-111 satumomab pendetide, diagnostic, per study dose, up to 6 millicuries N1
Use this code for Oncoscint.

MISCELLANEOUS SUPPLIES

N ☑ **A4648** Tissue marker, implantable, any type, each N1

Medical and Surgical Supplies

A4554 — A4648

Special Coverage Instructions | Noncovered by Medicare | Carrier Discretion | ☑ Quantity Alert | ● New Code | ○ Recycled/Reinstated | ▲ Revised Code

[N] **A4649** Surgical supply; miscellaneous
Determine if an alternative HCPCS Level II or a CPT code better describes the service being reported. This code should be used only if a more specific code is unavailable.

[N] ☑ **A4650** Implantable radiation dosimeter, each [N1]

[A] ☑ **A4651** Calibrated microcapillary tube, each ⊘

[A] **A4652** Microcapillary tube sealant ⊘

DIALYSIS SUPPLIES

[A] ☑ **A4653** Peritoneal dialysis catheter anchoring device, belt, each ⊘

[N] ☑ **A4657** Syringe, with or without needle, each ⊘

[N] **A4660** Sphygmomanometer/blood pressure apparatus with cuff and stethoscope ⊘

[N] **A4663** Blood pressure cuff only ⊘

[E] **A4670** Automatic blood pressure monitor ⊘
MED: 100-3,20.19

[B] ☑ **A4671** Disposable cycler set used with cycler dialysis machine, each ⊘

[B] ☑ **A4672** Drainage extension line, sterile, for dialysis, each ⊘

[B] **A4673** Extension line with easy lock connectors, used with dialysis ⊘

[B] ☑ **A4674** Chemicals/antiseptics solution used to clean/sterilize dialysis equipment, per 8 oz ⊘

[N] ☑ **A4680** Activated carbon filter for hemodialysis, each ⊘
MED: 100-3,230.7

[N] ☑ **A4690** Dialyzer (artificial kidneys), all types, all sizes, for hemodialysis, each ⊘

[N] ☑ **A4706** Bicarbonate concentrate, solution, for hemodialysis, per gallon ⊘

[N] ☑ **A4707** Bicarbonate concentrate, powder, for hemodialysis, per packet ⊘

[N] ☑ **A4708** Acetate concentrate solution, for hemodialysis, per gallon ⊘

[N] ☑ **A4709** Acid concentrate, solution, for hemodialysis, per gallon ⊘

[N] ☑ **A4714** Treated water (deionized, distilled, or reverse osmosis) for peritoneal dialysis, per gallon ⊘
MED: 100-3,230.7

[N] **A4719** "Y set" tubing for peritoneal dialysis ⊘

[N] ☑ **A4720** Dialysate solution, any concentration of dextrose, fluid volume greater than 249 cc, but less than or equal to 999 cc, for peritoneal dialysis ⊘

[N] ☑ **A4721** Dialysate solution, any concentration of dextrose, fluid volume greater than 999 cc but less than or equal to 1999 cc, for peritoneal dialysis ⊘

[N] ☑ **A4722** Dialysate solution, any concentration of dextrose, fluid volume greater than 1999 cc but less than or equal to 2999 cc, for peritoneal dialysis ⊘

[N] ☑ **A4723** Dialysate solution, any concentration of dextrose, fluid volume greater than 2999 cc but less than or equal to 3999 cc, for peritoneal dialysis ⊘

[N] ☑ **A4724** Dialysate solution, any concentration of dextrose, fluid volume greater than 3999 cc but less than or equal to 4999 cc, for peritoneal dialysis ⊘

[N] ☑ **A4725** Dialysate solution, any concentration of dextrose, fluid volume greater than 4999 cc but less than or equal to 5999 cc, for peritoneal dialysis ⊘

[N] ☑ **A4726** Dialysate solution, any concentration of dextrose, fluid volume greater than 5999 cc, for peritoneal dialysis ⊘

[B] ☑ **A4728** Dialysate solution, nondextrose containing, 500 ml ⊘

[N] ☑ **A4730** Fistula cannulation set for hemodialysis, each ⊘

[N] ☑ **A4736** Topical anesthetic, for dialysis, per gram ⊘

[N] ☑ **A4737** Injectable anesthetic, for dialysis, per 10 ml ⊘

[N] **A4740** Shunt accessory, for hemodialysis, any type, each ⊘

[N] ☑ **A4750** Blood tubing, arterial or venous, for hemodialysis, each ⊘

[N] ☑ **A4755** Blood tubing, arterial and venous combined, for hemodialysis, each ⊘

[N] ☑ **A4760** Dialysate solution test kit, for peritoneal dialysis, any type, each ⊘

[N] ☑ **A4765** Dialysate concentrate, powder, additive for peritoneal dialysis, per packet ⊘

[N] ☑ **A4766** Dialysate concentrate, solution, additive for peritoneal dialysis, per 10 ml ⊘

[N] ☑ **A4770** Blood collection tube, vacuum, for dialysis, per 50 ⊘

[N] ☑ **A4771** Serum clotting time tube, for dialysis, per 50 ⊘

[N] ☑ **A4772** Blood glucose test strips, for dialysis, per 50 ⊘

[N] ☑ **A4773** Occult blood test strips, for dialysis, per 50 ⊘

[N] ☑ **A4774** Ammonia test strips, for dialysis, per 50 ⊘

[N] ☑ **A4802** Protamine sulfate, for hemodialysis, per 50 mg ⊘

[N] ☑ **A4860** Disposable catheter tips for peritoneal dialysis, per 10 ⊘

[N] **A4870** Plumbing and/or electrical work for home hemodialysis equipment ⊘

[N] **A4890** Contracts, repair and maintenance, for hemodialysis equipment ⊘
MED: 100-2,15,110.2

[N] ☑ **A4911** Drain bag/bottle, for dialysis, each ⊘

[N] **A4913** Miscellaneous dialysis supplies, not otherwise specified ⊘
Pertinent documentation to evaluate medical appropriateness should be included when this code is reported. Determine if an alternative HCPCS Level II or a CPT code better describes the service being reported. This code should be used only if a more specific code is unavailable.

[N] ☑ **A4918** Venous pressure clamp, for hemodialysis, each ⊘

[N] ☑ **A4927** Gloves, nonsterile, per 100 ⊘

[N] ☑ **A4928** Surgical mask, per 20 ⊘

[N] ☑ **A4929** Tourniquet for dialysis, each ⊘

[N] ☑ **A4930** Gloves, sterile, per pair ⊘

[N] ☑ **A4931** Oral thermometer, reusable, any type, each ⊘

[E] ☑ **A4932** Rectal thermometer, reusable, any type, each

ADDITIONAL OSTOMY SUPPLIES

[A] ☑ **A5051** Ostomy pouch, closed; with barrier attached (1 piece), each ♿
MED: 100-2,15,120

[A] ☑ **A5052** Ostomy pouch, closed; without barrier attached (1 piece), each ♿
MED: 100-2,15,120

A ☑ **A5053** Ostomy pouch, closed; for use on faceplate, each ♿
MED: 100-2,15,120

A ☑ **A5054** Ostomy pouch, closed; for use on barrier with flange (2 piece), each ♿
MED: 100-2,15,120

A **A5055** Stoma cap ♿
MED: 100-2,15,120

A ☑ **A5061** Ostomy pouch, drainable; with barrier attached, (1 piece), each ♿

A ☑ **A5062** Ostomy pouch, drainable; without barrier attached (1 piece), each ♿
MED: 100-2,15,120

A ☑ **A5063** Ostomy pouch, drainable; for use on barrier with flange (2-piece system), each ♿
MED: 100-2,15,120

A ☑ **A5071** Ostomy pouch, urinary; with barrier attached (1 piece), each ♿
MED: 100-2,15,120

A ☑ **A5072** Ostomy pouch, urinary; without barrier attached (1 piece), each ♿
MED: 100-2,15,120

A ☑ **A5073** Ostomy pouch, urinary; for use on barrier with flange (2 piece), each ♿
MED: 100-2,15,120

A **A5081** Continent device; plug for continent stoma ♿
MED: 100-2,15,120

A **A5082** Continent device; catheter for continent stoma ♿
MED: 100-2,15,120

A **A5083** Continent device, stoma absorptive cover for continent stoma ♿

A **A5093** Ostomy accessory; convex insert ♿
MED: 100-2,15,120

ADDITIONAL INCONTINENCE APPLIANCES/SUPPLIES

A ☑ **A5102** Bedside drainage bottle with or without tubing, rigid or expandable, each ♿
MED: 100-2,15,120

A ☑ **A5105** Urinary suspensory with leg bag, with or without tube, each ♿
MED: 100-2,15,120

A **A5112** Urinary leg bag; latex ♿
MED: 100-2,15,120

A ☑ **A5113** Leg strap; latex, replacement only, per set ♿
MED: 100-2,15,120

A ☑ **A5114** Leg strap; foam or fabric, replacement only, per set ♿
MED: 100-2,15,120

SUPPLIES FOR EITHER INCONTINENCE OR OSTOMY APPLIANCES

For additional skin barrier codes see codes A4405-A4411.

A ☑ **A5120** Skin barrier, wipes or swabs, each
MED: 100-2,15,120

A ☑ **A5121** Skin barrier; solid, 6 x 6 or equivalent, each ♿
MED: 100-2,15,120

A ☑ **A5122** Skin barrier; solid, 8 x 8 or equivalent, each ♿
MED: 100-2,15,120

A **A5126** Adhesive or nonadhesive; disk or foam pad ♿
MED: 100-2,15,120

A ☑ **A5131** Appliance cleaner, incontinence and ostomy appliances, per 16 oz ♿
MED: 100-2,15,120

A **A5200** Percutaneous catheter/tube anchoring device, adhesive skin attachment ♿
MED: 100-2,15,120

DIABETIC SHOES, FITTING, AND MODIFICATIONS

According to Medicare, documentation from the prescribing physician must certify the diabetic patient has one of the following conditions: peripheral neuropathy with evidence of callus formation; history of preulcerative calluses; history of ulceration; foot deformity; previous amputation; or poor circulation. The footwear must be fitted and furnished by a podiatrist, pedorthist, orthotist, or prosthetist.

Y ☑ **A5500** For diabetics only, fitting (including follow-up), custom preparation and supply of off-the-shelf depth-inlay shoe manufactured to accommodate multidensity insert(s), per shoe
MED: 100-2,15,140

Y ☑ **A5501** For diabetics only, fitting (including follow-up), custom preparation and supply of shoe molded from cast(s) of patient's foot (custom molded shoe), per shoe
MED: 100-2,15,140

Y ☑ **A5503** For diabetics only, modification (including fitting) of off-the-shelf depth-inlay shoe or custom molded shoe with roller or rigid rocker bottom, per shoe
MED: 100-2,15,140

Y ☑ **A5504** For diabetics only, modification (including fitting) of off-the-shelf depth-inlay shoe or custom molded shoe with wedge(s), per shoe
MED: 100-2,15,140

Y ☑ **A5505** For diabetics only, modification (including fitting) of off-the-shelf depth-inlay shoe or custom molded shoe with metatarsal bar, per shoe
MED: 100-2,15,140

Y ☑ **A5506** For diabetics only, modification (including fitting) of off-the-shelf depth-inlay shoe or custom molded shoe with off-set heel(s), per shoe
MED: 100-2,15,140

Y ☑ **A5507** For diabetics only, not otherwise specified modification (including fitting) of off-the-shelf depth-inlay shoe or custom molded shoe, per shoe
MED: 100-2,15,140

Y ☑ **A5508** For diabetics only, deluxe feature of off-the-shelf depth-inlay shoe or custom molded shoe, per shoe
MED: 100-2,15,140

E ☑ **A5510** For diabetics only, direct formed, compression molded to patient's foot without external heat source, multiple-density insert(s) prefabricated, per shoe
MED: 100-2,15,140

Y ☑ **A5512** For diabetics only, multiple density insert, direct formed, molded to foot after external heat source of 230 degrees Fahrenheit or higher, total contact with patient's foot, including arch, base layer minimum of 1/4 inch material of shore a 35 durometer or 3/16 inch material of shore a 40 durometer (or higher), prefabricated, each ♿

Y ☑ **A5513** For diabetics only, multiple density insert, custom molded from model of patient's foot, total contact with patient's foot, including arch, base layer minimum of 3/16 inch material of shore a 35 durometer or higher), includes arch filler and other shaping material, custom fabricated, each ♿

Medical and Surgical Supplies

A5053 — A5513

DRESSINGS

E **A6000** Noncontact wound-warming wound cover for use with the noncontact wound-warming device and warming card
MED: 100-2,16,20

▲ A ☑ **A6010** Collagen based wound filler, dry form, sterile, per gram of collagen
MED: 100-2,15,100

▲ A ☑ **A6011** Collagen based wound filler, gel/paste, sterile, per gram of collagen
MED: 100-2,15,100

▲ A ☑ **A6021** Collagen dressing, sterile, pad size 16 sq in or less, each
MED: 100-2,15,100; 100-4,4,240

▲ A ☑ **A6022** Collagen dressing, sterile, pad size more than 16 sq in but less than or equal to 48 sq in, each
MED: 100-2,15,100; 100-4,4,240

▲ A ☑ **A6023** Collagen dressing, sterile, pad size more than 48 sq in, each
MED: 100-2,15,100; 100-4,4,240

▲ A ☑ **A6024** Collagen dressing wound filler, sterile, per 6 in
MED: 100-2,15,100; 100-4,4,240

E ☑ **A6025** Gel sheet for dermal or epidermal application, (e.g., silicone, hydrogel, other), each

A ☑ **A6154** Wound pouch, each
MED: 100-2,15,100

▲ A ☑ **A6196** Alginate or other fiber gelling dressing, wound cover, sterile, pad size 16 sq in or less, each dressing
MED: 100-2,15,100; 100-4,4,240

▲ A ☑ **A6197** Alginate or other fiber gelling dressing, wound cover, sterile, pad size more than 16 sq in but less than or equal to 48 sq in, each dressing
MED: 100-2,15,100; 100-4,4,240

▲ A ☑ **A6198** Alginate or other fiber gelling dressing, wound cover, sterile, pad size more than 48 sq in, each dressing
MED: 100-2,15,100; 100-4,4,240

▲ A ☑ **A6199** Alginate or other fiber gelling dressing, wound filler, sterile, per 6 in
MED: 100-2,15,100; 100-4,4,240

E ☑ **A6200** Composite dressing, pad size 16 sq in or less, without adhesive border, each dressing
MED: 100-2,15,100; 100-4,4,240

E ☑ **A6201** Composite dressing, pad size more than 16 sq in but less than or equal to 48 sq in, without adhesive border, each dressing
MED: 100-2,15,100; 100-4,4,240

E ☑ **A6202** Composite dressing, pad size more than 48 sq in, without adhesive border, each dressing
MED: 100-2,15,100; 100-4,4,240

▲ A ☑ **A6203** Composite dressing, sterile, pad size 16 sq in or less, with any size adhesive border, each dressing
MED: 100-2,15,100; 100-4,4,240

▲ A ☑ **A6204** Composite dressing, sterile, pad size more than 16 sq in, but less than or equal to 48 sq in, with any size adhesive border, each dressing
MED: 100-2,15,100; 100-4,4,240

▲ A ☑ **A6205** Composite dressing, sterile, pad size more than 48 sq in, with any size adhesive border, each dressing
MED: 100-2,15,100; 100-4,4,240

▲ A ☑ **A6206** Contact layer, sterile, 16 sq in or less, each dressing
MED: 100-2,15,100; 100-4,4,240

▲ A ☑ **A6207** Contact layer, sterile, more than 16 sq in but less than or equal to 48 sq in, each dressing
MED: 100-2,15,100; 100-4,4,240

▲ A ☑ **A6208** Contact layer, sterile, more than 48 sq in, each dressing
MED: 100-2,15,100; 100-4,4,240

▲ A ☑ **A6209** Foam dressing, wound cover, sterile, pad size 16 sq in or less, without adhesive border, each dressing
MED: 100-2,15,100; 100-4,4,240

▲ A ☑ **A6210** Foam dressing, wound cover, sterile, pad size more than 16 sq in but less than or equal to 48 sq in, without adhesive border, each dressing
MED: 100-2,15,100; 100-4,4,240

▲ A ☑ **A6211** Foam dressing, wound cover, sterile, pad size more than 48 sq in, without adhesive border, each dressing
MED: 100-2,15,100; 100-4,4,240

▲ A ☑ **A6212** Foam dressing, wound cover, sterile, pad size 16 sq in or less, with any size adhesive border, each dressing
MED: 100-2,15,100; 100-4,4,240

▲ A ☑ **A6213** Foam dressing, wound cover, sterile, pad size more than 16 sq in but less than or equal to 48 sq in, with any size adhesive border, each dressing
MED: 100-2,15,100; 100-4,4,240

▲ A ☑ **A6214** Foam dressing, wound cover, sterile, pad size more than 48 sq in, with any size adhesive border, each dressing
MED: 100-2,15,100; 100-4,4,240

▲ A ☑ **A6215** Foam dressing, wound filler, sterile, per gram
MED: 100-2,15,100; 100-4,4,240

A ☑ **A6216** Gauze, nonimpregnated, nonsterile, pad size 16 sq in or less, without adhesive border, each dressing
MED: 100-2,15,100; 100-4,4,240

A ☑ **A6217** Gauze, nonimpregnated, nonsterile, pad size more than 16 sq in but less than or equal to 48 sq in, without adhesive border, each dressing
MED: 100-2,15,100; 100-4,4,240

A ☑ **A6218** Gauze, nonimpregnated, nonsterile, pad size more than 48 sq in, without adhesive border, each dressing
MED: 100-2,15,100; 100-4,4,240

▲ A ☑ **A6219** Gauze, nonimpregnated, sterile, pad size 16 sq in or less, with any size adhesive border, each dressing
MED: 100-2,15,100; 100-4,4,240

▲ A ☑ **A6220** Gauze, nonimpregnated, sterile, pad size more than 16 sq in but less than or equal to 48 sq in, with any size adhesive border, each dressing
MED: 100-2,15,100; 100-4,4,240

▲ A ☑ **A6221** Gauze, nonimpregnated, sterile, pad size more than 48 sq in, with any size adhesive border, each dressing
MED: 100-2,15,100; 100-4,4,240

▲ A ☑ **A6222** Gauze, impregnated with other than water, normal saline, or hydrogel, sterile, pad size 16 sq in or less, without adhesive border, each dressing
MED: 100-2,15,100; 100-4,4,240

▲ A ☑ **A6223** Gauze, impregnated with other than water, normal saline, or hydrogel, sterile, pad size more than 16 sq in, but less than or equal to 48 sq in, without adhesive border, each dressing
MED: 100-2,15,100; 100-4,4,240

▲ A ☑ **A6224** Gauze, impregnated with other than water, normal saline, or hydrogel, sterile, pad size more than 48 sq in, without adhesive border, each dressing ♿
MED: 100-2,15,100; 100-4,4,240

▲ A ☑ **A6228** Gauze, impregnated, water or normal saline, sterile, pad size 16 sq in or less, without adhesive border, each dressing ♿
MED: 100-2,15,100; 100-4,4,240

▲ A ☑ **A6229** Gauze, impregnated, water or normal saline, sterile, pad size more than 16 sq in but less than or equal to 48 sq in, without adhesive border, each dressing ♿
MED: 100-2,15,100; 100-4,4,240

▲ A ☑ **A6230** Gauze, impregnated, water or normal saline, sterile, pad size more than 48 sq in, without adhesive border, each dressing
MED: 100-2,15,100; 100-4,4,240

▲ A ☑ **A6231** Gauze, impregnated, hydrogel, for direct wound contact, sterile, pad size 16 sq in or less, each dressing ♿
MED: 100-2,15,100; 100-4,4,240

▲ A ☑ **A6232** Gauze, impregnated, hydrogel, for direct wound contact, sterile, pad size greater than 16 sq in, but less than or equal to 48 sq in, each dressing ♿
MED: 100-2,15,100; 100-4,4,240

▲ A ☑ **A6233** Gauze, impregnated, hydrogel, for direct wound contact, sterile, pad size more than 48 sq in, each dressing ♿
MED: 100-2,15,100; 100-4,4,240

▲ A ☑ **A6234** Hydrocolloid dressing, wound cover, sterile, pad size 16 sq in or less, without adhesive border, each dressing ♿
MED: 100-2,15,100; 100-4,4,240

▲ A ☑ **A6235** Hydrocolloid dressing, wound cover, sterile, pad size more than 16 sq in but less than or equal to 48 sq in, without adhesive border, each dressing ♿
MED: 100-2,15,100; 100-4,4,240

▲ A ☑ **A6236** Hydrocolloid dressing, wound cover, sterile, pad size more than 48 sq in, without adhesive border, each dressing ♿
MED: 100-2,15,100; 100-4,4,240

▲ A ☑ **A6237** Hydrocolloid dressing, wound cover, sterile, pad size 16 sq in or less, with any size adhesive border, each dressing ♿
MED: 100-2,15,100; 100-4,4,240

▲ A ☑ **A6238** Hydrocolloid dressing, wound cover, sterile, pad size more than 16 sq in but less than or equal to 48 sq in, with any size adhesive border, each dressing ♿
MED: 100-2,15,100; 100-4,4,240

▲ A ☑ **A6239** Hydrocolloid dressing, wound cover, sterile, pad size more than 48 sq in, with any size adhesive border, each dressing
MED: 100-2,15,100; 100-4,4,240

▲ A ☑ **A6240** Hydrocolloid dressing, wound filler, paste, sterile, per oz ♿
MED: 100-2,15,100; 100-4,4,240

▲ A ☑ **A6241** Hydrocolloid dressing, wound filler, dry form, sterile, per gram ♿
MED: 100-2,15,100; 100-4,4,240

▲ A ☑ **A6242** Hydrogel dressing, wound cover, sterile, pad size 16 sq in or less, without adhesive border, each dressing ♿
MED: 100-2,15,100; 100-4,4,240

▲ A ☑ **A6243** Hydrogel dressing, wound cover, sterile, pad size more than 16 sq in but less than or equal to 48 sq in, without adhesive border, each dressing ♿
MED: 100-2,15,100; 100-4,4,240

▲ A ☑ **A6244** Hydrogel dressing, wound cover, sterile, pad size more than 48 sq in, without adhesive border, each dressing ♿
MED: 100-2,15,100; 100-4,4,240

▲ A ☑ **A6245** Hydrogel dressing, wound cover, sterile, pad size 16 sq in or less, with any size adhesive border, each dressing ♿
MED: 100-2,15,100; 100-4,4,240

▲ A ☑ **A6246** Hydrogel dressing, wound cover, sterile, pad size more than 16 sq in but less than or equal to 48 sq in, with any size adhesive border, each dressing ♿
MED: 100-2,15,100; 100-4,4,240

▲ A ☑ **A6247** Hydrogel dressing, wound cover, sterile, pad size more than 48 sq in, with any size adhesive border, each dressing ♿
MED: 100-2,15,100; 100-4,4,240

▲ A ☑ **A6248** Hydrogel dressing, wound filler, gel, sterile, per fl oz ♿
MED: 100-2,15,100; 100-4,4,240

A **A6250** Skin sealants, protectants, moisturizers, ointments, any type, any size
Surgical dressings applied by a physician are included as part of the professional service. Surgical dressings obtained by the patient to perform homecare as prescribed by the physician are covered.
MED: 100-2,15,100; 100-4,4,240

▲ A ☑ **A6251** Specialty absorptive dressing, wound cover, sterile, pad size 16 sq in or less, without adhesive border, each dressing ♿
MED: 100-2,15,100; 100-4,4,240

▲ A ☑ **A6252** Specialty absorptive dressing, wound cover, sterile, pad size more than 16 sq in but less than or equal to 48 sq in, without adhesive border, each dressing ♿
MED: 100-2,15,100; 100-4,4,240

▲ A ☑ **A6253** Specialty absorptive dressing, wound cover, sterile, pad size more than 48 sq in, without adhesive border, each dressing ♿
MED: 100-2,15,100; 100-4,4,240

▲ A ☑ **A6254** Specialty absorptive dressing, wound cover, sterile, pad size 16 sq in or less, with any size adhesive border, each dressing ♿
MED: 100-2,15,100; 100-4,4,240

▲ A ☑ **A6255** Specialty absorptive dressing, wound cover, sterile, pad size more than 16 sq in but less than or equal to 48 sq in, with any size adhesive border, each dressing ♿
MED: 100-2,15,100; 100-4,4,240

▲ A ☑ **A6256** Specialty absorptive dressing, wound cover, sterile, pad size more than 48 sq in, with any size adhesive border, each dressing
MED: 100-2,15,100; 100-4,4,240

▲ A ☑ **A6257** Transparent film, sterile, 16 sq in or less, each dressing ♿
Surgical dressings applied by a physician are included as part of the professional service. Surgical dressings obtained by the patient to perform homecare as prescribed by the physician are covered. Use this code for Polyskin, Tegaderm, and Tegaderm HP.
MED: 100-2,15,100; 100-4,4,240

▲ A ☑ **A6258** Transparent film, sterile, more than 16 sq in but less than or equal to 48 sq in, each dressing ♿
Surgical dressings applied by a physician are included as part of the professional service. Surgical dressings obtained by the patient to perform homecare as prescribed by the physician are covered.
MED: 100-2,15,100; 100-4,4,240

▲ A ☑ **A6259** Transparent film, sterile, more than 48 sq in, each dressing ♿
Surgical dressings applied by a physician are included as part of the professional service. Surgical dressings obtained by the patient to perform homecare as prescribed by the physician are covered.
MED: 100-2,15,100; 100-4,4,240

▲ A **A6260** Wound cleansers, sterile, any type, any size
Surgical dressings applied by a physician are included as part of the professional service. Surgical dressings obtained by the patient to perform homecare as prescribed by the physician are covered.
MED: 100-2,15,100; 100-4,4,240

▲ A ☑ **A6261** Wound filler, gel/paste, sterile, per fl oz, not otherwise specified
Surgical dressings applied by a physician are included as part of the professional service. Surgical dressings obtained by the patient to perform homecare as prescribed by the physician are covered.
MED: 100-2,15,100; 100-4,4,240

▲ A ☑ **A6262** Wound filler, dry form, sterile, per gram, not otherwise specified
MED: 100-2,15,100; 100-4,4,240

▲ A ☑ **A6266** Gauze, impregnated, other than water, normal saline, or zinc paste, sterile, any width, per linear yd ♿
Surgical dressings applied by a physician are included as part of the professional service. Surgical dressings obtained by the patient to perform homecare as prescribed by the physician are covered.
MED: 100-2,15,100; 100-4,4,240

A ☑ **A6402** Gauze, nonimpregnated, sterile, pad size 16 sq in or less, without adhesive border, each dressing ♿
Surgical dressings applied by a physician are included as part of the professional service. Surgical dressings obtained by the patient to perform homecare as prescribed by the physician are covered.
MED: 100-2,15,100; 100-4,4,240

A ☑ **A6403** Gauze, nonimpregnated, sterile, pad size more than 16 sq in, less than or equal to 48 sq in, without adhesive border, each dressing ♿
Surgical dressings applied by a physician are included as part of the professional service. Surgical dressings obtained by the patient to perform homecare as prescribed by the physician are covered.
MED: 100-2,15,100; 100-4,4,240

A ☑ **A6404** Gauze, nonimpregnated, sterile, pad size more than 48 sq in, without adhesive border, each dressing
MED: 100-2,15,100; 100-4,4,240

▲ A ☑ **A6407** Packing strips, nonimpregnated, sterile, up to 2 in in width, per linear yd ♿

A ☑ **A6410** Eye pad, sterile, each ♿
MED: 100-2,15,100

A ☑ **A6411** Eye pad, nonsterile, each ♿
MED: 100-2,15,100

E ☑ **A6412** Eye patch, occlusive, each

E ☑ **A6413** Adhesive bandage, first aid type, any size, each

A ☑ **A6441** Padding bandage, nonelastic, nonwoven/nonknitted, width greater than or equal to 3 in and less than 5 in, per yd ♿

A ☑ **A6442** Conforming bandage, nonelastic, knitted/woven, nonsterile, width less than 3 in, per yd ♿

A ☑ **A6443** Conforming bandage, nonelastic, knitted/woven, nonsterile, width greater than or equal to 3 in and less than 5 in, per yd ♿

A ☑ **A6444** Conforming bandage, nonelastic, knitted/woven, nonsterile, width greater than or equal to 5 in, per yd ♿

A ☑ **A6445** Conforming bandage, nonelastic, knitted/woven, sterile, width less than 3 in, per yd ♿

A ☑ **A6446** Conforming bandage, nonelastic, knitted/woven, sterile, width greater than or equal to 3 in and less than 5 in, per yd ♿

A ☑ **A6447** Conforming bandage, nonelastic, knitted/woven, sterile, width greater than or equal to 5 in, per yd ♿

A ☑ **A6448** Light compression bandage, elastic, knitted/woven, width less than 3 in, per yd ♿

A ☑ **A6449** Light compression bandage, elastic, knitted/woven, width greater than or equal to 3 in and less than 5 in, per yd ♿

A ☑ **A6450** Light compression bandage, elastic, knitted/woven, width greater than or equal to 5 in, per yd ♿

A ☑ **A6451** Moderate compression bandage, elastic, knitted/woven, load resistance of 1.25 to 1.34 ft lbs at 50% maximum stretch, width greater than or equal to 3 in and less than 5 in, per yd ♿

A ☑ **A6452** High compression bandage, elastic, knitted/woven, load resistance greater than or equal to 1.35 ft lbs at 50% maximum stretch, width greater than or equal to 3 in and less than 5 in, per yd ♿

A ☑ **A6453** Self-adherent bandage, elastic, nonknitted/nonwoven, width less than 3 in, per yd ♿

A ☑ **A6454** Self-adherent bandage, elastic, nonknitted/nonwoven, width greater than or equal to 3 in and less than 5 in, per yd ♿

A ☑ **A6455** Self-adherent bandage, elastic, nonknitted/nonwoven, width greater than or equal to 5 in, per yd ♿

A ☑ **A6456** Zinc paste impregnated bandage, nonelastic, knitted/woven, width greater than or equal to 3 in and less than 5 in, per yd ♿

A **A6457** Tubular dressing with or without elastic, any width, per linear yard

A **A6501** Compression burn garment, bodysuit (head to foot), custom fabricated ♿
MED: 100-2,15,100

A **A6502** Compression burn garment, chin strap, custom fabricated ♿
MED: 100-2,15,100

A **A6503** Compression burn garment, facial hood, custom fabricated ♿
MED: 100-2,15,100

A **A6504** Compression burn garment, glove to wrist, custom fabricated ♿
MED: 100-2,15,100

A **A6505** Compression burn garment, glove to elbow, custom fabricated ♿
MED: 100-2,15,100

A **A6506** Compression burn garment, glove to axilla, custom fabricated ♿
MED: 100-2,15,100

A **A6507** Compression burn garment, foot to knee length, custom fabricated ♿
MED: 100-2,15,100

A **A6508** Compression burn garment, foot to thigh length, custom fabricated ♿
MED: 100-2,15,100

Special Coverage Instructions | Noncovered by Medicare | Carrier Discretion | ☑ Quantity Alert | ● New Code | ○ Recycled/Reinstated | ▲ Revised Code

 A Age Edit | M Maternity Edit | ♀ Female Only | ♂ Male Only | A-Y OPPS Status Indicators

A A6509 Compression burn garment, upper trunk to waist including arm openings (vest), custom fabricated
MED: 100-2,15,100

A A6510 Compression burn garment, trunk, including arms down to leg openings (leotard), custom fabricated
MED: 100-2,15,100

A A6511 Compression burn garment, lower trunk including leg openings (panty), custom fabricated
MED: 100-2,15,100

A A6512 Compression burn garment, not otherwise classified
MED: 100-2,15,100

B A6513 Compression burn mask, face and/or neck, plastic or equal, custom fabricated

E ☑ A6530 Gradient compression stocking, below knee, 18-30 mm Hg, each

A ☑ A6531 Gradient compression stocking, below knee, 30-40 mm Hg, each
MED: 100-2,15,100

A ☑ A6532 Gradient compression stocking, below knee, 40-50 mm Hg, each
MED: 100-2,15,100

E ☑ A6533 Gradient compression stocking, thigh length, 18-30 mm Hg, each
MED: 100-2,15,130

E ☑ A6534 Gradient compression stocking, thigh length, 30-40 mm Hg, each
MED: 100-2,15,130

E ☑ A6535 Gradient compression stocking, thigh length, 40-50 mm Hg, each
MED: 100-2,15,130

E ☑ A6536 Gradient compression stocking, full-length/chap style, 18-30 mm Hg, each
MED: 100-2,15,130

E ☑ A6537 Gradient compression stocking, full-length/chap style, 30-40 mm Hg, each
MED: 100-2,15,130

E ☑ A6538 Gradient compression stocking, full-length/chap style, 40-50 mm Hg, each
MED: 100-2,15,130

E ☑ A6539 Gradient compression stocking, waist length, 18-30 mm Hg, each
MED: 100-2,15,130

E ☑ A6540 Gradient compression stocking, waist length, 30-40 mm Hg, each
MED: 100-2,15,130

E ☑ A6541 Gradient compression stocking, waist length, 40-50 mm Hg, each
MED: 100-2,15,130

E A6542 Gradient compression stocking, custom made
MED: 100-2,15,130

E A6543 Gradient compression stocking, lymphedema
MED: 100-2,15,130

E A6544 Gradient compression stocking, garter belt
MED: 100-2,15,130

● A ☑ A6545 Gradient compression wrap, nonelastic, below knee, 30-50 mm Hg, each

E A6549 Gradient compression stocking, not otherwise specified
MED: 100-2,15,130

Y ☑ A6550 Wound care set, for negative pressure wound therapy electrical pump, includes all supplies and accessories

MISCELLANEOUS SUPPLIES

Y ☑ A7000 Canister, disposable, used with suction pump, each

Y ☑ A7001 Canister, nondisposable, used with suction pump, each

Y ☑ A7002 Tubing, used with suction pump, each

Y A7003 Administration set, with small volume nonfiltered pneumatic nebulizer, disposable

Y A7004 Small volume nonfiltered pneumatic nebulizer, disposable

Y A7005 Administration set, with small volume nonfiltered pneumatic nebulizer, nondisposable

Y A7006 Administration set, with small volume filtered pneumatic nebulizer

Y A7007 Large volume nebulizer, disposable, unfilled, used with aerosol compressor

Y A7008 Large volume nebulizer, disposable, prefilled, used with aerosol compressor

Y A7009 Reservoir bottle, nondisposable, used with large volume ultrasonic nebulizer

Y ☑ A7010 Corrugated tubing, disposable, used with large volume nebulizer, 100 ft

Y ☑ A7011 Corrugated tubing, nondisposable, used with large volume nebulizer, 10 ft

Y A7012 Water collection device, used with large volume nebulizer

Y A7013 Filter, disposable, used with aerosol compressor

Y A7014 Filter, nondisposable, used with aerosol compressor or ultrasonic generator

Y A7015 Aerosol mask, used with DME nebulizer

Y A7016 Dome and mouthpiece, used with small volume ultrasonic nebulizer

Y A7017 Nebulizer, durable, glass or autoclavable plastic, bottle type, not used with oxygen
MED: 100-3,280.1

Y ☑ A7018 Water, distilled, used with large volume nebulizer, 1000 ml

Y ☑ A7025 High frequency chest wall oscillation system vest, replacement for use with patient-owned equipment, each

Y ☑ A7026 High frequency chest wall oscillation system hose, replacement for use with patient-owned equipment, each

Y ☑ A7027 Combination oral/nasal mask, used with continuous positive airway pressure device, each

Y ☑ A7028 Oral cushion for combination oral/nasal mask, replacement only, each

Y ☑ A7029 Nasal pillows for combination oral/nasal mask, replacement only, pair

Y ☑ A7030 Full face mask used with positive airway pressure device, each

Y ☑ A7031 Face mask interface, replacement for full face mask, each

Y ☑ A7032 Cushion for use on nasal mask interface, replacement only, each

Special Coverage Instructions | Noncovered by Medicare | Carrier Discretion | ☑ Quantity Alert | ● New Code | ○ Recycled/Reinstated | ▲ Revised Code

 A2-Z3 ASC Payment Indicators MED: Pub 100/NCD References DMEPOS Paid SNF Excluded PQRI

Y ☑ A7033 Pillow for use on nasal cannula type interface, replacement only, pair

Y A7034 Nasal interface (mask or cannula type) used with positive airway pressure device, with or without head strap

Y A7035 Headgear used with positive airway pressure device

Y A7036 Chinstrap used with positive airway pressure device

Y A7037 Tubing used with positive airway pressure device

Y A7038 Filter, disposable, used with positive airway pressure device

Y A7039 Filter, nondisposable, used with positive airway pressure device

A A7040 One way chest drain valve

A A7041 Water seal drainage container and tubing for use with implanted chest tube

N ☑ A7042 Implanted pleural catheter, each

A A7043 Vacuum drainage bottle and tubing for use with implanted catheter

Y ☑ A7044 Oral interface used with positive airway pressure device, each

Y A7045 Exhalation port with or without swivel used with accessories for positive airway devices, replacement only

MED: 100-3,230.17

Y ☑ A7046 Water chamber for humidifier, used with positive airway pressure device, replacement, each

MED: 100-3,230.17

A ☑ A7501 Tracheostoma valve, including diaphragm, each

MED: 100-2,15,120

A ☑ A7502 Replacement diaphragm/faceplate for tracheostoma valve, each

MED: 100-2,15,120

A ☑ A7503 Filter holder or filter cap, reusable, for use in a tracheostoma heat and moisture exchange system, each

MED: 100-2,15,120

A ☑ A7504 Filter for use in a tracheostoma heat and moisture exchange system, each

MED: 100-2,15,120

A ☑ A7505 Housing, reusable without adhesive, for use in a heat and moisture exchange system and/or with a tracheostoma valve, each

MED: 100-2,15,120

A ☑ A7506 Adhesive disc for use in a heat and moisture exchange system and/or with tracheostoma valve, any type each

MED: 100-2,15,120

A ☑ A7507 Filter holder and integrated filter without adhesive, for use in a tracheostoma heat and moisture exchange system, each

MED: 100-2,15,120

A ☑ A7508 Housing and integrated adhesive, for use in a tracheostoma heat and moisture exchange system and/or with a tracheostoma valve, each

MED: 100-2,15,120

A ☑ A7509 Filter holder and integrated filter housing, and adhesive, for use as a tracheostoma heat and moisture exchange system, each

MED: 100-2,15,120

A ☑ A7520 Tracheostomy/laryngectomy tube, noncuffed, polyvinylchloride (PVC), silicone or equal, each

A ☑ A7521 Tracheostomy/laryngectomy tube, cuffed, polyvinylchloride (PVC), silicone or equal, each

A ☑ A7522 Tracheostomy/laryngectomy tube, stainless steel or equal (sterilizable and reusable), each

A ☑ A7523 Tracheostomy shower protector, each

A ☑ A7524 Tracheostoma stent/stud/button, each

A ☑ A7525 Tracheostomy mask, each

A ☑ A7526 Tracheostomy tube collar/holder, each

A ☑ A7527 Tracheostomy/laryngectomy tube plug/stop, each

Y A8000 Helmet, protective, soft, prefabricated, includes all components and accessories

Y A8001 Helmet, protective, hard, prefabricated, includes all components and accessories

Y A8002 Helmet, protective, soft, custom fabricated, includes all components and accessories

Y A8003 Helmet, protective, hard, custom fabricated, includes all components and accessories

Y A8004 Soft interface for helmet, replacement only

ADMINISTRATIVE, MISCELLANEOUS & INVESTIGATIONAL A9000-A9999

This section of codes reports items such as nonprescription drugs, noncovered items/services, exercise equipment and, most notably, radiopharmaceutical diagnostic imaging agents.

B A9150 Nonprescription drugs

MED: 100-2,15,50

E ☑ A9152 Single vitamin/mineral/trace element, oral, per dose, not otherwise specified

E ☑ A9153 Multiple vitamins, with or without minerals and trace elements, oral, per dose, not otherwise specified

B A9155 Artificial saliva, 30 ml

E A9180 Pediculosis (lice infestation) treatment, topical, for administration by patient/caretaker

E A9270 Noncovered item or service

MED: 100-2,16,20

E ☑ A9274 External ambulatory insulin delivery system, disposable, each, includes all supplies and accessories

E A9275 Home glucose disposable monitor, includes test strips

E ☑ A9276 Sensor; invasive (e.g., subcutaneous), disposable, for use with interstitial continuous glucose monitoring system, 1 unit = 1 day supply

E A9277 Transmitter; external, for use with interstitial continuous glucose monitoring system

E A9278 Receiver (monitor); external, for use with interstitial continuous glucose monitoring system

E A9279 Monitoring feature/device, stand-alone or integrated, any type, includes all accessories, components and electronics, not otherwise classified

E A9280 Alert or alarm device, not otherwise classified

E ☑ A9281 Reaching/grabbing device, any type, any length, each

E ☑ A9282 Wig, any type, each

E ☑ A9283 Foot pressure off loading/supportive device, any type, each

● N A9284 Spirometer, nonelectronic, includes all accessories

E A9300 Exercise equipment
MED: 100-2,15,110.1; 100-3,280.1

RADIOPHARMACEUTICALS

N ☑ A9500 Technetium Tc-99m sestamibi, diagnostic, per study dose, up to 40 millicuries
Use this code for Cardiolite.

N ☑ A9501 Technetium Tc-99m teboroxime, diagnostic, per study dose

▲ N ☑ A9502 Technetium Tc-99m tetrofosmin, diagnostic, per study dose
Use this code for Myoview.

N ☑ A9503 Technetium Tc-99m medronate, diagnostic, per study dose, up to 30 millicuries
Use this code for CIS-MDP, Draximage MDP-10, Draximage MDP-25, MDP-Bracco, Technetium Tc-99m MPI-MDP
AHA: 2Q,'02,9

N ☑ A9504 Technetium Tc-99m apcitide, diagnostic, per study dose, up to 20 millicuries
Use this code for Acutect
AHA: 2Q,'02,9; 4Q,'01,5

N ☑ A9505 Thallium Tl-201 thallous chloride, diagnostic, per millicurie
Use this code for MIBG, Thallous Chloride USP.
AHA: 2Q,'02,9

N ☑ A9507 Indium In-111 capromab pendetide, diagnostic, per study dose, up to 10 millicuries
Use this code for Prostascint.

N ☑ A9508 Iodine I-131 iobenguane sulfate, diagnostic, per 0.5 millicurie
Use this code for MIBG.
AHA: 2Q,'02,9

N ☑ A9509 Iodine I-123 sodium iodide, diagnostic, per millicurie

N ☑ A9510 Technetium Tc-99m disofenin, diagnostic, per study dose, up to 15 millicuries
Use this code for Hepatolite.

N ☑ A9512 Technetium Tc-99m pertechnetate, diagnostic, per millicurie
Use this code for Technelite, Ultra-Technelow.

N ☑ A9516 Iodine I-123 sodium iodide, diagnostic, per 100 microcuries, up to 999 microcuries

H ☑ A9517 Iodine I-131 sodium iodide capsule(s), therapeutic, per millicurie

N ☑ A9521 Technetium Tc-99m exametazime, diagnostic, per study dose, up to 25 millicuries
Use this code for Ceretec.

N ☑ A9524 Iodine I-131 iodinated serum albumin, diagnostic, per 5 microcuries

N ☑ A9526 Nitrogen N-13 ammonia, diagnostic, per study dose, up to 40 millicuries
MED: 100-3,220.6; 100-4,13,60.3.1; 100-4,13,60.3.2

U ☑ A9527 Iodine I-125, sodium iodide solution, therapeutic, per millicurie

N ☑ A9528 Iodine I-131 sodium iodide capsule(s), diagnostic, per millicurie

N ☑ A9529 Iodine I-131 sodium iodide solution, diagnostic, per millicurie

H ☑ A9530 Iodine I-131 sodium iodide solution, therapeutic, per millicurie ⊘

N ☑ A9531 Iodine I-131 sodium iodide, diagnostic, per microcurie (up to 100 microcuries)

N ☑ A9532 Iodine I-125 serum albumin, diagnostic, per 5 microcuries

N ☑ A9535 Injection, methylene blue, 1 ml

N ☑ A9536 Technetium Tc-99m depreotide, diagnostic, per study dose, up to 35 millicuries

N ☑ A9537 Technetium Tc-99m mebrofenin, diagnostic, per study dose, up to 15 millicuries

N ☑ A9538 Technetium Tc-99m pyrophosphate, diagnostic, per study dose, up to 25 millicuries
Use this code for CIS-PYRO, Phosphostec, Technescan Pyp Kit

N ☑ A9539 Technetium Tc-99m pentetate, diagnostic, per study dose, up to 25 millicuries
Use this code for AN-DTPA, DTPA, Magnavist, MPI-DTPA Kit-Chelate, MPI Indium DTPA IN-111, Pentate Calcium Trisodium, Pentate Zinc Trisodium

N ☑ A9540 Technetium Tc-99m macroaggregated albumin, diagnostic, per study dose, up to 10 millicuries

N ☑ A9541 Technetium Tc-99m sulfur colloid, diagnostic, per study dose, up to 20 millicuries

N ☑ A9542 Indium In-111 ibritumomab tiuxetan, diagnostic, per study dose, up to 5 millicuries ⊘
Use this code for Zevalin

H ☑ A9543 Yttrium Y-90 ibritumomab tiuxetan, therapeutic, per treatment dose, up to 40 millicuries ⊘

N ☑ A9544 Iodine I-131 tositumomab, diagnostic, per study dose ⊘

H ☑ A9545 Iodine I-131 tositumomab, therapeutic, per treatment dose ⊘
Use this code for Bexxar.

N ☑ A9546 Cobalt Co-57/58, cyanocobalamin, diagnostic, per study dose, up to 1 microcurie

N ☑ A9547 Indium In-111 oxyquinoline, diagnostic, per 0.5 millicurie

N ☑ A9548 Indium In-111 pentetate, diagnostic, per 0.5 millicurie

N ☑ A9550 Technetium Tc-99m sodium gluceptate, diagnostic, per study dose, up to 25 millicurie

N ☑ A9551 Technetium Tc-99m succimer, diagnostic, per study dose, up to 10 millicuries
Use this code for MPI-DMSA Kidney Reagent.

N ☑ A9552 Fluorodeoxyglucose F-18 FDG, diagnostic, per study dose, up to 45 millicuries

N ☑ A9553 Chromium Cr-51 sodium chromate, diagnostic, per study dose, up to 250 microcuries
Use this code for Chromitope Sodium.

N ☑ A9554 Iodine I-125 sodium iothalamate, diagnostic, per study dose, up to 10 microcuries
Use this code for Glofil-125.

N ☑ A9555 Rubidium Rb-82, diagnostic, per study dose, up to 60 millicuries
Use this code for Cardiogen 82.

N ☑ A9556 Gallium Ga-67 citrate, diagnostic, per millicurie
Use this code for Ganite.

N ☑ **A9557** Technetium Tc-99m bicisate, diagnostic, per study dose, up to 25 millicuries N1
Use this code for Neurolite.

N ☑ **A9558** Xenon Xe-133 gas, diagnostic, per 10 millicuries N1

N ☑ **A9559** Cobalt Co-57 cyanocobalamin, oral, diagnostic, per study dose, up to 1 microcurie N1

N ☑ **A9560** Technetium Tc-99m labeled red blood cells, diagnostic, per study dose, up to 30 millicuries N1

N ☑ **A9561** Technetium Tc-99m oxidronate, diagnostic, per study dose, up to 30 millicuries N1
Use this code for TechneScan.

N ☑ **A9562** Technetium Tc-99m mertiatide, diagnostic, per study dose, up to 15 millicuries N1
Use this code for TechneScan MAG-3.

H ☑ **A9563** Sodium phosphate P-32, therapeutic, per millicurie

H ☑ **A9564** Chromic phosphate P-32 suspension, therapeutic, per millicurie
Use this code for Phosphocol (P32).

N ☑ **A9566** Technetium Tc-99m fanolesomab, diagnostic, per study dose, up to 25 millicuries N1

N ☑ **A9567** Technetium Tc-99m pentetate, diagnostic, aerosol, per study dose, up to 75 millicuries N1
Use this code for AN-DTPA, DTPA, MPI-DTPA Kit-Chelate, MPI Indium DTPA IN-111, Pentate Calcium Trisodium, Pentate Zinc Trisodium.

N ☑ **A9568** Technetium Tc-99m arcitumomab, diagnostic, per study dose, up to 45 millicuries N1
Use this code for CEA Scan.

N ☑ **A9569** Technetium Tc-99m exametazime labeled autologous white blood cells, diagnostic, per study dose N1
Use this code for Ceretec.

N ☑ **A9570** Indium In-111 labeled autologous white blood cells, diagnostic, per study dose N1

N ☑ **A9571** Indium In-111 labeled autologous platelets, diagnostic, per study dose N1

N ☑ **A9572** Indium In-111 pentetreotide, diagnostic, per study dose, up to 6 millicuries N1
Use this code for Ostreoscan.

N ☑ **A9576** Injection, gadoteridol, (ProHance multipack), per ml N1

N ☑ **A9577** Injection, gadobenate dimeglumine (MultiHance), per ml N1

N ☑ **A9578** Injection, gadobenate dimeglumine (MultiHance multipack), per ml N1

N ☑ **A9579** Injection, gadolinium-based magnetic resonance contrast agent, not otherwise specified (NOS), per ml N1
Use this code for Omniscan.

● N **A9580** Sodium fluoride F-18, diagnostic, per study dose, up to 30 millicuries N1

H ☑ **A9600** Strontium Sr-89 chloride, therapeutic, per millicurie
Use this code for Metastron.
AHA: 2Q,'02,9

H ☑ **A9605** Samarium Sm-153 lexidronamm, therapeutic, per 50 millicuries
Use this code for Quadramet.
AHA: 2Q,'02,9

N **A9698** Nonradioactive contrast imaging material, not otherwise classified, per study N1

N **A9699** Radiopharmaceutical, therapeutic, not otherwise classified

B **A9700** Supply of injectable contrast material for use in echocardiography, per study
AHA: 4Q,'01,5

MISCELLANEOUS

Y **A9900** Miscellaneous DME supply, accessory, and/or service component of another HCPCS code ♿

A **A9901** DME delivery, set up, and/or dispensing service component of another HCPCS code

Y **A9999** Miscellaneous DME supply or accessory, not otherwise specified

ENTERAL AND PARENTERAL THERAPY B4000-B9999

This section includes codes for supplies, formulae, nutritional solutions, and infusion pumps.

ENTERAL FORMULAE AND ENTERAL MEDICAL SUPPLIES

Certification of medical necessity is required for coverage. Submit a revision to the certification of medical necessity if the patient's daily volume changes by more than one liter; if there is a change in infusion method; or if there is a change from premix to home mix or parenteral to enteral therapy.

Y ☑ **B4034** Enteral feeding supply kit; syringe fed, per day ♿

MED: 100-2,15,120; 100-3,180.2; 100-4,20,100.2.2, 100-4,20,160.1

Y ☑ **B4035** Enteral feeding supply kit; pump fed, per day ♿

MED: 100-2,15,120; 100-3,180.2; 100-4,20,100.2.2; 100-4,20,160.1

Y ☑ **B4036** Enteral feeding supply kit; gravity fed, per day ♿

MED: 100-2,15,120; 100-3,180.2; 100-4,20,100.2.2; 100-4,20,160.1

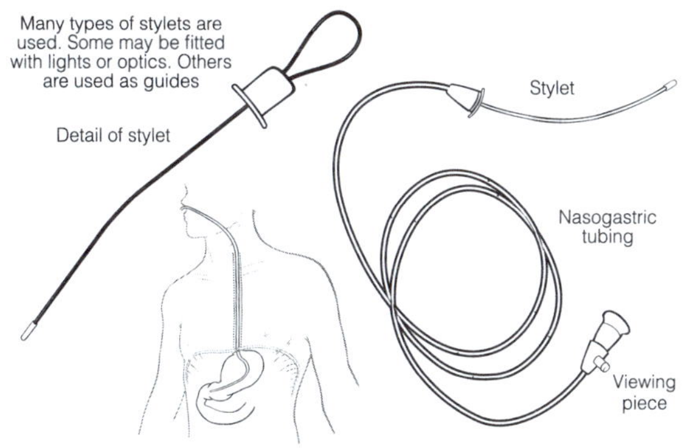

Y **B4081** Nasogastric tubing with stylet ♿

MED: 100-2,15,120; 100-3,180.2; 100-4,20,100.2.2; 100-4,20,160.1

Y **B4082** Nasogastric tubing without stylet ♿

MED: 100-2,15,120; 100-3,180.2; 100-4,20,100.2.2; 100-4,20,160.1

Y **B4083** Stomach tube — Levine type ♿

MED: 100-2,15,120; 100-3,180.2; 100-4,20,100.2.2

A ☑ **B4087** Gastrostomy/jejunostomy tube, standard, any material, any type, each

A ☑ **B4088** Gastrostomy/jejunostomy tube, low-profile, any material, any type, each

E ☑ **B4100** Food thickener, administered orally, per oz

Y ☑ **B4102** Enteral formula, for adults, used to replace fluids and electrolytes (e.g., clear liquids), 500 ml = 1 unit ♿

MED: 100-3,180.2; 100-4,20,160.1

Y ☑ **B4103** Enteral formula, for pediatrics, used to replace fluids and electrolytes (e.g., clear liquids), 500 ml = 1 unit ♿

MED: 100-3,180.2; 100-4,20,160.1

E **B4104** Additive for enteral formula (e.g., fiber)

MED: 100-3,180.2; 100-4,20,160.1

Y ☑ **B4149** Enteral formula, manufactured blenderized natural foods with intact nutrients, includes proteins, fats, carbohydrates, vitamins and minerals, may include fiber, administered through an enteral feeding tube, 100 calories = 1 unit ♿

MED: 100-2,15,120; 100-3,180.2; 100-4,20,100.2.2; 100-4,20,160.1

Y ☑ **B4150** Enteral formula, nutritionally complete with intact nutrients, includes proteins, fats, carbohydrates, vitamins and minerals, may include fiber, administered through an enteral feeding tube, 100 calories = 1 unit ♿

Use this code for Enrich, Ensure, Ensure HN, Ensure Powder, Isocal, Lonalac Powder, Meritene, Meritene Powder, Osmolite, Osmolite HN, Portagen Powder, Sustacal, Renu, Sustagen Powder, Travasorb.

MED: 100-2,15,120; 100-3,180.2; 100-4,20,100.2.2; 100-4,20,160.1

Y ☑ **B4152** Enteral formula, nutritionally complete, calorically dense (equal to or greater than 1.5 kcal/ml) with intact nutrients, includes proteins, fats, carbohydrates, vitamins and minerals, may include fiber, administered through an enteral feeding tube, 100 calories = 1 unit ♿

Use this code for Magnacal, Isocal HCN, Sustacal HC, Ensure Plus, Ensure Plus HN.

MED: 100-2,15,120; 100-3,180.2; 100-4,20,100.2.2; 100-4,20,160.1

Y ☑ **B4153** Enteral formula, nutritionally complete, hydrolyzed proteins (amino acids and peptide chain), includes fats, carbohydrates, vitamins and minerals, may include fiber, administered through an enteral feeding tube, 100 calories = 1 unit ♿

Use this code for Criticare HN, Vivonex t.e.n. (Total Enteral Nutrition), Vivonex HN, Vital (Vital HN), Travasorb HN, Isotein HN, Precision HN, Precision Isotonic.

MED: 100-2,15,120; 100-3,180.2; 100-4,20,100.2.2; 100-4,20,160.1

Y ☑ **B4154** Enteral formula, nutritionally complete, for special metabolic needs, excludes inherited disease of metabolism, includes altered composition of proteins, fats, carbohydrates, vitamins and/or minerals, may include fiber, administered through an enteral feeding tube, 100 calories = 1 unit ♿

Use this code for Hepatic-aid, Travasorb Hepatic, Travasorb MCT, Travasorb Renal, Traum-aid, Tramacal, Aminaid.

MED: 100-2,15,120; 100-3,180.2; 100-4,20,100.2.2; 100-4,20,160.1

Y ☑ **B4155** Enteral formula, nutritionally incomplete/modular nutrients, includes specific nutrients, carbohydrates (e.g., glucose polymers), proteins/amino acids (e.g., glutamine, arginine), fat (e.g., medium chain triglycerides) or combination, administered through an enteral feeding tube, 100 calories = 1 unit ♿

Use this code for Propac, Gerval Protein, Promix, Casec, Moducal, Controlyte, Polycose Liquid or Powder, Sumacal, Microlipids, MCT Oil, Nutri-source.

MED: 100-2,15,120; 100-3,180.2; 100-4,20,100.2.2; 100-4,20,160.1

Y ☑ **B4157** Enteral formula, nutritionally complete, for special metabolic needs for inherited disease of metabolism, includes proteins, fats, carbohydrates, vitamins and minerals, may include fiber, administered through an enteral feeding tube, 100 calories = 1 unit ♿

MED: 100-3,180.2; 100-4,20,160.1

Y ☑ **B4158** Enteral formula, for pediatrics, nutritionally complete with intact nutrients, includes proteins, fats, carbohydrates, vitamins and minerals, may include fiber and/or iron, administered through an enteral feeding tube, 100 calories = 1 unit ♿

MED: 100-3,180.2; 100-4,20,160.1

Y ☑ **B4159** Enteral formula, for pediatrics, nutritionally complete soy based with intact nutrients, includes proteins, fats, carbohydrates, vitamins and minerals, may include fiber and/or iron, administered through an enteral feeding tube, 100 calories = 1 unit ♿

MED: 100-3,180.2; 100-4,20,160.1

Y ☑ **B4160** Enteral formula, for pediatrics, nutritionally complete calorically dense (equal to or greater than 0.7 kcal/ml) with intact nutrients, includes proteins, fats, carbohydrates, vitamins and minerals, may include fiber, administered through an enteral feeding tube, 100 calories = 1 unit ♿
MED: 100-3,180.2; 100-4,20,160.1

Y ☑ **B4161** Enteral formula, for pediatrics, hydrolyzed/amino acids and peptide chain proteins, includes fats, carbohydrates, vitamins and minerals, may include fiber, administered through an enteral feeding tube, 100 calories = 1 unit ♿
MED: 100-3,180.2; 100-4,20,160.1

Y ☑ **B4162** Enteral formula, for pediatrics, special metabolic needs for inherited disease of metabolism, includes proteins, fats, carbohydrates, vitamins and minerals, may include fiber, administered through an enteral feeding tube, 100 calories = 1 unit ♿
MED: 100-3,180.2; 100-4,20,160.1

PARENTERAL NUTRITION SOLUTIONS AND SUPPLIES

Y ☑ **B4164** Parenteral nutrition solution: carbohydrates (dextrose), 50% or less (500 ml = 1 unit), home mix ♿
MED: 100-2,15,120; 100-3,180.2; 100-4,3,10.4; 100-4,20,100.2.2

Y ☑ **B4168** Parenteral nutrition solution; amino acid, 3.5%, (500 ml = 1 unit) — home mix ♿
MED: 100-2,15,120; 100-3,180.2; 100-4,3,10.4; 100-4,20,100.2.2

Y ☑ **B4172** Parenteral nutrition solution; amino acid, 5.5% through 7%, (500 ml = 1 unit) — home mix ♿
MED: 100-2,15,120; 100-3,180.2; 100-4,3,10.4; 100-4,20,100.2.2

Y ☑ **B4176** Parenteral nutrition solution; amino acid, 7% through 8.5%, (500 ml = 1 unit) — home mix ♿
MED: 100-2,15,120; 100-3,180.2; 100-4,3,10.4; 100-4,20,100.2.2

Y ☑ **B4178** Parenteral nutrition solution: amino acid, greater than 8.5% (500 ml = 1 unit), home mix ♿
MED: 100-2,15,120; 100-3,180.2; 100-4,3,10.4; 100-4,20,100.2.2

Y ☑ **B4180** Parenteral nutrition solution: carbohydrates (dextrose), greater than 50% (500 ml = 1 unit), home mix ♿
MED: 100-2,15,120; 100-3,180.2; 100-4,3,10.4; 100-4,20,100.2.2

B ☑ **B4185** Parenteral nutrition solution, per 10 grams lipids

Y ☑ **B4189** Parenteral nutrition solution: compounded amino acid and carbohydrates with electrolytes, trace elements, and vitamins, including preparation, any strength, 10 to 51 g of protein, premix ♿
MED: 100-2,15,120; 100-3,180.2; 100-4,3,10.4; 100-4,20,100.2.2

Y ☑ **B4193** Parenteral nutrition solution: compounded amino acid and carbohydrates with electrolytes, trace elements, and vitamins, including preparation, any strength, 52 to 73 g of protein, premix ♿
MED: 100-2,15,120; 100-3,180.2; 100-4,3,10.4; 100-4,20,100.2.2

Y ☑ **B4197** Parenteral nutrition solution; compounded amino acid and carbohydrates with electrolytes, trace elements and vitamins, including preparation, any strength, 74 to 100 grams of protein — premix ♿
MED: 100-2,15,120; 100-3,180.2; 100-4,3,10.4; 100-4,20,100.2.2

Y ☑ **B4199** Parenteral nutrition solution; compounded amino acid and carbohydrates with electrolytes, trace elements and vitamins, including preparation, any strength, over 100 grams of protein — premix ♿
MED: 100-2,15,120; 100-3,180.2; 100-4,3,10.4; 100-4,20,100.2.2

Y **B4216** Parenteral nutrition; additives (vitamins, trace elements, Heparin, electrolytes), home mix, per day ♿
MED: 100-2,15,120; 100-3,180.2; 100-4,3,10.4; 100-4,20,100.2.2

Y **B4220** Parenteral nutrition supply kit; premix, per day ♿
MED: 100-2,15,120; 100-3,180.2; 100-4,3,10.4; 100-4,20,100.2.2

Y **B4222** Parenteral nutrition supply kit; home mix, per day ♿
MED: 100-2,15,120; 100-3,180.2; 100-4,3,10.4; 100-4,20,100.2.2

Y **B4224** Parenteral nutrition administration kit, per day ♿
MED: 100-2,15,120; 100-3,180.2; 100-4,3,10.4; 100-4,20,100.2.2

Y **B5000** Parenteral nutrition solution: compounded amino acid and carbohydrates with electrolytes, trace elements, and vitamins, including preparation, any strength, renal - Amirosyn RF, NephrAmine, RenAmine - premix ♿
Use this code for Amirosyn-RF, NephrAmine, RenAmin.
MED: 100-2,15,120; 100-3,180.2; 100-4,3,10.4; 100-4,20,100.2.2

Y **B5100** Parenteral nutrition solution: compounded amino acid and carbohydrates with electrolytes, trace elements, and vitamins, including preparation, any strength, hepatic - FreAmine HBC, HepatAmine - premix ♿
Use this code for FreAmine HBC, HepatAmine.
MED: 100-2,15,120; 100-3,180.2; 100-4,3,10.4; 100-4,20,100.2.2

Y **B5200** Parenteral nutrition solution: compounded amino acid and carbohydrates with electrolytes, trace elements, and vitamins, including preparation, any strength, stress - branch chain amino acids - premix ♿
MED: 100-2,15,120; 100-3,180.2; 100-4,3,10.4; 100-4,20,100.2.2

ENTERAL AND PARENTERAL PUMPS

Submit documentation of the need for the infusion pump. Medicare will reimburse for the simplest model that meets the patient's needs.

Y **B9000** Enteral nutrition infusion pump — without alarm ♿
MED: 100-2,15,120; 100-3,180.2; 100-4,20,100.2.2

Y **B9002** Enteral nutrition infusion pump — with alarm ♿
MED: 100-2,15,120; 100-3,180.2; 100-4,20,100.2.2

Y **B9004** Parenteral nutrition infusion pump, portable ♿
MED: 100-2,15,120; 100-3,180.2; 100-4,3,10.4; 100-4,20,100.2.2

Y **B9006** Parenteral nutrition infusion pump, stationary ♿
MED: 100-2,15,120; 100-3,180.2; 100-4,3,10.4; 100-4,20,100.2.2

Y **B9998** NOC for enteral supplies ♿
MED: 100-2,15,120; 100-3,180.2; 100-4,3,10.4; 100-4,20,100.2.2

Y **B9999** NOC for parenteral supplies ♿
Determine if an alternative HCPCS Level II or a CPT code better describes the service being reported. This code should be used only if a more specific code is unavailable.
MED: 100-2,15,120; 100-3,180.2; 100-4,3,10.4; 100-4,20,100.2.2

OUTPATIENT PPS C1000-C9999

This section reports drugs, biologicals, and devices codes that must be used by OPPS hospitals. Non-OPPS hospitals, Critical Access Hospitals (CAHs), Indian Health Service Hospitals (HIS), hospitals located in American Samoa, Guam, Saipan, or the Virgin Islands, and Maryland waiver hospitals may report these codes at their discretion. The codes can only be reported for facility (technical) services.

The C series of HCPCS may include device catagories, new technology procedures, and drugs, biologicals and radiopharmaceuticals that do not have other HCPCS codes assigned. Some of these items and services are eligible for transitional pass-through payments for OPPS hospitals, have separate APC payments, or are items that are packaged. Hospitals are encouraged to report all appropriate C codes regardless of payment status.

S ☑ **C1300** Hyperbaric oxygen under pressure, full body chamber, per 30 minute interval
MED: 100-4,32,30.1

N **C1713** Anchor/screw for opposing bone-to-bone or soft tissue-to-bone (implantable) N1
MED: 100-4,4,61.1
AHA: 3Q,'02,5; 1Q,'01,5

N **C1714** Catheter, transluminal atherectomy, directional N1
MED: 100-4,4,61.1
AHA: 4Q,'03,8; 3Q,'02,5; 1Q,'01,5

N **C1715** Brachytherapy needle N1 ⊘
MED: 100-4,4,61.1
AHA: 3Q,'02,5; 1Q,'01,5

U ☑ **C1716** Brachytherapy source, nonstranded, gold-198, per source ⊘
MED: 100-4,4,61.1
AHA: 3Q,'02,5; 1Q,'01,5

U ☑ **C1717** Brachytherapy source, nonstranded, high dose rate iridium-192, per source ⊘
MED: 100-4,4,61.1
AHA: 3Q,'02,5; 1Q,'01,5

U ☑ **C1719** Brachytherapy source, nonstranded, nonhigh dose rate iridium-192, per source ⊘
MED: 100-4,4,61.1
AHA: 3Q,'02,5; 1Q,'01,5

N **C1721** Cardioverter-defibrillator, dual chamber (implantable) N1
MED: 100-4,4,61.1
AHA: 3Q,'02,5; 1Q,'01,5

N **C1722** Cardioverter-defibrillator, single chamber (implantable) N1
MED: 100-4,4,61.1
AHA: 3Q,'02,5; 1Q,'01,5

N **C1724** Catheter, transluminal atherectomy, rotational N1
MED: 100-4,4,61.1
AHA: 4Q,'03,8; 3Q,'02,5; 1Q,'01,5

N **C1725** Catheter, transluminal angioplasty, nonlaser (may include guidance, infusion/perfusion capability) N1
MED: 100-4,4,61.1
AHA: 4Q,'03,8; 3Q,'02,5; 1Q,'01,5

N **C1726** Catheter, balloon dilatation, nonvascular N1
MED: 100-4,4,61.1
AHA: 3Q,'02,5; 1Q,'01,5

N **C1727** Catheter, balloon tissue dissector, nonvascular (insertable) N1
MED: 100-4,4,61.1
AHA: 3Q,'02,5; 1Q,'01,5

○ N **C1728** Catheter, brachytherapy seed administration N1 ⊘
MED: 100-4,4,61.1
AHA: 3Q,'02,5; 1Q,'01,5

N **C1729** Catheter, drainage N1
MED: 100-4,4,61.1
AHA: 3Q,'02,5; 1Q,'01,5

N **C1730** Catheter, electrophysiology, diagnostic, other than 3D mapping (19 or fewer electrodes) N1
MED: 100-4,4,61.1
AHA: 3Q,'02,5; 1Q,'01,5

N **C1731** Catheter, electrophysiology, diagnostic, other than 3D mapping (20 or more electrodes) N1
MED: 100-4,4,61.1
AHA: 3Q,'02,5; 1Q,'01,5

N **C1732** Catheter, electrophysiology, diagnostic/ablation, 3D or vector mapping N1
MED: 100-4,4,61.1
AHA: 1Q,'01,5

N **C1733** Catheter, electrophysiology, diagnostic/ablation, other than 3D or vector mapping, other than cool-tip N1
MED: 100-4,4,61.1
AHA: 3Q,'02,5; 1Q,'01,5

N **C1750** Catheter, hemodialysis/peritoneal, long-term N1
MED: 100-4,4,61.1
AHA: 4Q,'03,8; 3Q,'02,5; 1Q,'01,5

N **C1751** Catheter, infusion, inserted peripherally, centrally or midline (other than hemodialysis) N1
MED: 100-4,4,61.1
AHA: 4Q,'03,8; 3Q,'02,5; 3Q,'01,5

N **C1752** Catheter, hemodialysis/peritoneal, short-term N1
MED: 100-4,4,61.1
AHA: 4Q,'03,8; 3Q,'02,5; 1Q,'01,5

N **C1753** Catheter, intravascular ultrasound N1
MED: 100-4,4,61.1
AHA: 4Q,'03,8; 3Q,'02,5; 1Q,'01,5

N **C1754** Catheter, intradiscal N1
MED: 100-4,4,61.1
AHA: 4Q,'03,8; 3Q,'02,5; 1Q,'01,5

N **C1755** Catheter, intraspinal N1
MED: 100-4,4,61.1
AHA: 4Q,'03,8; 3Q,'02,5; 1Q,'01,5

N **C1756** Catheter, pacing, transesophageal N1
MED: 100-4,4,61.1
AHA: 4Q,'03,8; 3Q,'02,5; 1Q,'01,5

N **C1757** Catheter, thrombectomy/embolectomy N1
MED: 100-4,4,61.1
AHA: 4Q,'03,8; 3Q,'02,5; 1Q,'01,5

N **C1758** Catheter, ureteral N1
MED: 100-4,4,61.1
AHA: 4Q,'03,8; 3Q,'02,5; 1Q,'01,6

N **C1759** Catheter, intracardiac echocardiography N1
MED: 100-4,4,61.1
AHA: 4Q,'03,8; 3Q,'02,5; 1Q,'01,5; 3Q,'01,4

N **C1760** Closure device, vascular (implantable/insertable) N1
MED: 100-4,4,61.1
AHA: 4Q,'03,8; 3Q,'02,5; 1Q,'01,6

N **C1762** Connective tissue, human (includes fascia lata) N1
MED: 100-4,4,61.1
AHA: 3Q,'03,12; 4Q,'03,8; 3Q,'02,5; 1Q,'01,6

N **C1763** Connective tissue, nonhuman (includes synthetic) N1
MED: 100-4,4,61.1
AHA: 3Q,'03,12; 4Q,'03,8; 3Q,'02,5; 1Q,'01,6

N **C1764** Event recorder, cardiac (implantable) N1
MED: 100-4,4,61.1
AHA: 4Q,'03,8; 3Q,'02,5; 1Q,'01,6

N **C1765** Adhesion barrier N1
MED: 100-4,4,61.1

N **C1766** Introducer/sheath, guiding, intracardiac electrophysiological, steerable, other than peel-away N1
MED: 100-4,4,61.1
AHA: 3Q,'02,5; 3Q,'01,5

N **C1767** Generator, neurostimulator (implantable), nonrechargeable N1
MED: 100-4,4,61.1
AHA: 4Q,'03,8; 1Q,'02,9; 3Q,'02,5

N **C1768** Graft, vascular N1
MED: 100-4,4,61.1
AHA: 4Q,'03,8; 3Q,'02,5; 1Q,'01,6

N **C1769** Guide wire N1
MED: 100-4,4,61.1
AHA: 4Q,'03,8; 3Q,'02,5; 1Q,'01,6; 3Q,'01,4

N **C1770** Imaging coil, magnetic resonance (insertable) N1
MED: 100-4,4,61.1
AHA: 4Q,'03,8; 3Q,'02,5; 1Q,'01,6

N **C1771** Repair device, urinary, incontinence, with sling graft N1
MED: 100-4,4,61.1
AHA: 4Q,'03,8; 3Q,'02,5; 1Q,'01,6

N **C1772** Infusion pump, programmable (implantable) N1
MED: 100-4,4,61.1
AHA: 3Q,'02,5; 1Q,'01,6

N **C1773** Retrieval device, insertable (used to retrieve fractured medical devices) N1
MED: 100-4,4,61.1
AHA: 4Q,'03,8; 3Q,'02,5; 1Q,'01,6

N **C1776** Joint device (implantable) N1
MED: 100-4,4,61.1
AHA: 3Q,'02,5; 1Q,'01,6; 3Q,'01,5

N **C1777** Lead, cardioverter-defibrillator, endocardial single coil (implantable) N1
MED: 100-4,4,61.1
AHA: 3Q,'02,5; 1Q,'01,6

N **C1778** Lead, neurostimulator (implantable) N1
MED: 100-4,4,61.1
AHA: 3Q,'02,5; 1Q,'02,9

N **C1779** Lead, pacemaker, transvenous VDD single pass N1
MED: 100-4,4,61.1
AHA: 3Q,'02,5; 1Q,'01,6

N **C1780** Lens, intraocular (new technology) N1
MED: 100-4,4,61.1
AHA: 3Q,'02,5; 1Q,'01,6

N **C1781** Mesh (implantable) N1
MED: 100-4,4,61.1
AHA: 3Q,'02,5; 1Q,'01,6

N **C1782** Morcellator N1
MED: 100-4,4,61.1
AHA: 3Q,'02,5; 1Q,'01,6

N **C1783** Ocular implant, aqueous drainage assist device N1
MED: 100-4,4,61.1

N **C1784** Ocular device, intraoperative, detached retina N1
MED: 100-4,4,61.1
AHA: 3Q,'02,5; 1Q,'01,6

N **C1785** Pacemaker, dual chamber, rate-responsive (implantable) N1
MED: 100-4,3,10.4; 100-4,4,61.1
AHA: 4Q,'03,8; 3Q,'02,5; 1Q,'01,6

N **C1786** Pacemaker, single chamber, rate-responsive (implantable) N1
MED: 100-4,4,61.1
AHA: 4Q,'03,8; 3Q,'02,5; 1Q,'01,6

N **C1787** Patient programmer, neurostimulator N1
MED: 100-4,4,61.1
AHA: 4Q,'03,8; 3Q,'02,5; 1Q,'01,6

N **C1788** Port, indwelling (implantable) N1
MED: 100-4,4,61.1
AHA: 4Q,'03,8; 3Q,'02,5; 1Q,'01,6; 3Q,'01,4

N **C1789** Prosthesis, breast (implantable) N1
MED: 100-4,4,61.1
AHA: 4Q,'03,8; 3Q,'02,5; 1Q,'01,6

N **C1813** Prosthesis, penile, inflatable N1
MED: 100-4,4,61.1
AHA: 4Q,'03,8; 3Q,'02,5; 1Q,'01,6

N **C1814** Retinal tamponade device, silicone oil N1
MED: 100-4,4,61.1

N **C1815** Prosthesis, urinary sphincter (implantable) N1
MED: 100-4,4,61.1
AHA: 4Q,'03,8; 3Q,'02,5; 1Q,'01,6

N **C1816** Receiver and/or transmitter, neurostimulator (implantable) N1
MED: 100-4,4,61.1
AHA: 4Q,'03,8; 3Q,'02,5; 1Q,'01,6

N **C1817** Septal defect implant system, intracardiac N1
MED: 100-4,4,61.1
AHA: 4Q,'03,8; 3Q,'02,5; 1Q,'01,6

N **C1818** Integrated keratoprosthesis N1
MED: 100-4,4,61.1
AHA: 4Q,'03,4

N **C1819** Surgical tissue localization and excision device (implantable) N1
MED: 100-4,4,61.1

N **C1820** Generator, neurostimulator (implantable), with rechargeable battery and charging system N1
MED: 100-4,4,10.12

N **C1821** Interspinous process distraction device (implantable) N1

N **C1874** Stent, coated/covered, with delivery system N1
MED: 100-4,4,61.1
AHA: 4Q,'03,8; 1Q,'01,6

N **C1875** Stent, coated/covered, without delivery system N1
MED: 100-4,4,61.1
AHA: 4Q,'03,8; 1Q,'01,6

N **C1876** Stent, noncoated/noncovered, with delivery system N1
MED: 100-4,4,61.1
AHA: 4Q,'03,8; 3Q,'02,5; 1Q,'01,6; 3Q,'01,4

N **C1877** Stent, noncoated/noncovered, without delivery system N1
MED: 100-4,4,61.1
AHA: 4Q,'03,8; 3Q,'02,5; 1Q,'01,6; 3Q,'01,4

N **C1878** Material for vocal cord medialization, synthetic (implantable) N1
MED: 100-4,4,61.1
AHA: 3Q,'02,5; 1Q,'01,6

N **C1879** Tissue marker (implantable) N1
MED: 100-4,4,61.1
AHA: 4Q,'03,8; 3Q,'02,5; 1Q,'01,6

N **C1880** Vena cava filter N1
MED: 100-4,4,61.1
AHA: 4Q,'03,8; 3Q,'02,5; 1Q,'01,6

N **C1881** Dialysis access system (implantable) N1
MED: 100-4,4,61.1
AHA: 4Q,'03,8; 3Q,'02,5; 1Q,'01,6

N **C1882** Cardioverter-defibrillator, other than single or dual chamber (implantable) N1
MED: 100-4,4,61.1
AHA: 3Q,'02,5; 1Q,'01,5

N **C1883** Adaptor/extension, pacing lead or neurostimulator lead (implantable) N1
MED: 100-4,4,61.1
AHA: 1Q,'02,9; 3Q,'02,5; 1Q,'01,5

N **C1884** Embolization protective system N1
MED: 100-4,4,61.1

N **C1885** Catheter, transluminal angioplasty, laser N1
MED: 100-4,4,61.1
AHA: 4Q,'03,8; 3Q,'02,5; 1Q,'01,5

N **C1887** Catheter, guiding (may include infusion/perfusion capability) N1
MED: 100-4,4,61.1
AHA: 3Q,'02,5; 1Q,'01,5

N **C1888** Catheter, ablation, noncardiac, endovascular (implantable) N1
MED: 100-4,4,61.1

N **C1891** Infusion pump, nonprogrammable, permanent (implantable) N1
MED: 100-4,4,61.1
AHA: 4Q,'03,8; 3Q,'02,5; 1Q,'01,6

N **C1892** Introducer/sheath, guiding, intracardiac electrophysiological, fixed-curve, peel-away N1
MED: 100-4,4,61.1
AHA: 3Q,'02,5; 1Q,'01,6

N **C1893** Introducer/sheath, guiding, intracardiac electrophysiological, fixed-curve, other than peel-away N1
MED: 100-4,4,61.1
AHA: 3Q,'02,5; 1Q,'01,6; 3Q,'01,4

N **C1894** Introducer/sheath, other than guiding, other than intracardiac electrophysiological, nonlaser N1
MED: 100-4,4,61.1
AHA: 3Q,'02,5

N **C1895** Lead, cardioverter-defibrillator, endocardial dual coil (implantable) N1
MED: 100-4,4,61.1
AHA: 3Q,'02,5; 1Q,'01,6

N **C1896** Lead, cardioverter-defibrillator, other than endocardial single or dual coil (implantable) N1
MED: 100-4,4,61.1
AHA: 3Q,'02,5; 1Q,'01,6

N **C1897** Lead, neurostimulator test kit (implantable) N1
MED: 100-4,4,61.1
AHA: 1Q,'02,9; 3Q,'02,5; 1Q,'01,6

N **C1898** Lead, pacemaker, other than transvenous VDD single pass N1
MED: 100-4,4,61.1
AHA: 1Q,'01,6; 3Q,'01,4

N **C1899** Lead, pacemaker/cardioverter-defibrillator combination (implantable) N1
MED: 100-4,4,61.1
AHA: 3Q,'02,5; 1Q,'01,6

N **C1900** Lead, left ventricular coronary venous system N1
MED: 100-4,4,61.1

N **C2614** Probe, percutaneous lumbar discectomy N1
MED: 100-4,4,61.1

N **C2615** Sealant, pulmonary, liquid N1
MED: 100-4,4,61.1
AHA: 3Q,'02,5; 1Q,'01,6

U ☑ **C2616** Brachytherapy source, nonstranded, yttrium-90, per source ⊘
MED: 100-4,4,61.1
AHA: 3Q,'03,11; 3Q,'02,5

N **C2617** Stent, noncoronary, temporary, without delivery system N1
MED: 100-4,4,61.1
AHA: 4Q,'03,8; 3Q,'02,5; 1Q,'01,6

N **C2618** Probe, cryoablation N1
MED: 100-4,4,61.1
AHA: 4Q,'03,8; 3Q,'02,5; 1Q,'01,6

N **C2619** Pacemaker, dual chamber, nonrate-responsive (implantable) N1
MED: 100-4,4,61.1
AHA: 3Q,'02,5; 1Q,'01,6; 3Q,'01,4

N **C2620** Pacemaker, single chamber, nonrate-responsive (implantable) N1
MED: 100-4,3,10.4; 100-4,4,61.1
AHA: 4Q,'03,8; 3Q,'02,5; 1Q,'01,6

N **C2621** Pacemaker, other than single or dual chamber (implantable) N1
MED: 100-4,3,10.4; 100-4,4,61.1
AHA: 4Q,'03,8; 1Q,'01,6

N **C2622** Prosthesis, penile, noninflatable N1
MED: 100-4,4,61.1
AHA: 4Q,'03,8; 3Q,'02,5; 1Q,'01,6

N **C2625** Stent, noncoronary, temporary, with delivery system N1
MED: 100-4,4,61.1
AHA: 4Q,'03,8; 3Q,'02,5; 1Q,'01,6

N **C2626** Infusion pump, nonprogrammable, temporary (implantable) N1
MED: 100-4,4,61.1
AHA: 3Q,'02,5; 1Q,'01,6

N **C2627** Catheter, suprapubic/cystoscopic N1
MED: 100-4,4,61.1
AHA: 4Q,'03,8; 3Q,'02,5; 1Q,'01,5

N **C2628** Catheter, occlusion N1
MED: 100-4,4,61.1
AHA: 4Q,'03,8; 3Q,'02,5; 1Q,'01,5

N **C2629** Introducer/sheath, other than guiding, intracardiac electrophysiological, laser N1
MED: 100-4,4,61.1
AHA: 3Q,'02,5; 1Q,'01,6

N **C2630** Catheter, electrophysiology, diagnostic/ablation, other than 3D or vector mapping, cool-tip N1
MED: 100-4,4,61.1
AHA: 3Q,'02,5; 1Q,'01,5

N **C2631** Repair device, urinary, incontinence, without sling graft N1
MED: 100-4,4,61.1
AHA: 4Q,'03,8; 3Q,'02,5; 1Q,'01,6

U ☑ **C2634** Brachytherapy source, nonstranded, high activity, iodine-125, greater than 1.01 mCi (NIST), per source ⊘
MED: 100-4,4,61.1
AHA: 2Q,'05,8

U ☑ **C2635** Brachytherapy source, nonstranded, high activity, palladium-103, greater than 2.2 mCi (NIST), per source ⊘
MED: 100-4,4,61.1
AHA: 2Q,'05,8

U ☑ **C2636** Brachytherapy linear source, nonstranded, palladium-103, per 1 mm ⊘
MED: 100-4,4,61.1

B ☑ **C2637** Brachytherapy source, nonstranded, ytterbium-169, per source ⊘
AHA: 3Q,'05,7

U ☑ **C2638** Brachytherapy source, stranded, iodine-125, per source

U ☑ **C2639** Brachytherapy source, nonstranded, iodine-125, per source

U ☑ **C2640** Brachytherapy source, stranded, palladium-103, per source

U ☑ **C2641** Brachytherapy source, nonstranded, palladium-103, per source

U ☑ **C2642** Brachytherapy source, stranded, cesium-131, per source

U ☑ **C2643** Brachytherapy source, nonstranded, cesium-131, per source

U ☑ **C2698** Brachytherapy source, stranded, not otherwise specified, per source

U ☑ **C2699** Brachytherapy source, nonstranded, not otherwise specified, per source

Q3 **C8900** Magnetic resonance angiography with contrast, abdomen Z2 ⊘

Q3 **C8901** Magnetic resonance angiography without contrast, abdomen Z2 ⊘

Q3 **C8902** Magnetic resonance angiography without contrast followed by with contrast, abdomen Z2 ⊘

Q3 **C8903** Magnetic resonance imaging with contrast, breast; unilateral Z2 ⊘

Q3 **C8904** Magnetic resonance imaging without contrast, breast; unilateral Z2 ⊘

Q3 **C8905** Magnetic resonance imaging without contrast followed by with contrast, breast; unilateral Z2 ⊘

Q3 **C8906** Magnetic resonance imaging with contrast, breast; bilateral Z2 ⊘

Q3 **C8907** Magnetic resonance imaging without contrast, breast; bilateral Z2 ⊘

Q3 **C8908** Magnetic resonance imaging without contrast followed by with contrast, breast; bilateral Z2 ⊘

Q3 **C8909** Magnetic resonance angiography with contrast, chest (excluding myocardium) Z2 ⊘

Q3 **C8910** Magnetic resonance angiography without contrast, chest (excluding myocardium) Z2 ⊘

Q3 **C8911** Magnetic resonance angiography without contrast followed by with contrast, chest (excluding myocardium) Z2 ⊘

Q3 **C8912** Magnetic resonance angiography with contrast, lower extremity Z2 ⊘

Q3 **C8913** Magnetic resonance angiography without contrast, lower extremity Z2 ⊘

Q3 **C8914** Magnetic resonance angiography without contrast followed by with contrast, lower extremity Z2 ⊘

Q3 **C8918** Magnetic resonance angiography with contrast, pelvis Z2 ⊘
AHA: 4Q,'03,4

Q3 **C8919** Magnetic resonance angiography without contrast, pelvis Z2 ⊘
AHA: 4Q,'03,4

Q3 **C8920** Magnetic resonance angiography without contrast followed by with contrast, pelvis Z2 ⊘
AHA: 4Q,'03,4

▲ S **C8921** Transthoracic echocardiography with contrast, or without contrast followed by with contrast, for congenital cardiac anomalies; complete

▲ S **C8922** Transthoracic echocardiography with contrast, or without contrast followed by with contrast, for congenital cardiac anomalies; follow-up or limited study

▲ S **C8923** Transthoracic echocardiography with contrast, or without contrast followed by with contrast, real-time with image documentation (2D) with or without M-mode recording; complete

▲ S **C8924** Transthoracic echocardiography with contrast, or without contrast followed by with contrast, real-time with image documentation (2D) with or without M-mode recording; follow-up or limited study

▲ S **C8925** Transesophageal echocardiography (TEE) with contrast, or without contrast followed by with contrast, real time with image documentation (2D) (with or without M-mode recording); including probe placement, image acquisition, interpretation and report

▲ S **C8926** Transesophageal echocardiography (TEE) with contrast, or without contrast followed by with contrast, for congenital cardiac anomalies; including probe placement, image acquisition, interpretation and report

▲ S **C8927** Transesophageal echocardiography (TEE) with contrast, or without contrast followed by with contrast, for monitoring purposes, including probe placement, real time 2-dimensional image acquisition and interpretation leading to ongoing (continuous) assessment of (dynamically changing) cardiac pumping function and to therapeutic measures on an immediate time basis

▲ S **C8928** Transthoracic echocardiography with contrast, or without contrast followed by with contrast, real-time with image documentation (2D), with or without M-mode recording, during rest and cardiovascular stress test using treadmill, bicycle exercise and/or pharmacologically induced stress, with interpretation and report

● S **C8929** Transthoracic echocardiography with contrast, or without contrast followed by with contrast, real-time with image documentation (2D), includes M-mode recording, when performed, complete, with spectral doppler echocardiography, and with color flow doppler echocardiography

● S **C8930** Transthoracic echocardiography, with contrast, or without contrast followed by with contrast, real-time with image documentation (2D), includes M-mode recording, when performed, during rest and cardiovascular stress test using treadmill, bicycle exercise and/or pharmacologically induced stress, with interpretation and report; including performance of continuous electrocardiographic monitoring, with physician supervision

S **C8957** Intravenous infusion for therapy/diagnosis; initiation of prolonged infusion (more than 8 hours), requiring use of portable or implantable pump
MED: 100-4,4,230.2.1; 100-4,4,230.2.3

~~C9003 Palivizumab-RSV-IgM, per 50 mg~~

N **C9113** Injection, pantoprazole sodium, per vial N1
Use this code for Protonix.

K ☑ **C9121** Injection, argatroban, per 5 mg K2

~~C9237 Injection, lanreotide acetate, 1 mg~~
See J1930

~~C9238 Injection, levetiracetam, 10 mg~~
See J1953

~~C9239 Injection, temsirolimus, 1 mg~~
See J9330

~~C9240 Injection, ixabepilone, 1 mg~~
See J9207

~~C9241 Injection, doripenem, 10 mg~~
See J1267

~~C9242 Injection, fosaprepitant, 1 mg~~
See J1453

~~C9243 Injection, bendamustine hcl, 1 mg~~
See J9033

~~C9244 Injection, regadenoson, 0.4 mg~~
See J2785

● G ☑ **C9245** Injection, romiplostim, 10 mcg K2
Use this code for Nplate

● G ☑ **C9246** Injection, gadoxetate disodium, per ml K2
Use this code for Eovist

● N **C9247** Iobenguane, I-123, diagnostic, per study dose, up to 10 millicuries N1

● G ☑ **C9248** Injection, clevidipine butyrate, 1 mg K2
Use this code for Cleviprex

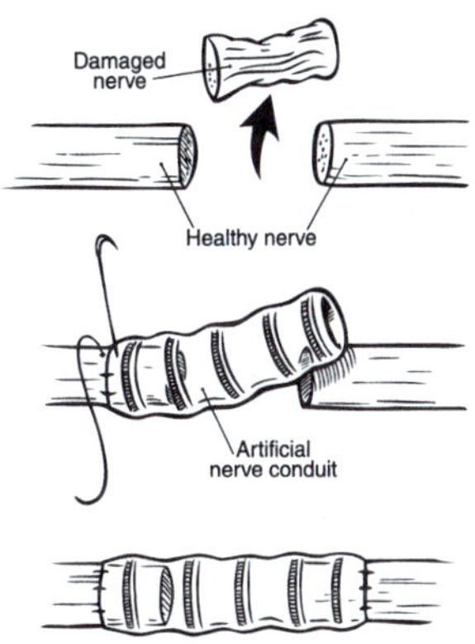

A synthetic "bridge" is affixed to each end of a severed nerve with sutures
This procedure is performed using an operating microscope

N ☑ **C9352** Microporous collagen implantable tube (NeuraGen Nerve Guide), per cm length N1

N ☑ **C9353** Microporous collagen implantable slit tube (NeuraWrap Nerve Protector), per cm length N1

G ☑ **C9354** Acellular pericardial tissue matrix of nonhuman origin (Veritas), per sq cm K2

G ☑ **C9355** Collagen nerve cuff (NeuroMatrix), per 0.5 cm length K2

● G ☑ **C9356** Tendon, porous matrix of cross-linked collagen and glycosaminoglycan matrix (TenoGlide Tendon Protector Sheet), per sq cm K2

~~C9357 Dermal substitute, granulated cross-linked collagen and glycosaminoglycan matrix (Flowable Wound Matrix), 1 cc~~
See Q4114

● G ☑ **C9358** Dermal substitute, native, nondenatured collagen (SurgiMend Collagen Matrix), per 0.5 square cm K2

● G ☑ **C9359** Porous purified collagen matrix bone void filler (Integra Mozaik Osteoconductive Scaffold Putty, Integra OS Osteoconductive Scaffold Putty), per 0.5 cc K2

A **C9399** Unclassified drugs or biologicals K7

T **C9716** Creations of thermal anal lesions by radiofrequency energy G2

~~C9723 Dynamic infrared blood perfusion imaging (DIRI)~~

T **C9724** Endoscopic full-thickness plication in the gastric cardia using endoscopic plication system (EPS); includes endoscopy G2

T **C9725** Placement of endorectal intracavitary applicator for high intensity brachytherapy G2 ⦸
AHA: 3Q,'05,7

T **C9726** Placement and removal (if performed) of applicator into breast for radiation therapy G2

T ☑ **C9727** Insertion of implants into the soft palate; minimum of 3 implants G2

X **C9728** Placement of interstitial device(s) for radiation therapy/surgery guidance (e.g., fiducial markers, dosimeter), other than prostate (any approach), single or multiple R2

● N **C9898** Radiolabeled product provided during a hospital inpatient stay

● A **C9899** Implanted prosthetic device, payable only for inpatients who do not have inpatient coverage

DENTAL PROCEDURES D0000-D9999

The D, or dental, codes are a separate category of national codes. The Current Dental Terminology code set is copyrighted by the American Dental Association (ADA). CDT is included in HCPCS Level II. Decisions regarding the modification, deletion, or addition of CDT codes are made by the ADA and not the national panel responsible for the administration of HCPCS.

The Department of Health and Human Services has an agreement with the AMA pertaining to the use of the CPT codes for physician services; it also has an agreement with the ADA to include as a set of HCPCS Level II codes for use in billing for dental services.

Please refer to you CPT book for possible alternate code(s).

DIAGNOSTIC D0100-D0999

CLINICAL ORAL EVALUATION

E **D0120** Periodic oral evaluation — established patient
This procedure is covered if its purpose is to identify a patient's existing infections prior to kidney transplantation.

E **D0140** Limited oral evaluation — problem focused

E **D0145** Oral evaluation for a patient under 3 years of age and counseling with primary caregiver

S **D0150** Comprehensive oral evaluation — new or established patient ⃠
This procedure is covered if its purpose is to identify a patient's existing infections prior to kidney transplantation.
MED: 100-2,15,150; 100-2,16,140; 100-3,260.6

E **D0160** Detailed and extensive oral evaluation — problem focused, by report
Pertinent documentation to evaluate medical appropriateness should be included when this code is reported.

E **D0170** Re-evaluation, limited, problem-focused (established patient, not postoperative visit)

E **D0180** Comprehensive periodontal evaluation — new or established patient

RADIOGRAPHS

E **D0210** Intraoral, complete series (including bitewings)

E ☑ **D0220** Intraoral, periapical, first film

E ☑ **D0230** Intraoral, periapical, each additional film

S **D0240** Intraoral — occlusal film ⃠
MED: 100-2,15,150; 100-2,16,140

S ☑ **D0250** Extraoral, first film ⃠
MED: 100-2,15,150; 100-2,16,140

S ☑ **D0260** Extraoral, each additional film ⃠
MED: 100-2,15,150; 100-2,16,140

S ☑ **D0270** Bitewing, single film ⃠
MED: 100-2,15,150; 100-2,16,140

S ☑ **D0272** Bitewings, 2 films ⃠
MED: 100-2,15,150; 100-2,16,140

E **D0273** Bitewings, 3 films

S ☑ **D0274** Bitewings, 4 films ⃠
MED: 100-2,15,150; 100-2,16,140

S ☑ **D0277** Vertical bitewings - 7 to 8 films
MED: 100-2,15,150; 100-2,16,140

E **D0290** Posterior-anterior or lateral skull and facial bone survey film

E **D0310** Sialography

E **D0320** Temporomandibular joint arthrogram, including injection

E **D0321** Other temporomandibular joint films, by report

E **D0322** Tomographic survey
MED: 100-3,260.6

E **D0330** Panoramic film

E **D0340** Cephalometric film

E **D0350** Oral/facial photographic images
This code excludes conventional radiographs.

E **D0360** Cone beam CT — craniofacial data capture

E **D0362** Cone beam, 2-dimensional image reconstruction using existing data, includes multiple images

E **D0363** Cone beam, 3-dimensional image reconstruction using existing data, includes multiple images

TEST AND LABORATORY EXAMINATIONS

E **D0415** Collection of microorganisms for culture and sensitivity
This procedure is covered if its purpose is to Identify a patient's existing infections prior to kidney transplantation.
See code(s): D0410

B **D0416** Viral culture

● D0417 Collection and preparation of saliva sample for laboratory diagnostic testing

● D0418 Analysis of saliva sample

B **D0421** Genetic test for susceptibility to oral diseases

E **D0425** Caries susceptibility tests
This procedure is covered by Medicare if its purpose is to identify a patient's existing infections prior to kidney transplantation.

B **D0431** Adjunctive prediagnostic test that aids in detection of mucosal abnormalities including premalignant and malignant lesions, not to include cytology or biopsy procedures

S **D0460** Pulp vitality tests ⃠
This procedure is covered by Medicare if its purpose is to identify a patient's existing infections prior to kidney transplantation.
MED: 100-2,15,150; 100-2,16,140; 100-3,260.6

E **D0470** Diagnostic casts

B **D0472** Accession of tissue, gross examination, preparation, and transmission of written report
MED: 100-2,15,150; 100-2,16,140; 100-3,260.6

B **D0473** Accession of tissue, gross and microscopic examination, preparation and transmission of written report
MED: 100-2,15,150; 100-2,16,140; 100-3,260.6

B **D0474** Accession of tissue, gross and microscopic examination, including assessment of surgical margins for presence of disease, preparation and transmission of written report
MED: 100-2,15,150; 100-2,16,140; 100-3,260.6

B **D0475** Decalcification procedure

B **D0476** Special stains for microorganisms

B **D0477** Special stains, not for microorganisms

B **D0478** Immunohistochemical stains

B **D0479** Tissue in-situ hybridization, including interpretation

B D0480 Accession of exfoliative cytologic smears, microscopic examination, preparation and transmission of written report
MED: 100-2,15,150; 100-2,16,140; 100-3,260.6

B D0481 Electron microscopy - diagnostic

B D0482 Direct immunofluorescence

B D0483 Indirect immunofluorescence

B D0484 Consultation on slides prepared elsewhere

B D0485 Consultation, including preparation of slides from biopsy material supplied by referring source

▲ E D0486 Laboratory accession of brush biopsy sample, microscopic examination, preparation and transmission of written report

B D0502 Other oral pathology procedures, by report ⊘
Pertinent documentation to evaluate medical appropriateness should be included when this code is reported. This procedure is covered by Medicare if its purpose is to identify a patient's existing infections prior to kidney transplantation.
MED: 100-2,15,150; 100-2,16,140; 100-3,260.6

B D0999 Unspecified diagnostic procedure, by report ⊘
Determine if an alternative HCPCS Level II or a CPT code better describes the service being reported. This code should be used only if a more specific code is unavailable.
MED: 100-2,15,150; 100-2,16,140; 100-3,260.6

PREVENTIVE D1000-D1999

DENTAL PROPHYLAXIS

E D1110 Prophylaxis, adult A

E D1120 Prophylaxis, child A

TOPICAL FLUORIDE TREATMENT (OFFICE PROCEDURE)

▲ E D1203 Topical application of fluoride, child A

▲ E D1204 Topical application of fluoride, adult A

E D1206 Topical fluoride varnish; therapeutic application for moderate to high caries risk patients

OTHER PREVENTIVE SERVICES

E D1310 Nutritional counseling for the control of dental disease
MED: 100-2,16,10

E D1320 Tobacco counseling for the control and prevention of oral disease
MED: 100-2,16,10

E D1330 Oral hygiene instruction
MED: 100-2,16,10

E ☑ D1351 Sealant, per tooth

SPACE MAINTENANCE (PASSIVE APPLIANCES)

S D1510 Space maintainer, fixed unilateral ⊘
MED: 100-2,16,140

S D1515 Space maintainer, fixed bilateral ⊘
MED: 100-2,15,150; 100-2,16,140

S D1520 Space maintainer, removable unilateral ⊘
MED: 100-2,15,150; 100-2,16,140

S D1525 Space maintainer, removable bilateral ⊘
MED: 100-2,15,150; 100-2,16,140

S D1550 Recementation of space maintainer ⊘
MED: 100-2,15,150; 100-2,16,140

E D1555 Removal of fixed space maintainer

E ☑ D2140 Amalgam—one surface, primary or permanent

E ☑ D2150 Amalgam, 2 surfaces, primary or permanent

E ☑ D2160 Amalgam, 3 surfaces, primary or permanent

E ☑ D2161 Amalgam, 4 or more surfaces, primary or permanent

RESIN RESTORATIONS

E ☑ D2330 Resin, one surface, anterior

E ☑ D2331 Resin, 2 surfaces, anterior

E ☑ D2332 Resin, 3 surfaces, anterior

E ☑ D2335 Resin, 4 or more surfaces or involving incisal angle (anterior)

E ☑ D2390 Resin-based composite crown, anterior

E ☑ D2391 Resin-based composite — one surface, posterior

E ☑ D2392 Resin-based composite, 2 surfaces, posterior

E ☑ D2393 Resin-based composite, 3 surfaces, posterior

E ☑ D2394 Resin-based composite, 4 or more surfaces, posterior

GOLD FOIL RESTORATIONS

E ☑ D2410 Gold foil, one surface

E ☑ D2420 Gold foil, 2 surfaces

E ☑ D2430 Gold foil, 3 surfaces

INLAY/ONLAY RESTORATIONS

E ☑ D2510 Inlay, metallic, one surface

E ☑ D2520 Inlay, metallic, 2 surfaces

E ☑ D2530 Inlay, metallic, 3 or more surfaces

E ☑ D2542 Onlay, metallic, 2 surfaces

E ☑ D2543 Onlay, metallic, 3 surfaces

E ☑ D2544 Onlay, metallic, 4 or more surfaces

E ☑ D2610 Inlay, porcelain/ceramic, one surface

E ☑ D2620 Inlay, porcelain/ceramic, 2 surfaces

E ☑ D2630 Inlay, porcelain/ceramic, 3 or more surfaces

E ☑ D2642 Onlay, porcelain/ceramic, 2 surfaces

E ☑ D2643 Onlay, porcelain/ceramic, 3 surfaces

E ☑ D2644 Onlay, porcelain/ceramic, 4 or more surfaces

E ☑ D2650 Inlay — resin-based composite — one surface

E ☑ D2651 Inlay, resin-based composite, 2 surfaces

E ☑ D2652 Inlay, resin-based composite, 3 or more surfaces

E ☑ D2662 Onlay, resin-based composite, 2 surfaces

E ☑ D2663 Onlay, resin-based composite, 3 surfaces

E ☑ D2664 Onlay, resin-based composite, 4 or more surfaces

CROWNS - SINGLE RESTORATION ONLY

E D2710 Crown — resin-based composite (indirect)

E D2712 Crown — 3/4 resin-based composite (indirect)

E D2720 Crown, resin with high noble metal

E D2721 Crown, resin with predominantly base metal

E D2722 Crown, resin with noble metal

E D2740 Crown, porcelain/ceramic substrate

E D2750 Crown, porcelain fused to high noble metal

E D2751 Crown — porcelain fused to predominantly base metal

E D2752 Crown, porcelain fused to noble metal

E D2780 Crown — 3/4 cast high noble metal

E D2781 Crown - 3/4 cast predominantly base metal

E D2782 Crown — 3/4 cast noble metal

E D2783 Crown - 3/4 porcelain/ceramic

E D2790 Crown, full cast high noble metal

E D2791 Crown, full cast predominantly base metal

E D2792 Crown, full cast noble metal

E D2794 Crown, titanium

E D2799 Provisional crown
Do not use this code to report a temporary crown for routine prosthetic restoration.

OTHER RESTORATIVE SERVICES

E D2910 Recement inlay, onlay or partial coverage restoration

E D2915 Recement cast or prefabricated post and core

E D2920 Recement crown

E D2930 Prefabricated stainless steel crown, primary tooth

E D2931 Prefabricated stainless steel crown, permanent tooth

E D2932 Prefabricated resin crown

E D2933 Prefabricated stainless steel crown with resin window

E D2934 Prefabricated esthetic coated stainless steel crown - primary tooth

E D2940 Sedative filling

E D2950 Core buildup, including any pins

E D2951 Pin retention, per tooth, in addition to restoration

E D2952 Post and core in addition to crown, indirectly fabricated

E D2953 Each additional indirectly fabricated post — same tooth
Report in addition to code D2952.

E D2954 Prefabricated post and core in addition to crown

E D2955 Post removal (not in conjunction with endodontic therapy)

E D2957 Each additional prefabricated post — same tooth
Report in addition to code D2954.

E D2960 Labial veneer (laminate)-chairside

E D2961 Labial veneer (resin laminate), laboratory

E D2962 Labial veneer (porcelain laminate), laboratory

○ E D2970 Temporary crown (fractured tooth)

E D2971 Additional procedures to construct new crown under existing partial denture framework

E D2975 Coping

E D2980 Crown repair, by report
Pertinent documentation to evaluate medical appropriateness should be included when this code is reported.

S D2999 Unspecified restorative procedure, by report ⊘
Determine if an alternative HCPCS Level II or a CPT code better describes the service being reported. This code should be used only if a more specific code is unavailable.
MED: 100-2,15,150; 100-2,16,140

ENDODONTICS D3000-D3999

PULP CAPPING

E D3110 Pulp cap, direct (excluding final restoration)

E D3120 Pulp cap, indirect (excluding final restoration)

PULPOTOMY

E D3220 Therapeutic pulpotomy (excluding final restoration), removal of pulp coronal to the dentinocemental junction and application of medicament
Do not use this code to report the first stage of root canal therapy.

E D3221 Pulpal debridement, primary and permanent teeth

● D3222 Partial pulpotomy for apexogenesis, permanent tooth with incomplete root development

PULPAL THERAPY ON PRIMARY TEETH (INCLUDES PRIMARY TEETH WITH SUCCEDANEOUS TEETH AND PLACEMENT OF RESORBABLE FILLING)

E D3230 Pulpal therapy (resorbable filling), anterior, primary tooth (excluding final restoration)

E D3240 Pulpal therapy (resorbable filling), posterior, primary tooth (excluding final restoration)

ROOT CANAL THERAPY (INCLUDING TREATMENT PLAN, CLINICAL PROCEDURES, AND FOLLOW-UP CARE, INCLUDES PRIMARY TEETH WITHOUT SUCCEDANEOUS TEETH AND PERMANENT TEETH)

▲ E D3310 Endodontic therapy, anterior tooth (excluding final restoration)

▲ E D3320 Endodontic therapy, bicuspid tooth (excluding final restoration)

▲ E D3330 Endodontic therapy, molar (excluding final restoration)

E D3331 Treatment of root canal obstruction; nonsurgical access

E D3332 Incomplete endodontic therapy; inoperable, unrestorable or fractured tooth

E D3333 Internal root repair of perforation defects

E D3346 Retreatment of previous root canal therapy, anterior

E D3347 Retreatment of previous root canal therapy, bicuspid

E D3348 Retreatment of previous root canal therapy, molar

E D3351 Apexification/recalcification, initial visit (apical closure/calcific repair of perforations, root resorption, etc.)

E D3352 Apexification/recalcification, interim medication replacement (apical closure/calcific repair of perforations, root resorption, etc.)

E D3353 Apexification/recalcification, final visit (includes completed root canal therapy, apical closure/calcific repair of perforations, root resorption, etc.)

APICOECTOMY/PERIRADICULAR SERVICES

E D3410 Apicoectomy/periradicular surgery, anterior

E D3421 Apicoectomy/periradicular surgery, bicuspid (first root)

E D3425 Apicoectomy/periradicular surgery, molar (first root)

E ☑ D3426 Apicoectomy/periradicular surgery (each additional root)

E ☑ D3430 Retrograde filling, per root

E ☑ D3450 Root amputation, per root

S D3460 Endodontic endosseous implant ⊘
MED: 100-2,15,150; 100-2,16,140

E D3470 Intentional replantation (including necessary splinting)

OTHER ENDODONTIC PROCEDURES

E D3910 Surgical procedure for isolation of tooth with rubber dam

E D3920 Hemisection (including any root removal), not including root canal therapy

E D3950 Canal preparation and fitting of preformed dowel or post

S D3999 Unspecified endodontic procedure, by report ⊘
Determine if an alternative HCPCS Level II or a CPT code better describes the service being reported. This code should be used only if a more specific code is unavailable.
MED: 100-2,15,150; 100-2,16,140

PERIODONTICS D4000-D4999

SURGICAL SERVICES (INCLUDING USUAL POSTOPERATIVE SERVICES)

▲ E ☑ D4210 Gingivectomy or gingivoplasty, 4 or more contiguous teeth or tooth bounded spaces per quadrant

▲ E ☑ D4211 Gingivectomy or gingivoplasty, 1 to 3 contiguous teeth or tooth bounded spaces per quadrant

E D4230 Anatomical crown exposure, 4 or more contiguous teeth per quadrant

E D4231 Anatomical crown exposure, 1 to 3 teeth per quadrant

▲ E ☑ D4240 Gingival flap procedure, including root planing, 4 or more contiguous teeth or tooth bounded spaces per quadrant

▲ E D4241 Gingival flap procedure, including root planing, 1 to 3 contiguous teeth or tooth bounded spaces per quadrant

E D4245 Apically positioned flap

E D4249 Clinical crown lengthening, hard tissue

▲ S ☑ D4260 Osseous surgery (including flap entry and closure), 4 or more contiguous teeth or tooth bounded spaces per quadrant ⊘
MED: 100-2,15,150; 100-2,16,140

▲ E D4261 Osseous surgery (including flap entry and closure), 1 to 3 contiguous teeth or tooth bounded spaces per quadrant

S ☑ D4263 Bone replacement graft — first site in quadrant ⊘
MED: 100-2,15,150; 100-2,16,140; 100-3,260.6

S ☑ D4264 Bone replacement graft — each additional site in quadrant ⊘
MED: 100-2,15,150; 100-2,16,140; 100-3,260.6

E D4265 Biologic materials to aid in soft and osseous tissue regeneration

E ☑ D4266 Guided tissue regeneration — resorbable barrier, per site

E ☑ D4267 Guided tissue regeneration, nonresorbable barrier, per site (includes membrane removal)

S ☑ D4268 Surgical revision procedure, per tooth
MED: 100-2,15,150; 100-2,16,140

S D4270 Pedicle soft tissue graft procedure ⊘
MED: 100-2,15,150; 100-2,16,140

S D4271 Free soft tissue graft procedure (including donor site surgery) ⊘
MED: 100-2,15,150; 100-2,16,140

S D4273 Subepithelial connective tissue graft procedures, per tooth ⊘
MED: 100-2,15,150; 100-2,16,140; 100-3,260.6

E D4274 Distal or proximal wedge procedure (when not performed in conjunction with surgical procedures in the same anatomical area)

E D4275 Soft tissue allograft

E D4276 Combined connective tissue and double pedicle graft, per tooth

ADJUNCTIVE PERIODONTAL SERVICES

E D4320 Provisional splinting, intracoronal

E D4321 Provisional splinting, extracoronal

E ☑ D4341 Periodontal scaling and root planing, 4 or more teeth per quadrant

E ☑ D4342 Periodontal scaling and root planing, 1 to 3 teeth, per quadrant

S D4355 Full mouth debridement to enable comprehensive evaluation and diagnosis ⊘
This procedure is covered by Medicare if its purpose is to identify a patient's existing infections prior to kidney transplantation.
MED: 100-2,15,150; 100-2,16,140; 100-3,260.6

S D4381 Localized delivery of antimicrobial agents via a controlled release vehicle into diseased crevicular tissue, per tooth, by report ⊘
Pertinent documentation to evaluate medical appropriateness should be included when this code is reported.
MED: 100-2,15,150; 100-2,16,140; 100-3,260.6

OTHER PERIODONTAL SERVICES

E D4910 Periodontal maintenance

E D4920 Unscheduled dressing change (by someone other than treating dentist)

E D4999 Unspecified periodontal procedure, by report
Determine if an alternative HCPCS Level II or a CPT code better describes the service being reported. This code should be used only if a more specific code is unavailable.

PROSTHODONTICS (REMOVABLE) D5000-D5899

COMPLETE DENTURES (INCLUDING ROUTINE POST DELIVERY CARE)

E D5110 Complete denture — maxillary

E D5120 Complete denture — mandibular

E D5130 Immediate denture — maxillary

E D5140 Immediate denture — mandibular

PARTIAL DENTURES (INCLUDING ROUTINE POST DELIVERY CARE)

▲ E D5211 Upper partial denture - resin base (including any conventional clasps, rests and teeth)

▲ E D5212 Lower partial denture - resin base (including any conventional clasps, rests and teeth)

E D5213 Maxillary partial denture — cast metal framework with resin denture bases (including any conventional clasps, rests and teeth)

E **D5214** Mandibular partial denture, cast metal framework with resin denture bases (including any conventional clasps, rests, and teeth)

E **D5225** Maxillary partial denture - flexible base (including any clasps, rests and teeth)

E **D5226** Mandibular partial denture — flexible base (including any clasps, rests and teeth)

E **D5281** Removable unilateral partial denture, 1 piece cast metal (including clasps and teeth)

ADJUSTMENTS TO REMOVABLE PROSTHESES

E **D5410** Adjust complete denture — maxillary

E **D5411** Adjust complete denture — mandibular

E **D5421** Adjust partial denture — maxillary

E **D5422** Adjust partial denture — mandibular

REPAIRS TO COMPLETE DENTURES

E **D5510** Repair broken complete denture base

E **D5520** Replace missing or broken teeth, complete denture (each tooth)

REPAIRS TO PARTIAL DENTURES

E **D5610** Repair resin denture base

E **D5620** Repair cast framework

E **D5630** Repair or replace broken clasp

E ☑ **D5640** Replace broken teeth, per tooth

E **D5650** Add tooth to existing partial denture

E **D5660** Add clasp to existing partial denture

E **D5670** Replace all teeth and acrylic on cast metal framework (maxillary)

E **D5671** Replace all teeth and acrylic on cast metal framework (mandibular)

DENTURE REBASE PROCEDURES

E **D5710** Rebase complete maxillary denture

E **D5711** Rebase complete mandibular denture

E **D5720** Rebase maxillary partial denture

E **D5721** Rebase mandibular partial denture

DENTURE RELINE PROCEDURES

E **D5730** Reline complete maxillary denture (chairside)

E **D5731** Reline lower complete mandibular denture (chairside)

E **D5740** Reline maxillary partial denture (chairside)

E **D5741** Reline mandibular partial denture (chairside)

E **D5750** Reline complete maxillary denture (laboratory)

E **D5751** Reline complete mandibular denture (laboratory)

E **D5760** Reline maxillary partial denture (laboratory)

E **D5761** Reline mandibular partial denture (laboratory)

OTHER REMOVABLE PROSTHETIC SERVICES

E **D5810** Interim complete denture (maxillary)

E **D5811** Interim complete denture (mandibular)

E **D5820** Interim partial denture (maxillary)

E **D5821** Interim partial denture (mandibular)

E **D5850** Tissue conditioning, maxillary

E **D5851** Tissue conditioning, mandibular

E **D5860** Overdenture, complete, by report

Pertinent documentation to evaluate medical appropriateness should be included when this code is reported.

E **D5861** Overdenture, partial, by report

Pertinent documentation to evaluate medical appropriateness should be included when this code is reported.

E **D5862** Precision attachment, by report

Pertinent documentation to evaluate medical appropriateness should be included when this code is reported.

E **D5867** Replacement of replaceable part of semi-precision or precision attachment (male or female component)

E **D5875** Modification of removable prosthesis following implant surgery

E **D5899** Unspecified removable prosthodontic procedure, by report

Determine if an alternative HCPCS Level II or a CPT code better describes the service being reported. This code should be used only if a more specific code is unavailable.

MAXILLOFACIAL PROSTHETICS D5900-D5999

S **D5911** Facial moulage (sectional) ⃠

MED: 100-2,15,120; 100-2,15,150

S **D5912** Facial moulage (complete) ⃠

MED: 100-2,15,120

E **D5913** Nasal prosthesis

E **D5914** Auricular prosthesis

E **D5915** Orbital prosthesis

See code(s): L8611

E **D5916** Ocular prosthesis

See code(s): V2623, V2629

E **D5919** Facial prosthesis

E **D5922** Nasal septal prosthesis

E **D5923** Ocular prosthesis, interim

E **D5924** Cranial prosthesis

E **D5925** Facial augmentation implant prosthesis

E **D5926** Nasal prosthesis, replacement

E **D5927** Auricular prosthesis, replacement

E **D5928** Orbital prosthesis, replacement

E **D5929** Facial prosthesis, replacement

E **D5931** Obturator prosthesis, surgical

E **D5932** Obturator prosthesis, definitive

E **D5933** Obturator prosthesis, modification

E **D5934** Mandibular resection prosthesis with guide flange

E **D5935** Mandibular resection prosthesis without guide flange

E **D5936** Obturator/prosthesis, interim

E **D5937** Trismus appliance (not for TM treatment)

MED: 100-2,15,120

E **D5951** Feeding aid ⃠

MED: 100-2,15,120; 100-2,16,140

E **D5952** Speech aid prosthesis, pediatric

E **D5953** Speech aid prosthesis, adult

E **D5954** Palatal augmentation prosthesis

E D5955 Palatal lift prosthesis, definitive

E D5958 Palatal lift prosthesis, interim

E D5959 Palatal lift prosthesis, modification

E D5960 Speech aid prosthesis, modification

E D5982 Surgical stent

S D5983 Radiation carrier ⊘
MED: 100-2,15,150; 100-2,16,140

S D5984 Radiation shield ⊘
MED: 100-2,15,150; 100-2,16,140

S D5985 Radiation cone locator ⊘
MED: 100-2,15,150; 100-2,16,140

E D5986 Fluoride gel carrier

S D5987 Commissure splint ⊘
MED: 100-2,15,150; 100-2,16,140; 100-4,4,240

E D5988 Surgical splint
MED: 100-4,4,240

● D5991 Topical medicament carrier

E D5999 Unspecified maxillofacial prosthesis, by report
Determine if an alternative HCPCS Level II or a CPT code better describes the service being reported. This code should be used only if a more specific code is unavailable.

IMPLANT SERVICES D6000-D6199

E D6010 Surgical placement of implant body: endosteal implant

E D6012 Surgical placement of interim implant body for transitional prosthesis: endosteal implant

E D6040 Surgical placement: eposteal implant

E D6050 Surgical placement: transosteal implant

E D6053 Implant/abutment supported removable denture for completely edentulous arch
MED: 100-2,15,150

E D6054 Implant/abutment supported removable denture for partially edentulous arch
MED: 100-2,15,150

E D6055 Dental implant supported connecting bar
MED: 100-2,15,150

E D6056 Prefabricated abutment - includes placement
MED: 100-2,15,150

E D6057 Custom abutment — includes placement
MED: 100-2,15,150

E D6058 Abutment supported porcelain/ceramic crown
MED: 100-2,15,150

E D6059 Abutment supported porcelain fused to metal crown (high noble metal)
MED: 100-2,15,150

E D6060 Abutment supported porcelain fused to metal crown (predominantly base metal)
MED: 100-2,15,150

E D6061 Abutment supported porcelain fused to metal crown (noble metal)
MED: 100-2,15,150

E D6062 Abutment supported cast metal crown (high noble metal)
MED: 100-2,15,150

E D6063 Abutment supported cast metal crown (predominantly base metal)
MED: 100-2,15,150

E D6064 Abutment supported cast metal crown (noble metal)
MED: 100-2,15,150

E D6065 Implant supported porcelain/ceramic crown
MED: 100-2,15,150

E D6066 Implant supported porcelain fused to metal crown (titanium, titanium alloy, high noble metal)
MED: 100-2,15,150

E D6067 Implant supported metal crown (titanium, titanium alloy, high noble metal)
MED: 100-2,15,150

E D6068 Abutment supported retainer for porcelain/ceramic FPD
MED: 100-2,15,150

E D6069 Abutment supported retainer for porcelain fused to metal FPD (high noble metal)
MED: 100-2,15,150

E D6070 Abutment supported retainer for porcelain fused to metal FPD (predominantly base metal)
MED: 100-2,15,150

E D6071 Abutment supported retainer for porcelain fused to metal FPD (noble metal)
MED: 100-2,15,150

E D6072 Abutment supported retainer for cast metal FPD (high noble metal)
MED: 100-2,15,150

E D6073 Abutment supported retainer for cast metal FPD (predominantly base metal)
MED: 100-2,15,150

E D6074 Abutment supported retainer for cast metal FPD (noble metal)
MED: 100-2,15,150

E D6075 Implant supported retainer for ceramic FPD
MED: 100-2,15,150

E D6076 Implant supported retainer for porcelain fused to metal FPD (titanium, titanium alloy, or high noble metal)
MED: 100-2,15,150

E D6077 Implant supported retainer for cast metal FPD (titanium, titanium alloy, or high noble metal)
MED: 100-2,15,150

E D6078 Implant/abutment supported fixed denture for completely edentulous arch
MED: 100-2,15,150

E D6079 Implant/abutment supported fixed denture for partially edentulous arch
MED: 100-2,15,150

E D6080 Implant maintenance procedures, including removal of prosthesis, cleansing of prosthesis and abutments, reinsertion of prosthesis
MED: 100-2,15,150

E D6090 Repair implant-supported prosthesis, by report
Pertinent documentation to evaluate medical appropriateness should be included when this code is reported.

E D6091 Replacement of semi-precision or precision attachment (male or female component) of implant/abutment supported prosthesis, per attachment

E D6092 Recement implant/abutment supported crown

E D6093 Recement implant/abutment supported fixed partial denture

E D6094 Abutment supported crown - (titanium)

E **D6095** Repair implant abutment, by report
Pertinent documentation to evaluate medical appropriateness should be included when this code is reported.

E **D6100** Implant removal, by report
Pertinent documentation to evaluate medical appropriateness should be included when this code is reported.

E **D6190** Radiographic/surgical implant index, by report

E **D6194** Abutment supported retainer crown for FPD - (titanium)

E **D6199** Unspecified implant procedure, by report

E **D6205** Pontic — indirect resin based composite

PROSTHODONTICS (FIXED) D6200-D6999

FIXED PARTIAL DENTURE PONTICS

E **D6210** Pontic, cast high noble metal
Each abutment and each pontic constitute a unit in a prosthesis. An alloy of at least 60 percent gold (Au), palladium (Pd), or platinum (Pt) is considered a high noble metal.

E **D6211** Pontic, cast predominantly base metal
Each abutment and each pontic constitute a unit in a prosthesis. An alloy of less than 25 percent gold (Au), palladium (Pd), or platinum (Pt) is considered a high noble metal.

E **D6212** Pontic, cast noble metal
Each abutment and each pontic constitute a unit in a prosthesis. An alloy of at least 25 percent gold (Au), palladium (Pd), or platinum (Pt) is considered a high noble metal.

E **D6214** Pontic — titanium

E **D6240** Pontic, porcelain fused to high noble metal
Each abutment and each pontic constitute a unit in a prosthesis. An alloy of at least 60 percent gold (Au), palladium (Pd), or platinum (Pt) is considered a high noble metal.

E **D6241** Pontic, porcelain fused to predominantly base metal
Each abutment and each pontic constitute a unit in a prosthesis. An alloy of less than 25 percent gold (Au), palladium (Pd), or platinum (Pt) is considered a high noble metal.

E **D6242** Pontic, porcelain fused to noble metal
Each abutment and each pontic constitute a unit in a prosthesis. An alloy of at least 60 percent gold (Au), palladium (Pd), or platinum (Pt) is considered a high noble metal.

E **D6245** Pontic — porcelain/ceramic
MED: 100-2,15,150

E **D6250** Pontic, resin with high noble metal
Each abutment and each pontic constitute a unit in a prosthesis. An alloy of at least 60 percent gold (Au), palladium (Pd), or platinum (Pt) is considered a high noble metal.

E **D6251** Pontic, resin with predominantly base metal
Each abutment and each pontic constitute a unit in a prosthesis. An alloy of less than 25 percent gold (Au), palladium (Pd), or platinum (Pt) is considered a high noble metal.

E **D6252** Pontic, resin with noble metal
Each abutment and each pontic constitute a unit in a prosthesis. An alloy of at least 25 percent gold (Au), palladium (Pd), or platinum (Pt) is considered a high noble metal.

E **D6253** Provisional pontic

E **D6545** Retainer, cast metal for resin bonded fixed prosthesis

E **D6548** Retainer — porcelain/ceramic for resin bonded fixed prosthesis
MED: 100-2,15,150

E **D6600** Inlay, porcelain/ceramic, 2 surfaces
MED: 100-2,15,150

E **D6601** Inlay, porcelain/ceramic, 3 or more surfaces
MED: 100-2,15,150

E **D6602** Inlay, cast high noble metal, 2 surfaces
MED: 100-2,15,150

E **D6603** Inlay, cast high noble metal, 3 or more surfaces
MED: 100-2,15,150

E **D6604** Inlay, cast predominantly base metal, 2 surfaces
MED: 100-2,15,150

E **D6605** Inlay, cast predominantly base metal, 3 or more surfaces
MED: 100-2,15,150

E **D6606** Inlay, cast noble metal, 2 surfaces
MED: 100-2,15,150

E **D6607** Inlay, cast noble metal, 3 or more surfaces
MED: 100-2,15,150

E **D6608** Onlay, porcelain/ceramic, 2 surfaces
MED: 100-2,15,150

E **D6609** Onlay, porcelain/ceramic, 3 or more surfaces
MED: 100-2,15,150

E **D6610** Onlay, cast high noble metal, 2 surfaces
MED: 100-2,15,150

E **D6611** Onlay, cast high noble metal, 3 or more surfaces
MED: 100-2,15,150

E **D6612** Onlay, cast predominantly base metal, 2 surfaces
MED: 100-2,15,150

E **D6613** Onlay, cast predominantly base metal, 3 or more surfaces
MED: 100-2,15,150

E **D6614** Onlay, cast noble metal, 2 surfaces
MED: 100-2,15,150

E **D6615** Onlay, cast noble metal, 3 or more surfaces
MED: 100-2,15,150

E **D6624** Inlay — titanium

E **D6634** Onlay — titanium

E **D6710** Crown — indirect resin based composite

FIXED PARTIAL DENTURE RETAINERS - CROWNS

E **D6720** Crown, resin with high noble metal
An alloy of at least 60 percent gold (Au), palladium (Pd), or platinum (Pt) is considered a high noble metal.

E **D6721** Crown, resin with predominantly base metal
An alloy of less than 25 percent gold (Au), palladium (Pd), or platinum (Pt) is considered a base metal.

E **D6722** Crown, resin with noble metal
An alloy of at least 25 percent gold (Au), palladium (Pd), or platinum (Pt) is considered a noble metal.

E D6740 Crown — porcelain/ceramic
MED: 100-2,15,150

E D6750 Crown, porcelain fused to high noble metal
An alloy of at least 60 percent gold (Au), palladium (Pd), or platinum (Pt) is considered a high noble metal.

E D6751 Crown, porcelain fused to predominantly base metal
An alloy of less than 25 percent gold (Au), palladium (Pd), or platinum (Pt) is considered a base metal.

E D6752 Crown, porcelain fused to noble metal
An alloy of at least 25 percent gold (Au), palladium (Pd), or platinum (Pt) is considered a noble metal.

E D6780 Crown, 3/4 cast high noble metal
An alloy of at least 60 percent gold (Au), palladium (Pd), or platinum (Pt) is considered a high noble metal.

E D6781 Crown - 3/4 cast predominantly base metal
An alloy of less than 25 percent gold (Au), palladium (Pd), or platinum (Pt) is considered a base metal.
MED: 100-2,15,150

E D6782 Crown — 3/4 cast noble metal
An alloy of at least 25 percent gold (Au), palladium (Pd), or platinum (Pt) is considered a noble metal.
MED: 100-2,15,150

E D6783 Crown — 3/4 porcelain/ceramic
MED: 100-2,15,150

E D6790 Crown, full cast high noble metal
An alloy of at least 60 percent gold (Au), palladium (Pd), or platinum (Pt) is considered a high noble metal.

E D6791 Crown, full cast predominantly base metal
An alloy of less than 25 percent gold (Au), palladium (Pd), or platinum (Pt) is considered a base metal.

E D6792 Crown, full cast noble metal
An alloy of at least 25 percent gold (Au), palladium (Pd), or platinum (Pt) is considered a noble metal.

E D6793 Provisional retainer crown

E D6794 Crown — titanium

OTHER FIXED PARTIAL DENTURE SERVICES

S D6920 Connector bar ⊘
MED: 100-2,15,150; 100-2,16,140; 100-3,260.6

E D6930 Recement bridge

E D6940 Stress breaker

E D6950 Precision attachment

E D6970 Post and core in addition to fixed partial denture retainer, indirectly fabricated

E D6972 Prefabricated post and core in addition to bridge retainer

E D6973 Core build up for retainer, including any pins

E D6975 Coping, metal

E D6976 Each additional indirectly fabricated post — same tooth
Report this code in addition to codes D6970.
MED: 100-2,15,150

E D6977 Each additional prefabricated post — same tooth
Report this code in addition to code D6972.
MED: 100-2,15,150

E D6980 Bridge repair, by report
Pertinent documentation to evaluate medical appropriateness should be included when this code is reported.

E D6985 Pediatric partial denture, fixed A

E D6999 Unspecified fixed prosthodontic procedure, by report
Determine if an alternative HCPCS Level II or a CPT code better describes the service being reported. This code should be used only if a more specific code is unavailable.

SURGICAL EXTRACTIONS (INCLUDES LOCAL ANESTHESIA AND ROUTINE POSTOPERATIVE CARE)

S D7111 Extraction, coronal remnants — deciduous tooth
MED: 100-2,16,140

S D7140 Extraction, erupted tooth or exposed root (elevation and/or forceps removal)
MED: 100-2,16,140

S D7210 Surgical removal of erupted tooth requiring elevation of mucoperiosteal flap and removal of bone and/or section of tooth ⊘
MED: 100-2,15,150; 100-2,16,140

S D7220 Removal of impacted tooth, soft tissue ⊘
MED: 100-2,15,150; 100-2,16,140

S D7230 Removal of impacted tooth, partially bony ⊘
MED: 100-2,15,150; 100-2,16,140

S D7240 Removal of impacted tooth, completely bony ⊘
MED: 100-2,15,150; 100-2,16,140

S D7241 Removal of impacted tooth, completely bony, with unusual surgical complications ⊘
MED: 100-2,15,150; 100-2,16,140

S D7250 Surgical removal of residual tooth roots (cutting procedure) ⊘
MED: 100-2,15,150; 100-2,16,140

OTHER SURGICAL PROCEDURES

S D7260 Oral antral fistula closure ⊘
MED: 100-2,15,150; 100-2,16,140

S D7261 Primary closure of a sinus perforation
See equivalent CPT code for repair of mucous membranes.
MED: 100-2,16,140

E D7270 Tooth reimplantation and/or stabilization of accidentally evulsed or displaced tooth

E D7272 Tooth transplantation (includes reimplantation from one site to another and splinting and/or stabilization)

E D7280 Surgical access of an unerupted tooth

E D7282 Mobilization of erupted or malpositioned tooth to aid eruption

B D7283 Placement of device to facilitate eruption of impacted tooth

E D7285 Biopsy of oral tissue — hard (bone, tooth)

E D7286 Biopsy of oral tissue — soft

E D7287 Exfoliative cytological sample collection

B D7288 Brush biopsy — transepithelial sample collection

E D7290 Surgical repositioning of teeth

S D7291 Transseptal fiberotomy/supra crestal fiberotomy, by report ⊘
Pertinent documentation to evaluate medical appropriateness should be included when this code is reported.
MED: 100-2,15,150; 100-2,16,140

E D7292 Surgical placement: temporary anchorage device (screw retained plate) requiring surgical flap

E D7293 Surgical placement: temporary anchorage device requiring surgical flap

E D7294 Surgical placement: temporary anchorage device without surgical flap

ALVEOLOPLASTY - SURGICAL PREPARATION OF RIDGE FOR DENTURES

E ☑ D7310 Alveoloplasty in conjunction with extractions, 4 or more teeth or tooth spaces, per quadrant

E ☑ D7311 Alveoloplasty in conjunction with extractions, 1 to 3 teeth or tooth spaces, per quadrant

E ☑ D7320 Alveoloplasty not in conjunction with extractions, 4 or more teeth or tooth spaces, per quadrant

B ☑ D7321 Alveoloplasty not in conjunction with extractions, 1 to 3 teeth or tooth spaces, per quadrant

VESTIBULOPLASTY

E D7340 Vestibuloplasty, ridge extension (second epithelialization)

E D7350 Vestibuloplasty, ridge extension (including soft tissue grafts, muscle re-attachments, revision of soft tissue attachment, and management of hypertrophied and hyperplastic tissue)

SURGICAL EXCISION OF REACTIVE INFLAMMATORY LESIONS (SCAR TISSUE OR LOCALIZED CONGENITAL LESIONS)

E D7410 Excision of benign lesion up to 1.25 cm

E D7411 Excision of benign lesion greater than 1.25 cm

E D7412 Excision of benign lesion, complicated

E D7413 Excision of malignant lesion up to 1.25 cm

E D7414 Excision of malignant lesion greater than 1.25 cm

E D7415 Excision of malignant lesion, complicated

E ☑ D7440 Excision of malignant tumor, lesion diameter up to 1.25 cm

E ☑ D7441 Excision of malignant tumor, lesion diameter greater than 1.25 cm

E ☑ D7450 Removal of benign odontogenic cyst or tumor — lesion diameter up to 1.25 cm

E ☑ D7451 Removal of benign odontogenic cyst or tumor, lesion diameter greater than 1.25 cm

E ☑ D7460 Removal of benign nonodontogenic cyst or tumor, lesion diameter up to 1.25 cm

E ☑ D7461 Removal of benign nonodontogenic cyst or tumor, lesion diameter greater than 1.25 cm

E D7465 Destruction of lesion(s) by physical or chemical methods, by report

Pertinent documentation to evaluate medical appropriateness should be included when this code is reported.

E ☑ D7471 Removal of lateral exostosis (maxilla or mandible)

E D7472 Removal of torus palatinus

E D7473 Removal of torus mandibularis

E D7485 Surgical reduction of osseous tuberosity

E D7490 Radical resection of maxilla or mandible

SURGICAL INCISION

E D7510 Incision and drainage of abscess, intraoral soft tissue

B D7511 Incision and drainage of abscess — intraoral soft tissue — complicated (includes drainage of multiple fascial spaces)

E D7520 Incision and drainage of abscess, extraoral soft tissue

B D7521 Incision and drainage of abscess — extraoral soft tissue — complicated (includes drainage of multiple fascial spaces)

E D7530 Removal of foreign body from mucosa, skin, or subcutaneous alveolar tissue

E D7540 Removal of reaction-producing foreign bodies, musculoskeletal system

E D7550 Partial ostectomy/sequestrectomy for removal of nonvital bone

E D7560 Maxillary sinusotomy for removal of tooth fragment or foreign body

TREATMENT OF FRACTURES - SIMPLE

E D7610 Maxilla, open reduction (teeth immobilized if present)

E D7620 Maxilla, closed reduction (teeth immobilized if present)

E D7630 Mandible, open reduction (teeth immobilized if present)

E D7640 Mandible, closed reduction (teeth immobilized if present)

E D7650 Malar and/or zygomatic arch, open reduction

E D7660 Malar and/or zygomatic arch, closed reduction

E D7670 Alveolus - closed reduction, may include stabilization of teeth

E D7671 Alveolus - open reduction, may include stabilization of teeth

E D7680 Facial bones, complicated reduction with fixation and multiple surgical approaches

TREATMENT OF FRACTURES - COMPOUND

E D7710 Maxilla, open reduction

E D7720 Maxilla, closed reduction

E D7730 Mandible, open reduction

E D7740 Mandible, closed reduction

E D7750 Malar and/or zygomatic arch, open reduction

E D7760 Malar and/or zygomatic arch, closed reduction

E D7770 Alveolus — open reduction stabilization of teeth

E D7771 Alveolus, closed reduction stabilization of teeth

E D7780 Facial bones, complicated reduction with fixation and multiple surgical approaches

REDUCTION OF DISLOCATION AND MANAGEMENT OF OTHER TEMPOROMANDIBULAR JOINT DYSFUNCTIONS

Procedures which are an integral part of a primary procedure should not be reported separately.

E D7810 Open reduction of dislocation

E D7820 Closed reduction of dislocation

E D7830 Manipulation under anesthesia

E D7840 Condylectomy

E D7850 Surgical discectomy; with/without implant

E D7852 Disc repair

E D7854 Synovectomy

E D7856 Myotomy

E D7858 Joint reconstruction

E **D7860** Arthrotomy
MED: 100-2,15,150; 100-2,16,140

E **D7865** Arthroplasty

E **D7870** Arthrocentesis

E **D7871** Nonarthroscopic lysis and lavage

E **D7872** Arthroscopy, diagnosis, with or without biopsy

E **D7873** Arthroscopy, surgical: lavage and lysis of adhesions

E **D7874** Arthroscopy, surgical: disc repositioning and stabilization

E **D7875** Arthroscopy, surgical: synovectomy

E **D7876** Arthroscopy, surgical: discectomy

E **D7877** Arthroscopy, surgical: debridement

E **D7880** Occlusal orthotic appliance

E **D7899** Unspecified TMD therapy, by report
Determine if an alternative HCPCS Level II or a CPT code better describes the service being reported. This code should be used only if a more specific code is unavailable.

REPAIR OF TRAUMATIC WOUNDS

E ☑ **D7910** Suture of recent small wounds up to 5 cm

COMPLICATED SUTURING (RECONSTRUCTION REQUIRING DELICATE HANDLING OF TISSUES AND WIDE UNDERMINING FOR METICULOUS CLOSURE)

E **D7911** Complicated suture, up to 5 cm

E **D7912** Complicated suture, greater than 5 cm

OTHER REPAIR PROCEDURES

E **D7920** Skin graft (identify defect covered, location, and type of graft)

S **D7940** Osteoplasty, for orthognathic deformities ⊘
MED: 100-2,15,150; 100-2,16,140

E **D7941** Osteotomy — mandibular rami

E **D7943** Osteotomy — mandibular rami with bone graft; includes obtaining the graft

E ☑ **D7944** Osteotomy-segmented or subapical

E **D7945** Osteotomy, body of mandible

E **D7946** LeFort I (maxilla, total)

E **D7947** LeFort I (maxilla, segmented)

E **D7948** LeFort II or LeFort III (osteoplasty of facial bones for midface hypoplasia or retrusion), without bone graft

E **D7949** LeFort II or LeFort III, with bone graft

E **D7950** Osseous, osteoperiosteal, or cartilage graft of the mandible or maxilla, autogenous or nonautogenous, by report
Pertinent documentation to evaluate medical appropriateness should be included when this code is reported.

E **D7951** Sinus augmentation with bone or bone substitutes

E ☑ **D7953** Bone replacement graft for ridge preservation - per site

E **D7955** Repair of maxillofacial soft and/or hard tissue defect

E **D7960** Frenulectomy (frenectomy or frenotomy), separate procedure

E **D7963** Frenuloplasty

E ☑ **D7970** Excision of hyperplastic tissue, per arch

E **D7971** Excision of pericoronal gingiva

E **D7972** Surgical reduction of fibrous tuberosity

E **D7980** Sialolithotomy

E **D7981** Excision of salivary gland, by report
Pertinent documentation to evaluate medical appropriateness should be included when this code is reported.

E **D7982** Sialodochoplasty

E **D7983** Closure of salivary fistula

E **D7990** Emergency tracheotomy

E **D7991** Coronoidectomy

E **D7995** Synthetic graft, mandible or facial bones, by report
Pertinent documentation to evaluate medical appropriateness should be included when this code is reported.

E **D7996** Implant, mandible for augmentation purposes (excluding alveolar ridge), by report
Pertinent documentation to evaluate medical appropriateness should be included when this code is reported.

E **D7997** Appliance removal (not by dentist who placed appliance), includes removal of archbar

E **D7998** Intraoral placement of a fixation device not in conjunction with a fracture

E **D7999** Unspecified oral surgery procedure, by report
Determine if an alternative HCPCS Level II or a CPT code better describes the service being reported. This code should be used only if a more specific code is unavailable.

ORTHODONTICS D8000-D8999

E **D8010** Limited orthodontic treatment of the primary dentition A

E **D8020** Limited orthodontic treatment of the transitional dentition

E **D8030** Limited orthodontic treatment of the adolescent dentition A

E **D8040** Limited orthodontic treatment of the adult dentition A

E **D8050** Interceptive orthodontic treatment of the primary dentition A

E **D8060** Interceptive orthodontic treatment of the transitional dentition

E **D8070** Comprehensive orthodontic treatment of the transitional dentition

E **D8080** Comprehensive orthodontic treatment of the adolescent dentition A

E **D8090** Comprehensive orthodontic treatment of the adult dentition A

MINOR TREATMENT TO CONTROL HARMFUL HABITS

E **D8210** Removable appliance therapy

E **D8220** Fixed appliance therapy

OTHER ORTHODONTIC SERVICES

E **D8660** Orthodontic treatment (alternative billing to a contract fee)

E **D8670** Periodic orthodontic treatment visit (as part of contract)

E **D8680** Orthodontic retention (removal of appliances, construction and placement of retainer(s))

E D8690 Orthodontic treatment (alternative billing to a contract fee)

E D8691 Repair of orthodontic appliance

E D8692 Replacement of lost or broken retainer

E D8693 Rebonding or recementing; and/or repair, as required, of fixed retainers

E D8999 Unspecified orthodontic procedure, by report
Determine if an alternative HCPCS Level II or a CPT code better describes the service being reported. This code should be used only if a more specific code is unavailable.

ADJUNCTIVE GENERAL SERVICES D9110-D9999

UNCLASSIFIED TREATMENT

N D9110 Palliative (emergency) treatment of dental pain-minor procedures ⦸
MED: 100-2,15,150; 100-2,16,140

E D9120 Fixed partial denture sectioning

ANESTHESIA

E D9210 Local anesthesia not in conjunction with operative or surgical procedures

E D9211 Regional block anesthesia

E D9212 Trigeminal division block anesthesia

E D9215 Local anesthesia

E ☑ D9220 Deep sedation/general anesthesia, first 30 minutes

E ☑ D9221 Deep sedation/general anesthesia, each additional 15 minutes
MED: 100-2,15,150; 100-2,16,140

N D9230 Analgesia, anxiolysis, inhalation of nitrous oxide ⦸
MED: 100-2,15,150; 100-2,16,140

E ☑ D9241 Intravenous conscious sedation/analgesia — first 30 minutes

E ☑ D9242 Intravenous conscious sedation/analgesia — each additional 15 minutes

N D9248 Nonintravenous conscious sedation

PROFESSIONAL CONSULTATION

E D9310 Consultation, diagnostic service provided by dentist or physician other than requesting dentist or physician

PROFESSIONAL VISITS

E D9410 House/extended care facility call

E D9420 Hospital call

E D9430 Office visit for observation (during regularly scheduled hours), no other services performed

E D9440 Office visit, after regularly scheduled hours

E D9450 Case presentation, detailed and extensive treatment planning

DRUGS

E D9610 Therapeutic parenteral drug, single administration
Pertinent documentation to evaluate medical appropriateness should be included when this code is reported.

E D9612 Therapeutic parenteral drugs, 2 or more administrations, different medications

S D9630 Other drugs and/or medicaments, by report ⦸
Determine if an alternative HCPCS Level II or a CPT code better describes the service being reported. This code should be used only if a more specific code is unavailable.
MED: 100-2,15,150; 100-2,16,140

MISCELLANEOUS SERVICES

E D9910 Application of desensitizing medicament

E ☑ D9911 Application of desensitizing resin for cervical and/or root surface, per tooth

E D9920 Behavior management, by report
Pertinent documentation to evaluate medical appropriateness should be included when this code is reported.

S D9930 Treatment of complications (postsurgical) — unusual circumstances, by report ⦸
MED: 100-2,15,150; 100-2,16,140

S D9940 Occlusal guards, by report ⦸
Pertinent documentation to evaluate medical appropriateness should be included when this code is reported.
MED: 100-2,15,150; 100-2,16,140

E D9941 Fabrication of athletic mouthguard

E D9942 Repair and/or reline of occlusal guard

S D9950 Occlusion analysis, mounted case ⦸
MED: 100-2,15,150; 100-2,16,140

S D9951 Occlusal adjustment, limited ⦸
MED: 100-2,15,150; 100-2,16,140

S D9952 Occlusal adjustment, complete ⦸
MED: 100-2,15,150; 100-2,16,140

E D9970 Enamel microabrasion

E ☑ D9971 Odontoplasty 1-2 teeth; includes removal of enamel projections

E ☑ D9972 External bleaching — per arch

E ☑ D9973 External bleaching — per tooth

E ☑ D9974 Internal bleaching — per tooth

E D9999 Unspecified adjunctive procedure, by report
Determine if an alternative HCPCS Level II or a CPT code better describes the service being reported. This code should be used only if a more specific code is unavailable.

DURABLE MEDICAL EQUIPMENT E0100-E9999

E codes include durable medical equipment such as canes, crutches, walkers, commodes, decubitus care, bath and toilet aids, hospital beds, oxygen and related respiratory equipment, monitoring equipment, pacemakers, patient lifts, safety equipment, restraints, traction equipment, fracture frames, wheelchairs, and artificial kidney machines.

CANES

Y **E0100** Cane, includes canes of all materials, adjustable or fixed, with tip ♿

White canes for the blind are not covered under Medicare.

MED: 100-2,15,110.1; 100-3,280.1; 100-3,280.2

Y **E0105** Cane, quad or 3-prong, includes canes of all materials, adjustable or fixed, with tips ♿

MED: 100-2,15,110.1; 100-3,280.1; 100-3,280.5

CRUTCHES

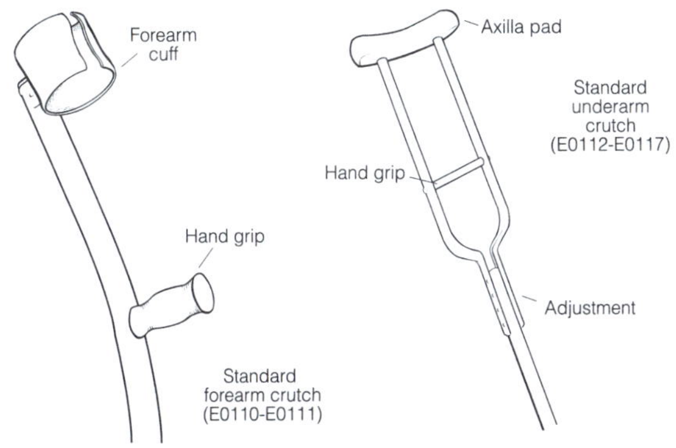

Y ☑ **E0110** Crutches, forearm, includes crutches of various materials, adjustable or fixed, pair, complete with tips and handgrips ♿

MED: 100-2,15,110.1; 100-3,280.1

Y ☑ **E0111** Crutch, forearm, includes crutches of various materials, adjustable or fixed, each, with tip and handgrips ♿

MED: 100-2,15,110.1; 100-3,280.1

Y ☑ **E0112** Crutches, underarm, wood, adjustable or fixed, pair, with pads, tips, and handgrips ♿

MED: 100-2,15,110.1; 100-3,280.1

Y ☑ **E0113** Crutch, underarm, wood, adjustable or fixed, each, with pad, tip, and handgrip ♿

MED: 100-2,15,110.1; 100-3,280.1

Y ☑ **E0114** Crutches, underarm, other than wood, adjustable or fixed, pair, with pads, tips, and handgrips ♿

MED: 100-2,15,110.1; 100-3,280.1

Y ☑ **E0116** Crutch, underarm, other than wood, adjustable or fixed, with pad, tip, handgrip, with or without shock absorber, each ♿

MED: 100-2,15,110.1; 100-3,280.1

Y ☑ **E0117** Crutch, underarm, articulating, spring assisted, each ♿

MED: 100-2,15,110.1

E ☑ **E0118** Crutch substitute, lower leg platform, with or without wheels, each

Medicare covers walkers if patient's ambulation is impaired.

WALKERS

Y **E0130** Walker, rigid (pickup), adjustable or fixed height

MED: 100-2,15,110.1; 100-3,280.1

Y **E0135** Walker, folding (pickup), adjustable or fixed height ♿

Medicare covers walkers if patient's ambulation is impaired.

MED: 100-2,15,110.1; 100-3,280.1

Y **E0140** Walker, with trunk support, adjustable or fixed height, any type ♿

MED: 100-2,15,110.1; 100-3,280.1

Y **E0141** Walker, rigid, wheeled, adjustable or fixed height ♿

Medicare covers walkers if patient's ambulation is impaired.

MED: 100-2,15,110.1; 100-3,280.1

Y **E0143** Walker, folding, wheeled, adjustable or fixed height ♿

Medicare covers walkers if patient's ambulation is impaired.

MED: 100-2,15,110.1; 100-3,280.1

Y **E0144** Walker, enclosed, 4 sided framed, rigid or folding, wheeled with posterior seat ♿

MED: 100-2,15,110.1; 100-3,280.1

Y **E0147** Walker, heavy duty, multiple braking system, variable wheel resistance ♿

Medicare covers safety roller walkers only in patients with severe neurological disorders or restricted use of one hand. In some cases, coverage will be extended to patients with a weight exceeding the limits of a standard wheeled walker.

MED: 100-2,15,110.1; 100-3,280.5

Y **E0148** Walker, heavy-duty, without wheels, rigid or folding, any type, each ♿

Y **E0149** Walker, heavy-duty, wheeled, rigid or folding, any type ♿

ATTACHMENTS

Y ☑ **E0153** Platform attachment, forearm crutch, each ♿

Y ☑ **E0154** Platform attachment, walker, each ♿

Y **E0155** Wheel attachment, rigid pick-up walker, per pair ♿

Y **E0156** Seat attachment, walker ♿

Y ☑ **E0157** Crutch attachment, walker, each ♿

Y ☑ **E0158** Leg extensions for walker, per set of 4 ♿

Y ☑ **E0159** Brake attachment for wheeled walker, replacement, each ♿

COMMODES

Y **E0160** Sitz type bath or equipment, portable, used with or without commode ♿

Medicare covers sitz baths if medical record indicates that the patient has an infection or injury of the perineal area and the sitz bath is prescribed by the physician.

MED: 100-3,280.1

Y **E0161** Sitz type bath or equipment, portable, used with or without commode, with faucet attachment(s) ♿

Medicare covers sitz baths if medical record indicates that the patient has an infection or injury of the perineal area and the sitz bath is prescribed by the physician.

MED: 100-3,280.1

Y **E0162** **Sitz bath chair**

Medicare covers sitz baths if medical record indicates that the patient has an infection or injury of the perineal area and the sitz bath is prescribed by the physician.

MED: 100-3,280.1

Y **E0163** **Commode chair, mobile or stationary, with fixed arms**

Medicare covers commodes for patients confined to their beds or rooms, for patients without indoor bathroom facilities, and to patients who cannot climb or descend the stairs necessary to reach the bathrooms in their homes.

MED: 100-2,15,110.1; 100-3,280.1

Y **E0165** **Commode chair, mobile or stationary, with detachable arms**

Medicare covers commodes for patients confined to their beds or rooms, for patients without indoor bathroom facilities, and to patients who cannot climb or descend the stairs necessary to reach the bathrooms in their homes.

MED: 100-2,15,110.1; 100-3,280.1

Y **E0167** **Pail or pan for use with commode chair, replacement only**

Medicare covers commodes for patients confined to their beds or rooms, for patients without indoor bathroom facilities, and to patients who cannot climb or descend the stairs necessary to reach the bathrooms in their homes.

MED: 100-3,280.1

Y **E0168** **Commode chair, extra wide and/or heavy-duty, stationary or mobile, with or without arms, any type, each**

Y **E0170** **Commode chair with integrated seat lift mechanism, electric, any type**

Y **E0171** **Commode chair with integrated seat lift mechanism, nonelectric, any type**

E **E0172** **Seat lift mechanism placed over or on top of toilet, any type**

Y ☑ **E0175** **Footrest, for use with commode chair, each**

DECUBITUS CARE EQUIPMENT

Y **E0181** **Powered pressure reducing mattress overlay/pad, alternating, with pump, includes heavy-duty**

Medicare covers pads if physicians supervise their use in patients who have decubitus ulcers or susceptibility to them. Prior authorization is required by Medicare for this item.

MED: 100-3,280.1; 100-8,5,5.2.3

Y **E0182** **Pump for alternating pressure pad, for replacement only**

Medicare covers pads if physicians supervise their use in patients who have decubitus ulcers or susceptibility to them. Prior authorization is required by Medicare for this item.

MED: 100-3,280.1; 100-8,5,5.2.3

Y **E0184** **Dry pressure mattress**

Medicare covers pads if physicians supervise their use in patients who have decubitus ulcers or susceptibility to them. Prior authorization is required by Medicare for this item.

MED: 100-3,280.1; 100-8,5,5.2.3

Y **E0185** **Gel or gel-like pressure pad for mattress, standard mattress length and width**

Medicare covers pads if physicians supervise their use in patients who have decubitus ulcers or susceptibility to them. Prior authorization is required by Medicare for this item.

MED: 100-3,280.1; 100-8,5,5.2.3

Y **E0186** **Air pressure mattress**

Medicare covers pads if physicians supervise their use in patients who have decubitus ulcers or susceptibility to them.

MED: 100-3,280.1

Y **E0187** **Water pressure mattress**

Medicare covers pads if physicians supervise their use in patients who have decubitus ulcers or susceptibility to them.

MED: 100-3,280.1

Y **E0188** **Synthetic sheepskin pad**

Medicare covers pads if physicians supervise their use in patients who have decubitus ulcers or susceptibility to them. Prior authorization is required by Medicare for this item.

MED: 100-3,280.1; 100-8,5,5.2.3

Y **E0189** **Lambswool sheepskin pad, any size**

Medicare covers pads if physicians supervise their use in patients who have decubitus ulcers or susceptibility to them. Prior authorization is required by Medicare for this item.

MED: 100-3,280.1; 100-8,5,5.2.3

E **E0190** **Positioning cushion/pillow/wedge, any shape or size, includes all components and accessories**

MED: 100-2,15,110.1

Y ☑ **E0191** **Heel or elbow protector, each**

Y **E0193** **Powered air flotation bed (low air loss therapy)**

Y **E0194** **Air fluidized bed**

An air fluidized bed is covered by Medicare if the patient has a stage 3 or stage 4 pressure sore and, without the bed, would require institutionalization. A physician's prescription is required.

MED: 100-3,280.8

Y **E0196** **Gel pressure mattress**

Medicare covers pads if physicians supervise their use in patients who have decubitus ulcers or susceptibility to them.

MED: 100-3,280.1

Y **E0197** **Air pressure pad for mattress, standard mattress length and width**

Medicare covers pads if physicians supervise their use in patients who have decubitus ulcers or susceptibility to them.

MED: 100-3,280.1

Y **E0198** **Water pressure pad for mattress, standard mattress length and width**

Medicare covers pads if physicians supervise their use in patients who have decubitus ulcers or susceptibility to them.

MED: 100-3,280.1

Y **E0199** **Dry pressure pad for mattress, standard mattress length and width**

Medicare covers pads if physicians supervise their use in patients who have decubitus ulcers or susceptibility to them.

MED: 100-3,280.1

HEAT/COLD APPLICATION

Y **E0200** Heat lamp, without stand (table model), includes bulb, or infrared element ♿
MED: 100-2,15,110.1; 100-3,280.1

Y **E0202** Phototherapy (bilirubin) light with photometer ♿

E **E0203** Therapeutic lightbox, minimum 10,000 lux, table top model

Y **E0205** Heat lamp, with stand, includes bulb, or infrared element ♿
MED: 100-2,15,110.1; 100-3,280.1

Y **E0210** Electric heat pad, standard ♿
MED: 100-3,280.1

Y **E0215** Electric heat pad, moist ♿
MED: 100-3,280.1

Y **E0217** Water circulating heat pad with pump ♿
MED: 100-3,280.1

Y **E0218** Water circulating cold pad with pump
MED: 100-3,280.1

Y **E0220** Hot water bottle ♿

Y **E0221** Infrared heating pad system ♿
MED: 100-3,270.2

Y **E0225** Hydrocollator unit, includes pads ♿
MED: 100-2,15,230; 100-3,280.1

Y **E0230** Ice cap or collar ♿

E **E0231** Noncontact wound-warming device (temperature control unit, AC adapter and power cord) for use with warming card and wound cover
MED: 100-2,16,20

E **E0232** Warming card for use with the noncontact wound-warming device and noncontact wound-warming wound cover
MED: 100-2,16,20

Y **E0235** Paraffin bath unit, portable (see medical supply code A4265 for paraffin) ♿
MED: 100-2,15,230; 100-3,280.1

Y **E0236** Pump for water circulating pad ♿
MED: 100-3,280.1

Y **E0238** Nonelectric heat pad, moist ♿
MED: 100-3,280.1

Y **E0239** Hydrocollator unit, portable ♿
MED: 100-2,15,230; 100-3,280.1

BATH AND TOILET AIDS

E **E0240** Bath/shower chair, with or without wheels, any size
MED: 100-3,280.1

E ☑ **E0241** Bathtub wall rail, each
MED: 100-2,15,110.1; 100-3,280.1

E **E0242** Bathtub rail, floor base
MED: 100-2,15,110.1; 100-3,280.1

E ☑ **E0243** Toilet rail, each
MED: 100-2,15,110.1; 100-3,280.1

E **E0244** Raised toilet seat
MED: 100-3,280.1

E **E0245** Tub stool or bench
MED: 100-3,280.1

E **E0246** Transfer tub rail attachment

E **E0247** Transfer bench for tub or toilet with or without commode opening
MED: 100-3,280.1

E **E0248** Transfer bench, heavy-duty, for tub or toilet with or without commode opening
MED: 100-3,280.1

Y **E0249** Pad for water circulating heat unit ♿
MED: 100-3,280.1

HOSPITAL BEDS AND ACCESSORIES

E **E0250** Hospital bed, fixed height, with any type side rails, with mattress ♿
MED: 100-2,15,110.1; 100-3,280.7

E **E0251** Hospital bed, fixed height, with any type side rails, without mattress ♿
MED: 100-2,15,110.1; 100-3,280.7

E **E0255** Hospital bed, variable height, hi-lo, with any type side rails, with mattress ♿
MED: 100-2,15,110.1; 100-3,280.7

E **E0256** Hospital bed, variable height, hi-lo, with any type side rails, without mattress ♿
MED: 100-2,15,110.1; 100-3,280.7

E **E0260** Hospital bed, semi-electric (head and foot adjustment), with any type side rails, with mattress ♿
MED: 100-2,15,110.1; 100-3,280.7

E **E0261** Hospital bed, semi-electric (head and foot adjustment), with any type side rails, without mattress ♿
MED: 100-2,15,110.1; 100-3,280.7

E **E0265** Hospital bed, total electric (head, foot, and height adjustments), with any type side rails, with mattress ♿
MED: 100-2,15,110.1; 100-3,280.7

E **E0266** Hospital bed, total electric (head, foot, and height adjustments), with any type side rails, without mattress ♿
MED: 100-2,15,110.1; 100-3,280.7

E **E0270** Hospital bed, institutional type includes: oscillating, circulating and Stryker frame, with mattress
MED: 100-3,280.1

E **E0271** Mattress, innerspring ♿
MED: 100-3,280.1; 100-3,280.7

E **E0272** Mattress, foam rubber ♿
MED: 100-3,280.1; 100-3,280.7

E **E0273** Bed board
MED: 100-3,280.1

E **E0274** Over-bed table
MED: 100-3,280.1

Y **E0275** Bed pan, standard, metal or plastic ♿
Reusable, autoclavable bedpans are covered by Medicare for bed-confined patients.
MED: 100-3,280.1

Y **E0276** Bed pan, fracture, metal or plastic ♿
Reusable, autoclavable bedpans are covered by Medicare for bed-confined patients.
MED: 100-3,280.1

Y **E0277** Powered pressure-reducing air mattress ♿
MED: 100-3,280.1

Y **E0280** Bed cradle, any type ♿

E **E0290** Hospital bed, fixed height, without side rails, with mattress ♿
MED: 100-2,15,110.1; 100-3,280.7

Special Coverage Instructions | Noncovered by Medicare | Carrier Discretion | ☑ Quantity Alert | ● New Code | ○ Recycled/Reinstated | ▲ Revised Code

Y **E0291** Hospital bed, fixed height, without side rails, without mattress ♿
MED: 100-2,15,110.1; 100-3,280.7

E **E0292** Hospital bed, variable height, hi-lo, without side rails, with mattress ♿
MED: 100-2,15,110.1; 100-3,280.7

Y **E0293** Hospital bed, variable height, hi-lo, without side rails, without mattress ♿
MED: 100-2,15,110.1; 100-3,280.7

E **E0294** Hospital bed, semi-electric (head and foot adjustment), without side rails, with mattress ♿
MED: 100-2,15,110.1; 100-3,280.7

Y **E0295** Hospital bed, semi-electric (head and foot adjustment), without side rails, without mattress ♿
MED: 100-2,15,110.1; 100-3,280.7

E **E0296** Hospital bed, total electric (head, foot, and height adjustments), without side rails, with mattress ♿
MED: 100-2,15,110.1; 100-3,280.7

Y **E0297** Hospital bed, total electric (head, foot, and height adjustments), without side rails, without mattress ♿
MED: 100-2,15,110.1; 100-3,280.7

Y **E0300** Pediatric crib, hospital grade, fully enclosed ♿

Y **E0301** Hospital bed, heavy-duty, extra wide, with weight capacity greater than 350 pounds, but less than or equal to 600 pounds, with any type side rails, without mattress ♿
MED: 100-3,280.7

Y **E0302** Hospital bed, extra heavy-duty, extra wide, with weight capacity greater than 600 pounds, with any type side rails, without mattress ♿
MED: 100-3,280.7

E **E0303** Hospital bed, heavy-duty, extra wide, with weight capacity greater than 350 pounds, but less than or equal to 600 pounds, with any type side rails, with mattress ♿
MED: 100-3,280.7

E **E0304** Hospital bed, extra heavy-duty, extra wide, with weight capacity greater than 600 pounds, with any type side rails, with mattress ♿
MED: 100-3,280.7

E **E0305** Bedside rails, half-length ♿
MED: 100-3,280.7

E **E0310** Bedside rails, full-length ♿
MED: 100-3,280.7

E **E0315** Bed accessory: board, table, or support device, any type
MED: 100-3,280.1

Y **E0316** Safety enclosure frame/canopy for use with hospital bed, any type ♿

Y **E0325** Urinal; male, jug-type, any material ♂ ♿
MED: 100-3,280.1

Y **E0326** Urinal; female, jug-type, any material ♀ ♿
MED: 100-3,280.1

Y **E0328** Hospital bed, pediatric, manual, 360 degree side enclosures, top of headboard, footboard and side rails up to 24 inches above the spring, includes mattress

Y **E0329** Hospital bed, pediatric, electric or semi-electric, 360 degree side enclosures, top of headboard, footboard and side rails up to 24 inches above the spring, includes mattress

E **E0350** Control unit for electronic bowel irrigation/evacuation system

E **E0352** Disposable pack (water reservoir bag, speculum, valving mechanism, and collection bag/box) for use with the electronic bowel irrigation/evacuation system

E **E0370** Air pressure elevator for heel

Y **E0371** Nonpowered advanced pressure reducing overlay for mattress, standard mattress length and width ♿

Y **E0372** Powered air overlay for mattress, standard mattress length and width ♿

Y **E0373** Nonpowered advanced pressure reducing mattress ♿

OXYGEN AND RELATED RESPIRATORY EQUIPMENT

Y **E0424** Stationary compressed gaseous oxygen system, rental; includes container, contents, regulator, flowmeter, humidifier, nebulizer, cannula or mask, and tubing ♿
For the first claim filed for home oxygen equipment or therapy, submit a certificate of medical necessity that includes the oxygen flow rate, anticipated frequency and duration of oxygen therapy, and physician signature. Medicare accepts oxygen therapy as medically necessary in cases documenting any of the following: erythocythemia with a hematocrit greater than 56 percent; a P pulmonale on EKG; or dependent edema consistent with congestive heart failure.
MED: 100-3,240.2

E **E0425** Stationary compressed gas system, purchase; includes regulator, flowmeter, humidifier, nebulizer, cannula or mask, and tubing
MED: 100-3,240.2

E **E0430** Portable gaseous oxygen system, purchase; includes regulator, flowmeter, humidifier, cannula or mask, and tubing
MED: 100-3,240.2

Y **E0431** Portable gaseous oxygen system, rental; includes portable container, regulator, flowmeter, humidifier, cannula or mask, and tubing ♿
MED: 100-3,240.2

Y **E0434** Portable liquid oxygen system, rental; includes portable container, supply reservoir, humidifier, flowmeter, refill adaptor, contents gauge, cannula or mask, and tubing ♿
MED: 100-3,240.2

E **E0435** Portable liquid oxygen system, purchase; includes portable container, supply reservoir, flowmeter, humidifier, contents gauge, cannula or mask, tubing and refill adaptor
MED: 100-3,240.2

Y **E0439** Stationary liquid oxygen system, rental; includes container, contents, regulator, flowmeter, humidifier, nebulizer, cannula or mask, & tubing ♿
MED: 100-3,240.2

E **E0440** Stationary liquid oxygen system, purchase; includes use of reservoir, contents indicator, regulator, flowmeter, humidifier, nebulizer, cannula or mask, and tubing
MED: 100-3,240.2

Y ☑ **E0441** Oxygen contents, gaseous (for use with owned gaseous stationary systems or when both a stationary and portable gaseous system are owned), 1 month's supply = 1 unit ♿
MED: 100-3,240.2

Y ☑ **E0442** Oxygen contents, liquid (for use with owned liquid stationary systems or when both a stationary and portable liquid system are owned), 1 month's supply = 1 unit ♿
MED: 100-3,240.2

Y ☑ **E0443** Portable oxygen contents, gaseous (for use only with portable gaseous systems when no stationary gas or liquid system is used), 1 month's supply = 1 unit ♿
MED: 100-3,240.2

Y ☑ **E0444** Portable oxygen contents, liquid (for use only with portable liquid systems when no stationary gas or liquid system is used), 1 month's supply = 1 unit ♿
MED: 100-3,240.2

N **E0445** Oximeter device for measuring blood oxygen levels noninvasively

Y **E0450** Volume control ventilator, without pressure support mode, may include pressure control mode, used with invasive interface (e.g., tracheostomy tube) ♿
MED: 100-3,280.1

Y **E0455** Oxygen tent, excluding croup or pediatric tents
MED: 100-3,240.2

Y **E0457** Chest shell (cuirass) ♿

Y **E0459** Chest wrap ♿

Y **E0460** Negative pressure ventilator; portable or stationary ♿
MED: 100-3,280.1

Y **E0461** Volume control ventilator, without pressure support mode, may include pressure control mode, used with noninvasive interface (e.g., mask) ♿
MED: 100-3,280.1

Y **E0462** Rocking bed, with or without side rails ♿

Y **E0463** Pressure support ventilator with volume control mode, may include pressure control mode, used with invasive interface (e.g., tracheostomy tube)

Y **E0464** Pressure support ventilator with volume control mode, may include pressure control mode, used with noninvasive interface (e.g., mask)

Y **E0470** Respiratory assist device, bi-level pressure capability, without backup rate feature, used with noninvasive interface, e.g., nasal or facial mask (intermittent assist device with continuous positive airway pressure device) ♿
MED: 100-3,280.1

Y **E0471** Respiratory assist device, bi-level pressure capability, with back-up rate feature, used with noninvasive interface, e.g., nasal or facial mask (intermittent assist device with continuous positive airway pressure device) ♿
MED: 100-3,280.1

Y **E0472** Respiratory assist device, bi-level pressure capability, with backup rate feature, used with invasive interface, e.g., tracheostomy tube (intermittent assist device with continuous positive airway pressure device) ♿
MED: 100-3,280.1

Y **E0480** Percussor, electric or pneumatic, home model ♿
MED: 100-3,280.1

E **E0481** Intrapulmonary percussive ventilation system and related accessories
MED: 100-3,240.5

Y **E0482** Cough stimulating device, alternating positive and negative airway pressure ♿

Y ☑ **E0483** High frequency chest wall oscillation air-pulse generator system, (includes hoses and vest), each ♿

Y ☑ **E0484** Oscillatory positive expiratory pressure device, nonelectric, any type, each ♿

Y **E0485** Oral device/appliance used to reduce upper airway collapsibility, adjustable or nonadjustable, prefabricated, includes fitting and adjustment

Y **E0486** Oral device/appliance used to reduce upper airway collapsibility, adjustable or nonadjustable, custom fabricated, includes fitting and adjustment

● N **E0487** Spirometer, electronic, includes all accessories

IPPB MACHINES

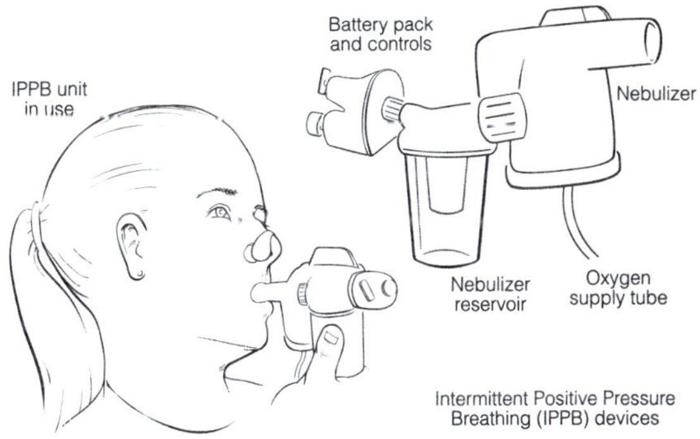

Intermittent Positive Pressure Breathing (IPPB) devices

Y **E0500** IPPB machine, all types, with built-in nebulization; manual or automatic valves; internal or external power source ♿
MED: 100-3,280.1

HUMIDIFIERS/COMPRESSORS/NEBULIZERS FOR USE WITH OXYGEN IPPB EQUIPMENT

Y **E0550** Humidifier, durable for extensive supplemental humidification during IPPB treatments or oxygen delivery ♿
MED: 100-3,280.1

Y **E0555** Humidifier, durable, glass or autoclavable plastic bottle type, for use with regulator or flowmeter ♿
MED: 100-3,280.1

Y **E0560** Humidifier, durable for supplemental humidification during IPPB treatment or oxygen delivery ♿
MED: 100-3,280.1

Y **E0561** Humidifier, nonheated, used with positive airway pressure device ♿

Y **E0562** Humidifier, heated, used with positive airway pressure device ♿

Y **E0565** Compressor, air power source for equipment which is not self-contained or cylinder driven ♿

Y **E0570** Nebulizer, with compressor ♿
MED: 100-3,280.1

Y **E0571** Aerosol compressor, battery powered, for use with small volume nebulizer ♿
MED: 100-3,280.1

Y **E0572** Aerosol compressor, adjustable pressure, light duty for intermittent use ♿

Y **E0574** Ultrasonic/electronic aerosol generator with small volume nebulizer ♿

Y **E0575** Nebulizer, ultrasonic, large volume ♿
MED: 100-3,280.1

Y **E0580** Nebulizer, durable, glass or autoclavable plastic, bottle type, for use with regulator or flowmeter ♿
MED: 100-3,280.1

Y **E0585** Nebulizer, with compressor and heater ♿
MED: 100-3,280.1

SUCTION PUMP/ROOM VAPORIZERS

Y **E0600** Respiratory suction pump, home model, portable or stationary, electric
MED: 100-3,280.1

Y **E0601** Continuous airway pressure (CPAP) device
MED: 100-3,240.4

Y **E0602** Breast pump, manual, any type M ♀

N **E0603** Breast pump, electric (AC and/or DC), any type M ♀

A **E0604** Breast pump, hospital grade, electric (AC and/or DC), any type M ♀

Y **E0605** Vaporizer, room type
MED: 100-3,280.1

Y **E0606** Postural drainage board
MED: 100-3,280.1

MONITORING EQUIPMENT

Y **E0607** Home blood glucose monitor
Medicare covers home blood testing devices for diabetic patients when the devices are prescribed by the patients' physicians. Many commercial payers provide this coverage to non-insulin dependent diabetics as well.
MED: 100.3,230.16

PACEMAKER MONITOR

Y **E0610** Pacemaker monitor, self-contained, (checks battery depletion, includes audible and visible check systems)
MED: 100-3,20.8; 100-3,20.8.1; 100-3,20.8.2

Y **E0615** Pacemaker monitor, self-contained, checks battery depletion and other pacemaker components, includes digital/visible check systems
MED: 100-3,20.8; 100-3,20.8.1; 100-3,20.8.2

N **E0616** Implantable cardiac event recorder with memory, activator, and programmer N1

Y **E0617** External defibrillator with integrated electrocardiogram analysis

Y **E0618** Apnea monitor, without recording feature

Y **E0619** Apnea monitor, with recording feature

Y **E0620** Skin piercing device for collection of capillary blood, laser, each

PATIENT LIFTS

Y **E0621** Sling or seat, patient lift, canvas or nylon
MED: 100-3,280.1

E **E0625** Patient lift, bathroom or toilet, not otherwise classified
MED: 100-3,280.1

Y **E0627** Seat lift mechanism incorporated into a combination lift-chair mechanism
MED: 100-3,280.4; 100-4,20,100; 100-4,20,130.2; 100-4,20,130.3; 100-4,20,130.4; 100-4,20,130.5

Y **E0628** Separate seat lift mechanism for use with patient-owned furniture, electric
MED: 100-3,280.4; 100-4,20,100; 100-4,20,130.2; 100-4,20,130.3; 100-4,20,130.4; 100-4,20,130.5

Y **E0629** Separate seat lift mechanism for use with patient-owned furniture, nonelectric
MED: 100-4,20,100; 100-4,20,130.2; 100-4,20,130.3; 100-4,20,130.4; 100-4,20,130.5

Y **E0630** Patient lift, hydraulic or mechanical, includes any seat, sling, strap(s), or pad(s)
MED: 100-3,280.1

Y **E0635** Patient lift, electric, with seat or sling
MED: 100-3,280.1

Y **E0636** Multipositional patient support system, with integrated lift, patient accessible controls

E **E0637** Combination sit to stand system, any size including pediatric, with seatlift feature, with or without wheels
MED: 100-3,280.1

E **E0638** Standing frame system, one position (e.g., upright, supine, or prone stander), any size including pediatric, with or without wheels
MED: 100-3,280.1

E **E0639** Patient lift, moveable from room to room with disassembly and reassembly, includes all components/accessories

E **E0640** Patient lift, fixed system, includes all components/accessories

E **E0641** Standing frame system, multi-position (e.g., 3-way stander), any size including pediatric, with or without wheels

E **E0642** Standing frame system, mobile (dynamic stander), any size including pediatric

PNEUMATIC COMPRESSOR AND APPLIANCES

Y **E0650** Pneumatic compressor, nonsegmental home model
MED: 100-3,280.6

Y **E0651** Pneumatic compressor, segmental home model without calibrated gradient pressure
MED: 100-3,280.6

Y **E0652** Pneumatic compressor, segmental home model with calibrated gradient pressure
MED: 100-3,280.6

Y **E0655** Nonsegmental pneumatic appliance for use with pneumatic compressor, half arm
MED: 100-3,280.6

● Y **E0656** Segmental pneumatic appliance for use with pneumatic compressor, trunk

● Y **E0657** Segmental pneumatic appliance for use with pneumatic compressor, chest

Y **E0660** Nonsegmental pneumatic appliance for use with pneumatic compressor, full leg
MED: 100-3,280.6

Y **E0665** Nonsegmental pneumatic appliance for use with pneumatic compressor, full arm
MED: 100-3,280.6

Y **E0666** Nonsegmental pneumatic appliance for use with pneumatic compressor, half leg
MED: 100-3,280.6

Y **E0667** Segmental pneumatic appliance for use with pneumatic compressor, full leg
MED: 100-3,280.6

Y **E0668** Segmental pneumatic appliance for use with pneumatic compressor, full arm
MED: 100-3,280.6

Y **E0669** Segmental pneumatic appliance for use with pneumatic compressor, half leg
MED: 100-3,280.6

Y **E0671** Segmental gradient pressure pneumatic appliance, full leg ♿
MED: 100-3,280.6

Y **E0672** Segmental gradient pressure pneumatic appliance, full arm ♿
MED: 100-3,280.6

Y **E0673** Segmental gradient pressure pneumatic appliance, half leg ♿
MED: 100-3,280.6

Y **E0675** Pneumatic compression device, high pressure, rapid inflation/deflation cycle, for arterial insufficiency (unilateral or bilateral system) ♿

Y **E0676** Intermittent limb compression device (includes all accessories), not otherwise specified ♿

Y **E0691** Ultraviolet light therapy system panel, includes bulbs/lamps, timer and eye protection, treatment area 2 sq ft or less ♿

Y **E0692** Ultraviolet light therapy system panel, includes bulbs/lamps, timer and eye protection, 4 ft panel ♿

Y **E0693** Ultraviolet light therapy system panel, includes bulbs/lamps, timer and eye protection, 6 ft panel ♿

Y **E0694** Ultraviolet multidirectional light therapy system in 6 ft cabinet, includes bulbs/lamps, timer, and eye protection ♿

SAFETY EQUIPMENT

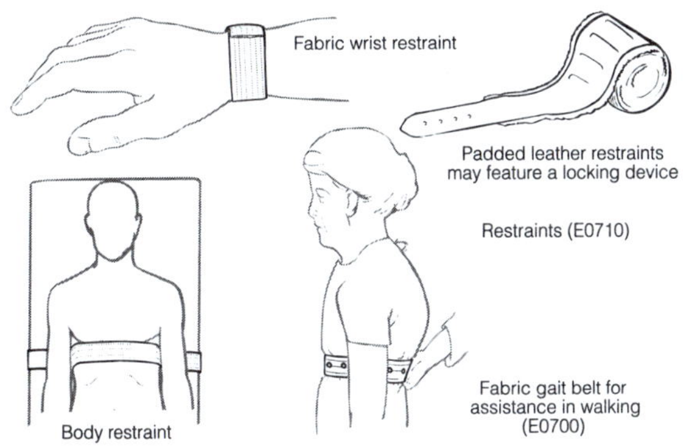

E **E0700** Safety equipment (e.g., belt, harness, or vest)

B ☑ **E0705** Transfer device, any type, each

RESTRAINTS

E **E0710** Restraints, any type (body, chest, wrist, or ankle)

TRANSCUTANEOUS AND/OR NEUROMUSCULAR ELECTRICAL NERVE STIMULATORS - TENS

Y **E0720** Transcutaneous electrical nerve stimulation (TENS) device, 2 lead, localized stimulation ♿
While TENS is covered when employed to control chronic pain, it is not covered for experimental treatment, as in motor function disorders like MS. Prior authorization is required by Medicare for this item.
MED: 100-3,40.5; 100-3,130.5; 100-3,130.6; 100-3,160.2; 100-3,160.7.1; 100-3,230.1; 100-8,5,5.2.3

Y **E0730** Transcutaneous electrical nerve stimulation (TENS) device, 4 or more leads, for multiple nerve stimulation ♿
While TENS is covered when employed to control chronic pain, it is not covered for experimental treatment, as in motor function disorders like MS. Prior authorization is required by Medicare for this item.
MED: 100-3,40.5; 100-3,130.5; 100-3,130.6; 100-3,160.2; 100-3,160.7.1; 100-3,230.1; 100-8,5,5.2.3

Y **E0731** Form-fitting conductive garment for delivery of TENS or NMES (with conductive fibers separated from the patient's skin by layers of fabric) ♿
MED: 100-3,160.13

Y **E0740** Incontinence treatment system, pelvic floor stimulator, monitor, sensor, and/or trainer ♿
MED: 100-3,230.8

Y **E0744** Neuromuscular stimulator for scoliosis ♿

Y **E0745** Neuromuscular stimulator, electronic shock unit ♿
MED: 100-3,160.12

N **E0746** Electromyography (EMG), biofeedback device
Biofeedback therapy is covered by Medicare only for re-education of specific muscles or for treatment of incapacitating muscle spasm or weakness. Medicare jurisdiction: local contractor.
MED: 100-3,30.1; 100-3,30.1.1

Y **E0747** Osteogenesis stimulator, electrical, noninvasive, other than spinal applications ♿
Medicare covers noninvasive osteogenic stimulation for nonunion of long bone fractures, failed fusion, or congenital pseudoarthroses.
MED: 100-3,150.2

Y **E0748** Osteogenesis stimulator, electrical, noninvasive, spinal applications ♿
Medicare covers noninvasive osteogenic stimulation as an adjunct to spinal fusion surgery for patients at high risk of pseudoarthroses due to previously failed spinal fusion, or for those undergoing fusion of three or more vertebrae.
MED: 100-3,150.2

N **E0749** Osteogenesis stimulator, electrical, surgically implanted N1 ♿
Medicare covers invasive osteogenic stimulation for nonunion of long bone fractures or as an adjunct to spinal fusion surgery for patients at high risk of pseudoarthroses due to previously failed spinal fusion, or for those undergoing fusion of three or more vertebrae.
MED: 100-3,150.2

E **E0755** Electronic salivary reflex stimulator (intraoral/noninvasive)

Y **E0760** Osteogenesis stimulator, low intensity ultrasound, noninvasive ♿
MED: 100-3,150.2

E **E0761** Nonthermal pulsed high frequency radiowaves, high peak power electromagnetic energy treatment device

B **E0762** Transcutaneous electrical joint stimulation device system, includes all accessories ♿

▲ Y **E0764** Functional neuromuscular stimulation, transcutaneous stimulation of sequential muscle groups of ambulation with computer control, used for walking by spinal cord injured, entire system, after completion of training program

Y **E0765** FDA approved nerve stimulator, with replaceable batteries, for treatment of nausea and vomiting ♿

B **E0769** Electrical stimulation or electromagnetic wound treatment device, not otherwise classified
MED: 100-4,32,11.1

● Y **E0770** Functional electrical stimulator, transcutaneous stimulation of nerve and/or muscle groups, any type, complete system, not otherwise specified

INFUSION SUPPLIES

Y **E0776** IV pole ♿

Y **E0779** Ambulatory infusion pump, mechanical, reusable, for infusion 8 hours or greater ♿

Y **E0780** Ambulatory infusion pump, mechanical, reusable, for infusion less than 8 hours ♿

Y **E0781** Ambulatory infusion pump, single or multiple channels, electric or battery operated, with administrative equipment, worn by patient ♿
MED: 100-3,280.14

N **E0782** Infusion pump, implantable, nonprogrammable (includes all components, e.g., pump, catheter, connectors, etc.) NI ♿
MED: 100-3,280.14

N **E0783** Infusion pump system, implantable, programmable (includes all components, e.g., pump, catheter, connectors, etc.) NI ♿
MED: 100-3,280.14

Y **E0784** External ambulatory infusion pump, insulin ♿
Covered by some commercial payers with preauthorization.
MED: 100-3,280.14

N **E0785** Implantable intraspinal (epidural/intrathecal) catheter used with implantable infusion pump, replacement NI ♿
Medicare jurisdiction: local contractor.
MED: 100-3,280.14

N **E0786** Implantable programmable infusion pump, replacement (excludes implantable intraspinal catheter) NI ♿
Medicare jurisdiction: local contractor.
MED: 100-3,280.14

Y **E0791** Parenteral infusion pump, stationary, single, or multichannel ♿
MED: 100-2,15,120; 100-3,180.2; 100-4,20,100.2.2

TRACTION - ALL TYPES

N **E0830** Ambulatory traction device, all types, each
MED: 100-3,280.1

TRACTION - CERVICAL

Y **E0840** Traction frame, attached to headboard, cervical traction ♿
MED: 100-3,280.1

Y **E0849** Traction equipment, cervical, free-standing stand/frame, pneumatic, applying traction force to other than mandible

Y **E0850** Traction stand, freestanding, cervical traction ♿
MED: 100-3,280.1

Y **E0855** Cervical traction equipment not requiring additional stand or frame ♿

Y **E0856** Cervical traction device, cervical collar with inflatable air bladder

TRACTION - OVERDOOR

Y **E0860** Traction equipment, overdoor, cervical ♿
MED: 100-3,280.1

TRACTION - EXTREMITY

Y **E0870** Traction frame, attached to footboard, extremity traction (e.g., Buck's) ♿
MED: 100-3,280.1

Y **E0880** Traction stand, freestanding, extremity traction (e.g., Buck's) ♿
MED: 100-3,280.1

TRACTION - PELVIC

Y **E0890** Traction frame, attached to footboard, pelvic traction ♿
MED: 100-3,280.1

Y **E0900** Traction stand, freestanding, pelvic traction (e.g., Buck's) ♿
MED: 100-3,280.1

TRAPEZE EQUIPMENT, FRACTURE FRAME, AND OTHER ORTHOPEDIC DEVICES

Y **E0910** Trapeze bars, also known as Patient Helper, attached to bed, with grab bar ♿
MED: 100-3,280.1

Y **E0911** Trapeze bar, heavy-duty, for patient weight capacity greater than 250 pounds, attached to bed, with grab bar

Y **E0912** Trapeze bar, heavy-duty, for patient weight capacity greater than 250 pounds, freestanding, complete with grab bar

Y **E0920** Fracture frame, attached to bed, includes weights ♿
MED: 100-3,280.1

Y **E0930** Fracture frame, freestanding, includes weights ♿
MED: 100-3,280.1

Y **E0935** Continuous passive motion exercise device for use on knee only ♿
MED: 100-3,280.1

E **E0936** Continuous passive motion exercise device for use other than knee

Y **E0940** Trapeze bar, freestanding, complete with grab bar ♿
MED: 100-3,280.1

Y **E0941** Gravity assisted traction device, any type ♿
MED: 100-3,280.1

Y **E0942** Cervical head harness/halter ♿

Y **E0944** Pelvic belt/harness/boot ♿

Y **E0945** Extremity belt/harness ♿

Y **E0946** Fracture frame, dual with cross bars, attached to bed (e.g., Balken, Four Poster) ♿
MED: 100-3,280.1

Y **E0947** Fracture frame, attachments for complex pelvic traction ♿
MED: 100-3,280.1

Y **E0948** Fracture frame, attachments for complex cervical traction ♿
MED: 100-3,280.1

WHEELCHAIR ACCESSORIES

Y **E0950** Wheelchair accessory, tray, each
MED: 100-3,280.1

Y ☑ **E0951** Heel loop/holder, any type, with or without ankle strap, each

Y ☑ **E0952** Toe loop/holder, any type, each ♿
MED: 100-3,280.1

Y ☑ **E0955** Wheelchair accessory, headrest, cushioned, any type, including fixed mounting hardware, each ♿

Y ☑ **E0956** Wheelchair accessory, lateral trunk or hip support, any type, including fixed mounting hardware, each ♿

Y ☑ **E0957** Wheelchair accessory, medial thigh support, any type, including fixed mounting hardware, each ♿

Y ☑ **E0958** Manual wheelchair accessory, one-arm drive attachment, each
MED: 100-3,280.1

B ☑ **E0959** Manual wheelchair accessory, adapter for amputee, each ♿
MED: 100-3,280.1

Y **E0960** Wheelchair accessory, shoulder harness/straps or chest strap, including any type mounting hardware ♿

B ☑ **E0961** Manual wheelchair accessory, wheel lock brake extension (handle), each ♿
MED: 100-3,280.1

B ☑ **E0966** Manual wheelchair accessory, headrest extension, each ♿
MED: 100-3,280.1

Y ☑ **E0967** Manual wheelchair accessory, hand rim with projections, any type, each ♿
MED: 100-3,280.1

Y **E0968** Commode seat, wheelchair ♿
MED: 100-3,280.1

Y **E0969** Narrowing device, wheelchair ♿
MED: 100-3,280.1

E **E0970** No. 2 footplates, except for elevating legrest ♿
See code(s): K0037, K0042
MED: 100-3,280.1

B ☑ **E0971** Manual wheelchair accessory, antitipping device, each ♿
DME fee schedule reflects a base billing unit of each.
MED: 100-3,280.1

B ☑ **E0973** Wheelchair accessory, adjustable height, detachable armrest, complete assembly, each ♿
MED: 100-3,280.1

B ☑ **E0974** Manual wheelchair accessory, antirollback device, each ♿
MED: 100-3,280.1

B ☑ **E0978** Wheelchair accessory, positioning belt/safety belt/pelvic strap, each ♿

Y **E0980** Safety vest, wheelchair ♿

Y ☑ **E0981** Wheelchair accessory, seat upholstery, replacement only, each ♿

Y ☑ **E0982** Wheelchair accessory, back upholstery, replacement only, each ♿

Y **E0983** Manual wheelchair accessory, power add-on to convert manual wheelchair to motorized wheelchair, joystick control ♿

Y **E0984** Manual wheelchair accessory, power add-on to convert manual wheelchair to motorized wheelchair, tiller control ♿

Y **E0985** Wheelchair accessory, seat lift mechanism ♿

Y ☑ **E0986** Manual wheelchair accessory, push activated power assist, each ♿

B ☑ **E0990** Wheelchair accessory, elevating legrest, complete assembly, each ♿
MED: 100-3,280.1

B **E0992** Manual wheelchair accessory, solid seat insert ♿

Y ☑ **E0994** Armrest, each ♿
MED: 100-3,280.1

B ☑ **E0995** Wheelchair accessory, calf rest/pad, each ♿
MED: 100-3,280.1

Y **E1002** Wheelchair accessory, power seating system, tilt only ♿

Y **E1003** Wheelchair accessory, power seating system, recline only, without shear reduction ♿

Y **E1004** Wheelchair accessory, power seating system, recline only, with mechanical shear reduction ♿

Y **E1005** Wheelchair accessory, power seatng System, recline only, with power shear reduction ♿

Y **E1006** Wheelchair accessory, power seating system, combination tilt and recline, without shear reduction ♿

Y **E1007** Wheelchair accessory, power seating system, combination tilt and recline, with mechanical shear reduction ♿

Y **E1008** Wheelchair accessory, power seating system, combination tilt and recline, with power shear reduction ♿

Y ☑ **E1009** Wheelchair accessory, addition to power seating system, mechanically linked leg elevation system, including pushrod and legrest, each ♿

Y ☑ **E1010** Wheelchair accessory, addition to power seating system, power leg elevation system, including legrest, pair ♿

Y **E1011** Modification to pediatric size wheelchair, width adjustment package (not to be dispensed with initial chair) ♿
MED: 100-3,280.1

Y **E1014** Reclining back, addition to pediatric size wheelchair ♿
MED: 100-3,280.1

Y **E1015** Shock absorber for manual wheelchair, each ♿
MED: 100-3,280.1

Y **E1016** Shock absorber for power wheelchair, each ♿
MED: 100-3,280.1

Y ☑ **E1017** Heavy-duty shock absorber for heavy-duty or extra heavy-duty manual wheelchair, each ♿
MED: 100-3,280.1

Y ☑ **E1018** Heavy-duty shock absorber for heavy-duty or extra heavy-duty power wheelchair, each ♿
MED: 100-3,280.1

Y **E1020** Residual limb support system for wheelchair ♿
MED: 100-3,280.3

Y **E1028** Wheelchair accessory, manual swingaway, retractable or removable mounting hardware for joystick, other control interface or positioning accessory ♿

Y **E1029** Wheelchair accessory, ventilator tray, fixed ♿

Y **E1030** Wheelchair accessory, ventilator tray, gimbaled ♿

ROLLABOUT CHAIR

Y **E1031** Rollabout chair, any and all types with castors 5 in or greater ♿
MED: 100-3,280.1

Y **E1035** Multi-positional patient transfer system, with integrated seat, operated by care giver ♿
MED: 100-2,15,110

Y **E1037** Transport chair, pediatric size ♿
MED: 100-3,280.1

Y **E1038** Transport chair, adult size, patient weight capacity up to and including 300 pounds ♿
MED: 100-3,280.1

Y **E1039** Transport chair, adult size, heavy-duty, patient weight capacity greater than 300 pounds ♿

WHEELCHAIRS - FULLY RECLINING

Y **E1050** Fully-reclining wheelchair, fixed full-length arms, swing-away detachable elevating legrests
MED: 100-3,280.1

Y **E1060** Fully-reclining wheelchair, detachable arms, desk or full-length, swing-away detachable elevating legrests
MED: 100-3,280.1

Y **E1070** Fully-reclining wheelchair, detachable arms (desk or full-length) swing-away detachable footrest
MED: 100-3,280.1

Y **E1083** Hemi-wheelchair; fixed full-length arms, swing-away, detachable, elevating legrests
MED: 100-3,280.1

Y **E1084** Hemi-wheelchair, detachable arms desk or full-length arms, swing-away detachable elevating legrests
MED: 100-3,280.1

E **E1085** Hemi-wheelchair, fixed full-length arms, swing-away detachable footrests
See code(s): K0002
MED: 100-3,280.1

E **E1086** Hemi-wheelchair, detachable arms, desk or full-length, swing-away detachable footrests
See code(s): K0002
MED: 100-3,280.1

Y **E1087** High strength lightweight wheelchair, fixed full-length arms, swing-away detachable elevating legrests
MED: 100-3,280.1

Y **E1088** High strength lightweight wheelchair, detachable arms desk or full-length, swing-away detachable elevating legrests
MED: 100-3,280.1

E **E1089** High-strength lightweight wheelchair, fixed-length arms, swing-away detachable footrest
See code(s): K0004
MED: 100-3,280.1

E **E1090** High-strength lightweight wheelchair, detachable arms, desk or full-length, swing-away detachable footrests
See code(s): K0004
MED: 100-3,280.1

Y **E1092** Wide heavy-duty wheel chair, detachable arms (desk or full-length), swing-away detachable elevating legrests
MED: 100-3,280.1

Y **E1093** Wide heavy-duty wheelchair, detachable arms, desk or full-length, swing-away detachable footrests
MED: 100-3,280.1

WHEELCHAIR - SEMI-RECLINING

Y **E1100** Semi-reclining wheelchair, fixed full-length arms, swing-away detachable elevating legrests
MED: 100-3,280.1

Y **E1110** Semi-reclining wheelchair, detachable arms (desk or full-length) elevating legrest
MED: 100-3,280.1

WHEELCHAIR - STANDARD

E **E1130** Standard wheelchair, fixed full-length arms, fixed or swing-away detachable footrests
See code(s): K0001
MED: 100-3,280.1

E **E1140** Wheelchair, detachable arms, desk or full-length, swing-away detachable footrests
See code(s): K0001
MED: 100-3,280.1

Y **E1150** Wheelchair, detachable arms, desk or full-length swing-away detachable elevating legrests ♿
MED: 100-3,280.1

Y **E1160** Wheelchair, fixed full-length arms, swing-away detachable elevating legrests
MED: 100-3,280.1

Y **E1161** Manual adult size wheelchair, includes tilt in space

WHEELCHAIR - AMPUTEE

Y **E1170** Amputee wheelchair, fixed full-length arms, swing-away detachable elevating legrests
MED: 100-3,280.1

Y **E1171** Amputee wheelchair, fixed full-length arms, without footrests or legrest
MED: 100-3,280.1

Y **E1172** Amputee wheelchair, detachable arms (desk or full-length) without footrests or legrest
MED: 100-3,280.1

Y **E1180** Amputee wheelchair, detachable arms (desk or full-length) swing-away detachable footrests
MED: 100-3,280.1

Y **E1190** Amputee wheelchair, detachable arms (desk or full-length) swing-away detachable elevating legrests
MED: 100-3,280.1

Y **E1195** Heavy-duty wheelchair, fixed full-length arms, swing-away detachable elevating legrests
MED: 100-3,280.1

Y **E1200** Amputee wheelchair, fixed full-length arms, swing-away detachable footrest
MED: 100-3,280.1

WHEELCHAIR - SPECIAL SIZE

Y **E1220** Wheelchair, specially sized or constructed (indicate brand name, model number, if any, and justification)
MED: 100-3,280.3

Y **E1221** Wheelchair with fixed arm, footrests
MED: 100-3,280.3

Y **E1222** Wheelchair with fixed arm, elevating legrests
MED: 100-3,280.3

Y **E1223** Wheelchair with detachable arms, footrests
MED: 100-3,280.3

Y **E1224** Wheelchair with detachable arms, elevating legrests
MED: 100-3,280.3

Y **E1225** Wheelchair accessory, manual semi-reclining back, (recline greater than 15 degrees, but less than 80 degrees), each ♿
MED: 100-3,280.3

B **E1226** Wheelchair accessory, manual fully reclining back, (recline greater than 80 degrees), each ♿
See also K0028
MED: 100-3,280.1

Y **E1227** Special height arms for wheelchair ♿
MED: 100-3,280.3

Y **E1228** Special back height for wheelchair ♿
MED: 100-3,280.3

Y **E1229** Wheelchair, pediatric size, not otherwise specified

Y **E1230** Power operated vehicle (3- or 4-wheel nonhighway, specify brand name and model number ♿
Prior authorization is required by Medicare for this item.
MED: 100-8,5,5.2.3

Y **E1231** Wheelchair, pediatric size, tilt-in-space, rigid, adjustable, with seating system ♿
MED: 100-3,280.1

Y **E1232** Wheelchair, pediatric size, tilt-in-space, folding, adjustable, with seating system ♿
MED: 100-3,280.1

Y **E1233** Wheelchair, pediatric size, tilt-in-space, rigid, adjustable, without seating system ♿
MED: 100-3,280.1

Y **E1234** Wheelchair, pediatric size, tilt-in-space, folding, adjustable, without seating system ♿
MED: 100-3,280.1

Y **E1235** Wheelchair, pediatric size, rigid, adjustable, with seating system ♿
MED: 100-3,280.1

Y **E1236** Wheelchair, pediatric size, folding, adjustable, with seating system ♿
MED: 100-3,280.1

Y **E1237** Wheelchair, pediatric size, rigid, adjustable, without seating system ♿
MED: 100-3,280.1

Y **E1238** Wheelchair, pediatric size, folding, adjustable, without seating system ♿
MED: 100-3,280.1

Y **E1239** Power wheelchair, pediatric size, not otherwise specified

WHEELCHAIR - LIGHTWEIGHT

Y **E1240** Lightweight wheelchair, detachable arms, (desk or full-length) swing-away detachable, elevating legrest
MED: 100-3,280.1

E **E1250** Lightweight wheelchair, fixed full-length arms, swing-away detachable footrest
See code(s): K0003
MED: 100-3,280.1

E **E1260** Lightweight wheelchair, detachable arms (desk or full-length) swing-away detachable footrest
See code(s): K0003
MED: 100-3,280.1

Y **E1270** Lightweight wheelchair, fixed full-length arms, swing-away detachable elevating legrests
MED: 100-3,280.1

WHEELCHAIR - HEAVY-DUTY

Y **E1280** Heavy-duty wheelchair, detachable arms (desk or full-length) elevating legrests
MED: 100-3,280.1

E **E1285** Heavy-duty wheelchair, fixed full-length arms, swing-away detachable footrest
See code(s): K0006
MED: 100-3,280.1

E **E1290** Heavy-duty wheelchair, detachable arms (desk or full-length) swing-away detachable footrest
See code(s): K0006
MED: 100-3,280.1

Y **E1295** Heavy-duty wheelchair, fixed full-length arms, elevating legrest
MED: 100-3,280.1

Y **E1296** Special wheelchair seat height from floor ♿
MED: 100-3,280.3

Y **E1297** Special wheelchair seat depth, by upholstery ♿
MED: 100-3,280.3

Y **E1298** Special wheelchair seat depth and/or width, by construction ♿
MED: 100-3,280.3

WHIRLPOOL - EQUIPMENT

E **E1300** Whirlpool, portable (overtub type)
MED: 100-3,280.1

Y **E1310** Whirlpool, nonportable (built-in type) ♿
MED: 100-3,280.1

REPAIRS AND REPLACEMENT SUPPLIES

Y ☑ **E1340** Repair or nonroutine service for durable medical equipment requiring the skill of a technician, labor component, per 15 minutes
Medicare jurisdiction: local contractor if repair or implanted DME.
MED: 100-2,15,110.2

ADDITIONAL OXYGEN RELATED EQUIPMENT

Y **E1353** Regulator ♿
MED: 100-3,240.2

● Y **E1354** Oxygen accessory, wheeled cart for portable cylinder or portable concentrator, any type, replacement only, each

Y **E1355** Stand/rack ♿
MED: 100-3,240.2

● Y **E1356** Oxygen accessory, battery pack/cartridge for portable concentrator, any type, replacement only, each

● Y **E1357** Oxygen accessory, battery charger for portable concentrator, any type, replacement only, each

● Y **E1358** Oxygen accessory, DC power adapter for portable concentrator, any type, replacement only, each

Y **E1372** Immersion external heater for nebulizer ♿
MED: 100-3,240.2

Y **E1390** Oxygen concentrator, single delivery port, capable of delivering 85 percent or greater oxygen concentration at the prescribed flow rate ♿
MED: 100-3,240.2

Durable Medical Equipment

E1225 — E1390

Y ☑ **E1391** Oxygen concentrator, dual delivery port, capable of delivering 85 percent or greater oxygen concentration at the prescribed flow rate, each
MED: 100-3,240.2

Y **E1392** Portable oxygen concentrator, rental

Y **E1399** Durable medical equipment, miscellaneous
Determine if an alternative HCPCS Level II or a CPT code better describes the service being reported. This code should be used only if a more specific code is unavailable. Medicare jurisdiction: local contractor if repair or implanted DME.

Y **E1405** Oxygen and water vapor enriching system with heated delivery
MED: 100-3,240.2; 100-4,20,20; 100-4,20,20.4

Y **E1406** Oxygen and water vapor enriching system without heated delivery
MED: 100-3,240.2; 100-4,20,20; 100-4,20,20.4

ARTIFICIAL KIDNEY MACHINES AND ACCESSORIES

A **E1500** Centrifuge, for dialysis

A **E1510** Kidney, dialysate delivery system kidney machine, pump recirculating, air removal system, flowrate meter, power off, heater and temp control with alarm, IV poles, pressure gauge, concentrate container

A **E1520** Heparin infusion pump for hemodialysis

A ☑ **E1530** Air bubble detector for hemodialysis, each, replacement

A ☑ **E1540** Pressure alarm for hemodialysis, each, replacement

A ☑ **E1550** Bath conductivity meter for hemodialysis, each

A ☑ **E1560** Blood leak detector for hemodialysis, each, replacement

A **E1570** Adjustable chair, for ESRD patients

A ☑ **E1575** Transducer protectors/fluid barriers, for hemodialysis, any size, per 10

A **E1580** Unipuncture control system for hemodialysis

A **E1590** Hemodialysis machine

A **E1592** Automatic intermittent peritoneal dialysis system

A **E1594** Cycler dialysis machine for peritoneal dialysis

A **E1600** Delivery and/or installation charges for hemodialysis equipment

A **E1610** Reverse osmosis water purification system, for hemodialysis
MED: 100-3,230.7

A **E1615** Deionizer water purification system, for hemodialysis
MED: 100-3,230.7

A **E1620** Blood pump for hemodialysis, replacement

A **E1625** Water softening system, for hemodialysis
MED: 100-3,230.7

A **E1630** Reciprocating peritoneal dialysis system

A ☑ **E1632** Wearable artificial kidney, each

B ☑ **E1634** Peritoneal dialysis clamps, each

A **E1635** Compact (portable) travel hemodialyzer system

A ☑ **E1636** Sorbent cartridges, for hemodialysis, per 10

A ☑ **E1637** Hemostats, each

A ☑ **E1639** Scale, each

A **E1699** Dialysis equipment, not otherwise specified
Determine if an alternative HCPCS Level II or a CPT code better describes the service being reported. This code should be used only if a more specific code is unavailable. Pertinent documentation to evaluate medical appropriateness should be included when this code is reported.

JAW MOTION REHABILITATION SYSTEM AND ACCESSORIES

Y **E1700** Jaw motion rehabilitation system
Medicare jurisdiction: local contractor.

Y ☑ **E1701** Replacement cushions for jaw motion rehabilitation system, package of 6
Medicare jurisdiction: local contractor.

Y ☑ **E1702** Replacement measuring scales for jaw motion rehabilitation system, package of 200
Medicare jurisdiction: local contractor.

OTHER ORTHOPEDIC DEVICES

Y **E1800** Dynamic adjustable elbow extension/flexion device, includes soft interface material

Y **E1801** Static progressive stretch elbow device, extension and/or flexion, with or without range of motion adjustment, includes all components and accessories

Y **E1802** Dynamic adjustable forearm pronation/supination device, includes soft interface material

Y **E1805** Dynamic adjustable wrist extension/flexion device, includes soft interface material

Y **E1806** Static progressive stretch wrist device, flexion and/or extension, with or without range of motion adjustment, includes all components and accessories

Y **E1810** Dynamic adjustable knee extension/flexion device, includes soft interface material

Y **E1811** Static progressive stretch knee device, extension and/or flexion, with or without range of motion adjustment, includes all components and accessories

Y **E1812** Dynamic knee, extension/flexion device with active resistance control

Y **E1815** Dynamic adjustable ankle extension/flexion device, includes soft interface material

Y **E1816** Static progressive stretch ankle device, flexion and/or extension, with or without range of motion adjustment, includes all components and accessories

Y **E1818** Static progressive stretch forearm pronation/supination device, with or without range of motion adjustment, includes all components and accessories

Y **E1820** Replacement soft interface material, dynamic adjustable extension/flexion device

Y **E1821** Replacement soft interface material/cuffs for bi-directional static progressive stretch device

Y **E1825** Dynamic adjustable finger extension/flexion device, includes soft interface material

Y **E1830** Dynamic adjustable toe extension/flexion device, includes soft interface material

Y **E1840** Dynamic adjustable shoulder flexion/abduction/rotation device, includes soft interface material

Y **E1841** Static progressive stretch shoulder device, with or without range of motion adjustment, includes all components and accessories

Y E1902 Communication board, nonelectronic augmentative or alternative communication device

Y E2000 Gastric suction pump, home model, portable or stationary, electric ♿

Y E2100 Blood glucose monitor with integrated voice synthesizer ♿
MED: 100.3,230.16

Y E2101 Blood glucose monitor with integrated lancing/blood sample ♿
MED: 100.3,230.16

Y E2120 Pulse generator system for tympanic treatment of inner ear endolymphatic fluid ♿

WHEELCHAIR ACCESSORY

Y ☑ E2201 Manual wheelchair accessory, nonstandard seat frame, width greater than or equal to 20 in and less than 24 in ♿

Y ☑ E2202 Manual wheelchair accessory, nonstandard seat frame width, 24-27 in ♿

Y ☑ E2203 Manual wheelchair accessory, nonstandard seat frame depth, 20 to less than 22 in ♿

Y ☑ E2204 Manual wheelchair accessory, nonstandard seat frame depth, 22 to 25 in ♿

Y ☑ E2205 Manual wheelchair accessory, handrim without projections (includes ergonomic or contoured), any type, replacement only, each

Y ☑ E2206 Manual wheelchair accessory, wheel Lock assembly, complete, each

Y ☑ E2207 Wheelchair accessory, crutch and cane holder, each

Y ☑ E2208 Wheelchair accessory, cylinder tank carrier, each

Y ☑ E2209 Accessory, arm trough, with or without hand support, each

Y ☑ E2210 Wheelchair accessory, bearings, any type, replacement only, each

Y ☑ E2211 Manual wheelchair accessory, pneumatic propulsion tire, any size, each

Y ☑ E2212 Manual wheelchair accessory, tube for pneumatic propulsion tire, any size, each

Y ☑ E2213 Manual wheelchair accessory, insert for pneumatic propulsion tire (removable), any type, any size, each

Y ☑ E2214 Manual wheelchair accessory, pneumatic caster tire, any size, each

Y ☑ E2215 Manual wheelchair accessory, tube for pneumatic caster tire, any size, each

Y ☑ E2216 Manual wheelchair accessory, foam filled propulsion tire, any size, each

Y ☑ E2217 Manual wheelchair accessory, foam filled caster tire, any size, each

Y ☑ E2218 Manual wheelchair accessory, foam propulsion tire, any size, each

Y ☑ E2219 Manual wheelchair accessory, foam caster tire, any size, each

Y ☑ E2220 Manual wheelchair accessory, solid (rubber/plastic) propulsion tire, any size, each

Y ☑ E2221 Manual wheelchair accessory, solid (rubber/plastic) caster tire (removable), any size, each

Y ☑ E2222 Manual wheelchair accessory, solid (rubber/plastic) caster tire with integrated wheel, any size, each

Y ☑ E2223 Manual wheelchair accessory, valve, any type, replacement only, each

Y ☑ E2224 Manual wheelchair accessory, propulsion wheel excludes tire, any size, each

Y ☑ E2225 Manual wheelchair accessory, caster wheel excludes tire, any size, replacement only, each

Y ☑ E2226 Manual wheelchair accessory, caster fork, any size, replacement only, each

Y ☑ E2227 Manual wheelchair accessory, gear reduction drive wheel, each ♿

Y ☑ E2228 Manual wheelchair accessory, wheel braking system and lock, complete, each ♿

● E E2230 Manual wheelchair accessory, manual standing system

● Y E2231 Manual wheelchair accessory, solid seat support base (replaces sling seat), includes any type mounting hardware

Y E2291 Back, planar, for pediatric size wheelchair including fixed attaching hardware

Y E2292 Seat, planar, for pediatric size wheelchair including fixed attaching hardware

Y E2293 Back, contoured, for pediatric size wheelchair including fixed attaching hardware

Y E2294 Seat, contoured, for pediatric size wheelchair including fixed attaching hardware

● Y E2295 Manual wheelchair accessory, for pediatric size wheelchair, dynamic seating frame, allows coordinated movement of multiple positioning features

Y E2300 Power wheelchair accessory, power seat elevation system

Y E2301 Power wheelchair accessory, power standing system

Y E2310 Power wheelchair accessory, electronic connection between wheelchair controller and one power seating system motor, including all related electronics, indicator feature, mechanical function selection switch, and fixed mounting hardware ♿

Y E2311 Power wheelchair accessory, electronic connection between wheelchair controller and 2 or more power seating system motors, including all related electronics, indicator feature, mechanical function selection switch, and fixed mounting hardware ♿

Y E2312 Power wheelchair accessory, hand or chin control interface, mini-proportional remote joystick, proportional, including fixed mounting hardware

Y E2313 Power wheelchair accessory, harness for upgrade to expandable controller, including all fasteners, connectors and mounting hardware, each

Y E2321 Power wheelchair accessory, hand control interface, remote joystick, nonproportional, including all related electronics, mechanical stop switch, and fixed mounting hardware ♿

Y E2322 Power wheelchair accessory, hand control interface, multiple mechanical switches, nonproportional, including all related electronics, mechanical stop switch, and fixed mounting hardware ♿

Y E2323 Power wheelchair accessory, specialty joystick handle for hand control interface, prefabricated ♿

Y E2324 Power wheelchair accessory, chin cup for chin control interface ♿

Y E2325 Power wheelchair accessory, sip and puff interface, nonproportional, including all related electronics, mechanical stop switch, and manual swingaway mounting hardware ♿

Y **E2326** Power wheelchair accessory, breath tube kit for sip and puff interface

Y **E2327** Power wheelchair accessory, head control interface, mechanical, proportional, including all related electronics, mechanical direction change switch, and fixed mounting hardware

Y **E2328** Power wheelchair accessory, head control or extremity control interface, electronic, proportional, including all related electronics and fixed mounting hardware

Y **E2329** Power wheelchair accessory, head control interface, contact switch mechanism, nonproportional, including all related electronics, mechanical stop switch, mechanical direction change switch, head array, and fixed mounting hardware

Y **E2330** Power wheelchair accessory, head control interface, proximity switch mechanism, nonproportional, including all related electronics, mechanical stop switch, mechanical direction change switch, head array, and fixed mounting hardware

Y **E2331** Power wheelchair accessory, attendant control, proportional, including all related electronics and fixed mounting hardware

Y ☑ **E2340** Power wheelchair accessory, nonstandard seat frame width, 20-23 in

Y ☑ **E2341** Power wheelchair accessory, nonstandard seat frame width, 24-27 in

Y ☑ **E2342** Power wheelchair accessory, nonstandard seat frame depth, 20 or 21 in

Y ☑ **E2343** Power wheelchair accessory, nonstandard seat frame depth, 22-25 in

Y **E2351** Power wheelchair accessory, electronic interface to operate speech generating device using power wheelchair control interface

Y ☑ **E2360** Power wheelchair accessory, 22 NF nonsealed lead acid battery, each

Y ☑ **E2361** Power wheelchair accessory, 22 NF sealed lead acid battery, each (e.g., gel cell, absorbed glassmat)

Y ☑ **E2362** Power wheelchair accessory, group 24 nonsealed lead acid battery, each

Y ☑ **E2363** Power wheelchair accessory, group 24 sealed lead acid battery, each (e.g., gel cell, absorbed glassmat)

Y ☑ **E2364** Power wheelchair accessory, U-1 nonsealed lead acid battery, each

Y ☑ **E2365** Power wheelchair accessory, U-1 sealed lead acid battery, each (e.g., gel cell, absorbed glassmat)

Y ☑ **E2366** Power wheelchair accessory, battery charger, single mode, for use with only one battery type, sealed or nonsealed, each

Y ☑ **E2367** Power wheelchair accessory, battery charger, dual mode, for use with either battery type, sealed or nonsealed, each

Y **E2368** Power wheelchair component, motor, replacement only

Y **E2369** Power wheelchair component, gear box, replacement only

Y **E2370** Power wheelchair component, motor and gear box combination, replacement only

Y ☑ **E2371** Power wheelchair accessory, group 27 sealed lead acid battery, (e.g., gel cell, absorbed glassmat), each

Y ☑ **E2372** Power wheelchair accessory, group 27 nonsealed lead acid battery, each

Y **E2373** Power wheelchair accessory, hand or chin control interface, compact remote joystick, proportional, including fixed mounting hardware

Y **E2374** Power wheelchair accessory, hand or chin control interface, standard remote joystick (not including controller), proportional, including all related electronics and fixed mounting hardware, replacement only

Y **E2375** Power wheelchair accessory, nonexpandable controller, including all related electronics and mounting hardware, replacement only

Y **E2376** Power wheelchair accessory, expandable controller, including all related electronics and mounting hardware, replacement only

Y **E2377** Power wheelchair accessory, expandable controller, including all related electronics and mounting hardware, upgrade provided at initial issue

Y ☑ **E2381** Power wheelchair accessory, pneumatic drive wheel tire, any size, replacement only, each

Y ☑ **E2382** Power wheelchair accessory, tube for pneumatic drive wheel tire, any size, replacement only, each

Y ☑ **E2383** Power wheelchair accessory, insert for pneumatic drive wheel tire (removable), any type, any size, replacement only, each

Y ☑ **E2384** Power wheelchair accessory, pneumatic caster tire, any size, replacement only, each

Y ☑ **E2385** Power wheelchair accessory, tube for pneumatic caster tire, any size, replacement only, each

Y ☑ **E2386** Power wheelchair accessory, foam filled drive wheel tire, any size, replacement only, each

Y ☑ **E2387** Power wheelchair accessory, foam filled caster tire, any size, replacement only, each

Y ☑ **E2388** Power wheelchair accessory, foam drive wheel tire, any size, replacement only, each

Y ☑ **E2389** Power wheelchair accessory, foam caster tire, any size, replacement only, each

Y ☑ **E2390** Power wheelchair accessory, solid (rubber/plastic) drive wheel tire, any size, replacement only, each

Y ☑ **E2391** Power wheelchair accessory, solid (rubber/plastic) caster tire (removable), any size, replacement only, each

Y ☑ **E2392** Power wheelchair accessory, solid (rubber/plastic) caster tire with integrated wheel, any size, replacement only, each

Y ☑ **E2393** Power wheelchair accessory, valve for pneumatic tire tube, any type, replacement only, each

Y ☑ **E2394** Power wheelchair accessory, drive wheel excludes tire, any size, replacement only, each

Y ☑ **E2395** Power wheelchair accessory, caster wheel excludes tire, any size, replacement only, each

Y ☑ **E2396** Power wheelchair accessory, caster fork, any size, replacement only, each

Y ☑ **E2397** Power wheelchair accessory, lithium-based battery, each

Y **E2399** Power wheelchair accessory, not otherwise classified interface, including all related electronics and any type mounting hardware

WOUND THERAPY

Y **E2402** Negative pressure wound therapy electrical pump, stationary or portable

SPEECH GENERATING DEVICE

Y ☑ **E2500** Speech generating device, digitized speech, using pre-recorded messages, less than or equal to eight minutes recording time ♿
MED: 100-3,50.1

Y ☑ **E2502** Speech generating device, digitized speech, using prerecorded messages, greater than 8 minutes but less than or equal to 20 minutes recording time ♿
MED: 100-3,50.1

Y ☑ **E2504** Speech generating device, digitized speech, using prerecorded messages, greater than 20 minutes but less than or equal to 40 minutes recording time ♿
MED: 100-3,50.1

Y ☑ **E2506** Speech generating device, digitized speech, using prerecorded messages, greater than 40 minutes recording time ♿
MED: 100-3,50.1

Y **E2508** Speech generating device, synthesized speech, requiring message formulation by spelling and access by physical contact with the device ♿
MED: 100-3,50.1

Y **E2510** Speech generating device, synthesized speech, permitting multiple methods of message formulation and multiple methods of device access ♿
MED: 100-3,50.1

Y **E2511** Speech generating software program, for personal computer or personal digital assistant ♿
MED: 100-3,50.1

Y **E2512** Accessory for speech generating device, mounting system ♿
MED: 100-3,50.1

Y **E2599** Accessory for speech generating device, not otherwise classified
MED: 100-3,50.1

WHEELCHAIR CUSHION

Y **E2601** General use wheelchair seat cushion, width less than 22 in, any depth

Y **E2602** General use wheelchair seat cushion, width 22 in or greater, any depth

Y **E2603** Skin protection wheelchair seat cushion, width less than 22 in, any depth

Y **E2604** Skin protection wheelchair seat cushion, width 22 in or greater, any depth

Y **E2605** Positioning wheelchair seat cushion, width less than 22 in, any depth

Y **E2606** Positioning wheelchair seat cushion, width 22 in or greater, any depth

Y **E2607** Skin protection and positioning wheelchair seat cushion, width less than 22 in, any depth

Y **E2608** Skin protection and positioning wheelchair seat cushion, width 22 in or greater, any depth

Y **E2609** Custom fabricated wheelchair seat cushion, any size

B **E2610** Wheelchair seat cushion, powered

Y **E2611** General use wheelchair back cushion, width less than 22 in, any height, including any type mounting hardware

Y **E2612** General use wheelchair back cushion, width 22 in or greater, any height, including any type mounting hardware

Y **E2613** Positioning wheelchair back cushion, posterior, width less than 22 in, any height, including any type mounting hardware

Y **E2614** Positioning wheelchair back cushion, posterior, width 22 in or greater, any height, including any type mounting hardware

Y **E2615** Positioning wheelchair back cushion, posterior-lateral, width less than 22 in, any height, including any type mounting hardware

Y **E2616** Positioning wheelchair back cushion, posterior-lateral, width 22 in or greater, any height, including any type mounting hardware

Y **E2617** Custom fabricated wheelchair back cushion, any size, including any type mounting hardware

Y **E2619** Replacement cover for wheelchair seat cushion or back cushion, each

Y **E2620** Positioning wheelchair back cushion, planar back with lateral supports, width less than 22 in, any height, including any type mounting hardware

Y **E2621** Positioning wheelchair back cushion, planar back with lateral supports, width 22 in or greater, any height, including any type mounting hardware

GAIT TRAINER

E **E8000** Gait trainer, pediatric size, posterior support, includes all accessories and components

E **E8001** Gait trainer, pediatric size, upright support, includes all accessories and components

E **E8002** Gait trainer, pediatric size, anterior support, includes all accessories and components

PROCEDURES/PROFESSIONAL SERVICES (TEMPORARY) G0000-G9999

The G codes are used to identify professional health care procedures and services that would otherwise be coded in CPT but for which there are no CPT codes.

Please refer to you CPT book for possible alternate code(s).

VACCINE ADMINISTRATION

S **G0008** Administration of influenza virus vaccine ⃠
MED: 100-2,6,10; 100-4,4,240

S **G0009** Administration of pneumococcal vaccine ⃠
MED: 100-2,6,10; 100-4,4,240

B **G0010** Administration of hepatitis B vaccine ⃠
MED: 100-2,6,10; 100-4,4,240

SEMEN ANALYSIS

A **G0027** Semen analysis; presence and/or motility of sperm excluding huhner ♂

SCREENING SERVICES

V **G0101** Cervical or vaginal cancer screening; pelvic and clinical breast examination ♀⃠
G0101 can be reported with an E/M code when a separately identifiable E/M service was provided.
MED: 100-2,6,10; 100-4,4,240
AHA: 4Q,'02,8; 3Q,'01,6

N **G0102** Prostate cancer screening; digital rectal examination ♂⃠
MED: 100-2,6,10; 100-3,210.1; 100-4,4,240

A **G0103** Prostate cancer screening; prostate specific antigen test (PSA) ♂⃠
MED: 100-2,6,10; 100-3,210.1; 100-4,4,240

S **G0104** Colorectal cancer screening; flexible sigmoidoscopy P3 ⃠
Medicare covers colorectal screening for cancer via flexible sigmoidoscopy once every four years for patients 50 years or older.
MED: 100-2,6,10; 100-4,4,240; 100-4,18,60.1

T **G0105** Colorectal cancer screening; colonoscopy on individual at high risk A2 ⃠
An individual with ulcerative enteritis or a history of a malignant neoplasm of the lower gastrointestinal tract is considered at high-risk for colorectal cancer, as defined by CMS.
MED: 100-2,6,10; 100-4,4,240; 100-4,18,60.1
AHA: 3Q,'01,6

S **G0106** Colorectal cancer screening; alternative to G0104, screening sigmoidoscopy, barium enema ⃠
MED: 100-2,6,10; 100-4,4,240; 100-4,18,60.1

A ☑ **G0108** Diabetes outpatient self-management training services, individual, per 30 minutes ⃠
MED: 100-2,6,10; 100-4,4,240

A ☑ **G0109** Diabetes outpatient self-management training services, group session (2 or more), per 30 minutes ⃠
MED: 100-2,6,10; 100-4,4,240

S **G0117** Glaucoma screening for high risk patients furnished by an optometrist or ophthalmologist ⃠
MED: 100-2,15,280.1
AHA: 1Q,'02,4; 3Q,'01,12

S **G0118** Glaucoma screening for high risk patient furnished under the direct supervision of an optometrist or ophthalmologist ⃠
MED: 100-2,15,280.1
AHA: 1Q,'02,4; 3Q,'01,12

S **G0120** Colorectal cancer screening; alternative to G0105, screening colonoscopy, barium enema ⃠
MED: 100-2,6,10; 100-4,18,60.1

T **G0121** Colorectal cancer screening; colonoscopy on individual not meeting criteria for high risk A2 ⃠
MED: 100-2,6,10; 100-4,4,240; 100-4,18,60.1
AHA: 1Q,'02,4; 3Q,'01,12

E **G0122** Colorectal cancer screening; barium enema

A **G0123** Screening cytopathology, cervical or vaginal (any reporting system), collected in preservative fluid, automated thin layer preparation, screening by cytotechnologist under physician supervision ♀⃠
See also P3000-P3001.
MED: 100-2,6,10; 100-3,190.2; 100-4,4,240

B **G0124** Screening cytopathology, cervical or vaginal (any reporting system), collected in preservative fluid, automated thin layer preparation, requiring interpretation by physician ♀⃠
See also P3000-P3001.
MED: 100-2,6,10; 100-3,190.2; 100-4,4,240

T **G0127** Trimming of dystrophic nails, any number P3 ⃠
MED: 100-2,15,290

B ☑ **G0128** Direct (face-to-face with patient) skilled nursing services of a registered nurse provided in a comprehensive outpatient rehabilitation facility, each 10 minutes beyond the first 5 minutes ⃠
MED: 100-4,5,100.3

▲ P **G0129** Occupational therapy services requiring the skills of a qualified occupational therapist, furnished as a component of a partial hospitalization treatment program, per session (45 minutes or more)

X **G0130** Single energy x-ray absorptiometry (SEXA) bone density study, one or more sites; appendicular skeleton (peripheral) (e.g., radius, wrist, heel) Z3
MED: 100-2,6,10; 100-3,150.3; 100-4,4,240; 100-4,13,140

B **G0141** Screening cytopathology smears, cervical or vaginal, performed by automated system, with manual rescreening, requiring interpretation by physician ♀⃠
MED: 100-2,6,10

A **G0143** Screening cytopathology, cervical or vaginal (any reporting system), collected in preservative fluid, automated thin layer preparation, with manual screening and rescreening by cytotechnologist under physician supervision ♀⃠
MED: 100-2,6,10

A **G0144** Screening cytopathology, cervical or vaginal (any reporting system), collected in preservative fluid, automated thin layer preparation, with screening by automated system, under physician supervision ♀⃠
MED: 100-2,6,10

A **G0145** Screening cytopathology, cervical or vaginal (any reporting system), collected in preservative fluid, automated thin layer preparation, with screening by automated system and manual rescreening under physician supervision ♀⃠
MED: 100-2,6,10

A **G0147** Screening cytopathology smears, cervical or vaginal, performed by automated system under physician supervision ♀⊘
MED: 100-2,6,10

A **G0148** Screening cytopathology smears, cervical or vaginal, performed by automated system with manual rescreening ♀⊘
MED: 100-2,6,10

B ☑ **G0151** Services of physical therapist in home health setting, each 15 minutes

B ☑ **G0152** Services of occupational therapist in home health setting, each 15 minutes

B ☑ **G0153** Services of speech and language pathologist in home health setting, each 15 minutes

B ☑ **G0154** Services of skilled nurse in home health setting, each 15 minutes

B ☑ **G0155** Services of clinical social worker in home health setting, each 15 minutes

B ☑ **G0156** Services of home health aide in home health setting, each 15 minutes

T ☑ **G0166** External counterpulsation, per treatment session ⊘
MED: 100-3,20.20

B **G0168** Wound closure utilizing tissue adhesive(s) only ⊘
AHA: 3Q,'01,13; 4Q,'01,12

S **G0173** Linear accelerator based stereotactic radiosurgery, complete course of therapy in one session Z2⊘

V **G0175** Scheduled interdisciplinary team conference (minimum of 3 exclusive of patient care nursing staff) with patient present

P **G0176** Activity therapy, such as music, dance, art or play therapies not for recreation, related to the care and treatment of patient's disabling mental health problems, per session (45 minutes or more)

N **G0177** Training and educational services related to the care and treatment of patient's disabling mental health problems per session (45 minutes or more)

M **G0179** Physician re-certification for Medicare-covered home health services under a home health plan of care (patient not present), including contacts with home health agency and review of reports of patient status required by physicians to affirm the initial implementation of the plan of care that meets patient's needs, per re-certification period ⊘
MED: 100-4,11,40.1.3.1; 100-4,12,180; 100-4,12,180.1

M **G0180** Physician certification for Medicare-covered home health services under a home health plan of care (patient not present), including contacts with home health agency and review of reports of patient status required by physicians to affirm the initial implementation of the plan of care that meets patient's needs, per certification period ⊘
MED: 100-4,11,40.1.3.1; 100-4,12,180; 100-4,12,180.1

M **G0181** Physician supervision of a patient receiving Medicare-covered services provided by a participating home health agency (patient not present) requiring complex and multidisciplinary care modalities involving regular physician development and/or revision of care plans, review of subsequent reports of patient status, review of laboratory and other studies, communication (including telephone calls) with other health care professionals involved in the patient's care, integration of new information into the medical treatment plan and/or adjustment of medical therapy, within a calendar month, 30 minutes or more ⊘
MED: 100-4,11,40.1.3.1; 100-4,12,180; 100-4,12,180.1

M **G0182** Physician supervision of a patient under a Medicare-approved hospice (patient not present) requiring complex and multidisciplinary care modalities involving regular physician development and/or revision of care plans, review of subsequent reports of patient status, review of laboratory and other studies, communication (including telephone calls) with other health care professionals involved in the patient's care, integration of new information into the medical treatment plan and/or adjustment of medical therapy, within a calendar month, 30 minutes or more ⊘
MED: 100-4,11,40.1.3.1; 100-4,12,180; 100-4,12,180.1

T **G0186** Destruction of localized lesion of choroid (for example, choroidal neovascularization); photocoagulation, feeder vessel technique (one or more sessions) R2⊘

A **G0202** Screening mammography, producing direct digital image, bilateral, all views ♀⊘
MED: 100-2,6,10; 100-4,4,240
AHA: 1Q,'02,3

A **G0204** Diagnostic mammography, producing direct digital image, bilateral, all views
AHA: 1Q,'03,7

A **G0206** Diagnostic mammography, producing direct digital image, unilateral, all views
AHA: 1Q,'03,7

E **G0219** PET imaging whole body; melanoma for noncovered indications
MED: 100-3,220.6
AHA: 1Q,'02,10

E **G0235** PET imaging, any site, not otherwise specified

S ☑ **G0237** Therapeutic procedures to increase strength or endurance of respiratory muscles, face-to-face, one-on-one, each 15 minutes (includes monitoring)

S ☑ **G0238** Therapeutic procedures to improve respiratory function, other than described by G0237, one-on-one, face-to-face, per 15 minutes (includes monitoring)

S **G0239** Therapeutic procedures to improve respiratory function or increase strength or endurance of respiratory muscles, 2 or more individuals (includes monitoring)

V **G0245** Initial physician evaluation and management of a diabetic patient with diabetic sensory neuropathy resulting in a loss of protective sensation (LOPS) which must include: (1) the diagnosis of LOPS, (2) a patient history, (3) a physical examination that consists of at least the following elements: (a) visual inspection of the forefoot, hindfoot, and toe web spaces, (b) evaluation of a protective sensation, (c) evaluation of foot structure and biomechanics, (d) evaluation of vascular status and skin integrity, and (e) evaluation and recommendation of footwear, and (4) patient education ⊘
MED: 100-3,70.2.1
AHA: 4Q,'02,9

V **G0246** Follow-up physician evaluation and management of a diabetic patient with diabetic sensory neuropathy resulting in a loss of protective sensation (LOPS) to include at least the following: (1) a patient history, (2) a physical examination that includes: (a) visual inspection of the forefoot, hindfoot, and toe web spaces, (b) evaluation of protective sensation, (c) evaluation of foot structure and biomechanics, (d) evaluation of vascular status and skin integrity, and (e) evaluation and recommendation of footwear, and (3) patient education ⊘
MED: 100-3,70.2.1
AHA: 4Q,'02,9

T **G0247** Routine foot care by a physician of a diabetic patient with diabetic sensory neuropathy resulting in a loss of protective sensation (LOPS) to include the local care of superficial wounds (i.e., superficial to muscle and fascia) and at least the following, if present: (1) local care of superficial wounds, (2) debridement of corns and calluses, and (3) trimming and debridement of nails P3 ⊘

MED: 100-3,70.2.1

AHA: 4Q,'02,9

▲ V **G0248** Demonstration, prior to initial use, of home INR monitoring for patient with either mechanical heart valve(s), chronic atrial fibrillation, or venous thromboembolism who meets Medicare coverage criteria, under the direction of a physician; includes: face-to-face demonstration of use and care of the INR monitor, obtaining at least one blood sample, provision of instructions for reporting home INR test results, and documentation of patient ability to perform testing prior to its use

MED: 100-3,210.1

AHA: 4Q,'02,9

V **G0249** Provision of test materials and equipment for home INR monitoring of patient with either mechanical heart valve(s), chronic atrial fibrillation, or venous thromboembolism who meets Medicare coverage criteria; includes provision of materials for use in the home and reporting of test results to physician; not occurring more frequently than once a week

MED: 100-3,210.1

AHA: 4Q,'02,9

▲ M **G0250** Physician review, interpretation, and patient management of home INR testing for a patient with either mechanical heart valve(s), chronic atrial fibrillation, or venous thromboembolism who meets Medicare coverage criteria; includes face-to-face verification by the physician at least once a year (e.g., during an evaluation and management service) that the patient uses the device in the context of the management of the anticoagulation therapy following initiation of the home INR monitoring; not occurring more frequently than once a week. ⊘

MED: 100-3,210.1

AHA: 4Q,'02,9

S ☑ **G0251** Linear accelerator based stereotactic radiosurgery, delivery including collimator changes and custom plugging, fractionated treatment, all lesions, per session, maximum 5 sessions per course of treatment Z2 ⊘

E **G0252** PET imaging, full and partial-ring PET scanners only, for initial diagnosis of breast cancer and/or surgical planning for breast cancer (e.g., initial staging of axillary lymph nodes)

MED: 100-3,220.6

E **G0255** Current perception threshold/sensory nerve conduction test, (SNCT) per limb, any nerve

MED: 100-3,160.23

AHA: 4Q,'02,9

S **G0257** Unscheduled or emergency dialysis treatment for an ESRD patient in a hospital outpatient department that is not certified as an ESRD facility

AHA: 1Q,'03,9; 4Q,'02,9

N **G0259** Injection procedure for sacroiliac joint; arthrography N1

AHA: 4Q,'02,9

T **G0260** Injection procedure for sacroiliac joint; provision of anesthetic, steroid and/or other therapeutic agent, with or without arthrography A2

AHA: 4Q,'02,9

N **G0268** Removal of impacted cerumen (one or both ears) by physician on same date of service as audiologic function testing N1 ⊘

AHA: 1Q,'03,12

N **G0269** Placement of occlusive device into either a venous or arterial access site, postsurgical or interventional procedure (e.g., angioseal plug, vascular plug) N1 ⊘

A ☑ **G0270** Medical nutrition therapy; reassessment and subsequent intervention(s) following second referral in same year for change in diagnosis, medical condition or treatment regimen (including additional hours needed for renal disease), individual, face-to-face with the patient, each 15 minutes ⊘ PQ

A ☑ **G0271** Medical nutrition therapy, reassessment and subsequent intervention(s) following second referral in same year for change in diagnosis, medical condition, or treatment regimen (including additional hours needed for renal disease), group (2 or more individuals), each 30 minutes ⊘ PQ

▲ N **G0275** Renal angiography, nonselective, one or both kidneys, performed at the same time as cardiac catheterization and/or coronary angiography, includes positioning or placement of any catheter in the abdominal aorta at or near the origins (ostia) of the renal arteries, injection of dye, flush aortogram, production of permanent images, and radiologic supervision and interpretation (List separately in addition to primary procedure) ⊘

▲ N **G0278** Iliac and/or femoral artery angiography, nonselective, bilateral or ipsilateral to catheter insertion, performed at the same time as cardiac catheterization and/or coronary angiography, includes positioning or placement of the catheter in the distal aorta or ipsilateral femoral or iliac artery, injection of dye, production of permanent images, and radiologic supervision and interpretation (List separately in addition to primary procedure) ⊘

A **G0281** Electrical stimulation, (unattended), to one or more areas, for chronic Stage III and Stage IV pressure ulcers, arterial ulcers, diabetic ulcers, and venous stasis ulcers not demonstrating measurable signs of healing after 30 days of conventional care, as part of a therapy plan of care

MED: 100-4,32,11.1

AHA: 1Q,'03,7; 2Q,'03,7

E **G0282** Electrical stimulation, (unattended), to one or more areas, for wound care other than described in G0281 ⊘

MED: 100-3,270.1

AHA: 1Q,'03,7; 2Q,'03,7

A **G0283** Electrical stimulation (unattended), to one or more areas for indication(s) other than wound care, as part of a therapy plan of care

AHA: 1Q,'03,7; 2Q,'03,7

N **G0288** Reconstruction, computed tomographic angiography of aorta for surgical planning for vascular surgery N1

N **G0289** Arthroscopy, knee, surgical, for removal of loose body, foreign body, debridement/shaving of articular cartilage (chondroplasty) at the time of other surgical knee arthroscopy in a different compartment of the same knee N1 ⊘

Special Coverage Instructions | Noncovered by Medicare | Carrier Discretion | ☑ Quantity Alert | ● New Code | ○ Recycled/Reinstated | ▲ Revised Code

T **G0290** Transcatheter placement of a drug eluting intracoronary stent(s), percutaneous, with or without other therapeutic intervention, any method; single vessel ⊘

AHA: 3Q,'03,11; 4Q,'03,7; 4Q,'02,9

T **G0291** Transcatheter placement of a drug eluting intracoronary stent(s), percutaneous, with or without other therapeutic intervention, any method; each additional vessel ⊘

AHA: 3Q,'03,11; 4Q,'03,7; 4Q,'02,9

X ☑ **G0293** Noncovered surgical procedure(s) using conscious sedation, regional, general, or spinal anesthesia in a Medicare qualifying clinical trial, per day ⊘

AHA: 4Q,'02,9

X ☑ **G0294** Noncovered procedure(s) using either no anesthesia or local anesthesia only, in a Medicare qualifying clinical trial, per day ⊘

AHA: 4Q,'02,9

E **G0295** Electromagnetic therapy, to one or more areas, for wound care other than described in G0329 or for other uses

MED: 100-3,270.1

AHA: 1Q,'03,7

S ☑ **G0302** Preoperative pulmonary surgery services for preparation for LVRS, complete course of services, to include a minimum of 16 days of services

S ☑ **G0303** Preoperative pulmonary surgery services for preparation for LVRS, 10 to 15 days of services

S ☑ **G0304** Preoperative pulmonary surgery services for preparation for LVRS, 1 to 9 days of services

S ☑ **G0305** Postdischarge pulmonary surgery services after LVRS, minimum of 6 days of services

A **G0306** Complete CBC, automated (HgB, HCT, RBC, WBC, without platelet count) and automated WBC differential count

A **G0307** Complete (CBC), automated (HgB, HCT, RBC, WBC, without platelet count)

~~G0308 ESRD related services during the course of treatment, for patients under 2 years of age to include monitoring for the adequacy of nutrition, assessment of growth and development, and counseling of parents; with 4 or more face-to-face physician visits per month.~~

~~G0309 ESRD related services during the course of treatment, for patients under 2 years of age to include monitoring for the adequacy of nutrition, assessment of growth and development, and counseling of parents; with 2 or 3 face-to-face physician visits per month.~~

~~G0310 ESRD related services during the course of treatment, for patients under 2 years of age to include monitoring for the adequacy of nutrition, assessment of growth and development, and counseling of parents; with 1 face-to-face physician visit per month~~

~~G0311 ESRD related services during the course of treatment, for patients between 2 and 11 years of age to include monitoring for the adequacy of nutrition, assessment of growth and development, and counseling of parents; with 4 or more face-to-face physician visits per month~~

~~G0312 ESRD related services during the course of treatment, for patients between 2 and 11 years of age to include monitoring for the adequacy of nutrition, assessment of growth and development, and counseling of parents; with 2 or 3 face-to-face physician visits per month~~

~~G0313 ESRD related services during the course of treatment, for patients between 2 and 11 years of age to include monitoring for the adequacy of nutrition, assessment of growth and development, and counseling of parents; with 1 face-to-face physician visit per month~~

~~G0314 ESRD related services during the course of treatment, for patients between 12 and 19 years of age to include monitoring for the adequacy of nutrition, assessment of growth and development, and counseling of parents; with 4 or more face-to-face physician visits per month~~

~~G0315 End Stage Renal disease (ESRD) related services during the course of treatment, for patients between 12 and 19 years of age to include monitoring for the adequacy of nutrition, assessment of growth and development, and counseling of parents; with two or three face-to-face physician visits per month~~

~~G0316 End Stage Renal disease (ESRD) related services during the course of treatment, for patients between 12 and 19 years of age to include monitoring for the adequacy of nutrition, assessment of growth and development, and counseling of parents; with one face-to-face physician visit per month~~

~~G0317 End Stage Renal disease (ESRD) related services during the course of treatment, for patients 20 years of age and over; with four or more face-to-face physician visits per month~~

~~G0318 ESRD related services during the course of treatment, for patients 20 years of age and over; with 2 or 3 face-to-face physician visits per month~~

~~G0319 End Stage Renal disease (ESRD) related services during the course of treatment, for patients 20 years of age and over; with one face-to-face physician visit per month~~

~~G0320 ESRD related services for home dialysis patients per full month; for patients under 2 years of age to include monitoring for adequacy of nutrition, assessment of growth and development, and counseling of parents~~

~~G0321 ESRD related services for home dialysis patients per full month; for patients 2 to 11 years of age to include monitoring for adequacy of nutrition, assessment of growth and development, and counseling of parents~~

~~G0322 End Stage Renal disease (ESRD) related services for home dialysis patients per full month; for patients 12 to 19 years of age to include monitoring for adequacy of nutrition, assessment of growth and development, and counseling of parents~~

~~G0323 End Stage Renal disease (ESRD) related services for home dialysis patients per full month; for patients 20 years of age and older~~

~~G0324 ESRD related services for home dialysis (less than full month), per day; for patients under 2 years of age~~

~~G0325 ESRD related services for home dialysis (less than full month), per day; for patients between 2 and 11 years of age~~

~~G0326 ESRD related services for home dialysis (less than full month), per day; for patients between twelve and nineteen years of age~~

~~G0327 ESRD related services for home dialysis (less than full month), per day; for patients twenty years of age and over~~

A **G0328** Colorectal cancer screening; fecal occult blood test, immunoassay, 1-3 simultaneous determinations ⊘

MED: 100-4,18,60.1

A **G0329** Electromagnetic therapy, to one or more areas for chronic Stage III and Stage IV pressure ulcers, arterial ulcers, diabetic ulcers and venous stasis ulcers not demonstrating measurable signs of healing after 30 days of conventional care as part of a therapy plan of care

MED: 100-4,32,11.2

~~G0332 Services for intravenous infusion of immunoglobulin prior to administration (this service is to be billed in conjunction with administration of immunoglobulin)~~

M **G0333** Pharmacy dispensing fee for inhalation drug(s); initial 30-day supply as a beneficiary

B **G0337** Hospice evaluation and counseling services, preelection

S **G0339** Image guided robotic linear accelerator-based stereotactic radiosurgery, complete course of therapy in one session, or first session of fractionated treatment

S **G0340** Image guided robotic linear accelerator-based stereotactic radiosurgery, delivery including collimator changes and custom plugging, fractionated treatment, all lesions, per session, second through fifth sessions, maximum 5 sessions per course of treatment

C **G0341** Percutaneous islet cell transplant, includes portal vein catheterization and infusion

MED: 100-3,260.3; 100-4,32,70

C **G0342** Laparoscopy for islet cell transplant, includes portal vein catheterization and infusion

MED: 100-3,260.3; 100-4,32,70

C **G0343** Laparotomy for islet cell transplant, includes portal vein catheterization and infusion

MED: 100-3,260.3; 100-4,32,70

~~G0344 Initial preventive physical examination; face-to-face visit, services limited to new beneficiary during the first six months of Medicare enrollment~~

See G0402

X **G0364** Bone marrow aspiration performed with bone marrow biopsy through the same incision on the same date of service

S **G0365** Vessel mapping of vessels for hemodialysis access (services for preoperative vessel mapping prior to creation of hemodialysis access using an autogenous hemodialysis conduit, including arterial inflow and venous outflow)

~~G0366 Electrocardiogram, routine ECG with 12 leads; performed as a component of the initial preventive examination with interpretation and report~~

See G0403

~~G0367 Tracing only, without interpretation and report, performed as a component of the initial preventive examination~~

See G0404

~~G0368 Interpretation and report only, performed as a component of the initial preventive examination~~

See G0405

M **G0372** Physician service required to establish and document the need for a power mobility device

N **G0378** Hospital observation service, per hour

MED: 100-2,6,20.6

Q3 **G0379** Direct admission of patient for hospital observation care

MED: 100-2,6,20.6

▲ V **G0380** Level 1 hospital emergency department visit provided in a type B emergency department; (the ED must meet at least one of the following requirements: (1) it is licensed by the state in which it is located under applicable state law as an emergency room or emergency department; (2) it is held out to the public (by name, posted signs, advertising, or other means) as a place that provides care for emergency medical conditions on an urgent basis without requiring a previously scheduled appointment; or (3) during the calendar year immediately preceding the calendar year in which a determination under 42 CFR 489.24 is being made, based on a representative sample of patient visits that occurred during that calendar year, it provides at least one-third of all of its outpatient visits for the treatment of emergency medical conditions on an urgent basis without requiring a previously scheduled appointment)

MED: 100-4,4,160

▲ V **G0381** Level 2 hospital emergency department visit provided in a type B emergency department; (the ED must meet at least one of the following requirements: (1) it is licensed by the state in which it is located under applicable state law as an emergency room or emergency department; (2) it is held out to the public (by name, posted signs, advertising, or other means) as a place that provides care for emergency medical conditions on an urgent basis without requiring a previously scheduled appointment; or (3) during the calendar year immediately preceding the calendar year in which a determination under 42 CFR 489.24 is being made, based on a representative sample of patient visits that occurred during that calendar year, it provides at least one-third of all of its outpatient visits for the treatment of emergency medical conditions on an urgent basis without requiring a previously scheduled appointment)

MED: 100-4,4,160

▲ V **G0382** Level 3 hospital emergency department visit provided in a type B emergency department; (the ED must meet at least one of the following requirements: (1) it is licensed by the state in which it is located under applicable state law as an emergency room or emergency department; (2) it is held out to the public (by name, posted signs, advertising, or other means) as a place that provides care for emergency medical conditions on an urgent basis without requiring a previously scheduled appointment; or (3) during the calendar year immediately preceding the calendar year in which a determination under 42 CFR 489.24 is being made, based on a representative sample of patient visits that occurred during that calendar year, it provides at least one-third of all of its outpatient visits for the treatment of emergency medical conditions on an urgent basis without requiring a previously scheduled appointment)

MED: 100-4,4,160

V **G0383** Level 4 hospital emergency department visit provided in a type B emergency department; (the ED must meet at least one of the following requirements: (1) it is licensed by the state in which it is located under applicable state law as an emergency room or emergency department; (2) it is held out to the public (by name, posted signs, advertising, or other means) as a place that provides care for emergency medical conditions on an urgent basis without requiring a previously scheduled appointment; or (3) during the calendar year immediately preceding the calendar year in which a determination under 42 CFR 489.24 is being made, based on a representative sample of patient visits that occurred during that calendar year, it provides at least one-third of all of its outpatient visits for the treatment of emergency medical conditions on an urgent basis without requiring a previously scheduled appointment)
MED: 100-4,4,160

▲ Q3 **G0384** Level 5 hospital emergency department visit provided in a type B emergency department; (the ED must meet at least one of the following requirements: (1) it is licensed by the state in which it is located under applicable state law as an emergency room or emergency department; (2) it is held out to the public (by name, posted signs, advertising, or other means) as a place that provides care for emergency medical conditions on an urgent basis without requiring a previously scheduled appointment; or (3) during the calendar year immediately preceding the calendar year in which a determination under 42 CFR 489.24 is being made, based on a representative sample of patient visits that occurred during that calendar year, it provides at least one-third of all of its outpatient visits for the treatment of emergency medical conditions on an urgent basis without requiring a previously scheduled appointment)
MED: 100-4,4,160

S **G0389** Ultrasound B-scan and/or real time with image documentation; for abdominal aortic aneurysm (AAA) screening ⊘

S **G0390** Trauma response team associated with hospital critical care service

T **G0392** Transluminal balloon angioplasty, percutaneous; for maintenance of hemodialysis access, arteriovenous fistula or graft; arterial A2

T **G0393** Transluminal balloon angioplasty, percutaneous; for maintenance of hemodialysis access, arteriovenous fistula or graft; venous A2

~~G0394 Blood occult test (e.g., guaiac), feces, for single determination for colorectal neoplasm (e.g., patient was provided three cards or single triple card for consecutive collection)~~

S **G0396** Alcohol and/or substance (other than tobacco) abuse structured assessment (e.g., AUDIT, DAST), and brief intervention 15 to 30 minutes

S **G0397** Alcohol and/or substance (other than tobacco) abuse structured assessment (e.g., AUDIT, DAST), and intervention, greater than 30 minutes

● S **G0398** Home sleep study test (HST) with type II portable monitor, unattended; minimum of 7 channels: EEG, EOG, EMG, ECG/heart rate, airflow, respiratory effort and oxygen saturation

● S **G0399** Home sleep test (HST) with type III portable monitor, unattended; minimum of 4 channels: 2 respiratory movement/airflow, 1 ECG/heart rate and 1 oxygen saturation

● S **G0400** Home sleep test (HST) with type IV portable monitor, unattended; minimum of 3 channels

● V **G0402** Initial preventive physical examination; face-to-face visit, services limited to new beneficiary during the first 12 months of Medicare enrollment

● M **G0403** Electrocardiogram, routine ECG with 12 leads; performed as a screening for the initial preventive physical examination with interpretation and report

● S **G0404** Electrocardiogram, routine ECG with 12 leads; tracing only, without interpretation and report, performed as a screening for the initial preventive physical examination

● B **G0405** Electrocardiogram, routine ECG with 12 leads; interpretation and report only, performed as a screening for the initial preventive physical examination

● C **G0406** Follow-up inpatient telehealth consultation, limited, physicians typically spend 15 minutes communicating with the patient via telehealth

● C **G0407** Follow-up inpatient telehealth consultation, intermediate, physicians typically spend 25 minutes communicating with the patient via telehealth

● C **G0408** Follow-up inpatient telehealth consultation, complex, physicians typically spend 35 minutes or more communicating with the patient via telehealth

● M **G0409** Social work and psychological services, directly relating to and/or furthering the patient's rehabilitation goals, each 15 minutes, face-to-face; individual (services provided by a CORF qualified social worker or psychologist in a CORF)

● P **G0410** Group psychotherapy other than of a multiple family group, in a partial hospitalization setting, approximately 45 to 50 minutes

● P **G0411** Interactive group psychotherapy, in a partial hospitalization setting, approximately 45 to 50 minutes

● C **G0412** Open treatment of iliac spine(s), tuberosity avulsion, or iliac wing fracture(s), unilateral or bilateral for pelvic bone fracture patterns which do not disrupt the pelvic ring, includes internal fixation, when performed

● T **G0413** Percutaneous skeletal fixation of posterior pelvic bone fracture and/or dislocation, for fracture patterns which disrupt the pelvic ring, unilateral or bilateral, (includes ilium, sacroiliac joint and/or sacrum)

● C **G0414** Open treatment of anterior pelvic bone fracture and/or dislocation for fracture patterns which disrupt the pelvic ring, unilateral or bilateral, includes internal fixation when performed (includes pubic symphysis and/or superior/inferior rami)

● C **G0415** Open treatment of posterior pelvic bone fracture and/or dislocation, for fracture patterns which disrupt the pelvic ring, unilateral or bilateral, includes internal fixation, when performed (includes ilium, sacroiliac joint and/or sacrum)

● S **G0416** Surgical pathology, gross and microscopic examination for prostate needle saturation biopsy sampling, 1-20 specimens

● S **G0417** Surgical pathology, gross and microscopic examination for prostate needle saturation biopsy sampling, 21-40 specimens

● S **G0418** Surgical pathology, gross and microscopic examination for prostate needle saturation biopsy sampling, 41-60 specimens

● S **G0419** Surgical pathology, gross and microscopic examination for prostate needle saturation biopsy sampling, greater than 60 specimens

S ☑ **G3001** Administration and supply of tositumomab, 450 mg ⃠

PHYSICIAN QUALITY REPORTING INDICATOR CODE (PQRI)

Physician Quality Reporting Indicator Codes (PQRI) are to be used for the physician Quality Reporting Indicator Code (PQRI) program in which CMS seeks to analyze the quality of care provided to Medicare beneficiaries. Reporting of these codes is voluntary. Physicians should not charge for these codes. Unless otherwise indicated, report these codes in addition to office visit, home visit, nursing facility, and domiciliary evaluation and management codes. For additional information, please visit the following website: http://www.cms.hhs.gov/providers/PQRI

M **G8006** Acute myocardial infarction: patient documented to have received aspirin at arrival

M **G8007** Acute myocardial infarction: patient not documented to have received aspirin at arrival

M **G8008** Clinician documented that acute myocardial infarction patient was not an eligible candidate to receive aspirin at arrival measure

M **G8009** Acute myocardial infarction: patient documented to have received beta-blocker at arrival PQ

M **G8010** Acute myocardial infarction: patient not documented to have received beta-blocker at arrival PQ

M **G8011** Clinician documented that acute myocardial infarction patient was not an eligible candidate for beta-blocker at arrival measure PQ

M **G8012** Pneumonia: patient documented to have received antibiotic within 4 hours of presentation

M **G8013** Pneumonia: patient not documented to have received antibiotic within 4 hours of presentation

M **G8014** Clinician documented that pneumonia patient was not an eligible candidate for antibiotic within 4 hours of presentation measure

M **G8015** Diabetic patient with most recent hemoglobin A1c level (within the last 6 months) documented as greater than 9%

M **G8016** Diabetic patient with most recent hemoglobin A1c level (within the last 6 months) documented as less than or equal to 9%

M **G8017** Clinician documented that diabetic patient was not eligible candidate for hemoglobin A1c measure

M **G8018** Clinician has not provided care for the diabetic patient for the required time for hemoglobin A1c measure (6 months)

M **G8019** Diabetic patient with most recent low-density lipoprotein (within the last 12 months) documented as greater than or equal to 100 mg/dl

M **G8020** Diabetic patient with most recent low-density lipoprotein (within the last 12 months) documented as less than 100 mg/dl

M **G8021** Clinician documented that diabetic patient was not eligible candidate for low-density lipoprotein measure

M **G8022** Clinician has not provided care for the diabetic patient for the required time for low-density lipoprotein measure (12 months)

M **G8023** Diabetic patient with most recent blood pressure (within the last 6 months) documented as equal to or greater than 140 systolic or equal to or greater than 80 mm Hg diastolic

M **G8024** Diabetic patient with most recent blood pressure (within the last 6 months) documented as less than 140 systolic and less than 80 diastolic

M **G8025** Clinician documented that the diabetic patient was not eligible candidate for blood pressure measure

M **G8026** Clinician has not provided care for the diabetic patient for the required time for blood pressure measure (within the last 6 months)

M **G8027** Heart failure patient with left ventricular systolic dysfunction (LVSD) documented to be on either angiotensin-converting enzyme-inhibitor or angiotensin-receptor blocker (ACE-1 or ARB) therapy

M **G8028** Heart failure patient with left ventricular systolic dysfunction (LVSD) not documented to be on either angiotensin-converting enzyme-inhibitor or angiotensin-receptor blocker (ACE-1 or ARB) therapy

M **G8029** Clinician documented that heart failure patient was not an eligible candidate for either angiotensin-converting enzyme-inhibitor or angiotensin-receptor blocker (ACE-1 or ARB) therapy measure

M **G8030** Heart failure patient with left ventricular systolic dysfunction (LVSD) documented to be on beta-blocker therapy

M **G8031** Heart failure patient with left ventricular systolic dysfunction (LVSD) not documented to be on beta-blocker therapy

M **G8032** Clinician documented that heart failure patient was not eligible candidate for beta-blocker therapy measure

M **G8033** Prior myocardial infarction, coronary artery disease patient documented to be on beta-blocker therapy

M **G8034** Prior myocardial infarction, coronary artery disease patient not documented to be on beta-blocker therapy

M **G8035** Clinician documented that prior myocardial infarction, coronary artery disease patient was not eligible candidate for beta-blocker therapy measure

M **G8036** Coronary artery disease patient documented to be on antiplatelet therapy

M **G8037** Coronary artery disease patient not documented to be on antiplatelet therapy

M **G8038** Clinician documented that coronary artery disease patient was not eligible candidate for antiplatelet therapy measure

M **G8039** Coronary artery disease patient with low-density lipoprotein documented to be greater than 100 mg/dl

M **G8040** Coronary artery disease patient with low-density lipoprotein documented to be less than or equal to 100 mg/dl

M **G8041** Clinician documented that coronary artery disease patient was not eligible candidate for low-density lipoprotein measure ♀

M **G8051** Patient (female) documented to have been assessed for osteoporosis ♀

M **G8052** Patient (female) not documented to have been assessed for osteoporosis ♀

M **G8053** Clinician documented that (female) patient was not an eligible candidate for osteoporosis assessment measure ♀

M **G8054** Patient not documented for the assessment for falls within last 12 months

M G8055 Patient documented for the assessment for falls within last 12 months

M G8056 Clinician documented that patient was not an eligible candidate for the falls assessment measure within the last 12 months

M G8057 Patient documented to have received hearing assessment

M G8058 Patient not documented to have received hearing assessment

M G8059 Clinician documented that patient was not an eligible candidate for hearing assessment measure

M G8060 Patient documented for the assessment of urinary incontinence

M G8061 Patient not documented for the assessment of urinary incontinence

M G8062 Clinician documented that patient was not an eligible candidate for urinary incontinence assessment measure

M G8075 ESRD patient with documented dialysis dose of URR greater than or equal to 65% (or Kt/ V greater than or equal to 1.2) A PQ

M G8076 ESRD patient with documented dialysis dose of URR less than 65% (or Kt/V less than 1.2) A PQ

M G8077 Clinician documented that ESRD patient was not an eligible candidate for URR or Kt/V measure A PQ

M G8078 ESRD patient with documented hematocrit greater than or equal to 33 (or hemoglobin greater than or equal to 11) A PQ

M G8079 ESRD patient with documented hematocrit less than 33 (or hemoglobin less than 11) A PQ

M G8080 Clinician documented that ESRD patient was not an eligible candidate for hematocrit (hemoglobin) measure A PQ

M G8081 ESRD patient requiring hemodialysis vascular access documented to have received autogenous AV fistula

M G8082 ESRD patient requiring hemodialysis documented to have received vascular access other than autogenous AV fistula

M G8085 ESRD patient requiring hemodialysis vascular access was not an eligible candidate for autogenous AV fistula

M G8093 Newly diagnosed chronic obstructive pulmonary disease (COPD) patient documented to have received smoking cessation intervention, within 3 months of diagnosis

M G8094 Newly diagnosed chronic obstructive pulmonary disease (COPD) patient not documented to have received smoking cessation intervention, within 3 months of diagnosis

M G8099 Osteoporosis patient documented to have been prescribed calcium and vitamin D supplements

M G8100 Clinician documented that osteoporosis patient was not an eligible candidate for calcium and vitamin D supplement measure

M G8103 Newly diagnosed osteoporosis patients documented to have been treated with antiresorptive therapy and/or PTH within 3 months of diagnosis

M G8104 Clinician documented that newly diagnosed osteoporosis patient was not an eligible candidate for antiresorptive therapy and/or PTH treatment measure within 3 months of diagnosis

M G8106 Within 6 months of suffering a nontraumatic fracture, female patient 65 years of age or older documented to have undergone bone mineral density testing or to have been prescribed a drug to treat or prevent osteoporosis

M G8107 Clinician documented that female patient 65 years of age or older who suffered a nontraumatic fracture within the last 6 months was not an eligible candidate for measure to test bone mineral density or drug to treat or prevent osteoporosis

M G8108 Patient documented to have received influenza vaccination during influenza season A

M G8109 Patient not documented to have received influenza vaccination during influenza season A

M G8110 Clinician documented that patient was not an eligible candidate for influenza vaccination measure A

M G8111 Patient (female) documented to have received a mammogram during the measurement year or prior year to the measurement year A ♀

M G8112 Patient (female) not documented to have received a mammogram during the measurement year or prior year to the measurement year A ♀

M G8113 Clinician documented that female patient was not an eligible candidate for mammography measure A

M G8114 Clinician did not provide care to patient for the required time of mammography measure (i.e., measurement year or prior year) A

M G8115 Patient documented to have received pneumococcal vaccination A

M G8116 Patient not documented to have received pneumococcal vaccination A

M G8117 Clinician documented that patient was not an eligible candidate for pneumococcal vaccination measure A

M G8126 Patient documented as being treated with antidepressant medication during the entire 12 week acute treatment phase A PQ

M G8127 Patient not documented as being treated with antidepressant medication during the entire 12 weeks acute treatment phase A PQ

M G8128 Clinician documented that patient was not an eligible candidate for antidepressant medication during the entire 12 week acute treatment phase measure A PQ

M G8129 Patient documented as being treated with antidepressant medication for at least 6 months continuous treatment phase A

M G8130 Patient not documented as being treated with antidepressant medication for at least 6 months continuous treatment phase A

M G8131 Clinician documented that patient was not an eligible candidate for antidepressant medication for continuous treatment phase A

M G8152 Patient documented to have received antibiotic prophylaxis one hour prior to incision time (2 hours for vancomycin)

M G8153 Patient not documented to have received antibiotic prophylaxis one hour prior to incision time (2 hours for vancomycin)

M G8154 Clinician documented that patient was not an eligible candidate for antibiotic prophylaxis one hour prior to incision time (2 hours for vancomycin) measure

M G8155 Patient with documented receipt of thromboembolism prophylaxis

M G8156 Patient without documented receipt of thromboembolism prophylaxis

M G8157 Clinician documented that patient was not an eligible candidate for thromboembolism prophylaxis measure

M G8159 Patient documented to have received coronary artery bypass graft without use of internal mammary artery

M G8162 Patient with isolated coronary artery bypass graft not documented to have received preoperative beta-blockade

M G8164 Patient with isolated coronary artery bypass graft documented to have prolonged intubation

M G8165 Patient with isolated coronary artery bypass graft not documented to have prolonged intubation

M G8166 Patient with isolated coronary artery bypass graft documented to have required surgical re-exploration

M G8167 Patient with isolated coronary artery bypass graft did not require surgical re-exploration

M G8170 Patient with isolated coronary artery bypass graft documented to have been discharged on aspirin or clopidogrel

M G8171 Patient with isolated coronary artery bypass graft not documented to have been discharged on aspirin or clopidogrel

M G8172 Clinician documented that patient with isolated coronary artery bypass graft was not an eligible candidate for antiplatelet therapy at discharge measure

M G8182 Clinician has not provided care for the cardiac patient for the required time for low-density lipoprotein measure (6 months)

M G8183 Patient with heart failure and atrial fibrillation documented to be on warfarin therapy

M G8184 Clinician documented that patient with heart failure and atrial fibrillation was not an eligible candidate for warfarin therapy measure

M G8185 Patients diagnosed with symptomatic osteoarthritis with documented annual assessment of function and pain

M G8186 Clinician documented that symptomatic osteoarthritis patient was not an eligible candidate for annual assessment of function and pain measure

M G8193 Clinician did not document that an order for prophylactic antibiotic to be given within one hour (if vancomycin, 2 hours) prior to surgical incision (or start of procedure when no incision is required) was given

M G8196 Clinician did not document a prophylactic antibiotic was administered within one hour (if vancomycin, 2 hours) prior to surgical incision (or start of procedure when no incision is required)

M G8200 Order for cefazolin or cefuroxime for antimicrobial prophylaxis not documented

M G8204 Clinician did not document an order was given to discontinue prophylactic antibiotics within 24 hours of surgical end time

M G8209 Clinician did not document an order was given to discontinue prophylactic antibiotics within 48 hours of surgical end time

M G8214 Clinician did not document an order was given for appropriate venous thromboembolism (VTE) prophylaxis to be given within 24 hrs prior to incision time or 24 hours after surgery end time

M G8217 Patient not documented to have received DVT prophylaxis by end of hospital day 2

M G8219 Patient documented to have received DVT prophylaxis by end of hospital day 2

M G8220 Patient not documented to have received DVT prophylaxis by end of hospital day 2

M G8221 Clinician documented that patient was not an eligible candidate for DVT prophylaxis by the end of hospital day 2, including physician documentation that patient is ambulatory

M G8223 Patient not documented to have received prescription for antiplatelet therapy at discharge

M G8226 Patient not documented to have received prescription for anticoagulant therapy at discharge

M G8231 Patient not documented to have received T-PA or not documented to have been considered a candidate for T-PA administration

M G8234 Patient not documented to have received dysphagia screening

M G8238 Patient not documented to have received order for or consideration for rehabilitation services

M G8240 Internal carotid stenosis patient in the 30-99% range, and no documentation of reference to measurements of distal internal carotid diameter as the denominator for stenosis measurement

M G8243 Patient not documented to have received CT or MRI and the presence or absence of hemorrhage, mass lesion and acute infarction not documented in the final report

M G8246 Patient was not an eligible candidate for medical history review with assessment of new or changing moles

M G8248 Patient with at least one alarm symptom not documented to have had upper endoscopy or referral for upper endoscopy

M G8251 Patient not documented to have received an esophageal biopsy when suspicion of Barrett's esophagus is indicated in the endoscopy report

M G8254 Patient with no documentation order for barium swallow test

M G8257 Clinician has not documented reconciliation of discharge medications with current medication list in medical record

M G8260 Patient not documented to have surrogate decision maker or advance care plan in medical record

M G8263 Patient not documented to have been assessed for presence or absence of urinary incontinence

M G8266 Patient not documented to have received characterization of urinary incontinence

M G8268 Patient not documented to have received plan of care for urinary incontinence

M G8271 Patient with no documentation of screening for fall risks (2 or more falls in the past year or any fall with injury in the past year)

M G8274 Clinician has not documented presence or absence of alarm symptoms

M G8276 Patient not documented to have received medical history with assessment of new or changing moles

M G8279 Patient not documented to have received a complete physical skin exam

M G8282 Patient not documented to have received counseling to perform a self-examination

M **G8285** Patient not documented to have received pharmacologic therapy

M **G8289** Patient with no documentation of calcium and vitamin D use or counseling regarding both calcium and vitamin D use, or exercise

M **G8293** COPD patient without spirometry results documented

M **G8296** COPD patient not documented to have inhaled bronchodilator therapy prescribed

M **G8298** Patient documented to have received optic nerve head evaluation

M **G8299** Patient not documented to have received optic nerve head evaluation

M **G8302** Patient documented to have a specific target intraocular pressure range goal

M **G8303** Patient not documented to have a specific target intraocular pressure range goal

M **G8304** Clinician documented that patient was not an eligible candidate for a specific target intraocular pressure range goal

M **G8305** Clinician has not provided care for the primary open-angle glaucoma patient for the required time for treatment range goal documentation measurement

M **G8306** Primary open-angle glaucoma patient with intraocular pressure above the target range goal documented to have received plan of care

M **G8307** Primary open-angle glaucoma patient with intraocular pressure at or below goal, no plan of care necessary

M **G8308** Primary open-angle glaucoma patient with intraocular pressure above the target range goal, and not documented to have received plan of care during the reporting year

M **G8310** Patient not documented to have been prescribed/recommended at least one antioxidant vitamin or mineral supplement during the reporting year

M **G8314** Patient not documented to have received macular exam with documentation of presence or absence of macular thickening or hemorrhage and no documentation of Level of macular degeneration severity

M **G8318** Patient documented not to have visual functional status assessed

M **G8322** Patient not documented to have had presurgical axial length, corneal power measurement and method of intraocular lens power calculation

M **G8326** Patient not documented to have received fundus evaluation within 6 months prior to cataract surgery

M **G8330** Patient not documented to have received dilated macular or fundus exam with level of severity of retinopathy and the presence or absence of macular edema not documented

M **G8334** Documentation of findings of macular or fundus exam not communicated to the physician managing the patient's ongoing diabetes care

M **G8338** Clinician has not documented that communication was sent to the physician managing ongoing care of patient that a fracture occurred and that the patient was or should be tested or treated for osteoporosis

M **G8341** Patient not documented to have had central DEXA measurement or pharmacologic therapy

M **G8345** Patient not documented to have had central DEXA measurement ordered or performed or pharmacologic therapy

M **G8351** Patient not documented to have had ECG

M **G8354** Patient not documented to have received or taken aspirin 24 hours before emergency department arrival or during emergency department stay

M **G8357** Patient not documented to have had ECG

M **G8360** Patient not documented to have vital signs recorded and reviewed

M **G8362** Patient not documented to have oxygen saturation assessed

M **G8365** Patient not documented to have mental status assessed

M **G8367** Patient not documented to have appropriate empiric antibiotic prescribed

M **G8370** Asthma patients with numeric frequency of symptoms or patient completion of an asthma assessment tool/survey/questionnaire not documented

M **G8371** Chemotherapy documented as not received or prescribed for Stage III colon cancer patients A PQ

M **G8372** Chemotherapy documented as received or prescribed for Stage III colon cancer patients A PQ

M **G8373** Chemotherapy plan documented prior to chemotherapy administration PQ

M **G8374** Chemotherapy plan not documented prior to chemotherapy administration PQ

M **G8375** Chronic lymphocytic leukemia (CLL) patient with no documentation of baseline flow cytometry performed

M **G8376** Clinician documentation that breast cancer patient was not eligible for tamoxifen or aromatase inhibitor therapy measure A ♀ PQ

M **G8377** Clinician documentation that colon cancer patient is not eligible for chemotherapy measure A PQ

M **G8378** Clinician documentation that patient was not an eligible candidate for radiation therapy measure A PQ

M **G8379** Documentation of radiation therapy recommended within 12 months of first office visit A PQ

M **G8380** For patients with ER or PR positive, Stage IC-III breast cancer, clinician did not document that the patient received or was prescribed tamoxifen or aromatase inhibitor A ♀ PQ

M **G8381** For patients with ER or PR positive, Stage IC-III breast cancer, clinician documented or prescribed that the patient is receiving tamoxifen or aromatase inhibitor A ♀ PQ

M **G8382** Multiple myeloma patients with no documentation of prescribed or received intravenous bisphosphonate therapy

M **G8383** No documentation of radiation therapy recommended within 12 months of first office visit A PQ

M **G8384** Baseline cytogenetic testing not performed in patients with myelodysplastic syndrome (MDS) or acute leukemias

M **G8385** Diabetic patients with no documentation of hemoglobin A1c level (within the last 12 months)

M **G8386** Diabetic patients with no documentation of low-density lipoprotein (within the last 12 months)

M **G8387** ESRD patient with a hematocrit or hemoglobin not documented A PQ

M **G8388** ESRD patient with URR or Kt/V value not documented, but otherwise eligible for measure A PQ

M **G8389** Myelodysplastic syndrome (MDS) patients with no documentation of iron stores prior to receiving erythropoietin therapy

M **G8390** Diabetic patients with no documentation of blood pressure measurement (within the last 12 months)

M **G8391** Patients with persistent asthma, no documentation of preferred long-term control medication or acceptable alternative treatment prescribed

M **G8395** Left ventricular ejection fraction (LVEF) >= 40% or documentation as normal or mildly depressed left ventricular systolic function

M **G8396** Left ventricular ejection fraction (LVEF) not performed or documented

M **G8397** Dilated macular or fundus exam performed, including documentation of the presence or absence of macular edema and level of severity of retinopathy

M **G8398** Dilated macular or fundus exam not performed

M **G8399** Patient with central dual-energy x-ray absorptiometry (DXA) results documented or ordered or pharmacologic therapy (other than minerals/vitamins) for osteoporosis prescribed

M **G8400** Patient with central dual-energy x-ray absorptiometry (DXA) results not documented or not ordered or pharmacologic therapy (other than minerals/vitamins) for osteoporosis not prescribed

M **G8401** Clinician documented that patient was not an eligible candidate for screening or therapy for osteoporosis for women measure ♀

M **G8402** Tobacco (smoke) use cessation intervention, counseling

M **G8403** Tobacco (smoke) use cessation intervention not counseled

M **G8404** Lower extremity neurological exam performed and documented

M **G8405** Lower extremity neurological exam not performed

M **G8406** Clinician documented that patient was not an eligible candidate for lower extremity neurological exam measure

M **G8407** ABI measured and documented

M **G8408** ABI measurement was not obtained

M **G8409** Clinician documented that patient was not an eligible candidate for ABI measurement measure

M **G8410** Footwear evaluation performed and documented

M **G8415** Footwear evaluation was not performed

M **G8416** Clinician documented that patient was not an eligible candidate for footwear evaluation measure

▲ M **G8417** Calculated BMI above the upper parameter and a follow-up plan was documented in the medical record

▲ M **G8418** Calculated BMI below the lower parameter and a follow-up plan was documented in the medical record

▲ M **G8419** Calculated BMI outside normal parameters, no follow-up plan was documented in the medical record

▲ M **G8420** Calculated BMI within normal parameters and documented

M **G8421** BMI not calculated

M **G8422** Patient not eligible for BMI calculation

M **G8423** Documented that patient was screened and either influenza vaccination status is current or patient was counseled

M **G8424** Influenza vaccine status was not screened

M **G8425** Influenza vaccine status screened, patient not current and counseling was not provided

M **G8426** Documented that patient was not appropriate for screening and/or counseling about the influenza vaccine (e.g., allergy to eggs)

▲ M **G8427** List of current medications with dosages (includes prescription, over-the-counter, herbals, vitamin/mineral/dietary nutritional supplements) and verification with the patient or authorized representative documented by the provider

▲ M **G8428** Provider documentation of current medications with dosages (includes prescription, over-the-counter, herbals, vitamin/mineral/dietary nutritional supplements) without documented patient verification

▲ M **G8429** Incomplete or no provider documentation that patient's current medications with dosages (includes prescription, over-the-counter, herbals, vitamin/mineral/dietary nutritional supplements were assessed

▲ M **G8430** Provider documentation that patient is not eligible for medication assessment

▲ M **G8431** Positive screen for clinical depression using a standardized tool and a follow-up plan documented

M **G8432** No documentation of clinical depression screening using a standardized tool

▲ M **G8433** Screening for clinical depression using a standardized tool not documented, patient not eligible/appropriate

M **G8434** Documentation of cognitive impairment screening using a standardized tool

M **G8435** No documentation of cognitive impairment screening using a standardized tool

M **G8436** Patient not eligible/not appropriate for cognitive impairment screening

▲ M **G8437** Documentation of clinician and patient involvement with the development of a plan of care including signature by the practitioner/therapist and either a co-signature by the patient or documented verbal agreement obtained from the patient or, when necessary, an authorized representative

▲ M **G8438** No documentation of clinician and patient involvement with the development of a plan of care including signature by the practitioner/therapist and either a co-signature by the patient or documented verbal agreement obtained from the patient or, when necessary, an authorized representative

▲ M **G8439** Documentation that patient is not eligible for co-developing a plan of care including signature by the practitioner/therapist and either a co-signature by the patient or documented verbal agreement obtained from the patient or, when necessary, an authorized representative

▲ M **G8440** Documentation of pain assessment (including location, intensity and description) prior to initiation of treatment or documentation of the absence of pain as a result of assessment through discussion with the patient including the use of a standardized tool and a follow-up plan is documented

M **G8441** No documentation of pain assessment (including location, intensity and description) prior to initiation of treatment

M **G8442** Documentation that patient is not eligible for pain assessment

M **G8443** All prescriptions created during the encounter were generated using a qualified e-prescribing system

M **G8445** No prescriptions were generated during the encounter, provider does have access to a qualified e-prescribing system

▲ M **G8446** Provider does have access to a qualified e-prescribing system and some or all of the prescriptions generated during the encounter were printed or phoned in as required by state or Federal law or regulations, patient request or pharmacy system being unable to receive electronic transmission; or because they were for narcotics or other controlled substances

▲ M **G8447** Patient encounter was documented using a CCHIT certified EHR

▲ M **G8448** Patient encounter was documented using a qualified (non-CCHIT certified) EHR

M **G8449** Patient encounter was not documented using an EMR due to system reasons such as, the system being inoperable at the time of the visit; use of this code implies that an EMR is in place and generally available

M **G8450** Beta-blocker therapy prescribed for patients with left ventricular ejection fraction (LVEF) <40% or documentation as moderately or severely depressed left ventricular systolic function

M **G8451** Clinician documented patient with left ventricular ejection fraction (LVEF) <40% or documentation as moderately or severely depressed left ventricular systolic function was not eligible candidate for beta-blocker therapy

M **G8452** Beta-blocker therapy not prescribed for patients with left ventricular ejection fraction (LVEF) <40% or documentation as moderately or severely depressed left ventricular systolic function

M **G8453** Tobacco use cessation intervention, counseling

M **G8454** Tobacco use cessation intervention not counseled, reason not specified

M **G8455** Current tobacco smoker

M **G8456** Current smokeless tobacco user

▲ M **G8457** Current tobacco nonuser

M **G8458** Clinician documented that patient is not an eligible candidate for genotype testing; patient not receiving antiviral treatment for hepatitis C

M **G8459** Clinician documented that patient is receiving antiviral treatment for hepatitis C

M **G8460** Clinician documented that patient is not an eligible candidate for quantitative RNA testing at week 12; patient not receiving antiviral treatment for hepatitis C

M **G8461** Patient receiving antiviral treatment for hepatitis C

M **G8462** Clinician documented that patient is not an eligible candidate for counseling regarding contraception prior to antiviral treatment; patient not receiving antiviral treatment for hepatitis C

M **G8463** Patient receiving antiviral treatment for hepatitis C documented

M **G8464** Clinician documented that prostate cancer patient is not an eligible candidate for adjuvant hormonal therapy; low or intermediate risk of recurrence or risk of recurrence not determined

M **G8465** High risk of recurrence of prostate cancer

M **G8466** Clinician documented that patient is not an eligible candidate for suicide risk assessment; major depressive disorder, in remission

M **G8467** Documentation of new diagnosis of initial or recurrent episode of major depressive disorder

M **G8468** Angiotensin converting enzyme (ACE) inhibitor or angiotensin receptor blocker (ARB) therapy prescribed for patients with a left ventricular ejection fraction (LVEF) <40% or documentation of moderately or severely depressed left ventricular systolic function

M **G8469** Clinician documented that patient with a left ventricular ejection fraction (LVEF) <40% or documentation of moderately or severely depressed left ventricular systolic function was not an eligible candidate for angiotensin converting enzyme (ACE) inhibitor or angiotensin receptor blocker (ARB) therapy

M **G8470** Patient with left ventricular ejection fraction (LVEF) >=40% or documentation as normal or mildly depressed left ventricular systolic function

M **G8471** Left ventricular ejection fraction (LVEF) was not performed or documented

M **G8472** Angiotensin converting enzyme (ACE) inhibitor or angiotensin receptor blocker (ARB) therapy not prescribed for patients with a left ventricular ejection fraction (LVEF) <40% or documentation of moderately or severely depressed left ventricular systolic function, reason not specified

M **G8473** Angiotensin converting enzyme (ACE) inhibitor or angiotensin receptor blocker (ARB) therapy prescribed

M **G8474** Angiotensin converting enzyme (ACE) inhibitor or angiotensin receptor blocker (ARB) therapy not prescribed for reasons documented by the clinician

M **G8475** Angiotensin converting enzyme (ACE) inhibitor or angiotensin receptor blocker (ARB) therapy not prescribed, reason not specified

M **G8476** Most recent blood pressure has a systolic measurement of <130 mm/Hg and a diastolic measurement of <80 mm/Hg

M **G8477** Most recent blood pressure has a systolic measurement of >=130 mm/Hg and/or a diastolic measurement of >=80 mm/Hg

M **G8478** Blood pressure measurement not performed or documented, reason not specified

M **G8479** Clinician prescribed angiotensin converting enzyme (ACE) inhibitor or angiotensin receptor blocker (ARB) therapy

M **G8480** Clinician documented that patient was not an eligible candidate for angiotensin converting enzyme (ACE) inhibitor or angiotensin receptor blocker (ARB) therapy

M **G8481** Clinician did not prescribe angiotensin converting enzyme (ACE) inhibitor or angiotensin receptor blocker (ARB) therapy, reason not specified

M **G8482** Influenza immunization was ordered or administered

M **G8483** Influenza immunization was not ordered or administered for reasons documented by clinician

M **G8484** Influenza immunization was not ordered or administered, reason not specified

● M **G8485** I intend to report the diabetes mellitus measures group

Special Coverage Instructions | Noncovered by Medicare | Carrier Discretion | ☑ Quantity Alert | ● New Code | ○ Recycled/Reinstated | ▲ Revised Code

A Age Edit | M Maternity Edit | ♀ Female Only | ♂ Male Only | A-Y OPPS Status Indicators

● M G8486 I intend to report the preventive care measures group

● M G8487 I intend to report the chronic kidney disease (CKD) measures group

● M G8488 Clinician intends to report the ESRD measure group

● M G8489 I intend to report the coronary artery disease (CAD) measures group

● M G8490 I intend to report the rheumatoid arthritis measures group

● M G8491 I intend to report the HIV/AIDS measures group

● M G8492 I intend to report the perioperative care measures group

● M G8493 I intend to report the back pain measures group

● M G8494 All quality actions for the applicable measures in the diabetes mellitus measures group have been performed for this patient

● M G8495 All quality actions for the applicable measures in the CKD measures group have been performed for this patient

● M G8496 All quality actions for the applicable measures in the preventive care measures group have been performed for this patient

● M G8497 All quality actions for the applicable measures in the coronary artery bypass graft (CABG) measures group have been performed for this patient

● M G8498 All quality actions for the applicable measures in the coronary artery disease (CAD) measures group have been performed for this patient

● M G8499 All quality actions for the applicable measures in the rheumatoid arthritis measures group have been performed for this patient

● M G8500 All quality actions for the applicable measures in the HIV/AIDS measures group have been performed for this patient

● M G8501 All quality actions for the applicable measures in the perioperative care measures group have been performed for this patient

● M G8502 All quality actions for the applicable measures in the back pain measures group have been performed for this patient

● M G8503 Documentation that prophylactic antibiotic was given within one hour (if fluoroquinolone or vancomycin, two hours) prior to surgical incision (or start of procedure when no incision is required)

● M G8504 Documentation of order for prophylactic antibiotics to be given within one hour (if fluoroquinolone or vancomycin, two hours) prior to surgical incision (or start of procedure when no incision is required)

● M G8505 Documentation that prophylactic antibiotic was not given within one hour (if fluoroquinolone or vancomycin, two hours) prior to surgical incision (or start of procedure when no incision is required), reason not specified

● M G8506 Patient receiving angiotensin converting enzyme (ACE) inhibitor or angiotensin receptor blocker (ARB) therapy

● M G8507 Provider documentation that patient is not eligible for patient verification of current medications

● M G8508 Documentation of pain assessment (including location, intensity and description) prior to initiation of treatment or documentation of the absence of pain as a result of assessment through discussion with the patient including the use of a standardized tool; no documentation of a follow-up plan, patient not eligible

● M G8509 Documentation of pain assessment (including location, intensity and description) prior to initiation of treatment or documentation of the absence of pain as a result of assessment through discussion with the patient including the use of a standardized tool; no documentation of a follow-up plan, reason not specified

● M G8510 Negative screen for clinical depression using a standardized tool, patient not eligible/appropriate for follow-up plan documented

● M G8511 Screen for clinical depression using a standardized tool documented, follow up plan not documented, reason not specified

● M G8512 Pain severity quantified; pain present

● M G8513 ABI measured and documented

● M G8514 Clinician documented that patient was not an eligible candidate for ABI measurement measure

● M G8515 ABI measurement was not obtained

● M G8516 Patient screened for future falls risk; documentation of two or more falls in the past year or any fall with injury in the past year

● M G8517 Patient screened for future fall risk; documentation of no falls in the past year or only one fall without injury in the past year

● M G8518 Clinical stage prior to surgery for lung cancer and esophageal cancer resection was recorded

● M G8519 Clinician documented that patient was not eligible for clinical stage prior to surgery for lung cancer and esophageal cancer resection measure

● M G8520 Clinician stage prior to surgery for lung cancer and esophageal cancer resection was not recorded, reason not specified

● M G8521 Antiplatelet therapy received (ASA [81-325 mg/day] and/or clopidogrel [75 mg/day]) within 48 hours of the initiation of surgery and at discharge

● M G8522 Clinician documented that patient was not an eligible candidate for antiplatelet therapy

● M G8523 Antiplatelet therapy not received 48 hours prior to CEA and at discharge, reason not specified

● M G8524 Patch closure used for patient undergoing conventional CEA

● M G8525 Clinician documented that patient did not receive conventional CEA

● M G8526 Patch closure not used for patient undergoing conventional CEA, reason not specified

● M G8527 Documentation of order for cefazolin or cefuroxime for antimicrobial prophylaxis

● M G8528 Clinician documented that patient was ineligible for prophylactic antibiotic selection measure

● M G8529 Order for cefazolin or cefuroxime for antimicrobial prophylaxis not documented, reason not specified

● M G8530 Autogenous AV fistula received

● M G8531 Clinician documented that patient was not an eligible candidate for autogenous AV fistula

● M **G8532** Clinician documented that patient received vascular access other than autogenous AV fistula, reason not specified

● M **G8533** Participation by a physician or other clinician in systematic clinical database registry that includes consensus-endorsed quality measures

● M **G8534** Documentation of an elder maltreatment screen and follow-up plan

● M **G8535** No documentation of an elder maltreatment screen, patient not eligible

● M **G8536** No documentation of an elder maltreatment screen, reason not specified

● M **G8537** Elder maltreatment screen documented, follow-up plan not documented, patient not eligible

● M **G8538** Elder maltreatment screen documented, follow-up plan not documented, reason not specified

● M **G8539** Documentation of a current functional outcome assessment using a standardized tool and care plan based on identified deficiencies

● M **G8540** Documentation that the patient is not eligible for a functional outcome assessment using a standardized tool

● M **G8541** No documentation of a current functional outcome assessment using a standardized tool, reason not specified

● M **G8542** Documentation of a current functional outcome assessment using a standardized tool; no documentation of a care plan, patient not eligible

● M **G8543** Documentation of a current functional outcome assessment using a standardized tool; no documentation of a care plan, reason not specified

● M **G8544** I intend to report the coronary artery bypass graft (CABG) measures group

B **G9001** Coordinated care fee, initial rate ⊘

B **G9002** Coordinated care fee, maintenance rate ⊘

B **G9003** Coordinated care fee, risk adjusted high, initial ⊘

B **G9004** Coordinated care fee, risk adjusted low, initial ⊘

B **G9005** Coordinated care fee, risk adjusted maintenance ⊘

B **G9006** Coordinated care fee, home monitoring ⊘

B **G9007** Coordinated care fee, scheduled team conference ⊘

B **G9008** Coordinated care fee, physician coordinated care oversight services ⊘

B **G9009** Coordinated care fee, risk adjusted maintenance, Level 3

B **G9010** Coordinated care fee, risk adjusted maintenance, Level 4 ⊘

B **G9011** Coordinated care fee, risk adjusted maintenance, Level 5 ⊘

B **G9012** Other specified case management service not elsewhere classified ⊘

E **G9013** ESRD demo basic bundle Level I

E **G9014** ESRD demo expanded bundle including venous access and related services

E **G9016** Smoking cessation counseling, individual, in the absence of or in addition to any other evaluation and management service, per session (6-10 minutes) [demo project code only] ⊘

A **G9017** Amantadine HCl, oral, per 100 mg (for use in a Medicare-approved demonstration project)

A **G9018** Zanamivir, inhalation powder, administered through inhaler, generic, per 10 mg (for use in a Medicare-approved demonstration project)

A **G9019** Oseltamivir phosphate, oral, generic, per 75 mg (for use in a Medicare-approved demonstration project)

A **G9020** Rimantadine HCl, oral, per 100 mg (for use in a Medicare-approved demonstration project)

A **G9033** Amantadine HCl, oral brand, per 100 mg (for use in a Medicare-approved demonstration project)

A **G9034** Zanamivir, inhalation powder, administered through inhaler, brand name, per 10 mg (for use in a Medicare-approved demonstration project)

A **G9035** Oseltamivir phosphate, oral, brand name, per 75 mg (for use in a Medicare-approved demonstration project)

A **G9036** Rimantadine HCl, oral, brand name, per 100 mg (for use in a Medicare-approved demonstration project)

A **G9041** Rehabilitation services for low vision by qualified occupational therapist, direct one-on-one contact, each 15 minutes

A **G9042** Rehabilitation services for low vision by certified orientation and mobility specialists, direct one-on-one contact, each 15 minutes

A **G9043** Rehabilitation services for low vision by certified low vision rehabilitation therapist, direct one-on-one contact, each 15 minutes

A **G9044** Rehabilitation services for low vision by certified low vision rehabilitation teacher, direct one-on-one contact, each 15 minutes

E **G9050** Oncology; primary focus of visit; work-up, evaluation, or staging at the time of cancer diagnosis or recurrence (for use in a Medicare-approved demonstration project)

E **G9051** Oncology; primary focus of visit; treatment decision-making after disease is staged or restaged, discussion of treatment options, supervising/coordinating active cancer-directed therapy or managing consequences of cancer-directed therapy (for use in a Medicare-approved demonstration project)

E **G9052** Oncology; primary focus of visit; surveillance for disease recurrence for patient who has completed definitive cancer-directed therapy and currently lacks evidence of recurrent disease; cancer-directed therapy might be considered in the future (for use in a Medicare-approved demonstration project)

E **G9053** Oncology; primary focus of visit; expectant management of patient with evidence of cancer for whom no cancer-directed therapy is being administered or arranged at present; cancer-directed therapy might be considered in the future (for use in a Medicare-approved demonstration project)

E **G9054** Oncology; primary focus of visit; supervising, coordinating or managing care of patient with terminal cancer or for whom other medical illness prevents further cancer treatment; includes symptom management, end-of-life care planning, management of palliative therapies (for use in a Medicare-approved demonstration project)

E **G9055** Oncology; primary focus of visit; other, unspecified service not otherwise listed (for use in a Medicare-approved demonstration project)

E **G9056** Oncology; practice guidelines; management adheres to guidelines (for use in a Medicare-approved demonstration project)

E G9057 Oncology; practice guidelines; management differs from guidelines as a result of patient enrollment in an institutional review board-approved clinical trial (for use in a Medicare-approved demonstration project)

E G9058 Oncology; practice guidelines; management differs from guidelines because the treating physician disagrees with guideline recommendations (for use in a Medicare-approved demonstration project)

E G9059 Oncology; practice guidelines; management differs from guidelines because the patient, after being offered treatment consistent with guidelines, has opted for alternative treatment or management, including no treatment (for use in a Medicare-approved demonstration project)

E G9060 Oncology; practice guidelines; management differs from guidelines for reason(s) associated with patient comorbid illness or performance status not factored into guidelines (for use in a Medicare-approved demonstration project)

E G9061 Oncology; practice guidelines; patient's condition not addressed by available guidelines (for use in a Medicare-approved demonstration project)

E G9062 Oncology; practice guidelines; management differs from guidelines for other reason(s) not listed (for use in a Medicare-approved demonstration project)

M G9063 Oncology; disease status; limited to nonsmall cell lung cancer; extent of disease initially established as Stage I (prior to neoadjuvant therapy, if any) with no evidence of disease progression, recurrence, or metastases (for use in a Medicare-approved demonstration project)

M G9064 Oncology; disease status; limited to nonsmall cell lung cancer; extent of disease initially established as Stage II (prior to neoadjuvant therapy, if any) with no evidence of disease progression, recurrence, or metastases (for use in a Medicare-approved demonstration project)

M G9065 Oncology; disease status; limited to nonsmall cell lung cancer; extent of disease initially established as Stage III a (prior to neoadjuvant therapy, if any) with no evidence of disease progression, recurrence, or metastases (for use in a Medicare-approved demonstration project)

M G9066 Oncology; disease status; limited to nonsmall cell lung cancer; Stage III B-IV at diagnosis, metastatic, locally recurrent, or progressive (for use in a Medicare-approved demonstration project)

M G9067 Oncology; disease status; limited to nonsmall cell lung cancer; extent of disease unknown, staging in progress, or not listed (for use in a Medicare-approved demonstration project)

M G9068 Oncology; disease status; limited to small cell and combined small cell/nonsmall cell; extent of disease initially established as limited with no evidence of disease progression, recurrence, or metastases (for use in a Medicare-approved demonstration project)

M G9069 Oncology; disease status; small cell lung cancer, limited to small cell and combined small cell/nonsmall cell; extensive Stage at diagnosis, metastatic, locally recurrent, or progressive (for use in a Medicare-approved demonstration project)

M G9070 Oncology; disease status; small cell lung cancer, limited to small cell and combined small cell/nonsmall; extent of disease unknown, staging in progress, or not listed (for use in a Medicare-approved demonstration project)

M G9071 Oncology; disease status; invasive female breast cancer (does not include ductal carcinoma in situ); adenocarcinoma as predominant cell type; stage I or stage IIA-IIB; or T3, N1, M0; and ER and/or PR positive; with no evidence of disease progression, recurrence, or metastases (for use in a Medicare-approved demonstration project) ♀

M G9072 Oncology; disease status; invasive female breast cancer (does not include ductal carcinoma in situ); adenocarcinoma as predominant cell type; stage I, or stage IIA-IIB; or T3, N1, M0; and ER and PR negative; with no evidence of disease progression, recurrence, or metastases (for use in a Medicare-approved demonstration project) ♀

M G9073 Oncology; disease status; invasive female breast cancer (does not include ductal carcinoma in situ); adenocarcinoma as predominant cell type; stage IIIA-IIIB; and not T3, N1, M0; and ER and/or PR positive; with no evidence of disease progression, recurrence, or metastases (for use in a Medicare-approved demonstration project) ♀

M G9074 Oncology; disease status; invasive female breast cancer (does not include ductal carcinoma in situ); adenocarcinoma as predominant cell type; stage IIIA-IIIB; and not T3, N1, M0; and ER and PR negative; with no evidence of disease progression, recurrence, or metastases (for use in a Medicare-approved demonstration project) ♀

M G9075 Oncology; disease status; invasive female breast cancer (does not include ductal carcinoma in situ); adenocarcinoma as predominant cell type; M1 at diagnosis, metastatic locally recurrent, or progressive (for use in a Medicare-approved demonstration project) ♀

M G9077 Oncology; disease status; prostate cancer, limited to adenocarcinoma as predominant cell type; T1-T2C and Gleason 2-7 and PSA < or equal to 20 at diagnosis with no evidence of disease progression, recurrence, or metastases (for use in a Medicare-approved demonstration project) ♂

M G9078 Oncology; disease status; prostate cancer, limited to adenocarcinoma as predominant cell type; T2 or T3a Gleason 8-10 or PSA >20 at diagnosis with no evidence of disease progression, recurrence, or metastases (for use in a Medicare-approved demonstration project) ♂

M G9079 Oncology; disease status; prostate cancer, limited to adenocarcinoma as predominant cell type; T3B-T4, any N; any T, N1 at diagnosis with no evidence of disease progression, recurrence, or metastases (for use in a Medicare-approved demonstration project) ♂

M G9080 Oncology; disease status; prostate cancer, limited to adenocarcinoma; after initial treatment with rising PSA or failure of PSA decline (for use in a Medicare-approved demonstration project) ♂

M G9083 Oncology; disease status; prostate cancer, limited to adenocarcinoma; extent of disease unknown, staging in progress, or not listed (for use in a Medicare-approved demonstration project) ♂

M G9084 Oncology; disease status; colon cancer, limited to invasive cancer, adenocarcinoma as predominant cell type; extent of disease initially established as T1-3, N0, M0 with no evidence of disease progression, recurrence or metastases (for use in a Medicare-approved demonstration project)

M **G9085** Oncology; disease status; colon cancer, limited to invasive cancer, adenocarcinoma as predominant cell type; extent of disease initially established as T4, N0, M0 with no evidence of disease progression, recurrence, or metastases (for use in a Medicare-approved demonstration project)

M **G9086** Oncology; disease status; colon cancer, limited to invasive cancer, adenocarcinoma as predominant cell type; extent of disease initially established as T1-4, N1-2, M0 with no evidence of disease progression, recurrence, or metastases (for use in a Medicare-approved demonstration project)

M **G9087** Oncology; disease status; colon cancer, limited to invasive cancer, adenocarcinoma as predominant cell type; M1 at diagnosis, metastatic locally recurrent, or progressive with current clinical, radiologic, or biochemical evidence of disease (for use in a Medicare-approved demonstration project)

M **G9088** Oncology; disease status; colon cancer, limited to invasive cancer, adenocarcinoma as predominant cell type; M1 at diagnosis, metastatic, locally recurrent, or progressive without current clinical, radiologic, or biochemical evidence of disease (for use in a Medicare-approved demonstration project)

M **G9089** Oncology; disease status; colon cancer, limited to invasive cancer, adenocarcinoma as predominant cell type; extent of disease unknown, staging in progress or not listed (for use in a Medicare-approved demonstration project)

M **G9090** Oncology; disease status; rectal cancer, limited to invasive cancer, adenocarcinoma as predominant cell type; extent of disease initially established as T1-2, N0, M0 (prior to neoadjuvant therapy, if any) with no evidence of disease progression, recurrence, or metastases (for use in a Medicare-approved demonstration project)

M **G9091** Oncology; disease status; rectal cancer, limited to invasive cancer, adenocarcinoma as predominant cell type; extent of disease initially established as T3, N0, M0 (prior to neoadjuvant therapy, if any) with no evidence of disease progression, recurrence, or metastases (for use in a Medicare-approved demonstration project)

M **G9092** Oncology; disease status; rectal cancer, limited to invasive cancer, adenocarcinoma as predominant cell type; extent of disease initially established as T1-3, N1-2, M0 (prior to neoadjuvant therapy, if any) with no evidence of disease progression, recurrence or metastases (for use in a Medicare-approved demonstration project)

M **G9093** Oncology; disease status; rectal cancer, limited to invasive cancer, adenocarcinoma as predominant cell type; extent of disease initially established as T4, any N, M0 (prior to neoadjuvant therapy, if any) with no evidence of disease progression, recurrence, or metastases (for use in a Medicare-approved demonstration project)

M **G9094** Oncology; disease status; rectal cancer, limited to invasive cancer, adenocarcinoma as predominant cell type; M1 at diagnosis, metastatic, locally recurrent, or progressive (for use in a Medicare-approved demonstration project)

M **G9095** Oncology; disease status; rectal cancer, limited to invasive cancer, adenocarcinoma as predominant cell type; extent of disease unknown, staging in progress or not listed (for use in a Medicare-approved demonstration project)

M **G9096** Oncology; disease status; esophageal cancer, limited to adenocarcinoma or squamous cell carcinoma as predominant cell type; extent of disease initially established as T1-T3, N0-N1 or NX (prior to neoadjuvant therapy, if any) with no evidence of disease progression, recurrence, or metastases (for use in a Medicare-approved demonstration project)

M **G9097** Oncology; disease status; esophageal cancer, limited to adenocarcinoma or squamous cell carcinoma as predominant cell type; extent of disease initially established as T4, any N, M0 (prior to neoadjuvant therapy, if any) with no evidence of disease progression, recurrence, or metastases (for use in a Medicare-approved demonstration project)

M **G9098** Oncology; disease status; esophageal cancer, limited to adenocarcinoma or squamous cell carcinoma as predominant cell type; M1 at diagnosis, metastatic, locally recurrent, or progressive (for use in a Medicare-approved demonstration project)

M **G9099** Oncology; disease status; esophageal cancer, limited to adenocarcinoma or squamous cell carcinoma as predominant cell type; extent of disease unknown, staging in progress, or not listed (for use in a Medicare-approved demonstration project)

M **G9100** Oncology; disease status; gastric cancer, limited to adenocarcinoma as predominant cell type; post R0 resection (with or without neoadjuvant therapy) with no evidence of disease recurrence, progression, or metastases (for use in a Medicare-approved demonstration project)

M **G9101** Oncology; disease status; gastric cancer, limited to adenocarcinoma as predominant cell type; post R1 or R2 resection (with or without neoadjuvant therapy) with no evidence of disease progression, or metastases (for use in a Medicare-approved demonstration project)

M **G9102** Oncology; disease status; gastric cancer, limited to adenocarcinoma as predominant cell type; clinical or pathologic M0, unresectable with no evidence of disease progression, or metastases (for use in a Medicare-approved demonstration project)

M **G9103** Oncology; disease status; gastric cancer, limited to adenocarcinoma as predominant cell type; clinical or pathologic M1 at diagnosis, metastatic, locally recurrent, or progressive (for use in a Medicare-approved demonstration project)

M **G9104** Oncology; disease status; gastric cancer, limited to adenocarcinoma as predominant cell type; extent of disease unknown, staging in progress, or not listed (for use in a Medicare-approved demonstration project)

M **G9105** Oncology; disease status; pancreatic cancer, limited to adenocarcinoma as predominant cell type; post R0 resection without evidence of disease progression, recurrence, or metastases (for use in a Medicare-approved demonstration project)

M **G9106** Oncology; disease status; pancreatic cancer, limited to adenocarcinoma; post R1 or R2 resection with no evidence of disease progression, or metastases (for use in a Medicare-approved demonstration project)

M **G9107** Oncology; disease status; pancreatic cancer, limited to adenocarcinoma; unresectable at diagnosis, M1 at diagnosis, metastatic, locally recurrent, or progressive (for use in a Medicare-approved demonstration project)

M **G9108** Oncology; disease status; pancreatic cancer, limited to adenocarcinoma; extent of disease unknown, staging in progress, or not listed (for use in a Medicare-approved demonstration project)

M **G9109** Oncology; disease status; head and neck cancer, limited to cancers of oral cavity, pharynx and larynx with squamous cell as predominant cell type; extent of disease initially established as T1-T2 and N0, M0 (prior to neoadjuvant therapy, if any) with no evidence of disease progression, recurrence, or metastases (for use in a Medicare-approved demonstration project)

M **G9110** Oncology; disease status; head and neck cancer, limited to cancers of oral cavity, pharynx and larynx with squamous cell as predominant cell type; extent of disease initially established as T3-4 and/or N1-3, M0 (prior to neoadjuvant therapy, if any) with no evidence of disease progression, recurrence, or metastases (for use in a Medicare-approved demonstration project)

M **G9111** Oncology; disease status; head and neck cancer, limited to cancers of oral cavity, pharynx and larynx with squamous cell as predominant cell type; M1 at diagnosis, metastatic, locally recurrent, or progressive (for use in a Medicare-approved demonstration project)

M **G9112** Oncology; disease status; head and neck cancer, limited to cancers of oral cavity, pharynx and larynx with squamous cell as predominant cell type; extent of disease unknown, staging in progress, or not listed (for use in a Medicare-approved demonstration project)

M **G9113** Oncology; disease status; ovarian cancer, limited to epithelial cancer; pathologic stage 1A-B (Grade 1) without evidence of disease progression, recurrence, or metastases (for use in a Medicare-approved demonstration project) ♀

M **G9114** Oncology; disease status; ovarian cancer, limited to epithelial cancer; pathologic stage IA-B (grade 2-3); or stage IC (all grades); or stage II; without evidence of disease progression, recurrence, or metastases (for use in a Medicare-approved demonstration project) ♀

M **G9115** Oncology; disease status; ovarian cancer, limited to epithelial cancer; pathologic stage III-IV; without evidence of progression, recurrence, or metastases (for use in a Medicare-approved demonstration project) ♀

M **G9116** Oncology; disease status; ovarian cancer, limited to epithelial cancer; evidence of disease progression, or recurrence, and/or platinum resistance (for use in a Medicare-approved demonstration project) ♀

M **G9117** Oncology; disease status; ovarian cancer, limited to epithelial cancer; extent of disease unknown, staging in progress, or not listed (for use in a Medicare-approved demonstration project) ♀

M **G9123** Oncology; disease status; chronic myelogenous leukemia, limited to Philadelphia chromosome positive and/or BCR-ABL positive; chronic phase not in hematologic, cytogenetic, or molecular remission (for use in a Medicare-approved demonstration project)

M **G9124** Oncology; disease status; chronic myelogenous leukemia, limited to Philadelphia chromosome positive and /or BCR-ABL positive; accelerated phase not in hematologic cytogenetic, or molecular remission (for use in a Medicare-approved demonstration project)

M **G9125** Oncology; disease status; chronic myelogenous leukemia, limited to Philadelphia chromosome positive and/or BCR-ABL positive; blast phase not in hematologic, cytogenetic, or molecular remission (for use in a Medicare-approved demonstration project)

M **G9126** Oncology; disease status; chronic myelogenous leukemia, limited to Philadelphia chromosome positive and/or BCR-ABL positive; in hematologic, cytogenetic, or molecular remission (for use in a Medicare-approved demonstration project)

M **G9128** Oncology; disease status; limited to multiple myeloma, systemic disease; smoldering, stage I (for use in a Medicare-approved demonstration project)

M **G9129** Oncology; disease status; limited to multiple myeloma, systemic disease; stage II or higher (for use in a Medicare-approved demonstration project)

M **G9130** Oncology; disease status; limited to multiple myeloma, systemic disease; extent of disease unknown, staging in progress, or not listed (for use in a Medicare-approved demonstration project)

M **G9131** Oncology; disease status; invasive female breast cancer (does not include ductal carcinoma in situ); adenocarcinoma as predominant cell type; extent of disease unknown, staging in progress, or not listed (for use in a Medicare-approved demonstration project) ♀

M **G9132** Oncology; disease status; prostate cancer, limited to adenocarcinoma; hormone-refractory/androgen-independent (e.g., rising PSA on antiandrogen therapy or postorchiectomy); clinical metastases (for use in a Medicare-approved demonstration project) ♂

M **G9133** Oncology; disease status; prostate cancer, limited to adenocarcinoma; hormone-responsive; clinical metastases or M1 at diagnosis (for use in a Medicare-approved demonstration project) ♂

M **G9134** Oncology; disease status; non-Hodgkin's lymphoma, any cellular classification; Stage I, II at diagnosis, not relapsed, not refractory (for use in a Medicare-approved demonstration project)

M **G9135** Oncology; disease status; non-Hodgkin's lymphoma, any cellular classification; Stage III, IV, not relapsed, not refractory (for use in a Medicare-approved demonstration project)

M **G9136** Oncology; disease status; non-Hodgkin's lymphoma, transformed from original cellular diagnosis to a second cellular classification (for use in a medicare-approved demonstration project)

M **G9137** Oncology; disease status; non-Hodgkin's lymphoma, any cellular classification; relapsed/refractory (for use in a medicare-approved demonstration project)

M **G9138** Oncology; disease status; non-Hodgkin's lymphoma, any cellular classification; diagnostic evaluation, stage not determined, evaluation of possible relapse or nonresponse to therapy, or not listed (for use in a Medicare-approved demonstration project)

M **G9139** Oncology; disease status; chronic myelogenous leukemia, limited to Philadelphia chromosome positive and/or BCR-ABL positive; extent of disease unknown, staging in progress, not listed (for use in a Medicare-approved demonstration project)

A ☑ **G9140** Frontier extended stay clinic demonstration; for a patient stay in a clinic approved for the CMS demonstration project; the following measures should be present: the stay must be equal to or greater than 4 hours; weather or other conditions must prevent transfer or the case falls into a category of monitoring and observation cases that are permitted by the rules of the demonstration; there is a maximum frontier extended stay clinic (FESC) visit of 48 hours, except in the case when weather or other conditions prevent transfer; payment is made on each period up to 4 hours, after the first 4 hours

ALCOHOL AND DRUG ABUSE TREATMENT SERVICES H0001-H2037

The H codes are used by those state Medicaid agencies that are mandated by state law to establish separate codes for identifying mental health services that include alcohol and drug treatment services.

H0001 Alcohol and/or drug assessment

H0002 Behavioral health screening to determine eligibility for admission to treatment program

H0003 Alcohol and/or drug screening; laboratory analysis of specimens for presence of alcohol and/or drugs

☑ H0004 Behavioral health counseling and therapy, per 15 minutes

H0005 Alcohol and/or drug services; group counseling by a clinician

H0006 Alcohol and/or drug services; case management

H0007 Alcohol and/or drug services; crisis intervention (outpatient)

H0008 Alcohol and/or drug services; subacute detoxification (hospital inpatient)

H0009 Alcohol and/or drug services; acute detoxification (hospital inpatient)

H0010 Alcohol and/or drug services; subacute detoxification (residential addiction program inpatient)

H0011 Alcohol and/or drug services; acute detoxification (residential addiction program inpatient)

H0012 Alcohol and/or drug services; subacute detoxification (residential addiction program outpatient)

H0013 Alcohol and/or drug services; acute detoxification (residential addiction program outpatient)

H0014 Alcohol and/or drug services; ambulatory detoxification

H0015 Alcohol and/or drug services; intensive outpatient (treatment program that operates at least 3 hours/day and at least 3 days/week and is based on an individualized treatment plan), including assessment, counseling; crisis intervention, and activity therapies or education

H0016 Alcohol and/or drug services; medical/somatic (medical intervention in ambulatory setting)

☑ H0017 Behavioral health; residential (hospital residential treatment program), without room and board, per diem

☑ H0018 Behavioral health; short-term residential (nonhospital residential treatment program), without room and board, per diem

☑ H0019 Behavioral health; long-term residential (nonmedical, nonacute care in a residential treatment program where stay is typically longer than 30 days), without room and board, per diem

H0020 Alcohol and/or drug services; methadone administration and/or service (provision of the drug by a licensed program)

H0021 Alcohol and/or drug training service (for staff and personnel not employed by providers)

H0022 Alcohol and/or drug intervention service (planned facilitation)

H0023 Behavioral health outreach service (planned approach to reach a targeted population)

H0024 Behavioral health prevention information dissemination service (one-way direct or nondirect contact with service audiences to affect knowledge and attitude)

H0025 Behavioral health prevention education service (delivery of services with target population to affect knowledge, attitude and/or behavior)

H0026 Alcohol and/or drug prevention process service, community-based (delivery of services to develop skills of impactors)

H0027 Alcohol and/or drug prevention environmental service (broad range of external activities geared toward modifying systems in order to mainstream prevention through policy and law)

H0028 Alcohol and/or drug prevention problem identification and referral service (e.g., student assistance and employee assistance programs), does not include assessment

H0029 Alcohol and/or drug prevention alternatives service (services for populations that exclude alcohol and other drug use e.g., alcohol free social events)

H0030 Behavioral health hotline service

H0031 Mental health assessment, by nonphysician

H0032 Mental health service plan development by nonphysician

H0033 Oral medication administration, direct observation

☑ H0034 Medication training and support, per 15 minutes

☑ H0035 Mental health partial hospitalization, treatment, less than 24 hours

☑ H0036 Community psychiatric supportive treatment, face-to-face, per 15 minutes

☑ H0037 Community psychiatric supportive treatment program, per diem

☑ H0038 Self-help/peer services, per 15 minutes

☑ H0039 Assertive community treatment, face-to-face, per 15 minutes

☑ H0040 Assertive community treatment program, per diem

☑ H0041 Foster care, child, nontherapeutic, per diem A

☑ H0042 Foster care, child, nontherapeutic, per month A

☑ H0043 Supported housing, per diem

☑ H0044 Supported housing, per month

☑ H0045 Respite care services, not in the home, per diem

H0046 Mental health services, not otherwise specified

H0047 Alcohol and/or other drug abuse services, not otherwise specified

H0048 Alcohol and/or other drug testing: collection and handling only, specimens other than blood

H0049 Alcohol and/or drug screening

☑ H0050 Alcohol and/or drug services, brief intervention, per 15 minutes

H1000 Prenatal care, at-risk assessment M ♀

H1001 Prenatal care, at-risk enhanced service; antepartum management M ♀

H1002 Prenatal care, at risk enhanced service; care coordination M ♀

H1003 Prenatal care, at-risk enhanced service; education M ♀

H1004 Prenatal care, at-risk enhanced service; follow-up home visit M ♀

H1005 Prenatal care, at-risk enhanced service package (includes H1001–H1004) M ♀

☑ H1010 Nonmedical family planning education, per session

H1011 Family assessment by licensed behavioral health professional for state defined purposes

H2000 Comprehensive multidisciplinary evaluation

☑ H2001 Rehabilitation program, per 1/2 day

☑ H2010 Comprehensive medication services, per 15 minutes

☑ H2011 Crisis intervention service, per 15 minutes

☑ H2012 Behavioral health day treatment, per hour

☑ H2013 Psychiatric health facility service, per diem

☑ H2014 Skills training and development, per 15 minutes

☑ H2015 Comprehensive community support services, per 15 minutes

☑ H2016 Comprehensive community support services, per diem

☑ H2017 Psychosocial rehabilitation services, per 15 minutes

☑ H2018 Psychosocial rehabilitation services, per diem

☑ H2019 Therapeutic behavioral services, per 15 minutes

☑ H2020 Therapeutic behavioral services, per diem

☑ H2021 Community-based wrap-around services, per 15 minutes

☑ H2022 Community-based wrap-around services, per diem

☑ H2023 Supported employment, per 15 minutes

☑ H2024 Supported employment, per diem

☑ H2025 Ongoing support to maintain employment, per 15 minutes

☑ H2026 Ongoing support to maintain employment, per diem

☑ H2027 Psychoeducational service, per 15 minutes

☑ H2028 Sexual offender treatment service, per 15 minutes

☑ H2029 Sexual offender treatment service, per diem

☑ H2030 Mental health clubhouse services, per 15 minutes

☑ H2031 Mental health clubhouse services, per diem

☑ H2032 Activity therapy, per 15 minutes

☑ H2033 Multisystemic therapy for juveniles, per 15 minutes

☑ H2034 Alcohol and/or drug abuse halfway house services, per diem

☑ H2035 Alcohol and/or other drug treatment program, per hour

☑ H2036 Alcohol and/or other drug treatment program, per diem

☑ H2037 Developmental delay prevention activities, dependent child of client, per 15 minutes A

DRUGS ADMINISTERED OTHER THAN ORAL METHOD J0000-J9999

J codes include drugs that ordinarily cannot be self-administered, chemotherapy drugs, immunosuppressive drugs, inhalation solutions, and other miscellaneous drugs and solutions.

N ☑ **J0120** Injection, tetracycline, up to 250 mg N1
MED: 100-2,15,50

K ☑ **J0128** Injection, abarelix, 10 mg ♂ K2
Use this code for Planaxis.

K ☑ **J0129** Injection, abatacept, 10 mg K2
Use this code for Orencia

K ☑ **J0130** Injection abciximab, 10 mg K2
Use this code for ReoPro.
MED: 100-2,15,50

K ☑ **J0132** Injection, acetylcysteine, 100 mg K2
Use this code for Acetadote.

N ☑ **J0133** Injection, acyclovir, 5 mg N1
Use this code for Zovirax

K ☑ **J0135** Injection, adalimumab, 20 mg K2
Use this code for Humira.

K ☑ **J0150** Injection, adenosine for therapeutic use, 6 mg (not to be used to report any adenosine phosphate compounds, instead use A9270) K2
Use this code for Adenocard.
MED: 100-2,15,50
AHA: 2Q,'02,10

K ☑ **J0152** Injection, adenosine for diagnostic use, 30 mg (not to be used to report any adenosine phosphate compounds; instead use A9270) K2
Use this code for Adenoscan.

N ☑ **J0170** Injection, adrenalin, epinephrine, up to 1 ml ampule N1
Use this code for Adrenalin Chloride, Epipen, Sus-Phrine.
MED: 100-2,15,50

K ☑ **J0180** Injection, agalsidase beta, 1 mg K2
Use this code for Fabrazyme.

N ☑ **J0190** Injection, biperiden lactate, per 5 mg N1
MED: 100-2,15,50

N ☑ **J0200** Injection, alatrofloxacin mesylate, 100 mg N1
MED: 100-2,15,50.5

K ☑ **J0205** Injection, alglucerase, per 10 units K2
Use this code for Ceredase.
MED: 100-2,15,50

K ☑ **J0207** Injection, amifostine, 500 mg K2
Use this code for Ethyol.
MED: 100-2,15,50

K ☑ **J0210** Injection, methyldopate HCl, up to 250 mg K2
Use this code for Aldomet.
MED: 100-2,15,50

K ☑ **J0215** Injection, alefacept, 0.5 mg K2
Use this for Amevive.

K ☑ **J0220** Injection, alglucosidase alfa, 10 mg K2
Use this code for Myozime

K ☑ **J0256** Injection, alpha 1-proteinase inhibitor — human, 10 mg K2
Use this code for Prolastin, Zemira.
MED: 100-2,15,50

▲ B **J0270** Injection, alprostadil, 1.25 mcg (code may be used for Medicare when drug administered under the direct supervision of a physician, not for use when drug is self-administered)
Use this code for Alprostadil, Caverject, Edex, Prostin VR Pediatric.
MED: 100-2,15,50

B **J0275** Alprostadil urethral suppository (code may be used for Medicare when drug administered under the direct supervision of a physician, not for use when drug is self-administered)
Use this code for Muse.
MED: 100-2,15,50

N ☑ **J0278** Injection, amikacin sulfate, 100 mg N1
Use this code for Amikin.

N ☑ **J0280** Injection, aminophyllin, up to 250 mg N1
MED: 100-2,15,50

N ☑ **J0282** Injection, amiodarone HCl, 30 mg N1
Use this code for Cordarone IV.
MED: 100-2,15,50

N ☑ **J0285** Injection, amphotericin B, 50 mg N1
Use this for Abelcet, Amphocin, Fungizone
MED: 100-2,15,50

K ☑ **J0287** Injection, amphotericin B lipid complex, 10 mg K2
MED: 100-2,15,50

K ☑ **J0288** Injection, amphotericin B cholesteryl sulfate complex, 10 mg K2
Use this code for Amphotec.
MED: 100-2,15,50

K ☑ **J0289** Injection, amphotericin B liposome, 10 mg K2
Use this code for Ambisome.
MED: 100-2,15,50

N ☑ **J0290** Injection, ampicillin sodium, 500 mg N1
MED: 100-2,15,50

N ☑ **J0295** Injection, ampicillin sodium/sulbactam sodium, per 1.5 g N1
Use this code for Unasyn.
MED: 100-2,15,50

N ☑ **J0300** Injection, amobarbital, up to 125 mg N1
Use this code for Amytal.
MED: 100-2,15,50

N ☑ **J0330** Injection, succinylcholine chloride, up to 20 mg N1
Use this code for Anectine, Quelicin.
MED: 100-2,15,50

▲ K ☑ **J0348** Injection, anidulafungin, 1 mg K2
Use this code for Eraxis.

N ☑ **J0350** Injection, anistreplase, per 30 units N1
Use this code for Eminase.
MED: 100-2,15,50

N ☑ **J0360** Injection, hydralazine HCl, up to 20 mg N1
MED: 100-2,15,50

N ☑ **J0364** Injection, apomorphine HCl, 1 mg N1
Use this code for Apokyn.

K ☑ **J0365** Injection, aprotonin, 10,000 kiu K2
Use this code for Trasylol.
MED: 100-2,15,50

N ☑ **J0380** Injection, metaraminol bitartrate, per 10 mg N1
Use this code for Aramine.
MED: 100-2,15,50

N ☑ **J0390** Injection, chloroquine HCl, up to 250 mg N1
Use this code for Aralen.
MED: 100-2,15,50

N ☑ **J0395** Injection, arbutamine HCl, 1 mg N1
MED: 100-2,15,50

N ☑ **J0400** Injection, aripiprazole, intramuscular, 0.25 mg N1
Use this code for Abilify.

N ☑ **J0456** Injection, azithromycin, 500 mg N1
Use this code for Zithromax.
MED: 100-2,15,50.5

N ☑ **J0460** Injection, atropine sulfate, up to 0.3 mg N1
Use this code for Atropen.
MED: 100-2,15,50

K ☑ **J0470** Injection, dimercaprol, per 100 mg K2
Use this code for BAL
MED: 100-2,15,50

K ☑ **J0475** Injection, baclofen, 10 mg K2
Use this code for Lioresal.
MED: 100-2,15,50

K ☑ **J0476** Injection, baclofen, 50 mcg for intrathecal trial K2
Use this code for Lioresal for intrathecal trial.
MED: 100-2,15,50

K **J0480** Injection, basiliximab, 20 mg K2
Use this code for Simulect.
MED: 100-2,15,50; 100-4,4,240

N ☑ **J0500** Injection, dicyclomine HCl, up to 20 mg N1
Use this code for Bentyl.
MED: 100-2,15,50

N ☑ **J0515** Injection, benztropine mesylate, per 1 mg N1
Use this code for Cogentin.
MED: 100-2,15,50

N ☑ **J0520** Injection, bethanechol chloride, Myotonachol or Urecholine, up to 5 mg N1
MED: 100-2,15,50

N ☑ **J0530** Injection, penicillin G benzathine and penicillin G procaine, up to 600,000 units N1
Use this code for Bicillin C-R.
MED: 100-2,15,50

N ☑ **J0540** Injection, penicillin G benzathine and penicillin G procaine, up to 1,200,000 units N1
Use this code for Bicillin C-R, Bicillin C-R 900/300.
MED: 100-2,15,50

K ☑ **J0550** Injection, penicillin G benzathine and penicillin G procaine, up to 2,400,000 units K2
Use this code for Bicillin C-R.
MED: 100-2,15,50

N ☑ **J0560** Injection, penicillin G benzathine, up to 600,000 units N1
Use this code for Bicillin L-A, Permapen.
MED: 100-2,15,50

N ☑ **J0570** Injection, penicillin G benzathine, up to 1,200,000 units N1
Use this code for Bicillin L-A, Permapen.
MED: 100-2,15,50

N ☑ **J0580** Injection, penicillin G benzathine, up to 2,400,000 units N1
Use this code for Bicillin L-A, Permapen.
MED: 100-2,15,50

K ☑ **J0583** Injection, bivalirudin, 1 mg K2
Use this code for Angiomax.

K ☑ **J0585** Botulinum toxin type A, per unit K2
Use this code for Botox.
MED: 100-2,15,50

K ☑ **J0587** Botulinum toxin type B, per 100 units K2
Use this code for Myobloc.
MED: 100-2,15,50
AHA: 2Q,'02,8

N ☑ **J0592** Injection, buprenorphine HCl, 0.1 mg N1
Use this code for Buprenex.
MED: 100-2,15,50

K ☑ **J0594** Injection, busulfan, 1 mg K2
Use this code for Busulfex.

N ☑ **J0595** Injection, butorphanol tartrate, 1 mg N1
Use this code for Stadol.

K ☑ **J0600** Injection, edetate calcium disodium, up to 1,000 mg K2
Use this code for Calcium Disodium Versenate, Calcium EDTA.
MED: 100-2,15,50

N ☑ **J0610** Injection, calcium gluconate, per 10 ml N1
MED: 100-2,15,50

N ☑ **J0620** Injection, calcium glycerophosphate and calcium lactate, per 10 ml N1
MED: 100-2,15,50

K ☑ **J0630** Injection, calcitonin salmon, up to 400 units K2
Use this code for Calcimar, Miacalcin.
MED: 100-2,15,50

N ☑ **J0636** Injection, calcitriol, 0.1 mcg N1
Use this code for Calcijex.
MED: 100-2,15,50

K **J0637** Injection, caspofungin acetate, 5 mg K2
Use this code for Cancidas.

N ☑ **J0640** Injection, leucovorin calcium, per 50 mg N1
MED: 100-2,15,50

● K ☑ **J0641** Injection, levoleucovorin calcium, 0.5 mg K2
Use this code for Fusilev

N ☑ **J0670** Injection, mepivacaine HCl, per 10 ml N1
Use this code for Carbocaine, Polocaine, Isocaine HCl, Scandonest
MED: 100-2,15,50

N ☑ **J0690** Injection, cefazolin sodium, 500 mg N1
Use this code for Ancef, Kefzol
MED: 100-2,15,50

N ☑ **J0692** Injection, cefepime HCl, 500 mg N1
Use this code for Maxipime.

N ☑ **J0694** Injection, cefoxitin sodium, 1 g N1
MED: 100-2,15,50

N ☑ **J0696** Injection, ceftriaxone sodium, per 250 mg N1
Use this code for Rocephin.
MED: 100-2,15,50

N ☑ **J0697** Injection, sterile cefuroxime sodium, per 750 mg N1
Use this code for Zinacef.
MED: 100-2,15,50

N ☑ **J0698** Injection, cefotaxime sodium, per g N1
Use this code for Claforan.
MED: 100-2,15,50

N ☑ **J0702** Injection, betamethasone acetate 3 mg and betamethasone sodium phosphate 3 mg N1
Use this code for Celestone Soluspan.
MED: 100-2,15,50

N ☑ **J0704** Injection, betamethasone sodium phosphate, per 4 mg N1
MED: 100-2,15,50

N ☑ **J0706** Injection, caffeine citrate, 5 mg N1
Use this code for Cafcit.
AHA: 2Q,'02,8

N ☑ **J0710** Injection, cephapirin sodium, up to 1 g N1
MED: 100-2,15,50

N ☑ **J0713** Injection, ceftazidime, per 500 mg N1
Use this code for Ceptax, Fortaz, Tazicef
MED: 100-2,15,50

N ☑ **J0715** Injection, ceftizoxime sodium, per 500 mg N1
Use this code for Cefizox.
MED: 100-2,15,50

N ☑ **J0720** Injection, chloramphenicol sodium succinate, up to 1 g N1
Use this code for Chlormycetin.
MED: 100-2,15,50

N ☑ **J0725** Injection, chorionic gonadotropin, per 1,000 USP units N1
MED: 100-2,15,50

K ☑ **J0735** Injection, clonidine HCl, 1 mg K2
Use this code for Clorpres, Duraclon, Iopidine
MED: 100-2,15,50

K ☑ **J0740** Injection, cidofovir, 375 mg K2
Use this code for Vistide.
MED: 100-2,15,50

N ☑ **J0743** Injection, cilastatin sodium; imipenem, per 250 mg N1
Use this code for Primaxin I.M., Primaxin I.V.
MED: 100-2,15,50

N ☑ **J0744** Injection, ciprofloxacin for intravenous infusion, 200 mg N1
Use this code for Cipro.

N ☑ **J0745** Injection, codeine phosphate, per 30 mg N1
MED: 100-2,15,50

N ☑ **J0760** Injection, colchicine, per 1 mg N1
MED: 100-2,15,50

N ☑ **J0770** Injection, colistimethate sodium, up to 150 mg N1
Use this code for Coly-Mycin M.
MED: 100-2,15,50

N ☑ **J0780** Injection, prochlorperazine, up to 10 mg N1
Use this code for Compazine, Cotranzine, Compa-Z, Ultrazine-10.
MED: 100-2,15,50

K ☑ **J0795** Injection, corticorelin ovine triflutate, 1 mcg K2
Use this code for Acthrel.
MED: 100-2,15,50

K ☑ **J0800** Injection, corticotropin, up to 40 units K2
Use this code for H.P. Acthar gel
MED: 100-2,15,50

K ☑ **J0835** Injection, cosyntropin, per 0.25 mg K2
Use this code for Cortrosyn.
MED: 100-2,15,50

K ☑ **J0850** Injection, cytomegalovirus immune globulin intravenous (human), per vial K2
Use this code for Cytogam.
MED: 100-2,15,50; 100-4,4,240

K ☑ **J0878** Injection, daptomycin, 1 mg K2
Use this code for Cubicin.

K ☑ **J0881** Injection, darbepoetin alfa, 1 mcg (non-ESRD use) K2
Use this code for Aranesp.
MED: 100-2,6,10; 100-4,4,240

A ☑ **J0882** Injection, darbepoetin alfa, 1 mcg (for ESRD on dialysis) ⊘
Use this code for Aranesp.
MED: 100-2,6,10; 100-4,4,240

K ☑ **J0885** Injection, epoetin alfa, (for non-ESRD use), 1000 units K2
Use this code for Epogen/Procrit.
MED: 100-2,6,10; 100-2,15,50; 100-4,4,240

A ☑ **J0886** Injection, epoetin alfa, 1000 units (for ESRD on dialysis) ⊘
Use this code for Epogen/Procrit.
MED: 100-2,6,10; 100-4,4,240

K ☑ **J0894** Injection, decitabine, 1 mg K2
Use this code for Dacogen.

N ☑ **J0895** Injection, deferoxamine mesylate, 500 mg N1
Use this code for Desferal.
MED: 100-2,15,50

N ☑ **J0900** Injection, testosterone enanthate and estradiol valerate, up to 1 cc N1
MED: 100-2,15,50

N ☑ **J0945** Injection, brompheniramine maleate, per 10 mg N1
MED: 100-2,15,50

N ☑ **J0970** Injection, estradiol valerate, up to 40 mg N1
Use this code for Clinagen LA, Clinagen, LA-10, Clinagen LA-20, Clinagen LA-40, Delestrogen
MED: 100-2,15,50

N ☑ **J1000** Injection, depo-estradiol cypionate, up to 5 mg N1
Use this code for depGynogen, Depogen, Estradiol Cypionate
MED: 100-2,15,50

N ☑ **J1020** Injection, methylprednisolone acetate, 20 mg N1
Use this code for Depo-Medrol.
MED: 100-2,15,50; 100-4,4,240

N ☑ **J1030** Injection, methylprednisolone acetate, 40 mg N1
Use this code for DepoMedalone40, Depo-Medrol, Sano-Drol
MED: 100-2,15,50; 100-4,4,240

N ☑ **J1040** Injection, methylprednisolone acetate, 80 mg N1
Use this code for Cortimed, DepMedalone, DepoMedalone 80, Depo-Medrol, Duro Cort, Methylcotolone, Pri-Methylate, Sano-Drol
MED: 100-2,15,50; 100-4,4,240

N ☑ **J1051** Injection, medroxyprogesterone acetate, 50 mg ♀ N1
Use this code for Depo-Provera.
MED: 100-2,15,50

E **J1055** Injection, medroxyprogesterone acetate for contraceptive use, 150 mg ♀
Use this code for Depo-Provera.

E **J1056** Injection, medroxyprogesterone acetate/estradiol cypionate, 5 mg/25 mg ♀
Use this code for Lunelle monthly contraceptive.

N ☑ **J1060** Injection, testosterone cypionate and estradiol cypionate, up to 1 ml N1
Use this code for Depo-Testadiol, Duo-Span, Duo-Span II.
MED: 100-2,15,50

Special Coverage Instructions | Noncovered by Medicare | Carrier Discretion | ☑ Quantity Alert | ● New Code | ○ Recycled/Reinstated | ▲ Revised Code

N ☑ **J1070** **Injection, testosterone cypionate, up to 100 mg** N1
Use this code for Depo Testosterone Cypionate
MED: 100-2,15,50

N ☑ **J1080** **Injection, testosterone cypionate, 1 cc, 200 mg** N1
Use this code for Depandrante, Depo-Testosterone, Virilon
MED: 100-2,15,50

N **J1094** **Injection, dexamethasone acetate, 1 mg** N1
Use this code for Cortastat LA, Dalalone L.A., Dexamethasone Acetate Anhydrous, Dexone LA.
MED: 100-2,15,50

N ☑ **J1100** **Injection, dexamethasone sodium phosphate, 1 mg** N1
Use this code for Cortastat, Dalalone, Decaject, Dexone, Solurex, Adrenocort, Primethasone, Dexasone, Dexim, Medidex, Spectro-Dex.
MED: 100-2,15,50

N ☑ **J1110** **Injection, dihydroergotamine mesylate, per 1 mg** N1
Use this code for D.H.E. 45.
MED: 100-2,15,50

N ☑ **J1120** **Injection, acetazolamide sodium, up to 500 mg** N1
Use this code for Diamox.
MED: 100-2,15,50

N ☑ **J1160** **Injection, digoxin, up to 0.5 mg** N1
Use this code for Lanoxin.
MED: 100-2,15,50

K ☑ **J1162** **Injection, digoxin immune fab (ovine), per vial** K2
Use this code for Digibind, Digifab.
MED: 100-2,15,50

N ☑ **J1165** **Injection, phenytoin sodium, per 50 mg** N1
Use this code for Dilantin.
MED: 100-2,15,50

N ☑ **J1170** **Injection, hydromorphone, up to 4 mg** N1
Use this code for Dilaudid, Dilaudid-HP.
MED: 100-2,15,50

N ☑ **J1180** **Injection, dyphylline, up to 500 mg** N1
MED: 100-2,15,50

K ☑ **J1190** **Injection, dexrazoxane HCl, per 250 mg** K2
Use this code for Totect, Zinecard.
MED: 100-2,15,50

N ☑ **J1200** **Injection, diphenhydramine HCl, up to 50 mg** N1
Use this code for Benadryl, Benahist 10, Benahist 50, Benoject-10, Benoject-50, Bena-D 10, Bena-D 50, Nordryl, Dihydrex, Dimine, Diphenacen-50, Hyrexin-50, Truxadryl, Wehdryl.
MED: 100-2,15,50
AHA: 1Q,'02,2

K ☑ **J1205** **Injection, chlorothiazide sodium, per 500 mg** K2
Use this code for Diuril Sodium.
MED: 100-2,15,50

K ☑ **J1212** **Injection, DMSO, dimethyl sulfoxide, 50%, 50 ml** K2
Use this code for Rimso 50. DMSO is covered only as a treatment of interstitial cystitis.
MED: 100-2,15,50; 100-3,230.12

N ☑ **J1230** **Injection, methadone HCl, up to 10 mg** N1
Use this code for Dolophine HCl.
MED: 100-2,15,50

N ☑ **J1240** **Injection, dimenhydrinate, up to 50 mg** N1
Use this code for Dramamine, Dinate, Dommanate, Dramanate, Dramilin, Dramocen, Dramoject, Dymenate, Hydrate, Marmine, Wehamine.
MED: 100-2,15,50

N ☑ **J1245** **Injection, dipyridamole, per 10 mg** N1
Use this code for Persantine IV.
MED: 100-2,15,50

N ☑ **J1250** **Injection, Dobutamine HCl, per 250 mg** N1
MED: 100-2,15,50

K ☑ **J1260** **Injection, dolasetron mesylate, 10 mg** K2
Use this code for Anzemet.
MED: 100-2,15,50

N ☑ **J1265** **Injection, dopamine HCl, 40 mg** N1

● G **J1267** **Injection, doripenem, 10 mg** K2
Use this code for Doribax

N ☑ **J1270** **Injection, doxercalciferol, 1 mcg** N1
Use this code for Hectorol.

G ☑ **J1300** **Injection, eculizumab, 10 mg** K2
Use this code for Soliris.

N ☑ **J1320** **Injection, amitriptyline HCl, up to 20 mg** N1
Use this code for Elavil
MED: 100-2,15,50

N ☑ **J1324** **Injection, enfuvirtide, 1 mg** N1
Use this code for Fuzeon.

N ☑ **J1325** **Injection, epoprostenol, 0.5 mg** N1
Use this code for Flolan. See K0455 for infusion pump for epoprosterol.
MED: 100-2,15,50

K ☑ **J1327** **Injection, eptifibatide, 5 mg** K2
Use this code for Integrilin.
MED: 100-2,15,50

N ☑ **J1330** **Injection, ergonovine maleate, up to 0.2 mg** N1
Medicare jurisdiction: local contractor. Use this code for Ergotrate Maleate.
MED: 100-2,15,50

N ☑ **J1335** **Injection, ertapenem sodium, 500 mg** N1
Use this code for Invanz.

N ☑ **J1364** **Injection, erythromycin lactobionate, per 500 mg** N1
MED: 100-2,15,50

N ☑ **J1380** **Injection, estradiol valerate, up to 10 mg** N1
Use this code for Delestrogen, Dioval, Dioval XX, Dioval 40, Duragen-10, Duragen-20, Duragen-40, Estradiol L.A., Estradiol L.A. 20, Estradiol L.A. 40, Gynogen L.A. 10, Gynogen L.A. 20, Gynogen L.A. 40, Valergen 10, Valergen 20, Valergen 40, Estra-L 20, Estra-L 40, L.A.E. 20.
MED: 100-2,15,50

N ☑ **J1390** **Injection, estradiol valerate, up to 20 mg** N1
Use this code for Delestrogen, Dioval, Dioval XX, Dioval 40, Duragen-10, Duragen-20, Duragen-40, Estradiol L.A., Estradiol L.A. 20, Estradiol L.A. 40, Gynogen L.A. 10, Gynogen L.A. 20, Gynogen L.A. 40, Valergen 10, Valergen 20, Valergen 40, Estra-L 20, Estra-L 40, L.A.E. 20.
MED: 100-2,15,50

K ☑ **J1410** **Injection, estrogen conjugated, per 25 mg** K2
Use this code for Natural Estrogenic Substance, Premarin Intravenous, Primestrin Aqueous.
MED: 100-2,15,50

K **J1430** **Injection, ethanolamine oleate, 100 mg** K2
Use this code for Ethamiolin.
MED: 100-2,15,50

N ☑ **J1435** **Injection, estrone, per 1 mg** N1
Use this code for Estone Aqueous, Estragyn, Estro-A, Estrone, Estronol, Theelin Aqueous, Estone 5, Kestrone 5.
MED: 100-2,15,50

K ☑ **J1436** Injection, etidronate disodium, per 300 mg K2
Use this code for Didronel.
MED: 100-2,15,50

K ☑ **J1438** Injection, etanercept, 25 mg (code may be used for Medicare when drug administered under the direct supervision of a physician, not for use when drug is self-administered) K2
Use this code for Enbrel.
MED: 100-2,15,50

K ☑ **J1440** Injection, filgrastim (G-CSF), 300 mcg K2
Use this code for Neupogen.
MED: 100-2,15,50

K ☑ **J1441** Injection, filgrastim (G-CSF), 480 mcg K2
Use this code for Neupogen.
MED: 100-2,15,50

N ☑ **J1450** Injection, fluconazole, 200 mg N1
Use this code for Diflucan.
MED: 100-2,15,50.5

K ☑ **J1451** Injection, fomepizole, 15 mg K2
Use this code for Antizol.
MED: 100-2,15,50

N ☑ **J1452** Injection, fomivirsen sodium, intraocular, 1.65 mg N1
Use this code for Vitavene.
MED: 100-2,15,50.4.2

● G **J1453** Injection, fosaprepitant, 1 mg K2
Use this code for Emend

K ☑ **J1455** Injection, foscarnet sodium, per 1,000 mg K2
Use this code for Foscavir.

K ☑ **J1457** Injection, gallium nitrate, 1 mg K2
Use this code for Ganite.

K ☑ **J1458** Injection, galsulfase, 1 mg K2
Use this code for Naglazyme.

● G **J1459** Injection, immune globulin (Privigen), intravenous, nonlyophilized (e.g., liquid), 500 mg K2

K ☑ **J1460** Injection, gamma globulin, intramuscular, 1 cc K2
Use this code for GamaSTAN SD.
MED: 100-2,15,50

K ☑ **J1470** Injection, gamma globulin, intramuscular, 2 cc K2
Use this code for GamaSTAN SD.
MED: 100-2,15,50

K ☑ **J1480** Injection, gamma globulin, intramuscular, 3 cc K2
Use this code for GamaSTAN SD.
MED: 100-2,15,50

K ☑ **J1490** Injection, gamma globulin, intramuscular, 4 cc K2
Use this code for GamaSTAN SD.
MED: 100-2,15,50

K ☑ **J1500** Injection, gamma globulin, intramuscular, 5 cc K2
Use this code for GamaSTAN SD.
MED: 100-2,15,50

K ☑ **J1510** Injection, gamma globulin, intramuscular, 6 cc K2
Use this code for GamaSTAN SD.
MED: 100-2,15,50

K ☑ **J1520** Injection, gamma globulin, intramuscular, 7 cc K2
Use this code for GamaSTAN SD.
MED: 100-2,15,50

K ☑ **J1530** Injection, gamma globulin, intramuscular, 8 cc K2
Use this code for GamaSTAN SD.
MED: 100-2,15,50

K ☑ **J1540** Injection, gamma globulin, intramuscular, 9 cc K2
Use this code for GamaSTAN SD.
MED: 100-2,15,50

K ☑ **J1550** Injection, gamma globulin, intramuscular, 10 cc K2
Use this code for GamaSTAN SD.
MED: 100-2,15,50

K ☑ **J1560** Injection, gamma globulin, intramuscular, over 10 cc K2
Use this code for GamaSTAN SD.
MED: 100-2,15,50

K ☑ **J1561** Injection, immune globulin, (Gamunex), intravenous, nonlyophilized (e.g., liquid), 500 mg K2

K ☑ **J1562** Injection, immune globulin (Vivaglobin), 100 mg K2

K ☑ **J1565** Injection, respiratory syncytial virus immune globulin, intravenous, 50 mg K2
Use this code for Respigam.
MED: 100-2,15,50

K ☑ **J1566** Injection, immune globulin, intravenous, lyophilized (e.g., powder), not otherwise specified, 500 mg K2
Use this code for Carimune.
MED: 100-2,15,50

K ☑ **J1568** Injection, immune globulin, (Octagam), intravenous, nonlyophilized (e.g., liquid), 500 mg K2

K ☑ **J1569** Injection, immune globulin, (Gammagard liquid), intravenous, nonlyophilized, (e.g., liquid), 500 mg K2

N ☑ **J1570** Injection, ganciclovir sodium, 500 mg N1
Use this code for Cytovene.
MED: 100-2,15,50

G ☑ **J1571** Injection, hepatitis B immune globulin (Hepagam B), intramuscular, 0.5 ml K2

▲ K ☑ **J1572** Injection, immune globulin, (Flebogamma/Flebogamma Dif), intravenous, nonlyophilized (e.g., liquid), 500 mg K2

G ☑ **J1573** Injection, hepatitis B immune globulin (Hepagam B), intravenous, 0.5 ml K2

N ☑ **J1580** Injection, garamycin, gentamicin, up to 80 mg N1
Use this code for Gentamicin Sulfate, Jenamicin.
MED: 100-2,15,50

N ☑ **J1590** Injection, gatifloxacin, 10 mg N1

K ☑ **J1595** Injection, glatiramer acetate, 20 mg K2
Use this code for Copaxone.
MED: 100-2,15,50

N ☑ **J1600** Injection, gold sodium thiomalate, up to 50 mg N1
Use this code for Myochrysine.
MED: 100-2,15,50

K ☑ **J1610** Injection, glucagon HCl, per 1 mg K2
Use this code for Glucagen.
MED: 100-2,15,50

K ☑ **J1620** Injection, gonadorelin HCl, per 100 mcg K2
Use this code for Factrel, Lutrepulse.
MED: 100-2,15,50

K ☑ **J1626** Injection, granisetron HCl, 100 mcg K2
Use this code for Kytril.
MED: 100-2,15,50

N ☑ **J1630** Injection, haloperidol, up to 5 mg N1
Use this code for Haldol.
MED: 100-2,15,50

N ☑ **J1631** Injection, haloperidol decanoate, per 50 mg N1
Use this code for Haldol Decanoate-50.
MED: 100-2,15,50

K ☑ **J1640** Injection, hemin, 1 mg K2
Use this code for Panhematin.
MED: 100-2,15,50

N ☑ **J1642** Injection, heparin sodium, (heparin lock flush), per 10 units N1
Use this code for Hep-Lock, Hep-Lock U/P, Hep-Pak, Lok-Pak.
MED: 100-2,15,50

N ☑ **J1644** Injection, Heparin sodium, per 1000 units N1
Use this code for Heparin Sodium, Liquaemin Sodium.
MED: 100-2,15,50

N ☑ **J1645** Injection, dalteparin sodium, per 2500 IU N1
Use this code for Fragmin.
MED: 100-2,15,50

N ☑ **J1650** Injection, enoxaparin sodium, 10 mg N1
Use this code for Lovenox.

K ☑ **J1652** Injection, fondaparinux sodium, 0.5 mg K2
Use this code for Atrixtra.
MED: 100-2,15,50

N ☑ **J1655** Injection, tinzaparin sodium, 1000 IU N1
Use this code for Innohep.

K ☑ **J1670** Injection, tetanus immune globulin, human, up to 250 units K2
Use this code for HyperTET SD.
MED: 100-2,15,50

B **J1675** Injection, histrelin acetate, 10 mcg
Use this code for Supprelin LA.
MED: 100-2,15,50

N ☑ **J1700** Injection, hydrocortisone acetate, up to 25 mg N1
Use this code for Hydrocortone Acetate.
MED: 100-2,15,50

N ☑ **J1710** Injection, hydrocortisone sodium phosphate, up to 50 mg N1
Use this code for Hydrocortone Phosphate.
MED: 100-2,15,50

N ☑ **J1720** Injection, hydrocortisone sodium succinate, up to 100 mg N1
Use this code for Solu-Cortef, A-Hydrocort.
MED: 100-2,15,50

K ☑ **J1730** Injection, diazoxide, up to 300 mg K2
MED: 100-2,15,50

K ☑ **J1740** Injection, ibandronate sodium, 1 mg K2
Use this code for Boniva.

K ☑ **J1742** Injection, ibutilide fumarate, 1 mg K2
Use this code for Corvert.
MED: 100-2,15,50

K **J1743** Injection, idursulfase, 1 mg K2
Use this code for Elaprase.

K ☑ **J1745** Injection infliximab, 10 mg K2
Use this code for Remicade.
MED: 100-2,15,50

○ K **J1750** Injection, iron dextran, 50 mg K2
Use this code for INFeD.

~~J1751~~ ~~Injection, iron dextran 165, 50 mg~~
See J1750

~~J1752~~ ~~Injection, iron dextran 267, 50 mg~~
See J1750

K ☑ **J1756** Injection, iron sucrose, 1 mg K2
Use this code for Venofer.

K ☑ **J1785** Injection, imiglucerase, per unit K2
Use this code for Cerezyme.
MED: 100-2,15,50

N ☑ **J1790** Injection, droperidol, up to 5 mg N1
Use this code for Inapsine.
MED: 100-2,15,50

N ☑ **J1800** Injection, propranolol HCl, up to 1 mg N1
Use this code for Inderal.
MED: 100-2,15,50

E ☑ **J1810** Injection, droperidol and fentanyl citrate, up to 2 ml ampule
MED: 100-2,15,50
AHA: 2Q,'02,8

N ☑ **J1815** Injection, insulin, per 5 units N1
Use this code for Humalog, Humulin, Iletin, Insulin Lispo, Novo Nordisk, NPH, Pork insulin, Regular insulin, Ultralente, Velosulin, Humulin R, Iletin II Regular Port, Insulin Purified Pork, Relion, Lente Iletin I, Novolin R, Humulin R U-500.
MED: 100-2,15,50; 100-3,280.14

N ☑ **J1817** Insulin for administration through DME (i.e., insulin pump) per 50 units N1
Use this code for Humalog, Humulin, Vesolin BR, Iletin II NPH Pork, Lantus, Lispro-PFC, Novolin, Novolog, Novolog Flexpen, Novolog Mix, Relion Novolin.

E ☑ **J1825** Injection, interferon beta-1a, 33 mcg
Use this code for Avonex, Rebif.

K ☑ **J1830** Injection interferon beta-1b, 0.25 mg (code may be used for Medicare when drug administered under the direct supervision of a physician, not for use when drug is self-administered) K2
Use this code for Betaseron.
MED: 100-2,15,50

K ☑ **J1835** Injection, itraconazole, 50 mg K2
Use this code for Sporonox IV.

N ☑ **J1840** Injection, kanamycin sulfate, up to 500 mg N1
Use this code for Kantrex
MED: 100-2,15,50

N ☑ **J1850** Injection, kanamycin sulfate, up to 75 mg N1
Use this code for Kantrex
MED: 100-2,15,50

N ☑ **J1885** Injection, ketorolac tromethamine, per 15 mg N1
MED: 100-2,15,50

N ☑ **J1890** Injection, cephalothin sodium, up to 1 g N1
MED: 100-2,15,50

● K ☑ **J1930** Injection, lanreotide, 1 mg K2
Use this code for Somatuline

K ☑ **J1931** Injection, laronidase, 0.1 mg K2
Use this code for Aldurazyme.

N ☑ **J1940** Injection, furosemide, up to 20 mg N1
Use this code for Lasix
MED: 100-2,15,50

K ☑ **J1945** Injection, lepirudin, 50 mg K2
Use this code for Refludan.
This drug is used for patients with heparin induced thrombocytopenia.
MED: 100-2,15,50

K ☑ **J1950** Injection, leuprolide acetate (for depot suspension), per 3.75 mg K2
Use this code for Eliguard, Lupron, Lupron-3, Lupron-4, Lupron Depot.
MED: 100-2,15,50

● G ☑ **J1953** Injection, levetiracetam, 10 mg K2
Use this code for Keppra

B ☑ **J1955** Injection, levocarnitine, per 1 g
Use this code for Carnitor
MED: 100-2,15,50

N ☑ **J1956** Injection, levofloxacin, 250 mg N1
Use this code for Levaquin.
MED: 100-2,15,50

N ☑ **J1960** Injection, levorphanol tartrate, up to 2 mg N1
Use this code for Levo-Dromoran.
MED: 100-2,15,50

N ☑ **J1980** Injection, hyoscyamine sulfate, up to 0.25 mg N1
Use this code for Levsin.
MED: 100-2,15,50

N ☑ **J1990** Injection, chlordiazepoxide HCl, up to 100 mg N1
Use this code for Librium.
MED: 100-2,15,50

N ☑ **J2001** Injection, lidocaine HCl for intravenous infusion, 10 mg N1
Use this code for Xylocaine.
MED: 100-2,15,50

N ☑ **J2010** Injection, lincomycin HCl, up to 300 mg N1
Use this code for Lincocin
MED: 100-2,15,50

K ☑ **J2020** Injection, linezolid, 200 mg K2
Use this code for Zyvok.
AHA: 2Q,'02,8

N ☑ **J2060** Injection, lorazepam, 2 mg N1
Use this code for Ativan.
MED: 100-2,15,50

N ☑ **J2150** Injection, mannitol, 25% in 50 ml N1
Use this code for Osmitrol.
MED: 100-2,15,50

N ☑ **J2170** Injection, mecasermin, 1 mg N1
Use this code for Iplex, Increlex.

N ☑ **J2175** Injection, meperidine HCl, per 100 mg N1
Use this code for Demerol.
MED: 100-2,15,50

N ☑ **J2180** Injection, meperidine and promethazine HCl, up to 50 mg N1
Use this code for Mepergan Injection.
MED: 100-2,15,50

N ☑ **J2185** Injection, meropenem, 100 mg N1
Use this code for Merrem

N ☑ **J2210** Injection, methylergonovine maleate, up to 0.2 mg N1
Use this code for Methergine.
MED: 100-2,15,50

K ☑ **J2248** Injection, micafungin sodium, 1 mg K2
Use this code for Mycamine.

N ☑ **J2250** Injection, midazolam HCl, per 1 mg N1
Use this code for Versed.
MED: 100-2,15,50

N ☑ **J2260** Injection, milrinone lactate, 5 mg N1
Use this code for Primacor.
MED: 100-2,15,50

N ☑ **J2270** Injection, morphine sulfate, up to 10 mg N1
Use this code for Depodur, Infumorph
MED: 100-2,15,50

N ☑ **J2271** Injection, morphine sulfate, 100 mg N1
Use this code for Depodur, Infumorph
MED: 100-2,15,50; 100-3,280.14

N ☑ **J2275** Injection, morphine sulfate (preservative-free sterile solution), per 10 mg N1
Use this code for Astramorph PF, Duramorph, Infumorph.
MED: 100-2,15,50; 100-3,280.14

K ☑ **J2278** Injection, ziconotide, 1 mcg K2
Use this code for Prialt

N ☑ **J2280** Injection, moxifloxacin, 100 mg N1
Use this code for Avelox.

N ☑ **J2300** Injection, nalbuphine HCl, per 10 mg N1
Use this code for Nubain.
MED: 100-2,15,50

N ☑ **J2310** Injection, naloxone HCl, per 1 mg N1
Use this code for Narcan.
MED: 100-2,15,50

K ☑ **J2315** Injection, naltrexone, depot form, 1 mg K2
Use this code for Vivitrol.

N ☑ **J2320** Injection, nandrolone decanoate, up to 50 mg N1
MED: 100-2,15,50

N ☑ **J2321** Injection, nandrolone decanoate, up to 100 mg N1
MED: 100-2,15,50

N ☑ **J2322** Injection, nandrolone decanoate, up to 200 mg N1
MED: 100-2,15,50

K **J2323** Injection, natalizumab, 1 mg K2
Use this code for Tysabri.

K ☑ **J2325** Injection, nesiritide, 0.1 mg K2
Use this code for Natrecor.
MED: 100-2,15,50

K ☑ **J2353** Injection, octreotide, depot form for intramuscular injection, 1 mg K2
Use this code for Sandostatin LAR.

N ☑ **J2354** Injection, octreotide, nondepot form for subcutaneous or intravenous injection, 25 mcg N1
Use this code for Sandostatin.

K ☑ **J2355** Injection, oprelvekin, 5 mg K2
Use this code for Neumega.
MED: 100-2,15,50

K ☑ **J2357** Injection, omalizumab, 5 mg K2
Use this code for Xolair.

N ☑ **J2360** Injection, orphenadrine citrate, up to 60 mg N1
Use this code for Norflex
MED: 100-2,15,50

N ☑ **J2370** Injection, phenylephrine HCl, up to 1 ml N1
MED: 100-2,15,50

N ☑ **J2400** Injection, chloroprocaine HCl, per 30 ml N1
Use this code for Nesacaine, Nesacaine-MPF.
MED: 100-2,15,50

K ☑ **J2405** Injection, ondansetron HCl, per 1 mg K2
Use this code for Zofran.
MED: 100-2,15,50

N ☑ **J2410** Injection, oxymorphone HCl, up to 1 mg N1
Use this code for Numorphan, Oxymorphone HCl.
MED: 100-2,15,50

K ☑ **J2425** Injection, palifermin, 50 mcg K2
Use this code for Kepivance.

K ☑ J2430 Injection, pamidronate disodium, per 30 mg K2
Use this code for Aredia
MED: 100-2,15,50

N ☑ J2440 Injection, papaverine HCl, up to 60 mg N1
MED: 100-2,15,50

K ☑ J2460 Injection, oxytetracycline HCl, up to 50 mg K2
Use this code for Terramycin IM.
MED: 100-2,15,50

K ☑ J2469 Injection, palonosetron HCl, 25 mcg K2
Use this code for Aloxi.

N ☑ J2501 Injection, paricalcitol, 1 mcg N1
Use this code For Zemplar.
MED: 100-2,15,50

K J2503 Injection, pegaptanib sodium, 0.3 mg K2
Use this code for Mucagen.

K ☑ J2504 Injection, pegademase bovine, 25 IU K2
Use this code for Adagen.
MED: 100-2,15,50

K ☑ J2505 Injection, pegfilgrastim, 6 mg K2
Use this code for Neulasta.

N ☑ J2510 Injection, penicillin G procaine, aqueous, up to 600,000 units N1
Use this code for Wycillin, Duracillin A.S., Pfizerpen A.S., Crysticillin 300 A.S., Crysticillin 600 A.S.
MED: 100-2,15,50

K J2513 Injection, pentastarch, 10% solution, 100 ml K2
MED: 100-2,15,50

K ☑ J2515 Injection, pentobarbital sodium, per 50 mg K2
Use this code for Nembutal Sodium Solution.
MED: 100-2,15,50

N ☑ J2540 Injection, penicillin G potassium, up to 600,000 units N1
Use this code for Pfizerpen.
MED: 100-2,15,50

N ☑ J2543 Injection, piperacillin sodium/tazobactam sodium, 1 g/0.125 g (1.125 g) N1
Use this code for Zosyn.
MED: 100-2,15,50

B ☑ J2545 Pentamidine isethionate, inhalation solution, FDA-approved final product, noncompounded, administered through DME, unit dose form, per 300 mg
Use this code for Nebupent, Pentam 300

N ☑ J2550 Injection, promethazine HCl, up to 50 mg N1
Use this code for Phenergan
MED: 100-2,15,50

N ☑ J2560 Injection, phenobarbital sodium, up to 120 mg N1
MED: 100-2,15,50

N ☑ J2590 Injection, oxytocin, up to 10 units N1
Use this code for Pitocin, Syntocinon.
MED: 100-2,15,50

N ☑ J2597 Injection, desmopressin acetate, per 1 mcg N1
Use this code for DDAVP.
MED: 100-2,15,50

N ☑ J2650 Injection, prednisolone acetate, up to 1 ml N1
MED: 100-2,15,50; 100-4,4,240

N ☑ J2670 Injection, tolazoline HCl, up to 25 mg N1
MED: 100-2,15,50

N J2675 Injection, progesterone, per 50 mg N1
Use this code for Gesterone, Gestrin.
MED: 100-2,15,50

N ☑ J2680 Injection, fluphenazine decanoate, up to 25 mg N1
MED: 100-2,15,50

N ☑ J2690 Injection, procainamide HCl, up to 1 g N1
Use this code for Pronestyl.
MED: 100-2,15,50

N ☑ J2700 Injection, oxacillin sodium, up to 250 mg N1
Use this code for Bactocill
MED: 100-2,15,50

N ☑ J2710 Injection, neostigmine methylsulfate, up to 0.5 mg N1
Use this code for Prostigmin.
MED: 100-2,15,50

N ☑ J2720 Injection, protamine sulfate, per 10 mg N1
MED: 100-2,15,50

K J2724 Injection, protein C concentrate, intravenous, human, 10 IU K2

N ☑ J2725 Injection, protirelin, per 250 mcg N1
Use this code for Thyrel TRH
MED: 100-2,15,50

K ☑ J2730 Injection, pralidoxime chloride, up to 1 g K2
Use this code for Protopam Chloride.
MED: 100-2,15,50

N ☑ J2760 Injection, phentolamine mesylate, up to 5 mg N1
Use this code for Regitine.
MED: 100-2,15,50

N ☑ J2765 Injection, metoclopramide HCl, up to 10 mg N1
Use this code for Reglan
MED: 100-2,15,50

K ☑ J2770 Injection, quinupristin/dalfopristin, 500 mg (150/350) K2
Use this code for Synercid.
MED: 100-2,15,50

K ☑ J2778 Injection, ranibizumab, 0.1 mg K2
Use this code for Lucentis.

N ☑ J2780 Injection, ranitidine HCl, 25 mg N1
Use this code for Zantac.
MED: 100-2,15,50

K ☑ J2783 Injection, rasburicase, 0.5 mg K2
Use this code for Elitek.

● G ☑ J2785 Injection, regadenoson, 0.1 mg K2
Use this code for Lexiscan

▲ K ☑ J2788 Injection, Rho D immune globulin, human, minidose, 50 mcg (250 i.u.) K2
Use this code for RhoGam, MiCRhoGAM.
MED: 100-2,15,50

▲ K ☑ J2790 Injection, Rho D immune globulin, human, full dose, 300 mcg (1500 i.u.) K2
Use this code for RhoGam, Rhophylac.
MED: 100-2,15,50

K J2791 Injection, Rho(D) immune globulin (human), (Rhophylac), intramuscular or intravenous, 100 IU K2
Use this for HypRho SD, WINRho SDF.

K ☑ J2792 Injection, Rho D immune globulin, intravenous, human, solvent detergent, 100 IU K2
MED: 100-2,15,50

K ☑ J2794 Injection, risperidone, long acting, 0.5 mg K2
Use this code for Risperidal Consta Long Acting.

N ☑ **J2795** Injection, ropivacaine HCl, 1 mg N1
Use this code for Naropin.

N ☑ **J2800** Injection, methocarbamol, up to 10 ml N1
Use this code for Robaxin
MED: 100-2,15,50

K **J2805** Injection, sincalide, 5 mcg K2
Use this code for Kinevac.

N ☑ **J2810** Injection, theophylline, per 40 mg N1
MED: 100-2,15,50

K ☑ **J2820** Injection, sargramostim (GM-CSF), 50 mcg K2
Use this code for Leukine
MED: 100-2,15,50

K ☑ **J2850** Injection, secretin, synthetic, human, 1 mcg K2
MED: 100-2,15,50

N ☑ **J2910** Injection, aurothioglucose, up to 50 mg N1
Use this code for Solganal.
MED: 100-2,15,50

N ☑ **J2916** Injection, sodium ferric gluconate complex in sucrose injection, 12.5 mg N1
MED: 100-2,15,50.2

N ☑ **J2920** Injection, methylprednisolone sodium succinate, up to 40 mg N1
Use this code for Solu-Medrol, A-methaPred.
MED: 100-2,15,50; 100-4,4,240

N ☑ **J2930** Injection, methylprednisolone sodium succinate, up to 125 mg N1
Use this code for Solu-Medrol, A-methaPred.
MED: 100-2,15,50; 100-4,4,240

K ☑ **J2940** Injection, somatrem, 1 mg K2
Use this code for Protropin.
MED: 100-2,15,50
AHA: 2Q,'02,8

K ☑ **J2941** Injection, somatropin, 1 mg K2
Use this code for Humatrope, Genotropin Nutropin, Biotropin, Genotropin, Genotropin Miniquick, Norditropin, Nutropin, Nutropin AQ, Saizen, Saizen Somatropin RDNA Origin, Serostim, Serostim RDNA Origin, Zorbtive.
MED: 100-2,15,50
AHA: 2Q,'02,8

N ☑ **J2950** Injection, promazine HCl, up to 25 mg N1
Use this code for Sparine, Prozine-50.
MED: 100-2,15,50

K ☑ **J2993** Injection, reteplase, 18.1 mg K2
Use this code for Retavase
MED: 100-2,15,50

K ☑ **J2995** Injection, streptokinase, per 250,000 IU K2
Use this code for Streptase
MED: 100-2,15,50

K ☑ **J2997** Injection, alteplase recombinant, 1 mg K2
Use this code for Activase, Cathflo.
MED: 100-2,15,50

N ☑ **J3000** Injection, streptomycin, up to 1 g N1
Use this code for Streptomycin Sulfate.
MED: 100-2,15,50

N ☑ **J3010** Injection, fentanyl citrate, 0.1 mg N1
Use this code for Sublimaze.
MED: 100-2,15,50

K ☑ **J3030** Injection, sumatriptan succinate, 6 mg (code may be used for Medicare when drug administered under the direct supervision of a physician, not for use when drug is self-administered) K2
Use this code for Imitrex.
MED: 100-2,15,50

N ☑ **J3070** Injection, pentazocine, 30 mg N1
Use this code for Talwin.
MED: 100-2,15,50

~~J3100 Injection, tenecteplase, 50 mg~~
See J3101

● K ☑ **J3101** Injection, tenecteplase, 1 mg K2
Use this code for TNKase.

N ☑ **J3105** Injection, terbutaline sulfate, up to 1 mg N1
For terbutaline in inhalation solution, see K0525 and K0526.
MED: 100-2,15,50

B ☑ **J3110** Injection, teriparatide, 10 mcg
Use this code for Forteo.

N ☑ **J3120** Injection, testosterone enanthate, up to 100 mg N1
Use this code for Delatestryl.
MED: 100-2,15,50

N ☑ **J3130** Injection, testosterone enanthate, up to 200 mg N1
Use this code for Delatestryl.
MED: 100-2,15,50

N ☑ **J3140** Injection, testosterone suspension, up to 50 mg N1
MED: 100-2,15,50

N ☑ **J3150** Injection, testosterone propionate, up to 100 mg N1
MED: 100-2,15,50

N ☑ **J3230** Injection, chlorpromazine HCl, up to 50 mg N1
Use this code for Thorazine.
MED: 100-2,15,50

K ☑ **J3240** Injection, thyrotropin alpha, 0.9 mg, provided in 1.1 mg vial K2
Use this code for Thyrogen.
MED: 100-2,15,50

K ☑ **J3243** Injection, tigecycline, 1 mg K2
Use this code for Tygacil.

K ☑ **J3246** Injection, tirofiban HCl, 0.25 mg K2
Use this code for Aggrastat.

N ☑ **J3250** Injection, trimethobenzamide HCl, up to 200 mg N1
Use this code for Tigan, Tiject-20, Arrestin.
MED: 100-2,15,50

N ☑ **J3260** Injection, tobramycin sulfate, up to 80 mg N1
Use this code for Nebcin.
MED: 100-2,15,50

N ☑ **J3265** Injection, torsemide, 10 mg/ml N1
Use this code for Demadex, Torsemide.
MED: 100-2,15,50

N ☑ **J3280** Injection, thiethylperazine maleate, up to 10 mg N1
MED: 100-2,15,50

K ☑ **J3285** Injection, treprostinil, 1 mg K2
Use this code for Remodulin.

● N **J3300** Injection, triamcinolone acetonide, preservative free, 1 mg N1
Use this code for TRIVARIS.

▲ N ☑ **J3301** Injection, triamcinolone acetonide, not otherwise specified, 10 mg N1
Use this code for Kenalog-10, Kenalog-40, Tri-Kort, Kenaject-40, Cenacort A-40, Triam-A, Trilog.
MED: 100-2,15,50

N ☑ **J3302** Injection, triamcinolone diacetate, per 5 mg N1
Use this code for Aristocort, Aristocort Intralesional, Aristocort Forte, Amcort, Trilone, Cenacort Forte.
MED: 100-2,15,50

N ☑ **J3303** Injection, triamcinolone hexacetonide, per 5 mg N1
Use this code for Aristospan Intralesional, Aristospan Intra-articular.
MED: 100-2,15,50

K ☑ **J3305** Injection, trimetrexate glucuronate, per 25 mg K2
Use this code for Neutrexin.
MED: 100-2,15,50

N ☑ **J3310** Injection, perphenazine, up to 5 mg N1
Use this code for Trilafon.
MED: 100-2,15,50

K ☑ **J3315** Injection, triptorelin pamoate, 3.75 mg ♂ K2
Use this code for Trelstar Depot, Trelstar Depot Plus Debioclip Kit, Trelstar LA.
MED: 100-2,15,50

N ☑ **J3320** Injection, spectinomycin dihydrochloride, up to 2 g N1
Use this code for Trobicin.
MED: 100-2,15,50

K ☑ **J3350** Injection, urea, up to 40 g K2
MED: 100-2,15,50

K **J3355** Injection, urofollitropin, 75 IU K2
Use this code for Metrodin, Bravelle, Fertinex.
MED: 100-2,15,50

N ☑ **J3360** Injection, diazepam, up to 5 mg N1
Use this code for Diastat, Dizac, Valium.
MED: 100-2,15,50

N ☑ **J3364** Injection, urokinase, 5,000 IU vial N1
Use this code for Kinlytic
MED: 100-2,15,50

K ☑ **J3365** Injection, IV, urokinase, 250,000 IU vial K2
Use this code for Kinlytic
MED: 100-2,15,50

N ☑ **J3370** Injection, vancomycin HCl, 500 mg N1
Use this code for Vancocin.
MED: 100-2,15,50; 100-3,280.14

K ☑ **J3396** Injection, verteporfin, 0.1 mg K2
Use this code for Visudyne.
MED: 100-3,80.2; 100-3,80.3

K ☑ **J3400** Injection, triflupromazine HCl, up to 20 mg K2
MED: 100-2,15,50

N ☑ **J3410** Injection, hydroxyzine HCl, up to 25 mg N1
Use this code for Vistaril, Vistaject-25, Hyzine, Hyzine-50.
MED: 100-2,15,50

N ☑ **J3411** Injection, thiamine HCl, 100 mg N1

N ☑ **J3415** Injection, pyridoxine HCl, 100 mg N1

N ☑ **J3420** Injection, vitamin B-12 cyanocobalamin, up to 1,000 mcg N1
Use this code for Sytobex, Redisol, Rubramin PC, Betalin 12, Berubigen, Cobex, Cobal, Crystal B12, Cyano, Cyanocobalamin, Hydroxocobalamin, Hydroxycobal, Nutri-Twelve.
MED: 100-2,15,50; 100-3,150.6

N ☑ **J3430** Injection, phytonadione (vitamin K), per 1 mg N1
Use this code for AquaMephyton, Konakion, Menadione, Phytonadione.
MED: 100-2,15,50

K ☑ **J3465** Injection, voriconazole, 10 mg K2
MED: 100-2,15,50

N ☑ **J3470** Injection, hyaluronidase, up to 150 units N1
MED: 100-2,15,50

N ☑ **J3471** Injection, hyaluronidase, ovine, preservative free, per 1 USP unit (up to 999 USP units) N1

K ☑ **J3472** Injection, hyaluronidase, ovine, preservative free, per 1,000 USP units K2

K ☑ **J3473** Injection, hyaluronidase, recombinant, 1 USP unit K2

N ☑ **J3475** Injection, magnesium sulfate, per 500 mg N1
Use this code for Mag Sul, Sulfa Mag.
MED: 100-2,15,50

N ☑ **J3480** Injection, potassium chloride, per 2 mEq N1
MED: 100-2,15,50

N ☑ **J3485** Injection, zidovudine, 10 mg N1
Use this code for Retrovir, Zidovudine.
MED: 100-2,15,50

N ☑ **J3486** Injection, ziprasidone mesylate, 10 mg N1
Use this code for Geodon.

K ☑ **J3487** Injection, zoledronic acid (Zometa), 1 mg K2

G ☑ **J3488** Injection, zoledronic acid (Reclast), 1 mg K2

N **J3490** Unclassified drugs N1
MED: 100-2,15,50

E ☑ **J3520** Edetate disodium, per 150 mg
Use this code for Endrate, Disotate, Meritate, Chealamide, E.D.T.A. This drug is used in chelation therapy, a treatment for atherosclerosis that is not covered by Medicare.
MED: 100-3,20.21; 100-3,20.22

N **J3530** Nasal vaccine inhalation N1
MED: 100-2,15,50

E **J3535** Drug administered through a metered dose inhaler
MED: 100-2,15,50

E **J3570** Laetrile, amygdalin, vitamin B-17
The FDA has found Laetrile to have no safe or effective therapeutic purpose.
MED: 100-3,30.7

N **J3590** Unclassified biologics N1

MISCELLANEOUS DRUGS AND SOLUTIONS

N ☑ **J7030** Infusion, normal saline solution, 1,000 cc N1
MED: 100-2,15,50

N ☑ **J7040** Infusion, normal saline solution, sterile (500 ml=1 unit) N1
MED: 100-2,15,50

N ☑ **J7042** 5% dextrose/normal saline (500 ml = 1 unit) N1
MED: 100-2,15,50

N ☑ **J7050** Infusion, normal saline solution, 250 cc N1
MED: 100-2,15,50

N ☑ **J7060** 5% dextrose/water (500 ml = 1 unit) N1
MED: 100-2,15,50

N ☑ **J7070** Infusion, D-5-W, 1,000 cc N1
MED: 100-2,15,50

N ☑ **J7100** Infusion, dextran 40, 500 ml N1
Use this code for Gentran, 10% LMD, Rheomacrodex.
MED: 100-2,15,50

N ☑ **J7110** Infusion, dextran 75, 500 ml N1
Use this code for Gentran 75.
MED: 100-2,15,50

N ☑ **J7120** Ringers lactate infusion, up to 1,000 cc N1
MED: 100-2,15,50

N ☑ **J7130** Hypertonic saline solution, 50 or 100 mEq, 20 cc vial N1
MED: 100-2,15,50

● K **J7186** Injection, antihemophilic factor VIII/von Willebrand factor complex (human), per factor VIII i.u. K2
Use this code for Alphanate.

K **J7187** Injection, von Willebrand factor complex (Humate-P), per IU vWF-RCO K2

K ☑ **J7189** Factor VIIa (antihemophilic factor, recombinant), per 1 mcg K2
MED: 100-1,1,10.1; 100-2,6,10; 100-2,15,50; 100-4,3,20.7.3

K ☑ **J7190** Factor VIII (antihemophilic factor, human) per IU K2
Use this code for Koate-DVI, Monarc-M, Monoclate-P.
MED: 100-1,1,10.1; 100-2,6,10; 100-2,15,50; 100-4,3,20.7.3; 100-4,4,240; 100-4,17,80.4

K ☑ **J7191** Factor VIII (antihemophilic factor (porcine)), per IU K2
MED: 100-1,1,10.1; 100-2,6,10; 100-2,15,50; 100-4,3,20.7.3; 100-4,4,240; 100-4,17,80.4

K ☑ **J7192** Factor VIII (antihemophilic factor, recombinant) per IU K2
Use this code for Recombinate, Kogenate FS, Helixate FX, Advate rAHF-PFM, Antihemophilic Factor Human Method M Monoclonal Purified, Refacto.
MED: 100-1,1,10.1; 100-2,6,10; 100-2,15,50; 100-4,3,20.7.3; 100-4,4,240; 100-4,17,80.4

K ☑ **J7193** Factor IX (antihemophilic factor, purified, nonrecombinant) per IU K2
Use this code for AlphaNine SD, Mononine.
MED: 100-1,1,10.1; 100-2,6,10; 100-2,15,50; 100-4,3,20.7.3; 100-4,4,240; 100-4,17,80.4
AHA: 2Q,'02,8

K ☑ **J7194** Factor IX complex, per IU K2
Use this code for Konyne-80, Profilnine SD, Proplex T, Proplex T, Bebulin VH, factor IX+ complex, Profilnine SD.
MED: 100-1,1,10.1; 100-2,6,10; 100-2,15,50; 100-4,3,20.7.3; 100-4,4,240; 100-4,17,80.4

K ☑ **J7195** Factor IX (antihemophilic factor, recombinant) per IU K2
Use this code for Benefix.
MED: 100-1,1,10.1; 100-2,6,10; 100-2,15,50; 100-4,3,20.7.3; 100-4,4,240; 100-4,17,80.4
AHA: 2Q,'02,8

N ☑ **J7197** Antithrombin III (human), per IU N1
Use this code for Thrombate III, ATnativ.
MED: 100-2,15,50

K ☑ **J7198** Antiinhibitor, per IU K2
Medicare jurisdiction: local contractor. Use this code for Autoplex T, Feiba VH AICC.

B **J7199** Hemophilia clotting factor, not otherwise classified
Medicare jurisdiction: local contractor.

E **J7300** Intrauterine copper contraceptive
Use this code for Paragard T380A.

E ☑ **J7302** Levonorgestrel-releasing intrauterine contraceptive system, 52 mg ♀
Use this code for Mirena.

E ☑ **J7303** Contraceptive supply, hormone containing vaginal ring, each ♀
Use this code for Nuvaring Vaginal Ring.

E ☑ **J7304** Contraceptive supply, hormone containing patch, each

E **J7306** Levonorgestrel (contraceptive) implant system, including implants and supplies
Use this code for Norplant II.

E **J7307** Etonogestrel (contraceptive) implant system, including implant and supplies
Use this code for Implanon.

K ☑ **J7308** Aminolevulinic acid HCl for topical administration, 20%, single unit dosage form (354 mg) K2

K ☑ **J7310** Ganciclovir, 4.5 mg, long-acting implant K2
Use this code for Vitrasert.
MED: 100-2,15,50

K **J7311** Fluocinolone acetonide, intravitreal implant K2
Use this code for Retisert.

K ☑ **J7321** Hyaluronan or derivative, Hyalgan or Supartz, for intra-articular injection, per dose K2

K ☑ **J7322** Hyaluronan or derivative, Synvisc, for intra-articular injection, per dose K2

K ☑ **J7323** Hyaluronan or derivative, Euflexxa, for intra-articular injection, per dose K2

K ☑ **J7324** Hyaluronan or derivative, Orthovisc, for intra-articular injection, per dose K2

B ☑ **J7330** Autologous cultured chondrocytes, implant
Medicare jurisdiction: local contractor. Use this code for Carticel.

~~J7340 Dermal and epidermal, (substitute) tissue of human origin, with or without bioengineered or processed elements, with metabolically active elements, per square centimeter~~
See Q4100-Q4111

~~J7341 Dermal (substitute) tissue of nonhuman origin, with or without other bioengineered or processed elements, with metabolically active elements, per square centimeter~~
See Q4100-Q4111

~~J7342 Dermal (substitute) tissue of human origin, with or without other bioengineered or processed elements, with metabolically active elements, per square centimeter~~
See Q4100-Q4111

~~J7343 Dermal and epidermal, (substitute) tissue of nonhuman origin, with or without other bioengineered or processed elements, without metabolically active elements, per square centimeter~~
See Q4100-Q4111

~~J7344 Dermal (substitute) tissue of human origin, with or without other bioengineered or processed elements, without metabolically active elements, per square centimeter~~
See Q4100-Q4111

~~J7346 Dermal (substitute) tissue of human origin, injectable, with or without other bioengineered or processed elements, but without metabolically active elements, 1 cc~~
See Q4100-Q4111

~~J7347 Dermal (substitute) tissue of nonhuman origin, with or without other bioengineered or processed elements, without metabolically active elements (Integra Matrix), per sq. cm.~~
See Q4100-Q4111

~~J7348 Dermal (substitute) tissue of nonhuman origin, with or without other bioengineered or processed elements, without metabolically active elements (TissueMend), per sq. cm.~~
See Q4100-Q4111

~~J7349 Dermal (substitute) tissue of nonhuman origin, with or without other bioengineered or processed elements, without metabolically active elements (PriMatrix), per sq. cm.~~
See Q4100-Q4111

N ☑ J7500 Azathioprine, oral, 50 mg N1
Use this code for Azasan, Imuran.
MED: 100-2,15,50.5; 100-4,4,240; 100-4,17,80.3

K ☑ J7501 Azathioprine, parenteral, 100 mg K2
MED: 100-2,6,10; 100-2,15,50; 100-4,4,240; 100-4,17,80.3

K ☑ J7502 Cyclosporine, oral, 100 mg K2
Use this code for Neoral, Sandimmune, Gengraf, Sangcya
MED: 100-2,15,50.5; 100-4,4,240; 100-4,17,80.3

K ☑ J7504 Lymphocyte immune globulin, antithymocyte globulin, equine, parenteral, 250 mg K2
Use this code for Atgam.
MED: 100-2,6,10; 100-2,15,50; 100-3,260.7; 100-4,4,240; 100-4,17,80.3

K ☑ J7505 Muromonab-CD3, parenteral, 5 mg K2
Use this code for Orthoclone OKT3.
MED: 100-2,6,10; 100-2,15,50; 100-4,4,240; 100-4,17,80.3

N ☑ J7506 Prednisone, oral, per 5 mg N1
Use this code for Deltasone, Liquid Pred Syrup, Levoxyl, Predone, Prednicot, Sterapred.
MED: 100-2,15,50.5; 100-4,4,240; 100-4,17,80.3

K ☑ J7507 Tacrolimus, oral, per 1 mg K2
Use this code for Prograf.
MED: 100-2,15,50.5; 100-4,4,240; 100-4,17,80.3

N ☑ J7509 Methylprednisolone, oral, per 4 mg N1
Use this code for Medrol, Methylpred.
MED: 100-2,15,50.5; 100-4,4,240; 100-4,17,80.3

N ☑ J7510 Prednisolone, oral, per 5 mg N1
Use this code for Delta-Cortef, Cotolone, Pediapred, Prednoral, Prelone.
MED: 100-2,15,50.5; 100-4,4,240; 100-4,17,80.3

K ☑ J7511 Lymphocyte immune globulin, antithymocyte globulin, rabbit, parenteral, 25 mg K2
Use this code for Thymoglobulin.
MED: 100-2,6,10; 100-4,4,240; 100-4,17,80.3
AHA: 2Q,'02,8

K ☑ J7513 Daclizumab, parenteral, 25 mg K2
Use this code for Zenapax.
MED: 100-2,6,10; 100-2,15,50.5; 100-4,4,240; 100-4,17,80.3

N ☑ J7515 Cyclosporine, oral, 25 mg N1
Use this code for Neoral, Sandimmune, Gengraf, Sangcya.
MED: 100-4,4,240; 100-4,17,80.3

K ☑ J7516 Cyclosporine, parenteral, 250 mg K2
Use this code for Neoral, Sandimmune, Gengraf, Sangcya.
MED: 100-2,6,10; 100-4,4,240; 100-4,17,80.3

K ☑ J7517 Mycophenolate mofetil, oral, 250 mg K2
Use this code for CellCept.
MED: 100-4,4,240; 100-4,17,80.3

K ☑ J7518 Mycophenolic acid, oral, 180 mg K2
Use this code for Myfortic Delayed Release.
MED: 100-4,4,240; 100-4,17,80.3.1

K ☑ J7520 Sirolimus, oral, 1 mg K2
Use this code for Rapamune.
MED: 100-2,15,50.5; 100-4,4,240; 100-4,17,80.3

K ☑ J7525 Tacrolimus, parenteral, 5 mg K2
Use this code for Prograf.
MED: 100-2,6,10; 100-2,15,50.5; 100-4,4,240; 100-4,17,80.3

N J7599 Immunosuppressive drug, not otherwise classified N1
Determine if an alternative HCPCS Level II or a CPT code better describes the service being reported. This code should be used only if a more specific code is unavailable.
MED: 100-2,6,10; 100-2,15,50.5; 100-4,4,240; 100-4,17,80.3

INHALATION SOLUTIONS

~~J7602 Albuterol, all formulations including separated isomers, inhalation solution, FDA-approved final product, noncompounded, administered through DME, concentrated form, per 1 mg (Albuterol) or per 0.5 mg Levalbuterol)~~

~~J7603 Albuterol, all formulations including separated isomers, inhalation solution, FDA-approved final product, noncompounded, administered through DME, unit dose, per 1 mg (Albuterol) or per 0.5 mg Levalbuterol)~~

M ☑ J7604 Acetylcysteine, inhalation solution, compounded product, administered through DME, unit dose form, per g

M ☑ J7605 Arformoterol, inhalation solution, FDA approved final product, noncompounded, administered through DME, unit dose form, 15 mcg

● M J7606 Formoterol fumarate, inhalation solution, FDA approved final product, noncompounded, administered through DME, unit dose form, 20 mcg
Use this code for Perforomist.

M ☑ J7607 Levalbuterol, inhalation solution, compounded product, administered through DME, concentrated form, 0.5 mg

M ☑ J7608 Acetylcysteine, inhalation solution, FDA-approved final product, noncompounded, administered through DME, unit dose form, per g
Use this code for Acetadote, Mucomyst, Mucosil.
MED: 100-2,15,110.3

M ☑ J7609 Albuterol, inhalation solution, compounded product, administered through DME, unit dose, 1 mg

M ☑ J7610 Albuterol, inhalation solution, compounded product, administered through DME, concentrated form, 1 mg

○ M ☑ J7611 Albuterol, inhalation solution, FDA-approved final product, noncompounded, administered through DME, concentrated form, 1 mg
Use this code for Accuneb, Proventil, Respirol, Ventolin.
MED: 100-2,15,110.3

○ M ☑ J7612 Levalbuterol, inhalation solution, FDA-approved final product, noncompounded, administered through DME, concentrated form, 0.5 mg
Use this code for Xopenex HFA.
MED: 100-2,15,110.3

○ M ☑ J7613 Albuterol, inhalation solution, FDA-approved final product, noncompounded, administered through DME, unit dose, 1 mg
Use this code for Accuneb, Proventil, Respirol, Ventolin.
MED: 100-2,15,110.3

○ M ☑ **J7614** Levalbuterol, inhalation solution, FDA-approved final product, noncompounded, administered through DME, unit dose, 0.5 mg
Use this code for Xopenex.
MED: 100-2,15,110.3

M ☑ **J7615** Levalbuterol, inhalation solution, compounded product, administered through DME, unit dose, 0.5 mg

M ☑ **J7620** Albuterol, up to 2.5 mg and ipratropium bromide, up to 0.5 mg, FDA-approved final product, noncompounded, administered through DME
MED: 100-2,15,110.3

M ☑ **J7622** Beclomethasone, inhalation solution, compounded product, administered through DME, unit dose form, per mg
Use this code for Beclovent, Beconase.

M ☑ **J7624** Betamethasone, inhalation solution, compounded product, administered through DME, unit dose form, per mg

M ☑ **J7626** Budesonide, inhalation solution, FDA-approved final product, noncompounded, administered through DME, unit dose form, up to 0.5 mg
Use this code for Pulmicort, Pulmicort Flexhaler, Pulmicort Respules, Vanceril.

M ☑ **J7627** Budesonide, inhalation solution, compounded product, administered through DME, unit dose form, up to 0.5 mg

M ☑ **J7628** Bitolterol mesylate, inhalation solution, compounded product, administered through DME, concentrated form, per mg
MED: 100-2,15,110.3

M ☑ **J7629** Bitolterol mesylate, inhalation solution, compounded product, administered through DME, unit dose form, per mg
MED: 100-2,15,110.3

M ☑ **J7631** Cromolyn sodium, inhalation solution, FDA-approved final product, noncompounded, administered through DME, unit dose form, per 10 mg
Use this code for Intal, Nasalcrom
MED: 100-2,15,110.3

M ☑ **J7632** Cromolyn sodium, inhalation solution, compounded product, administered through DME, unit dose form, per 10 mg

M ☑ **J7633** Budesonide, inhalation solution, FDA-approved final product, noncompounded, administered through DME, concentrated form, per 0.25 mg
Use this code for Pulmicort, Pulmicort Flexhaler, Pulmicort Respules, Vanceril

M ☑ **J7634** Budesonide, inhalation solution, compounded product, administered through DME, concentrated form, per 0.25 mg

M ☑ **J7635** Atropine, inhalation solution, compounded product, administered through DME, concentrated form, per mg
MED: 100-2,15,110.3

M ☑ **J7636** Atropine, inhalation solution, compounded product, administered through DME, unit dose form, per mg
MED: 100-2,15,110.3

M ☑ **J7637** Dexamethasone, inhalation solution, compounded product, administered through DME, concentrated form, per mg
MED: 100-2,15,110.3

M ☑ **J7638** Dexamethasone, inhalation solution, compounded product, administered through DME, unit dose form, per mg
MED: 100-2,15,110.3

▲ M ☑ **J7639** Dornase alfa, inhalation solution, FDA-approved final product, noncompounded, administered through DME, unit dose form, per mg
Use this code for Pulmozyme.
MED: 100-2,15,110.3

E ☑ **J7640** Formoterol, inhalation solution, compounded product, administered through DME, unit dose form, 12 mcg

M ☑ **J7641** Flunisolide, inhalation solution, compounded product, administered through DME, unit dose, per mg
Use this code for Aerobid, Flunisolide.

M ☑ **J7642** Glycopyrrolate, inhalation solution, compounded product, administered through DME, concentrated form, per mg
MED: 100-2,15,110.3

M ☑ **J7643** Glycopyrrolate, inhalation solution, compounded product, administered through DME, unit dose form, per mg
MED: 100-2,15,110.3

M ☑ **J7644** Ipratropium bromide, inhalation solution, FDA-approved final product, noncompounded, administered through DME, unit dose form, per mg
Use this code for Atrovent.
MED: 100-2,15,110.3

M ☑ **J7645** Ipratropium bromide, inhalation solution, compounded product, administered through DME, unit dose form, per mg

M ☑ **J7647** Isoetharine HCl, inhalation solution, compounded product, administered through DME, concentrated form, per mg

M ☑ **J7648** Isoetharine HCl, inhalation solution, FDA-approved final product, noncompounded, administered through DME, concentrated form, per mg
Use this code for Beta-2.
MED: 100-2,15,110.3

M ☑ **J7649** Isoetharine HCl, inhalation solution, FDA-approved final product, noncompounded, administered through DME, unit dose form, per mg
MED: 100-2,15,110.3

M ☑ **J7650** Isoetharine HCl, inhalation solution, compounded product, administered through DME, unit dose form, per mg

M ☑ **J7657** Isoproterenol HCl, inhalation solution, compounded product, administered through DME, concentrated form, per mg

M ☑ **J7658** Isoproterenol HCl, inhalation solution, FDA-approved final product, noncompounded, administered through DME, concentrated form, per mg
Use this code for Isuprel HCl.
MED: 100-2,15,110.3

M ☑ **J7659** Isoproterenol HCl, inhalation solution, FDA-approved final product, noncompounded, administered through DME, unit dose form, per mg
Use this code for Isuprel HCl
MED: 100-2,15,110.3

M ☑ **J7660** Isoproterenol HCl, inhalation solution, compounded product, administered through DME, unit dose form, per mg

M ☑ **J7667** Metaproterenol sulfate, inhalation solution, compounded product, concentrated form, per 10 mg

M ☑ **J7668** Metaproterenol sulfate, inhalation solution, FDA-approved final product, noncompounded, administered through DME, concentrated form, per 10 mg
Use this code for Alupent
MED: 100-2,15,110.3

M ☑ **J7669** Metaproterenol sulfate, inhalation solution, FDA-approved final product, noncompounded, administered through DME, unit dose form, per 10 mg
Use this code for Alupent.
MED: 100-2,15,110.3

M ☑ **J7670** Metaproterenol sulfate, inhalation solution, compounded product, administered through DME, unit dose form, per 10 mg

N ☑ **J7674** Methacholine chloride administered as inhalation solution through a nebulizer, per 1 mg N1

M ☑ **J7676** Pentamidine isethionate, inhalation solution, compounded product, administered through DME, unit dose form, per 300 mg

M ☑ **J7680** Terbutaline sulfate, inhalation solution, compounded product, administered through DME, concentrated form, per mg
Use this code for Brethine.
MED: 100-2,15,110.3

M ☑ **J7681** Terbutaline sulfate, inhalation solution, compounded product, administered through DME, unit dose form, per mg
Use this code for Brethine.
MED: 100-2,15,110.3

M ☑ **J7682** Tobramycin, inhalation solution, FDA-approved final product, noncompounded, unit dose form, administered through DME, per 300 mg
Use this code for Tobi.
MED: 100-2,15,110.3

M ☑ **J7683** Triamcinolone, inhalation solution, compounded product, administered through DME, concentrated form, per mg
Use this code for Azmacort.
MED: 100-2,15,110.3

M ☑ **J7684** Triamcinolone, inhalation solution, compounded product, administered through DME, unit dose form, per mg
Use this code for Azmacort.
MED: 100-2,15,110.3

M ☑ **J7685** Tobramycin, inhalation solution, compounded product, administered through DME, unit dose form, per 300 mg

M **J7699** NOC drugs, inhalation solution administered through DME
MED: 100-2,15,110.3

N **J7799** NOC drugs, other than inhalation drugs, administered through DME N1
MED: 100-2,15,110.3

B **J8498** Antiemetic drug, rectal/suppository, not otherwise specified

E **J8499** Prescription drug, oral, nonchemotherapeutic, NOS
MED: 100-2,15,50

K ☑ **J8501** Aprepitant, oral, 5 mg K2
Use this code for Emend.
MED: 100-4,4,240; 100-4,17,80.2; 100-4,17,80.2.1; 100-4,17,80.2.4

K ☑ **J8510** Busulfan; oral, 2 mg K2
Use this code for Busulfex, Myleran.
MED: 100-2,15,50.5; 100-4,4,240; 100-4,17,80.1.1

E ☑ **J8515** Cabergoline, oral, 0.25 mg
Use this code for Dostinex.
MED: 100-2,15,50.5; 100-4,4,240

K ☑ **J8520** Capecitabine, oral, 150 mg K2
Use this code for Xeloda.
MED: 100-2,15,50.5; 100-4,4,240; 100-4,17,80.1.1

K ☑ **J8521** Capecitabine, oral, 500 mg K2
Use this code for Xeloda.
MED: 100-2,15,50.5; 100-4,4,240; 100-4,17,80.1.1

N ☑ **J8530** Cyclophosphamide; oral, 25 mg N1
Use this code for Cytoxan.
MED: 100-2,15,50.5; 100-4,4,240; 100-4,17,80.1.1

N ☑ **J8540** Dexamethasone, oral, 0.25 mg N1
Use this code for Decadron.

K ☑ **J8560** Etoposide; oral, 50 mg K2
Use this code for VePesid.
MED: 100-2,15,50.5; 100-4,4,240; 100-4,17,80.1.1

E ☑ **J8565** Gefitinib, oral, 250 mg
Use this code for Iressa.
MED: 100-4,4,240; 100-4,17,80.1.1

N **J8597** Antiemetic drug, oral, not otherwise specified N1

N ☑ **J8600** Melphalan; oral, 2 mg N1
Use this code for Alkeran.
MED: 100-2,15,50.5; 100-4,4,240; 100-4,17,80.1.1

N ☑ **J8610** Methotrexate; oral, 2.5 mg N1
Use this code for Trexall.
Methotrexate is an anti-metabolite used in the treatment of certain neoplastic diseases, severe psoriasis, and adult rheumatoid arthritis.
MED: 100-2,15,50.5; 100-4,4,240; 100-4,17,80.1.1

K ☑ **J8650** Nabilone, oral, 1 mg K2
Use this code for Cesamet

K ☑ **J8700** Temozolomide, oral, 5 mg K2
Use this code for Temodar.
MED: 100-2,15,50.5; 100-4,4,240

● K ☑ **J8705** Topotecan, oral, 0.25 mg K2
Use this code for Hycamtin.

B **J8999** Prescription drug, oral, chemotherapeutic, NOS
Determine if an alternative HCPCS Level II or a CPT code better describes the service being reported. This code should be used only if a more specific code is unavailable.
MED: 100-2,15,50.5; 100-4,4,240; 100-4,17,80.1.1; 100-4,17,80.1.2

CHEMOTHERAPY DRUGS J9000-J9999

These codes cover the cost of the chemotherapy drug only, not the administration.

▲ N ☑ **J9000** Injection, doxorubicin HCl, 10 mg N1 ⊘
Use this code for Adriamycin PFS, Adriamycin RDF, Rubex.
MED: 100-2,15,50; 100-4,17,80.2

▲ K ☑ **J9001** Injection, doxorubicin HCl, all lipid formulations, 10 mg K2 ⊘
Use this code for Doxil.
MED: 100-2,15,50; 100-4,17,80.2

▲ K ☑ **J9010** Injection, alemtuzumab, 10 mg K2 ⊘
Use this code for Campath.

▲ K ☑ **J9015** Injection, aldesleukin, per single use vial K2 ⊘
Use this code for Proleukin, IL-2, Interleukin.
MED: 100-2,15,50

▲ K ☑ **J9017** Injection, arsenic trioxide, 1 mg K2 ⊘
Use this code for Trisenox.
AHA: 2Q,'02,8

▲ K ☑ **J9020** Injection, asparaginase, 10,000 units K2 ⊘
Use this code for Elspar.
MED: 100-2,15,50

K ☑ **J9025** Injection, azacitidine, 1 mg K2 ⊘
Use this code for Vidaza.

K ☑ **J9027** Injection, clofarabine, 1 mg K2 ⊘
Use this code for Clolar.

K ☑ **J9031** BCG (intravesical) per instillation K2
Use this code for Tice BCG, PACIS BCG, TheraCys.
MED: 100-2,15,50

● G ☑ **J9033** Injection, bendamustine HCl, 1 mg K2
Use this code for TREANDA.

K ☑ **J9035** Injection, bevacizumab, 10 mg K2 ⊘
Use this code for Avastin.

▲ N ☑ **J9040** Injection, bleomycin sulfate, 15 units N1 ⊘
Use this code for Blenoxane.
MED: 100-2,15,50

K ☑ **J9041** Injection, bortezomib, 0.1 mg K2 ⊘
Use this code for Velcade.

▲ N ☑ **J9045** Injection, carboplatin, 50 mg N1 ⊘
Use this code for Paraplatin, Platinol AQ.
MED: 100-2,15,50

▲ K ☑ **J9050** Injection, carmustine, 100 mg K2 ⊘
Use this code for BiCNU.
MED: 100-2,15,50; 100-4,17,80.2

K ☑ **J9055** Injection, cetuximab, 10 mg K2 ⊘
Use this code for Erbitux.

N ☑ **J9060** Cisplatin, powder or solution, per 10 mg N1 ⊘
Use this code for Plantinol AQ.
MED: 100-2,15,50; 100-4,17,80.2

N ☑ **J9062** Cisplatin, 50 mg N1 ⊘
Use this code for Plantinol AQ.
MED: 100-2,15,50; 100-4,17,80.2

K ☑ **J9065** Injection, cladribine, per 1 mg K2 ⊘
Use this code for Leustatin.
MED: 100-2,15,50

N ☑ **J9070** Cyclophosphamide, 100 mg N1 ⊘
Use this code for Endoxan-Asta.
MED: 100-2,15,50; 100-4,17,80.2

N ☑ **J9080** Cyclophosphamide, 200 mg N1 ⊘
Use this code for Cytoxan, Neosar.
MED: 100-2,15,50; 100-4,17,80.2

N ☑ **J9090** Cyclophosphamide, 500 mg N1 ⊘
Use this code for Cytoxan, Neosar.
MED: 100-2,15,50; 100-4,17,80.2

N ☑ **J9091** Cyclophosphamide, 1 g N1 ⊘
Use this code for Cytoxan, Neosar.
MED: 100-2,15,50; 100-4,17,80.2

N ☑ **J9092** Cyclophosphamide, 2 g N1 ⊘
Use this code for Cytoxan, Neosar.
MED: 100-2,15,50; 100-4,17,80.2

N ☑ **J9093** Cyclophosphamide, lyophilized, 100 mg N1 ⊘
Use this code for Cytoxan Lyophilized.
MED: 100-2,15,50; 100-4,17,80.2

N ☑ **J9094** Cyclophosphamide, lyophilized, 200 mg N1 ⊘
Use this code for Cytoxan Lyophilized.
MED: 100-2,15,50; 100-4,17,80.2

N ☑ **J9095** Cyclophosphamide, lyophilized, 500 mg N1 ⊘
Use this code for Cytoxan Lyophilized.
MED: 100-2,15,50; 100-4,17,80.2

N ☑ **J9096** Cyclophosphamide, lyophilized, 1 g N1 ⊘
Use this code for Cytoxan Lyophilized.
MED: 100-2,15,50; 100-4,17,80.2

N ☑ **J9097** Cyclophosphamide, lyophilized, 2 g N1 ⊘
Use this code for Cytoxan Lyophilized.
MED: 100-2,15,50; 100-4,17,80.2

▲ K ☑ **J9098** Injection, cytarabine liposome, 10 mg K2 ⊘
Use this code for Depocyt.

▲ N ☑ **J9100** Injection, cytarabine, 100 mg N1 ⊘
Use this code for Cytosar-U, Ara-C, Tarabin CFS.
MED: 100-2,15,50

▲ N ☑ **J9110** Injection cytarabine 500 mg N1 ⊘
Use this code for Cytosar-U.
MED: 100-2,15,50

▲ K ☑ **J9120** Injection, dactinomycin, 0.5 mg K2 ⊘
Use this code for Cosmegen.
MED: 100-2,15,50

N ☑ **J9130** Dacarbazine, 100 mg N1 ⊘
Use this code for DTIC-Dome.
MED: 100-2,15,50; 100-4,17,80.2

N ☑ **J9140** Dacarbazine, 200 mg N1 ⊘
Use this code for DTIC-Dome.
MED: 100-2,15,50; 100-4,17,80.2

▲ K ☑ **J9150** Injection, daunorubicin, 10 mg K2 ⊘
Use this code for Cerubidine.
MED: 100-2,15,50

▲ K ☑ **J9151** Injection, daunorubicin citrate, liposomal formulation, 10 mg K2 ⊘
Use this code for Daunoxome.
MED: 100-2,15,50

▲ K ☑ **J9160** Injection, denileukin diftitox, 300 mcg K2 ⊘
Use this code for Ontak.

▲ K ☑ **J9165** Injection, diethylstilbestrol diphosphate, 250 mg K2
MED: 100-2,15,50

▲ K ☑ **J9170** Injection, docetaxel, 20 mg K2 ⊘
Use this code for Taxotere.
MED: 100-2,15,50

N ☑ **J9175** Injection, Elliotts' B solution, 1 ml N1
MED: 100-2,15,50

K ☑ **J9178** Injection, epirubicin HCl, 2 mg K2 ⊘
Use this code for Ellence.
MED: 100-4,17,80.2

▲ N ☑ **J9181** Injection, etoposide, 10 mg N1 ⊘
Use this code for VePesid, Toposar.
MED: 100-2,15,50

~~J9182 Etoposide, 100 mg~~
See J9181

▲ K ☑ **J9185** Injection, fludarabine phosphate, 50 mg K2 ⊘
Use this code for Fludara.
MED: 100-2,15,50

▲ N ☑ **J9190** Injection, fluorouracil, 500 mg N1
Use this code for Adrucil.
MED: 100-2,15,50

▲ K ☑ **J9200** Injection, floxuridine, 500 mg K2 ⊘
Use this code for FUDR.
MED: 100-2,15,50

▲ K ☑ **J9201** Injection, gemcitabine HCl, 200 mg K2 ⊘
Use this code for Gemzar.
MED: 100-2,15,50

K ☑ **J9202** Goserelin acetate implant, per 3.6 mg K2
Use this code for Zoladex.
MED: 100-2,15,50

▲ K ☑ **J9206** Injection, irinotecan, 20 mg K2 ⊘
Use this code for Camptosar.
MED: 100-2,15,50

● G ☑ **J9207** Injection, ixabepilone, 1 mg K2
Use this code for IXEMPRA.

▲ K ☑ **J9208** Injection, ifosfamide, 1 g K2 ⊘
Use this code for IFEX, Mitoxana.
MED: 100-2,15,50

▲ K ☑ **J9209** Injection, mesna, 200 mg K2
Use this code for Mesnex.
MED: 100-2,15,50

▲ K ☑ **J9211** Injection, idarubicin HCl, 5 mg K2 ⊘
Use this code for Idamycin.
MED: 100-2,15,50

N ☑ **J9212** Injection, interferon alfacon-1, recombinant, 1 mcg N1
Use this code for Infergen.
MED: 100-2,15,50

▲ K ☑ **J9213** Injection, interferon, alfa-2a, recombinant, 3 million units K2
Use this code for Roferon-A.
MED: 100-2,15,50

▲ K ☑ **J9214** Injection, interferon, alfa-2b, recombinant, 1 million units K2
Use this code for Intron A, Rebetron Kit.
MED: 100-2,15,50

▲ K ☑ **J9215** Injection, interferon, alfa-N3, (human leukocyte derived), 250,000 IU K2
Use this code for Alferon N.
MED: 100-2,15,50

▲ K ☑ **J9216** Injection, interferon, gamma-1b, 3 million units K2
Use this code for Actimmune.
MED: 100-2,15,50

K ☑ **J9217** Leuprolide acetate (for depot suspension), 7.5 mg K2
Use this code for Lupron Depot, Eligard.
MED: 100-2,15,50

K ☑ **J9218** Leuprolide acetate, per 1 mg K2
Use this code for Lupron.
MED: 100-2,15,50

K ☑ **J9219** Leuprolide acetate implant, 65 mg K2
Use this code for Lupron Implant.
MED: 100-2,15,50
AHA: 4Q,'01,5

G ☑ **J9225** Histrelin implant (Vantas), 50 mg K2 ⊘
MED: 100-2,15,50

G ☑ **J9226** Histrelin implant (Supprelin LA), 50 mg K2

▲ K ☑ **J9230** Injection, mechlorethamine HCl, (nitrogen mustard), 10 mg K2 ⊘
Use this code for Mustargen.
MED: 100-2,15,50; 100-4,17,80.2

K ☑ **J9245** Injection, melphalan HCl, 50 mg K2 ⊘
Use this code for Alkeran, L-phenylalanine mustard.
MED: 100-2,15,50

N ☑ **J9250** Methotrexate sodium, 5 mg N1
Use this code for Folex, Folex PFS, Methotrexate LPF.
MED: 100-2,15,50

N ☑ **J9260** Methotrexate sodium, 50 mg N1
Use this code for Folex, Folex PFS, Methotrexate LPF.
MED: 100-2,15,50

G ☑ **J9261** Injection, nelarabine, 50 mg K2 ⊘
Use this code for Arranon

K ☑ **J9263** Injection, oxaliplatin, 0.5 mg K2 ⊘
Use this code for Eloxatin.

K ☑ **J9264** Injection, paclitaxel protein-bound particles, 1 mg K2 ⊘
Use this code for Abraxane.

▲ K ☑ **J9265** Injection, paclitaxel, 30 mg K2 ⊘
Use this code for Taxol, Nov-Onxol.
MED: 100-2,15,50

▲ K ☑ **J9266** Injection, pegaspargase, per single dose vial K2 ⊘
Use this code for Oncaspar.
MED: 100-2,15,50
AHA: 2Q,'02,8

▲ K ☑ **J9268** Injection, pentostatin, 10 mg K2 ⊘
Use this code for Nipent.
MED: 100-2,15,50

▲ K ☑ **J9270** Injection, plicamycin, 2.5 mg K2 ⊘
Use this code for Mithacin.
MED: 100-2,15,50

K ☑ **J9280** Mitomycin, 5 mg K2 ⊘
Use this code for Mutamycin.
MED: 100-2,15,50

K ☑ **J9290** Mitomycin, 20 mg K2 ⊘
Use this code for Mutamycin.
MED: 100-2,15,50

K ☑ **J9291** Mitomycin, 40 mg K2 ⊘
Use this code for Mutamycin.
MED: 100-2,15,50

K ☑ **J9293** Injection, mitoxantrone HCl, per 5 mg K2 ⊘
Use this code for Navantrone.
MED: 100-2,15,50

▲ K ☑ **J9300** Injection, gemtuzumab ozogamicin, 5 mg K2 ⊘
Use this code for Mylotarg.
AHA: 2Q,'02,8

K ☑ **J9303** Injection, panitumumab, 10 mg K2 ⊘
Use this code for Vectibix.

K ☑ **J9305** Injection, pemetrexed, 10 mg K2 ⊘
Use this code for Alimta.

▲ K ☑ **J9310** Injection, rituximab, 100 mg K2 ⊘
Use this code for RituXan.
MED: 100-2,15,50

▲ K ☑ **J9320** Injection, streptozocin, 1 g K2 ⊘
Use this code for Zanosar.
MED: 100-2,15,50; 100-4,17,80.2

● G ☑ **J9330** Injection, temsirolimus, 1 mg K2
Use this code for TORISEL.

▲ K ☑ **J9340** Injection, thiotepa, 15 mg K2 ⊘
Use this code for Thioplex.
MED: 100-2,15,50

▲ K ☑ **J9350** Injection, topotecan, 4 mg K2 ⊘
Use this code for Hycamtin.
MED: 100-2,15,50

▲ K ☑ **J9355** Injection, trastuzumab, 10 mg K2 ⊘
Use this code for Herceptin.

▲ K ☑ **J9357** Injection, valrubicin, intravesical, 200 mg K2 ⊘
Use this code for Valstar.
MED: 100-2,15,50

▲ N ☑ **J9360** Injection, vinblastine sulfate, 1 mg N1 ⊘
Use this code for Velban.
MED: 100-2,15,50

N ☑ **J9370** Vincristine sulfate, 1 mg N1 ⊘
Use this code for Oncovin, Vincasar PFS.
MED: 100-2,15,50

N ☑ **J9375** Vincristine sulfate, 2 mg N1 ⊘
Use this code for Oncovin, Vincasar PFS.
MED: 100-2,15,50

N ☑ **J9380** Vincristine sulfate, 5 mg N1 ⊘
Use this code for Oncovin.
MED: 100-2,15,50

▲ K ☑ **J9390** Injection, vinorelbine tartrate, 10 mg K2 ⊘
Use this code for Navelbine.
MED: 100-2,15,50

K ☑ **J9395** Injection, fulvestrant, 25 mg K2 ⊘
Use this code for Fastodex.

▲ K ☑ **J9600** Injection, porfimer sodium, 75 mg K2 ⊘
Use this code for Photofrin.
MED: 100-2,15,50

N **J9999** Not otherwise classified, antineoplastic drugs N1
Determine if an alternative HCPCS Level II or a CPT code better describes the service being reported. This code should be used only if a more specific code is unavailable.
MED: 100-2,15,50; 100-3,110.2

TEMPORARY CODES K0000-K9999

The K codes were established for use by the DME Medicare Administrative Contractors (DME MACs). The K codes are developed when the currently existing permanent national codes for supplies and certain product categories do not include the codes needed to implement a DME MAC medical review policy.

K CODES ASSIGNED TO DURABLE MEDICAL EQUIPMENT ADMINISTRATIVE CONTRACTORS (DME MACS)

WHEELCHAIR AND WHEELCHAIR ACCESSORIES

- Y **K0001** Standard wheelchair
- Y **K0002** Standard hemi (low seat) wheelchair
- Y **K0003** Lightweight wheelchair
- Y **K0004** High strength, lightweight wheelchair
- Y **K0005** Ultralightweight wheelchair
- Y **K0006** Heavy-duty wheelchair
- Y **K0007** Extra heavy-duty wheelchair
- Y **K0009** Other manual wheelchair/base
- Y **K0010** Standard-weight frame motorized/power wheelchair
- Y **K0011** Standard-weight frame motorized/power wheelchair with programmable control parameters for speed adjustment, tremor dampening, acceleration control and braking
- Y **K0012** Lightweight portable motorized/power wheelchair
- Y **K0014** Other motorized/power wheelchair base
- Y ☑ **K0015** Detachable, nonadjustable height armrest, each
- Y ☑ **K0017** Detachable, adjustable height armrest, base, each
- Y ☑ **K0018** Detachable, adjustable height armrest, upper portion, each
- Y ☑ **K0019** Arm pad, each
- Y ☑ **K0020** Fixed, adjustable height armrest, pair
- Y ☑ **K0037** High mount flip-up footrest, each
- Y ☑ **K0038** Leg strap, each
- Y ☑ **K0039** Leg strap, H style, each
- Y ☑ **K0040** Adjustable angle footplate, each
- Y ☑ **K0041** Large size footplate, each
- Y ☑ **K0042** Standard size footplate, each
- Y ☑ **K0043** Footrest, lower extension tube, each
- Y ☑ **K0044** Footrest, upper hanger bracket, each
- Y **K0045** Footrest, complete assembly
- Y ☑ **K0046** Elevating legrest, lower extension tube, each
- Y ☑ **K0047** Elevating legrest, upper hanger bracket, each
- Y **K0050** Ratchet assembly
- Y ☑ **K0051** Cam release assembly, footrest or legrest, each
- Y ☑ **K0052** Swingaway, detachable footrests, each
- Y ☑ **K0053** Elevating footrests, articulating (telescoping), each
- Y ☑ **K0056** Seat height less than 17 in or equal to or greater than 21 in for a high-strength, lightweight, or ultralightweight wheelchair
- Y ☑ **K0065** Spoke protectors, each
- Y ☑ **K0069** Rear wheel assembly, complete, with solid tire, spokes or molded, each
- Y ☑ **K0070** Rear wheel assembly, complete, with pneumatic tire, spokes or molded, each
- Y ☑ **K0071** Front caster assembly, complete, with pneumatic tire, each
- Y ☑ **K0072** Front caster assembly, complete, with semipneumatic tire, each
- Y ☑ **K0073** Caster pin lock, each
- Y ☑ **K0077** Front caster assembly, complete, with solid tire, each
- Y **K0098** Drive belt for power wheelchair
- Y ☑ **K0105** IV hanger, each
- Y **K0108** Wheelchair component or accessory, not otherwise specified
- Y **K0195** Elevating legrests, pair (for use with capped rental wheelchair base)
  MED: 100-3,230.10
- Y **K0455** Infusion pump used for uninterrupted parenteral administration of medication, (e.g., epoprostenol or treprostinol)
  MED: 100-3,280.14
- Y **K0462** Temporary replacement for patient-owned equipment being repaired, any type
  MED: 100-4,20,40.1
- Y ☑ **K0552** Supplies for external drug infusion pump, syringe type cartridge, sterile, each
  MED: 100-3,280.14
- Y ☑ **K0601** Replacement battery for external infusion pump owned by patient, silver oxide, 1.5 volt, each
  AHA: 2Q,'03,7
- Y ☑ **K0602** Replacement battery for external infusion pump owned by patient, silver oxide, 3 volt, each
  AHA: 2Q,'03,7
- Y ☑ **K0603** Replacement battery for external infusion pump owned by patient, alkaline, 1.5 volt, each
  AHA: 2Q,'03,7
- Y ☑ **K0604** Replacement battery for external infusion pump owned by patient, lithium, 3.6 volt, each
  AHA: 2Q,'03,7
- Y ☑ **K0605** Replacement battery for external infusion pump owned by patient, lithium, 4.5 volt, each
  AHA: 2Q,'03,7
- Y **K0606** Automatic external defibrillator, with integrated electrocardiogram analysis, garment type
  AHA: 4Q,'03,4
- Y ☑ **K0607** Replacement battery for automated external defibrillator, garment type only, each
  AHA: 4Q,'03,4
- Y ☑ **K0608** Replacement garment for use with automated external defibrillator, each
  AHA: 4Q,'03,4
- Y ☑ **K0609** Replacement electrodes for use with automated external defibrillator, garment type only, each
  AHA: 4Q,'03,4
- ▲ Y **K0669** Wheelchair accessory, wheelchair seat or back cushion, does not meet specific code criteria or no written coding verification from DME PDAC
- ● A ☑ **K0672** Addition to lower extremity orthotic, removable soft interface, all components, replacement only, each
- Y **K0730** Controlled dose inhalation drug delivery system

Y **K0733** Power wheelchair accessory, 12 to 24 amp hour sealed lead acid battery, each (e.g., gel cell, absorbed glassmat) ♿

Y **K0734** Skin protection wheelchair seat cushion, adjustable, width less than 22 in, any depth

Y **K0735** Skin protection wheelchair seat cushion, adjustable, width 22 in or greater, any depth

Y **K0736** Skin protection and positioning wheelchair seat cushion, adjustable, width less than 22 in, any depth

Y **K0737** Skin protection and positioning wheelchair seat cushion, adjustable, width 22 in or greater, any depth

Y **K0738** Portable gaseous oxygen system, rental; home compressor used to fill portable oxygen cylinders; includes portable containers, regulator, flowmeter, humidifier, cannula or mask, and tubing

Y **K0800** Power operated vehicle, group 1 standard, patient weight capacity up to and including 300 pounds ♿

Y **K0801** Power operated vehicle, group 1 heavy-duty, patient weight capacity 301 to 450 pounds ♿

Y **K0802** Power operated vehicle, group 1 very heavy-duty, patient weight capacity 451 to 600 pounds ♿

Y **K0806** Power operated vehicle, group 2 standard, patient weight capacity up to and including 300 pounds ♿

Y **K0807** Power operated vehicle, group 2 heavy-duty, patient weight capacity 301 to 450 pounds ♿

Y **K0808** Power operated vehicle, group 2 very heavy-duty, patient weight capacity 451 to 600 pounds ♿

Y **K0812** Power operated vehicle, not otherwise classified ♿

Y **K0813** Power wheelchair, group 1 standard, portable, sling/solid seat and back, patient weight capacity up to and including 300 pounds ♿

Y **K0814** Power wheelchair, group 1 standard, portable, captain's chair, patient weight capacity up to and including 300 pounds ♿

Y **K0815** Power wheelchair, group 1 standard, sling/solid seat and back, patient weight capacity up to and including 300 pounds ♿

Y **K0816** Power wheelchair, group 1 standard, captain's chair, patient weight capacity up to and including 300 pounds ♿

Y **K0820** Power wheelchair, group 2 standard, portable, sling/solid seat/back, patient weight capacity up to and including 300 pounds ♿

Y **K0821** Power wheelchair, group 2 standard, portable, captain's chair, patient weight capacity up to and including 300 pounds ♿

Y **K0822** Power wheelchair, group 2 standard, sling/solid seat/back, patient weight capacity up to and including 300 pounds ♿

Y **K0823** Power wheelchair, group 2 standard, captain's chair, patient weight capacity up to and including 300 pounds ♿

Y **K0824** Power wheelchair, group 2 heavy-duty, sling/solid seat/back, patient weight capacity 301 to 450 pounds ♿

Y **K0825** Power wheelchair, group 2 heavy-duty, captain's chair, patient weight capacity 301 to 450 pounds ♿

Y **K0826** Power wheelchair, group 2 very heavy-duty, sling/solid seat/back, patient weight capacity 451 to 600 pounds ♿

Y **K0827** Power wheelchair, group 2 very heavy-duty, captain's chair, patient weight capacity 451 to 600 pounds ♿

Y **K0828** Power wheelchair, group 2 extra heavy-duty, sling/solid seat/back, patient weight capacity 601 pounds or more ♿

Y **K0829** Power wheelchair, group 2 extra heavy-duty, captain's chair, patient weight 601 pounds or more ♿

Y **K0830** Power wheelchair, group 2 standard, seat elevator, sling/solid seat/back, patient weight capacity up to and including 300 pounds ♿

Y **K0831** Power wheelchair, group 2 standard, seat elevator, captain's chair, patient weight capacity up to and including 300 pounds ♿

Y **K0835** Power wheelchair, group 2 standard, single power option, sling/solid seat/back, patient weight capacity up to and including 300 pounds ♿

Y **K0836** Power wheelchair, group 2 standard, single power option, captain's chair, patient weight capacity up to and including 300 pounds ♿

Y **K0837** Power wheelchair, group 2 heavy-duty, single power option, sling/solid seat/back, patient weight capacity 301 to 450 pounds ♿

Y **K0838** Power wheelchair, group 2 heavy-duty, single power option, captain's chair, patient weight capacity 301 to 450 pounds ♿

Y **K0839** Power wheelchair, group 2 very heavy-duty, single power option sling/solid seat/back, patient weight capacity 451 to 600 pounds ♿

Y **K0840** Power wheelchair, group 2 extra heavy-duty, single power option, sling/solid seat/back, patient weight capacity 601 pounds or more ♿

Y **K0841** Power wheelchair, group 2 standard, multiple power option, sling/solid seat/back, patient weight capacity up to and including 300 pounds ♿

Y **K0842** Power wheelchair, group 2 standard, multiple power option, captain's chair, patient weight capacity up to and including 300 pounds ♿

Y **K0843** Power wheelchair, group 2 heavy-duty, multiple power option, sling/solid seat/back, patient weight capacity 301 to 450 pounds ♿

Y **K0848** Power wheelchair, group 3 standard, sling/solid seat/back, patient weight capacity up to and including 300 pounds ♿

Y **K0849** Power wheelchair, group 3 standard, captain's chair, patient weight capacity up to and including 300 pounds ♿

Y **K0850** Power wheelchair, group 3 heavy-duty, sling/solid seat/back, patient weight capacity 301 to 450 pounds ♿

Y **K0851** Power wheelchair, group 3 heavy-duty, captain's chair, patient weight capacity 301 to 450 pounds ♿

Y **K0852** Power wheelchair, group 3 very heavy-duty, sling/solid seat/back, patient weight capacity 451 to 600 pounds ♿

Y **K0853** Power wheelchair, group 3 very heavy-duty, captain's chair, patient weight capacity 451 to 600 pounds ♿

Y **K0854** Power wheelchair, group 3 extra heavy-duty, sling/solid seat/back, patient weight capacity 601 pounds or more ♿

Y **K0855** Power wheelchair, group 3 extra heavy duty, captain's chair, patient weight capacity 601 pounds or more ♿

Y **K0856** Power wheelchair, group 3 standard, single power option, sling/solid seat/back, patient weight capacity up to and including 300 pounds ♿

Y **K0857** Power wheelchair, group 3 standard, single power option, captain's chair, patient weight capacity up to and including 300 pounds ♿

Y **K0858** Power wheelchair, group 3 heavy-duty, single power option, sling/solid seat/back, patient weight 301 to 450 pounds ♿

Y **K0859** Power wheelchair, group 3 heavy-duty, single power option, captain's chair, patient weight capacity 301 to 450 pounds ♿

Y **K0860** Power wheelchair, group 3 very heavy-duty, single power option, sling/solid seat/back, patient weight capacity 451 to 600 pounds ♿

Y **K0861** Power wheelchair, group 3 standard, multiple power option, sling/solid seat/back, patient weight capacity up to and including 300 pounds ♿

Y **K0862** Power wheelchair, group 3 heavy-duty, multiple power option, sling/solid seat/back, patient weight capacity 301 to 450 pounds ♿

Y **K0863** Power wheelchair, group 3 very heavy-duty, multiple power option, sling/solid seat/back, patient weight capacity 451 to 600 pounds ♿

Y **K0864** Power wheelchair, group 3 extra heavy-duty, multiple power option, sling/solid seat/back, patient weight capacity 601 pounds or more ♿

Y **K0868** Power wheelchair, group 4 standard, sling/solid seat/back, patient weight capacity up to and including 300 pounds ♿

Y **K0869** Power wheelchair, group 4 standard, captain's chair, patient weight capacity up to and including 300 pounds ♿

Y **K0870** Power wheelchair, group 4 heavy-duty, sling/solid seat/back, patient weight capacity 301 to 450 pounds ♿

Y **K0871** Power wheelchair, group 4 very heavy-duty, sling/solid seat/back, patient weight capacity 451 to 600 pounds ♿

Y **K0877** Power wheelchair, group 4 standard, single power option, sling/solid seat/back, patient weight capacity up to and including 300 pounds ♿

Y **K0878** Power wheelchair, group 4 standard, single power option, captain's chair, patient weight capacity up to and including 300 pounds ♿

Y **K0879** Power wheelchair, group 4 heavy-duty, single power option, sling/solid seat/back, patient weight capacity 301 to 450 pounds ♿

Y **K0880** Power wheelchair, group 4 very heavy-duty, single power option, sling/solid seat/back, patient weight 451 to 600 pounds ♿

Y **K0884** Power wheelchair, group 4 standard, multiple power option, sling/solid seat/back, patient weight capacity up to and including 300 pounds ♿

Y **K0885** Power wheelchair, group 4 standard, multiple power option, captain's chair, patient weight capacity up to and including 300 pounds ♿

Y **K0886** Power wheelchair, group 4 heavy-duty, multiple power option, sling/solid seat/back, patient weight capacity 301 to 450 pounds ♿

Y **K0890** Power wheelchair, group 5 pediatric, single power option, sling/solid seat/back, patient weight capacity up to and including 125 pounds ♿

Y **K0891** Power wheelchair, group 5 pediatric, multiple power option, sling/solid seat/back, patient weight capacity up to and including 125 pounds ♿

Y **K0898** Power wheelchair, not otherwise classified ♿

▲ Y **K0899** Power mobility device, not coded by DME PDAC or does not meet criteria ♿

ORTHOTIC PROCEDURES AND DEVICES L0000-L4999

L codes include orthotic and prosthetic procedures and devices, as well as scoliosis equipment, orthopedic shoes, and prosthetic implants.

ORTHOTIC DEVICES - SPINAL

CERVICAL

A **L0112** Cranial cervical orthotic, congenital torticollis type, with or without soft interface material, adjustable range of motion joint, custom fabricated

● A **L0113** Cranial cervical orthotic, torticollis type, with or without joint, with or without soft interface material, prefabricated, includes fitting and adjustment

A **L0120** Cervical, flexible, nonadjustable (foam collar)

A **L0130** Cervical, flexible, thermoplastic collar, molded to patient

A **L0140** Cervical, semi-rigid, adjustable (plastic collar)

A **L0150** Cervical, semi-rigid, adjustable molded chin cup (plastic collar with mandibular/occipital piece)

A **L0160** Cervical, semi-rigid, wire frame occipital/mandibular support

A **L0170** Cervical, collar, molded to patient model

A **L0172** Cervical, collar, semi-rigid thermoplastic foam, 2 piece

A **L0174** Cervical, collar, semi-rigid, thermoplastic foam, 2 piece with thoracic extension

MULTIPLE POST COLLAR

A **L0180** Cervical, multiple post collar, occipital/mandibular supports, adjustable

A **L0190** Cervical, multiple post collar, occipital/mandibular supports, adjustable cervical bars (SOMI, Guilford, Taylor types)

A **L0200** Cervical, multiple post collar, occipital/mandibular supports, adjustable cervical bars, and thoracic extension

THORACIC

A **L0210** Thoracic, rib belt

A **L0220** Thoracic, rib belt, custom fabricated

A **L0430** Spinal orthotic, anterior-posterior-lateral control, with interface material, custom fitted (DeWall Posture Protector only)

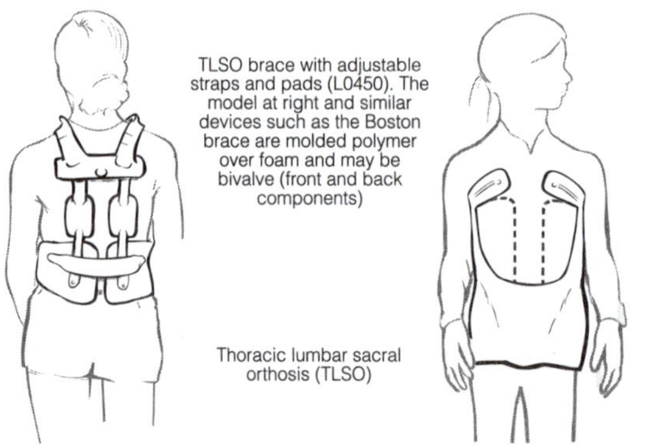

TLSO brace with adjustable straps and pads (L0450). The model at right and similar devices such as the Boston brace are molded polymer over foam and may be bivalve (front and back components)

Thoracic lumbar sacral orthosis (TLSO)

A **L0450** Thoracic-lumbar-sacral orthotic (TLSO), flexible, provides trunk support, upper thoracic region, produces intracavitary pressure to reduce load on the intervertebral disks with rigid stays or panel(s), includes shoulder straps and closures, prefabricated, includes fitting and adjustment

A **L0452** Thoracic-lumbar-sacral orthotic (TLSO), flexible, provides trunk support, upper thoracic region, produces intracavitary pressure to reduce load on the intervertebral disks with rigid stays or panel(s), includes shoulder straps and closures, custom fabricated

A **L0454** Thoracic-lumbar-sacral orthotic (TLSO) flexible, provides trunk support, extends from sacrococcygeal junction to above T-9 vertebra, restricts gross trunk motion in the sagittal plane, produces intracavitary pressure to reduce load on the intervertebral disks with rigid stays or panel(s), includes shoulder straps and closures, prefabricated, includes fitting and adjustment

A **L0456** Thoracic-lumbar-sacral orthotic (TLSO), flexible, provides trunk support, thoracic region, rigid posterior panel and soft anterior apron, extends from the sacrococcygeal junction and terminates just inferior to the scapular spine, restricts gross trunk motion in the sagittal plane, produces intracavitary pressure to reduce load on the intervertebral disks, includes straps and closures, prefabricated, includes fitting and adjustment

A **L0458** Thoracic-lumbar-sacral orthotic (TLSO), triplanar control, modular segmented spinal system, 2 rigid plastic shells, posterior extends from the sacrococcygeal junction and terminates just inferior to the scapular spine, anterior extends from the symphysis pubis to the xiphoid, soft liner, restricts gross trunk motion in the sagittal, coronal, and transverse planes, lateral strength is provided by overlapping plastic and stabilizing closures, includes straps and closures, prefabricated, includes fitting and adjustment

A **L0460** Thoracic-lumbar-sacral orthotic (TLSO), triplanar control, modular segmented spinal system, 2 rigid plastic shells, posterior extends from the sacrococcygeal junction and terminates just inferior to the scapular spine, anterior extends from the symphysis pubis to the sternal notch, soft liner, restricts gross trunk motion in the sagittal, coronal, and transverse planes, lateral strength is provided by overlapping plastic and stabilizing closures, includes straps and closures, prefabricated, includes fitting and adjustment ♿

A **L0462** Thoracic-lumbar-sacral orthotic (TLSO), triplanar control, modular segmented spinal system, 3 rigid plastic shells, posterior extends from the sacrococcygeal junction and terminates just inferior to the scapular spine, anterior extends from the symphysis pubis to the sternal notch, soft liner, restricts gross trunk motion in the sagittal, coronal, and transverse planes, lateral strength is provided by overlapping plastic and stabilizing closures, includes straps and closures, prefabricated, includes fitting and adjustment ♿

A **L0464** Thoracic-lumbar-sacral orthotic (TLSO), triplanar control, modular segmented spinal system, 4 rigid plastic shells, posterior extends from sacrococcygeal junction and terminates just inferior to scapular spine, anterior extends from symphysis pubis to the sternal notch, soft liner, restricts gross trunk motion in sagittal, coronal, and transverse planes, lateral strength is provided by overlapping plastic and stabilizing closures, includes straps and closures, prefabricated, includes fitting and adjustment ♿

A **L0466** Thoracic-lumbar-sacral orthotic (TLSO), sagittal control, rigid posterior frame and flexible soft anterior apron with straps, closures and padding, restricts gross trunk motion in sagittal plane, produces intracavitary pressure to reduce load on intervertebral disks, includes fitting and shaping the frame, prefabricated, includes fitting and adjustment ♿

A **L0468** Thoracic-lumbar-sacral orthotic (TLSO), sagittal-coronal control, rigid posterior frame and flexible soft anterior apron with straps, closures and padding, extends from sacrococcygeal junction over scapulae, lateral strength provided by pelvic, thoracic, and lateral frame pieces, restricts gross trunk motion in sagittal, and coronal planes, produces intracavitary pressure to reduce load on intervertebral disks, includes fitting and shaping the frame, prefabricated, includes fitting and adjustment ♿

A **L0470** Thoracic-lumbar-sacral orthotic (TLSO), triplanar control, rigid posterior frame and flexible soft anterior apron with straps, closures and padding, extends from sacrococcygeal junction to scapula, lateral strength provided by pelvic, thoracic, and lateral frame pieces, rotational strength provided by subclavicular extensions, restricts gross trunk motion in sagittal, coronal, and transverse planes, produces intracavitary pressure to reduce load on the intervertebral disks, includes fitting and shaping the frame, prefabricated, includes fitting and adjustment ♿

A **L0472** Thoracic-lumbar-sacral orthotic (TLSO), triplanar control, hyperextension, rigid anterior and lateral frame extends from symphysis pubis to sternal notch with 2 anterior components (one pubic and one sternal), posterior and lateral pads with straps and closures, limits spinal flexion, restricts gross trunk motion in sagittal, coronal, and transverse planes, includes fitting and shaping the frame, prefabricated, includes fitting and adjustment ♿

A **L0480** Thoracic-lumbar-sacral orthotic (TLSO), triplanar control, 1 piece rigid plastic shell without interface liner, with multiple straps and closures, posterior extends from sacrococcygeal junction and terminates just inferior to scapular spine, anterior extends from symphysis pubis to sternal notch, anterior or posterior opening, restricts gross trunk motion in sagittal, coronal, and transverse planes, includes a carved plaster or CAD-CAM model, custom fabricated ♿

A **L0482** Thoracic-lumbar-sacral orthotic (TLSO), triplanar control, 1 piece rigid plastic shell with interface liner, multiple straps and closures, posterior extends from sacrococcygeal junction and terminates just inferior to scapular spine, anterior extends from symphysis pubis to sternal notch, anterior or posterior opening, restricts gross trunk motion in sagittal, coronal, and transverse planes, includes a carved plaster or CAD-CAM model, custom fabricated ♿

A **L0484** Thoracic-lumbar-sacral orthotic TLSO, triplanar control, 2 piece rigid plastic shell without interface liner, with multiple straps and closures, posterior extends from sacrococcygeal junction and terminates just inferior to scapular spine, anterior extends from symphysis pubis to sternal notch, lateral strength is enhanced by overlapping plastic, restricts gross trunk motion in the sagittal, coronal, and transverse planes, includes a carved plaster or CAD-CAM model, custom fabricated ♿

A **L0486** Thoracic-lumbar-sacral orthotic (TLSO), triplanar control, 2 piece rigid plastic shell with interface liner, multiple straps and closures, posterior extends from sacrococcygeal junction and terminates just inferior to scapular spine, anterior extends from symphysis pubis to sternal notch, lateral strength is enhanced by overlapping plastic, restricts gross trunk motion in the sagittal, coronal, and transverse planes, includes a carved plaster or CAD-CAM model, custom fabricated ♿

A **L0488** Thoracic-lumbar-sacral orthotic (TLSO), triplanar control, 1 piece rigid plastic shell with interface liner, multiple straps and closures, posterior extends from sacrococcygeal junction and terminates just inferior to scapular spine, anterior extends from symphysis pubis to sternal notch, anterior or posterior opening, restricts gross trunk motion in sagittal, coronal, and transverse planes, prefabricated, includes fitting and adjustment ♿

A **L0490** Thoracic-lumbar-sacral orthotic (TLSO), sagittal-coronal control, 1 piece rigid plastic shell, with overlapping reinforced anterior, with multiple straps and closures, posterior extends from sacrococcygeal junction and terminates at or before the T-9 vertebra, anterior extends from symphysis pubis to xiphoid, anterior opening, restricts gross trunk motion in sagittal and coronal planes, prefabricated, includes fitting and adjustment ♿

A **L0491** Thoracic-lumbar-sacral orthotic (TLSO), sagittal-coronal control, modular segmented spinal system, 2 rigid plastic shells, posterior extends from the sacrococcygeal junction and terminates just inferior to the scapular spine, anterior extends from the symphysis pubis to the xiphoid, soft liner, restricts gross trunk motion in the sagittal and coronal planes, lateral strength is provided by overlapping plastic and stabilizing closures, includes straps and closures, prefabricated, includes fitting and adjustment

A **L0492** Thoracic-lumbar-sacral orthotic (TLSO), sagittal-coronal control, modular segmented spinal system, 3 rigid plastic shells, posterior extends from the sacrococcygeal junction and terminates just inferior to the scapular spine, anterior extends from the symphysis pubis to the xiphoid, soft liner, restricts gross trunk motion in the sagittal and coronal planes, lateral strength is provided by overlapping plastic and stabilizing closures, includes straps and closures, prefabricated, includes fitting and adjustment

CERVICAL-THORACIC-LUMBAR-SACRAL ORTHOTIC (CTLSO)

A **L0621** Sacroiliac orthotic, flexible, provides pelvic-sacral support, reduces motion about the sacroiliac joint, includes straps, closures, may include pendulous abdomen design, prefabricated, includes fitting and adjustment

A **L0622** Sacroiliac orthotic, flexible, provides pelvic-sacral support, reduces motion about the sacroiliac joint, includes straps, closures, may include pendulous abdomen design, custom fabricated

A **L0623** Sacroiliac orthotic, provides pelvic-sacral support, with rigid or semi-rigid panels over the sacrum and abdomen, reduces motion about the sacroiliac joint, includes straps, closures, may include pendulous abdomen design, prefabricated, includes fitting and adjustment

A **L0624** Sacroiliac orthotic, provides pelvic-sacral support, with rigid or semi-rigid panels placed over the sacrum and abdomen, reduces motion about the sacroiliac joint, includes straps, closures, may include pendulous abdomen design, custom fabricated

A **L0625** Lumbar orthotic, flexible, provides lumbar support, posterior extends from L-1 to below L-5 vertebra, produces intracavitary pressure to reduce load on the intervertebral discs, includes straps, closures, may include pendulous abdomen design, shoulder straps, stays, prefabricated, includes fitting and adjustment

A **L0626** Lumbar orthotic, sagittal control, with rigid posterior panel(s), posterior extends from L-1 to below L-5 vertebra, produces intracavitary pressure to reduce load on the intervertebral discs, includes straps, closures, may include padding, stays, shoulder straps, pendulous abdomen design, prefabricated, includes fitting and adjustment

A **L0627** Lumbar orthotic, sagittal control, with rigid anterior and posterior panels, posterior extends from L-1 to below L-5 vertebra, produces intracavitary pressure to reduce load on the intervertebral discs, includes straps, closures, may include padding, shoulder straps, pendulous abdomen design, prefabricated, includes fitting and adjustment

A **L0628** Lumbar-sacral orthotic, flexible, provides lumbo-sacral support, posterior extends from sacrococcygeal junction to T-9 vertebra, produces intracavitary pressure to reduce load on the intervertebral discs, includes straps, closures, may include stays, shoulder straps, pendulous abdomen design, prefabricated, includes fitting and adjustment

A **L0629** Lumbar-sacral orthotic, flexible, provides lumbo-sacral support, posterior extends from sacrococcygeal junction to T-9 vertebra, produces intracavitary pressure to reduce load on the intervertebral discs, includes straps, closures, may include stays, shoulder straps, pendulous abdomen design, custom fabricated

A **L0630** Lumbar-sacral orthotic, sagittal control, with rigid posterior panel(s), posterior extends from sacrococcygeal junction to T-9 vertebra, produces intracavitary pressure to reduce load on the intervertebral discs, includes straps, closures, may include padding, stays, shoulder straps, pendulous abdomen design, prefabricated, includes fitting and adjustment

A **L0631** Lumbar-sacral orthotic, sagittal control, with rigid anterior and posterior panels, posterior extends from sacrococcygeal junction to T-9 vertebra, produces intracavitary pressure to reduce load on the intervertebral discs, includes straps, closures, may include padding, shoulder straps, pendulous abdomen design, prefabricated, includes fitting and adjustment

A **L0632** Lumbar-sacral orthotic (LSO), sagittal control, with rigid anterior and posterior panels, posterior extends from sacrococcygeal junction to T-9 vertebra, produces intracavitary pressure to reduce load on the intervertebral discs, includes straps, closures, may include padding, shoulder straps, pendulous abdomen design, custom fabricated

A **L0633** Lumbar-sacral orthotic (LSO), sagittal-coronal control, with rigid posterior frame/panel(s), posterior extends from sacrococcygeal junction to T-9 vertebra, lateral strength provided by rigid lateral frame/panels, produces intracavitary pressure to reduce load on intervertebral discs, includes straps, closures, may include padding, stays, shoulder straps, pendulous abdomen design, prefabricated, includes fitting and adjustment

A **L0634** Lumbar-sacral orthotic (LSO), sagittal-coronal control, with rigid posterior frame/panel(s), posterior extends from sacrococcygeal junction to T-9 vertebra, lateral strength provided by rigid lateral frame/panel(s), produces intracavitary pressure to reduce load on intervertebral discs, includes straps, closures, may include padding, stays, shoulder straps, pendulous abdomen design, custom fabricated

A **L0635** Lumbar-sacral orthotic (LSO), sagittal-coronal control, lumbar flexion, rigid posterior frame/panel(s), lateral articulating design to flex the lumbar spine, posterior extends from sacrococcygeal junction to T-9 vertebra, lateral strength provided by rigid lateral frame/panel(s), produces intracavitary pressure to reduce load on intervertebral discs, includes straps, closures, may include padding, anterior panel, pendulous abdomen design, prefabricated, includes fitting and adjustment

A **L0636** Lumbar-sacral orthotic (LSO), sagittal-coronal control, lumbar flexion, rigid posterior frame/panels, lateral articulating design to flex the lumbar spine, posterior extends from sacrococcygeal junction to T-9 vertebra, lateral strength provided by rigid lateral frame/panels, produces intracavitary pressure to reduce load on intervertebral discs, includes straps, closures, may include padding, anterior panel, pendulous abdomen design, custom fabricated

A **L0637** Lumbar-sacral orthotic (LSO), sagittal-coronal control, with rigid anterior and posterior frame/panels, posterior extends from sacrococcygeal junction to T-9 vertebra, lateral strength provided by rigid lateral frame/panels, produces intracavitary pressure to reduce load on intervertebral discs, includes straps, closures, may include padding, shoulder straps, pendulous abdomen design, prefabricated, includes fitting and adjustment

A **L0638** Lumbar-sacral orthotic (LSO), sagittal-coronal control, with rigid anterior and posterior frame/panels, posterior extends from sacrococcygeal junction to T-9 vertebra, lateral strength provided by rigid lateral frame/panels, produces intracavitary pressure to reduce load on intervertebral discs, includes straps, closures, may include padding, shoulder straps, pendulous abdomen design, custom fabricated

A **L0639** Lumbar-sacral orthotic (LSO), sagittal-coronal control, rigid shell(s)/panel(s), posterior extends from sacrococcygeal junction to T-9 vertebra, anterior extends from symphysis pubis to xyphoid, produces intracavitary pressure to reduce load on the intervertebral discs, overall strength is provided by overlapping rigid material and stabilizing closures, includes straps, closures, may include soft interface, pendulous abdomen design, prefabricated, includes fitting and adjustment

A **L0640** Lumbar-sacral orthotic (LSO), sagittal-coronal control, rigid shell(s)/panel(s), posterior extends from sacrococcygeal junction to T-9 vertebra, anterior extends from symphysis pubis to xyphoid, produces intracavitary pressure to reduce load on the intervertebral discs, overall strength is provided by overlapping rigid material and stabilizing closures, includes straps, closures, may include soft interface, pendulous abdomen design, custom fabricated

ANTERIOR-POSTERIOR-LATERAL CONTROL

A **L0700** Cervical-thoracic-lumbar-sacral orthosis (CTLSO), anterior-posterior-lateral control, molded to patient model, (Minerva type) ♿

A **L0710** Cervical-thoracic-lumbar-sacral orthotic (CTLSO), anterior-posterior-lateral-control, molded to patient model, with interface material, (Minerva type) ♿

HALO PROCEDURE

A **L0810** Halo procedure, cervical halo incorporated into jacket vest ♿

A **L0820** Halo procedure, cervical halo incorporated into plaster body jacket ♿

A **L0830** Halo procedure, cervical halo incorporated into Milwaukee type orthotic ♿

A **L0859** Addition to halo procedure, magnetic resonance image compatible systems, rings and pins, any material

A **L0861** Addition to halo procedure, replacement liner/interface material ♿

ADDITIONS TO SPINAL ORTHOTIC

A **L0970** Thoracic-lumbar-sacral orthotic (TLSO), corset front ♿

A **L0972** Lumbar-sacral orthotic (LSO), corset front ♿

A **L0974** Thoracic-lumbar-sacral orthotic (TLSO), full corset ♿

A **L0976** Lumbar-sacral orthotic (LSO), full corset ♿

A **L0978** Axillary crutch extension ♿

A ☑ **L0980** Peroneal straps, pair ♿

A ☑ **L0982** Stocking supporter grips, set of 4 ♿

A ☑ **L0984** Protective body sock, each ♿

A **L0999** Addition to spinal orthotic, not otherwise specified
Determine if an alternative HCPCS Level II or a CPT code better describes the service being reported. This code should be used only if a more specific code is unavailable.

ORTHOTIC DEVICES - SCOLIOSIS PROCEDURES

The orthotic care of scoliosis differs from other orthotic care in that the treatment is more dynamic in nature and uses continual modification of the orthosis to the patient's changing condition. This coding structure uses the proper names - or eponyms - of the procedures because they have historic and universal acceptance in the profession. It should be recognized that variations to the basic procedures described by the founders/developers are accepted in various medical and orthotic practices throughout the country. All procedures include model of patient when indicated.

CERVICAL-THORACIC-LUMBAR-SACRAL ORTHOTIC (CTLSO)

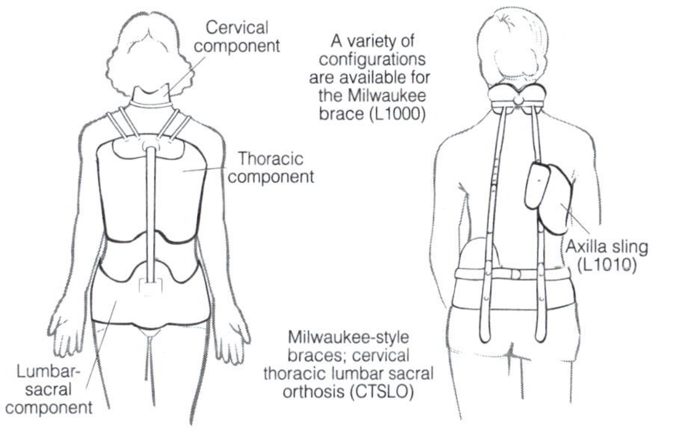

A **L1000** Cervical-thoracic-lumbar-sacral orthotic (CTLSO) (Milwaukee), inclusive of furnishing initial orthotic, including model ♿

A **L1001** Cervical-thoracic-lumbar-sacral orthotic (CTLSO), immobilizer, infant size, prefabricated, includes fitting and adjustment A

A **L1005** Tension based scoliosis orthotic and accessory pads, includes fitting and adjustment ♿

A **L1010** Addition to cervical-thoracic-lumbar-sacral orthotic (CTLSO) or scoliosis orthotic, axilla sling ♿

A **L1020** Addition to cervical-thoracic-lumbar-sacral orthotic (CTLSO) or scoliosis orthotic, kyphosis pad ♿

A **L1025** Addition to cervical-thoracic-lumbar-sacral orthotic (CTLSO) or scoliosis orthotic, kyphosis pad, floating ♿

A **L1030** Addition to cervical-thoracic-lumbar-sacral orthotic (CTLSO) or scoliosis orthotic, lumbar bolster pad ♿

A **L1040** Addition to cervical-thoracic-lumbar-sacral orthotic (CTLSO) or scoliosis orthotic, lumbar or lumbar rib pad ♿

A **L1050** Addition to cervical-thoracic-lumbar-sacral orthotic (CTLSO) or scoliosis orthotic, sternal pad ♿

A **L1060** Addition to cervical-thoracic-lumbar-sacral orthotic (CTLSO) or scoliosis orthotic, thoracic pad ♿

A **L1070** Addition to cervical-thoracic-lumbar-sacral orthotic (CTLSO) or scoliosis orthotic, trapezius sling ♿

A **L1080** Addition to cervical-thoracic-lumbar-sacral orthotic (CTLSO) or scoliosis orthotic, outrigger ♿

A **L1085** Addition to cervical-thoracic-lumbar-sacral orthotic (CTLSO) or scoliosis orthotic, outrigger, bilateral with vertical extensions ♿

A **L1090** Addition to cervical-thoracic-lumbar-sacral orthotic (CTLSO) or scoliosis orthotic, lumbar sling ♿

A **L1100** Addition to cervical-thoracic-lumbar-sacral orthotic (CTLSO) or scoliosis orthotic, ring flange, plastic or leather ♿

A **L1110** Addition to cervical-thoracic-lumbar-sacral orthotic (CTLSO) or scoliosis orthotic, ring flange, plastic or leather, molded to patient model ♿

A ☑ **L1120** Addition to cervical-thoracic-lumbar-sacral orthotic (CTLSO), scoliosis orthotic, cover for upright, each ♿

THORACIC-LUMBAR-SACRAL ORTHOSIS (TLSO) (LOW PROFILE)

A L1200 Thoracic-lumbar-sacral orthotic (TLSO), inclusive of furnishing initial orthotic only ♿

A L1210 Addition to thoracic-lumbar-sacral orthotic (TLSO), (low profile), lateral thoracic extension ♿

A L1220 Addition to thoracic-lumbar-sacral orthotic (TLSO), (low profile), anterior thoracic extension ♿

A L1230 Addition to thoracic-lumbar-sacral orthotic (TLSO), (low profile), Milwaukee type superstructure ♿

A L1240 Addition to thoracic-lumbar-sacral orthotic (TLSO), (low profile), lumbar derotation pad ♿

A L1250 Addition to thoracic-lumbar-sacral orthotic (TLSO), (low profile), anterior ASIS pad ♿

A L1260 Addition to thoracic-lumbar-sacral orthotic (TLSO), (low profile), anterior thoracic derotation pad ♿

A L1270 Addition to thoracic-lumbar-sacral orthotic (TLSO), (low profile), abdominal pad ♿

A ☑ L1280 Addition to thoracic-lumbar-sacral orthotic (TLSO), (low profile), rib gusset (elastic), each ♿

A L1290 Addition to thoracic-lumbar-sacral orthotic (TLSO), (low profile), lateral trochanteric pad ♿

OTHER SCOLIOSIS PROCEDURES

A L1300 Other scoliosis procedure, body jacket molded to patient model ♿

A L1310 Other scoliosis procedure, postoperative body jacket ♿

A L1499 Spinal orthotic, not otherwise specified

Determine if an alternative HCPCS Level II or a CPT code better describes the service being reported. This code should be used only if a more specific code is unavailable.

THORACIC-HIP-KNEE-ANKLE ORTHOTIC (THKAO)

A L1500 Thoracic-hip-knee-ankle orthotic (THKAO), mobility frame (Newington, Parapodium types) ♿

A L1510 Thoracic-hip-knee-ankle orthotic (THKAO), standing frame, with or without tray and accessories ♿

A L1520 Thoracic-hip-knee-ankle orthotic (THKAO), swivel walker ♿

ORTHOTIC DEVICES - LOWER LIMB

The procedures in L1600-L2999 are considered as "base" or "basic procedures" and may be modified by listing procedure from the "additions" sections and adding them to the base procedures.

HIP ORTHOTIC (HO) - FLEXIBLE

A L1600 Hip orthotic (HO), abduction control of hip joints, flexible, Frejka type with cover, prefabricated, includes fitting and adjustment ♿

A L1610 Hip orthotic (HO), abduction control of hip joints, flexible, (Frejka cover only), prefabricated, includes fitting and adjustment ♿

A L1620 Hip orthosis (HO), abduction control of hip joints, flexible, (Pavlik harness), prefabricated, includes fitting and adjustment ♿

A L1630 Hip orthotic (HO), abduction control of hip joints, semi-flexible (Von Rosen type), custom fabricated ♿

A L1640 Hip orthotic (HO), abduction control of hip joints, static, pelvic band or spreader bar, thigh cuffs, custom fabricated ♿

A L1650 Hip orthotic (HO), abduction control of hip joints, static, adjustable, (Ilfled type), prefabricated, includes fitting and adjustment ♿

A L1652 Hip orthotic, bilateral thigh cuffs with adjustable abductor spreader bar, adult size, prefabricated, includes fitting and adjustment, any type ♿

A L1660 Hip orthotic (HO), abduction control of hip joints, static, plastic, prefabricated, includes fitting and adjustment ♿

A L1680 Hip orthotic (HO), abduction control of hip joints, dynamic, pelvic control, adjustable hip motion control, thigh cuffs (Rancho hip action type), custom fabricated ♿

A L1685 Hip orthosis (HO), abduction control of hip joint, postoperative hip abduction type, custom fabricated ♿

A L1686 Hip orthotic (HO), abduction control of hip joint, postoperative hip abduction type, prefabricated, includes fitting and adjustment ♿

A L1690 Combination, bilateral, lumbo-sacral, hip, femur orthotic providing adduction and internal rotation control, prefabricated, includes fitting and adjustment ♿

LEGG PERTHES

A L1700 Legg Perthes orthotic, (Toronto type), custom fabricated ♿

A L1710 Legg Perthes orthotic, (Newington type), custom fabricated ♿

A L1720 Legg Perthes orthotic, trilateral, (Tachdijan type), custom fabricated ♿

A L1730 Legg Perthes orthotic, (Scottish Rite type), custom fabricated ♿

A L1755 Legg Perthes orthotic, (Patten bottom type), custom fabricated ♿

KNEE ORTHOTIC (KO)

A L1800 Knee orthotic (KO), elastic with stays, prefabricated, includes fitting and adjustment ♿

A L1810 Knee orthotic (KO), elastic with joints, prefabricated, includes fitting and adjustment ♿

A L1815 Knee orthotic (KO), elastic or other elastic type material with condylar pad(s), prefabricated, includes fitting and adjustment ♿

A L1820 Knee orthotic, elastic with condylar pads and joints, with or without patellar control, prefabricated, includes fitting and adjustment ♿

A L1825 Knee orthotic (KO), elastic knee cap, prefabricated, includes fitting and adjustment ♿

A L1830 Knee orthotic (KO), immobilizer, canvas longitudinal, prefabricated, includes fitting and adjustment ♿

A L1831 Knee orthotic, locking knee joint(s), positional orthotic, prefabricated, includes fitting and adjustment ♿

A L1832 Knee orthotic, adjustable knee joints (unicentric or polycentric), positional orthotic, rigid support, prefabricated, includes fitting and adjustment ♿

A L1834 Knee orthotic (KO), without knee joint, rigid, custom fabricated ♿

A L1836 Knee orthotic, rigid, without joint(s), includes soft interface material, prefabricated, includes fitting and adjustment ♿

L1840 Knee orthotic (KO), derotation, medial-lateral, anterior cruciate ligament, custom fabricated

L1843 Knee orthotic (KO), single upright, thigh and calf, with adjustable flexion and extension joint (unicentric or polycentric), medial-lateral and rotation control, with or without varus/valgus adjustment, prefabricated, includes fitting and adjustment

L1844 Knee orthotic (KO), single upright, thigh and calf, with adjustable flexion and extension joint (unicentric or polycentric), medial-lateral and rotation control, with or without varus/valgus adjustment, custom fabricated

L1845 Knee orthotic, double upright, thigh and calf, with adjustable flexion and extension joint (unicentric or polycentric), medial-lateral and rotation control, with or without varus/valgus adjustment, prefabricated, includes fitting and adjustment

L1846 Knee orthotic, double upright, thigh and calf, with adjustable flexion and extension joint (unicentric or polycentric), medial-lateral and rotation control, with or without varus/valgus adjustment, custom fabricated

L1847 Knee orthotic (KO), double upright with adjustable joint, with inflatable air support chamber(s), prefabricated, includes fitting and adjustment

L1850 Knee orthotic (KO), Swedish type, prefabricated, includes fitting and adjustment

L1860 Knee orthotic (KO), modification of supracondylar prosthetic socket, custom fabricated (SK)

ANKLE-FOOT ORTHOTIC (AFO)

L1900 Ankle-foot orthotic (AFO), spring wire, dorsiflexion assist calf band, custom fabricated

L1901 Ankle orthotic, elastic, prefabricated, includes fitting and adjustment (e.g., neoprene, Lycra)

L1902 Ankle-foot orthotic (AFO), ankle gauntlet, prefabricated, includes fitting and adjustment

L1904 Ankle-foot orthotic (AFO), molded ankle gauntlet, custom fabricated

L1906 Ankle-foot orthosis (AFO), multiligamentus ankle support, prefabricated, includes fitting and adjustment

L1907 AFO, supramalleolar with straps, with or without interface/pads, custom fabricated

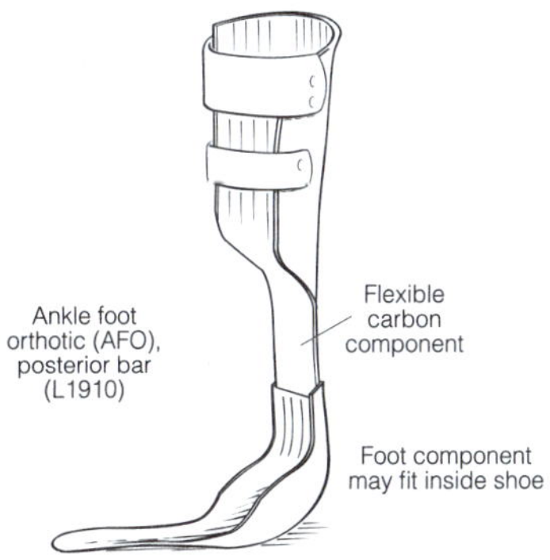

L1910 Ankle-foot orthotic (AFO), posterior, single bar, clasp attachment to shoe counter, prefabricated, includes fitting and adjustment

L1920 Ankle-foot orthotic (AFO), single upright with static or adjustable stop (Phelps or Perlstein type), custom fabricated

L1930 Ankle-foot orthotic (AFO), plastic or other material, prefabricated, includes fitting and adjustment

L1932 AFO, rigid anterior tibial section, total carbon fiber or equal material, prefabricated, includes fitting and adjustment

L1940 Ankle-foot orthotic (AFO), plastic or other material, custom fabricated

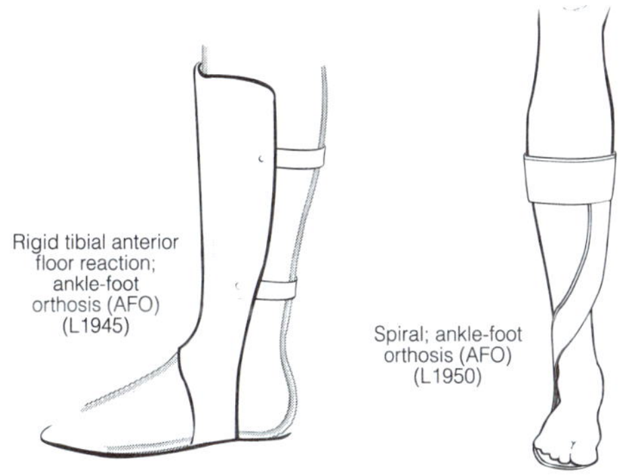

L1945 Ankle-foot orthotic (AFO), plastic, rigid anterior tibial section (floor reaction), custom fabricated

L1950 Ankle-foot orthotic (AFO), spiral, (Institute of Rehabilitative Medicine type), plastic, custom fabricated

L1951 Ankle-foot orthotic (AFO), spiral, (Institute of rehabilitative Medicine type), plastic or other material, prefabricated, includes fitting and adjustment

L1960 Ankle-foot orthotic (AFO), posterior solid ankle, plastic, custom fabricated

L1970 Ankle-foot orthotic (AFO), plastic with ankle joint, custom fabricated

L1971 Ankle-foot orthotic (AFO), plastic or other material with ankle joint, prefabricated, includes fitting and adjustment

L1980 Ankle-foot orthotic (AFO), single upright free plantar dorsiflexion, solid stirrup, calf band/cuff (single bar 'BK' orthotic), custom fabricated

L1990 Ankle-foot orthotic (AFO), double upright free plantar dorsiflexion, solid stirrup, calf band/cuff (double bar 'BK' orthotic), custom fabricated

KNEE-ANKLE-FOOT ORTHOTIC (KAFO) - OR ANY COMBINATION

L2000 Knee-ankle-foot orthotic (KAFO), single upright, free knee, free ankle, solid stirrup, thigh and calf bands/cuffs (single bar 'AK' orthotic), custom fabricated

L2005 Knee-ankle-foot orthotic (KAFO), any material, single or double upright, stance control, automatic lock and swing phase release, mechanical activation, includes ankle joint, any type, custom fabricated

L2010 Knee-ankle-foot orthotic (KAFO), single upright, free ankle, solid stirrup, thigh and calf bands/cuffs (single bar 'AK' orthotic), without knee joint, custom fabricated

L2020 Knee-ankle-foot orthotic (KAFO), double upright, free ankle, solid stirrup, thigh and calf bands/cuffs (double bar 'AK' orthotic), custom fabricated

L2030 Knee-ankle-foot orthotic (KAFO), double upright, free ankle, solid stirrup, thigh and calf bands/cuffs, (double bar 'AK' orthotic), without knee joint, custom fabricated

A L2034 Knee-ankle-foot orthotic (KAFO), full plastic, single upright, with or without free motion knee, medial-lateral rotation control, with or without free motion ankle, custom fabricated

A L2035 Knee-ankle-foot orthotic (KAFO), full plastic, static (pediatric size), without free motion ankle, prefabricated, includes fitting and adjustment ♿

A L2036 Knee-ankle-foot orthotic (KAFO), full plastic, double upright, with or without free motion knee, with or without free motion ankle, custom fabricated ♿

A L2037 Knee-ankle-foot orthotic (KAFO), full plastic, single upright, with or without free motion knee, with or without free motion ankle, custom fabricated ♿

A L2038 Knee-ankle-foot orthotic (KAFO), full plastic, with or without free motion knee, multi-axis ankle, custom fabricated ♿

TORSION CONTROL: HIP-KNEE-ANKLE-FOOT ORTHOTIC (HKAFO)

A L2040 Hip-knee-ankle-foot orthotic (HKAFO), torsion control, bilateral rotation straps, pelvic band/belt, custom fabricated ♿

A L2050 Hip-knee-ankle-foot orthotic (HKAFO), torsion control, bilateral torsion cables, hip joint, pelvic band/belt, custom fabricated ♿

A L2060 Hip-knee-ankle-foot orthotic (HKAFO), torsion control, bilateral torsion cables, ball bearing hip joint, pelvic band/ belt, custom fabricated ♿

A L2070 Hip-knee-ankle-foot orthotic (HKAFO), torsion control, unilateral rotation straps, pelvic band/belt, custom fabricated ♿

A L2080 Hip-knee-ankle-foot orthotic (HKAFO), torsion control, unilateral torsion cable, hip joint, pelvic band/belt, custom fabricated ♿

A L2090 Hip-knee-ankle-foot orthotic (HKAFO), torsion control, unilateral torsion cable, ball bearing hip joint, pelvic band/ belt, custom fabricated ♿

A L2106 Ankle-foot orthotic (AFO), fracture orthotic, tibial fracture cast orthotic, thermoplastic type casting material, custom fabricated ♿

A L2108 Ankle-foot orthotic (AFO), fracture orthotic, tibial fracture cast orthotic, custom fabricated ♿

A L2112 Ankle-foot orthotic (AFO), fracture orthotic, tibial fracture orthotic, soft, prefabricated, includes fitting and adjustment ♿

A L2114 Ankle-foot orthosis (AFO), fracture orthosis, tibial fracture orthosis, semi-rigid, prefabricated, includes fitting and adjustment ♿

A L2116 Ankle-foot orthotic (AFO), fracture orthotic, tibial fracture orthotic, rigid, prefabricated, includes fitting and adjustment ♿

A L2126 Knee-ankle-foot orthotic (KAFO), fracture orthotic, femoral fracture cast orthotic, thermoplastic type casting material, custom fabricated ♿

A L2128 Knee-ankle-foot orthotic (KAFO), fracture orthotic, femoral fracture cast orthotic, custom fabricated ♿

A L2132 Knee-ankle-foot orthotic (KAFO), fracture orthotic, femoral fracture cast orthotic, soft, prefabricated, includes fitting and adjustment ♿

A L2134 Knee-ankle-foot orthotic (KAFO), fracture orthotic, femoral fracture cast orthotic, semi-rigid, prefabricated, includes fitting and adjustment ♿

A L2136 KAFO, fracture orthotic, femoral fracture cast orthotic, rigid, prefabricated, includes fitting and adjustment ♿

ADDITIONS TO FRACTURE ORTHOTIC

A L2180 Addition to lower extremity fracture orthotic, plastic shoe insert with ankle joints ♿

A L2182 Addition to lower extremity fracture orthotic, drop lock knee joint ♿

A L2184 Addition to lower extremity fracture orthotic, limited motion knee joint ♿

A L2186 Addition to lower extremity fracture orthotic, adjustable motion knee joint, Lerman type ♿

A L2188 Addition to lower extremity fracture orthotic, quadrilateral brim ♿

A L2190 Addition to lower extremity fracture orthotic, waist belt ♿

A L2192 Addition to lower extremity fracture orthotic, hip joint, pelvic band, thigh flange, and pelvic belt ♿

ADDITIONS TO LOWER EXTREMITY ORTHOTIC: SHOE-ANKLE-SHIN-KNEE

A ☑ L2200 Addition to lower extremity, limited ankle motion, each joint ♿

A ☑ L2210 Addition to lower extremity, dorsiflexion assist (plantar flexion resist), each joint ♿

A ☑ L2220 Addition to lower extremity, dorsiflexion and plantar flexion assist/resist, each joint ♿

A L2230 Addition to lower extremity, split flat caliper stirrups and plate attachment ♿

A L2232 Addition to lower extremity orthotic, rocker bottom for total contact ankle-foot orthotic (AFO), for custom fabricated orthotic only

A L2240 Addition to lower extremity, round caliper and plate attachment ♿

A L2250 Addition to lower extremity, foot plate, molded to patient model, stirrup attachment ♿

A L2260 Addition to lower extremity, reinforced solid stirrup (Scott-Craig type) ♿

A L2265 Addition to lower extremity, long tongue stirrup ♿

A L2270 Addition to lower extremity, varus/valgus correction (T) strap, padded/lined or malleolus pad ♿

A L2275 Addition to lower extremity, varus/valgus correction, plastic modification, padded/lined ♿

A L2280 Addition to lower extremity, molded inner boot ♿

A L2300 Addition to lower extremity, abduction bar (bilateral hip involvement), jointed, adjustable ♿

A L2310 Addition to lower extremity, abduction bar, straight ♿

A L2320 Addition to lower extremity, nonmolded lacer, for custom fabricated orthotic only ♿

A L2330 Addition to lower extremity, lacer molded to patient model, for custom fabricated orthotic only ♿

A L2335 Addition to lower extremity, anterior swing band ♿

A L2340 Addition to lower extremity, pretibial shell, molded to patient model ♿

A L2350 Addition to lower extremity, prosthetic type, (BK) socket, molded to patient model, (used for PTB, AFO orthoses) ♿

A L2360 Addition to lower extremity, extended steel shank ♿

A L2370 Addition to lower extremity, Patten bottom

A L2375 Addition to lower extremity, torsion control, ankle joint and half solid stirrup

A ☑ L2380 Addition to lower extremity, torsion control, straight knee joint, each joint

A ☑ L2385 Addition to lower extremity, straight knee joint, heavy-duty, each joint

A L2387 Addition to lower extremity, polycentric knee joint, for custom fabricated knee-ankle-foot orthotic(KAFO), each joint

A ☑ L2390 Addition to lower extremity, offset knee joint, each joint

A ☑ L2395 Addition to lower extremity, offset knee joint, heavy-duty, each joint

A L2397 Addition to lower extremity orthotic, suspension sleeve

ADDITIONS TO STRAIGHT KNEE OR OFFSET KNEE JOINTS

A ☑ L2405 Addition to knee joint, drop lock, each

A ☑ L2415 Addition to knee lock with integrated release mechanism (bail, cable, or equal), any material, each joint

A ☑ L2425 Addition to knee joint, disc or dial lock for adjustable knee flexion, each joint

A ☑ L2430 Addition to knee joint, ratchet lock for active and progressive knee extension, each joint

A L2492 Addition to knee joint, lift loop for drop lock ring

ADDITIONS: THIGH/WEIGHT BEARING - GLUTEAL/ISCHIAL WEIGHT BEARING

A L2500 Addition to lower extremity, thigh/weight bearing, gluteal/ischial weight bearing, ring

A L2510 Addition to lower extremity, thigh/weight bearing, quadri-lateral brim, molded to patient model

A L2520 Addition to lower extremity, thigh/weight bearing, quadri-lateral brim, custom fitted

A L2525 Addition to lower extremity, thigh/weight bearing, ischial containment/narrow M-L brim molded to patient model

A L2526 Addition to lower extremity, thigh/weight bearing, ischial containment/narrow M-L brim, custom fitted

A L2530 Addition to lower extremity, thigh/weight bearing, lacer, nonmolded

A L2540 Addition to lower extremity, thigh/weight bearing, lacer, molded to patient model

A L2550 Addition to lower extremity, thigh/weight bearing, high roll cuff

ADDITIONS: PELVIC AND THORACIC CONTROL

A ☑ L2570 Addition to lower extremity, pelvic control, hip joint, Clevis type, 2-position joint, each

A L2580 Addition to lower extremity, pelvic control, pelvic sling

A ☑ L2600 Addition to lower extremity, pelvic control, hip joint, Clevis type, or thrust bearing, free, each

A ☑ L2610 Addition to lower extremity, pelvic control, hip joint, Clevis or thrust bearing, lock, each

A ☑ L2620 Addition to lower extremity, pelvic control, hip joint, heavy-duty, each

A ☑ L2622 Addition to lower extremity, pelvic control, hip joint, adjustable flexion, each

A ☑ L2624 Addition to lower extremity, pelvic control, hip joint, adjustable flexion, extension, abduction control, each

A L2627 Addition to lower extremity, pelvic control, plastic, molded to patient model, reciprocating hip joint and cables

A L2628 Addition to lower extremity, pelvic control, metal frame, reciprocating hip joint and cables

A L2630 Addition to lower extremity, pelvic control, band and belt, unilateral

A L2640 Addition to lower extremity, pelvic control, band and belt, bilateral

A ☑ L2650 Addition to lower extremity, pelvic and thoracic control, gluteal pad, each

A L2660 Addition to lower extremity, thoracic control, thoracic band

A L2670 Addition to lower extremity, thoracic control, paraspinal uprights

A L2680 Addition to lower extremity, thoracic control, lateral support uprights

ADDITIONS: GENERAL

A ☑ L2750 Addition to lower extremity orthotic, plating chrome or nickel, per bar

A L2755 Addition to lower extremity orthotic, high strength, lightweight material, all hybrid lamination/prepreg composite, per segment, for custom fabricated orthotic only

A ☑ L2760 Addition to lower extremity orthotic, extension, per extension, per bar (for lineal adjustment for growth)

A ☑ L2768 Orthotic side bar disconnect device, per bar

A ☑ L2770 Addition to lower extremity orthotic, any material, per bar or joint

A ☑ L2780 Addition to lower extremity orthotic, noncorrosive finish, per bar

A ☑ L2785 Addition to lower extremity orthotic, drop lock retainer, each

A L2795 Addition to lower extremity orthotic, knee control, full kneecap

A L2800 Addition to lower extremity orthotic, knee control, knee cap, medial or lateral pull, for use with custom fabricated orthotic only

A L2810 Addition to lower extremity orthotic, knee control, condylar pad

A L2820 Addition to lower extremity orthotic, soft interface for molded plastic, below knee section

A L2830 Addition to lower extremity orthotic, soft interface for molded plastic, above knee section

A ☑ L2840 Addition to lower extremity orthotic, tibial length sock, fracture or equal, each

A ☑ L2850 Addition to lower extremity orthotic, femoral length sock, fracture or equal, each

~~L2860 Addition to lower extremity joint, knee or ankle, concentric adjustable torsion style mechanism, each~~

A **L2999** Lower extremity orthoses, not otherwise specified
Determine if an alternative HCPCS Level II or a CPT code better describes the service being reported. This code should be used only if a more specific code is unavailable.

ORTHOPEDIC SHOES

INSERTS

A ☑ **L3000** Foot insert, removable, molded to patient model, UCB type, Berkeley shell, each
MED: 100-2,15,290

A ☑ **L3001** Foot, insert, removable, molded to patient model, Spenco, each
MED: 100-2,15,290

A ☑ **L3002** Foot insert, removable, molded to patient model, Plastazote or equal, each
MED: 100-2,15,290

A ☑ **L3003** Foot insert, removable, molded to patient model, silicone gel, each
MED: 100-2,15,290

A ☑ **L3010** Foot insert, removable, molded to patient model, longitudinal arch support, each
MED: 100-2,15,290

A ☑ **L3020** Foot insert, removable, molded to patient model, longitudinal/metatarsal support, each
MED: 100-2,15,290

A ☑ **L3030** Foot insert, removable, formed to patient foot, each
MED: 100-2,15,290

A ☑ **L3031** Foot, insert/plate, removable, addition to lower extremity orthotic, high strength, lightweight material, all hybrid lamination/prepreg composite, each

ARCH SUPPORT, REMOVABLE, PREMOLDED

A ☑ **L3040** Foot, arch support, removable, premolded, longitudinal, each
MED: 100-2,15,290

A ☑ **L3050** Foot, arch support, removable, premolded, metatarsal, each
MED: 100-2,15,290

A ☑ **L3060** Foot, arch support, removable, premolded, longitudinal/metatarsal, each
MED: 100-2,15,290

ARCH SUPPORT, NONREMOVABLE, ATTACHED TO SHOE

A ☑ **L3070** Foot, arch support, nonremovable, attached to shoe, longitudinal, each
MED: 100-2,15,290

A ☑ **L3080** Foot, arch support, nonremovable, attached to shoe, metatarsal, each
MED: 100-2,15,290

A ☑ **L3090** Foot, arch support, nonremovable, attached to shoe, longitudinal/metatarsal, each
MED: 100-2,15,290

A **L3100** Hallus-valgus night dynamic splint
MED: 100-2,15,290; 100-4,4,240

ABDUCTION AND ROTATION BARS

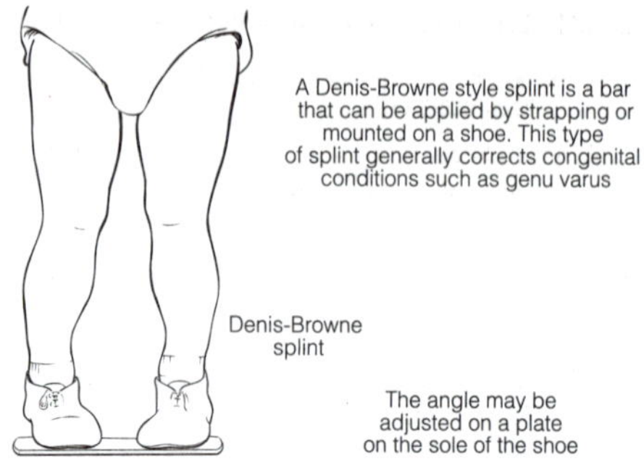

A **L3140** Foot, abduction rotation bar, including shoes
MED: 100-2,15,290

A **L3150** Foot, abduction rotation bar, without shoes
MED: 100-2,15,290

A **L3160** Foot, adjustable shoe-styled positioning device

A **L3170** Foot, plastic, silicone or equal, heel stabilizer, each
MED: 100-2,15,290

ORTHOPEDIC FOOTWEAR

A **L3201** Orthopedic shoe, Oxford with supinator or pronator, infant A
MED: 100-2,15,290

A **L3202** Orthopedic shoe, Oxford with supinator or pronator, child A
MED: 100-2,15,290

A **L3203** Orthopedic shoe, Oxford with supinator or pronator, junior A
MED: 100-2,15,290

A **L3204** Orthopedic shoe, hightop with supinator or pronator, infant A
MED: 100-2,15,290

A **L3206** Orthopedic shoe, hightop with supinator or pronator, child A
MED: 100-2,15,290

A **L3207** Orthopedic shoe, hightop with supinator or pronator, junior A
MED: 100-2,15,290

A ☑ **L3208** Surgical boot, each, infant A
MED: 100-2,15,100

A ☑ **L3209** Surgical boot, each, child A
MED: 100-2,15,100

A ☑ **L3211** Surgical boot, each, junior A
MED: 100-2,15,100

A ☑ **L3212** Benesch boot, pair, infant A
MED: 100-2,15,100

A ☑ **L3213** Benesch boot, pair, child A
MED: 100-2,15,100

A ☑ **L3214** Benesch boot, pair, junior A
MED: 100-2,15,100

E ☑ **L3215** Orthopedic footwear, ladies shoe, oxford, each A ♀

E ☑ **L3216** Orthopedic footwear, ladies shoe, depth inlay, each A ♀

E ☑ **L3217** Orthopedic footwear, ladies shoe, hightop, depth inlay, each A ♀

E ☑ **L3219** Orthopedic footwear, mens shoe, oxford, each A ♂

E ☑ **L3221** Orthopedic footwear, mens shoe, depth inlay, each A ♂

E ☑ **L3222** Orthopedic footwear, mens shoe, hightop, depth inlay, each A ♂

Special Coverage Instructions | Noncovered by Medicare | Carrier Discretion | ☑ Quantity Alert | ● New Code | ○ Recycled/Reinstated | ▲ Revised Code

 A Age Edit | M Maternity Edit | ♀ Female Only | ♂ Male Only | A-Y OPPS Status Indicators

A L3224 Orthopedic footwear, woman's shoe, oxford, used as an integral part of a brace (orthotic) ♀ ♿
MED: 100-2,15,290

A L3225 Orthopedic footwear, man's shoe, oxford, used as an integral part of a brace (orthotic) ♂ ♿
MED: 100-2,15,290

A L3230 Orthopedic footwear, custom shoe, depth inlay, each
MED: 100-2,15,290

A ☑ L3250 Orthopedic footwear, custom molded shoe, removable inner mold, prosthetic shoe, each
MED: 100-2,15,290

A ☑ L3251 Foot, shoe molded to patient model, silicone shoe, each
MED: 100-2,15,290

A ☑ L3252 Foot, shoe molded to patient model, Plastazote (or similar), custom fabricated, each
MED: 100-2,15,290

A ☑ L3253 Foot, molded shoe, Plastazote (or similar), custom fitted, each
MED: 100-2,15,290

A L3254 Nonstandard size or width
MED: 100-2,15,290

A L3255 Nonstandard size or length
MED: 100-2,15,290

A L3257 Orthopedic footwear, additional charge for split size
MED: 100-2,15,290

E ☑ L3260 Surgical boot/shoe, each
MED: 100-2,15,100

A ☑ L3265 Plastazote sandal, each

SHOE MODIFICATION - LIFTS

A ☑ L3300 Lift, elevation, heel, tapered to metatarsals, per in
MED: 100-2,15,290

A ☑ L3310 Lift, elevation, heel and sole, neoprene, per in
MED: 100-2,15,290

A ☑ L3320 Lift, elevation, heel and sole, cork, per in
MED: 100-2,15,290

A L3330 Lift, elevation, metal extension (skate)
MED: 100-2,15,290

A ☑ L3332 Lift, elevation, inside shoe, tapered, up to one-half in
MED: 100-2,15,290

A ☑ L3334 Lift, elevation, heel, per in
MED: 100-2,15,290

SHOE MODIFICATION - WEDGES

A L3340 Heel wedge, SACH
MED: 100-2,15,290

A L3350 Heel wedge
MED: 100-2,15,290

A L3360 Sole wedge, outside sole
MED: 100-2,15,290

A L3370 Sole wedge, between sole
MED: 100-2,15,290

A L3380 Clubfoot wedge
MED: 100-2,15,290

A L3390 Outflare wedge
MED: 100-2,15,290

A L3400 Metatarsal bar wedge, rocker
MED: 100-2,15,290

A L3410 Metatarsal bar wedge, between sole
MED: 100-2,15,290

A L3420 Full sole and heel wedge, between sole
MED: 100-2,15,290

SHOE MODIFICATIONS - HEELS

A L3430 Heel, counter, plastic reinforced
MED: 100-2,15,290

A L3440 Heel, counter, leather reinforced
MED: 100-2,15,290

A L3450 Heel, SACH cushion type
MED: 100-2,15,290

A L3455 Heel, new leather, standard
MED: 100-2,15,290

A L3460 Heel, new rubber, standard
MED: 100-2,15,290

A L3465 Heel, Thomas with wedge
MED: 100-2,15,290

A L3470 Heel, Thomas extended to ball
MED: 100-2,15,290

A L3480 Heel, pad and depression for spur
MED: 100-2,15,290

A L3485 Heel, pad, removable for spur
MED: 100-2,15,290

MISCELLANEOUS SHOE ADDITIONS

A L3500 Orthopedic shoe addition, insole, leather
MED: 100-2,15,290

A L3510 Orthopedic shoe addition, insole, rubber
MED: 100-2,15,290

A L3520 Orthopedic shoe addition, insole, felt covered with leather
MED: 100-2,15,290

A L3530 Orthopedic shoe addition, sole, half
MED: 100-2,15,290

A L3540 Orthopedic shoe addition, sole, full
MED: 100-2,15,290

A L3550 Orthopedic shoe addition, toe tap, standard
MED: 100-2,15,290

A L3560 Orthopedic shoe addition, toe tap, horseshoe
MED: 100-2,15,290

A L3570 Orthopedic shoe addition, special extension to instep (leather with eyelets)
MED: 100-2,15,290

A L3580 Orthopedic shoe addition, convert instep to Velcro closure
MED: 100-2,15,290

A L3590 Orthopedic shoe addition, convert firm shoe counter to soft counter
MED: 100-2,15,290

A L3595 Orthopedic shoe addition, March bar
MED: 100-2,15,290

TRANSFER OR REPLACEMENT

A L3600 Transfer of an orthotic from one shoe to another, caliper plate, existing
MED: 100-2,15,290

A L3610 Transfer of an orthotic from one shoe to another, caliper plate, new
MED: 100-2,15,290

A L3620 Transfer of an orthotic from one shoe to another, solid stirrup, existing
MED: 100-2,15,290

A L3630 Transfer of an orthotic from one shoe to another, solid stirrup, new
MED: 100-2,15,290

A L3640 Transfer of an orthotic from one shoe to another, Dennis Browne splint (Riveton), both shoes
MED: 100-2,15,290

A L3649 Orthopedic shoe, modification, addition or transfer, not otherwise specified
Determine if an alternative HCPCS Level II or a CPT code better describes the service being reported. This code should be used only if a more specific code is unavailable.
MED: 100-2,15,290

ORTHOTIC DEVICES - UPPER LIMB

The procedures in this section are considered as "base" or "basic procedures" and may be modified by listing procedures from the "additions" sections and adding them to the base procedure.

SHOULDER ORTHOTIC (SO)

A L3650 Shoulder orthotic (SO), figure of eight design abduction restrainer, prefabricated, includes fitting and adjustment ♿

A L3651 Shoulder orthotic (SO), single shoulder, elastic, prefabricated, includes fitting and adjustment (e.g., neoprene, Lycra) ♿

A L3652 Shoulder orthotic (SO), double shoulder, elastic, prefabricated, includes fitting and adjustment (e.g., neoprene, Lycra) ♿

A L3660 Shoulder orthotic (SO), figure of eight design abduction restrainer, canvas and webbing, prefabricated, includes fitting and adjustment ♿

A L3670 Shoulder orthotic (SO), acromio/clavicular (canvas and webbing type), prefabricated, includes fitting and adjustment ♿

A L3671 Shoulder orthotic (SO), shoulder cap design, without joints, may include soft interface, straps, custom fabricated, includes fitting and adjustment

A L3672 Shoulder orthotic (SO), abduction positioning (airplane design), thoracic component and support bar, without joints, may inlcude soft interface, straps, custom fabricated, includes fitting and adjustment

A L3673 Shoulder orthotic (SO), abduction positioning (airplane design), thoracic component and support bar, includes nontorsion joint/turnbuckle, may include soft interface, straps, custom fabricated, includes fitting and adjustment

A L3675 Shoulder orthotic (SO), vest type abduction restrainer, canvas webbing type or equal, prefabricated, includes fitting and adjustment ♿

E L3677 Shoulder orthotic (SO), hard plastic, shoulder stabilizer, prefabricated, includes fitting and adjustment
MED: 100-2,15,120

ELBOW ORTHOTIC (EO)

A L3700 Elbow orthotic (EO), elastic with stays, prefabricated, includes fitting and adjustment ♿

A L3701 Elbow orthotic (EO), elastic, prefabricated, includes fitting and adjustment (e.g., neoprene, Lycra) ♿

A L3702 Elbow orthotic (EO), without joints, may include soft interface, straps, custom fabricated, includes fitting and adjustment

A L3710 Elbow orthotic (EO), elastic with metal joints, prefabricated, includes fitting and adjustment ♿

A L3720 Elbow orthotic (EO), double upright with forearm/arm cuffs, free motion, custom fabricated ♿

A L3730 Elbow orthotic (EO), double upright with forearm/arm cuffs, extension/ flexion assist, custom fabricated ♿

A L3740 Elbow orthotic (EO), double upright with forearm/arm cuffs, adjustable position lock with active control, custom fabricated ♿

A L3760 Elbow orthotic (EO), with adjustable position locking joint(s), prefabricated, includes fitting and adjustments, any type ♿

A L3762 Elbow orthotic (EO), rigid, without joints, includes soft interface material, prefabricated, includes fitting and adjustment ♿

A L3763 Elbow-wrist-hand orthotic (EWHO), rigid, without joints, may include soft interface, straps, custom fabricated, includes fitting and adjustment

A L3764 Elbow-wrist-hand orthotic (EWHO), includes one or more nontorsion joints, elastic bands, turnbuckles, may include soft interface, straps, custom fabricated, includes fitting and adjustment

A L3765 Elbow-wrist-hand-finger orthotic (EWHFO), rigid, without joints, may include soft interface, straps, custom fabricated, includes fitting and adjustment

A L3766 Elbow-wrist-hand-finger orthotic, includes one or more nontorsion joints, elastic bands (EWHFO), turnbuckles, may include soft interface, straps, custom fabricated, includes fitting and adjustment

WRIST-HAND-FINGER ORTHOTIC (WHFO)

A L3806 Wrist-hand-finger orthotic (WHFO), includes one or more nontorsion joint(s), turnbuckles, elastic bands/springs, may include soft interface material, straps, custom fabricated, includes fitting and adjustment ♿

A L3807 Wrist-hand-finger orthotic (WHFO), without joint(s), prefabricated, includes fitting and adjustments, any type ♿

A L3808 Wrist-hand-finger orthotic (WHFO), rigid without joints, may include soft interface material; straps, custom fabricated, includes fitting and adjustment ♿

ADDITIONS

~~L3890 Addition to upper extremity joint, wrist or elbow, concentric adjustable torsion style mechanism, each~~

DYNAMIC FLEXOR HINGE, RECIPROCAL WRIST EXTENSION/FLEXION, FINGER FLEXION/EXTENSION

A L3900 Wrist-hand-finger orthotic (WHFO), dynamic flexor hinge, reciprocal wrist extension/ flexion, finger flexion/extension, wrist or finger driven, custom fabricated ♿

A L3901 Wrist-hand-finger orthotic (WHFO), dynamic flexor hinge, reciprocal wrist extension/ flexion, finger flexion/extension, cable driven, custom fabricated ♿

EXTERNAL POWER

A L3904 Wrist-hand-finger orthotic (WHFO), external powered, electric, custom fabricated ♿

OTHER - CUSTOM FITTED

▲ A **L3905** Wrist-hand orthotic (WHO), includes one or more nontorsion joints, elastic bands, turnbuckles, may include soft interface, straps, custom fabricated, includes fitting and adjustment

A **L3906** Wrist-hand orthosis (WHO), without joints, may include soft interface, straps, custom fabricated, includes fitting and adjustment ♿

A **L3908** Wrist-hand orthotic (WHO), wrist extension control cock-up, nonmolded, prefabricated, includes fitting and adjustment ♿

A **L3909** Wrist orthotic (WO), elastic, prefabricated, includes fitting and adjustment (e.g., neoprene, Lycra) ♿

A **L3911** Wrist hand finger orthotic (WHFO), elastic, prefabricated, includes fitting and adjustment (e.g., neoprene, Lycra) ♿

A **L3912** Hand-finger orthotic (HFO), flexion glove with elastic finger control, prefabricated, includes fitting and adjustment ♿

A **L3913** Hand finger orthotic (HFO), without joints, may include soft interface, straps, custom fabricated, includes fitting and adjustment

A **L3915** Wrist hand orthotic (WHO), includes one or more nontorsion joint(s), elastic bands, turnbuckles, may include soft interface, straps, prefabricated, includes fitting and adjustment ♿

A **L3917** Hand orthotic (HO), metacarpal fracture orthotic, prefabricated, includes fitting and adjustment ♿

A **L3919** Hand orthotic (HO), without joints, may include soft interface, straps, custom fabricated, includes fitting and adjustment

A **L3921** Hand finger orthotic (HFO), includes one or more nontorsion joints, elastic bands, turnbuckles, may include soft interface, straps, custom fabricated, includes fitting and adjustment

A **L3923** Hand finger orthotic (HFO), without joints, may include soft interface, straps, prefabricated, includes fitting and adjustment ♿

A **L3925** Finger orthotic (FO), proximal interphalangeal (PIP)/distal interphalangeal (DIP), nontorsion joint/spring, extension/flexion, may include soft interface material, prefabricated, includes fitting and adjustment

A **L3927** Finger orthotic (FO), proximal interphalangeal (PIP)/distal interphalangeal (DIP), without joint/spring, extension/flexion (e.g., static or ring type), may include soft interface material, prefabricated, includes fitting and adjustment

A **L3929** Hand-finger orthotic (HFO), includes one or more nontorsion joint(s), turnbuckles, elastic bands/springs, may include soft interface material, straps, prefabricated, includes fitting and adjustment

A **L3931** Wrist-hand-finger orthotic (WHFO), includes one or more nontorsion joint(s), turnbuckles, elastic bands/springs, may include soft interface material, straps, prefabricated, includes fitting and adjustment

A **L3933** Finger orthotic (FO), without joints, may include soft interface, custom fabricated, includes fitting and adjustment

A **L3935** Finger orthotic, nontorsion joint, may include soft interface, custom fabricated, includes fitting and adjustment

A ☑ **L3956** Addition of joint to upper extremity orthotic, any material; per joint ♿

SHOULDER-ELBOW-WRIST-HAND ORTHOTIC (SEWHO)

ABDUCTION POSITION, CUSTOM FITTED

A **L3960** Shoulder-elbow-wrist-hand orthotic (SEWHO), abduction positioning, airplane design, prefabricated, includes fitting and adjustment ♿

A **L3961** Shoulder elbow wrist hand orthotic (SEWHO), shoulder cap design, without joints, may include soft interface, straps, custom fabricated, includes fitting and adjustment

A **L3962** Shoulder-elbow-wrist-hand orthotic (SEWHO), abduction positioning, Erb's palsy design, prefabricated, includes fitting and adjustment ♿

Y **L3964** Shoulder-elbow orthotic (SEO), mobile arm support attached to wheelchair, balanced, adjustable, prefabricated, includes fitting and adjustment ♿

Y **L3965** Shoulder-elbow orthotic (SEO), mobile arm support attached to wheelchair, balanced, adjustable Rancho type, prefabricated, includes fitting and adjustment ♿

Y **L3966** Shoulder-elbow orthotic (SEO), mobile arm support attached to wheelchair, balanced, reclining, prefabricated, includes fitting and adjustment ♿

A **L3967** Shoulder-elbow-wrist-hand orthotic (SEWHO), abduction positioning (airplane design), thoracic component and support bar, without joints, may include soft interface, straps, custom fabricated, includes fitting and adjustment

Y **L3968** Shoulder-elbow orthotic (SEO), mobile arm support attached to wheelchair, balanced, friction arm support (friction dampening to proximal and distal joints), prefabricated, includes fitting and adjustment ♿

Y **L3969** Shoulder-elbow orthotic (SEO), mobile arm support, monosuspension arm and hand support, overhead elbow forearm hand sling support, yoke type suspension support, prefabricated, includes fitting and adjustment ♿

ADDITIONS TO MOBILE ARM SUPPORTS

Y **L3970** Shoulder-elbow orthotic (SEO), addition to mobile arm support, elevating proximal arm ♿

A **L3971** Shoulder-elbow-wrist-hand orthotic (SEWHO), shoulder cap design, includes one or more nontorsion joints, elastic bands, turnbuckles, may include soft interface, straps, custom fabricated, includes fitting and adjustment

Y **L3972** Shoulder-elbow orthotic (SEO), addition to mobile arm support, offset or lateral rocker arm with elastic balance control ♿

A **L3973** Shoulder-elbow-wrist-hand orthotic (SEWHO), abduction positioning (airplane design), thoracic component and support bar, includes one or more nontorsion joints, elastic bands, turnbuckles, may include soft interface, straps, custom fabricated, includes fitting and adjustment

Y **L3974** Shoulder-elbow orthotic (SEO), addition to mobile arm support, supinator ♿

A **L3975** Shoulder-elbow-wrist-hand-finger orthotic (SEWHO), shoulder cap design, without joints, may include soft interface, straps, custom fabricated, includes fitting and adjustment

A L3976 Shoulder-elbow-wrist-hand-finger orthotic (SEWHO), abduction positioning (airplane design), thoracic component and support bar, without joints, may include soft interface, straps, custom fabricated, includes fitting and adjustment

A L3977 Shoulder-elbow-wrist-hand-finger orthotic (SEWHO), shoulder cap design, includes one or more nontorsion joints, elastic bands, turnbuckles, may include soft interface, straps, custom fabricated, includes fitting and adjustment

A L3978 Shoulder-elbow-wrist-hand-finger orthotic (SEWHO), abduction positioning (airplane design), thoracic component and support bar, includes one or more nontorsion joints, elastic bands, turnbuckles, may include soft interface, straps, custom fabricated, includes fitting and adjustment

FRACTURE ORTHOTIC

A L3980 Upper extremity fracture orthotic, humeral, prefabricated, includes fitting and adjustment ♿

A L3982 Upper extremity fracture orthotic, radius/ulnar, prefabricated, includes fitting and adjustment ♿

A L3984 Upper extremity fracture orthotic, wrist, prefabricated, includes fitting and adjustment ♿

A ☑ L3995 Addition to upper extremity orthotic, sock, fracture or equal, each ♿

A L3999 Upper limb orthosis, not otherwise specified

SPECIFIC REPAIR

A L4000 Replace girdle for spinal orthotic (cervical-thoracic-lumbar-sacral orthotic (CTLSO) or spinal orthotic SO) ♿

A L4002 Replacement strap, any orthotic, includes all components, any length, any type

A L4010 Replace trilateral socket brim ♿

A L4020 Replace quadrilateral socket brim, molded to patient model ♿

A L4030 Replace quadrilateral socket brim, custom fitted ♿

A L4040 Replace molded thigh lacer, for custom fabricated orthotic only ♿

A L4045 Replace nonmolded thigh lacer, for custom fabricated orthotic only ♿

A L4050 Replace molded calf lacer, for custom fabricated orthotic only ♿

A L4055 Replace nonmolded calf lacer, for custom fabricated orthotic only ♿

A L4060 Replace high roll cuff ♿

A L4070 Replace proximal and distal upright for KAFO ♿

A L4080 Replace metal bands KAFO, proximal thigh ♿

A L4090 Replace metal bands KAFO-AFO, calf or distal thigh ♿

A L4100 Replace leather cuff KAFO, proximal thigh ♿

A L4110 Replace leather cuff KAFO-AFO, calf or distal thigh ♿

A L4130 Replace pretibial shell ♿

REPAIRS

A ☑ L4205 Repair of orthotic device, labor component, per 15 minutes

MED: 100-2,15,110.2

A L4210 Repair of orthotic device, repair or replace minor parts

MED: 100-2,15,110.2; 100-2,15,120

A L4350 Ankle control orthotic, stirrup style, rigid, includes any type interface (e.g., pneumatic, gel), prefabricated, includes fitting and adjustment ♿

▲ A L4360 Walking boot, pneumatic and/or vacuum, with or without joints, with or without interface material, prefabricated, includes fitting and adjustment ♿

A L4370 Pneumatic full leg splint, prefabricated, includes fitting and adjustment ♿

MED: 100-4,4,240

A L4380 Pneumatic knee splint, prefabricated, includes fitting and adjustment ♿

MED: 100-4,4,240

A L4386 Walking boot, nonpneumatic, with or without joints, with or without interface material, prefabricated, includes fitting and adjustment ♿

A L4392 Replacement, soft interface material, static AFO ♿

A L4394 Replace soft interface material, foot drop splint ♿

A L4396 Static ankle-foot orthotic (AFO), including soft interface material, adjustable for fit, for positioning, pressure reduction, may be used for minimal ambulation, prefabricated, includes fitting and adjustment ♿

A L4398 Foot drop splint, recumbent positioning device, prefabricated, includes fitting and adjustment ♿

MED: 100-4,4,240

PROSTHETIC PROCEDURES L5000-L9999

LOWER LIMB

The procedures in this section are considered as "base" or "basic procedures" and may be modified by listing items/procedures or special materials from the "additions" sections and adding them to the base procedure.

PARTIAL FOOT

A L5000 Partial foot, shoe insert with longitudinal arch, toe filler

MED: 100-2,15,290; 100-4,3,10.4

A L5010 Partial foot, molded socket, ankle height, with toe filler

MED: 100-2,15,290; 100-4,3,10.4

A L5020 Partial foot, molded socket, tibial tubercle height, with toe filler

MED: 100-2,15,290; 100-4,3,10.4

ANKLE

A L5050 Ankle, Symes, molded socket, SACH foot ⊘ ♿

MED: 100-4,3,10.4

A L5060 Ankle, Symes, metal frame, molded leather socket, articulated ankle/foot ⊘ ♿

MED: 100-4,3,10.4

BELOW KNEE

A L5100 Below knee, molded socket, shin, SACH foot ⊘ ♿

MED: 100-4,3,10.4

A L5105 Below knee, plastic socket, joints and thigh lacer, SACH foot ⊘ ♿

MED: 100-4,3,10.4

KNEE DISARTICULATION

A **L5150** Knee disarticulation (or through knee), molded socket, external knee joints, shin, SACH foot ⊘ ♿

MED: 100-4,3,10.4

A **L5160** Knee disarticulation (or through knee), molded socket, bent knee configuration, external knee joints, shin, SACH foot ⊘ ♿

MED: 100-4,3,10.4

ABOVE KNEE

A **L5200** Above knee, molded socket, single axis constant friction knee, shin, SACH foot ⊘ ♿

MED: 100-4,3,10.4

A ☑ **L5210** Above knee, short prosthesis, no knee joint (stubbies), with foot blocks, no ankle joints, each ⊘ ♿

MED: 100-4,3,10.4

A ☑ **L5220** Above knee, short prosthesis, no knee joint (stubbies), with articulated ankle/foot, dynamically aligned, each ⊘ ♿

MED: 100-4,3,10.4

A **L5230** Above knee, for proximal femoral focal deficiency, constant friction knee, shin, SACH foot ⊘ ♿

MED: 100-4,3,10.4

HIP DISARTICULATION

A **L5250** Hip disarticulation, Canadian type; molded socket, hip joint, single axis constant friction knee, shin, SACH foot ⊘ ♿

MED: 100-4,3,10.4

A **L5270** Hip disarticulation, tilt table type; molded socket, locking hip joint, single axis constant friction knee, shin, SACH foot ⊘ ♿

MED: 100-4,3,10.4

HEMIPELVECTOMY

A **L5280** Hemipelvectomy, Canadian type; molded socket, hip joint, single axis constant friction knee, shin, SACH foot ⊘ ♿

MED: 100-4,3,10.4

A **L5301** Below knee, molded socket, shin, SACH foot, endoskeletal system ⊘ ♿

MED: 100-4,3,10.4

A **L5311** Knee disarticulation (or through knee), molded socket, external knee joints, shin, SACH foot, endoskeletal system ⊘ ♿

MED: 100-4,3,10.4

A **L5321** Above knee, molded socket, open end, SACH foot, endoskeletal system, single axis knee ⊘ ♿

MED: 100-4,3,10.4

A **L5331** Hip disarticulation, Canadian type, molded socket, endoskeletal system, hip joint, single axis knee, SACH foot ⊘ ♿

MED: 100-4,3,10.4

A **L5341** Hemipelvectomy, Canadian type, molded socket, endoskeletal system, hip joint, single axis knee, SACH foot ⊘ ♿

MED: 100-4,3,10.4

IMMEDIATE POSTSURGICAL OR EARLY FITTING PROCEDURES

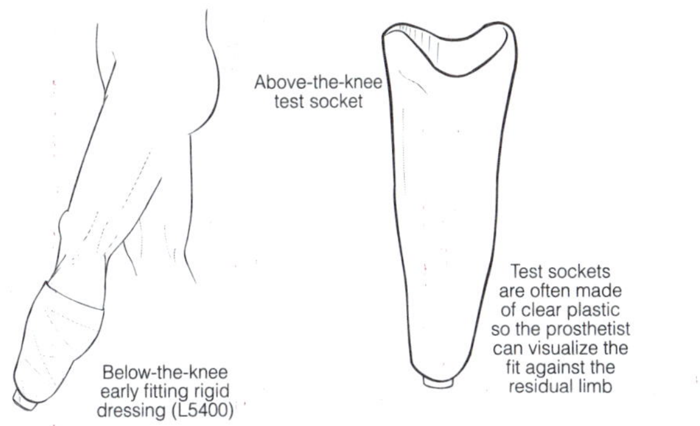

A ☑ **L5400** Immediate postsurgical or early fitting, application of initial rigid dressing, including fitting, alignment, suspension, and one cast change, below knee

A ☑ **L5410** Immediate postsurgical or early fitting, application of initial rigid dressing, including fitting, alignment and suspension, below knee, each additional cast change and realignment ⊘ ♿

A ☑ **L5420** Immediate postsurgical or early fitting, application of initial rigid dressing, including fitting, alignment and suspension and one cast change AK or knee disarticulation ⊘ ♿

A ☑ **L5430** Immediate postsurgical or early fitting, application of initial rigid dressing, including fitting, alignment and suspension, AK or knee disarticulation, each additional cast change and realignment ⊘ ♿

A **L5450** Immediate postsurgical or early fitting, application of nonweight bearing rigid dressing, below knee ⊘ ♿

A **L5460** Immediate postsurgical or early fitting, application of nonweight bearing rigid dressing, above knee ⊘ ♿

INITIAL PROSTHESIS

A **L5500** Initial, below knee PTB type socket, nonalignable system, pylon, no cover, SACH foot, plaster socket, direct formed ⊘ ♿

MED: 100-4,3,10.4

A **L5505** Initial, above knee, knee disarticulation, ischial level socket, nonalignable system, pylon, no cover, SACH foot, plaster socket, direct formed ⊘ ♿

MED: 100-4,3,10.4

PREPARATORY PROSTHESIS

A **L5510** Preparatory, below knee PTB type socket, nonalignable system, pylon, no cover, SACH foot, plaster socket, molded to model ⊘ ♿

A **L5520** Preparatory, below knee PTB type socket, nonalignable system, pylon, no cover, SACH foot, thermoplastic or equal, direct formed ⊘ ♿

A **L5530** Preparatory, below knee PTB type socket, nonalignable system, pylon, no cover, SACH foot, thermoplastic or equal, molded to model ⊘ ♿

A **L5535** Preparatory, below knee PTB type socket, nonalignable system, pylon, no cover, SACH foot, prefabricated, adjustable open end socket ⊘ ♿

A **L5540** Preparatory, below knee PTB type socket, nonalignable system, pylon, no cover, SACH foot, laminated socket, molded to model ⊘ ♿

A **L5560** Preparatory, above knee, knee disarticulation, ischial level socket, nonalignable system, pylon, no cover, SACH foot, plaster socket, molded to model ⊘ ♿

A L5570 Preparatory, above knee — knee disarticulation, ischial level socket, nonalignable system, pylon, no cover, SACH foot, thermoplastic or equal, direct formed

A L5580 Preparatory, above knee, knee disarticulation, ischial level socket, nonalignable system, pylon, no cover, SACH foot, thermoplastic or equal, molded to model

A L5585 Preparatory, above knee — knee disarticulation, ischial level socket, nonalignable system, pylon, no cover, SACH foot, prefabricated adjustable open end socket

A L5590 Preparatory, above knee, knee disarticulation, ischial level socket, nonalignable system, pylon, no cover, SACH foot, laminated socket, molded to model

A L5595 Preparatory, hip disarticulation/hemipelvectomy, pylon, no cover, SACH foot, thermoplastic or equal, molded to patient model

A L5600 Preparatory, hip disarticulation/hemipelvectomy, pylon, no cover, SACH foot, laminated socket, molded to patient model

ADDITIONS: LOWER EXTREMITY

A L5610 Addition to lower extremity, endoskeletal system, above knee, hydracadence system

A L5611 Addition to lower extremity, endoskeletal system, above knee, knee disarticulation, 4-bar linkage, with friction swing phase control

A L5613 Addition to lower extremity, endoskeletal system, above knee, knee disarticulation, 4-bar linkage, with hydraulic swing phase control

A L5614 Addition to lower extremity, exoskeletal system, above knee-knee disarticulation, 4 bar linkage, with pneumatic swing phase control

A L5616 Addition to lower extremity, endoskeletal system, above knee, universal multiplex system, friction swing phase control

A ☑ L5617 Addition to lower extremity, quick change self-aligning unit, above knee or below knee, each

ADDITIONS: TEST SOCKETS

A L5618 Addition to lower extremity, test socket, Symes

A L5620 Addition to lower extremity, test socket, below knee

A L5622 Addition to lower extremity, test socket, knee disarticulation

A L5624 Addition to lower extremity, test socket, above knee

A L5626 Addition to lower extremity, test socket, hip disarticulation

A L5628 Addition to lower extremity, test socket, hemipelvectomy

A L5629 Addition to lower extremity, below knee, acrylic socket

ADDITIONS: SOCKET VARIATIONS

A L5630 Addition to lower extremity, Symes type, expandable wall socket

A L5631 Addition to lower extremity, above knee or knee disarticulation, acrylic socket

A L5632 Addition to lower extremity, Symes type, PTB brim design socket

A L5634 Addition to lower extremity, Symes type, posterior opening (Canadian) socket

A L5636 Addition to lower extremity, Symes type, medial opening socket

A L5637 Addition to lower extremity, below knee, total contact

A L5638 Addition to lower extremity, below knee, leather socket

A L5639 Addition to lower extremity, below knee, wood socket

A L5640 Addition to lower extremity, knee disarticulation, leather socket

A L5642 Addition to lower extremity, above knee, leather socket

A L5643 Addition to lower extremity, hip disarticulation, flexible inner socket, external frame

A L5644 Addition to lower extremity, above knee, wood socket

A L5645 Addition to lower extremity, below knee, flexible inner socket, external frame

A L5646 Addition to lower extremity, below knee, air, fluid, gel or equal, cushion socket

A L5647 Addition to lower extremity, below knee, suction socket

A L5648 Addition to lower extremity, above knee, air, fluid, gel or equal, cushion socket

A L5649 Addition to lower extremity, ischial containment/narrow M-L socket

A L5650 Additions to lower extremity, total contact, above knee or knee disarticulation socket

A L5651 Addition to lower extremity, above knee, flexible inner socket, external frame

A L5652 Addition to lower extremity, suction suspension, above knee or knee disarticulation socket

A L5653 Addition to lower extremity, knee disarticulation, expandable wall socket

ADDITIONS: SOCKET INSERT AND SUSPENSION

A L5654 Addition to lower extremity, socket insert, Symes, (Kemblo, Pelite, Aliplast, Plastazote) or equal

A L5655 Addition to lower extremity, socket insert, below knee (Kemblo, Pelite, Aliplast, Plastazote or equal)

A L5656 Addition to lower extremity, socket insert, knee disarticulation (Kemblo, Pelite, Aliplast, Plastazote or equal)

A L5658 Addition to lower extremity, socket insert, above knee (Kemblo, Pelite, Aliplast, Plastazote or equal)

A L5661 Addition to lower extremity, socket insert, multidurometer Symes

A L5665 Addition to lower extremity, socket insert, multidurometer, below knee

A L5666 Addition to lower extremity, below knee, cuff suspension

A L5668 Addition to lower extremity, below knee, molded distal cushion

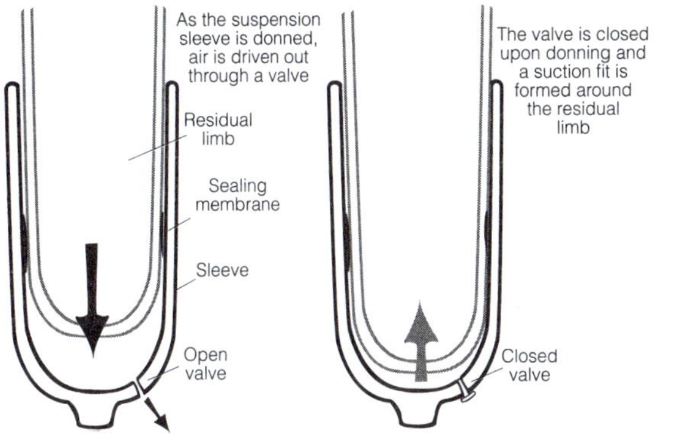

A L5670 Addition to lower extremity, below knee, molded supracondylar suspension (PTS or similar) ⊘ ♿

A L5671 Addition to lower extremity, below knee / above knee suspension locking mechanism (shuttle, lanyard, or equal), excludes socket insert ⊘ ♿

A L5672 Addition to lower extremity, below knee, removable medial brim suspension ⊘ ♿

A L5673 Addition to lower extremity, below knee/above knee, custom fabricated from existing mold or prefabricated, socket insert, silicone gel, elastomeric or equal, for use with locking mechanism ⊘ ♿

A ☑ L5676 Additions to lower extremity, below knee, knee joints, single axis, pair ⊘ ♿

A ☑ L5677 Additions to lower extremity, below knee, knee joints, polycentric, pair ⊘ ♿

A ☑ L5678 Additions to lower extremity, below knee, joint covers, pair ⊘ ♿

A L5679 Addition to lower extremity, below knee/above knee, custom fabricated from existing mold or prefabricated, socket insert, silicone gel, elastomeric or equal, not for use with locking mechanism ⊘ ♿

A L5680 Addition to lower extremity, below knee, thigh lacer, nonmolded ⊘ ♿

A L5681 Addition to lower extremity, below knee/above knee, custom fabricated socket insert for congenital or atypical traumatic amputee, silicone gel, elastomeric or equal, for use with or without locking mechanism, initial only (for other than initial, use code L5673 or L5679) ⊘ ♿

A L5682 Addition to lower extremity, below knee, thigh lacer, gluteal/ischial, molded ⊘ ♿

A L5683 Addition to lower extremity, below knee/above knee, custom fabricated socket insert for other than congenital or atypical traumatic amputee, silicone gel, elastomeric or equal, for use with or without locking mechanism, initial only (for other than initial, use code L5673 or L5679) ⊘ ♿

A L5684 Addition to lower extremity, below knee, fork strap ⊘ ♿

A L5685 Addition to lower extremity prosthesis, below knee, suspension/sealing sleeve, with or without valve, any material, each ⊘

A L5686 Addition to lower extremity, below knee, back check (extension control) ⊘ ♿

A L5688 Addition to lower extremity, below knee, waist belt, webbing ⊘ ♿

A L5690 Addition to lower extremity, below knee, waist belt, padded and lined ⊘ ♿

A L5692 Addition to lower extremity, above knee, pelvic control belt, light ⊘ ♿

A L5694 Addition to lower extremity, above knee, pelvic control belt, padded and lined ⊘ ♿

A ☑ L5695 Addition to lower extremity, above knee, pelvic control, sleeve suspension, neoprene or equal, each ⊘

A L5696 Addition to lower extremity, above knee or knee disarticulation, pelvic joint ⊘

A L5697 Addition to lower extremity, above knee or knee disarticulation, pelvic band ⊘

A L5698 Addition to lower extremity, above knee or knee disarticulation, Silesian bandage ⊘

A L5699 All lower extremity prostheses, shoulder harness ⊘

REPLACEMENTS

A L5700 Replacement, socket, below knee, molded to patient model ⊘

A L5701 Replacement, socket, above knee/knee disarticulation, including attachment plate, molded to patient model ⊘

A L5702 Replacement, socket, hip disarticulation, including hip joint, molded to patient model ⊘

A L5703 Ankle, Symes, molded to patient model, socket without solid ankle cushion heel (SACH) foot, replacement only ⊘

A L5704 Custom shaped protective cover, below knee ⊘

A L5705 Custom shaped protective cover, above knee ⊘

A L5706 Custom shaped protective cover, knee disarticulation ⊘

A L5707 Custom shaped protective cover, hip disarticulation ⊘

ADDITIONS: EXOSKELETAL KNEE-SHIN SYSTEM

A L5710 Addition, exoskeletal knee-shin system, single axis, manual lock ⊘

A L5711 Additions exoskeletal knee-shin system, single axis, manual lock, ultra-light material ⊘

A L5712 Addition, exoskeletal knee-shin system, single axis, friction swing and stance phase control (safety knee) ⊘

A L5714 Addition, exoskeletal knee-shin system, single axis, variable friction swing phase control ⊘

A L5716 Addition, exoskeletal knee-shin system, polycentric, mechanical stance phase lock ⊘

A L5718 Addition, exoskeletal knee-shin system, polycentric, friction swing and stance phase control ⊘

A L5722 Addition, exoskeletal knee-shin system, single axis, pneumatic swing, friction stance phase control ⊘

A L5724 Addition, exoskeletal knee-shin system, single axis, fluid swing phase control ⊘

A L5726 Addition, exoskeletal knee/shin system, single axis, external joints, fluid swing phase control ⊘

A L5728 Addition, exoskeletal knee-shin system, single axis, fluid swing and stance phase control ⊘

A L5780 Addition, exoskeletal knee-shin system, single axis, pneumatic/hydra pneumatic swing phase control ⊘

A L5781 Addition to lower limb prosthesis, vacuum pump, residual limb volume management and moisture evacuation system ⊘

A L5782 Addition to lower limb prosthesis, vacuum pump, residual limb volume management and moisture evacuation system, heavy-duty ⊘

COMPONENT MODIFICATION

A **L5785** Addition, exoskeletal system, below knee, ultra-light material (titanium, carbon fiber or equal) ⊘

A **L5790** Addition, exoskeletal system, above knee, ultra-light material (titanium, carbon fiber or equal) ⊘

A **L5795** Addition, exoskeletal system, hip disarticulation, ultra-light material (titanium, carbon fiber or equal) ⊘

ADDITIONS: ENDOSKELETAL KNEE-SHIN SYSTEM

A **L5810** Addition, endoskeletal knee-shin system, single axis, manual lock ⊘

A **L5811** Addition, endoskeletal knee-shin system, single axis, manual lock, ultra-light material ⊘

A **L5812** Addition, endoskeletal knee-shin system, single axis, friction swing and stance phase control (safety knee) ⊘

A **L5814** Addition, endoskeletal knee-shin system, polycentric, hydraulic swing phase control, mechanical stance phase lock ⊘

A **L5816** Addition, endoskeletal knee-shin system, polycentric, mechanical stance phase lock ⊘

A **L5818** Addition, endoskeletal knee/shin system, polycentric, friction swing and stance phase control ⊘

A **L5822** Addition, endoskeletal knee-shin system, single axis, pneumatic swing, friction stance phase control ⊘

A **L5824** Addition, endoskeletal knee-shin system, single axis, fluid swing phase control ⊘

A **L5826** Addition, endoskeletal knee-shin system, single axis, hydraulic swing phase control, with miniature high activity frame ⊘

A **L5828** Addition, endoskeletal knee-shin system, single axis, fluid swing and stance phase control ⊘

A **L5830** Addition, endoskeletal knee/shin system, single axis, pneumatic/swing phase control ⊘

A **L5840** Addition, endoskeletal knee/shin system, 4-bar linkage or multiaxial, pneumatic swing phase control ⊘

A **L5845** Addition, endoskeletal knee/shin system, stance flexion feature, adjustable ⊘

A **L5848** Addition to endoskeletal knee-shin system, fluid stance extension, dampening feature, with or without adjustability ⊘

A **L5850** Addition, endoskeletal system, above knee or hip disarticulation, knee extension assist ⊘

A **L5855** Addition, endoskeletal system, hip disarticulation, mechanical hip extension assist ⊘

A **L5856** Addition to lower extremity prosthesis, endoskeletal knee-shin system, microprocessor control feature, swing and stance phase, includes electronic sensor(s), any type ⊘

A **L5857** Addition to lower extremity prosthesis, endoskeletal knee-shin system, microprocessor control feature, swing phase only, includes electronic sensor(s), any type ⊘

A **L5858** Addition to lower extremity prosthesis, endoskeletal knee shin system, microprocessor control feature, stance phase only, includes electronic sensor(s), any type ⊘

A **L5910** Addition, endoskeletal system, below knee, alignable system ⊘

A **L5920** Addition, endoskeletal system, above knee or hip disarticulation, alignable system ⊘

A **L5925** Addition, endoskeletal system, above knee, knee disarticulation or hip disarticulation, manual lock ⊘

A **L5930** Addition, endoskeletal system, high activity knee control frame ⊘

A **L5940** Addition, endoskeletal system, below knee, ultra-light material (titanium, carbon fiber or equal) ⊘

A **L5950** Addition, endoskeletal system, above knee, ultra-light material (titanium, carbon fiber or equal) ⊘

A **L5960** Addition, endoskeletal system, hip disarticulation, ultra-light material (titanium, carbon fiber or equal) ⊘

A **L5962** Addition, endoskeletal system, below knee, flexible protective outer surface covering system ⊘

A **L5964** Addition, endoskeletal system, above knee, flexible protective outer surface covering system ⊘

A **L5966** Addition, endoskeletal system, hip disarticulation, flexible protective outer surface covering system ⊘

A **L5968** Addition to lower limb prosthesis, multiaxial ankle with swing phase active dorsiflexion feature ⊘

A **L5970** All lower extremity prostheses, foot, external keel, SACH foot ⊘

A **L5971** All lower extremity prosthesis, solid ankle cushion heel (SACH) foot, replacement only ⊘

A **L5972** All lower extremity prostheses, flexible keel foot (SAFE, STEN, Bock Dynamic or equal) ⊘

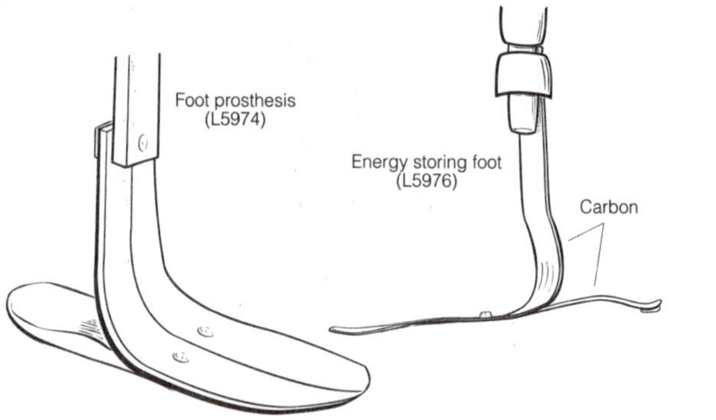

A **L5974** All lower extremity prostheses, foot, single axis ankle/foot ⊘

A **L5975** All lower extremity prosthesis, combination single axis ankle and flexible keel foot ⊘

A **L5976** All lower extremity prostheses, energy storing foot (Seattle Carbon Copy II or equal) ⊘

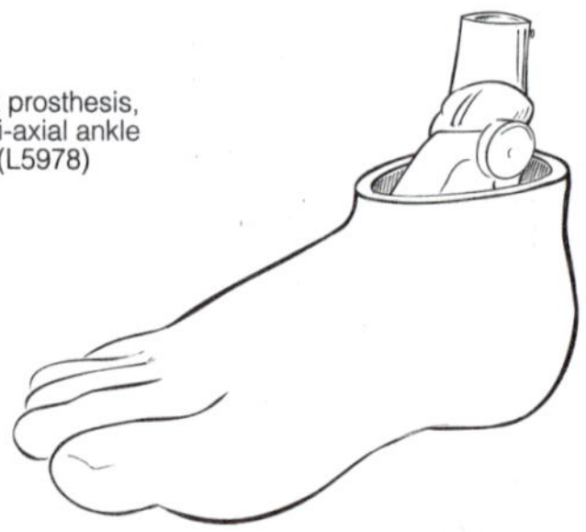

A **L5978** All lower extremity prostheses, foot, multiaxial ankle/foot ⊘

A **L5979** All lower extremity prostheses, multiaxial ankle, dynamic response foot, one piece system ⊘

A **L5980** All lower extremity prostheses, flex-foot system ⊘

A **L5981** All lower extremity prostheses, flex-walk system or equal ⊘

A **L5982** All exoskeletal lower extremity prostheses, axial rotation unit ⊘

A **L5984** All endoskeletal lower extremity prosthesis, axial rotation unit, with or without adjustability ⊘

A **L5985** All endoskeletal lower extremity prostheses, dynamic prosthetic pylon ⊘

A **L5986** All lower extremity prostheses, multiaxial rotation unit (MCP or equal) ⊘

A **L5987** All lower extremity prosthesis, shank foot system with vertical loading pylon

A **L5988** Addition to lower limb prosthesis, vertical shock reducing pylon feature ⊘

A **L5990** Addition to lower extremity prosthesis, user adjustable heel height ⊘

~~L5993 Addition to lower extremity prosthesis, heavy duty feature, foot only, (for patient weight greater than 300 lbs)~~

~~L5994 Addition to lower extremity prosthesis, heavy duty feature, knee only, (for patient weight greater than 300 lbs)~~

~~L5995 Addition to lower extremity prosthesis, heavy duty feature, other than foot or knee, (for patient weight greater than 300 lbs)~~

A **L5999** Lower extremity prosthesis, not otherwise specified
Determine if an alternative HCPCS Level II or a CPT code better describes the service being reported. This code should be used only if a more specific code is unavailable.

UPPER LIMB

The procedures in L6000-L6590 are considered as "base" or "basic procedures" and may be modified by listing procedures from the "addition" sections. The base procedures include only standard friction wrist and control cable system unless otherwise specified.

PARTIAL HAND

A **L6000** Partial hand, Robin-Aids, thumb remaining (or equal)

A **L6010** Partial hand, Robin-Aids, little and/or ring finger remaining (or equal)

A **L6020** Partial hand, Robin-Aids, no finger remaining (or equal)

A **L6025** Transcarpal/metacarpal or partial hand disarticulation prosthesis, external power, self-suspended, inner socket with removable forearm section, electrodes and cables, 2 batteries, charger, myoelectric control of terminal device

WRIST DISARTICULATION

A **L6050** Wrist disarticulation, molded socket, flexible elbow hinges, triceps pad ⊘

A **L6055** Wrist disarticulation, molded socket with expandable interface, flexible elbow hinges, triceps pad ⊘

BELOW ELBOW

A **L6100** Below elbow, molded socket, flexible elbow hinge, triceps pad ⊘

A **L6110** Below elbow, molded socket (Muenster or Northwestern suspension types) ⊘

A **L6120** Below elbow, molded double wall split socket, step-up hinges, half cuff ⊘

A **L6130** Below elbow, molded double wall split socket, stump activated locking hinge, half cuff ⊘

ELBOW DISARTICULATION

A **L6200** Elbow disarticulation, molded socket, outside locking hinge, forearm ⊘

A **L6205** Elbow disarticulation, molded socket with expandable interface, outside locking hinges, forearm ⊘ ♿

ABOVE ELBOW

A **L6250** Above elbow, molded double wall socket, internal locking elbow, forearm ⊘ ♿

SHOULDER DISARTICULATION

A **L6300** Shoulder disarticulation, molded socket, shoulder bulkhead, humeral section, internal locking elbow, forearm ⊘ ♿

A **L6310** Shoulder disarticulation, passive restoration (complete prosthesis) ⊘ ♿

A **L6320** Shoulder disarticulation, passive restoration (shoulder cap only) ⊘ ♿

INTERSCAPULAR THORACIC

A **L6350** Interscapular thoracic, molded socket, shoulder bulkhead, humeral section, internal locking elbow, forearm ⊘ ♿

A **L6360** Interscapular thoracic, passive restoration (complete prosthesis) ⊘ ♿

A **L6370** Interscapular thoracic, passive restoration (shoulder cap only) ⊘ ♿

IMMEDIATE AND EARLY POSTSURGICAL PROCEDURES

A **L6380** Immediate postsurgical or early fitting, application of initial rigid dressing, including fitting alignment and suspension of components, and one cast change, wrist disarticulation or below elbow ♿

A ☑ **L6382** Immediate postsurgical or early fitting, application of initial rigid dressing including fitting alignment and suspension of components, and one cast change, elbow disarticulation or above elbow ♿

A ☑ **L6384** Immediate postsurgical or early fitting, application of initial rigid dressing including fitting alignment and suspension of components, and one cast change, shoulder disarticulation or interscapular thoracic ♿

A ☑ **L6386** Immediate postsurgical or early fitting, each additional cast change and realignment ♿

A **L6388** Immediate postsurgical or early fitting, application of rigid dressing only ♿

ENDOSKELETAL: BELOW ELBOW

A **L6400** Below elbow, molded socket, endoskeletal system, including soft prosthetic tissue shaping ⊘ ♿

ENDOSKELETAL: ELBOW DISARTICULATION

A **L6450** Elbow disarticulation, molded socket, endoskeletal system, including soft prosthetic tissue shaping ⊘ ♿

ENDOSKELETAL: ABOVE ELBOW

A **L6500** Above elbow, molded socket, endoskeletal system, including soft prosthetic tissue shaping ⊘ ♿

ENDOSKELETAL: SHOULDER DISARTICULATION

A L6550 Shoulder disarticulation, molded socket, endoskeletal system, including soft prosthetic tissue shaping ⊘ ♿

ENDOSKELETAL: INTERSCAPULAR THORACIC

A L6570 Interscapular thoracic, molded socket, endoskeletal system, including soft prosthetic tissue shaping ⊘ ♿

A L6580 Preparatory, wrist disarticulation or below elbow, single wall plastic socket, friction wrist, flexible elbow hinges, figure of eight harness, humeral cuff, Bowden cable control, USMC or equal pylon, no cover, molded to patient model ⊘ ♿

A L6582 Preparatory, wrist disarticulation or below elbow, single wall socket, friction wrist, flexible elbow hinges, figure of eight harness, humeral cuff, Bowden cable control, USMC or equal pylon, no cover, direct formed ⊘ ♿

A L6584 Preparatory, elbow disarticulation or above elbow, single wall plastic socket, friction wrist, locking elbow, figure of eight harness, fair lead cable control, USMC or equal pylon, no cover, molded to patient model ⊘ ♿

A L6586 Preparatory, elbow disarticulation or above elbow, single wall socket, friction wrist, locking elbow, figure of eight harness, fair lead cable control, USMC or equal pylon, no cover, direct formed ⊘ ♿

A L6588 Preparatory, shoulder disarticulation or interscapular thoracic, single wall plastic socket, shoulder joint, locking elbow, friction wrist, chest strap, fair lead cable control, USMC or equal pylon, no cover, molded to patient model ⊘ ♿

A L6590 Preparatory, shoulder disarticulation or interscapular thoracic, single wall socket, shoulder joint, locking elbow, friction wrist, chest strap, fair lead cable control, USMC or equal pylon, no cover, direct formed ⊘ ♿

ADDITIONS: UPPER LIMB

The following procedures/modifications/components may be added to other base procedures. The items in this section should reflect the additional complexity of each modification procedure, in addition to the base procedure, at the time of the original order.

A ☑ L6600 Upper extremity additions, polycentric hinge, pair ⊘ ♿

A ☑ L6605 Upper extremity additions, single pivot hinge, pair ⊘ ♿

A ☑ L6610 Upper extremity additions, flexible metal hinge, pair ⊘ ♿

A L6611 Addition to upper extremity prosthesis, external powered, additional switch, any type ⊘ ♿

A L6615 Upper extremity addition, disconnect locking wrist unit ⊘ ♿

A ☑ L6616 Upper extremity addition, additional disconnect insert for locking wrist unit, each ⊘ ♿

A L6620 Upper extremity addition, flexion/extension wrist unit, with or without friction ⊘ ♿

A L6621 Upper extremity prosthesis addition, flexion/extension wrist with or without friction, for use with external powered terminal device ⊘

A L6623 Upper extremity addition, spring assisted rotational wrist unit with latch release ⊘ ♿

A L6624 Upper extremity addition, flexion/extension and rotation wrist unit ⊘ ♿

A L6625 Upper extremity addition, rotation wrist unit with cable lock ⊘ ♿

A L6628 Upper extremity addition, quick disconnect hook adapter, Otto Bock or equal ⊘ ♿

A L6629 Upper extremity addition, quick disconnect lamination collar with coupling piece, Otto Bock or equal ⊘ ♿

A L6630 Upper extremity addition, stainless steel, any wrist ⊘ ♿

A ☑ L6632 Upper extremity addition, latex suspension sleeve, each ⊘ ♿

A L6635 Upper extremity addition, lift assist for elbow ⊘ ♿

A L6637 Upper extremity addition, nudge control elbow lock ⊘ ♿

A L6638 Upper extremity addition to prosthesis, electric locking feature, only for use with manually powered elbow ⊘ ♿

A L6639 Upper extremity addition, heavy-duty feature, any elbow ⊘ ♿

A ☑ L6640 Upper extremity additions, shoulder abduction joint, pair ⊘ ♿

A L6641 Upper extremity addition, excursion amplifier, pulley type ⊘ ♿

A L6642 Upper extremity addition, excursion amplifier, lever type ⊘ ♿

A ☑ L6645 Upper extremity addition, shoulder flexion-abduction joint, each ⊘ ♿

A L6646 Upper extremity addition, shoulder joint, multipositional locking, flexion, adjustable abduction friction control, for use with body powered or external powered system ⊘ ♿

A L6647 Upper extremity addition, shoulder lock mechanism, body powered actuator ⊘ ♿

A L6648 Upper extremity addition, shoulder lock mechanism, external powered actuator ⊘ ♿

A ☑ L6650 Upper extremity addition, shoulder universal joint, each ⊘ ♿

A L6655 Upper extremity addition, standard control cable, extra ⊘ ♿

A L6660 Upper extremity addition, heavy-duty control cable ⊘ ♿

A L6665 Upper extremity addition, Teflon, or equal, cable lining ⊘ ♿

A L6670 Upper extremity addition, hook to hand, cable adapter ⊘ ♿

A L6672 Upper extremity addition, harness, chest or shoulder, saddle type ⊘ ♿

A L6675 Upper extremity addition, harness, (e.g., figure of eight type), single cable design ⊘ ♿

A L6676 Upper extremity addition, harness, (e.g., figure of eight type), dual cable design ⊘ ♿

A L6677 Upper extremity addition, harness, triple control, simultaneous operation of terminal device and elbow ⊘

A L6680 Upper extremity addition, test socket, wrist disarticulation or below elbow ⊘ ♿

A L6682 Upper extremity addition, test socket, elbow disarticulation or above elbow ⊘ ♿

A L6684 Upper extremity addition, test socket, shoulder disarticulation or interscapular thoracic ⊘ ♿

A L6686 Upper extremity addition, suction socket ⊘ ♿

A L6687 Upper extremity addition, frame type socket, below elbow or wrist disarticulation ⊘ ♿

A L6688 Upper extremity addition, frame type socket, above elbow or elbow disarticulation ⊘ ♿

A L6689 Upper extremity addition, frame type socket, shoulder disarticulation ⊘ ♿

A L6690 Upper extremity addition, frame type socket, interscapular-thoracic ⊘ ♿

A ☑ L6691 Upper extremity addition, removable insert, each ⊘ ♿

A ☑ L6692 Upper extremity addition, silicone gel insert or equal, each ⊘ ♿

A L6693 Upper extremity addition, locking elbow, forearm counterbalance ⊘ ♿

A L6694 Addition to upper extremity prosthesis, below elbow/above elbow, custom fabricated from existing mold or prefabricated, socket insert, silicone gel, elastomeric or equal, for use with locking mechanism ⊘

A L6695 Addition to upper extremity prosthesis, below elbow/above elbow, custom fabricated from existing mold or prefabricated, socket insert, silicone gel, elastomeric or equal, not for use with locking mechanism ⊘

A L6696 Addition to upper extremity prosthesis, below elbow/above elbow, custom fabricated socket insert for congenital or atypical traumatic amputee, silicone gel, elastomeric or equal, for use with or without locking mechanism, initial only (for other than initial, use code L6694 or L6695) ⊘

A L6697 Addition to upper extremity prosthesis, below elbow/above elbow, custom fabricated socket insert for other than congenital or atypical traumatic amputee, silicone gel, elastomeric or equal, for use with or without locking mechanism, initial only (for other than initial, use code L6694 or L6695) ⊘

A L6698 Addition to upper extremity prosthesis, below elbow/above elbow, lock mechanism, excludes socket insert ⊘

TERMINAL DEVICES

HOOKS AND HANDS

A L6703 Terminal device, passive hand/mitt, any material, any size ⊘

A L6704 Terminal device, sport/recreational/work attachment, any material, any size ⊘

A L6706 Terminal device, hook, mechanical, voluntary opening, any material, any size, lined or unlined ⊘

A L6707 Terminal device, hook, mechanical, voluntary closing, any material, any size, lined or unlined ⊘

A L6708 Terminal device, hand, mechanical, voluntary opening, any material, any size ⊘

A L6709 Terminal device, hand, mechanical, voluntary closing, any material, any size ⊘

● A L6711 Terminal device, hook, mechanical, voluntary opening, any material, any size, lined or unlined, pediatric

● A L6712 Terminal device, hook, mechanical, voluntary closing, any material, any size, lined or unlined, pediatric

● A L6713 Terminal device, hand, mechanical, voluntary opening, any material, any size, pediatric

● A L6714 Terminal device, hand, mechanical, voluntary closing, any material, any size, pediatric

● A L6721 Terminal device, hook or hand, heavy-duty, mechanical, voluntary opening, any material, any size, lined or unlined

● A L6722 Terminal device, hook or hand, heavy-duty, mechanical, voluntary closing, any material, any size, lined or unlined

A L6805 Addition to terminal device, modifier wrist unit ⊘ ♿

MED: 100-2,15,120; 100-4,3,10.4

A L6810 Addition to terminal device, precision pinch device ⊘ ♿

MED: 100-2,15,120; 100-4,3,10.4

A L6881 Automatic grasp feature, addition to upper limb electric prosthetic terminal device ⊘ ♿

A L6882 Microprocessor control feature, addition to upper limb prosthetic terminal device ⊘ ♿

MED: 100-2,15,120; 100-4,3,10.4

A L6883 Replacement socket, below elbow/wrist disarticulation, molded to patient model, for use with or without external power

A L6884 Replacement socket, above elbow/elbow disarticulation, molded to patient model, for use with or without external power

A L6885 Replacement socket, shoulder disarticulation/interscapular thoracic, molded to patient model, for use with or without external power

GLOVES FOR ABOVE HANDS

A L6890 Addition to upper extremity prosthesis, glove for terminal device, any material, prefabricated, includes fitting and adjustment ♿

A L6895 Addition to upper extremity prosthesis, glove for terminal device, any material, custom fabricated ♿

HAND RESTORATION

A L6900 Hand restoration (casts, shading and measurements included), partial hand, with glove, thumb or one finger remaining ♿

A L6905 Hand restoration (casts, shading and measurements included), partial hand, with glove, multiple fingers remaining ♿

A L6910 Hand restoration (casts, shading and measurements included), partial hand, with glove, no fingers remaining ♿

A L6915 Hand restoration (shading and measurements included), replacement glove for above ♿

EXTERNAL POWER

BASE DEVICES

A L6920 Wrist disarticulation, external power, self-suspended inner socket, removable forearm shell, Otto Bock or equal switch, cables, 2 batteries and 1 charger, switch control of terminal device ⊘ ♿

A L6925 Wrist disarticulation, external power, self-suspended inner socket, removable forearm shell, Otto Bock or equal electrodes, cables, 2 batteries and one charger, myoelectronic control of terminal device ⊘ ♿

A L6930 Below elbow, external power, self-suspended inner socket, removable forearm shell, Otto Bock or equal switch, cables, 2 batteries and one charger, switch control of terminal device

A L6935 Below elbow, external power, self-suspended inner socket, removable forearm shell, Otto Bock or equal electrodes, cables, 2 batteries and one charger, myoelectronic control of terminal device

A L6940 Elbow disarticulation, external power, molded inner socket, removable humeral shell, outside locking hinges, forearm, Otto Bock or equal switch, cables, 2 batteries and one charger, switch control of terminal device

A L6945 Elbow disarticulation, external power, molded inner socket, removable humeral shell, outside locking hinges, forearm, Otto Bock or equal electrodes, cables, 2 batteries and one charger, myoelectronic control of terminal device

A L6950 Above elbow, external power, molded inner socket, removable humeral shell, internal locking elbow, forearm, Otto Bock or equal switch, cables, 2 batteries and one charger, switch control of terminal device

A L6955 Above elbow, external power, molded inner socket, removable humeral shell, internal locking elbow, forearm, Otto Bock or equal electrodes, cables, 2 batteries and one charger, myoelectronic control of terminal device

A L6960 Shoulder disarticulation, external power, molded inner socket, removable shoulder shell, shoulder bulkhead, humeral section, mechanical elbow, forearm, Otto Bock or equal switch, cables, 2 batteries and one charger, switch control of terminal device

A L6965 Shoulder disarticulation, external power, molded inner socket, removable shoulder shell, shoulder bulkhead, humeral section, mechanical elbow, forearm, Otto Bock or equal electrodes, cables, 2 batteries and one charger, myoelectronic control of terminal device

A L6970 Interscapular-thoracic, external power, molded inner socket, removable shoulder shell, shoulder bulkhead, humeral section, mechanical elbow, forearm, Otto Bock or equal switch, cables, 2 batteries and one charger, switch control of terminal device

A L6975 Interscapular-thoracic, external power, molded inner socket, removable shoulder shell, shoulder bulkhead, humeral section, mechanical elbow, forearm, Otto Bock or equal electrodes, cables, 2 batteries and one charger, myoelectronic control of terminal device

A L7007 Electric hand, switch or myoelectric controlled, adult

A L7008 Electric hand, switch or myoelectric, controlled, pediatric

A L7009 Electric hook, switch or myoelectric controlled, adult

A L7040 Prehensile actuator, switch controlled

A L7045 Electric hook, switch or myoelectric controlled, pediatric

ELBOW

A L7170 Electronic elbow, Hosmer or equal, switch controlled

A L7180 Electronic elbow, microprocessor sequential control of elbow and terminal device

A L7181 Electronic elbow, microprocessor simultaneous control of elbow and terminal device

A L7185 Electronic elbow, adolescent, Variety Village or equal, switch controlled

A L7186 Electronic elbow, child, Variety Village or equal, switch controlled

A L7190 Electronic elbow, adolescent, Variety Village or equal, myoelectronically controlled

A L7191 Electronic elbow, child, Variety Village or equal, myoelectronically controlled

A L7260 Electronic wrist rotator, Otto Bock or equal

A L7261 Electronic wrist rotator, for Utah arm

A L7266 Servo control, Steeper or equal

A L7272 Analogue control, UNB or equal

A L7274 Proportional control, 6–12 volt, Liberty, Utah or equal

BATTERY COMPONENTS

A ☑ L7360 Six volt battery, each

A ☑ L7362 Battery charger, 6 volt, each

A ☑ L7364 Twelve volt battery, each

A ☑ L7366 Battery charger, twelve volt, each

A L7367 Lithium ion battery, replacement

A L7368 Lithium ion battery charger

A L7400 Addition to upper extremity prosthesis, below elbow/wrist disarticulation, ultralight material (titanium, carbon fiber or equal)

A L7401 Addition to upper extremity prosthesis, above elbow disarticulation, ultralight material (titanium, carbon fiber or equal)

A L7402 Addition to upper extremity prosthesis, shoulder disarticulation/interscapular thoracic, ultralight material (titanium, carbon fiber or equal)

A L7403 Addition to upper extremity prosthesis, below elbow/wrist disarticulation, acrylic material

A L7404 Addition to upper extremity prosthesis, above elbow disarticulation, acrylic material

A L7405 Addition to upper extremity prosthesis, shoulder disarticulation/interscapular thoracic, acrylic material

A L7499 Upper extremity prosthesis, not otherwise specified

REPAIRS

A L7500 Repair of prosthetic device, hourly rate (excludes V5335 repair of oral or laryngeal prosthesis or artificial larynx)

Medicare jurisdiction: local contractor if repair of implanted prosthetic device.

MED: 100-2,15,110.2; 100-2,15,120; 100-4,32,100

A L7510 Repair of prosthetic device, repair or replace minor parts

Medicare jurisdiction: local contractor if repair of implanted prosthetic device.

MED: 100-2,15,110.2; 100-2,15,120; 100-4,32,100

A ☑ L7520 Repair prosthetic device, labor component, per 15 minutes

Medicare jurisdiction: local contractor if repair of implanted prosthetic device.

E ☑ L7600 Prosthetic donning sleeve, any material, each

TERMINAL DEVICES

~~L7611 Terminal device, hook, mechanical, voluntary opening, any material, any size, lined or unlined, pediatric~~
See L6711

~~L7612 Terminal device, hook, mechanical, voluntary closing, any material, any size, lined or unlined, pediatric~~
See L6712

~~L7613 Terminal device, hand, mechanical, voluntary opening, any material, any size, pediatric~~
See L6713

~~L7614 Terminal device, hand, mechanical, voluntary closing, any material, any size, pediatric~~
See L6714

~~L7621 Terminal device, hook or hand, heavy duty, mechanical, voluntary opening, any material, any size, lined or unlined~~
See L6721

~~L7622 Terminal device, hook or hand, heavy duty, mechanical, voluntary closing, any material, any size, lined or unlined~~
See L6722

GENERAL

A **L7900** Male vacuum erection system A ♂

PROSTHESIS

A **L8000** Breast prosthesis, mastectomy bra A ♀
MED: 100-2,15,120

A **L8001** Breast prosthesis, mastectomy bra, with integrated breast prosthesis form, unilateral A ♀
MED: 100-2,15,120

A **L8002** Breast prosthesis, mastectomy bra, with integrated breast prosthesis form, bilateral A ♀
MED: 100-2,15,120

A **L8010** Breast prosthesis, mastectomy sleeve A ♀
MED: 100-2,15,120

A **L8015** External breast prosthesis garment, with mastectomy form, postmastectomy A ♀
MED: 100-2,15,120

A **L8020** Breast prosthesis, mastectomy form A ♀
MED: 100-2,15,120

A **L8030** Breast prosthesis, silicone or equal A ♀
MED: 100-2,15,120

A **L8035** Custom breast prosthesis, post mastectomy, molded to patient model A ♀
MED: 100-2,15,120

A **L8039** Breast prosthesis, not otherwise specified A ♀

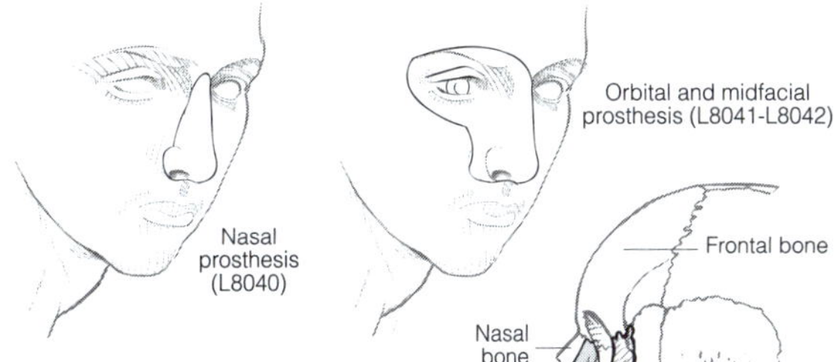

Facial prosthetics are typically custom manufactured from polymers and carefully matched to the original features. The maxilla, zygoma, frontal, and nasal bones are often involved, either singly or in combination (L8040-L8044)

A **L8040** Nasal prosthesis, provided by a nonphysician

A **L8041** Midfacial prosthesis, provided by a nonphysician

A **L8042** Orbital prosthesis, provided by a nonphysician

A **L8043** Upper facial prosthesis, provided by a nonphysician

A **L8044** Hemi-facial prosthesis, provided by a nonphysician

A **L8045** Auricular prosthesis, provided by a nonphysician

A **L8046** Partial facial prosthesis, provided by a nonphysician

A **L8047** Nasal septal prosthesis, provided by a nonphysician

A **L8048** Unspecified maxillofacial prosthesis, by report, provided by a nonphysician

A **L8049** Repair or modification of maxillofacial prosthesis, labor component, 15 minute increments, provided by a nonphysician

TRUSSES

A **L8300** Truss, single with standard pad
MED: 100-2,15,120; 100-3,280.11; 100-3,280.12; 100-4,4,240

A **L8310** Truss, double with standard pads
MED: 100-2,15,120; 100-3,280.11; 100-3,280.12; 100-4,4,240

A **L8320** Truss, addition to standard pad, water pad
MED: 100-2,15,120; 100-3,280.11; 100-3,280.12; 100-4,4,240

A **L8330** Truss, addition to standard pad, scrotal pad ♂
MED: 100-2,15,120; 100-3,280.11; 100-3,280.12; 100-4,4,240

PROSTHETIC SOCKS

A ☑ **L8400** Prosthetic sheath, below knee, each
MED: 100-2,15,120

A ☑ **L8410** Prosthetic sheath, above knee, each
MED: 100-2,15,120

A ☑ **L8415** Prosthetic sheath, upper limb, each
MED: 100-2,15,120

A ☑ **L8417** Prosthetic sheath/sock, including a gel cushion layer, below knee or above knee, each

A ☑ **L8420** Prosthetic sock, multiple ply, below knee, each
MED: 100-2,15,120

A ☑ **L8430** Prosthetic sock, multiple ply, above knee, each
MED: 100-2,15,120

A ☑ **L8435** Prosthetic sock, multiple ply, upper limb, each
MED: 100-2,15,120

A ☑ **L8440** Prosthetic shrinker, below knee, each
MED: 100-2,15,120

A ☑ **L8460** Prosthetic shrinker, above knee, each
MED: 100-2,15,120

A ☑ **L8465** Prosthetic shrinker, upper limb, each
MED: 100-2,15,120

A ☑ **L8470** Prosthetic sock, single ply, fitting, below knee, each
MED: 100-2,15,120

A ☑ **L8480** Prosthetic sock, single ply, fitting, above knee, each
MED: 100-2,15,120

A ☑ **L8485** Prosthetic sock, single ply, fitting, upper limb, each
MED: 100-2,15,120

A **L8499** Unlisted procedure for miscellaneous prosthetic services
Determine if an alternative HCPCS Level II or a CPT code better describes the service being reported. This code should be used only if a more specific code is unavailable.

PROSTHETIC IMPLANTS

INTEGUMENTARY SYSTEM

A **L8500** Artificial larynx, any type
MED: 100-2,15,120; 100-3,50.2; 100-4,4,240

A **L8501** Tracheostomy speaking valve
MED: 100-3,50.4

A **L8505** Artificial larynx replacement battery/accessory, any type

A ☑ **L8507** Tracheo-esophageal voice prosthesis, patient inserted, any type, each

A **L8509** Tracheo-esophageal voice prosthesis, inserted by a licensed health care provider, any type

A **L8510** Voice amplifier
MED: 100-3,50.2

A ☑ **L8511** Insert for indwelling tracheoesophageal prosthesis, with or without valve, replacement only, each

A ☑ **L8512** Gelatin capsules or equivalent, for use with tracheoesophageal voice prosthesis, replacement only, per 10

A ☑ **L8513** Cleaning device used with tracheoesophageal voice prosthesis, pipet, brush, or equal, replacement only, each

A ☑ **L8514** Tracheoesophageal puncture dilator, replacement only, each

A ☑ **L8515** Gelatin capsule, application device for use with tracheoesophageal voice prosthesis, each

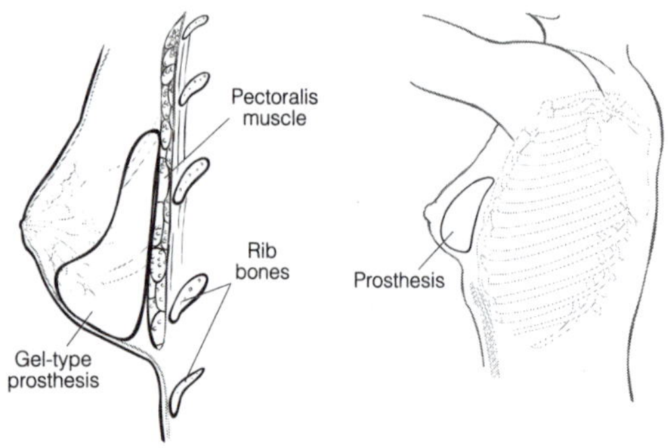

N **L8600** Implantable breast prosthesis, silicone or equal
Medicare covers implants inserted in post-mastectomy reconstruction in a breast cancer patient. Always report concurrent to the implant procedure.
MED: 100-2,15,120; 100-3,140.2; 100-4,4,240

N ☑ **L8603** Injectable bulking agent, collagen implant, urinary tract, 2.5 ml syringe, includes shipping and necessary supplies
Medicare covers up to five separate collagen implant treatments in patients with intrinsic sphincter deficiency. Who have passed a collagen sensitivity test.
MED: 100-3,230.10

● N **L8604** Injectable bulking agent, dextranomer/hyaluronic acid copolymer implant, urinary tract, 1 ml, includes shipping and necessary supplies

N ☑ **L8606** Injectable bulking agent, synthetic implant, urinary tract, 1 ml syringe, includes shipping and necessary supplies
MED: 100-3,230.10

N **L8609** Artificial cornea

HEAD: SKULL, FACIAL BONES, AND TEMPOROMANDIBULAR JOINT

N **L8610** Ocular implant
MED: 100-2,15,120; 100-4,4,240

N **L8612** Aqueous shunt
MED: 100-2,15,120; 100-4,4,240

N **L8613** Ossicula implant
MED: 100-2,15,120; 100-4,4,240

N **L8614** Cochlear device, includes all internal and external components
A cochlear implant is covered by Medicare when the patient has bilateral sensorineural deafness.
MED: 100-2,15,120; 100-3,50.3; 100-4,4,240; 100-4,32,100
AHA: 4Q,'03,8; 3Q,'02,5

A **L8615** Headset/headpiece for use with cochlear implant device, replacement

A **L8616** Microphone for use with cochlear implant device, replacement

A **L8617** Transmitting coil for use with cochlear implant device, replacement

A **L8618** Transmitter cable for use with cochlear implant device, replacement

A **L8619** Cochlear implant external speech processor, replacement
Medicare jurisdiction: local contractor.
MED: 100-3,50.3; 100-4,32,100

A ☑ **L8621** Zinc air battery for use with cochlear implant device, replacement, each

A ☑ **L8622** Alkaline battery for use with cochlear implant device, any size, replacement, each

A ☑ **L8623** Lithium ion battery for use with cochlear implant device speech processor, other than ear level, replacement, each

A ☑ **L8624** Lithium ion battery for use with cochlear implant device speech processor, ear level, replacement, each

UPPER EXTREMITY

N **L8630** Metacarpophalangeal joint implant
MED: 100-2,15,120; 100-4,4,240

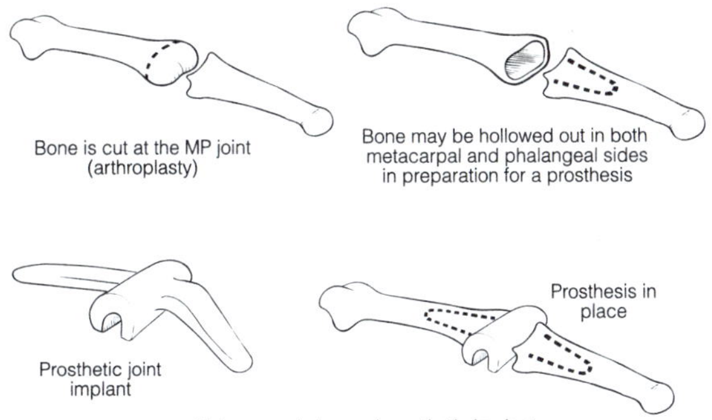

Metacarpophalangeal prosthetic implant

[N] **L8631** Metacarpal phalangeal joint replacement, 2 or more pieces, metal (e.g., stainless steel or cobalt chrome), ceramic-like material (e.g., pyrocarbon), for surgical implantation (all sizes, includes entire system) N1 ♿

MED: 100-2,15,120; 100-4,4,240

LOWER EXTREMITY - JOINT: KNEE, ANKLE, TOE

[N] **L8641** Metatarsal joint implant N1 ♿

MED: 100-2,15,120; 100-4,4,240

[N] **L8642** Hallux implant N1 ♿

MED: 100-2,15,120; 100-4,4,240

MISCELLANEOUS MUSCULAR-SKELETAL

[N] ☑ **L8658** Interphalangeal joint spacer, silicone or equal, each N1 ♿

MED: 100-2,15,120; 100-4,4,240

[N] **L8659** Interphalangeal finger joint replacement, 2 or more pieces, metal (e.g., stainless steel or cobalt chrome), ceramic-like material (e.g., pyrocarbon) for surgical implantation, any size N1 ♿

MED: 100-2,15,120; 100-4,4,240

CARDIOVASCULAR SYSTEM

[N] **L8670** Vascular graft material, synthetic, implant N1 ♿

MED: 100-2,15,120; 100-4,4,240

GENERAL

[B] ☑ **L8680** Implantable neurostimulator electrode, each

MED: 100-4,32,50

▲ [A] **L8681** Patient programmer (external) for use with implantable programmable neurostimulator pulse generator, replacement only

[N] **L8682** Implantable neurostimulator radiofrequency receiver N1

[A] **L8683** Radiofrequency transmitter (external) for use with implantable neurostimulator radiofrequency receiver

[A] **L8684** Radiofrequency transmitter (external) for use with implantable sacral root neurostimulator receiver for bowel and bladder management, replacement

[N] **L8685** Implantable neurostimulator pulse generator, single array, rechargeable, includes extension

MED: 100-4,32,50

[N] **L8686** Implantable neurostimulator pulse generator, single array, nonrechargeable, includes extension

MED: 100-4,32,50

[N] **L8687** Implantable neurostimulator pulse generator, dual array, rechargeable, includes extension

MED: 100-4,32,50

[N] **L8688** Implantable neurostimulator pulse generator, dual array, nonrechargeable, includes extension

MED: 100-4,32,50

▲ [A] **L8689** External recharging system for battery (internal) for use with implantable neurostimulator, replacement only

[N] **L8690** Auditory osseointegrated device, includes all internal and external components N1

[A] **L8691** Auditory osseointegrated device, external sound processor, replacement

▲ [A] **L8695** External recharging system for battery (external) for use with implantable neurostimulator, replacement only

[N] **L8699** Prosthetic implant, not otherwise specified N1

Determine if an alternative HCPCS Level II or a CPT code better describes the service being reported. This code should be used only if a more specific code is unavailable.

[N] **L9900** Orthotic and prosthetic supply, accessory, and/or service component of another HCPCS L code

MEDICAL SERVICES M0000-M0301

OTHER MEDICAL SERVICES

M codes include office services, cellular therapy, prolotherapy, intragastric hypothermia, IV chelation therapy, and fabric wrapping of an abdominal aneurysm.

Q3 **M0064** Brief office visit for the sole purpose of monitoring or changing drug prescriptions used in the treatment of mental psychoneurotic and personality disorders ⊘

MED: 100-4,12,210.1

E **M0075** Cellular therapy

The therapeutic efficacy of injecting foreign proteins has not been established.

MED: 100-3,30.8

E **M0076** Prolotherapy

The therapeutic efficacy of prolotherapy and joint sclerotherapy has not been established.

MED: 100-3,150.7

E **M0100** Intragastric hypothermia using gastric freezing

Code with caution: This procedure is considered obsolete.

MED: 100-3,100.6

CARDIOVASCULAR SERVICES

E **M0300** IV chelation therapy (chemical endarterectomy)

Chelation therapy is considered experimental in the United States.

MED: 100-3,20.21

E **M0301** Fabric wrapping of abdominal aneurysm

Code with caution: This procedure has largely been replaced with more effective treatment modalities. Submit documentation.

MED: 100-3,20.23

PATHOLOGY AND LABORATORY SERVICES P0000-P9999

P codes include chemistry, toxicology, and microbiology tests, screening Papanicolaou procedures, and various blood products.

CHEMISTRY AND TOXICOLOGY TESTS

A **P2028** Cephalin floculation, blood
Code with caution: This test is considered obsolete. Submit documentation.
MED: 100-3,300.1

A **P2029** Congo red, blood
Code with caution: This test is considered obsolete. Submit documentation.
MED: 100-3,300.1

E **P2031** Hair analysis (excluding arsenic)
MED: 100-3,190.6

A **P2033** Thymol turbidity, blood
Code with caution: This test is considered obsolete. Submit documentation.
MED: 100-3,300.1

A **P2038** Mucoprotein, blood (seromucoid) (medical necessity procedure)
Code with caution: This test is considered obsolete. Submit documentation.
MED: 100-3,300.1

PATHOLOGY SCREENING TESTS

A **P3000** Screening Papanicolaou smear, cervical or vaginal, up to 3 smears, by technician under physician supervision A ♀ ⊘
One Pap test is covered by Medicare every two years, unless the physician suspects cervical abnormalities and shortens the interval. See also G0123-G0124.
MED: 100-2,6,10; 100-3,190.2; 100-4,4,240

B **P3001** Screening Papanicolaou smear, cervical or vaginal, up to 3 smears, requiring interpretation by physician A ♀ ⊘
One Pap test is covered by Medicare every two years, unless the physician suspects cervical abnormalities and shortens the interval. See also G0123-G0124.
MED: 100-2,6,10; 100-3,190.2; 100-4,4,240

MICROBIOLOGY TESTS

E **P7001** Culture, bacterial, urine; quantitative, sensitivity study

MISCELLANEOUS

R ☑ **P9010** Blood (whole), for transfusion, per unit
MED: 100-1,3,20.5; 100-2,1,10; 100-4,3,40.2.2

R ☑ **P9011** Blood, split unit
MED: 100-1,3,20.5; 100-2,1,10; 100-4,3,40.2.2

R ☑ **P9012** Cryoprecipitate, each unit
MED: 100-1,3,20.5; 100-2,1,10; 100-4,3,40.2.2

R ☑ **P9016** Red blood cells, leukocytes reduced, each unit
MED: 100-1,3,20.5; 100-2,1,10; 100-4,3,40.2.2

R ☑ **P9017** Fresh frozen plasma (single donor), frozen within 8 hours of collection, each unit
MED: 100-1,3,20.5; 100-2,1,10; 100-4,3,40.2.2

R ☑ **P9019** Platelets, each unit
MED: 100-1,3,20.5; 100-2,1,10; 100-4,3,40.2.2

R ☑ **P9020** Platelet rich plasma, each unit
MED: 100-1,3,20.5; 100-4,3,40.2.2

R ☑ **P9021** Red blood cells, each unit
MED: 100-1,3,20.5; 100-2,1,10; 100-4,3,40.2.2

R ☑ **P9022** Red blood cells, washed, each unit
MED: 100-1,3,20.5; 100-2,1,10; 100-4,3,40.2.2

R ☑ **P9023** Plasma, pooled multiple donor, solvent/detergent treated, frozen, each unit
MED: 100-1,3,20.5; 100-2,1,10; 100-4,3,40.2.2

R ☑ **P9031** Platelets, leukocytes reduced, each unit
MED: 100-1,3,20.5; 100-1,3,20.5.2; 100-1,3,20.5.3; 100-2,1,10; 100-4,3,40.2.2

R ☑ **P9032** Platelets, irradiated, each unit
MED: 100-1,3,20.5; 100-1,3,20.5.2; 100-1,3,20.5.3; 100-2,1,10; 100-4,3,40.2.2

R ☑ **P9033** Platelets, leukocytes reduced, irradiated, each unit
MED: 100-1,3,20.5; 100-1,3,20.5.2; 100-1,3,20.5.3; 100-2,1,10; 100-4,3,40.2.2

R ☑ **P9034** Platelets, pheresis, each unit
MED: 100-1,3,20.5; 100-1,3,20.5.2; 100-1,3,20.5.3; 100-2,1,10; 100-4,3,40.2.2

R ☑ **P9035** Platelets, pheresis, leukocytes reduced, each unit
MED: 100-1,3,20.5; 100-1,3,20.5.2; 100-1,3,20.5.3; 100-2,1,10; 100-4,3,40.2.2

R ☑ **P9036** Platelets, pheresis, irradiated, each unit
MED: 100-1,3,20.5; 100-1,3,20.5.2; 100-1,3,20.5.3; 100-2,1,10; 100-4,3,40.2.2

R ☑ **P9037** Platelets, pheresis, leukocytes reduced, irradiated, each unit
MED: 100-1,3,20.5; 100-1,3,20.5.2; 100-1,3,20.5.3; 100-2,1,10; 100-4,3,40.2.2

R ☑ **P9038** Red blood cells, irradiated, each unit
MED: 100-1,3,20.5; 100-1,3,20.5.2; 100-1,3,20.5.3; 100-2,1,10; 100-4,3,40.2.2

R ☑ **P9039** Red blood cells, deglycerolized, each unit
MED: 100-1,3,20.5; 100-1,3,20.5.2; 100-1,3,20.5.3; 100-2,1,10; 100-4,3,40.2.2

R ☑ **P9040** Red blood cells, leukocytes reduced, irradiated, each unit
MED: 100-1,3,20.5; 100-1,3,20.5.2; 100-1,3,20.5.3; 100-2,1,10; 100-4,3,40.2.2

K ☑ **P9041** Infusion, albumin (human), 5%, 50 ml K2
Not considered a blood product for OPPS effective July 1, 2005.
MED: 100-2,1,10; 100-4,3,40.2.2

R ☑ **P9043** Infusion, plasma protein fraction (human), 5%, 50 ml
MED: 100-1,3,20.5; 100-2,1,10; 100-4,3,40.2.2

R ☑ **P9044** Plasma, cryoprecipitate reduced, each unit
MED: 100-1,3,20.5; 100-2,1,10; 100-4,3,40.2.2

K ☑ **P9045** Infusion, albumin (human), 5%, 250 ml K2
Not considered a blood product for OPPS effective July 1, 2005.
MED: 100-2,1,10; 100-4,3,40.2.2

K ☑ **P9046** Infusion, albumin (human), 25%, 20 ml K2
Not considered a blood product for OPPS effective July 1, 2005.
MED: 100-2,1,10; 100-4,3,40.2.2

K ☑ **P9047** Infusion, albumin (human), 25%, 50 ml K2
Not considered a blood product for OPPS effective July 1, 2005.
MED: 100-2,1,10; 100-4,3,40.2.2

R ☑ **P9048** Infusion, plasma protein fraction (human), 5%, 250 ml
MED: 100-2,1,10; 100-4,3,40.2.2

R ☑ **P9050** Granulocytes, pheresis, each unit
MED: 100-2,1,10; 100-4,3,40.2.2

R ☑ **P9051** Whole blood or red blood cells, leukocytes reduced, CMV-negative, each unit
MED: 100-2,1,10; 100-4,3,40.2.2

R ☑ **P9052** Platelets, HLA-matched leukocytes reduced, apheresis/pheresis, each unit
MED: 100-2,1,10; 100-4,3,40.2.2

R ☑ **P9053** Platelets, pheresis, leukocytes reduced, CMV-negative, irradiated, each unit
MED: 100-2,1,10; 100-4,3,40.2.2

R ☑ **P9054** Whole blood or red blood cells, leukocytes reduced, frozen, deglycerol, washed, each unit
MED: 100-2,1,10; 100-4,3,40.2.2

R ☑ **P9055** Platelets, leukocytes reduced, CMV-negative, apheresis/pheresis, each unit
MED: 100-2,1,10; 100-4,3,40.2.2

R ☑ **P9056** Whole blood, leukocytes reduced, irradiated, each unit
MED: 100-2,1,10; 100-4,3,40.2.2

R ☑ **P9057** Red blood cells, frozen/deglycerolized/washed, leukocytes reduced, irradiated, each unit
MED: 100-2,1,10; 100-4,3,40.2.2

R ☑ **P9058** Red blood cells, leukocytes reduced, CMV-negative, irradiated, each unit
MED: 100-2,1,10; 100-4,3,40.2.2

R ☑ **P9059** Fresh frozen plasma between 8-24 hours of collection, each unit
MED: 100-2,1,10; 100-4,3,40.2.2

R ☑ **P9060** Fresh frozen plasma, donor retested, each unit
MED: 100-2,1,10; 100-4,3,40.2.2

A ☑ **P9603** Travel allowance, one way in connection with medically necessary laboratory specimen collection drawn from homebound or nursing homebound patient; prorated miles actually travelled.
MED: 100-4,16,60

A ☑ **P9604** Travel allowance, one way in connection with medically necessary laboratory specimen collection drawn from homebound or nursing homebound patient; prorated trip charge
MED: 100-4,16,60

A **P9612** Catheterization for collection of specimen, single patient, all places of service
MED: 100-4,16,60

N **P9615** Catheterization for collection of specimen(s) (multiple patients)
MED: 100-4,16,60

Q CODES (TEMPORARY) Q0000-Q9999

New temporary Q codes to pay health care providers for the supplies used in creating casts were established to replace the removal of the practice expense for all HCPCS codes, including the CPT codes for fracture management and for casts and splints. Coders should continue to use the appropriate CPT code to report the work and practice expenses involved with creating the cast or splint; the temporary Q codes replace less specific coding for the casting and splinting supplies.

X **Q0035** Cardiokymography
Covered only in conjunction with electrocardiographic stress testing in male patients with atypical angina or nonischemic chest pain, or female patients with angina.
MED: 100-3,20.24

B **Q0081** Infusion therapy, using other than chemotherapeutic drugs, per visit
MED: 100-3,280.14
AHA: 1Q,'02,7; 4Q,'02,7

B ☑ **Q0083** Chemotherapy administration by other than infusion technique only (e.g., subcutaneous, intramuscular, push), per visit ⊘

B ☑ **Q0084** Chemotherapy administration by infusion technique only, per visit ⊘
MED: 100-3,280.14

B ☑ **Q0085** Chemotherapy administration by both infusion technique and other technique(s) (e.g., subcutaneous, intramuscular, push), per visit ⊘

T **Q0091** Screening Papanicolaou smear; obtaining, preparing and conveyance of cervical or vaginal smear to laboratory A ♀ ⊘
One pap test is covered by Medicare every two years for low risk patients and every one year for high risk patients. Q0091 can be reported with an E/M code when a separately identifiable E/M service is provided.
MED: 100-3,190.2
AHA: 4Q,'02,8

N **Q0092** Set-up portable x-ray equipment

A **Q0111** Wet mounts, including preparations of vaginal, cervical or skin specimens

A **Q0112** All potassium hydroxide (KOH) preparations

A **Q0113** Pinworm examinations

A **Q0114** Fern test ♀

A **Q0115** Postcoital direct, qualitative examinations of vaginal or cervical mucous A ♀

E ☑ **Q0144** Azithromycin dihydrate, oral, capsules/powder, 1 g
Use this code for Zithromax, Zithromax Z-PAK.

N ☑ **Q0163** Diphenhydramine HCl, 50 mg, oral, FDA approved prescription antiemetic, for use as a complete therapeutic substitute for an IV antiemetic at time of chemotherapy treatment not to exceed a 48-hour dosage regimen N1
See also J1200. Medicare covers at the time of chemotherapy if regimen doesn't exceed 48 hours. Submit on the same claim as the chemotherapy. Use this code for Truxadryl.
MED: 100-2,6,10; 100-4,4,240; 100-4,17,80.2
AHA: 1Q,'02,2

N ☑ **Q0164** Prochlorperazine maleate, 5 mg, oral, FDA approved prescription antiemetic, for use as a complete therapeutic substitute for an IV antiemetic at the time of chemotherapy treatment, not to exceed a 48-hour dosage regimen N1
Medicare covers at the time of chemotherapy if regimen doesn't exceed 48 hours. Submit on the same claim as the chemotherapy. Use this code for Compazine.
MED: 100-2,6,10; 100-4,4,240; 100-4,17,80.2

N ☑ **Q0165** Prochlorperazine maleate, 10 mg, oral, FDA approved prescription antiemetic, for use as a complete therapeutic substitute for an IV antiemetic at the time of chemotherapy treatment, not to exceed a 48-hour dosage regimen
Medicare covers at the time of chemotherapy if regimen doesn't exceed 48 hours. Submit on the same claim as the chemotherapy. Use this code for Compazine.
MED: 100-2,6,10; 100-4,4,240; 100-4,17,80.2

K ☑ **Q0166** Granisetron HCl, 1 mg, oral, FDA approved prescription antiemetic, for use as a complete therapeutic substitute for an IV antiemetic at the time of chemotherapy treatment, not to exceed a 24-hour dosage regimen K2
Medicare covers at the time of chemotherapy if regimen doesn't exceed 48 hours. Submit on the same claim as the chemotherapy. Use this code for Kytril.
MED: 100-2,6,10; 100-4,4,240; 100-4,17,80.2

N ☑ **Q0167** Dronabinol, 2.5 mg, oral, FDA approved prescription antiemetic, for use as a complete therapeutic substitute for an IV antiemetic at the time of chemotherapy treatment, not to exceed a 48-hour dosage regimen N1
Medicare covers at the time of chemotherapy if regimen doesn't exceed 48 hours. Submit on the same claim as the chemotherapy. Use this code for Marinol.
MED: 100-2,6,10; 100-4,4,240; 100-4,17,80.2

N ☑ **Q0168** Dronabinol, 5 mg, oral, FDA approved prescription antiemetic, for use as a complete therapeutic substitute for an IV antiemetic at the time of chemotherapy treatment, not to exceed a 48-hour dosage regimen
Use this code for Marinol.
MED: 100-2,6,10; 100-4,4,240; 100-4,17,80.2

N ☑ **Q0169** Promethazine HCl, 12.5 mg, oral, FDA approved prescription antiemetic, for use as a complete therapeutic substitute for an IV antiemetic at the time of chemotherapy treatment, not to exceed a 48-hour dosage regimen N1
Medicare covers at the time of chemotherapy if regimen doesn't exceed 48 hours. Submit on the same claim as the chemotherapy. Use this code for Phenergan, Amergan.
MED: 100-2,6,10; 100-4,4,240; 100-4,17,80.2

N ☑ **Q0170** Promethazine HCl, 25 mg, oral, FDA approved prescription antiemetic, for use as a complete therapeutic substitute for an IV antiemetic at the time of chemotherapy treatment, not to exceed a 48-hour dosage regimen
Medicare covers at the time of chemotherapy if regimen doesn't exceed 48 hours. Submit on the same claim as the chemotherapy. Use this code for Phenergan, Amergan.
MED: 100-2,6,10; 100-4,4,240; 100-4,17,80.2

N ☑ **Q0171** Chlorpromazine HCl, 10 mg, oral, FDA approved prescription antiemetic, for use as a complete therapeutic substitute for an IV antiemetic at the time of chemotherapy treatment, not to exceed a 48-hour dosage regimen N1

Medicare covers at the time of chemotherapy if regimen doesn't exceed 48 hours. Submit on the same claim as the chemotherapy. Use this code for Thorazine.

MED: 100-2,6,10; 100-4,4,240; 100-4,17,80.2

N ☑ **Q0172** Chlorpromazine HCl, 25 mg, oral, FDA approved prescription antiemetic, for use as a complete therapeutic substitute for an IV antiemetic at the time of chemotherapy treatment, not to exceed a 48-hour dosage regimen

Medicare covers at the time of chemotherapy if regimen doesn't exceed 48 hours. Submit on the same claim as the chemotherapy. Use this code for Thorazine.

MED: 100-2,6,10; 100-4,4,240; 100-4,17,80.2

N ☑ **Q0173** Trimethobenzamide HCl, 250 mg, oral, FDA approved prescription antiemetic, for use as a complete therapeutic substitute for an IV antiemetic at the time of chemotherapy treatment, not to exceed a 48-hour dosage regimen N1

Medicare covers at the time of chemotherapy if regimen doesn't exceed 48 hours. Submit on the same claim as the chemotherapy. Use this code for Tebamide, T-Gen, Ticon, Tigan, Triban, Thimazide.

MED: 100-2,6,10; 100-4,4,240; 100-4,17,80.2

N ☑ **Q0174** Thiethylperazine maleate, 10 mg, oral, FDA approved prescription antiemetic, for use as a complete therapeutic substitute for an IV antiemetic at the time of chemotherapy treatment, not to exceed a 48-hour dosage regimen N1

Medicare covers at the time of chemotherapy if regimen doesn't exceed 48 hours. Submit on the same claim as the chemotherapy. Use this code for Torecan.

MED: 100-2,6,10; 100-4,4,240; 100-4,17,80.2

N ☑ **Q0175** Perphenazine, 4 mg, oral, FDA approved prescription antiemetic, for use as a complete therapeutic substitute for an IV antiemetic at the time of chemotherapy treatment, not to exceed a 48 hour dosage regimen N1

Medicare covers at the time of chemotherapy if regimen doesn't exceed 48 hours. Submit on the same claim as the chemotherapy. Use this code for Trilifon.

MED: 100-2,6,10; 100-4,4,240; 100-4,17,80.2

N ☑ **Q0176** Perphenazine, 8 mg, oral, FDA approved prescription antiemetic, for use as a complete therapeutic substitute for an IV antiemetic at the time of chemotherapy treatment, not to exceed a 48 hour dosage regimen

Medicare covers at the time of chemotherapy if regimen doesn't exceed 48 hours. Submit on the same claim as the chemotherapy. Use this code for Trilifon.

MED: 100-2,6,10; 100-4,4,240; 100-4,17,80.2

N ☑ **Q0177** Hydroxyzine pamoate, 25 mg, oral, FDA approved prescription antiemetic, for use as a complete therapeutic substitute for an IV antiemetic at the time of chemotherapy treatment, not to exceed a 48-hour dosage regimen N1

Medicare covers at the time of chemotherapy if regimen doesn't exceed 48 hours. Submit on the same claim as the chemotherapy. Use this code for Vistaril.

MED: 100-2,6,10; 100-4,4,240; 100-4,17,80.2

N ☑ **Q0178** Hydroxyzine pamoate, 50 mg, oral, FDA approved prescription antiemetic, for use as a complete therapeutic substitute for an IV antiemetic at the time of chemotherapy treatment, not to exceed a 48-hour dosage regimen

Medicare covers at the time of chemotherapy if regimen doesn't exceed 48 hours. Submit on the same claim as the chemotherapy.

MED: 100-2,6,10; 100-4,4,240; 100-4,17,80.2

K ☑ **Q0179** Ondansetron HCl 8 mg, oral, FDA approved prescription antiemetic, for use as a complete therapeutic substitute for an IV antiemetic at the time of chemotherapy treatment, not to exceed a 48-hour dosage regimen K2

Medicare covers at the time of chemotherapy if regimen doesn't exceed 48 hours. Submit on the same claim as the chemotherapy. Use this code for Zofran.

MED: 100-2,6,10; 100-4,4,240; 100-4,17,80.2

K ☑ **Q0180** Dolasetron mesylate, 100 mg, oral, FDA approved prescription antiemetic, for use as a complete therapeutic substitute for an IV antiemetic at the time of chemotherapy treatment, not to exceed a 24-hour dosage regimen K2

Medicare covers at the time of chemotherapy if regimen doesn't exceed 24 hours. Submit on the same claim as the chemotherapy. Use this code for Anzemet.

MED: 100-2,6,10; 100-4,4,240; 100-4,17,80.2

E ☑ **Q0181** Unspecified oral dosage form, FDA approved prescription antiemetic, for use as a complete therapeutic substitute for an IV antiemetic at the time of chemotherapy treatment, not to exceed a 48-hour dosage regimen

Medicare covers at the time of chemotherapy if regimen doesn't exceed 48-hours. Submit on the same claim as the chemotherapy.

MED: 100-2,6,10; 100-4,4,240; 100-4,17,80.2

A **Q0480** Driver for use with pneumatic ventricular assist device, replacement only ♿

AHA: 3Q,'05,2

A **Q0481** Microprocessor control unit for use with electric ventricular assist device, replacement only ♿

AHA: 3Q,'05,2

A **Q0482** Microprocessor control unit for use with electric/pneumatic combination ventricular assist device, replacement only ♿

AHA: 3Q,'05,2

A **Q0483** Monitor/display module for use with electric ventricular assist device, replacement only ♿

AHA: 3Q,'05,2

A **Q0484** Monitor/display module for use with electric or electric/pneumatic ventricular assist device, replacement only ♿

AHA: 3Q,'05,2

A **Q0485** Monitor control cable for use with electric ventricular assist device, replacement only ♿

AHA: 3Q,'05,2

A **Q0486** Monitor control cable for use with electric/pneumatic ventricular assist device, replacement only ♿

AHA: 3Q,'05,2

A **Q0487** Leads (pneumatic/electrical) for use with any type electric/pneumatic ventricular assist device, replacement only ♿

AHA: 3Q,'05,2

A **Q0488** Power pack base for use with electric ventricular assist device, replacement only

AHA: 3Q,'05,2

A **Q0489** Power pack base for use with electric/pneumatic ventricular assist device, replacement only ♿
AHA: 3Q,'05,2

A **Q0490** Emergency power source for use with electric ventricular assist device, replacement only ♿
AHA: 3Q,'05,2

A **Q0491** Emergency power source for use with electric/pneumatic ventricular assist device, replacement only ♿
AHA: 3Q,'05,2

A **Q0492** Emergency power supply cable for use with electric ventricular assist device, replacement only ♿
AHA: 3Q,'05,2

A **Q0493** Emergency power supply cable for use with electric/pneumatic ventricular assist device, replacement only ♿
AHA: 3Q,'05,2

A **Q0494** Emergency hand pump for use with electric or electric/pneumatic ventricular assist device, replacement only ♿
AHA: 3Q,'05,2

A **Q0495** Battery/power pack charger for use with electric or electric/pneumatic ventricular assist device, replacement only ♿
AHA: 3Q,'05,2

A **Q0496** Battery for use with electric or electric/pneumatic ventricular assist device, replacement only ♿
AHA: 3Q,'05,2

A **Q0497** Battery clips for use with electric or electric/pneumatic ventricular assist device, replacement only ♿
AHA: 3Q,'05,2

A **Q0498** Holster for use with electric or electric/pneumatic ventricular assist device, replacement only ♿
AHA: 3Q,'05,2

A **Q0499** Belt/vest for use with electric or electric/pneumatic ventricular assist device, replacement only ♿
AHA: 3Q,'05,2

A ☑ **Q0500** Filters for use with electric or electric/pneumatic ventricular assist device, replacement only ♿
The base unit for this code is for each filter.
AHA: 3Q,'05,2

A **Q0501** Shower cover for use with electric or electric/pneumatic ventricular assist device, replacement only ♿
AHA: 3Q,'05,2

A **Q0502** Mobility cart for pneumatic ventricular assist device, replacement only ♿
AHA: 3Q,'05,2

A ☑ **Q0503** Battery for pneumatic ventricular assist device, replacement only, each ♿
AHA: 3Q,'05,2

A **Q0504** Power adapter for pneumatic ventricular assist device, replacement only, vehicle type ♿
AHA: 3Q,'05,2

A **Q0505** Miscellaneous supply or accessory for use with ventricular assist device
AHA: 3Q,'05,2

B **Q0510** Pharmacy supply fee for initial immunosuppressive drug(s), first month following transplant
MED: 100-4,4,240

B **Q0511** Pharmacy supply fee for oral anticancer, oral antiemetic, or immunosuppressive drug(s); for the first prescription in a 30-day period
MED: 100-4,4,240

B **Q0512** Pharmacy supply fee for oral anticancer, oral antiemetic, or immunosuppressive drug(s); for a subsequent prescription in a 30-day period
MED: 100-4,4,240

B **Q0513** Pharmacy dispensing fee for inhalation drug(s); per 30 days

B **Q0514** Pharmacy dispensing fee for inhalation drug(s); per 90 days

K ☑ **Q0515** Injection, sermorelin acetate, 1 mcg K2
MED: 100-2,15,50

N **Q1003** New technology, intraocular lens, category 3 (reduced spherical aberration) L6 ⊘

E **Q1004** New technology intraocular lens category 4 as defined in Federal Register notice

E **Q1005** New technology intraocular lens category 5 as defined in Federal Register notice

N ☑ **Q2004** Irrigation solution for treatment of bladder calculi, for example renacidin, per 500 ml N1
MED: 100-2,15,50

N ☑ **Q2009** Injection, fosphenytoin, 50 mg N1
Use this code for Cerebyx.

K ☑ **Q2017** Injection, teniposide, 50 mg K2
Use this code for Vumon.
MED: 100-2,15,50

B ☑ **Q3001** Radioelements for brachytherapy, any type, each ⊘

A **Q3014** Telehealth originating site facility fee

K ☑ **Q3025** Injection, interferon beta-1a, 11 mcg for intramuscular use K2
Use this code for Avonex, Rebif. See also J1825.
MED: 100-2,15,50

E ☑ **Q3026** Injection, interferon beta-1a, 11 mcg for subcutaneous use
Use this code for Avonex, Rebif. See also J1825.

N **Q3031** Collagen skin test
MED: 100-3,230.10

B **Q4001** Casting supplies, body cast adult, with or without head, plaster A
MED: 100-4,4,240; 100-4,20,170

B **Q4002** Cast supplies, body cast adult, with or without head, fiberglass A
MED: 100-4,4,240; 100-4,20,170

B **Q4003** Cast supplies, shoulder cast, adult (11 years +), plaster A
MED: 100-4,4,240; 100-4,20,170

B **Q4004** Cast supplies, shoulder cast, adult (11 years +), fiberglass A
MED: 100-4,4,240; 100-4,20,170

B **Q4005** Cast supplies, long arm cast, adult (11 years +), plaster A
MED: 100-4,4,240; 100-4,20,170

B **Q4006** Cast supplies, long arm cast, adult (11 years +), fiberglass A
MED: 100-4,4,240; 100-4,20,170

B **Q4007** Cast supplies, long arm cast, pediatric (0–10 years), plaster A
MED: 100-4,4,240; 100-4,20,170

B **Q4008** Cast supplies, long arm cast, pediatric (0–10 years), fiberglass A
MED: 100-4,4,240; 100-4,20,170

Special Coverage Instructions | Noncovered by Medicare | Carrier Discretion | ☑ Quantity Alert | ● New Code | ○ Recycled/Reinstated | ▲ Revised Code

A Age Edit | M Maternity Edit | ♀ Female Only | ♂ Male Only | A-Y OPPS Status Indicators

Q4009 Cast supplies, short arm cast, adult (11 years +), plaster
MED: 100-4,4,240; 100-4,20,170

Q4010 Cast supplies, short arm cast, adult (11 years +), fiberglass
MED: 100-4,4,240; 100-4,20,170

Q4011 Cast supplies, short arm cast, pediatric (0–10 years), plaster
MED: 100-4,4,240; 100-4,20,170

Q4012 Cast supplies, short arm cast, pediatric (0–10 years), fiberglass
MED: 100-4,4,240; 100-4,20,170

Q4013 Cast supplies, gauntlet cast (includes lower forearm and hand), adult (11 years +), plaster
MED: 100-4,4,240; 100-4,20,170

Q4014 Cast supplies, gauntlet cast (includes lower forearm and hand), adult (11 years +), fiberglass
MED: 100-4,4,240; 100-4,20,170

Q4015 Cast supplies, gauntlet cast (includes lower forearm and hand), pediatric (0–10 years), plaster
MED: 100-4,4,240; 100-4,20,170

Q4016 Cast supplies, gauntlet cast (includes lower forearm and hand), pediatric (0–10 years), fiberglass
MED: 100-4,4,240; 100-4,20,170

Q4017 Cast supplies, long arm splint, adult (11 years +), plaster
MED: 100-4,4,240; 100-4,20,170

Q4018 Cast supplies, long arm splint, adult (11 years +), fiberglass
MED: 100-4,4,240; 100-4,20,170

Q4019 Cast supplies, long arm splint, pediatric (0–10 years), plaster
MED: 100-4,4,240; 100-4,20,170

Q4020 Cast supplies, long arm splint, pediatric (0–10 years), fiberglass
MED: 100-4,4,240; 100-4,20,170

Q4021 Cast supplies, short arm splint, adult (11 years +), plaster
MED: 100-4,4,240; 100-4,20,170

Q4022 Cast supplies, short arm splint, adult (11 years +), fiberglass
MED: 100-4,4,240; 100-4,20,170

Q4023 Cast supplies, short arm splint, pediatric (0–10 years), plaster
MED: 100-4,4,240; 100-4,20,170

Q4024 Cast supplies, short arm splint, pediatric (0–10 years), fiberglass
MED: 100-4,4,240; 100-4,20,170

Q4025 Cast supplies, hip spica (one or both legs), adult (11 years +), plaster
MED: 100-4,4,240; 100-4,20,170

Q4026 Cast supplies, hip spica (one or both legs), adult (11 years +), fiberglass
MED: 100-4,4,240; 100-4,20,170

Q4027 Cast supplies, hip spica (one or both legs), pediatric (0–10 years), plaster
MED: 100-4,4,240; 100-4,20,170

Q4028 Cast supplies, hip spica (one or both legs), pediatric (0–10 years), fiberglass
MED: 100-4,4,240; 100-4,20,170

Q4029 Cast supplies, long leg cast, adult (11 years +), plaster
MED: 100-4,4,240; 100-4,20,170

Q4030 Cast supplies, long leg cast, adult (11 years +), fiberglass
MED: 100-4,4,240; 100-4,20,170

Q4031 Cast supplies, long leg cast, pediatric (0–10 years), plaster
MED: 100-4,4,240; 100-4,20,170

Q4032 Cast supplies, long leg cast, pediatric (0–10 years), fiberglass
MED: 100-4,4,240; 100-4,20,170

Q4033 Cast supplies, long leg cylinder cast, adult (11 years +), plaster
MED: 100-4,4,240; 100-4,20,170

Q4034 Cast supplies, long leg cylinder cast, adult (11 years +), fiberglass
MED: 100-4,4,240; 100-4,20,170

Q4035 Cast supplies, long leg cylinder cast, pediatric (0–10 years), plaster
MED: 100-4,4,240; 100-4,20,170

Q4036 Cast supplies, long leg cylinder cast, pediatric (0–10 years), fiberglass
MED: 100-4,4,240; 100-4,20,170

Q4037 Cast supplies, short leg cast, adult (11 years +), plaster
MED: 100-4,4,240; 100-4,20,170

Q4038 Cast supplies, short leg cast, adult (11 years +), fiberglass
MED: 100-4,4,240; 100-4,20,170

Q4039 Cast supplies, short leg cast, pediatric (0–10 years), plaster
MED: 100-4,4,240; 100-4,20,170

Q4040 Cast supplies, short leg cast, pediatric (0–10 years), fiberglass
MED: 100-4,4,240; 100-4,20,170

Q4041 Cast supplies, long leg splint, adult (11 years +), plaster
MED: 100-4,4,240; 100-4,20,170

Q4042 Cast supplies, long leg splint, adult (11 years +), fiberglass
MED: 100-4,4,240; 100-4,20,170

Q4043 Cast supplies, long leg splint, pediatric (0–10 years), plaster
MED: 100-4,4,240; 100-4,20,170

Q4044 Cast supplies, long leg splint, pediatric (0–10 years), fiberglass
MED: 100-4,4,240; 100-4,20,170

Q4045 Cast supplies, short leg splint, adult (11 years +), plaster
MED: 100-4,4,240; 100-4,20,170

Q4046 Cast supplies, short leg splint, adult (11 years +), fiberglass
MED: 100-4,4,240; 100-4,20,170

Q4047 Cast supplies, short leg splint, pediatric (0–10 years), plaster
MED: 100-4,4,240; 100-4,20,170

Q4048 Cast supplies, short leg splint, pediatric (0–10 years), fiberglass
MED: 100-4,4,240; 100-4,20,170

B **Q4049** Finger splint, static
MED: 100-4,4,240; 100-4,20,170

B **Q4050** Cast supplies, for unlisted types and materials of casts
MED: 100-4,4,240; 100-4,20,170

B **Q4051** Splint supplies, miscellaneous (includes thermoplastics, strapping, fasteners, padding and other supplies)
MED: 100-4,4,240; 100-4,20,170

Y ☑ **Q4080** Iloprost, inhalation solution, FDA-approved final product, noncompounded, administered through DME, unit dose form, 20 mcg
AHA: 3Q,'05,7

A ☑ **Q4081** Injection, epoetin alfa, 100 units (for ESRD on dialysis)

B **Q4082** Drug or biological, not otherwise classified, Part B drug competitive acquisition program (CAP)

~~Q4096 Injection, von Willebrand factor complex human, ristocetin cofactor (not otherwise specified), per I.U. VWF:RCO~~

~~Q4097 Injection, immune globulin (Privigen), intravenous, nonlyophilized (e.g., liquid), 500 mg~~
See J1459

~~Q4098 Injection, iron dextran, 50 mg~~
See J1750

~~Q4099 Formoterol fumarate, inhalation solution, FDA approved final product, noncompounded, administered through DME, unit dose form, 20 micrograms~~
See J7606

● N **Q4100** Skin substitute, not otherwise specified N1

● K **Q4101** Skin substitute, Apligraf, per sq cm K2

● K **Q4102** Skin substitute, Oasis wound matrix, per sq cm K2

● K **Q4103** Skin substitute, Oasis burn matrix, per sq cm K2

● K **Q4104** Skin substitute, Integra bilayer matrix wound dressing (BMWD), per sq cm K2

● K **Q4105** Skin substitute, Integra dermal regeneration template (DRT), per sq cm K2

● K **Q4106** Skin substitute, Dermagraft, per sq cm K2

● K **Q4107** Skin substitute, GRAFTJACKET, per sq cm K2

● K **Q4108** Skin substitute, Integra matrix, per sq cm K2

● N **Q4109** Skin substitute, TissueMend, per sq cm N1

● K **Q4110** Skin substitute, PriMatrix, per sq cm K2

● **Q4111** Skin substitute, GammaGraft, per sq cm

● K **Q4112** Allograft, Cymetra, injectable, 1 cc K2

● K **Q4113** Allograft, GRAFTJACKET express, injectable, 1cc K2

● G **Q4114** Integra flowable wound matrix, injectable, 1 cc K2

B **Q5001** Hospice care provided in patient's home/residence

B **Q5002** Hospice care provided in assisted living facility

B **Q5003** Hospice care provided in nursing long-term care facility (LTC) or nonskilled nursing facility (NF)

B **Q5004** Hospice care provided in skilled nursing facility (SNF)

B **Q5005** Hospice care provided in inpatient hospital

B **Q5006** Hospice care provided in inpatient hospice facility

B **Q5007** Hospice care provided in long-term care facility

B **Q5008** Hospice care provided in inpatient psychiatric facility

B **Q5009** Hospice care provided in place not otherwise specified (NOS)

N ☑ **Q9951** Low osmolar contrast material, 400 or greater mg/ml iodine concentration, per ml N1

N ☑ **Q9953** Injection, iron-based magnetic resonance contrast agent, per ml N1

N ☑ **Q9954** Oral magnetic resonance contrast agent, per 100 ml N1

N ☑ **Q9955** Injection, perflexane lipid microspheres, per ml N1

N ☑ **Q9956** Injection, octafluoropropane microspheres, per ml N1

N ☑ **Q9957** Injection, perflutren lipid microspheres, per ml N1

N ☑ **Q9958** High osmolar contrast material, up to 149 mg/ml iodine concentration, per ml N1
AHA: 3Q,'05,7

N ☑ **Q9959** High osmolar contrast material, 150–199 mg/ml iodine concentration, per ml N1
AHA: 3Q,'05,7

N ☑ **Q9960** High osmolar contrast material, 200–249 mg/ml iodine concentration, per ml N1
AHA: 3Q,'05,7

N ☑ **Q9961** High osmolar contrast material, 250–299 mg/ml iodine concentration, per ml N1
AHA: 3Q,'05,7

N ☑ **Q9962** High osmolar contrast material, 300–349 mg/ml iodine concentration, per ml N1
AHA: 3Q,'05,7

N ☑ **Q9963** High osmolar contrast material, 350–399 mg/ml iodine concentration, per ml N1
AHA: 3Q,'05,7

N ☑ **Q9964** High osmolar contrast material, 400 or greater mg/ml iodine concentration, per ml N1
AHA: 3Q,'05,7

N ☑ **Q9965** Low osmolar contrast material, 100–199 mg/ml iodine concentration, per ml N1
Use this code for Omnipaque 140, Omnipaque 180, Optiray 160, Optiray 140.

N ☑ **Q9966** Low osmolar contrast material, 200–299 mg/ml iodine concentration, per ml N1
Use this code for Omnipaque 240, Optiray 240.

N ☑ **Q9967** Low osmolar contrast material, 300–399 mg/ml iodine concentration, per ml N1
Use this code for Omnipaque 300, Omnipaque 350, Optiray, Optiray 300, Optiray 320, Oxilan 300, Oxilan 350.

DIAGNOSTIC RADIOLOGY SERVICES R0000-R5999

R codes are used for the transportation of portable x-ray and/or EKG equipment.

B ☑ **R0070 Transportation of portable x-ray equipment and personnel to home or nursing home, per trip to facility or location, one patient seen**

Only a single, reasonable transportation charge is allowed for each trip the portable x-ray supplier makes to a location. When more than one patient is x-rayed at the same location, prorate the single allowable transport charge among all patients.

B ☑ **R0075 Transportation of portable x-ray equipment and personnel to home or nursing home, per trip to facility or location, more than one patient seen**

Only a single, reasonable transportation charge is allowed for each trip the portable x-ray supplier makes to a location. When more than one patient is x-rayed at the same location, prorate the single allowable transport charge among all patients.

B ☑ **R0076 Transportation of portable EKG to facility or location, per patient**

Only a single, reasonable transportation charge is allowed for each trip the portable EKG supplier makes to a location. When more than one patient is tested at the same location, prorate the single allowable transport charge among all patients.

MED: 100-1,5,90.2; 100-3,20.15

TEMPORARY NATIONAL CODES (NON-MEDICARE) S0000-S9999

The S codes are used by the Blue Cross/Blue Shield Association (BCBSA) and the Health Insurance Association of America (HIAA) to report drugs, services, and supplies for which there are no national codes but for which codes are needed by the private sector to implement policies, programs, or claims processing. They are for the purpose of meeting the particular needs of the private sector. These codes are also used by the Medicaid program, but they are not payable by Medicare.

☑ **S0012** Butorphanol tartrate, nasal spray, 25 mg
Use this code for Stadol NS.

☑ **S0014** Tacrine HCl, 10 mg
Use this code for Cognex.

☑ **S0017** Injection, aminocaproic acid, 5 g
Use this code for Amicar.

☑ **S0020** Injection, bupivicaine HCl, 30 ml
Use this code for Marcaine, Sensorcaine.

☑ **S0021** Injection, cefoperazone sodium, 1 g
Use this code for Cefobid.

☑ **S0023** Injection, cimetidine HCl, 300 mg
Use this code for Tagamet HCl.

☑ **S0028** Injection, famotidine, 20 mg
Use this code for Pepcid.

☑ **S0030** Injection, metronidazole, 500 mg
Use this code for Flagyl IV RTU.

☑ **S0032** Injection, nafcillin sodium, 2 g
Use this code for Nallpen, Unipen.

☑ **S0034** Injection, ofloxacin, 400 mg
Use this code for Floxin IV.

☑ **S0039** Injection, sulfamethoxazole and trimethoprim, 10 ml
Use this code for Bactrim IV, Septra IV, SMZ-TMP, Sulfutrim.

☑ **S0040** Injection, ticarcillin disodium and clavulanate potassium, 3.1 g
Use this code for Timentin.

☑ **S0073** Injection, aztreonam, 500 mg
Use this code for Azactam.

☑ **S0074** Injection, cefotetan disodium, 500 mg
Use this code for Cefotan.

☑ **S0077** Injection, clindamycin phosphate, 300 mg
Use this code for Cleocin Phosphate.

☑ **S0078** Injection, fosphenytoin sodium, 750 mg
Use this code for Cerebryx.

☑ **S0080** Injection, pentamidine isethionate, 300 mg
Use this code for NebuPent, Pentam 300, Pentacarinat. See also code J2545.

☑ **S0081** Injection, piperacillin sodium, 500 mg
Use this code for Pipracil.

▲ ☑ **S0088** Imatinib, 100 mg
Use this code for Gleevec.

☑ **S0090** Sildenafil citrate, 25 mg A
Use this code for Viagra.

☑ **S0091** Granisetron HCl, 1 mg (for circumstances falling under the Medicare statute, use Q0166)
Use this code for Kytril.

☑ **S0092** Injection, hydromorphone HCl, 250 mg (loading dose for infusion pump)
Use this code for Dilaudid, Hydromophone. See also J1170.

☑ **S0093** Injection, morphine sulfate, 500 mg (loading dose for infusion pump)
Use this code for Duramorph, MS Contin, Morphine Sulfate. See also J2270, J2271, J2275.

S0104 Zidovudine, oral, 100 mg
See also J3485 for Retrovir.

☑ **S0106** Bupropion HCl sustained release tablet, 150 mg, per bottle of 60 tablets
Use this code for Wellbutrin SR tablets.

☑ **S0108** Mercaptopurine, oral, 50 mg
Use this code for Purinethol oral.

☑ **S0109** Methadone, oral, 5 mg
Use this code for Dolophine.

☑ **S0117** Tretinoin, topical, 5 g

☑ **S0122** Injection, menotropins, 75 IU
Use this code for Humegon, Pergonal, Repronex.

☑ **S0126** Injection, follitropin alfa, 75 IU
Use this code for Gonal-F.

☑ **S0128** Injection, follitropin beta, 75 IU ♀
Use this code for Follistim.

☑ **S0132** Injection, ganirelix acetate, 250 mcg ♀
Use this code for Antagon.

☑ **S0136** Clozapine, 25 mg
Use this code for Clozaril.

☑ **S0137** Didanosine (ddI), 25 mg
Use this code for Videx.

☑ **S0138** Finasteride, 5 mg ♂
Use this code for Propecia (oral), Proscar (oral).

☑ **S0139** Minoxidil, 10 mg
Use this code for Loniten (oral).

☑ **S0140** Saquinavir, 200 mg
Use this code for Fortovase (oral), Invirase (oral).

~~S0141 Zalcitabine (ddC), 0.375 mg~~

☑ **S0142** Colistimethate sodium, inhalation solution administered through DME, concentrated form, per mg

~~S0143 Aztreonam, inhalation solution administered through DME, concentrated form, per g~~

☑ **S0145** Injection, pegylated interferon alfa-2a, 180 mcg per ml
Use this code for Pegasys.

☑ **S0146** Injection, pegylated interferon alfa-2b, 10 mcg per 0.5 ml

☑ **S0155** Sterile dilutant for epoprostenol, 50 ml
Use this code for Flolan.

☑ **S0156** Exemestane, 25 mg
Use this code for Aromasin.

☑ **S0157** Becaplermin gel 0.01%, 0.5 gm
Use this code for Regraex Gel.

☑ **S0160** Dextroamphetamine sulfate, 5 mg

☑ **S0161** Calcitrol, 0.25 mg

☑ **S0162** Injection, efalizumab, 125 mg
Use this code for Raptiva.

☑ **S0164** Injection, pantoprazole sodium, 40 mg
Use this code for Protonix IV.

☑ **S0166** Injection, olanzapine, 2.5 mg
Use this code for Zyprexa.

☑ **S0170** Anastrozole, oral, 1 mg
Use this code for Arimidex.

☑ **S0171** Injection, bumetanide, 0.5 mg
Use this code for Bumex.

☑ **S0172** Chlorambucil, oral, 2 mg
Use this code for Leukeran.

☑ **S0174** Dolasetron mesylate, oral 50 mg (for circumstances falling under the Medicare statute, use Q0180)
Use this code for Anzemet.

☑ **S0175** Flutamide, oral, 125 mg
Use this code for Eulexin.

☑ **S0176** Hydroxyurea, oral, 500 mg
Use this code for Droxia, Hydrea, Mylocel.

☑ **S0177** Levamisole HCl, oral, 50 mg
Use this code for Ergamisol.

☑ **S0178** Lomustine, oral, 10 mg
Use this code for Ceenu.
MED: 100-4,17,80.2

☑ **S0179** Megestrol acetate, oral, 20 mg
Use this code for Megace.

☑ **S0181** Ondansetron HCl, oral, 4 mg (for circumstances falling under the Medicare statute, use Q0179)
Use this code for Zofran.

☑ **S0182** Procarbazine HCl, oral, 50 mg
Use this code for Matulane.

☑ **S0183** Prochlorperazine maleate, oral, 5 mg (for circumstances falling under the Medicare statute, use Q0164-Q0165)
Use this code for Compazine.

☑ **S0187** Tamoxifen citrate, oral, 10 mg
Use this code for Nolvadex.

☑ **S0189** Testosterone pellet, 75 mg

☑ **S0190** Mifepristone, oral, 200 mg ♀
Use this code for Mifoprex 200 mg oral.

☑ **S0191** Misoprostol, oral, 200 mcg

☑ **S0194** Dialysis/stress vitamin supplement, oral, 100 capsules

S0195 Pneumococcal conjugate vaccine, polyvalent, intramuscular, for children from 5 years to 9 years of age who have not previously received the vaccine A
Use this code for Pneumovax II.

☑ **S0196** Injectable poly-l-lactic acid, restorative implant, 1 ml, face (deep dermis, subcutaneous layers)

☑ **S0197** Prenatal vitamins, 30-day supply M♀

S0199 Medically induced abortion by oral ingestion of medication including all associated services and supplies (e.g., patient counseling, office visits, confirmation of pregnancy by HCG, ultrasound to confirm duration of pregnancy, ultrasound to confirm completion of abortion) except drugs ♀

S0201 Partial hospitalization services, less than 24 hours, per diem

S0207 Paramedic intercept, nonhospital-based ALS service (nonvoluntary), nontransport

S0208 Paramedic intercept, hospital-based ALS service (nonvoluntary), nontransport

S0209 Wheelchair van, mileage, per mile

☑ **S0215** Nonemergency transportation; mileage, per mile
See also codes A0021-A0999 for transportation.

☑ **S0220** Medical conference by a physician with interdisciplinary team of health professionals or representatives of community agencies to coordinate activities of patient care (patient is present); approximately 30 minutes

☑ **S0221** Medical conference by a physician with interdisciplinary team of health professionals or representatives of community agencies to coordinate activities of patient care (patient is present); approximately 60 minutes

S0250 Comprehensive geriatric assessment and treatment planning performed by assessment team A

S0255 Hospice referral visit (advising patient and family of care options) performed by nurse, social worker, or other designated staff

S0257 Counseling and discussion regarding advance directives or end of life care planning and decisions, with patient and/or surrogate (list separately in addition to code for appropriate evaluation and management service)

S0260 History and physical (outpatient or office) related to surgical procedure (list separately in addition to code for appropriate evaluation and management service)

☑ **S0265** Genetic counseling, under physician supervision, each 15 minutes

☑ **S0270** Physician management of patient home care, standard monthly case rate (per 30 days)

☑ **S0271** Physician management of patient home care, hospice monthly case rate (per 30 days)

☑ **S0272** Physician management of patient home care, episodic care monthly case rate (per 30 days)

S0273 Physician visit at member's home, outside of a capitation arrangement

S0274 Nurse practitioner visit at member's home, outside of a capitation arrangement

S0302 Completed early periodic screening diagnosis and treatment (EPSDT) service (list in addition to code for appropriate evaluation and management service)

S0310 Hospitalist services (list separately in addition to code for appropriate evaluation and management service)

S0315 Disease management program; initial assessment and initiation of the program

S0316 Disease management program, follow-up/reassessment

☑ **S0317** Disease management program; per diem

S0320 Telephone calls by a registered nurse to a disease management program member for monitoring purposes; per month

S0340 Lifestyle modification program for management of coronary artery disease, including all supportive services; first quarter/stage

S0341 Lifestyle modification program for management of coronary artery disease, including all supportive services; second or third quarter/stage

S0342 Lifestyle modification program for management of coronary artery disease, including all supportive services; 4th quarter / stage

☑ **S0345** Electrocardiographic monitoring utilizing a home computerized telemetry station with automatic activation and real-time notification of monitoring station, 24-hour attended monitoring, including recording, monitoring, receipt of transmissions, analysis, and physician review and interpretation; per 24-hour period

☑ **S0346** Electrocardiographic monitoring utilizing a home computerized telemetry station with automatic activation and real-time notification of monitoring station, 24-hour attended monitoring, including recording, monitoring, receipt of transmissions, and analysis; per 24-hour period

☑ **S0347** Electrocardiographic monitoring utilizing a home computerized telemetry station with automatic activation and real-time notification of monitoring station, 24-hour attended monitoring, including physician review and interpretation; 24-hour period

S0390 Routine foot care; removal and/or trimming of corns, calluses and/or nails and preventive maintenance in specific medical conditions (e.g., diabetes), per visit

S0395 Impression casting of a foot performed by a practitioner other than the manufacturer of the orthotic

S0400 Global fee for extracorporeal shock wave lithotripsy treatment of kidney stone(s)

☑ **S0500** Disposable contact lens, per lens

☑ **S0504** Single vision prescription lens (safety, athletic, or sunglass), per lens

☑ **S0506** Bifocal vision prescription lens (safety, athletic, or sunglass), per lens

☑ **S0508** Trifocal vision prescription lens (safety, athletic, or sunglass), per lens

☑ **S0510** Nonprescription lens (safety, athletic, or sunglass), per lens

☑ **S0512** Daily wear specialty contact lens, per lens

☑ **S0514** Color contact lens, per lens

S0515 Scleral lens, liquid bandage device, per lens

S0516 Safety eyeglass frames

S0518 Sunglasses frames

S0580 Polycarbonate lens (list this code in addition to the basic code for the lens)

S0581 Nonstandard lens (list this code in addition to the basic code for the lens)

S0590 Integral lens service, miscellaneous services reported separately

S0592 Comprehensive contact lens evaluation

S0595 Dispensing new spectacle lenses for patient supplied frame

S0601 Screening proctoscopy ♂

MED: 100-4,4,240

S0605 Digital rectal examination, annual

S0610 Annual gynecological examination, new patient ♀

MED: 100-4,4,240

S0612 Annual gynecological examination, established patient ♀

MED: 100-4,4,240

S0613 Annual gynecological examination; clinical breast examination without pelvic evaluation ♀

S0618 Audiometry for hearing aid evaluation to determine the level and degree of hearing loss

S0620 Routine ophthalmological examination including refraction; new patient

S0621 Routine ophthalmological examination including refraction; established patient

S0622 Physical exam for college, new or established patient (list separately in addition to appropriate evaluation and management code) A

S0625 Retinal telescreening by digital imaging of multiple different fundus areas to screen for vision-threatening conditions, including imaging, interpretation and report

S0630 Removal of sutures; by a physician other than the physician who originally closed the wound

S0800 Laser in situ keratomileusis (LASIK)

S0810 Photorefractive keratectomy (PRK)

S0812 Phototherapeutic keratectomy (PTK)

S1001 Deluxe item, patient aware (list in addition to code for basic item)

MED: 100-2,1,10.1.4

S1002 Customized item (list in addition to code for basic item)

S1015 IV tubing extension set

S1016 Non-PVC (polyvinyl chloride) intravenous administration set, for use with drugs that are not stable in PVC e.g., Paclitaxel

S1030 Continuous noninvasive glucose monitoring device, purchase (for physician interpretation of data, use CPT code)

S1031 Continuous noninvasive glucose monitoring device, rental, including sensor, sensor replacement, and download to monitor (for physician interpretation of data, use CPT code)

S1040 Cranial remolding orthotic, pediatric, rigid, with soft interface material, custom fabricated, includes fitting and adjustment(s)

S2053 Transplantation of small intestine and liver allografts

S2054 Transplantation of multivisceral organs

S2055 Harvesting of donor multivisceral organs, with preparation and maintenance of allografts; from cadaver donor

S2060 Lobar lung transplantation

S2061 Donor lobectomy (lung) for transplantation, living donor

S2065 Simultaneous pancreas kidney transplantation

S2066 Breast reconstruction with gluteal artery perforator (GAP) flap, including harvesting of the flap, microvascular transfer, closure of donor site and shaping the flap into a breast, unilateral ♀

S2067 Breast reconstruction of a single breast with "stacked" deep inferior epigastric perforator (DIEP) flap(s) and/or gluteal artery perforator (GAP) flap(s), including harvesting of the flap(s), microvascular transfer, closure of donor site(s) and shaping the flap into a breast, unilateral ♀

S2068 Breast reconstruction with deep inferior epigastric perforator (DIEP) flap or superficial inferior epigastric artery (SIEA) flap, including harvesting of the flap, microvascular transfer, closure of donor site and shaping the flap into a breast, unilateral ♀

S2070 Cystourethroscopy, with ureteroscopy and/or pyeloscopy; with endoscopic laser treatment of ureteral calculi (includes ureteral catheterization)

~~S2075 Laparoscopy, surgical; repair incisional or ventral hernia~~

~~S2076 Laparoscopy, surgical; repair umbilical hernia~~

~~S2077 Laparoscopy, surgical; implantation of mesh or other prosthesis for incisional or ventral hernia repair (List separately in addition to code for the incisional or ventral hernia repair)~~

S2079 Laparoscopic esophagomyotomy (Heller type)

S2080 Laser-assisted uvulopalatoplasty (LAUP)

S2083 Adjustment of gastric band diameter via subcutaneous port by injection or aspiration of saline

S2095 Transcatheter occlusion or embolization for tumor destruction, percutaneous, any method, using yttrium-90 microspheres

S2102 Islet cell tissue transplant from pancreas; allogeneic

S2103 Adrenal tissue transplant to brain

S2107 Adoptive immunotherapy i.e. development of specific antitumor reactivity (e.g., tumor-infiltrating lymphocyte therapy) per course of treatment

S2112 Arthroscopy, knee, surgical for harvesting of cartilage (chondrocyte cells)

S2115 Osteotomy, periacetabular, with internal fixation

S2117 Arthroereisis, subtalar

● S2118 Metal-on-metal total hip resurfacing, including acetabular and femoral components

S2120 Low density lipoprotein (LDL) apheresis using heparin-induced extracorporeal LDL precipitation

~~S2135 Neurolysis, by injection, of metatarsal neuroma/interdigital neuritis, any interspace of the foot~~

S2140 Cord blood harvesting for transplantation, allogeneic

S2142 Cord blood-derived stem-cell transplantation, allogeneic

S2150 Bone marrow or blood-derived stem cells (peripheral or umbilical), allogeneic or autologous, harvesting, transplantation, and related complications including pheresis and cell preparation/storage; marrow ablative therapy; drugs, supplies, hospitalization with outpatient follow-up; medical/surgical, diagnostic, emergency, and rehabilitative services; and the number of days of pre- and posttransplant care in the global definition

S2152 Solid organ(s), complete or segmental, single organ or combination of organs; deceased or living donor (s), procurement, transplantation, and related complications; including: drugs; supplies; hospitalization with outpatient follow-up; medical/surgical, diagnostic, emergency, and rehabilitative services, and the number of days of pre and posttransplant care in the global definition

S2202 Echosclerotherapy

S2205 Minimally invasive direct coronary artery bypass surgery involving mini-thoracotomy or mini-sternotomy surgery, performed under direct vision; using arterial graft(s), single coronary arterial graft

S2206 Minimally invasive direct coronary artery bypass surgery involving mini-thoracotomy or mini-sternotomy surgery, performed under direct vision; using arterial graft(s), 2 coronary arterial grafts

S2207 Minimally invasive direct coronary artery bypass surgery involving mini-thoracotomy or mini-sternotomy surgery, performed under direct vision; using venous graft only, single coronary venous graft

S2208 Minimally invasive direct coronary artery bypass surgery involving mini-thoracotomy or mini-sternotomy surgery, performed under direct vision; using single arterial and venous graft(s), single venous graft

S2209 Minimally invasive direct coronary artery bypass surgery involving mini-thoracotomy or mini-sternotomy surgery, performed under direct vision; using 2 arterial grafts and single venous graft

S2225 Myringotomy, laser-assisted

S2230 Implantation of magnetic component of semi-implantable hearing device on ossicles in middle ear

S2235 Implantation of auditory brain stem implant

S2260 Induced abortion, 17 to 24 weeks M ♀

S2265 Induced abortion, 25 to 28 weeks M ♀

S2266 Induced abortion, 29 to 31 weeks M ♀

S2267 Induced abortion, 32 weeks or greater M ♀

● S2270 Insertion of vaginal cylinder for application of radiation source or clinical brachytherapy (report separately in addition to radiation source delivery)

S2300 Arthroscopy, shoulder, surgical; with thermally-induced capsulorrhaphy

S2325 Hip core decompression

S2340 Chemodenervation of abductor muscle(s) of vocal cord

S2341 Chemodenervation of adductor muscle(s) of vocal cord

S2342 Nasal endoscopy for postoperative debridement following functional endoscopic sinus surgery, nasal and/or sinus cavity(s), unilateral or bilateral

S2344 Nasal/sinus endoscopy, surgical; with enlargement of sinus ostium opening using inflatable device (i.e., balloon sinuplasty)

S2348 Decompression procedure, percutaneous, of nucleus pulposus of intervertebral disc, using radiofrequency energy, single or multiple levels, lumbar

S2350 Diskectomy, anterior, with decompression of spinal cord and/or nerve root(s), including osteophytectomy; lumbar, single interspace

S2351 Diskectomy, anterior, with decompression of spinal cord and/or nerve root(s), including osteophytectomy; lumbar, each additional interspace (list separately in addition to code for primary procedure)

S2360 Percutaneous vertebroplasty, one vertebral body, unilateral or bilateral injection; cervical

S2361 Each additional cervical vertebral body (list separately in addition to code for primary procedure)

S2400 Repair, congenital diaphragmatic hernia in the fetus using temporary tracheal occlusion, procedure performed in utero M ♀

S2401 Repair, urinary tract obstruction in the fetus, procedure performed in utero M ♀

S2402 Repair, congenital cystic adenomatoid malformation in the fetus, procedure performed in utero M ♀

S2403 Repair, extralobar pulmonary sequestration in the fetus, procedure performed in utero M ♀

S2404 Repair, myelomeningocele in the fetus, procedure performed in utero M ♀

S2405 Repair of sacrococcygeal teratoma in the fetus, procedure performed in utero M ♀

S2409 Repair, congenital malformation of fetus, procedure performed in utero, not otherwise classified M ♀

S2411 Fetoscopic laser therapy for treatment of twin-to-twin transfusion syndrome M ♀

S2900 Surgical techniques requiring use of robotic surgical system (list separately in addition to code for primary procedure)

S3000 Diabetic indicator; retinal eye exam, dilated, bilateral

S3005 Performance measurement, evaluation of patient self assessment, depression

S3600 STAT laboratory request (situations other than S3601)

S3601 Emergency STAT laboratory charge for patient who is homebound or residing in a nursing facility

S3620 Newborn metabolic screening panel, includes test kit, postage and the laboratory tests specified by the state for inclusion in this panel (e.g., galactose; hemoglobin, electrophoresis; hydroxyprogesterone, 17-d; phenylanine (PKU); and thyroxine, total) A

S3625 Maternal serum triple marker screen including alpha-fetoprotein (AFP), estriol, and human chorionic gonadotropin (HCG) M ♀

S3626 Maternal serum quadruple marker screen including alpha-fetoprotein (AFP), estriol, human chorionic gonadotropin hCG) and inhibin A

● **S3628** Placental alpha microglobulin-1 rapid immunoassay for detection of rupture of fetal membranes M ♀

S3630 Eosinophil count, blood, direct

S3645 HIV-1 antibody testing of oral mucosal transudate

S3650 Saliva test, hormone level; during menopause A ♀

S3652 Saliva test, hormone level; to assess preterm labor risk M ♀

S3655 Antisperm antibodies test (immunobead) A ♀

S3708 Gastrointestinal fat absorption study

● **S3711** Circulating tumor cell test

S3800 Genetic testing for amyotrophic lateral sclerosis (ALS)

S3818 Complete gene sequence analysis; BRCA1 gene

S3819 Complete gene sequence analysis; BRCA2 gene

S3820 Complete BRCA1 and BRCA2 gene sequence analysis for susceptibility to breast and ovarian cancer ♀

S3822 Single mutation analysis (in individual with a known BRCA1 or BRCA2 mutation in the family) for susceptibility to breast and ovarian cancer ♀

S3823 Three-mutation BRCA1 and BRCA2 analysis for susceptibility to breast and ovarian cancer in Ashkenazi individuals ♀

S3828 Complete gene sequence analysis; MLH1 gene

S3829 Complete gene sequence analysis; MLH2 gene

S3830 Complete MLH1 and MLH2 gene sequence analysis for hereditary nonpolyposis colorectal cancer (HNPCC) genetic testing

S3831 Single-mutation analysis (in individual with a known MLH1 and MLH2 mutation in the family) for hereditary nonpolyposis colorectal cancer (HNPCC) genetic testing

S3833 Complete APC gene sequence analysis for susceptibility to familial adenomatous polyposis (FAP) and attenuated fap

S3834 Single-mutation analysis (in individual with a known APC mutation in the family) for susceptibility to familial adenomatous polyposis (FAP) and attenuated FAP

S3835 Complete gene sequence analysis for cystic fibrosis genetic testing

S3837 Complete gene sequence analysis for hemochromatosis genetic testing

S3840 DNA analysis for germline mutations of the RET proto-oncogene for susceptibility to multiple endocrine neoplasia type 2

S3841 Genetic testing for retinoblastoma

S3842 Genetic testing for Von Hippel-Lindau disease

S3843 DNA analysis of the F5 gene for susceptibility to factor V Leiden thrombophilia

S3844 DNA analysis of the connexin 26 gene (GJB2) for susceptibility to congenital, profound deafness

S3845 Genetic testing for alpha-thalassemia

S3846 Genetic testing for hemoglobin E beta-thalassemia

S3847 Genetic testing for Tay-Sachs disease

S3848 Genetic testing for Gaucher disease

S3849 Genetic testing for Niemann-Pick disease

S3850 Genetic testing for sickle cell anemia

S3851 Genetic testing for Canavan disease

S3852 DNA analysis for APOE epsilon 4 allele for susceptibility to Alzheimer's disease

S3853 Genetic testing for myotonic muscular dystrophy

S3854 Gene expression profiling panel for use in the management of breast cancer treatment

S3855 Genetic testing for detection of mutations in the presenilin - 1 gene

● **S3860** Genetic testing, comprehensive cardiac ion channel analysis, for variants in 5 major cardiac ion channel genes for individuals with high index of suspicion for familial long QT syndrome (LQTS) or related syndromes

● **S3861** Genetic testing, sodium channel, voltage-gated, type V, alpha subunit (SCN5A) and variants for suspected Brugada Syndrome

● **S3862** Genetic testing, family-specific ion channel analysis, for blood-relatives of individuals (index case) who have previously tested positive for a genetic variant of a cardiac ion channel syndrome using either one of the above test configurations or confirmed results from another laboratory

S3890 DNA analysis, fecal, for colorectal cancer screening

S3900 Surface electromyography (EMG)

S3902 Ballistocardiogram

S3904 Masters 2 step

S3905 Noninvasive electrodiagnostic testing with automatic computerized hand-held device to stimulate and measure neuromuscular signals in diagnosing and evaluating systemic and entrapment neuropathies

S4005 Interim labor facility global (labor occurring but not resulting in delivery) M ♀

S4011 In vitro fertilization; including but not limited to identification and incubation of mature oocytes, fertilization with sperm, incubation of embryo(s), and subsequent visualization for determination of development M ♀

S4013 Complete cycle, gamete intrafallopian transfer (GIFT), case rate M ♀

S4014 Complete cycle, zygote intrafallopian transfer (ZIFT), case rate M ♀

S4015 Complete in vitro fertilization cycle, not otherwise specified, case rate M ♀

S4016 Frozen in vitro fertilization cycle, case rate ♀

S4017 Incomplete cycle, treatment cancelled prior to stimulation, case rate ♀

S4018 Frozen embryo transfer procedure cancelled before transfer, case rate ♀

S4020 In vitro fertilization procedure cancelled before aspiration, case rate ♀

S4021 In vitro fertilization procedure cancelled after aspiration, case rate ♀

S4022 Assisted oocyte fertilization, case rate ♀

S4023 Donor egg cycle, incomplete, case rate ♀

S4025 Donor services for in vitro fertilization (sperm or embryo), case rate A

S4026 Procurement of donor sperm from sperm bank ♂

S4027 Storage of previously frozen embryos ♀

S4028 Microsurgical epididymal sperm aspiration (MESA) A ♂

S4030 Sperm procurement and cryopreservation services; initial visit A ♂

S4031 Sperm procurement and cryopreservation services; subsequent visit A ♂

S4035 Stimulated intrauterine insemination (IUI), case rate ♀

S4037 Cryopreserved embryo transfer, case rate ♀

S4040 Monitoring and storage of cryopreserved embryos, per 30 days ♀

S4042 Management of ovulation induction (interpretation of diagnostic tests and studies, nonface-to-face medical management of the patient), per cycle

S4981 Insertion of levonorgestrel-releasing intrauterine system ♀

S4989 Contraceptive intrauterine device (e.g., Progestacert IUD), including implants and supplies ♀

☑ **S4990** Nicotine patches, legend

☑ **S4991** Nicotine patches, nonlegend

S4993 Contraceptive pills for birth control ♀

S4995 Smoking cessation gum

☑ **S5000** Prescription drug, generic

☑ **S5001** Prescription drug, brand name

☑ **S5010** 5% dextrose and 0.45% normal saline, 1000 ml

☑ **S5011** 5% dextrose in lactated ringer's, 1000 ml

☑ **S5012** 5% dextrose with potassium chloride, 1000 ml

☑ **S5013** 5% dextrose/0.45% normal saline with potassium chloride and magnesium sulfate, 1000 ml

☑ **S5014** 5% dextrose/0.45% normal saline with potassium chloride and magnesium sulfate, 1500 ml

S5035 Home infusion therapy, routine service of infusion device (e.g., pump maintenance)

S5036 Home infusion therapy, repair of infusion device (e.g., pump repair)

☑ **S5100** Day care services, adult; per 15 minutes A

☑ **S5101** Day care services, adult; per half day A

☑ **S5102** Day care services, adult; per diem A

☑ **S5105** Day care services, center-based; services not included in program fee, per diem

☑ **S5108** Home care training to home care client, per 15 minutes

☑ **S5109** Home care training to home care client, per session

☑ **S5110** Home care training, family; per 15 minutes

S5111 Home care training, family; per session

☑ **S5115** Home care training, nonfamily; per 15 minutes

☑ **S5116** Home care training, nonfamily; per session

☑ **S5120** Chore services; per 15 minutes

☑ **S5121** Chore services; per diem

☑ **S5125** Attendant care services; per 15 minutes

☑ **S5126** Attendant care services; per diem

☑ **S5130** Homemaker service, NOS; per 15 minutes

☑ **S5131** Homemaker service, NOS; per diem

☑ **S5135** Companion care, adult (e.g., IADL/ADL); per 15 minutes A

☑ **S5136** Companion care, adult (e.g., IADL/ADL); per diem A

☑ **S5140** Foster care, adult; per diem A

S5141 Foster care, adult; per month A

S5145 Foster care, therapeutic, child; per diem A

S5146 Foster care, therapeutic, child; per month A

☑ **S5150** Unskilled respite care, not hospice; per 15 minutes

S5151 Unskilled respite care, not hospice; per diem

S5160 Emergency response system; installation and testing

S5161 Emergency response system; service fee, per month (excludes installation and testing)

S5162 Emergency response system; purchase only

S5165 Home modifications; per service

S5170 Home delivered meals, including preparation; per meal

S5175 Laundry service, external, professional; per order

S5180 Home health respiratory therapy, initial evaluation

S5181 Home health respiratory therapy, NOS, per diem

S5185 Medication reminder service, nonface-to-face; per month

S5190 Wellness assessment, performed by nonphysician

S5199 Personal care item, NOS, each

S5497 Home infusion therapy, catheter care/maintenance, not otherwise classified; includes administrative services, professional pharmacy services, care coordination, and all necessary supplies and equipment (drugs and nursing visits coded separately), per diem

S5498 Home infusion therapy, catheter care/maintenance, simple (single lumen), includes administrative services, professional pharmacy services, care coordination and all necessary supplies and equipment, (drugs and nursing visits coded separately), per diem

S5501 Home infusion therapy, catheter care/maintenance, complex (more than one lumen), includes administrative services, professional pharmacy services, care coordination, and all necessary supplies and equipment (drugs and nursing visits coded separately), per diem

S5502 Home infusion therapy, catheter care/maintenance, implanted access device, includes administrative services, professional pharmacy services, care coordination and all necessary supplies and equipment (drugs and nursing visits coded separately), per diem (use this code for interim maintenance of vascular access not currently in use)

S5517 Home infusion therapy, all supplies necessary for restoration of catheter patency or declotting

S5518 Home infusion therapy, all supplies necessary for catheter repair

S5520 Home infusion therapy, all supplies (including catheter) necessary for a peripherally inserted central venous catheter (PICC) line insertion

S5521 Home infusion therapy, all supplies (including catheter) necessary for a midline catheter insertion

S5522 Home infusion therapy, insertion of peripherally inserted central venous catheter (PICC), nursing services only (no supplies or catheter included)

S5523 Home infusion therapy, insertion of midline venous catheter, nursing services only (no supplies or catheter included)

☑ S5550 Insulin, rapid onset, 5 units

☑ S5551 Insulin, most rapid onset (Lispro or Aspart); 5 units

☑ S5552 Insulin, intermediate acting (NPH or LENTE); 5 units

☑ S5553 Insulin, long acting; 5 units

☑ S5560 Insulin delivery device, reusable pen; 1.5 ml size

☑ S5561 Insulin delivery device, reusable pen; 3 ml size

☑ S5565 Insulin cartridge for use in insulin delivery device other than pump; 150 units

☑ S5566 Insulin cartridge for use in insulin delivery device other than pump; 300 units

☑ S5570 Insulin delivery device, disposable pen (including insulin); 1.5 ml size

☑ S5571 Insulin delivery device, disposable pen (including insulin); 3 ml size

S8030 Scleral application of tantalum ring(s) for localization of lesions for proton beam therapy

S8035 Magnetic source imaging

S8037 Magnetic resonance cholangiopancreatography (MRCP)

S8040 Topographic brain mapping

S8042 Magnetic resonance imaging (MRI), low-field

S8049 Intraoperative radiation therapy (single administration)

S8055 Ultrasound guidance for multifetal pregnancy reduction(s), technical component (only to be used when the physician doing the reduction procedure does not perform the ultrasound, guidance is included in the CPT code for multifetal pregnancy reduction (59866) M ♀

S8080 Scintimammography (radioimmunoscintigraphy of the breast), unilateral, including supply of radiopharmaceutical

S8085 Fluorine-18 fluorodeoxyglucose (F-18 FDG) imaging using dual-head coincidence detection system (nondedicated PET scan)

S8092 Electron beam computed tomography (also known as ultrafast CT, cine CT)

S8096 Portable peak flow meter

☑ S8097 Asthma kit (including but not limited to portable peak expiratory flow meter, instructional video, brochure, and/or spacer)

S8100 Holding chamber or spacer for use with an inhaler or nebulizer; without mask

S8101 Holding chamber or spacer for use with an inhaler or nebulizer; with mask

S8110 Peak expiratory flow rate (physician services)

☑ S8120 Oxygen contents, gaseous, 1 unit equals 1 cubic foot

☑ S8121 Oxygen contents, liquid, 1 unit equals 1 pound

S8185 Flutter device

S8186 Swivel adaptor

S8189 Tracheostomy supply, not otherwise classified

S8190 Electronic spirometer (or microspirometer)

S8210 Mucus trap

S8262 Mandibular orthopedic repositioning device, each

S8265 Haberman feeder for cleft lip/palate

S8270 Enuresis alarm, using auditory buzzer and/or vibration device

S8301 Infection control supplies, not otherwise specified

S8415 Supplies for home delivery of infant M ♀

S8420 Gradient pressure aid (sleeve and glove combination), custom made

S8421 Gradient pressure aid (sleeve and glove combination), ready made

S8422 Gradient pressure aid (sleeve), custom made, medium weight

S8423 Gradient pressure aid (sleeve), custom made, heavy weight

S8424 Gradient pressure aid (sleeve), ready made

S8425 Gradient pressure aid (glove), custom made, medium weight

S8426 Gradient pressure aid (glove), custom made, heavy weight

S8427 Gradient pressure aid (glove), ready made

S8428 Gradient pressure aid (gauntlet), ready made

S8429 Gradient pressure exterior wrap

☑ S8430 Padding for compression bandage, roll

☑ S8431 Compression bandage, roll

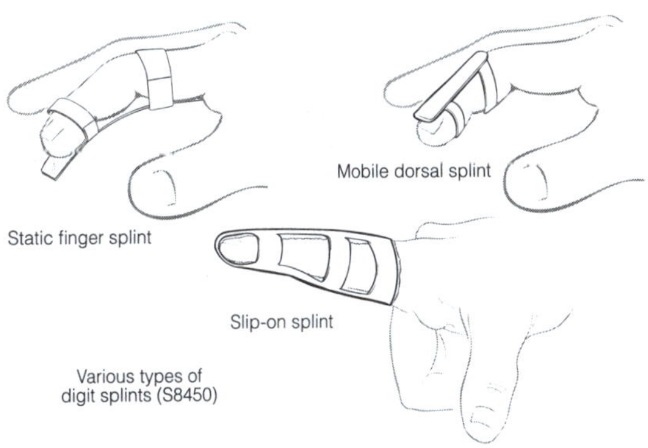

Various types of digit splints (S8450)

☑ S8450 Splint, prefabricated, digit (specify digit by use of modifier)

☑ S8451 Splint, prefabricated, wrist or ankle

☑ S8452 Splint, prefabricated, elbow

S8460 Camisole, postmastectomy

☑ S8490 Insulin syringes (100 syringes, any size)

S8940 Equestrian/hippotherapy, per session

☑ S8948 Application of a modality (requiring constant provider attendance) to one or more areas; low-level laser; each 15 minutes

☑ S8950 Complex lymphedema therapy, each 15 minutes

S8990 Physical or manipulative therapy performed for maintenance rather than restoration

S8999 Resuscitation bag (for use by patient on artificial respiration during power failure or other catastrophic event)

S9001 Home uterine monitor with or without associated nursing services M ♀

S9007 Ultrafiltration monitor

S9015 Automated EEG monitoring

S9024 Paranasal sinus ultrasound

S9025 Omnicardiogram/cardiointegram

S9034 Extracorporeal shockwave lithotripsy for gall stones (if performed with ERCP, use 43265)

S9055 Procuren or other growth factor preparation to promote wound healing

S9056 Coma stimulation per diem

S9061 Home administration of aerosolized drug therapy (e.g., Pentamidine); administrative services, professional pharmacy services, care coordination, all necessary supplies and equipment (drugs and nursing visits coded separately), per diem

S9075 Smoking cessation treatment

S9083 Global fee urgent care centers

S9088 Services provided in an urgent care center (list in addition to code for service)

☑ S9090 Vertebral axial decompression, per session

~~S9092 Canolith repositioning, per visit~~

S9097 Home visit for wound care

S9098 Home visit, phototherapy services (e.g., Bili-lite), including equipment rental, nursing services, blood draw, supplies, and other services, per diem

S9109 Congestive heart failure telemonitoring, equipment rental, including telescale, computer system and software, telephone connections, and maintenance, per month

☑ S9117 Back school, per visit

☑ S9122 Home health aide or certified nurse assistant, providing care in the home; per hour

☑ S9123 Nursing care, in the home; by registered nurse, per hour (use for general nursing care only, not to be used when CPT codes 99500-99602 can be used)

☑ S9124 Nursing care, in the home; by licensed practical nurse, per hour

☑ S9125 Respite care, in the home, per diem

☑ S9126 Hospice care, in the home, per diem

☑ S9127 Social work visit, in the home, per diem

☑ S9128 Speech therapy, in the home, per diem

☑ S9129 Occupational therapy, in the home, per diem

☑ S9131 Physical therapy; in the home, per diem

☑ S9140 Diabetic management program, follow-up visit to non-MD provider

☑ S9141 Diabetic management program, follow-up visit to MD provider

S9145 Insulin pump initiation, instruction in initial use of pump (pump not included)

S9150 Evaluation by ocularist

S9152 Speech therapy, re-evaluation

S9208 Home management of preterm labor, including administrative services, professional pharmacy services, care coordination, and all necessary supplies or equipment (drugs and nursing visits coded separately), per diem (do not use this code with any home infusion per diem code) M ♀

S9209 Home management of preterm premature rupture of membranes (PPROM), including administrative services, professional pharmacy services, care coordination, and all necessary supplies or equipment (drugs and nursing visits coded separately), per diem (do not use this code with any home infusion per diem code) M ♀

S9211 Home management of gestational hypertension, includes administrative services, professional pharmacy services, care coordination and all necessary supplies and equipment (drugs and nursing visits coded separately); per diem (do not use this code with any home infusion per diem code) M ♀

S9212 Home management of postpartum hypertension, includes administrative services, professional pharmacy services, care coordination, and all necessary supplies and equipment (drugs and nursing visits coded separately), per diem (do not use this code with any home infusion per diem code) ♀

S9213 Home management of preeclampsia, includes administrative services, professional pharmacy services, care coordination, and all necessary supplies and equipment (drugs and nursing services coded separately); per diem (do not use this code with any home infusion per diem code) M ♀

S9214 Home management of gestational diabetes, includes administrative services, professional pharmacy services, care coordination, and all necessary supplies and equipment (drugs and nursing visits coded separately); per diem (do not use this code with any home infusion per diem code) M ♀

S9325 Home infusion therapy, pain management infusion; administrative services, professional pharmacy services, care coordination, and all necessary supplies and equipment, (drugs and nursing visits coded separately), per diem (do not use this code with S9326, S9327 or S9328)

S9326 Home infusion therapy, continuous (24 hours or more) pain management infusion; administrative services, professional pharmacy services, care coordination and all necessary supplies and equipment (drugs and nursing visits coded separately), per diem

S9327 Home infusion therapy, intermittent (less than 24 hours) pain management infusion; administrative services, professional pharmacy services, care coordination, and all necessary supplies and equipment (drugs and nursing visits coded separately), per diem

S9328 Home infusion therapy, implanted pump pain management infusion; administrative services, professional pharmacy services, care coordination, and all necessary supplies and equipment (drugs and nursing visits coded separately), per diem

S9329 Home infusion therapy, chemotherapy infusion; administrative services, professional pharmacy services, care coordination, and all necessary supplies and equipment (drugs and nursing visits coded separately), per diem (do not use this code with S9330 or S9331)

S9330 Home infusion therapy, continuous (24 hours or more) chemotherapy infusion; administrative services, professional pharmacy services, care coordination, and all necessary supplies and equipment (drugs and nursing visits coded separately), per diem

S9331 Home infusion therapy, intermittent (less than 24 hours) chemotherapy infusion; administrative services, professional pharmacy services, care coordination, and all necessary supplies and equipment (drugs and nursing visits coded separately), per diem

S9335 Home therapy, hemodialysis; administrative services, professional pharmacy services, care coordination, and all necessary supplies and equipment (drugs and nursing services coded separately), per diem

S9336 Home infusion therapy, continuous anticoagulant infusion therapy (e.g., Heparin), administrative services, professional pharmacy services, care coordination and all necessary supplies and equipment (drugs and nursing visits coded separately), per diem

S9338 Home infusion therapy, immunotherapy, administrative services, professional pharmacy services, care coordination, and all necessary supplies and equipment (drugs and nursing visits coded separately), per diem

S9339 Home therapy; peritoneal dialysis, administrative services, professional pharmacy services, care coordination and all necessary supplies and equipment (drugs and nursing visits coded separately), per diem

S9340 Home therapy; enteral nutrition; administrative services, professional pharmacy services, care coordination, and all necessary supplies and equipment (enteral formula and nursing visits coded separately), per diem

S9341 Home therapy; enteral nutrition via gravity; administrative services, professional pharmacy services, care coordination, and all necessary supplies and equipment (enteral formula and nursing visits coded separately), per diem

S9342 Home therapy; enteral nutrition via pump; administrative services, professional pharmacy services, care coordination, and all necessary supplies and equipment (enteral formula and nursing visits coded separately), per diem

S9343 Home therapy; enteral nutrition via bolus; administrative services, professional pharmacy services, care coordination, and all necessary supplies and equipment (enteral formula and nursing visits coded separately), per diem

S9345 Home infusion therapy, antihemophilic agent infusion therapy (e.g., factor VIII); administrative services, professional pharmacy services, care coordination, and all necessary supplies and equipment (drugs and nursing visits coded separately), per diem

S9346 Home infusion therapy, alpha-1-proteinase inhibitor (e.g., Prolastin); administrative services, professional pharmacy services, care coordination, and all necessary supplies and equipment (drugs and nursing visits coded separately), per diem

S9347 Home infusion therapy, uninterrupted, long-term, controlled rate intravenous or subcutaneous infusion therapy (e.g., epoprostenol); administrative services, professional pharmacy services, care coordination, and all necessary supplies and equipment (drugs and nursing visits coded separately), per diem

S9348 Home infusion therapy, sympathomimetic/inotropic agent infusion therapy (e.g., Dobutamine); administrative services, professional pharmacy services, care coordination, all necessary supplies and equipment (drugs and nursing visits coded separately), per diem

S9349 Home infusion therapy, tocolytic infusion therapy; administrative services, professional pharmacy services, care coordination, and all necessary supplies and equipment (drugs and nursing visits coded separately), per diem M ♀

S9351 Home infusion therapy, continuous or intermittent antiemetic infusion therapy; administrative services, professional pharmacy services, care coordination, and all necessary supplies and equipment (drugs and visits coded separately), per diem

S9353 Home infusion therapy, continuous insulin infusion therapy; administrative services, professional pharmacy services, care coordination, and all necessary supplies and equipment (drugs and nursing visits coded separately), per diem

S9355 Home infusion therapy, chelation therapy; administrative services, professional pharmacy services, care coordination, and all necessary supplies and equipment (drugs and nursing visits coded separately), per diem

S9357 Home infusion therapy, enzyme replacement intravenous therapy; (e.g., Imiglucerase); administrative services, professional pharmacy services, care coordination, and all necessary supplies and equipment (drugs and nursing visits coded separately), per diem

S9359 Home infusion therapy, antitumor necrosis factor intravenous therapy; (e.g., Infliximab); administrative services, professional pharmacy services, care coordination, and all necessary supplies and equipment (drugs and nursing visits coded separately), per diem

S9361 Home infusion therapy, diuretic intravenous therapy; administrative services, professional pharmacy services, care coordination, and all necessary supplies and equipment (drugs and nursing visits coded separately), per diem

S9363 Home infusion therapy, antispasmotic therapy; administrative services, professional pharmacy services, care coordination, and all necessary supplies and equipment (drugs and nursing visits coded separately), per diem

S9364 Home infusion therapy, total parenteral nutrition (TPN); administrative services, professional pharmacy services, care coordination, and all necessary supplies and equipment including standard TPN formula (lipids, specialty amino acid formulas, drugs other than in standard formula and nursing visits coded separately), per diem (do not use with home infusion codes S9365–S9368 using daily volume scales)

S9365 Home infusion therapy, total parenteral nutrition (TPN); 1 liter per day, administrative services, professional pharmacy services, care coordination, and all necessary supplies and equipment including standard TPN formula (lipids, specialty amino acid formulas, drugs other than in standard formula and nursing visits coded separately), per diem

S9366 Home infusion therapy, total parenteral nutrition (TPN); more than 1 liter but no more than 2 liters per day, administrative services, professional pharmacy services, care coordination, and all necessary supplies and equipment including standard TPN formula (lipids, specialty amino acid formulas, drugs other than in standard formula and nursing visits coded separately), per diem

S9367 Home infusion therapy, total parenteral nutrition (TPN); more than 2 liters but no more than 3 liters per day, administrative services, professional pharmacy services, care coordination, and all necessary supplies and equipment including standard TPN formula (lipids, specialty amino acid formulas, drugs other than in standard formula and nursing visits coded separately), per diem

S9368 Home infusion therapy, total parenteral nutrition (TPN); more than 3 liters per day, administrative services, professional pharmacy services, care coordination, and all necessary supplies and equipment including standard TPN formula (lipids, specialty amino acid formulas, drugs other than in standard formula and nursing visits coded separately), per diem

S9370 Home therapy, intermittent antiemetic injection therapy; administrative services, professional pharmacy services, care coordination, and all necessary supplies and equipment (drugs and nursing visits coded separately), per diem

S9372 Home therapy; intermittent anticoagulant injection therapy (e.g., Heparin); administrative services, professional pharmacy services, care coordination, and all necessary supplies and equipment (drugs and nursing visits coded separately), per diem (do not use this code for flushing of infusion devices with Heparin to maintain patency)

S9373 Home infusion therapy, hydration therapy; administrative services, professional pharmacy services, care coordination, and all necessary supplies and equipment (drugs and nursing visits coded separately), per diem (do not use with hydration therapy codes S9374–S9377 using daily volume scales)

S9374 Home infusion therapy, hydration therapy; 1 liter per day, administrative services, professional pharmacy services, care coordination, and all necessary supplies and equipment (drugs and nursing visits coded separately), per diem

S9375 Home infusion therapy, hydration therapy; more than 1 liter but no more than 2 liters per day, administrative services, professional pharmacy services, care coordination, and all necessary supplies and equipment (drugs and nursing visits coded separately), per diem

S9376 Home infusion therapy, hydration therapy; more than 2 liters but no more than 3 liters per day, administrative services, professional pharmacy services, care coordination, and all necessary supplies and equipment (drugs and nursing visits coded separately), per diem

S9377 Home infusion therapy, hydration therapy; more than 3 liters per day, administrative services, professional pharmacy services, care coordination, and all necessary supplies (drugs and nursing visits coded separately), per diem

S9379 Home infusion therapy, infusion therapy, not otherwise classified; administrative services, professional pharmacy services, care coordination, and all necessary supplies and equipment (drugs and nursing visits coded separately), per diem

S9381 Delivery or service to high risk areas requiring escort or extra protection, per visit

S9401 Anticoagulation clinic, inclusive of all services except laboratory tests, per session

S9430 Pharmacy compounding and dispensing services

● **S9433** Medical food nutritionally complete, administered orally, providing 100% of nutritional intake

S9434 Modified solid food supplements for inborn errors of metabolism

S9435 Medical foods for inborn errors of metabolism

☑ **S9436** Childbirth preparation/Lamaze classes, nonphysician provider, per session M ♀

S9437 Childbirth refresher classes, nonphysician provider, per session M ♀

☑ **S9438** Cesarean birth classes, nonphysician provider, per session M ♀

☑ **S9439** VBAC (vaginal birth after cesarean) classes, nonphysician provider, per session M ♀

☑ **S9441** Asthma education, nonphysician provider, per session

☑ **S9442** Birthing classes, nonphysician provider, per session M ♀

☑ **S9443** Lactation classes, nonphysician provider, per session M ♀

☑ **S9444** Parenting classes, nonphysician provider, per session

☑ **S9445** Patient education, not otherwise classified, nonphysician provider, individual, per session

☑ **S9446** Patient education, not otherwise classified, nonphysician provider, group, per session

☑ **S9447** Infant safety (including CPR) classes, nonphysician provider, per session

☑ **S9449** Weight management classes, nonphysician provider, per session

S9451 Exercise classes, nonphysician provider, per session

S9452 Nutrition classes, nonphysician provider, per session

S9453 Smoking cessation classes, nonphysician provider, per session

S9454 Stress management classes, nonphysician provider, per session

S9455 Diabetic management program, group session

S9460 Diabetic management program, nurse visit

S9465 Diabetic management program, dietitian visit

S9470 Nutritional counseling, dietitian visit

S9472 Cardiac rehabilitation program, nonphysician provider, per diem

S9473 Pulmonary rehabilitation program, nonphysician provider, per diem

S9474 Enterostomal therapy by a registered nurse certified in enterostomal therapy, per diem

S9475 Ambulatory setting substance abuse treatment or detoxification services, per diem

S9476 Vestibular rehabilitation program, nonphysician provider, per diem

S9480 Intensive outpatient psychiatric services, per diem

☑ **S9482** Family stabilization services, per 15 minutes

☑ **S9484** Crisis intervention mental health services, per hour

S9485 Crisis intervention mental health services, per diem

Special Coverage Instructions | Noncovered by Medicare | Carrier Discretion | ☑ Quantity Alert | ● New Code | ○ Recycled/Reinstated | ▲ Revised Code

 A Age Edit | M Maternity Edit | ♀ Female Only | ♂ Male Only | A-Y OPPS Status Indicators

S9490 Home infusion therapy, corticosteroid infusion; administrative services, professional pharmacy services, care coordination, and all necessary supplies and equipment (drugs and nursing visits coded separately), per diem

S9494 Home infusion therapy, antibiotic, antiviral, or antifungal therapy; administrative services, professional pharmacy services, care coordination, and all necessary supplies and equipment (drugs and nursing visits coded separately, per diem) (do not use this code with home infusion codes for hourly dosing schedules S9497–S9504)

S9497 Home infusion therapy, antibiotic, antiviral, or antifungal therapy; once every 3 hours; administrative services, professional pharmacy services, care coordination, and all necessary supplies and equipment (drugs and nursing visits coded separately), per diem

S9500 Home infusion therapy, antibiotic, antiviral, or antifungal therapy; once every 24 hours; administrative services, professional pharmacy services, care coordination, and all necessary supplies and equipment (drugs and nursing visits coded separately), per diem

S9501 Home infusion therapy, antibiotic, antiviral, or antifungal therapy; once every 12 hours; administrative services, professional pharmacy services, care coordination, and all necessary supplies and equipment (drugs and nursing visits coded separately), per diem

S9502 Home infusion therapy, antibiotic, antiviral, or antifungal therapy; once every 8 hours, administrative services, professional pharmacy services, care coordination, and all necessary supplies and equipment (drugs and nursing visits coded separately), per diem

S9503 Home infusion therapy, antibiotic, antiviral, or antifungal; once every 6 hours; administrative services, professional pharmacy services, care coordination, and all necessary supplies and equipment (drugs and nursing visits coded separately), per diem

S9504 Home infusion therapy, antibiotic, antiviral, or antifungal; once every 4 hours; administrative services, professional pharmacy services, care coordination, and all necessary supplies and equipment (drugs and nursing visits coded separately), per diem

S9529 Routine venipuncture for collection of specimen(s), single homebound, nursing home, or skilled nursing facility patient

S9537 Home therapy; hematopoietic hormone injection therapy (e.g., erythropoietin, G-CSF, GM-CSF); administrative services, professional pharmacy services, care coordination, and all necessary supplies and equipment (drugs and nursing visits coded separately), per diem

S9538 Home transfusion of blood product(s); administrative services, professional pharmacy services, care coordination and all necessary supplies and equipment (blood products, drugs, and nursing visits coded separately), per diem

S9542 Home injectable therapy, not otherwise classified, including administrative services, professional pharmacy services, care coordination, and all necessary supplies and equipment (drugs and nursing visits coded separately), per diem

S9558 Home injectable therapy; growth hormone, including administrative services, professional pharmacy services, care coordination, and all necessary supplies and equipment (drugs and nursing visits coded separately), per diem

S9559 Home injectable therapy, interferon, including administrative services, professional pharmacy services, care coordination, and all necessary supplies and equipment (drugs and nursing visits coded separately), per diem

S9560 Home injectable therapy; hormonal therapy (e.g., leuprolide, goserelin), including administrative services, professional pharmacy services, care coordination, and all necessary supplies and equipment (drugs and nursing visits coded separately), per diem

S9562 Home injectable therapy, palivizumab, including administrative services, professional pharmacy services, care coordination, and all necessary supplies and equipment (drugs and nursing visits coded separately), per diem

S9590 Home therapy, irrigation therapy (e.g., sterile irrigation of an organ or anatomical cavity); including administrative services, professional pharmacy services, care coordination, and all necessary supplies and equipment (drugs and nursing visits coded separately), per diem

S9810 Home therapy; professional pharmacy services for provision of infusion, specialty drug administration, and/or disease state management, not otherwise classified, per hour (do not use this code with any per diem code)

S9900 Services by authorized Christian Science practitioner for the process of healing, per diem; not to be used for rest or study; excludes in-patient services

S9970 Health club membership, annual

S9975 Transplant related lodging, meals and transportation, per diem

S9976 Lodging, per diem, not otherwise classified

S9977 Meals, per diem, not otherwise specified

S9981 Medical records copying fee, administrative

☑ **S9982** Medical records copying fee, per page

S9986 Not medically necessary service (patient is aware that service not medically necessary)

S9988 Services provided as part of a Phase I clinical trial

S9989 Services provided outside of the United States of America (list in addition to code(s) for services(s))

S9990 Services provided as part of a Phase II clinical trial

S9991 Services provided as part of a Phase III clinical trial

S9992 Transportation costs to and from trial location and local transportation costs (e.g., fares for taxicab or bus) for clinical trial participant and one caregiver/companion

S9994 Lodging costs (e.g., hotel charges) for clinical trial participant and one caregiver/companion

S9996 Meals for clinical trial participant and one caregiver/companion

S9999 Sales tax

NATIONAL T CODES ESTABLISHED FOR STATE MEDICAID AGENCIES T1000-T9999

The T codes are designed for use by Medicaid state agencies to establish codes for items for which there are no permanent national codes but for which codes are necessary to administer the Medicaid program (T codes are not accepted by Medicare but can be used by private insurers). This range of codes describes nursing and home health-related services, substance abuse treatment, and certain training-related procedures.

☑ **T1000** Private duty/independent nursing service(s), licensed, up to 15 minutes

T1001 Nursing assessment/evaluation

☑ **T1002** RN services, up to 15 minutes

☑ **T1003** LPN/LVN services, up to 15 minutes

☑ **T1004** Services of a qualified nursing aide, up to 15 minutes

☑ **T1005** Respite care services, up to 15 minutes

T1006 Alcohol and/or substance abuse services, family/couple counseling

T1007 Alcohol and/or substance abuse services, treatment plan development and/or modification

T1009 Child sitting services for children of the individual receiving alcohol and/or substance abuse services

T1010 Meals for individuals receiving alcohol and/or substance abuse services (when meals not included in the program)

T1012 Alcohol and/or substance abuse services, skills development

☑ **T1013** Sign language or oral interpretive services, per 15 minutes

T1014 Telehealth transmission, per minute, professional services bill separately

T1015 Clinic visit/encounter, all-inclusive

☑ **T1016** Case management, each 15 minutes

☑ **T1017** Targeted case management, each 15 minutes

T1018 School-based individualized education program (IEP) services, bundled

☑ **T1019** Personal care services, per 15 minutes, not for an inpatient or resident of a hospital, nursing facility, ICF/MR or IMD, part of the individualized plan of treatment (code may not be used to identify services provided by home health aide or certified nurse assistant)

T1020 Personal care services, per diem, not for an inpatient or resident of a hospital, nursing facility, ICF/MR or IMD, part of the individualized plan of treatment (code may not be used to identify services provided by home health aide or certified nurse assistant)

T1021 Home health aide or certified nurse assistant, per visit

T1022 Contracted home health agency services, all services provided under contract, per day

T1023 Screening to determine the appropriateness of consideration of an individual for participation in a specified program, project or treatment protocol, per encounter

T1024 Evaluation and treatment by an integrated, specialty team contracted to provide coordinated care to multiple or severely handicapped children, per encounter A

T1025 Intensive, extended multidisciplinary services provided in a clinic setting to children with complex medical, physical, mental and psychosocial impairments, per diem A

T1026 Intensive, extended multidisciplinary services provided in a clinic setting to children with complex medical, physical, medical and psychosocial impairments, per hour A

☑ **T1027** Family training and counseling for child development, per 15 minutes

T1028 Assessment of home, physical and family environment, to determine suitability to meet patient's medical needs

T1029 Comprehensive environmental lead investigation, not including laboratory analysis, per dwelling

☑ **T1030** Nursing care, in the home, by registered nurse, per diem

☑ **T1031** Nursing care, in the home, by licensed practical nurse, per diem

☑ **T1502** Administration of oral, intramuscular and/or subcutaneous medication by health care agency/professional, per visit

☑ **T1503** Administration of medication, other than oral and/or injectable, by a health care agency/professional, per visit

T1999 Miscellaneous therapeutic items and supplies, retail purchases, not otherwise classified; identify product in "remarks"

T2001 Nonemergency transportation; patient attendant/escort

☑ **T2002** Nonemergency transportation; per diem

T2003 Nonemergency transportation; encounter/trip

T2004 Nonemergency transport; commercial carrier, multipass

T2005 Nonemergency transportation; stretcher van

☑ **T2007** Transportation waiting time, air ambulance and nonemergency vehicle, one-half (1/2) hour increments

☑ **T2010** Preadmission screening and resident review (PASRR) level I identification screening, per screen

T2011 Preadmission screening and resident review (PASRR) level II evaluation, per evaluation

☑ **T2012** Habilitation, educational; waiver, per diem

☑ **T2013** Habilitation, educational, waiver; per hour

☑ **T2014** Habilitation, prevocational, waiver; per diem

☑ **T2015** Habilitation, prevocational, waiver; per hour

☑ **T2016** Habilitation, residential, waiver; per diem

☑ **T2017** Habilitation, residential, waiver; 15 minutes

☑ **T2018** Habilitation, supported employment, waiver; per diem

☑ **T2019** Habilitation, supported employment, waiver; per 15 minutes

☑ **T2020** Day habilitation, waiver; per diem

☑ **T2021** Day habilitation, waiver; per 15 minutes

☑ **T2022** Case management, per month

☑ **T2023** Targeted case management; per month

T2024 Service assessment/plan of care development, waiver

T2025 Waiver services; not otherwise specified (NOS)

☑ **T2026** Specialized childcare, waiver; per diem

☑ **T2027** Specialized childcare, waiver; per 15 minutes

T2028 Specialized supply, not otherwise specified, waiver

T2029 Specialized medical equipment, not otherwise specified, waiver

☑ **T2030** Assisted living, waiver; per month

☑ **T2031** Assisted living; waiver, per diem

☑ **T2032** Residential care, not otherwise specified (NOS), waiver; per month

☑ **T2033** Residential care, not otherwise specified (NOS), waiver; per diem

☑ **T2034** Crisis intervention, waiver; per diem

T2035 Utility services to support medical equipment and assistive technology/devices, waiver

☑ **T2036** Therapeutic camping, overnight, waiver; each session

☑ **T2037** Therapeutic camping, day, waiver; each session

☑ **T2038** Community transition, waiver; per service

☑ **T2039** Vehicle modifications, waiver; per service

☑ **T2040** Financial management, self-directed, waiver; per 15 minutes

☑ **T2041** Supports brokerage, self-directed, waiver; per 15 minutes

☑ **T2042** Hospice routine home care; per diem

☑ **T2043** Hospice continuous home care; per hour

☑ **T2044** Hospice inpatient respite care; per diem

☑ **T2045** Hospice general inpatient care; per diem

☑ **T2046** Hospice long-term care, room and board only; per diem

☑ **T2048** Behavioral health; long-term care residential (nonacute care in a residential treatment program where stay is typically longer than 30 days), with room and board, per diem

☑ **T2049** Nonemergency transportation; stretcher van, mileage; per mile

T2101 Human breast milk processing, storage and distribution only ♀

☑ **T4521** Adult sized disposable incontinence product, brief/diaper, small, each
MED: 100-3,230.10

☑ **T4522** Adult sized disposable incontinence product, brief/diaper, medium, each
MED: 100-3,230.10

☑ **T4523** Adult sized disposable incontinence product, brief/diaper, large, each
MED: 100-3,230.10

☑ **T4524** Adult sized disposable incontinence product, brief/diaper, extra large, each
MED: 100-3,230.10

☑ **T4525** Adult sized disposable incontinence product, protective underwear/pull-on, small size, each
MED: 100-3,230.10

☑ **T4526** Adult sized disposable incontinence product, protective underwear/pull-on, medium size, each
MED: 100-3,230.10

☑ **T4527** Adult sized disposable incontinence product, protective underwear/pull-on, large size, each
MED: 100-3,230.10

☑ **T4528** Adult sized disposable incontinence product, protective underwear/pull-on, extra large size, each
MED: 100-3,230.10

☑ **T4529** Pediatric sized disposable incontinence product, brief/diaper, small/medium size, each
MED: 100-3,230.10

☑ **T4530** Pediatric sized disposable incontinence product, brief/diaper, large size, each
MED: 100-3,230.10

☑ **T4531** Pediatric sized disposable incontinence product, protective underwear/pull-on, small/medium size, each
MED: 100-3,230.10

☑ **T4532** Pediatric sized disposable incontinence product, protective underwear/pull-on, large size, each
MED: 100-3,230.10

☑ **T4533** Youth sized disposable incontinence product, brief/diaper, each
MED: 100-3,230.10

☑ **T4534** Youth sized disposable incontinence product, protective underwear/pull-on, each
MED: 100-3,230.10

☑ **T4535** Disposable liner/shield/guard/pad/undergarment, for incontinence, each
MED: 100-3,230.10

☑ **T4536** Incontinence product, protective underwear/pull-on, reusable, any size, each
MED: 100-3,230.10

☑ **T4537** Incontinence product, protective underpad, reusable, bed size, each
MED: 100-3,230.10

☑ **T4538** Diaper service, reusable diaper, each diaper
MED: 100-3,230.10

☑ **T4539** Incontinence product, diaper/brief, reusable, any size, each
MED: 100-3,230.10

☑ **T4540** Incontinence product, protective underpad, reusable, chair size, each
MED: 100-3,230.10

☑ **T4541** Incontinence product, disposable underpad, large, each

☑ **T4542** Incontinence product, disposable underpad, small size, each

☑ **T4543** Disposable incontinence product, brief/diaper, bariatric, each

T5001 Positioning seat for persons with special orthopedic needs

T5999 Supply, not otherwise specified

Special Coverage Instructions | Noncovered by Medicare | Carrier Discretion | ☑ Quantity Alert | ● New Code | ○ Recycled/Reinstated | ▲ Revised Code

 A Age Edit | M Maternity Edit | ♀ Female Only | ♂ Male Only | A-Y OPPS Status Indicators

VISION SERVICES V0000-V2999

These V codes include vision-related supplies, including spectacles, lenses, contact lenses, prostheses, intraocular lenses, and miscellaneous lenses.

FRAMES

A **V2020** Frames, purchases ♿
MED: 100-2,15,120; 100-4,3,10.4

E **V2025** Deluxe frame
MED: 100-4,1,30.3.5

SPECTACLE LENSES

See S0500-S0592 for temporary vision codes.

SINGLE VISION, GLASS, OR PLASTIC

Monofocal spectacles (V2100-V2114)

Trifocal spectacles (V2300-V2314)

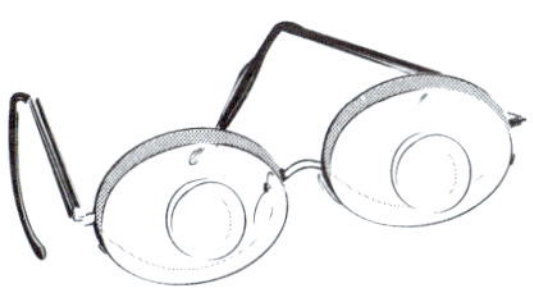
Low vision aids mounted to spectacles (V2610)

Telescopic or other compound lens fitted on spectacles as a low vision aid (V2615)

A ☑ **V2100** Sphere, single vision, plano to plus or minus 4.00, per lens ♿

A ☑ **V2101** Sphere, single vision, plus or minus 4.12 to plus or minus 7.00d, per lens ♿

A ☑ **V2102** Sphere, single vision, plus or minus 7.12 to plus or minus 20.00d, per lens ♿

A ☑ **V2103** Spherocylinder, single vision, plano to plus or minus 4.00d sphere, 0.12 to 2.00d cylinder, per lens ♿

A ☑ **V2104** Spherocylinder, single vision, plano to plus or minus 4.00d sphere, 2.12 to 4.00d cylinder, per lens ♿

A ☑ **V2105** Spherocylinder, single vision, plano to plus or minus 4.00d sphere, 4.25 to 6.00d cylinder, per lens ♿

A ☑ **V2106** Spherocylinder, single vision, plano to plus or minus 4.00d sphere, over 6.00d cylinder, per lens ♿

A ☑ **V2107** Spherocylinder, single vision, plus or minus 4.25 to plus or minus 7.00 sphere, 0.12 to 2.00d cylinder, per lens ♿

A ☑ **V2108** Spherocylinder, single vision, plus or minus 4.25d to plus or minus 7.00d sphere, 2.12 to 4.00d cylinder, per lens ♿

A ☑ **V2109** Spherocylinder, single vision, plus or minus 4.25 to plus or minus 7.00d sphere, 4.25 to 6.00d cylinder, per lens ♿

A ☑ **V2110** Spherocylinder, single vision, plus or minus 4.25 to 7.00d sphere, over 6.00d cylinder, per lens ♿

A ☑ **V2111** Spherocylinder, single vision, plus or minus 7.25 to plus or minus 12.00d sphere, 0.25 to 2.25d cylinder, per lens ♿

A ☑ **V2112** Spherocylinder, single vision, plus or minus 7.25 to plus or minus 12.00d sphere, 2.25d to 4.00d cylinder, per lens ♿

A ☑ **V2113** Spherocylinder, single vision, plus or minus 7.25 to plus or minus 12.00d sphere, 4.25 to 6.00d cylinder, per lens ♿

A ☑ **V2114** Spherocylinder, single vision, sphere over plus or minus 12.00d, per lens ♿

A ☑ **V2115** Lenticular (myodisc), per lens, single vision ♿

A **V2118** Aniseikonic lens, single vision ♿

A ☑ **V2121** Lenticular lens, per lens, single ♿
MED: 100-2,15,120; 100-4,3,10.4

A **V2199** Not otherwise classified, single vision lens

BIFOCAL, GLASS, OR PLASTIC

A ☑ **V2200** Sphere, bifocal, plano to plus or minus 4.00d, per lens ♿

A ☑ **V2201** Sphere, bifocal, plus or minus 4.12 to plus or minus 7.00d, per lens ♿

A ☑ **V2202** Sphere, bifocal, plus or minus 7.12 to plus or minus 20.00d, per lens ♿

A ☑ **V2203** Spherocylinder, bifocal, plano to plus or minus 4.00d sphere, 0.12 to 2.00d cylinder, per lens ♿

A ☑ **V2204** Spherocylinder, bifocal, plano to plus or minus 4.00d sphere, 2.12 to 4.00d cylinder, per lens ♿

A ☑ **V2205** Spherocylinder, bifocal, plano to plus or minus 4.00d sphere, 4.25 to 6.00d cylinder, per lens ♿

A ☑ **V2206** Spherocylinder, bifocal, plano to plus or minus 4.00d sphere, over 6.00d cylinder, per lens ♿

A ☑ **V2207** Spherocylinder, bifocal, plus or minus 4.25 to plus or minus 7.00d sphere, 0.12 to 2.00d cylinder, per lens ♿

A ☑ **V2208** Spherocylinder, bifocal, plus or minus 4.25 to plus or minus 7.00d sphere, 2.12 to 4.00d cylinder, per lens ♿

A ☑ **V2209** Spherocylinder, bifocal, plus or minus 4.25 to plus or minus 7.00d sphere, 4.25 to 6.00d cylinder, per lens ♿

A ☑ **V2210** Spherocylinder, bifocal, plus or minus 4.25 to plus or minus 7.00d sphere, over 6.00d cylinder, per lens ♿

A ☑ **V2211** Spherocylinder, bifocal, plus or minus 7.25 to plus or minus 12.00d sphere, 0.25 to 2.25d cylinder, per lens ♿

A ☑ **V2212** Spherocylinder, bifocal, plus or minus 7.25 to plus or minus 12.00d sphere, 2.25 to 4.00d cylinder, per lens ♿

A ☑ **V2213** Spherocylinder, bifocal, plus or minus 7.25 to plus or minus 12.00d sphere, 4.25 to 6.00d cylinder, per lens ♿

A ☑ **V2214** Spherocylinder, bifocal, sphere over plus or minus 12.00d, per lens ♿

A ☑ **V2215** Lenticular (myodisc), per lens, bifocal ♿

A ☑ **V2218** Aniseikonic, per lens, bifocal ♿

A ☑ **V2219** Bifocal seg width over 28mm ♿

A ☑ **V2220** Bifocal add over 3.25d ♿

A **V2221** Lenticular lens, per lens, bifocal ♿
MED: 100-2,15,120; 100-4,3,10.4

A **V2299** Specialty bifocal (by report)
Pertinent documentation to evaluate medical appropriateness should be included when this code is reported.

TRIFOCAL, GLASS, OR PLASTIC

A ☑ **V2300** Sphere, trifocal, plano to plus or minus 4.00d, per lens

A ☑ **V2301** Sphere, trifocal, plus or minus 4.12 to plus or minus 7.00d per lens

A ☑ **V2302** Sphere, trifocal, plus or minus 7.12 to plus or minus 20.00, per lens

A ☑ **V2303** Spherocylinder, trifocal, plano to plus or minus 4.00d sphere, 0.12 to 2.00d cylinder, per lens

A ☑ **V2304** Spherocylinder, trifocal, plano to plus or minus 4.00d sphere, 2.25 to 4.00d cylinder, per lens

A ☑ **V2305** Spherocylinder, trifocal, plano to plus or minus 4.00d sphere, 4.25 to 6.00 cylinder, per lens

A ☑ **V2306** Spherocylinder, trifocal, plano to plus or minus 4.00d sphere, over 6.00d cylinder, per lens

A ☑ **V2307** Spherocylinder, trifocal, plus or minus 4.25 to plus or minus 7.00d sphere, 0.12 to 2.00d cylinder, per lens

A ☑ **V2308** Spherocylinder, trifocal, plus or minus 4.25 to plus or minus 7.00d sphere, 2.12 to 4.00d cylinder, per lens

A ☑ **V2309** Spherocylinder, trifocal, plus or minus 4.25 to plus or minus 7.00d sphere, 4.25 to 6.00d cylinder, per lens

A ☑ **V2310** Spherocylinder, trifocal, plus or minus 4.25 to plus or minus 7.00d sphere, over 6.00d cylinder, per lens

A ☑ **V2311** Spherocylinder, trifocal, plus or minus 7.25 to plus or minus 12.00d sphere, 0.25 to 2.25d cylinder, per lens

A ☑ **V2312** Spherocylinder, trifocal, plus or minus 7.25 to plus or minus 12.00d sphere, 2.25 to 4.00d cylinder, per lens

A ☑ **V2313** Spherocylinder, trifocal, plus or minus 7.25 to plus or minus 12.00d sphere, 4.25 to 6.00d cylinder, per lens

A ☑ **V2314** Spherocylinder, trifocal, sphere over plus or minus 12.00d, per lens

A ☑ **V2315** Lenticular, (myodisc), per lens, trifocal

A **V2318** Aniseikonic lens, trifocal

A ☑ **V2319** Trifocal seg width over 28 mm

A ☑ **V2320** Trifocal add over 3.25d

A **V2321** Lenticular lens, per lens, trifocal
MED: 100-2,15,120; 100-4,3,10.4

A **V2399** Specialty trifocal (by report)
Pertinent documentation to evaluate medical appropriateness should be included when this code is reported.

VARIABLE ASPHERICITY LENS, GLASS, OR PLASTIC

A ☑ **V2410** Variable asphericity lens, single vision, full field, glass or plastic, per lens

A ☑ **V2430** Variable asphericity lens, bifocal, full field, glass or plastic, per lens

A **V2499** Variable sphericity lens, other type

CONTACT LENS

If procedure code 92391 or 92396 is reported, recode with specific lens type listed below (per lens).

A ☑ **V2500** Contact lens, PMMA, spherical, per lens

A ☑ **V2501** Contact lens, PMMA, toric or prism ballast, per lens

A ☑ **V2502** Contact lens PMMA, bifocal, per lens

A ☑ **V2503** Contact lens, PMMA, color vision deficiency, per lens

A ☑ **V2510** Contact lens, gas permeable, spherical, per lens

A ☑ **V2511** Contact lens, gas permeable, toric, prism ballast, per lens

A ☑ **V2512** Contact lens, gas permeable, bifocal, per lens

A ☑ **V2513** Contact lens, gas permeable, extended wear, per lens

A ☑ **V2520** Contact lens, hydrophilic, spherical, per lens
Hydrophilic contact lenses are covered by Medicare only for aphakic patients. Local contractor if incident to physician services.
MED: 100-3,80.1; 100-3,80.4

A ☑ **V2521** Contact lens, hydrophilic, toric, or prism ballast, per lens
Hydrophilic contact lenses are covered by Medicare only for aphakic patients. Local contractor if incident to physician services.
MED: 100-3,80.1; 100-3,80.4

A ☑ **V2522** Contact lens, hydrophilic, bifocal, per lens
Hydrophilic contact lenses are covered by Medicare only for aphakic patients. Local contractor if incident to physician services.
MED: 100-3,80.1; 100-3,80.4

A ☑ **V2523** Contact lens, hydrophilic, extended wear, per lens
Hydrophilic contact lenses are covered by Medicare only for aphakic patients.
MED: 100-3,80.1; 100-3,80.4

A ☑ **V2530** Contact lens, scleral, gas impermeable, per lens (for contact lens modification, see 92325)

A ☑ **V2531** Contact lens, scleral, gas permeable, per lens (for contact lens modification, see 92325)
MED: 100-3,80.5

A **V2599** Contact lens, other type
Local contractor if incident to physician services.

VISION AIDS

A **V2600** Hand held low vision aids and other nonspectacle mounted aids

A **V2610** Single lens spectacle mounted low vision aids

A **V2615** Telescopic and other compound lens system, including distance vision telescopic, near vision telescopes and compound microscopic lens system

PROSTHETIC EYE

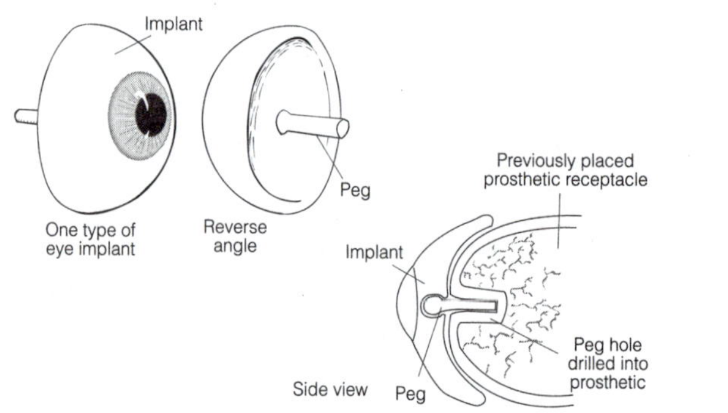

A V2623 Prosthetic eye, plastic, custom
MED: 100-2,15,120; 100-4,3,10.4

A V2624 Polishing/resurfacing of ocular prosthesis

A V2625 Enlargement of ocular prosthesis

A V2626 Reduction of ocular prosthesis

A V2627 Scleral cover shell
A scleral shell covers the cornea and the anterior sclera. Medicare covers a scleral shell when it is prescribed as an artificial support to a shrunken and sightless eye or as a barrier in the treatment of severe dry eye.
MED: 100-3,80.5

A V2628 Fabrication and fitting of ocular conformer

A V2629 Prosthetic eye, other type

INTRAOCULAR LENSES

N V2630 Anterior chamber intraocular lens N1
The IOL must be FDA-approved for reimbursement. Medicare payment for an IOL is included in the payment for ASC facility services. Medicare jurisdiction: local contractor.
MED: 100-2,15,120; 100-4,3,10.4

N V2631 Iris supported intraocular lens N1
The IOL must be FDA-approved for reimbursement. Medicare payment for an IOL is included in the payment for ASC facility services. Medicare jurisdiction: local contractor.
MED: 100-2,15,120; 100-4,3,10.4

N V2632 Posterior chamber intraocular lens N1
The IOL must be FDA-approved for reimbursement. Medicare payment for an IOL is included in the payment for ASC facility services. Medicare jurisdiction: local contractor.
MED: 100-2,15,120; 100-4,3,10.4

MISCELLANEOUS

A ☑ V2700 Balance lens, per lens

E V2702 Deluxe lens feature
MED: 100-2,15,120; 100-4,3,10.4

A ☑ V2710 Slab off prism, glass or plastic, per lens

A ☑ V2715 Prism, per lens

A ☑ V2718 Press-on lens, Fresnel prism, per lens

A ☑ V2730 Special base curve, glass or plastic, per lens

A ☑ V2744 Tint, photochromatic, per lens
MED: 100-2,15,120; 100-4,3,10.4

A ☑ V2745 Addition to lens; tint, any color, solid, gradient or equal, excludes photochromatic, any lens material, per lens
MED: 100-2,15,120; 100-4,3,10.4

A ☑ V2750 Antireflective coating, per lens
MED: 100-2,15,120; 100-4,3,10.4

A ☑ V2755 U-V lens, per lens
MED: 100-2,15,120; 100-4,3,10.4

E V2756 Eye glass case

A ☑ V2760 Scratch resistant coating, per lens

B ☑ V2761 Mirror coating, any type, solid, gradient or equal, any lens material, per lens
MED: 100-2,15,120; 100-4,3,10.4

A ☑ V2762 Polarization, any lens material, per lens
MED: 100-2,15,120; 100-4,3,10.4

A ☑ V2770 Occluder lens, per lens

A ☑ V2780 Oversize lens, per lens

B ☑ V2781 Progressive lens, per lens

A ☑ V2782 Lens, index 1.54 to 1.65 plastic or 1.60 to 1.79 glass, excludes polycarbonate, per lens
MED: 100-2,15,120; 100-4,3,10.4

A ☑ V2783 Lens, index greater than or equal to 1.66 plastic or greater than or equal to 1.80 glass, excludes polycarbonate, per lens
MED: 100-2,15,120; 100-4,3,10.4

A ☑ V2784 Lens, polycarbonate or equal, any index, per lens
MED: 100-2,15,120; 100-4,3,10.4

F V2785 Processing, preserving and transporting corneal tissue F4
Medicare jurisdiction: local contractor.

A ☑ V2786 Specialty occupational multifocal lens, per lens
MED: 100-2,15,120; 100-4,3,10.4

E V2787 Astigmatism correcting function of intraocular lens

E V2788 Presbyopia correcting function of intraocular lens

N V2790 Amniotic membrane for surgical reconstruction, per procedure N1
Medicare jurisdiction: local contractor.

A V2797 Vision supply, accessory and/or service component of another HCPCS vision code

A V2799 Vision service, miscellaneous
Determine if an alternative HCPCS Level II or a CPT code better describes the service being reported. This code should be used only if a more specific code is unavailable.

HEARING SERVICES V5000-V5999

This range of codes describes hearing tests and related supplies and equipment, speech-language pathology screenings, and repair of augmentative communicative system.

E V5008 Hearing screening
MED: 100-2,16,90

E V5010 Assessment for hearing aid

E V5011 Fitting/orientation/checking of hearing aid

E V5014 Repair/modification of a hearing aid

E V5020 Conformity evaluation

E V5030 Hearing aid, monaural, body worn, air conduction

E V5040 Hearing aid, monaural, body worn, bone conduction

E V5050 Hearing aid, monaural, in the ear

E V5060 Hearing aid, monaural, behind the ear

E V5070 Glasses, air conduction

E V5080 Glasses, bone conduction

E V5090 Dispensing fee, unspecified hearing aid

E V5095 Semi-implantable middle ear hearing prosthesis

E V5100 Hearing aid, bilateral, body worn

E V5110 Dispensing fee, bilateral

E V5120 Binaural, body

E V5130 Binaural, in the ear

E V5140 Binaural, behind the ear

E V5150 Binaural, glasses

E V5160 Dispensing fee, binaural

E V5170 Hearing aid, CROS, in the ear

E V5180 Hearing aid, CROS, behind the ear

E V5190 Hearing aid, CROS, glasses

E V5200 Dispensing fee, CROS

E V5210 Hearing aid, BICROS, in the ear

E V5220 Hearing aid, BICROS, behind the ear

E V5230 Hearing aid, BICROS, glasses

E V5240 Dispensing fee, BICROS

E V5241 Dispensing fee, monaural hearing aid, any type

E V5242 Hearing aid, analog, monaural, CIC (completely in the ear canal)

E V5243 Hearing aid, analog, monaural, ITC (in the canal)

E V5244 Hearing aid, digitally programmable analog, monaural, CIC

E V5245 Hearing aid, digitally programmable, analog, monaural, ITC

E V5246 Hearing aid, digitally programmable analog, monaural, ITE (in the ear)

E V5247 Hearing aid, digitally programmable analog, monaural, BTE (behind the ear)

E V5248 Hearing aid, analog, binaural, CIC

E V5249 Hearing aid, analog, binaural, ITC

E V5250 Hearing aid, digitally programmable analog, binaural, CIC

E V5251 Hearing aid, digitally programmable analog, binaural, ITC

E V5252 Hearing aid, digitally programmable, binaural, ITE

E V5253 Hearing aid, digitally programmable, binaural, BTE

E V5254 Hearing aid, digital, monaural, CIC

E V5255 Hearing aid, digital, monaural, ITC

E V5256 Hearing aid, digital, monaural, ITE

E V5257 Hearing aid, digital, monaural, BTE

E V5258 Hearing aid, digital, binaural, CIC

E V5259 Hearing aid, digital, binaural, ITC

E V5260 Hearing aid, digital, binaural, ITE

E V5261 Hearing aid, digital, binaural, BTE

E V5262 Hearing aid, disposable, any type, monaural

E V5263 Hearing aid, disposable, any type, binaural

E V5264 Ear mold/insert, not disposable, any type

E V5265 Ear mold/insert, disposable, any type

E V5266 Battery for use in hearing device

E V5267 Hearing aid supplies/accessories

E V5268 Assistive listening device, telephone amplifier, any type

E V5269 Assistive listening device, alerting, any type

E V5270 Assistive listening device, television amplifier, any type

E V5271 Assistive listening device, television caption decoder

E V5272 Assistive listening device, TDD

E V5273 Assistive listening device, for use with cochlear implant

E V5274 Assistive listening device, not otherwise specified

E ☑ V5275 Ear impression, each

E V5298 Hearing aid, not otherwise classified

B V5299 Hearing service, miscellaneous ⊘

Determine if an alternative HCPCS Level II or a CPT code better describes the service being reported. This code should be used only if a more specific code is unavailable.

MED: 100-2,16,90

SPEECH-LANGUAGE PATHOLOGY SERVICES

E V5336 Repair/modification of augmentative communicative system or device (excludes adaptive hearing aid)

Medicare jurisdiction: DME regional contractor.

E V5362 Speech screening

E V5363 Language screening

E V5364 Dysphagia screening

APPENDIX 1 — TABLE OF DRUGS

Introduction and Directions

The HCPCS 2009 Table of Drugs is designed to quickly and easily direct the user to drug names and their corresponding codes. Both generic and brand or trade names are alphabetically listed in the "Drug Name" column of the table. The associated A, C, J, K, Q, or S code is given only for the generic name of the drug.

The "Unit Per" column lists the stated amount for the referenced generic drug as provided by CMS. "Up to" listings are inclusive of all quantities up to and including the listed amount. All other listings are for the amount of the drug as listed. The editors recognize that the availability of some drugs in the quantities listed is dependent on many variables beyond the control of the clinical ordering clerk. The availability in your area of regularly used drugs in the most cost-effective quantities should be relayed to your third-party payers.

The "Route of Administration" column addresses the most common methods of delivering the referenced generic drug as described in current pharmaceutical literature. The official definitions for Level II drug codes generally describe administration other than by oral method. Therefore, with a handful of exceptions, oral-delivered options for most drugs are omitted from the Route of Administration column.

Intravenous administration includes all methods, such as gravity infusion, injections, and timed pushes. When several routes of administration are listed, the first listing is simply the first, or most common, method as described in current reference literature. The "VAR" posting denotes various routes of administration and is used for drugs that are commonly administered into joints, cavities, tissues, or topical applications, in addition to other parenteral administrations. Listings posted with "OTH" alert the user to other administration methods, such as suppositories or catheter injections.

Please be reminded that the Table of Drugs, as well as all HCPCS Level II national definitions and listings, constitutes a post-treatment medical reference for billing purposes only. Although the editors have exercised all normal precautions to ensure the accuracy of the table and related material, the use of any of this information to select medical treatment is entirely inappropriate. Do not code directly from the table of drugs. Refer to the tabular section for complete information.

See Appendix 3 for abbreviations.

Drug Name	*Unit Per*	*Route*	*Code*
10% LMD	500 ML	IV	J7100
5% DEXTROSE/NORMAL SALINE	5%	VAR	J7042
5% DEXTROSE/WATER	500 ML	IV	J7060
ABARELIX	10 MG	IM	J0128
ABATACEPT	10 MG	IV	J0129
ABCIXIMAB	10 MG	IV	J0130
ABELCET	50 MG	IV	J0285
ABILIFY	0.25 MG	IM	J0400
ABRAXANE	1 MG	IV	J9264
ACCELULAR PERICARDIAL TISSUE MATRIX NONHUMAN	SQ CM	OTH	C9354
ACCUNEB NONCOMPOUNDED, CONCENTRATED	1 MG	INH	J7611
ACCUNEB NONCOMPOUNDED, UNIT DOSE	1 MG	INH	J7613
ACETADOTE	1 G	INH	J7608
ACETADOTE	100 MG	IV	J0132
ACETAZOLAMIDE SODIUM	500 MG	IM, IV	J1120
ACETYLCYSTEINE COMPOUNDED	PER G	INH	J7604
ACETYLCYSTEINE NONCOMPOUNDED	1 G	INH	J7608
ACTHREL	1 MCG	IV	J0795
ACTIMMUNE	0.25 MG	SC	J1830
ACTIMMUNE	3 MU	SC	J9216
ACTIVASE	1 MG	IV	J2997
ACUTECT	DOSE	IV	A9504
ACYCLOVIR	5 MG	IV	J0133
ADAGEN	25 IU	IM	J2504
ADALIMUMAB	20 MG	SC	J0135
ADBEON	4 MG	IM, IV	J0704
ADENOCARD	6 MG	IV	J0150
ADENOSCAN	30 MG	IV	J0152
ADENOSINE	30 MG	IV	J0152
ADENOSINE	6 MG	IV	J0150
ADRENALIN	1 MG	IM, IV, SC	J0170
ADRENALIN CHLORIDE	1 MG	IM, IV, SC	J0170
ADRENOCORT	1 MG	IM, IV, OTH	J1100
ADRIAMYCIN	10 MG	IV	J9000
ADRUCIL	500 MG	IV	J9190
AEROBID	1 MG	INH	J7641
AGALSIDASE BETA	1 MG	IV	J0180
AGGRASTAT	12.5 MG	IM, IV	J3246
A-HYDROCORT	100 MG	IV, IM, SC	J1720
ALATROFLOXACIN MESYLATE	100 MG	IV	J0200
ALBUTEROL AND IPRATROPIUM BROMIDE NONCOMPOUNDED	2.5MG/0.5 MG	INH	J7620
ALBUTEROL COMPOUNDED, CONCENTRATED	1 MG	INH	J7610
ALBUTEROL COMPOUNDED, UNIT DOSE	1 MG	INH	J7609
~~ALBUTEROL NONCOMPOUNDED, UNIT DOSE~~	~~PER 1 MG~~	~~INH~~	~~J7603~~
ALBUTEROL NONCOMPOUNDED, UNIT DOSE	PER 1 MG	INH	J7613
~~ALBUTEROL, NONCOMPOUNDED, CONCENTRATED FORM~~	~~PER 1 MG~~	~~INH~~	~~J7602~~
ALBUTEROL, NONCOMPOUNDED, CONCENTRATED FORM	PER 1 MG	INH	J7611
ALDESLEUKIN	1 VIAL	IV	J9015
ALDURAZYME	0.1 MG	IV	J1931
ALEFACEPT	0.5 MG	IV, IM	J0215
ALEMTUZUMAB	10 MG	IV	J9010
ALFERON N	250,000 IU	IM	J9215
ALGLUCERASE	10 U	IV	J0205
ALGLUCOSIDASE ALFA	10 MG	IV	J0220
ALIMTA	10 MG	IV	J9305
ALKERAN	2 MG	ORAL	J8600
ALKERAN	50 MG	IV	J9245
ALLOGRAFT, CYMETRA	1 CC	INJ	Q4112
ALLOGRAFT, GRAFTJACKET EXPRESS	1 CC	INJ	Q4113
ALOXI	25 MCG	IV	J2469
ALPHA 1 - PROTEINASE INHIBITOR — HUMAN	10 MG	IV	J0256
ALPHANATE	PER FACTOR IU	IV	J7186
ALPHANINE SD	1 IU	IV	J7193
ALPROSTADIL	1.25 MCG	INJ	J0270
ALPROSTADIL	EA	OTH	J0275
ALTEPLASE RECOMBINANT	1 MG	IV	J2997
ALUPENT, NONCOMPOUNDED, CONCENTRATED	10 MG	INH	J7668
ALUPENT, NONCOMPOUNDED, UNIT DOSE	10 MG	INH	J7669
AMANTADINE HYDROCHLORIDE (BRAND NAME)	100 MG	ORAL	G9033

Drug Name	Unit Per	Route	Code
AMANTADINE HYDROCHLORIDE (GENERIC)	100 MG	ORAL	G9017
AMBISOME	10 MG	IV	J0289
AMCORT	5 MG	IM	J3302
AMERGAN	12.5 MG	ORAL	Q0169
A-METHAPRED	125 MG	IM, IV	J2930
A-METHAPRED	40 MG	IM, IV	J2920
AMEVIVE	0.5 MG	IV, IM	J0215
AMICAR	5 G	IV	S0017
AMIFOSTINE	500 MG	IV	J0207
AMIKACIN SULFATE	100 MG	IM, IV	J0278
~~AMIKIN~~	~~100 MG~~	~~IM, IV~~	
AMINOCAPRIOC ACID	5 G	IV	S0017
AMINOPHYLLINE	250 MG	IV	J0280
AMIODARONE HCL	30 MG	IV	J0282
AMITRIPTYLINE HCL	20 MG	IM	J1320
AMMONIA N-13	DOSE	IV	A9526
AMOBARBITAL	125 MG	IM, IV	J0300
AMPHOCIN	50 MG	IV	J0285
AMPHOTEC	10 MG	IV	J0287
AMPHOTERICIN B	50 MG	IV	J0285
AMPHOTERICIN B CHOLESTERYL SULFATE COMPLEX	10 MG	IV	J0288
AMPHOTERICIN B LIPID COMPLEX	10 MG	IV	J0287
AMPHOTERICIN B LIPOSOME	10 MG	IV	J0289
AMPICILLIN SODIUM	500 MG	IM, IV	J0290
AMPICILLIN SODIUM/SULBACTAM SODIUM	1.5 G	IM, IV	J0295
AMYTAL	125 MG	IM, IV	J0300
ANASTROZOLE	1 MG	ORAL	S0170
ANCEF	500 MG	IV, IM	J0690
AN-DTPA DIAGNOSTIC	UP TO 25 MCI	IV	A9539
AN-DTPA THERAPEUTIC	UP TO 25 MCI	IV	A9567
ANECTINE	20 MG	IM, IV	J0330
ANGIOMAX	1 MG	IV	J0583
ANIDULAFUNGIN	1 MG	IV	J0348
ANISTREPLASE	30 U	IV	J0350
ANTAGON	250 MCG	SC	S0132
ANTIHEMOPHILIC FACTOR HUMAN METHOD M MONOCLONAL PURIFIED	1 IU	IV	J7192
ANTIHEMOPHILIC FACTOR PORCINE	1 IU	IV	J7191
ANTIHEMOPHILIC FACTOR VIII/VON WILLEBRAND FACTOR COMPLEX, HUMAN	PER FACTOR VIII IU	IV	J7186
ANTI-INHIBITOR	1 IU	IV	J7198
ANTITHROMBIN III	1 IU	IV	J7195
ANTI-THYMOCYTE GLOBULIN,EQUINE	250 MG	OTH	J7504
ANTIZOL	15 MG	IV	J1451
ANZEMET	10 MG	IV	J1260
~~ANZEMET~~	~~50 MG~~	~~ORAL~~	~~S0174~~
ANZEMET	100 MG	ORAL	Q0180
~~APLIGRAF~~	~~SQ CM~~	~~OTH~~	~~J7340~~
APLIGRAF	SQ CM	OTH	Q4101
APOKYN	1 MG	SC	J0364
~~APOKYN~~	~~1 MG~~	~~SC~~	
~~APOMORPHINE HYDROCHLORIDE~~	~~1 MG~~	~~SC~~	
APOMORPHINE HYDROCHLORIDE	1 MG	SC	J0364
APREPITANT, ORAL, 5 MG	5 MG	ORAL	J8501
APROTININ	10,000 KIU	IV	J0365
AQUAMEPHYTON	1 MG	IM, SC, IV	J3430
ARA-C	100 MG	SC, IV	J9100
ARAMINE	10 MG	IV, IM, SC	J0380
ARANESP, ESRD USE	1 MCG	SC, IV	J0882
ARANESP, NON-ESRD USE	1 MCG	SC, IV	J0881
ARBUTAMINE HCL	1 MG	IV	J0395
AREDIA	30 MG	IV	J2430
ARFORMOTEROL	15 MCG	INH	J7605
ARIMIDEX	1 MG	ORAL	S0170
ARIPIPRAZOLE	0.25 MG	IM	J0400
ARISTOCORT	5 MG	IM	J3302
ARISTOCORTE FORTE	5 MG	IM	J3302
ARISTOCORTE INTRALESIONAL	5 MG	OTH	J3302
ARISTOSPAN	5 MG	VAR	J3303
ARIXTRA	0.5 MG	SC	J1652
AROMASIN	25 MG	ORAL	S0156
ARRANON	50 MG	IV	J9261
ARRESTIN	200 MG	IM	J3250
ARSENIC TRIOXIDE	1 MG	IV	J9017
ASPARAGINASE	10,000 U	VAR	J9020
ASTRAMORPH PF	10 MG	IM, IV, SC	J2275
ATGAM	250 MG	OTH	J7504
ATIVAN	2 MG	IM, IV	J2060
ATOPICLAIR	ANY SIZE	OTH	A6250
ATROPEN	0.3 MG	IV, IM, SC	J0460
ATROPINE SULFATE	0.3 MG	IV, IM, SC	J0460
ATROPINE, COMPOUNDED, CONCENTRATED	I MG	INH	J7635
ATROPINE, COMPOUNDED, UNIT DOSE	1 MG	INH	J7636
ATROVENT, NONCOMPOUNDED, UNIT DOSE	1 MG	INH	J7644
AUROTHIOGLUCOSE	50 MG	IM	J2910
AUTOPLEX T	1 IU	IV	J7198
AVASTIN	10 MG	IV	J9035
AVELOX	100 MG	IV	J2280
AVONEX	11 MCG	IM	Q3025
AVONEX	33 MCG	IM	J1825
AZACITIDINE	1 MG	SC	J9025
AZACTAM	500 MG	IV	S0073
AZASAN	50 MG	ORAL	J7500
AZATHIOPRINE	100 MG	OTH	J7501
AZATHIOPRINE	50 MG	ORAL	J7500
AZITHROMYCIN	500 MG	IV	J0456
AZMACORT	PER MG	INH	J7684
AZMACORT CONCENTRATED	PER MG	INH	J7683
AZTREONAM	500 MG	IV	S0073
~~AZTREONAM~~	~~PER MG~~	~~INH~~	~~S0143~~
BACLOFEN	10 MG	IT	J0475
BACLOFEN	50 MCG	OTH	J0476
~~BACTERIOSTATIC WATER~~	~~5%~~	~~VAR~~	

APPENDIX 1 — TABLE OF DRUGS

Drug Name	Unit Per	Route	Code
BACTOCILL	250 MG	IM, IV	J2700
BACTRIM IV	10 ML	IV	S0039
BAL	100 MG	IM	J0470
BASILIXIMAB	20 MG	IV	J0480
~~BAYGAM~~	~~1 CC~~	~~IM~~	~~J1460~~
BAYRHO-D	300 MCG	IM	J2790
~~BAYTET~~	~~250 U~~	~~IM~~	~~J1670~~
BCG VACCINE LIVE	VIAL	IV	J9031
BEBULIN VH	1 IU	IV	J7194
BECAPLERMIN GEL 0.01%	0.5 G	OTH	S0157
BECLOMETHASONE COMPOUNDED	1 MG	INH	J7622
BECLOVENT COMPOUNDED	1 MG	INH	J7622
BECONASE COMPOUNDED	1 MG	INH	J7622
BENA-D 10	50 MG	IV, IM	J1200
BENA-D 50	50 MG	IV, IM	J1200
BENADRYL	50 MG	IV, IM	J1200
BENAHIST 10	50 MG	IV, IM	J1200
BENAHIST 50	50 MG	IV, IM	J1200
~~BENDAMUSTINE HCL~~	~~1 MG~~	~~IV~~	~~C9243~~
BENDAMUSTINE HCL	1 MG	IV	J9033
BENEFIX	1 IU	IV	J7195
BENOJECT-10	50 MG	IV, IM	J1200
BENOJECT-50	50 MG	IV, IM	J1200
BENTYL	20 MG	IM	J0500
BENZTROPINE MESYLATE	1 MG	IM, IV	J0515
BERUBIGEN	1,000 MCG	SC, IM	J3420
BETA-2	1 MG	INH	J7648
BETALIN 12	1,000 MCG	SC, IM	J3420
BETAMETHASONE ACETATE AND BETAMETHASONE SODIUM PHOSPHATE	3 MG, OF EACH	IM	J0702
BETAMETHASONE COMPOUNDED, UNIT DOSE	1 MG	INH	J7624
BETAMETHASONE SODIUM PHOSPHATE	4 MG	IM, IV	J0704
BETASERON	0.25 MG	SC	J1830
BETHANECHOL CHLORIDE, MYOTONACHOL OR URECHOLINE	5 MG	SC	J0520
BEVACIZUMAB	10 MG	IV	J9035
BEXXAR THERAPEUTIC	TX DOSE	IV	A9545
BICILLIN CR	1,200,000 U	IM	J0540
BICILLIN CR	600,000 U	IM	J0530
BICILLIN CR 900/300	1,200,000 U	IM, IV	J0540
BICILLIN CR 900/300	2,400,000 U	IM, IV	J0550
BICILLIN LA	1,200,000 U	IM	J0570
BICILLIN LA	600,000 U	IM	J0560
BICILLIN LA	2,400,000 U	INJ	J0580
BICNU	100 MG	IV	J9050
BIOCLATE	1 IU	IV	J7192
BIOTROPIN	1 MG	SC	J2941
BITOLTEROL MESYLATE, COMPOUNDED CONCENTRATED	PER MG	INH	J7628
BITOLTEROL MESYLATE, COMPOUNDED UNIT DOSE	PER MG	INH	J7629
BIVALIRUDIN	1 MG	IV	J0583
BLENOXANE	15 U	IM, IV, SC	J9040
BLEOMYCIN LYOPHILLIZED	15 U	IM, IV, SC	J9040
BLEOMYCIN SULFATE	15 U	IM, IV, SC	J9040
BONIVA	1 MG	IV	J1740
BORTEZOMIB	0.1 MG	IV	J9041
BOTOX	1 U	IM	J0585
BOTULINUM TOXIN TYPE A	1 U	OTH	J0585
BOTULINUM TOXIN TYPE B	100 U	OTH	J0587
BRAVELLE	75 IU	SC, IM	J3355
BRETHINE	PER MG	INH	J7681
BRETHINE CONCENTRATED	PER MG	INH	J7680
BRICANYL	PER MG	INH	J7681
BRICANYL CONCENTRATED	PER MG	INH	J7680
BROM-A-COT	10 MG	IM, SC, IV	J0945
BROMPHENIRAMINE MALEATE	10 MG	IM, SC, IV	J0945
~~BRONCHO SALINE~~	~~5 CC~~	~~VAR~~	
BUDESONIDE COMPOUNDED, CONCETRATED	0.25 MG	INH	J7634
BUDESONIDE, COMPOUNDED, UNIT DOSE	0.5 MG	INH	J7627
BUDESONIDE, NONCOMPOUNDED, CONCENTRATED	0.25 MG	INH	J7633
BUDESONIDE, NONCOMPOUNDED, UNIT DOSE	0.5 MG	INH	J7626
BUMETANIDE	0.5 MG	IM, IV	S0171
BUPIVACAINE HCL	30 ML	OTH	S0020
BUPRENEX	0.1 MG	IM, IV	J0592
BUPRENORPHINE HCL	0.1 MG	IM, IV	J0592
BUPROPION HCL	150 MG	ORAL	S0106
BUSULFAN	1 MG	IV	J0594
BUSULFAN	2 MG	OTH	J8510
BUSULFEX	1 MG	IV	J0594
BUSULFEX	2 MG	ORAL	J8510
BUTORPHANOL TARTRATE	2 MG	IM, IV	J0595
BUTORPHANOL TARTRATE	25 MG	OTH	S0012
CABERGOLINE	0.25 MG	ORAL	J8515
CAFCIT	5 MG	IV	J0706
CAFFEINE CITRATE	5 MG	IV	J0706
CALCIJEX	0.1 MCG	IM	J0636
CALCIMAR	UP TO 400 U	SC, IM	J0630
CALCITONIN SALMON	400 U	SC, IM	J0630
CALCITRIOL	0.1 MCG	IM	J0636
CALCITROL	0.25 MG	IM	S0161
CALCIUM DISODIUM VERSENATE	1,000 MG	IV, SC, IM	J0600
CALCIUM GLUCONATE	10 ML	IV	J0610
CALCIUM GLYCEROPHOSPHATE AND CALCIUM LACTATE	10 ML	IM, SC	J0620
CAMPATH	10 MG	IV	J9010
CAMPTOSAR	20 MG	IV	J9206
CANCIDAS	5 MG	IV	J0637
CAPECITABINE	150 MG	ORAL	J8520
CAPROMAB PENDETIDE	DOSE	IV	A9507
CARBOCAINE	10 ML	VAR	J0670
CARBOPLATIN	50 MG	IV	J9045
CARDIOGEN 82	60 MCI	IV	A9555
CARDIOLITE	DOSE	IV	A9500
CARIMUNE	500 MG	IV	J1566
CARMUSTINE	100 MG	IV	J9050

Drug Name	Unit Per	Route	Code
CARNITOR	1 G	IV	J1955
CARTICEL		OTH	J7330
CASPOFUNGIN ACETATE	5 MG	IV	J0637
CATAPRES	1 MG	OTH	J0735
CATHFLO	1 MG	IV	J2997
CAVERJECT	1.25 MCG	VAR	J0270
CEA SCAN	UP TO 45 MCI	IV	A9568
CEENU	10 MG	ORAL	S0178
CEFEPIME HCL	500 MG	IV	J0692
CEFIZOX	500 MG	IV, IM	J0715
CEFOBID	1 G	IV	S0021
CEFOPERAZONE SODIUM	1 G	IV	S0021
CEFOTAN	500 MG	IM, IV	S0074
CEFOTAXIME SODIUM	1 GM	IV, IM	J0698
CEFOTETAN DISODIUM	500 MG	IM. IV	S0074
CEFOXITIN SODIUM	1 GM	IV, IM	J0694
CEFTAZIDIME	500 MG	IM, IV	J0713
CEFTIZOXIME SODIUM	500 MG	IV, IM	J0715
CEFTRIAXONE	250 MG	IV, IM	J0696
CEFTRIAXONE SODIUM	250 MG	IV, IM	J0696
CEFUROXIME	750 MG	IM, IV	J0697
CEFUROXIME SODIUM STERILE	750 MG	IM, IV	J0697
CELESTONE SOLUSPAN	3 MG	IM	J0702
CELLCEPT	250 MG	ORAL	J7517
CENACORT A-40	10 MG	IM	J3301
CENACORT FORTE	5 MG	IM	J3302
CEPHAPIRIN SODIUM	1 G	IV	J0710
CEPTAZ	500 MG	IM, IV	J0713
CEREBRYX	50 MG	IM, IV	Q2009
CEREBRYX	750 MG	IM, IV	S0078
CEREDASE	10 U	IV	J0205
CERETEC	DOSE	IV	A9521
CERETEC	PER STUDY DOSE	IV	A9569
CEREZYME	1 U	IV	J1785
CERUBIDINE	10 MG	IV	J9150
CESAMET	1 MG	ORAL	J8650
CETUXIMAB	10 MG	IV	J9055
CHEALAMIDE	150 MG	IV	J3520
CHLORAMBUCIL	2 MG	ORAL	S0172
CHLORAMPHENICOL SODIUM SUCCINATE	1 G	IV	J0720
CHLORDIAZEPOXIDE HCL	100 MG	IM, IV	J1990
CHLOROMYCETIN	1 G	IV	J0720
CHLOROPROCAINE HCL	30 ML	VAR	J2400
CHLOROTHIAZIDE SODIUM	500 MG	IV	J1205
CHLORPROMAZINE HCL	10 MG	ORAL	Q0171
CHLORPROMAZINE HCL	50 MG	IM, IV	J3230
CHLORPROMAZINE HCL	25 MG	ORAL	Q0172
CHOLETEC	UP TO 35 MCI	IV	A9537
CHORIONIC GONADOTROPIN	1,000 USP U	IM	J0725
CHROMIC PHOSPHATE P32	1 MCI	IV	A9564
CHROMITOPE SODIUM	250 UCI	IV	A9553
CHROMIUM CR-51 SODIUM IOTHALAMATE, DIAGNOSTIC	10 UCI	IV	A9553
CIDOFOVIR	375 MG	IV	J0740
CILASTATIN SODIUM	250 MG	IV, IM	J0743
CIMETIDINE HCL	300 MG	IM, IV	S0023
CIPRO	200 MG	IV	J0744
CIPROFLOXACIN FOR INTRAVENOUS INFUSION	200 MG	IV	J0744
CIS-MDP	30 MCI	IV	A9503
CISPLATIN	10 MG	IV	J9060
CIS-PYRO	UP TO 25 MCI	IV	A9538
CLADRIBINE	1 MG	IV	J9065
CLAFORAN	1 GM	IV, IM	J0698
CLEOCIN PHOSPHATE	300 MG	IV	S0077
CLEVIDIPINE BUTYRATE	1 MG	IV	C9248
CLEVIPREX	1 MG	IV	C9248
CLINAGEN LA	UP TO 40 MG	IM	J0970
CLINDAMYCIN PHOSPHATE	300 MG	IV	S0077
CLOFARABINE	1 MG	IV	J9027
CLOLAR	1 MG	IV	J9027
CLONIDINE HCL	1 MG	OTH	J0735
CLOSTRIDIUM BOTULINUM TOXIN	1 U	OTH	J0585
CLOZAPINE	25 MG	ORAL	S0136
CLOZARIL	25 MG	ORAL	S0136
COBAL	1,000 MCG	IM, SC	J3420
COBALT CO-57 CYNOCOBALAMIN, DIAGNOSTIC	1 UCI	ORAL	A9559
COBATOPE 57	1 UCI	ORAL	A9559
COBEX	1,000 MCG	SC, IM	J3420
CODEINE PHOSPHATE	30 MG	IM, IV, SC	J0745
COGENTIN	1 MG	IM, IV	J0515
COGNEX	10 MG	ORAL	S0014
COLCHICINE	1 MG	IV	J0760
COLHIST	10 MG	IM, SC, IV	J0945
COLISTIMETHATE SODIUM	150 MG	IM, IV	J0770
COLISTIMETHATE SODIUM	PER MG	INH	S0142
COLLAGEN BASED WOUND FILLER DRY FOAM	1 GM	OTH	A6010
COLLAGEN NERVE CUFF	0.5 CM LENGTH	OTH	C9355
~~COLLAGEN, MICROPOROUS NONHUMAN~~	~~SQ CM~~	~~OTH~~	
~~COLLAGEN-GLYCOSAMINOGLYCAN SKIN SUBSTITUTE~~	~~SQ CM~~	~~OTH~~	~~J7343~~
COLLAGEN BASED WOUND FILLER, GEL/PASTE	1 GM	OTH	A6011
COLY-MYCIN M	150 MG	IM, IV	J0770
COMPAZINE	10 MG	IM, IV	J0780
COMPAZINE	5 MG	ORAL	S0183
COMPAZINE	10 MG	ORAL	Q0165
COMPAZINE	5 MG	ORAL	Q0164
CONTRACEPTIVE SUPPLY, HORMONE CONTAINING PATCH	EACH	OTH	J7304
COPAXONE	20 MG	SC	J1595
COPPER T MODEL TCU380A IUD COPPER WIRE/COPPER COLLAR	EA	OTH	J7300
CORDARONE	30 MG	IV	J0282
CORTASTAT	1 MG	IM, IV, OTH	J1100
CORTASTAT LA	1 MG	IM	J1094
CORTICORELIN OVINE TRIFLUTATE	1 MCG	IV	J0795

Drug Name	Unit Per	Route	Code
CORTICOTROPIN	40 U	IV, IM, SC	J0800
CORTIMED	80 MG	IM	J1040
CORTROSYN	0.25 MG	IM, IV	J0835
CORVERT	1 MG	IV	J1742
COSMEGEN	0.5 MG	IV	J9120
COSYNTROPIN	0.25 MG	IM, IV	J0835
COTOLONE	5 MG	ORAL	J7510
CROMOLYN SODIUM COMPOUNDED	PER 10 MG	INH	J7632
CROMOLYN SODIUM NONCOMPOUNDED	10 MG	INH	J7631
CRYSTAL B12	1,000 MCG	IM, SC	J3420
CRYSTICILLIN 300 A.S.	600,000 UNITS	IM, IV	J2510
CRYSTICILLIN 600 A.S.	600,000 UNITS	IM, IV	J2510
CUBICIN	1 MG	IV	J0878
CYANO	1,000 MCG	IM, SC	J3420
CYANOCOBALAMIN	1,000 MCG	IM, SC	J3420
CYANOCOBALAMIN COBALT 58/57	1 UCI	IV	A9546
CYANOCOBALAMIN COBALT CO-57	1 UCI	ORAL	A9559
CYCLOPHOSPHAMIDE	1 G	IV	J9091
CYCLOPHOSPHAMIDE	200 MG	IV	J9080
CYCLOPHOSPHAMIDE	25 MG	ORAL	J8530
CYCLOPHOSPHAMIDE	500 MG	IV	J9090
CYCLOPHOSPHAMIDE	2 G	IV	J9092
CYCLOPHOSPHAMIDE	100 MG	IV	J9070
CYCLOPHOSPHAMIDE LYOPHILIZED	1 G	IV	J9096
CYCLOPHOSPHAMIDE LYOPHILIZED	2 G	IV	J9097
CYCLOPHOSPHAMIDE LYOPHILIZED	500 MG	IV	J9095
CYCLOPHOSPHAMIDE LYOPHILIZED	100 MG	IV	J9093
CYCLOPHOSPHAMIDE LYOPHILIZED	200 MG	IV	J9094
CYCLOSPORINE	100 MG	ORAL	J7502
CYCLOSPORINE	25 MG	ORAL	J7515
CYCLOSPORINE	250 MG	IV	J7516
CYMETRA	1 CC	INJ	Q4112
CYTARABINE	100 MG	SC, IV	J9100
CYTARABINE	500 MG	SC, IV	J9110
CYTARABINE LIPOSOME	10 MG	IT	J9098
CYTOGAM	VIAL	IV	J0850
CYTOMEGALOVIRUS IMMUNE GLOB	VIAL	IV	J0850
CYTOSAR-U	100 MG	SC, IV	J9100
CYTOSAR-U	500 MG	SC, IV	J9110
CYTOTEC	200 MCG	ORAL	S0191
CYTOVENE	500 MG	IV	J1570
CYTOXAN	1 G	IV	J9091
CYTOXAN	100 MG	IV	J9070
CYTOXAN	500 MG	IV	J9090
CYTOXAN	200 MG	IV	J9080
CYTOXAN	2 G	IV	J9092
CYTOXAN	25 MG	ORAL	J8530
CYTOXAN LYOPHILIZED	1 G	IV	J9096
CYTOXAN LYOPHILIZED	500 MG	IV	J9095
CYTOXAN LYOPHILIZED	2 G	IV	J9097
CYTOXAN LYOPHILIZED	200 MG	IV	J9094
CYTOXAN LYOPHILIZED	100 MG	IV	J9093

Drug Name	Unit Per	Route	Code
D.H.E. 45	1 MG	IM, IV	J1110
DACARBAZINE	100 MG	IV	J9130
DACARBAZINE	200 MG	IV	J9140
DACLIZUMAB	25 MG	OTH	J7513
DACOGEN	1 MG	IV	J0894
DACTINOMYCIN	0.5 MG	IV	J9120
DALALONE	1 MG	IM, IV, OTH	J1100
DALALONE LA	1 MG	IM	J1094
DALTEPARIN SODIUM	2,500 IU	SC	J1645
DAPTOMYCIN	1 MG	IV	J0878
DARBEPOETIN ALFA, ESRD USE	1 MCG	SC, IV	J0882
DARBEPOETIN ALFA, NON-ESRD USE	1 MCG	SC, IV	J0881
DAUNORUBICIN	10 MG	IV	J9150
DAUNORUBICIN CITRATE, LIPOOSOMAL FORMULATION	10 MG	IV	J9151
DAUNOXOME	10 MG	IV	J9151
DDAVP	1 MCG	IV, SC	J2597
DECADRON	0.25 MG	ORAL	J8540
DECAJECT	1 MG	IM, IV, OTH	J1100
DECITABINE	1 MG	IV	J0894
DECOLONE-50	50 MG	IM	J2320
DEFEROXAMINE MESYLATE	500 MG	IM, SC, IV	J0895
DELATESTRYL	100 MG	IM	J3120
DELATESTRYL	200 MG	IM	J3130
DELESTROGEN	10 MG	IM	J1380
DELESTROGEN	20 MG	IM	J1390
DELESTROGEN	UP TO 40 MG	IM	J0970
DELTA-CORTEF	5 MG	ORAL	J7510
DELTASONE	5 MG	ORAL	J7506
DELTASONE	5 MG	OTH	J7506
DEMADEX	10 MG	IV	J3265
DEMEROL	100 MG	IM, IV, SC	J2175
DENILEUKIN DIFTITOX	300 MCG	IV	J9160
DEPANDRATE	1 CC, 200 MG	IM	J1080
DEPANDROGYN	1 ML	IM	J1060
DEPGYNOGEN	UP TO 5 MG	IM	J1000
DEPHENACEN-50	50 MG	IM, IV	J1200
DEPMEDALONE	40 MG	IM	J1030
DEPMEDALONE	80 MG	IM	J1040
DEPOCYT	10 MG	IT	J9098
DEPODUR	UP TO 10 MG	IV	J2270
DEPODUR	UP TO 10 MG	IV	J2271
DEPO-ESTRADIOL CYPIONATE	UP TO 5 MG	IM	J1000
DEPOGEN	UP TO 5 MG	IM	J1000
DEPO-MEDROL	20 MG	IM	J1020
DEPO-MEDROL	40 MG	IM	J1030
DEPO-MEDROL	80 MG	IM	J1040
DEPO-PROVERA	150 MG	IM	J1055
DEPO-PROVERA	50 MG	IM	J1051
DEPO-TESTADIOL	1 ML	IM	J1060
DEPO-TESTOSTERONE	1 CC, 200 MG	IM	J1080
DEPO-TESTOSTERONE	UP TO 100 MG	IM	J1070
DEPO-TESTOSTERONE CYPIONATE	UP TO 100 MG	IM	J1070

Drug Name	Unit Per	Route	Code
DEPTESTROGEN	UP TO 100 MG	IM	J1070
~~DERMAGRAFT~~	~~SQ CM~~	~~OTH~~	~~J7342~~
DERMAGRAFT	SQ CM	OTH	Q4106
~~DERMAL (SUBSTITUTE) TISSUE OF NONHUMAN ORIGIN, WITH OR WITHOUT OTHER BIOENGINEERED OR PROCESSED ELEMENTS, WITHOUT METABOLICALLY ACTIVE ELEMENTS (INTEGRA MATRIX)~~	~~UNIT PER SQ CM~~	~~OTH~~	~~J7347~~
~~DERMAL (SUBSTITUTE) TISSUE OF NONHUMAN ORIGIN, WITH OR WITHOUT OTHER BIOENGINEERED OR PROCESSED ELEMENTS, WITHOUT METABOLICALLY ACTIVE ELEMENTS (PRIMATRIX)~~	~~SQ CM~~	~~OTH~~	~~J7349~~
~~DERMAL (SUBSTITUTE) TISSUE OF NONHUMAN ORIGIN, WITH OR WITHOUT OTHER BIOENGINEERED OR PROCESSED ELEMENTS, WITHOUT METABOLICALLY ACTIVE ELEMENTS (TISSUEMEND)~~	~~SQ CM~~	~~OTH~~	~~J7348~~
~~DERMAL AND EPIDERMAL, TISSUE OF NONHUMAN ORIGIN, WITH OR WITHOUT OTHER BIOENGINEERED OR PROCESSED ELEMENTS, WITHOUT METABOLICALLY ACTIVE ELEMENTS~~	~~SQ CM~~	~~OTH~~	~~J7343~~
~~DERMAL SUBSTITUTE, GRANULATED CROSS-LINKED COLLAGEN AND GLYCOSAMINOGLYCAN MATRIX~~	~~1 CC~~	~~OTH~~	~~C9357~~
DERMAL SUBSTITUTE, NATIVE, NONDENATURED	0.5 SQ CM	OTH	C9358
DERMAL SUBSTITUTE, NATIVE, NONDENTURED COLLAGEN	0.5 SQ CM	OTH	C9358
~~DERMAL TISSUE, OF HUMAN ORIGIN, WITH OR WITHOUT OTHER BIOENGINEERED OR PROCESSED ELEMENTS, WITH METABOLICALLY ACTIVE ELEMENTS~~	~~SQ CM~~	~~OTH~~	~~J7342~~
DERMAL TISSUE, OF HUMAN ORIGIN, WITH OR WITHOUT OTHER BIOENGINEERED OR PROCESSED ELEMENTS, WITHOUT METABOLICALLY ACTIVE ELEMENTS	~~SQ CM~~	~~OTH~~	~~J7344~~
DESFERAL	500 MG	IM, SC, IV	J0895
DESMOPRESSIN ACETATE	1 MCG	IV, SC	J2597
DEXAMETHASONE	0.25 MG	ORAL	J8540
DEXAMETHASONE ACETATE	1 MG	IM	J1094
DEXAMETHASONE ACETATE ANHYDROUS	1 MG	IM	J1094
DEXAMETHASONE SODIUM PHOSPHATE	1 MG	IM, IV, OTH	J1100
DEXAMETHASONE, COMPOUNDED, CONCENTRATED	PER MG	INH	J7637
DEXAMETHASONE, COMPOUNDED, UNIT DOSE	PER MG	INH	J7638
DEXASONE	1 MG	IM, IV, OTH	J1100
DEXEDRINE	5 MG	ORAL	S0160
~~DEXFERRUM~~	~~50 MG~~	~~IM, IV~~	~~J1752~~
DEXIM	1 MG	IM, IV, OTH	J1100
DEXONE	0.25 MG	ORAL	J8540
DEXONE	1 MG	IM, IV, OTH	J1100
DEXONE LA	1 MG	IM	J1094
DEXRAZOXANE	250 MG	IV	J1190
DEXRAZOXANE HYDROCHLORIDE	250 MG	IV	J1190
DEXTRAN 40	500 ML	IV	J7100
DEXTROAMPHETAMINE SULFATE	5 MG	ORAL	S0160
DEXTROSE	500 ML	IV	J7060
DEXTROSE, STERILE WATER, AND/OR DEXTROSE DILUENT/FLUSH	10 ML	VAR	A4216
DEXTROSE/SODIUM CHLORIDE	5%	VAR	J7042
DEXTROSE/THEOPHYLLINE	40 MG	IV	J2810
DEXTROSTAT	5 MG	ORAL	S0160
DIALYSIS/STRESS VITAMINS	100 CAPS	ORAL	S0194
DIAMOX	500 MG	IM, IV	J1120
DIASTAT	5 MG	IV, IM	J3360
DIAZEPAM	5 MG	IV, IM	J3360
DIAZOXIDE	300 MG	IV	J1730
DICYCLOMINE HCL	20 MG	IM	J0500
DIDANOSINE (DDI)	25 MG	ORAL	S0137
DIDRONEL	300 MG	IV	J1436
DIETHYLSTILBESTROL DIPHOSPHATE	250 MG	INJ	J9165
DIFLUCAN	200 MG	IV	J1450
DIGIBIND	VIAL	IV	J1162
DIGIFAB	VIAL	IV	J1162
DIGOXIN	0.5 MG	IM, IV	J1160
DIGOXIN IMMUNE FAB	VIAL	IV	J1162
DIHYDROERGOTAMINE MESYLATE	1 MG	IM, IV	J1110
DILANTIN	50 MG	IM, IV	J1165
DILAUDID	250 MG	OTH	S0092
DILAUDID	4 MG	SC, IM, IV	J1170
DIMENHYDRINATE	50 MG	IM, IV	J1240
DIMERCAPROL	100 MG	IM	J0470
DIMINE	50 MG	IV, IM	J1200
DINATE	50 MG	IM, IV	J1240
DIOVAL	10 MG	IM	J1380
DIOVAL	20 MG	IM	J1390
DIOVAL 40	10 MG	IM	J1380
DIOVAL 40	20 MG	IM	J1390
DIOVAL XX	10 MG	IM	J1380
DIOVAL XX	20 MG	IM	J1390
DIPHENHYDRAMINE HCL	50 MG	IV, IM	J1200
DIPHENHYDRAMINE HCL	50 MG	ORAL	Q0163
DIPYRIDAMOLE	10 MG	IV	J1245
DISOTATE	150 MG	IV	J3520
DIURIL	500 MG	IV	J1205
DIURIL SODIUM	500 MG	IV	J1205
DIZAC	5 MG	IV, IM	J3360
~~DMSA~~	~~VIAL~~	~~IV~~	
~~DMSA KIT~~	~~VIAL~~	~~IV~~	
DMSO, DIMETHYL SULFOXIDE	50%, 50 ML	OTH	J1212
DOBUTAMINE HCL	250 MG	IV	J1250
DOCETAXEL	20 MG	IV	J9170
DOLASETRON MESYLATE	10 MG	IV	J1260
DOLASETRON MESYLATE	50 MG	ORAL	S0174
DOLASETRON MESYLATE	100 MG	ORAL	Q0180
DOLOPHINE	5 MG	ORAL	S0109
DOLOPHINE HCL	10 MG	IM, SC	J1230
DOMMANATE	50 MG	IM, IV	J1240
DOPAMINE HCL	40 MG	IV	J1265

APPENDIX 1 — TABLE OF DRUGS

Drug Name	Unit Per	Route	Code
DORIBAX	10 MG	IV	J1267
DORIPENEM	10 MG	IV	J1267
DORNASE ALPHA, NONCOMPOUNDED, UNIT DOSE	PER MG	INH	J7639
DOSTINEX	0.25 MG	ORAL	J8515
DOXERCALCIFEROL	1 MG	IV	J1270
DOXIL	10 MG	IV	J9001
DOXORUBICIN HCL	10 MG	IV	J9000
DOXORUBICIN HCL, ALL LIPID FORMULATIONS	10 MG	IV	J9001
DRAMAMINE	50 MG	IM, IV	J1240
DRAMILIN	50 MG	IM, IV	J1240
DRAMOCEN	50 MG	IM, IV	J1240
DRAMOJECT	50 MG	IM, IV	J1240
DRAXIMAGE MDP-10	30 MCI	IV	A9503
DRAXIMAGE MDP-25	30 MCI	IV	A9503
DRONABINAL	2.5 MG	ORAL	Q0167
DRONABINAL	5 MG	ORAL	Q0168
DROPERIDOL	5 MG	IM, IV	J1790
DROPERIDOL AND FENTANYL CITRATE	2 ML	IM, IV	J1810
DROXIA	500 MG	ORAL	S0176
DTIC-DOME	100 MG	IV	J9130
DTIC-DOME	200 MG	IV	J9140
DTPA	UP TO 25 MCI	IV	A9539
DTPA	UP TO 25 MCI	INH	A9567
DUO-SPAN	1 ML	IM	J1060
DUO-SPAN II	1 ML	IM	J1060
DURACILLIN A.S.	600,000 UNITS	IM, IV	J2510
DURACLON	1 MG	OTH	J0735
DURAGEN-10	10 MG	IM	J1380
DURAGEN-10	20 MG	IM	J1390
DURAGEN-20	10 MG	IM	J1380
DURAGEN-20	20 MG	IM	J1390
DURAGEN-40	10 MG	IM	J1380
DURAGEN-40	20 MG	IM	J1390
DURAMORPH	10 MG	IM, IV, SC	J2275
DURAMORPH	500 MG	OTH	S0093
DURO CORT	80 MG	IM	J1040
DYMENATE	50 MG	IM, IV	J1240
DYPHYLLINE	500 MG	IM	J1180
E.D.T.A	150 MG	IV	J3520
ECHOCARDIOGRAM IMAGE ENHANCER	1 ML	IV	Q9955
ECHOCARDIOGRAM IMAGE ENHANCER	1 ML	INJ	Q9956
ECULIZUMAB	10 MG	IV	J1300
EDETATE CALCIUM DISODIUM	1,000 MG	IV, SC, IM	J0600
EDETATE DISODIUM	150 MG	IV	J3520
EDEX	1.25 MCG	VAR	J0270
EFALIZUMAB	125 MG	SC	S0162
~~ELAPRASE~~	~~1 MG~~	~~IV~~	~~Q9205~~
ELAPRASE	1 MG	IV	J1743
ELAVIL	20 MG	IM	J1320
ELIGARD	7.5 MG	IM	J9217
ELIGARD	PER 3.75 MG	SC	J1950
ELITEK	50 MCG	IM	J2783
ELLENCE	2 MG	IV	J9178
ELLIOTTS B SOLUTION	1 ML	IV, IT	J9175
ELOXATIN	0.5 MG	IV	J9263
ELSPAR	10,000 U	VAR	J9020
EMEND	5 MG	ORAL	J8501
EMEND	1 MG	IV	J1453
EMINASE	30 U	IV	J0350
ENBREL	25 MG	IM, IV	J1438
ENDOXAN-ASTA	1 G	IV	J9091
ENDOXAN-ASTA	200 MG	IV	J9080
ENDOXAN-ASTA	100 MG	IV	J9070
ENDOXAN-ASTA	500 MG	IV	J9090
ENDRATE	150 MG	IV	J3520
ENFUVIRTIDE	1 MG	SC	J1324
ENOXAPARIN SODIUM	10 MG	SC	J1650
EOVIST	1 ML	IV	C9246
EPINEPHRINE	1 MG	IM, IV, SC, VAR	J0170
EPIPEN	0.3 MG	IM	J0170
EPIRUBICIN HCL	2 MG	IV	J9178
EPOETIN ALFA, ESRD USE	1,000 U	SC, IV	J0886
EPOETIN ALFA, NON-ESRD USE	1,000 U	SC, IV	J0885
EPOGEN/ESRD	1,000 U	SC, IV	J0886
EPOGEN/NON-ESRD	1,000 U	SC, IV	J0885
EPOPROSTENOL	0.5 MG	IV	J1325
EPOPROSTENOL STERILE DILUTANT	50 ML	IV	S0155
EPTIFIBATIDE	5 MG	IM, IV	J1327
ERAXIS	1 MG	IV	J0348
ERBITUX	10 MG	IV	J9055
ERGAMISOL	50 MG	ORAL	S0177
ERGONOVINE MALEATE	0.2 MG	IM, IV	J1330
ERTAPENEM SODIUM	500 MG	IM, IV	J1335
ERYTHROCIN LACTOBIONATE	500 MG	IV	J1364
ESTONE AQUEOUS	1 MG	IM, IV	J1435
ESTRADIOL CYPIONATE	UP TO 5 MG	IM	J1000
ESTRADIOL L.A.	10 MG	IM	J1380
ESTRADIOL L.A.	20 MG	IM	J1390
ESTRADIOL L.A. 20	10 MG	IM	J1380
ESTRADIOL L.A. 20	20 MG	IM	J1390
ESTRADIOL L.A. 40	10 MG	IM	J1380
ESTRADIOL L.A. 40	20 MG	IM	J1390
ESTRADIOL VALERATE	10 MG	IM	J1380
ESTRADIOL VALERATE	UP TO 40 MG	IM	J0970
ESTRADIOL VALERATE	20 MG	IM	J1390
ESTRAGYN	1 MG	IV, IM	J1435
ESTRA-L 20	10 MG	IM	J1380
ESTRA-L 20	20 MG	IM	J1390
ESTRA-L 40	10 MG	IM	J1380
ESTRA-L 40	20 MG	IM	J1390
ESTRO-A	1 MG	IV, IM	J1435
ESTROGEN CONJUGATED	25 MG	IV, IM	J1410
ESTRONE	1 MG	IV, IM	J1435
ESTRONOL	1 MG	IM, IV	J1435

Drug Name	Unit Per	Route	Code
ETANERCEPT	25 MG	IM, IV	J1438
ETHAMOLIN	100 MG	IV	J1430
ETHANOLAMINE OLEATE	100 MG	IV	J1430
ETHYOL	500 MG	IV	J0207
ETIDRONATE DISODIUM	300 MG	IV	J1436
ETONOGESTREL	PER IMPLANT	OTH	J7307
ETOPOSIDE	10 MG	IV	J9181
~~ETOPOSIDE~~	~~100 MG~~	~~IV~~	~~J9182~~
ETOPOSIDE	50 MG	ORAL	J8560
EUFLEXXA	PER DOSE	OTH	J7323
EULEXIN	125 MG	ORAL	S0175
EXAMETAZIME LABELED AUTOLOGOUS WHITE BLOOD CELLS, TECHNETIUM TC-99M	PER STUDY DOSE	IV	A9569
EXMESTANE	25 MG	ORAL	S0156
FABRAZYME	1 MG	IV	J0180
FACTOR IX NON-RECOMBINANT	1 IU	IV	J7193
FACTOR IX RECOMBINANT	1 IU	IV	J7195
FACTOR IX+ COMPLEX	1 IU	IV	J7194
FACTOR VIIA RECOMBINANT	1 MCG	IV	J7189
FACTOR VIII PORCINE	1 IU	IV	J7191
FACTOR VIII RECOMBINANT	1 IU	IV	J7192
FACTOR VIII, HUMAN	1 IU	IV	J7190
FACTREL	100 MCG	SC, IV	J1620
FAMOTIDINE	20 MG	IV	S0028
FASLODEX	25 MG	IM	J9395
FDG	STUDY DOSE		A9552
FEIBA-VH AICC	1 IU	IV	J7198
FENTANYL CITRATE	0.1 MG	IM, IV	J3010
FERIDEX IV	1 ML	IV	Q9953
FERRLECIT	12.5 MG	IV	J2916
FERTINEX	75 IU	SC	J3355
FILGRASTIM	300 MCG	SC, IV	J1440
FILGRASTIM	480 MCG	SC, IV	J1441
FINASTERIDE	5 MG	ORAL	S0138
FLAGYL	500 MG	IV	S0030
FLEBOGAMMA	500 MG	IV	J1572
FLEXON	60 MG	IV, IM	J2360
FLOLAN	0.5 MG	IV	J1325
~~FLOWABLE WOUND MATRIX~~	~~1 CC~~	~~OTH~~	~~C9357~~
FLOXIN IV	400 MG	IV	S0034
FLOXURIDINE	500 MG	IV	J9200
FLUCONAZOLE	200 MG	IV	J1450
FLUDARA	50 MG	IV	J9185
FLUDARABINE PHOSPHATE	50 MG	IV	J9185
FLUDEOXYGLUCOSE F18	STUDY DOSE	IV	A9552
FLUNISOLIDE, COMPOUNDED, UNIT DOSE	1 MG	INH	J7641
FLUOCINOLONE ACETONIDE INTRAVITREAL	IMPLANT	OTH	J7311
FLUORODEOXYGLUCOSE F-18 FDG, DIAGNOSTIC	45 MCI	IV	A9552
FLUOROURACIL	500 MG	IV	J9190
FLUPHENAZINE DECANOATE	25 MG	SC, IM	J2680
FLUTAMIDE	125 MG	ORAL	S0175

Drug Name	Unit Per	Route	Code
FOLEX	5 MG	IV, IM, IT, IA	J9250
FOLEX	50 MG	IV, IM, IT, IA	J9260
FOLEX PFS	5 MG	IV, IM, IT, IA	J9250
FOLEX PFS	50 MG	IV, IM, IT, IA	J9260
FOLLISTIM	75 IU	SC, IM	S0128
FOLLITROPIN ALFA	75 IU	SC	S0126
FOLLITROPIN BETA	75 IU	SC, IM	S0128
FOMEPIZOLE	15 MG	IV	J1451
FOMIVIRSEN SODIUM	1.65 MG	OTH	J1452
FONDAPARINUX SODIUM	0.5 MG	SC	J1652
~~FORMOTEROL FUMARATE~~	~~20 MCG~~	~~INH~~	~~Q4099~~
FORMOTEROL FUMERATE NONCOMPOUNDED UNIT DOSE FORM	20 MCG	INH	J7606
FORMOTEROL, COMPOUNDED, UNIT DOSE	12 MCG	INH	J7640
FORTAZ	500 MG	IM, IV	J0713
FORTEO	10 MCG	SC	J3110
FORTOVASE	200 MG	ORAL	S0140
FOSAPREPITANT	1 MG	IV	J1453
FOSCARNET SODIUM	1,000 MG	IV	J1455
FOSCAVIR	1,000 MG	IV	J1455
FOSPHENYTOIN	50 MG	IM, IV	Q2009
FOSPHENYTOIN SODIUM	750 MG	IM, IV	S0078
FRAGMIN	2,500 IU	SC	J1645
FUDR	500 MG	IV	J9200
FULVESTRANT	25 MG	IM	J9395
FUNGIZONE	50 MG	IV	J0285
FUROSEMIDE	20 MG	IM, IV	J1940
FUSILEV	0.5 MG	IV	J0641
FUZEON	1 MG	SC	J1324
GADOBENATE DIMEGLUMINE (MULTIHANCE MULTIPACK)	PER ML	IV	A9577
GADOTERIDOL (PROHANCE MULTIPACK)	PER ML	IV	A9576
GADOXETATE DISODIUM	1 ML	IV	C9246
GALLIUM GA-67	1 MCI	IV	A9556
GALLIUM NITRATE	1 MG	IV	J1457
GALSULFASE	1 MG	IV	J1458
GAMASTAN	1 CC	IM	J1460
GAMASTAN	2 CC	IM	J1470
GAMASTAN	5 CC	IM	J1500
GAMASTAN	6 CC	IM	J1510
GAMASTAN	4 CC	IM	J1490
GAMASTAN	3 CC	IM	J1480
GAMASTAN	7 CC	IM	J1520
GAMASTAN	9 CC	IM	J1540
GAMASTAN	OVER 10 CC	IM	J1560
GAMASTAN	10 CC	IM	J1550
GAMASTAN	8 CC	IM	J1530
GAMASTAN SD	1 CC	IM	J1460
GAMASTAN SD	OVER 10 CC	IM	J1560
GAMASTAN SD	10 CC	IM	J1550
GAMASTAN SD	9 CC	IM	J1540
GAMASTAN SD	4 CC	IM	J1490
GAMASTAN SD	5 CC	IM	J1500

Drug Name	*Unit Per*	*Route*	*Code*
GAMASTAN SD	6 CC	IM	**J1510**
GAMASTAN SD	8 CC	IM	**J1530**
GAMASTAN SD	7 CC	IM	**J1520**
GAMASTAN SD	3 CC	IM	**J1480**
GAMASTAN SD	2 CC	IM	**J1470**
~~**GAMIMMUNE N**~~	~~500 MG~~	~~IV~~	
GAMMA GLOBULIN	1 CC	IM	**J1460**
GAMMA GLOBULIN	2 CC	IM	**J1470**
GAMMA GLOBULIN	3 CC	IM	**J1480**
GAMMA GLOBULIN	5 CC	IM	**J1500**
GAMMA GLOBULIN	OVER 10 CC	IM	**J1560**
GAMMA GLOBULIN	10 CC	IM	**J1550**
GAMMA GLOBULIN	9 CC	IM	**J1540**
GAMMA GLOBULIN	8 CC	IM	**J1530**
GAMMA GLOBULIN	7 CC	IM	**J1520**
GAMMA GLOBULIN	6 CC	IM	**J1510**
GAMMA GLOBULIN	4 CC	IM	**J1490**
GAMMAGARD	500 MG	IV	**J1569**
GAMMAGARD S/D	500 MG	IV	**J1566**
GAMMAGRAFT	SQ CM	OTH	**Q4111**
~~**GAMMAR**~~	~~1 CC~~	~~IM~~	~~**J1460**~~
~~**GAMMAR**~~	~~2 CC~~	~~IM~~	~~**J1470**~~
~~**GAMMAR**~~	~~4 CC~~	~~IM~~	~~**J1490**~~
~~**GAMMAR**~~	~~7 CC~~	~~IM~~	~~**J1520**~~
~~**GAMMAR**~~	~~6 CC~~	~~IM~~	~~**J1510**~~
~~**GAMMAR**~~	~~5 CC~~	~~IM~~	~~**J1500**~~
~~**GAMMAR**~~	~~3 CC~~	~~IM~~	~~**J1480**~~
~~**GAMMAR**~~	~~8 CC~~	~~IM~~	~~**J1530**~~
~~**GAMMAR**~~	~~OVER 10 CC~~	~~IM~~	~~**J1560**~~
~~**GAMMAR**~~	~~10 CC~~	~~IM~~	~~**J1550**~~
~~**GAMMAR**~~	~~9 CC~~	~~IM~~	~~**J1540**~~
~~**GAMMAR P**~~	~~500 MG~~	~~IV~~	~~**J1566**~~
~~**GAMULIN RH**~~	~~300 MCG~~	~~IM~~	~~**J2790**~~
~~**GAMUNEX**~~	~~500 MG~~	~~IV~~	
GAMUNEX	500 MG	IV	**J1561**
GANCICLOVIR	4.5 MG	OTH	**J7310**
GANCICLOVIR SODIUM	500 MG	IV	**J1570**
GANIRELIX ACETATE	250 MCG	SC	**S0132**
GANITE	1 MG	IV	**J1457**
GANITE	PER MCI	IV	**A9556**
GARAMYCIN	80 MG	IM, IV	**J1580**
GASTROCROM	10 MG	INH	**J7631**
GASTROMARK	1 ML	ORAL	**Q9954**
GATIFLOXACIN	10 MG	IV	**J1590**
GEFITINIB	250 MG	ORAL	**J8565**
GEMCITABINE HCL	200 MG	IV	**J9201**
GEMTUZUMAB	5 MG	IV	**J9300**
GEMZAR	200 MG	IV	**J9201**
~~**GENARC**~~	~~1 IU~~	~~IV~~	~~**J7192**~~
GENGRAF	100 MG	ORAL	**J7502**
GENGRAF	25 MG	ORAL	**J7515**
GENOTROPIN	1 MG	SC	**J2941**
GENOTROPIN MINIQUICK	1 MG	SC	**J2941**
GENOTROPIN NUTROPIN	1 MG	SC	**J2941**
GENTAMICIN	80 MG	IM, IV	**J1580**
GENTRAN	500 ML	IV	**J7100**
GENTRAN 75	500 ML	IV	**J7110**
GEODON	10 MG	IM	**J3486**
GEREF	1MCG	SC	**Q0515**
GLATIRAMER ACETATE	20 MG	SC	**J1595**
GLEEVEC	100 MG	ORAL	**S0088**
GLOFIL-125	10 UCI	IV	**A9554**
GLUCAGEN	1 MG	SC, IM, IV	**J1610**
GLUCAGON	1 MG	SC, IM, IV	**J1610**
GLUCOTOPE	STUDY DOSE	IV	**A9552**
GLYCOPYRROLATE, COMPOUNDED CONCENTRATED	PER MG	INH	**J7642**
GLYCOPYRROLATE, COMPOUNDED, UNIT DOSE	1 MG	INH	**J7643**
GOLD SODIUM THIOMALATE	50 MG	IM	**J1600**
GONADORELIN HCL	100 MCG	SC, IV	**J1620**
GONAL-F	75 IU	SC	**S0126**
GOSERELIN ACETATE	3.6 MG	SC	**J9202**
GRAFTJACKET	SQ CM	OTH	**Q4107**
GRAFTJACKET EXPRESS	1 CC	INJ	**Q4113**
~~**GRAFTJACKET REGULAR MATRIX**~~	~~PER 16 SQ CM~~	~~OTH~~	
~~**GRAFTJACKET SOFT TISSUE MATRIX**~~	~~1 CC~~	~~OTH~~	
GRANISETRON HCL	1 MG	ORAL	**Q0166**
GRANISETRON HCL	1 MG	IV	**S0091**
GRANISETRON HCL	100 MCG	IV	**J1626**
GYNOGEN L.A. 10	10 MG	IM	**J1380**
GYNOGEN L.A. 10	20 MG	IM	**J1390**
GYNOGEN L.A. 20	10 MG	IM	**J1380**
GYNOGEN L.A. 20	20 MG	IM	**J1390**
GYNOGEN L.A. 40	10 MG	IM	**J1380**
GYNOGEN L.A. 40	20 MG	IM	**J1390**
GYNOGEN LA	20 MG	IM	**J1390**
H.P. ACTHAR GEL	UP TO 40 UNITS	OTH	**J0800**
HALDOL	5 MG	IM, IV	**J1630**
HALDOL DECANOATE	50 MG	IM	**J1631**
HALOPERIDOL	5 MG	IM, IV	**J1630**
~~**HAVID**~~	~~0.375 MG~~	~~ORAL~~	~~**S0141**~~
HECTOROL	1 MG	IV	**J1270**
HELIXATE FS	1 IU	IV	**J7192**
HEMIN	1 MG	IV	**J1640**
HEMOFIL-M	1 IU	IV	**J7190**
HEP LOCK	10 U	IV	**J1642**
HEPAGAM B	0.5 ML	IM	**J1571**
HEPAGAM B	0.5 ML	IV	**J1571**
HEPARIN SODIUM	1,000 U	IV, SC	**J1644**
HEPARIN SODIUM	10 U	IV	**J1642**
HEPATOLITE	UP TO 15 MCI	IV	**A9510**
HEP-PAK	10 UNITS	IV	**J1642**
HERCEPTIN	10 MG	IV	**J9355**
~~**HEXABRIX 320**~~	~~1 ML~~	~~IV~~	~~**Q9201**~~
HEXADROL	0.25 MG	ORAL	**J8540**

Drug Name	Unit Per	Route	Code
HIGH OSMOLAR CONTRAST MATERIAL, UP TO 149 MG/ML IODINE CONCENTRATION	1 ML	IV	Q9958
HIGH OSMOLAR CONTRAST MATERIAL, UP TO 150-199 MG/ML IODINE CONCENTRATION	1 ML	IV	Q9959
HIGH OSMOLAR CONTRAST MATERIAL, UP TO 200-249 MG/ML IODINE CONCENTRATION	1 ML	IV	Q9960
HIGH OSMOLAR CONTRAST MATERIAL, UP TO 250-299 MG/ML IODINE CONCENTRATION	1 ML	IV	Q9961
HIGH OSMOLAR CONTRAST MATERIAL, UP TO 300-349 MG/ML IODINE CONCENTRATION	1 ML	IV	Q9962
HIGH OSMOLAR CONTRAST MATERIAL, UP TO 350-399 MG/ML IODINE CONCENTRATION	1 ML	IV	Q9963
HIGH OSMOLAR CONTRAST MATERIAL, UP TO 400 OR GREATER MG/ML IODINE CONCENTRATION	1 ML	IV	Q9964
HISTERLIN IMPLANT	50 MG	OTH	J9225
HISTRELIN ACETATE	10 MG	INJ	J1675
HUMALOG	5 U	SC	J1815
HUMALOG	5 U	SC	S5551
HUMALOG	50 U	SC	J1817
HUMATE-P	1 IU	IV	J7187
HUMATROPE	1 MG	SC	J2941
HUMIRA	20 MG	SC	J0135
HUMULIN	5 U	SC	J1815
HUMULIN	50 U	SC	J1817
HUMULIN R	5 U	SC	J1815
HUMULIN R U-500	5 U	SC	J1815
HYALGAN	DOSE	OTH	J7321
HYALURONAN, EUFLEXXA	PER DOSE	OTH	J7323
HYALURONAN, HYALGAN OR SUPARTZ	PER DOSE	OTH	J7321
HYALURONAN, ORTHOVISC	PER DOSE	OTH	J7324
HYALURONAN, SYNVISC	PER DOSE	OTH	J7322
HYALURONIDASE	150 UNITS	VAR	J3470
HYALURONIDASE RECOMBINANT	1 USP UNIT	SC	J3473
HYALURONIDASE, OVINE, PRESERVATIVE FREE	1 USP	OTH	J3471
HYALURONIDASE, OVINE, PRESERVATIVE FREE	1000 USP	OTH	J3472
~~HYATE C~~	~~1 IU~~	~~IV~~	~~J7191~~
HYCAMTIN	4 MG	IV	J9350
HYCAMTIN	0.25 MG	ORAL	J8705
HYCAMTIN	0.25 MG	ORAL	J8705
HYDRALAZINE HCL	20 MG	IV, IM	J0360
HYDRATE	50 MG	IM, IV	J1240
HYDREA	500 MG	ORAL	S0176
HYDROCORTISONE ACETATE	25 MG	IV, IM, SC	J1700
HYDROCORTISONE SODIUM PHOSPHATE	50 MG	IV, IM, SC	J1710
HYDROCORTISONE SODIUM SUCCINATE	100 MG	IV, IM, SC	J1720
HYDROCORTONE PHOSPHATE	50 MG	SC, IM, IV	J1710
HYDROMORPHONE HCL	4 MG	SC, IM, IV	J1170
HYDROMORPHONE HYDROCHLORIDE	250 MG	OTH	S0092
HYDROXOCOBALAMIN	1,000 MCG	IM, SC	J3420
HYDROXYCOBAL	1,000 MCG	IM, SC	J3420
HYDROXYUREA	500 MG	ORAL	S0176
HYDROXYZINE HCL	25 MG	IM	J3410
HYDROXYZINE PAMOATE	25 MG	ORAL	Q0177
HYDROXYZINE PAMOATE	50 MG	ORAL	Q0178
HYOSCYAMINE SULFATE	0.25 MG	SC, IM, IV	J1980
HYPERTET SD	UP TO 250 MG	IM	J1670
~~HYPRHO-D~~	~~300 MCG~~	~~IM~~	~~J2790~~
HYREXIN	50 MG	IV, IM	J1200
HYZINE	25 MG	IM	J3410
HYZINE-50	25 MG	IM	J3410
I-131 TOSITUMOMAB DIAGNOSTIC	DOSE	IV	A9544
I-131 TOSITUMOMAB THERAPEUTIC	DOSE	IV	A9545
IBANDRONATE SODIUM	1 MG	IV	J1740
IBRITUMOMAB TUXETAN	5 MCI	IV	A9542
IBUTILIDE FUMARATE	1 MG	IV	J1742
IDAMYCIN	5 MG	IV	J9211
IDAMYCIN PFS	5 MG	IV	J9211
IDARUBICIN HCL	5 MG	IV	J9211
IDURSULFASE	1 MG	IV	J1743
IFEX	1 G	IV	J9208
IFOSFAMIDE	1 G	IV	J9208
IL-2	1 VIAL	IV	J9015
ILETIN	5 UNITS	SC	J1815
ILETIN II NPH PORK	50 U	SC	J1817
ILETIN II REGULAR PORK	5 U	SC	J1815
ILOPROST INHALATION SOLUTION	20 UCI	INH	Q4080
IMAGENT	1 ML	IV	Q9955
IMATINIB	100 MG	ORAL	S0088
IMIGLUCERASE	1 U	IV	J1785
IMITREX	6 MG	SC	J3030
IMMUNE GLOBULIN (FLEBOGAMMA, FLEBOGAMMA DIF	500 MG	IV	J1572
IMMUNE GLOBULIN (GAMMAGARD LIQUID)	500 MG	IV	J1569
IMMUNE GLOBULIN (GAMUNEX)	500 MG	IV	J1561
IMMUNE GLOBULIN (OCTAGAM)	500 MG	IV	J1568
IMMUNE GLOBULIN (PRIVIGEN) NONLYOPHILIZED	500 MG	IV	J1459
IMMUNE GLOBULIN (RHOPHYLAC)	100 IU	IM, IV	J2791
IMMUNE GLOBULIN LYOPHILIZED	500 MG	IV	J1566
IMMUNE GLOBULIN SUBCUTANEOUS	100 MG	SC	J1562
IMPLANON	PER IMPLANT	OTH	J7307
IMURAN	50 MG	ORAL	J7500
IN-111 SATUMOMAB PENDETIDE	DOSE	IV	A4642
INAPSINE	5 MG	IM, IV	J1790
INDERAL	1 MG	IV	J1800
INDIUM IN-111 IBRITUMOMAB TIUXETAN, DIAGNOSTIC	5 MCI	IV	A9542
INDIUM IN-111 LABELED AUTOLOGOUS PLATELETS	PER STUDY DOSAGE	IV	A9571
INDIUM IN-111 LABELED AUTOLOGOUS WHITE BLOOD CELLS	PER STUDY DOSE	IV	A9570
INDIUM IN-111 OXYQUINOLINE	0.5 MCI	IV	A9547

APPENDIX 1 — TABLE OF DRUGS

Drug Name	Unit Per	Route	Code
INDIUM IN-111PENTETREOTIDE	PER STUDY DOSE	IV	A9572
INDURSALFASE	1 MG	IV	J1743
~~INFED~~	~~50 MG~~	~~IM, IV~~	~~J1751~~
INFED	50 MG	IM, IV	J1750
INFERGEN	1 MCG	SC	J9212
INFLIXIMAB	100 MG	IV	J1745
INFUMORPH	10 MG	IM, IV, SC	J2270
INFUMORPH	10 MG	OTH	J2275
INFUMORPH PRESERVATIVE FREE	100 MG	IM, IV, SC	J2271
INNOHEP	1,000 IU	SC	J1655
INSULIN	5 U	SC	J1815
INSULIN	50 U	SC	J1817
INSULIN LISPRO	5 U	SC	J1815
INSULIN LISPRO	5 U	SC	S5551
INSULIN PURIFIED REGULAR PORK	5 U	SC	J1815
INTAL	10 MG	INH	J7631
INTEGRA BILAYER MATRIX DRESSING	SQ CM	OTH	Q4104
INTEGRA DERMAL REGENERATION TEMPLATE	SQ CM	OTH	Q4105
INTEGRA FLOWABLE WOUND MATRIC	1 CC	INJ	Q4114
INTEGRA FLOWABLE WOUND MATRIX	1 CC	INJ	Q4114
INTEGRA MATRIX	PER SQ. CM.	OTH	J7347
INTEGRA MATRIX	SQ CM	OTH	Q4108
INTEGRA MOZAIK OSTEOCONDUCTIVE SCAFFOLD PUTTY	0.5 CC	OTH	C9359
INTEGRA MOZAIK OSTEOCONDUCTIVE SCAFFOLD PUTTY	0.5 CC	OTH	C9359
INTEGRA OS OSTEOCONDUCTIVE SCAFFOLD PUTTY	0.5 CC	OTH	C9359
INTEGRA OS OSTEOCONDUCTIVE SCAFFOLD PUTTY	0.5 CC	OTH	C9359
INTEGRILIN	5 MG	IM, IV	J1327
INTERFERON ALFA-2A	3,000,000 U	SC, IM	J9213
INTERFERON ALFA-2B	1,000,000 U	SC, IM	J9214
INTERFERON ALFACON-1	1 MCG	SC	J9212
INTERFERON ALFA-N3	250,000 IU	IM	J9215
INTERFERON BETA-1A	11 MCG	IM	Q3025
INTERFERON BETA-1A	33 MCG	IM	J1825
INTERFERON BETA-1A	11 MCG	SC	Q3026
INTERFERON BETA-1B	0.25 MG	SC	J1830
INTERFERON, ALFA-2A, RECOMBINANT	3,000,000 U	SC, IM	J9213
INTERFERON, ALFA-2B, RECOMBINANT	1,000,000 U	SC, IM	J9214
INTERFERON, ALFA-N3, (HUMAN LEUKOCYTE DERIVED)	250,000 IU	IM	J9215
INTERFERON, GAMMA 1-B	3,000,000 U	SC	J9216
INTERLUEKIN	1 VIAL	IV	J9015
INTRON A	1,000,000 U	SC, IM	J9214
INVANZ	500 MG	IM, IV	J1335
INVIRASE	200 MG	ORAL	S0140
IOBENGUANE SULFATE I-131	0.5 MCI	IV	A9508

Drug Name	Unit Per	Route	Code
IOBENGUANE, I-123, DIAGNOSTIC	PER STUDY DOSE UP TO 10 MCI	IV	C9247
IODINE I-123 SODIUM IODIDE	PER MCI	IV	A9509
IODINE I-123 SODIUM IODIDE CAPSULE(S), DIAGNOSTIC	100 UCI	ORAL	A9516
IODINE I-125 SERUM ALBUMIN, DIAGNOSTIC	10 UCI	IV	A9554
IODINE I-125 SODIUM IOTHALAMATE, DIAGNOSTIC	10 UCI	IV	A9554
IODINE I-125, SODIUM IODIDE SOLUTION, THERAPEUTIC	1 UCI	ORAL	A9527
IODINE I-131 IODINATED SERIUM ALBUMIN, DIAGNOSTIC	PER 5 UCI	ORAL	A9524
IODINE I-131 SERUM ALBUMIN, DIAGNOSTIC	5 UCI	IV	A9532
IODINE I-131 SODIUM IODIDE CAPSULE(S), DIAGNOSTIC	1 MCI	ORAL	A9528
IODINE I-131 SODIUM IODIDE CAPSULE(S), THERAPEUTIC	1 MCI	ORAL	A9517
IODINE I-131 SODIUM IODIDE SOLUTION, DIAGNOSTIC	1 MCI	ORAL	A9529
IODINE I-131 SODIUM IODIDE SOLUTION, THERAPEUTIC	1 MCI	ORAL	A9530
IODINE I-131 SODIUM IODIDE, DIAGNOSTIC	100 UCI	IV	A9531
IODINE I-131 TOSITUMOMAB, DIAGNOSTIC	STUDY DOSE	IV	A9544
IODINE I-131 TOSITUMOMAB, THERAPEUTIC	STUDY DOSE	IV	A9545
IODOTOPE THERAPEUTIC CAPSULE(S)	1 MCI	ORAL	A9517
IODOTOPE THERAPEUTIC SOLUTION	1 MCI	ORAL	A9530
ION-BASED MAGNETIC RESONANCE CONTRAST AGENT	1 ML	IV	Q9953
IOTHALAMATE SODIUM I-125	STUDY DOSE	IV	A9554
IPLEX	1 MG	SC	J2170
IPRATROPIUM BROMIDE, NONCOMPOUNDED, UNIT DOSE	1 MG	INH	J7644
IPTRATROPIUM BROMIDE COMPOUNDED, UNIT DOSE	1 MG	INH	J7645
IRESSA	250 MG	ORAL	J8565
IRINOTECAN	20 MG	IV	J9206
~~IRON DEXTRAN 165~~	~~50 MG~~	~~IM, IV~~	~~J1751~~
~~IRON DEXTRAN 237~~	~~50 MG~~	~~IM, IV~~	~~J1752~~
IRON DEXTRAN, 50 MG	50 MG	IM, IV	J1750
IRON SUCROSE	1 MG	IV	J1756
ISOCAINE	10 ML	VAR	J0670
ISOETHARINE HCL COMPOUNDED, CONCENTRATED	1 MG	INH	J7647
ISOETHARINE HCL NONCOMPOUNDED, CONCENTRATED	1 MG	INH	J7650
ISOETHARINE HCL, NONCOMPOUNDED CONCENTRATED	PER MG	INH	J7648
ISOETHARINE HCL, NONCOMPOUNDED, UNIT DOSE	1 MG	INH	J7649
ISOJEX	5 MCI	IV	A9532
ISOPROTERENOL HCL COMPOUNDED, CONCENTRATED	1 MG	INH	J7657
ISOPROTERENOL HCL COMPOUNDED, UNIT DOSE	1 MG	INH	J7660
ISOPROTERENOL HCL, NONCOMPOUNDED CONCENTRATED	1 MG	INH	J7658

Drug Name	Unit Per	Route	Code
ISOPROTERNOL HCL, NONCOMPOUNDED, UNIT DOSE	PER MG	INH	J7659
ITRACONAZOLE	50 MG	IV	J1835
IVEEGAM	500 MG	IV	J1566
IXABEPILONE	1 MG	IV	J9207
IXEMPRA	1 MG	IV	J9207
KANAMYCIN	500 MG	IM, IV	J1840
KANTREX	500 MG	IM, IV	J1840
KANTREX	75 MG	IM, IV	J1850
KEFZOL	500 MG	IV, IM	J0690
KENAJECT-40	10 MG	IM	J3301
KENALOG-10	10 MG	IM	J3301
KENALOG-40	10 MG	IM	J3301
KEPIVANCE	50 MCG	IV	J2425
KEPIVANCE	60 MCG	IV	J2425
KEPPRA	10 MG	IV	J1953
KESTRONE	1 MG	IV, IM	J1435
KETOROLAC TROMETHAMINE	15 MG	IM, IV	J1885
KINEVAC	5 MCG	IV	J2805
KOATE-DVI	1 IU	IV	J7190
~~KOGENATE~~	~~1 IU~~	~~IV~~	~~J7190~~
KOGENATE FS	1 IU	IV	J7192
KONAKION	1 MG	SC, IM, IV	J3430
KONYNE 80	1 IU	IV	J7194
KYTRIL	1 MG	ORAL	Q0166
KYTRIL	1 MG	IV	S0091
KYTRIL	100 MCG	IV	J1626
L.A.E. 20	10 MG	IM	J1380
L.A.E. 20	20 MG	IM	J1390
LANOXIN	0.5 MG	IM, IV	J1160
LANREOTIDE	1 MG	SC	J1930
LANTUS	50 U	SC	J1817
LARONIDASE	0.1 MG	IV	J1931
LASIX	20 MG	IM, IV	J1940
LENTE ILETIN I	5 U	SC	J1815
LEPIRUDIN	50 MG	IV	J1945
LEUCOVORIN CALCIUM	50 MG	IM, IV	J0640
LEUKERAN	2 MG	ORAL	S0172
LEUKINE	50 MCG	IV	J2820
LEUPROLIDE ACETATE	1 MG	IM	J9218
LEUPROLIDE ACETATE	7.5 MG	IM	J9217
LEUPROLIDE ACETATE (FOR DEPOT SUSPENSION)	3.75 MG	IM	J1950
LEUPROLIDE ACETATE DEPOT	7.5 MG	IM	J9217
LEUPROLIDE ACETATE IMPLANT	65 MG	OTH	J9219
LEUSTATIN	1 MG	IV	J9065
LEVABUTEROL COMPOUNDED, UNIT DOSE	1 MG	INH	J7615
LEVABUTEROL, COMPOUNDED, CONCENTRATED	0.5 MG	INH	J7607
LEVALBUTEROL NONCOMPOUNDED, CONCENTRATED FORM	0.5 MG	INH	J7612
~~LEVALBUTEROL, NONCOMPOUNDED, CONCENTRATED FORM~~	~~PER 0.5 MG~~	~~INH~~	~~J7602~~
LEVALBUTEROL, NONCOMPOUNDED, CONCENTRATED FORM	PER 0.5 MG	INH	J7612
~~LEVALBUTEROL, NONCOMPOUNDED, UNIT DOSE~~	~~PER 0.5 MG~~	~~INH~~	~~J7603~~
LEVALBUTEROL, NONCOMPOUNDED, UNIT DOSE	PER 0.5 MG	INH	J7614
LEVAMISOLE HCL	50 MG	ORAL	S0177
LEVAQUIN	250 MG	IV	J1956
LEVETIRACETAM	10 MG	IV	J1953
LEVOCARNITINE	1 G	IV	J1955
LEVOFLOXACIN	250 MG	IV	J1956
LEVOLEUCOVORIN CALCIUM	0.5 MG	IV	J0641
LEVONORGESTREL	52 MG	OTH	J7302
LEVORPHANOL TARTRATE	2 MG	SC, IV, IM	J1960
LEVOXYL	5 MG	ORAL	J7506
LEVSIN	0.25 MG	SC, IM, IV	J1980
LEVULAN KERASTICK	SINGLE UNIT DOSE (354 MG)	OTH	J7308
~~LEXISCAN~~	~~0.4 MG~~	~~IV~~	~~C9244~~
LEXISCAN	0.1 MG	IV	J2785
LIBRIUM	100 MG	IM, IV	J1990
LIDOCAINE HCL	10 MG	IV	J2001
LINCOCIN HCL	300 MG	IV	J2010
LINCOMYCIN HCL	300 MG	IM, IV	J2010
LINEZOLID	200 MG	IV	J2020
LIORESAL	10 MG	IT	J0475
LIORESAL INTRATHECAL REFILL	50 MCG	IT	J0476
LIQUAEMIN SODIUM	1,000 UNITS	SC, IV	J1644
LIQUID PRED SYRUP	5 MG	OTH	J7506
LISPRO-PFC	50 U	SC	J1817
LOK-PAK	10 UNITS	IV	J1642
LOMUSTINE	10 MG	ORAL	S0178
LONITEN	10 MG	ORAL	S0139
LORAZEPAM	2 MG	IM, IV	J2060
LOVENOX	10 MG	SC	J1650
LOW OSMOLAR CONTRAST MATERIAL, 100-199 MG/ML IODINE CONCENTRATIONS	PER ML	IV	Q9965
LOW OSMOLAR CONTRAST MATERIAL, 200-299 MG/ML IODINE CONCENTRATION	PER ML	IV	Q9966
LOW OSMOLAR CONTRAST MATERIAL, 300-399 MG/ML IODINE CONCENTRATION	PER ML	IV	Q9967
LOW OSMOLAR CONTRAST MATERIAL, 400 OR GREATER MG/ML IODINE CONCENTRATION	1 ML	IV	Q9951
L-PHENYLALANINE MUSTARD	50 MG	IV	J9245
LUCENTIS	0.1 MG	IV	J2778
LUNELLE	5 MG/25 MG	IM	J1056
LUPRON	1 MG	IM	J9218
LUPRON	PER 3.75 MG	SC	J1950
LUPRON	7.5 MG	IM	J9217
LUPRON DEPOT	3.75 MG	IM	J1950
LUPRON DEPOT	7.5 MG	IM	J9217
LUPRON IMPLANT	65 MG	OTH	J9219
LUPRON-3	PER 3.75 MG	SC	J1950

Drug Name	Unit Per	Route	Code
LUPRON-4	PER 3.75 MG	SC	J1950
LUTREPULSE	100 MCG	SC, IV	J1620
LYMPHOCYTE IMMUNE GLOBULIN, ANTITHYMOCYTE GLOBULIN, EQUINE	250 MG	OTH	J7504
LYMPHOCYTE IMMUNE GLOBULIN, ANTITHYMOCYTE GLOBULIN, RABBIT	25 MG	OTH	J7511
MACUGEN	0.3 MG	OTH	J2503
MAGNAVIST	UP TO 25 MCI	INH	A9567
MAGNESIUM SULFATE	500 MG	IV	J3475
MAGNETIC RESONANCE CONTRAST AGENT	1 ML	ORAL	Q9954
MAGNEVIST	UP TO 25 MCI	IV	A9539
MAGROTEC	10 MCI	IV	A9540
MANNITOL	25% IN 50 ML	IV	J2150
MARCAINE HCL	30 ML	VAR	S0020
MARINOL	2.5 MG	ORAL	Q0167
MARINOL	5 MG	ORAL	Q0168
MARMINE	50 MG	IM, IV	J1240
MATULANE	50 MG	ORAL	S0182
MAXIPIME	500 MG	IV	J0692
MDP-BRACCO	30 MCI	IV	A9503
MECASERMIN	1 MG	SC	J2170
MECHLORETHAMINE HYDROCHLORIDE (NITROGEN MUSTARD)	10 MG	IV	J9230
MEDIDEX	1 MG	IM, IV, OTH	J1100
MEDROL	4 MG	ORAL	J7509
MEDROXYPROGESTERONE ACETATE	150 MG	IM	J1055
MEDROXYPROGESTERONE ACETATE	50 MG	IM	J1051
MEDROXYPROGESTERONE ACETATE/ESTRADIOL CYPIONATE	5 MG/25 MG	IM	J1056
MEFOXIN	1 G	IV	J0694
MEGACE	20 MG	ORAL	S0179
MEGESTROL ACETATE	20 MG	ORAL	S0179
MELPHALAN HCL	2 MG	ORAL	J8600
MELPHALAN HCL	50 MG	IV	J9245
MENADIONE	1 MG	IM, SC, IV	J3430
MENOTROPINS	75 IU	SC, IM, IV	S0122
MEPERGAN	50 MG	IM, IV	J2180
MEPERIDINE AND PROMETHAZINE HCL	50 MG	IM, IV	J2180
MEPERIDINE HCL	100 MG	IM, IV, SC	J2175
MEPIVACAINE HCL	10 ML	VAR	J0670
MERCAPTOPURINE	50 MG	ORAL	S0108
MERITATE	150 MG	IV	J3520
MEROPENEM	100 MG	IV	J2185
MERREM	100 MG	IV	J2185
MESNA	200 MG	IV	J9209
MESNEX	200 MG	IV	J9209
METAPROTERENOL SULFATE COMPOUNDED, UNIT DOSE	10 MG	INH	J7670
METAPROTERENOL SULFATE, NONCOMPOUNDED, CONCENTRATED	10 MG	INH	J7668
METAPROTERENOL SULFATE, NONCOMPOUNDED, UNIT DOSE	10 MG	INH	J7669
METARAMINOL BITARTRATE	10 MG	IV, IM, SC	J0380
METASTRON STRONTIUM 89 CHLORIDE	1 MCI	IV	A9600
METATRACE	STUDY DOSE	IV	A9552
METHACHOLINE CHLORIDE	1 MG	INH	J7674
METHADONE	5 MG	ORAL	S0109
METHADONE HCL	10 MG	IM, SC	J1230
METHAPREL, COMPOUNDED, UNIT DOSE	10 MG	INH	J7670
METHAPREL, NONCOMPOUNDED, CONCENTRATED	10 MG	INH	J7668
METHAPREL, NONCOMPOUNDED, UNIT DOSE	10 MG	INH	J7669
METHERGINE	0.2 MG	IM, IV	J2210
METHOTREXATE	5 MG	IV, IM, IT, IA	J9250
METHOTREXATE	50 MG	IV, IM, IT, IA	J9260
METHOTREXATE LPF	5 MG	IV, IM, IT, IA	J9250
METHOTREXATE LPF	50 MG	IV, IM, IT, IA	J9260
METHOTREXATE SODIUM	2.5 MG	ORAL	J8610
METHOTREXATE SODIUM	5 MG	IV, IM, IT, IA	J9250
METHOTREXATE SODIUM	50 MG	IV, IM, IT, IA	J9260
METHYLCOTOLONE	80 MG	IM	J1040
METHYLDOPA HCL	250 MG	IV	J0210
METHYLDOPATE HCL	5 MG	IV	J0210
METHYLENE BLUE	1 ML	IV	A9535
METHYLERGONOVINE MALEATE	0.2 MG	IM, IV	J2210
METHYLPRED	4 MG	ORAL	J7509
METHYLPREDNISOLONE	125 MG	IM, IV	J2930
METHYLPREDNISOLONE	4 MG	ORAL	J7509
METHYLPREDNISOLONE	UP TO 40 MG	IM, IV	J2920
METHYLPREDNISOLONE ACETATE	20 MG	IM	J1020
METHYLPREDNISOLONE ACETATE	40 MG	IM	J1030
METHYLPREDNISOLONE ACETATE	80 MG	IM	J1040
METOCLOPRAMIDE	10 MG	IV	J2765
METRONIDAZOLE	500 MG	IV	S0030
MIACALCIN	400 U	SC, IM	J0630
MIBG	0.5 MCI	IV	A9508
MICAFUNGIN SODIUM	1 MG	IV	J2248
MICRHOGAM	50 MCG	IV	J2788
MICROPOROUS COLLAGEN IMPLANTABLE SLIT TUBE	1 CM LENGTH	OTH	C9353
MICROPOROUS COLLAGGEN IMPLANTABLE TUBE	1 CM LENGTH	OTH	C9352
MIDAZOLAM HCI	1 MG	IM, IV	J2250
MIFEPRISTONE	200 MG	ORAL	S0190
MILRINONE LACTATE	5 MG	IV	J2260
MINOXIDIL	10 MG	ORAL	S0139
MIRENA	52 MG	OTH	J7302
MISOPROSTOL	200 MG	ORAL	S0191
MITHRACIN	2.5 MG	IV	J9270
MITOMYCIN	20 MG	IV	J9290
MITOMYCIN	5 MG	IV	J9280
MITOMYCIN	40 MG	IV	J9291
MITOXANA	1 G	IV	J9208
MITOXANTRONE HYDROCHLORIDE	5 MG	IV	J9293
MONARC-M	1 IU	IV	J7190

Drug Name	Unit Per	Route	Code
MONOCLATE-P	1 IU	IV	J7190
MONONINE	1 IU	IV	J7193
MONOPUR	75 IU	SC, IM	S0122
MORPHINE SULFATE	10 MG	IM, IV, SC	J2270
MORPHINE SULFATE	500 MG	OTH	S0093
MORPHINE SULFATE	100 MG	IM, IV, SC	J2271
MORPHINE SULFATE, PRESERVATIVE FREE, STERILE SOLUTION	10 MG	IM, IV, SC	J2275
MOXIFLOXACIN	100 MG	IV	J2280
MPI INDIUM DTPA	0.5 MCI	IV	A9548
MS CONTIN	500 MG	OTH	S0093
MUCOMYST	1 G	INH	J7608
MUCOSIL	1 G	INH	J7608
MULTIHANCE	1 ML	IV	A9577
MULTIHANCE MULTIPACK	1 ML	IV	A9578
MUROMONAB-CD3	5 MG	OTH	J7505
MUSE	EA	OTH	J0275
MUSTARGEN	10 MG	IV	J9230
MUTAMYCIN	20 MG	IV	J9290
MUTAMYCIN	5 MG	IV	J9280
MUTAMYCIN	40 MG	IV	J9291
MYCAMINE	1 MG	IV	J2248
MYCOPHENOLATE MOFETIL	250 MG	ORAL	J7517
MYCOPHENOLIC ACID	180 MG	ORAL	J7518
MYFORTIC DELAYED RELEASE	180 MG	ORAL	J7518
MYLERAN	2 MG	ORAL	J8510
MYLOCEL	500 MG	ORAL	S0176
MYLOTARG	5 MG	IV	J9300
MYOBLOC	100 U	IM	J0587
MYOCHRYSINE	50 MG	IM	J1600
NABILONE	1 MG	ORAL	J8650
NAFCILLIN SODIUM	2 GM	IM, IV	S0032
NAGLAZYME	1 MG	IV	J1458
NALBUPHINE HCL	10 MG	IM, IV, SC	J2300
NALLPEN	2 GM	IM, IV	S0032
NALOXONE HCL	1 MG	IM, IV, SC	J2310
NALTREXONE, DEPOT FORM	1 MG	IM	J2315
NANDROLONE DECANOATE	100 MG	IM	J2321
NANDROLONE DECANOATE	200 MG	IM	J2322
NANDROLONE DECANOATE	50 MG	IM	J2320
NARCAN	1 MG	IM, IV, SC	J2310
NAROPIN	1 MG	VAR	J2795
NASAHIST B	10 MG	IM	J0945
NASALCROM	10 MG	INH	J7631
NATALIZUMAB	1 MG	IV	J2323
NATRECOR	0.1 MG	IV	J2325
NATURAL ESTROGENIC SUBSTANCE	1 MG	IM, IV	J1410
NAVELBINE	10 MG	IV	J9390
ND-STAT	10 MG	IM, SC, IV	J0945
NEBCIN	80 MG	IM, IV	J3260
NEBUPENT	300 MG	INH	J2545
NEBUPENT	300 MG	IM, IV	S0080
NELARABINE	50 MG	IV	J9261
NEMBUTAL SODIUM	50 MG	IM, IV, OTH	J2515
NEORAL	25 MG	ORAL	J7515
NEORAL	250 MG	ORAL	J7516
NEOSAR	1 G	IV	J9091
NEOSAR	2 G	IV	J9092
NEOSAR	200 MG	IV	J9080
NEOSAR	100 MG	IV	J9070
NEOSAR	500 MG	IV	J9090
NEOSCAN	1 MCI	IV	A9556
NEOSTIGMINE METHYLSULFATE	250 MG	IM, IV	J2710
NEOTECT	STUDY DOSE	IV	A9536
NESACAINE	30 ML	VAR	J2400
NESACAINE-MPF	30 ML	VAR	J2400
NESIRITIDE	0.1 MG	IV	J2325
NEULASTA	6 MG	SC, SQ	J2505
NEUMEGA	5 MG	SC	J2355
NEUPOGEN	300 MCG	SC, IV	J1440
NEUPOGEN	480 MCG	SC, IV	J1441
NEURAGEN NERVE GUIDE	1 CM LENGTH	OTH	C9352
NEUROLITE	25 MCI	IV	A9557
NEUROMATRIX	0.5 CM LENGTH	OTH	C9355
NEUROWRAP NERVE PROTECTOR	1 CM LENGTH	OTH	C9353
NEUTREXIN	25 MG	IV	J3305
NEUTROSPEC	25 MCI	IV	A9566
NIPENT	10 MG	IV	J9268
NITROGEN MUSTARD	10 MG	IV	J9230
NITROGEN N-13 AMMONIA, DIAGNOSTIC	STUDY DOSE, UP TO 40 MCI	INJ	A9526
NOC DRUGS, INHALATION SOLUTION ADMINISTERED THROUGH DME	1 EA		J7699
NOLVADEX	10 MG	ORAL	S0187
NOLVADEX	10 MG	ORAL	S0187
NORDITROPIN	1 MG	SC	J2941
NORDYL	50 MG	IV, IM	J1200
NORFLEX	60 MG	IV, IM	J2360
NORPLANT II	PER IMPLANT	OTH	J7306
NOT OTHERWISE CLASSIFIED, ANTINEOPLASTIC DRUGS			J9999
NOVANTRONE	5 MG	IV	J9293
NOVAREL	1,000 USP U	IM	J0725
NOVASTAN	5 MG	IV	C9121
NOVO NORDISK	5 UNITS	SC	J1815
NOVOLIN	50 U	SC	J1817
NOVOLIN R	5 U	SC	J1815
NOVOLOG	50 U	SC	J1817
NOV-ONXOL	30 MG	IV	J9265
NOVOSEVEN	1 MCG	IV	J7189
NPH	5 UNITS	SC	J1815
NPLATE	10 MCG	SC	C9245
NUBAIN	10 MG	IM, IV, SC	J2300
NUMORPHAN	1 MG	IV, SC, IM	J2410
NUTRI-TWELVE	1,000 MCG	IM, SC	J3420
NUTROPIN	1 MG	SC	J2941

APPENDIX 1 — TABLE OF DRUGS

Drug Name	Unit Per	Route	Code
NUTROPIN A.Q.	1 MG	SC	J2941
NUVARING VAGINAL RING	EA	OTH	J7303
OASIS BURN MATRIX	SQ CM	OTH	Q4103
OASIS WOUND MATRIX	SQ CM	OTH	Q4102
OCTAFLUOROPROPANE UCISPHERES	1 ML	IV	Q9956
OCTAGAM	500 MG	IV	J1568
~~OCTAGAM IMMUNE GLOBULIN~~	~~1 GM~~	~~IV~~	
OCTREOSCAN	1 MCI	IV	A9572
OCTREOTIDE ACETATE DEPOT	1 MG	IM	J2353
OCTREOTIDE, NON-DEPOT FORM	25 MCG	SC, IV	J2354
OFLOXACIN	400 MG	IV	S0034
OLANZAPINE	2.5 MG	IM	S0166
OMALIZUMAB	5 MG	SC	J2357
OMNIPAQUE 140	PER ML	IV	Q9965
OMNIPAQUE 180	PER ML	IV	Q9965
OMNIPAQUE 240	PER ML	IV	Q9966
OMNIPAQUE 300	PER ML	IV	Q9966
OMNIPAQUE 350	PER ML	IV	Q9967
OMNISCAN	PER ML	IV	A9579
ONCASPAR	VIAL	IM, IV	J9266
ONCOSCINT	DOSE	IV	A4642
ONDANSETRON HCL	4 MG	ORAL	S0181
ONDANSETRON HCL	8 MG	ORAL	Q0179
ONDANSETRON HYDROCHLORIDE	1 MG	IV	J2405
ONTAK	300 MCG	IV	J9160
ONXOL	30 MG	IV	J9265
OPRELVEKIN	5 MG	SC	J2355
OPTIRAY	PER ML	IV	Q9967
OPTIRAY 160	PER ML	IV	Q9965
OPTIRAY 240	PER ML	IV	Q9966
OPTIRAY 300	PER ML	IV	Q9967
OPTIRAY 320	PER ML	IV	Q9967
OPTISON	1 ML	IV	Q9957
ORAL MAGNETIC RESONANCE CONTRAST AGENT, PER 100 ML	100 ML	ORAL	Q9954
~~ORCEL~~	~~SQ CM~~	~~OTH~~	~~J7340~~
ORENCIA	10 MG	IV	J0129
ORPHENADRINE CITRATE	60 MG	IV, IM	J2360
ORTHOCLONE OKT3	5 MG	OTH	J7505
ORTHOVISC	PER DOSE	OTH	J7324
OSELTAMIVIR PHOSPHATE (BRAND NAME)	75 MG	ORAL	G9035
OSELTAMIVIR PHOSPHATE (GENERIC)	75 MG	ORAL	G9019
OSMITROL	25% IN 50 ML	IV	J2150
OSTREOSCAN	UP TO 6 MCI	IV	A9572
OXACILLIN SODIUM	250 MG	IM, IV	J2700
OXALIPLATIN	0.5 MG	IV	J9263
OXILAN 300	PER ML	IV	Q9967
OXILAN 350	PER ML	IV	Q9967
OXYMORPHONE HCL	1 MG	IV, SC, IM	J2410
OXYTETRACYCLINE HCL	50 MG	IM	J2460
OXYTOCIN	10 U	IV, IM	J2590
PACIS BCG	VIAL	OTH	J9031

Drug Name	Unit Per	Route	Code
PACLITAXEL	30 MG	IV	J9265
PACLITAXEL PROTEIN-BOUND PARTICLES	1 MG	IV	J9264
PALIFERMIN	50 MCG	IV	J2425
~~PALIVIZUMAB-RSV-IGM~~	~~50 MG~~	~~IM~~	~~C9003~~
PALONOSETRON HCL	25 MCG	IV	J2469
PAMIDRONATE DISODIUM	30 MG	IV	J2430
~~PANGLOBULIN~~	~~1 G~~	~~IV~~	~~S0045~~
PANHEMATIN	1 MG	IV	J1640
PANITUMUMAB	10 MG	IV	J9303
PANTOPRAZOLE SODIUM	40 MG	IV	S0164
PANTOPRAZOLE SODIUM	VIAL	IV	C9113
PAPAVERINE HCL	60 MG	IV, IM	J2440
PARAGARD T380A	EA	OTH	J7300
PARAPLANTIN	50 MG	IV	J9045
PARICALCITOL	1 MCG	IV, IM	J2501
PEDIAPRED	5 MG	ORAL	J7510
PEGADEMASE BOVINE	25 IU	IM	J2504
PEGAPTANIB SODIUM	0.3 MG	OTH	J2503
PEGASPARGASE	VIAL	IM, IV	J9266
PEGASYS	10 MCG	SC	S0146
PEGFILGRASTIM	6 MG	SC	J2505
PEGINTERFERON ALFA-2A	180 MCG	SC	S0145
PEG-INTRON	10 MCG	SC	S0146
PEG-INTRON	180 MCG	SC	S0145
PEGYLATED INTERFERON ALFA-2A	180 MCG	SC	S0145
PEGYLATED INTERFERON ALFA-2B	10 MCG	SC	S0146
PEMETREXED	10 MG	IV	J9305
PEN G BENZ/PEN G PROCAINE	600,000 U	IM	J0530
PENICILLIN G BENZATHINE	1,200,000 U	IM	J0570
PENICILLIN G BENZATHINE	600,000 U	IM	J0560
PENICILLIN G BENZATHINE	2,400,000 U	IM	J0580
PENICILLIN G BENZATHINE AND PENICILLIN G PROCAINE	1,200,000 U	IM	J0540
PENICILLIN G POTASSIUM	600,000 U	IM, IV	J2540
PENICILLIN G PROCAINE	600,000 U	IM, IV	J2510
PENTACARINAT	300 MG	INH	S0080
PENTAM	300 MG	IM, IV	J2545
PENTAM 300	300 MG	IM, IV	S0080
PENTAMIDINE ISETHIONATE	300 MG	IM, IV	S0080
PENTAMIDINE ISETHIONATE COMPOUNDED	PER 300 MG	INH	J7676
PENTAMIDINE ISETHIONATE NONCOMPOUNDED	300 MG	INH	J2545
PENTASPAN	100 ML	IV	J2513
PENTASTARCH 10% SOLUTION	100 ML	IV	J2513
PENTATE CALCIUM TRISODIUM	UP TO 25 MCI	IV	A9539
PENTATE CALCIUM TRISODIUM	UP TO 25 MCI	INH	A9567
PENTATE ZINC TRISODIUM	UP TO 25 MCI	IV	A9539
PENTATE ZINC TRISODIUM	UP TO 25 MCI	INH	A9567
PENTAZOCINE	30 MG	IM, SC, IV	J3070
PENTOBARBITAL SODIUM	50 MG	IM, IV, OTH	J2515
PENTOSTATIN	10 MG	IV	J9268
PEPCID	20 MG	IV	S0028
PERFLEXANE LIPID UCISPHERE	1 ML	IV	Q9955
PERFLUTREN LIPID UCISPHERE	1 ML	IV	Q9957

Drug Name	Unit Per	Route	Code
PERFOROMIST	20 MCG	INH	J7606
~~PERFOROMIST~~	~~20 MCG~~	~~INH~~	~~Q4099~~
PERMAPEN	>1,200,000 U	IM	J0570
PERMAPEN	600,000	IM	J0560
PERMAPEN	> 2,400,000 U	IM	J0580
PERPHENAZINE	4 MG	ORAL	Q0175
PERPHENAZINE	5 MG	IM, IV	J3310
PERSANTINE	10 MG	IV	J1245
PFIZERPEN A.S.	600,000 U	IM, IV	J2510
PHENERGAN	12.5 MG	ORAL	Q0169
PHENERGAN	50 MG	IM, IV	J2550
PHENOBARBITAL SODIUM	120 MG	IM, IV	J2560
PHENTOLAMINE MESYLATE	5 MG	IM, IV	J2760
PHENYLEPHRINE HCL	1 ML	SC, IM, IV	J2370
PHENYTOIN SODIUM	50 MG	IM, IV	J1165
PHOSPHOCOL	1 MCI	IV	A9563
PHOSPHOTEC	25 MCI	IV	A9538
PHOTOFRIN	75 MG	IV	J9600
PHYTONADIONE	1 MG	IM, SC, IV	J3430
PIPERACILLIN SODIUM	500 MG	IM, IV	S0081
PIPERACILLIN SODIUM/TAZOBACTAM SODIUM	1 G/1.125 GM	IV	J2543
PITOCIN	10 U	IV, IM	J2590
PLATINOL AQ	10 MG	IV	J9060
PLATINOL AQ	50 MG	IV	J9062
PLENAXIS	10 MG	IM	J0128
PLICAMYCIN	2.5 MG	IV	J9270
PNEUMOCOCCAL CONJUGATE	EA	IM	S0195
PNEUMOVAX II	EA	IM	S0195
POLOCAINE	10 ML	VAR	J0670
POLYGAM	500 MG	IV	J1566
POLYGAM S/D	500 MG	IV	J1566
POLY-L-LACTIC ACID	1 ML	SC	S0196
PORFIMER SODIUM	75 MG	IV	J9600
PORK INSULIN	5 U	SC	J1815
POROUS PURIFIED COLLAGEN MATRIX BONE VOID FILLER	0.5 CC	OTH	C9359
POROUS PURIFIED COLLAGEN MATRIX BONE VOID FILLER	0.5 CC	OTH	C9359
POTASSIUM CHLORIDE	2 MEQ	IV	J3480
PRALIDOXIME CHLORIDE	1 MG	IV, IM, SC	J2730
PREDNICOT	5 ML	ORAL	J7506
PREDNISOLONE	5 MG	ORAL	J7510
PREDNISOLONE ACETATE	1 ML	IM	J2650
PREDNISONE	5 MG	ORAL	J7506
PREDNORAL	5 MG	ORAL	J7510
PREDONE	5 MG	ORAL	J7506
PREGNYL	1,000 USP U	IM	J0725
PRELONE	5 MG	ORAL	J7510
PREMARIN	25 MG	IV, IM	J1410
PRENATAL VITAMINS	30 TABS	ORAL	S0197
PRIALT	1 MCG	OTH	J2278
PRIMACOR	5 MG	IV	J2260
~~PRIMATRIX~~	~~PER SQ. CM.~~	~~OTH~~	~~J7349~~
PRIMATRIX	SQ CM	OTH	Q4110
PRIMAXIN	250 MG	IV, IM	J0743
PRIMESTRIN AQUEOUS	1 MG	IM, IV	J1410
PRIMETHASONE	1 MG	IM, IV, OTH	J1100
PRI-METHYLATE	80 MG	IM	J1040
PRIVIGEN	500 MG	IV	J1459
PROCAINAMIDE HCL	1 G	IM, IV	J2690
PROCARBAZINE HCL	50 MG	ORAL	S0182
PROCHLOPERAZINE MALEATE	5 MG	ORAL	S0183
PROCHLORPERAZINE	10 MG	IM, IV	J0780
PROCHLORPERAZINE MALEATE	10 MG	ORAL	Q0165
PROCHLORPERAZINE MALEATE	5 MG	ORAL	Q0164
PROCRIT, ESRD USE	1,000 U	SC, IV	J0886
PROCRIT, NON-ESRD USE	1,000 U	SC, IV	J0885
PROFILNINE HEAT-TREATED	1 IU	IV	J7194
PROFILNINE SD	1 IU	IV	J7194
PROFONIX	VIAL	INJ	C9113
PROGESTERONE	50 MG	IM	J2675
PROGRAF	1 MG	ORAL	J7507
PROGRAF	5 MG	OTH	J7525
PROHANCE	1 ML	IV	5005F
~~PROHANCE MULTIPACK (GADOTERIDOL)~~	~~PER ML~~	~~IV~~	~~A9576~~
PROLASTIN	10 MG	IV	J0256
PROLEUKIN	1 VIAL	VAR	J9015
PROLIXIN DECANOATE	25 MG	SC, IM	J2680
PROMAZINE HCL	25 MG	IM	J2950
PROMETHAZINE HCL	12.5 MG	ORAL	Q0169
PROMETHAZINE HCL	50 MG	IM, IV	J2550
PRONESTYL	1 G	IM, IV	J2690
PROPECIA	5 MG	ORAL	S0138
PROPLEX SX-T	1 IU	IV	J7194
PROPLEX T	1 IU	IV	J7194
PROPRANOLOL HCL	1 MG	IV	J1800
PROREX	50 MG	IM, IV	J2550
PROSCAR	5 MG	ORAL	S0138
PROSTASCINT	DOSE	IV	A9507
PROSTIGMIN	0.5 MG	IM, IV	J2710
PROSTIN VR	1.25 MCG	INJ	J0270
PROTAMINE SULFATE	10 MG	IV	J2720
PROTEIN C CONCENTRATE	10 IU	IV	J2724
PROTEINASE INHIBITOR (HUMAN)	10 MG	IV	J0256
PROTIRELIN	250 MCG	IV	J2725
PROTONIX IV	40 MG	IV	S0164
PROTONIX IV	VIAL	IV	C9113
PROTOPAM CHLORIDE	1 G	SC, IM, IV	J2730
PROTROPIN	1 MG	SC, IM	J2940
PROVENTIL NONCOMPOUNDED, CONCENTRATED	1 MG	INH	J7611
PROVENTIL NONCOMPOUNDED, UNIT DOSE	1 MG	INH	J7613
PROVOCHOLINE POWDER	1 MG	INH	J7674
PROZINE-50	25 MG	IM	J2950
PULMICORT	0.25 MG	INH	J7633
PULMICORT RESPULES	0.5 MG	INH	J7627
PULMICORT RESPULES NONCOMPOUNDED, CONCETRATED	0.25 MG	INH	J7626

Drug Name	Unit Per	Route	Code
PULMOZYME	1 MG	INH	J7639
PURINETHOL	50 MG	ORAL	S0108
PYRIDOXINE HCL	100 MG	INJ	J3415
QUADRAMET	50 MCI	IV	A9605
QUELICIN	20 MG	IM, IV	J0330
QUINUPRISTIN/DALFOPRISTIN	500 MG	IV	J2770
RANIBIZUMAB	0.5 MG	OTH	J2778
RANITIDINE HCL	25 MG	INJ	J2780
RAPAMUNE	1 MG	ORAL	J7520
RAPTIVA	125 MG	SC	S0162
RASBURICASE	50 MCG	IM	J2783
REBETRON KIT	1,000,000 U	SC, IM	J9214
REBIF	11 MCG	SC	Q3026
REBIF	33 MCG	SC	J1825
RECLAST	1 MG	IV	J3488
RECOMBINATE	1 IU	IV	J7192
REDISOL	1,000 MCG	SC. IM	J3420
REFACTO	1 IU	IV	J7192
REFLUDAN	50 MG	IM, IV	J1945
~~REGADENOSON~~	~~0.4 MG~~	~~IV~~	~~C9244~~
REGADENOSON	0.1 MG	IV	J2785
REGITINE	5 MG	IM, IV	J2760
REGLAN	10 MG	IV	J2765
~~REGRANEX GEL~~	~~0.5 G~~	~~OTH~~	~~S0065~~
REGRANEX GEL	0.5 G	OTH	S0157
REGULAR INSULIN	5 UNITS	SC	J1815
RELAXIN	10 ML	IV, IM	J2800
RELION	5 U	SC	J1815
RELION NOVOLIN	50 U	SC	J1817
REMICADE	10 MG	IV	J1745
REMODULIN	1 MG	SC	J3285
REODULIN	1 MG	SC	J3285
REOPRO	10 MG	IV	J0130
REPRONEX	75 IU	SC, IM, IV	S0122
RESP SYNCYTIAL VIR IMMUNE GLOB	50 MG	IV	J1565
RESPIGAM	50 MG	IV	J1565
RESPIROL NONCOMPOUNDED, CONCENTRATED	1 MG	INH	J7611
RESPIROL NONCOMPOUNDED, UNIT DOSE	1 MG	INH	J7613
RETAVASE	18.1 MG	IV	J2993
RETEPLASE	18.1 MG	IV	J2993
RETISERT	IMPLANT	OTH	J7311
RETROVIR	10 MG	IV	J3485
RETROVIR	100 MG	ORAL	S0104
RHEOMACRODEX	500 ML	IV	J7100
RHEUMATREX DOSE PACK	2.5 MG	ORAL	J8610
RHO D IMMUNE GLOBULIN	300 MCG	IV	J2790
RHO D IMMUNE GLOBULIN (RHOPHYLAC)	100 IU	IM, IV	J2791
RHO D IMMUNE GLOBULIN MINIDOSE	50 MCG	IM	J2788
RHO D IMMUNE GLOBULIN SOLVENT DETERGENT	100 IU	IV	J2792
RHOGAM	300 MCG	IM	J2790
RHOGAM	50 MCG	IM	J2788
RHOPHYLAC	100 IU	IM, IV	J2791
RIMANTADINE HYDROCHLORIDE	100 MG	ORAL	G9036
RIMANTADINE HYDROCHLORIDE (GENERIC)	100 MG	ORAL	G9020
RIMSO 50	50 ML	IV	J1212
RINGERS LACTATE INFUSION	1,000 ML	VAR	J7120
RISPERDAL COSTA LONG ACTING	0.5 MG	IM	J2794
RISPERIDONE, LONG ACTING	0.5 MG	IM	J2794
RITUXAN	100 MG	IV	J9310
RITUXIMAB	100 MG	IV	J9310
ROBAXIN	10 ML	IV, IM	J2800
ROCEPHIN	250 MG	IV, IM	J0696
ROFERON-A	3,000,000 U	SC, IM	J9213
ROMIPLOSTIM	10 MCG	SC	C9245
ROPIVACAINE HYDROCHLORIDE	1 MG	VAR	J2795
RUBEX	10 MG	IV	J9000
RUBIDIUM RB-82	60 MCI	IV	A9555
RUBRAMIN PC	1,000 MCG	SC, IM	J3420
RUBRATOPE 57	1 MCI	ORAL	A9559
SAIZEN	1 MG	SC	J2941
SAIZEN SOMATROPIN RDNA ORIGIN	1 MG	SC	J2941
SALINE OR STERILE WATER, METERED DOSE DISPENSER	10 ML	INH	A4218
SALINE, STERILE WATER, AND/OR DEXTROSE DILUENT/FLUSH	10 ML	VAR	A4216
SALINE/STERILE WATER	500 ML	VAR	A4217
SAMARIUM LEXIDRONAMM	50 MCI	IV	A9605
SANDIMMUNE	100 MG	ORAL	J7502
SANDIMMUNE	25 MG	ORAL	J7515
SANDIMMUNE	250 MG	IV	J7516
~~SANDOGLOBULIN~~	~~1 G~~	~~IV~~	~~S0045~~
SANDOSTATIN	25 MCG	SC, IV	J2354
SANDOSTATIN LAR	1 MG	IM	J2353
SANGCYA	100 MG	ORAL	J7502
SANO-DROL	40 MG	IM	J1030
SANO-DROL	80 MG	IM	J1040
SAQUINAVIR	200 MG	ORAL	S0140
SARGRAMOSTIM (GM-CSF)	50 MCG	IV	J2820
SCANDONEST	PER 10 ML	IV	J0670
SECREFLO	1 MCG	IV	J2850
SECRETIN, SYNTHETIC, HUMAN	1 MCG	IV	J2850
SENSORCAINE	30 ML	VAR	S0020
SEPTRA IV	10 ML	IV	S0039
SERMORELIN ACETATE	1 MCG	IV	Q0515
SEROSTIM	1 MG	SC	J2941
SEROSTIM RDNA ORIGIN	1 MG	SC	J2941
SILDENAFIL CITRATE	25 MG	ORAL	S0090
SIMULECT	20 MG	IV	J0480
SINCALIDE	5 MCG	IV	J2805
SIROLIMUS	1 MG	ORAL	J7520
SKIN SUBSTITUTE, APLIGRAF	SQ CM	OTH	Q4101
SKIN SUBSTITUTE, DERMAGRAFT	SQ CM	OTH	Q4106
SKIN SUBSTITUTE, GAMMAGRAFT	SQ CM	OTH	Q4111
SKIN SUBSTITUTE, GRAFTJACKET	SQ CM	OTH	Q4107

Drug Name	Unit Per	Route	Code
SKIN SUBSTITUTE, INTEGRA BILAYER MATRIX WOUND DRESSING	SQ CM	OTH	Q4104
SKIN SUBSTITUTE, INTEGRA DERMAL REGENERATION TEMPLATE	SQ CM	OTH	Q4105
SKIN SUBSTITUTE, INTEGRA MATRIX	SQ CM	OTH	Q4108
SKIN SUBSTITUTE, OASIS BURN MATRIX	SQ CM	OTH	Q4103
SKIN SUBSTITUTE, OASIS WOUND MATRIX	SQ CM	OTH	Q4102
SKIN SUBSTITUTE, PRIMATRIX	SQ CM	OTH	Q4110
SKIN SUBSTITUTE, TISSUEMEND	SQ CM	OTH	Q4109
SMZ-TMP	10 ML	IV	S0039
SODIUM FERRIC GLUCONATE COMPLEX IN SUCROSE	12.5 MG	IV	J2916
SODIUM FLUORIDE F-18, DIAGNOSTIC	STUDY DOSE UP TO 30 MCI	IV	A9580
~~SODIUM HYALURONATE~~	~~1 MG~~	~~OTH~~	~~C0000~~
~~SODIUM HYALURONATE~~	~~INJ~~	~~OTH~~	~~C0000~~
SODIUM IODIDE I-131 CAPSULE DIAGNOSTIC	1 MCI	ORAL	A9528
SODIUM IODIDE I-131 CAPSULE THERAPEUTIC	1 MCI	ORAL	A9517
SODIUM IODIDE I-131 SOLUTION THERAPEUTIC	1 MCI	ORAL	A9530
SODIUM PHOSPHATE P32	1 MCI	IV	A9563
SOLGANAL	50 MG	IM	J2910
SOLIRIS	10 MG	IV	J1300
SOLTAMOX	10 MG	ORAL	S0187
SOLU-CORTEF	100 MG	IV, IM, SC	J1720
SOLU-MEDROL	125 MG	IM, IV	J2930
SOLU-MEDROL	40 MG	IM, IV	J2920
SOLUREX	1 MG	IM, IV, OTH	J1100
SOMATREM	1 MG	SC, IM	J2940
SOMATROPIN	1 MG	SC	J2941
~~SOMATULINE~~	~~1 MG~~	~~INJ~~	~~C9237~~
SOMATULINE	1 MG	SC	J1930
SPECTINOMYCIN DIHYDROCHLORIDE	2 G	IM	J3320
SPECTRO-DEX	1 MG	IM, IV, OTH	J1100
SPORANOX	50 MG	IV	J1835
STADOL	1 MG	IM, IV	J0595
STADOL NS	25 MG	OTH	S0012
STERAPRED	5 MG	ORAL	J7506
STERILE WATER OR SALINE, METERED DOSE DISPENSER	10 ML	INH	A4218
STERILE WATER, SALINE, AND/OR DEXTROSE DILUENT/FLUSH	10 ML	VAR	A4216
STERILE WATER/SALINE	500 ML	VAR	A4217
STREPTASE	250,000 IU	IV	J2995
STREPTOKINASE	250,000 IU	IV	J2995
STREPTOMYCIN	1 G	IM	J3000
STREPTOZOCIN	1 GM	IV	J9320
STRONTIUM 89 CHLORIDE	1 MCI	IV	A9600
SUBLIMAZE	0.1 MG	IM, IV	J3010
SUCCINYLCHOLINE CHLORIDE	20 MG	IM, IV	J0330

Drug Name	Unit Per	Route	Code
SULFAMETHOXAZOLE AND TRIMETHOPRIM	10 ML	IV	S0039
SULFAMETHOXAZOLE-TRIMETHOPRIM	400-80 MG	ORAL	J8499
SULFUTRIM	10 ML	IV	S0039
SUMATRIPTAN SUCCINATE	6 MG	SC	J3030
SUPARTZ	PER DOSE	OTH	J7321
SUPPRELIN LA	10 MCG	OTH	J1675
SURGIMEND COLLAGEN MATRIX	0.5 SQ CM	OTH	C9358
SUS-PHRINE	UP TO 1 ML	VAR	J0170
~~SYNAGIS~~	~~50 MG~~	~~IM~~	~~C9003~~
SYNERCID	500 MG	IV	J2770
SYNTOCINON	10 UNITS	IV	J2590
SYNVISC	PER DOSE	OTH	J7322
SYTOBEX	1,000 MCG	SC, IM	J3420
TACRINE HCL	10 MG	ORAL	S0014
TACROLIMUS	1 MG	ORAL	J7507
TACROLIMUS	5 MG	OTH	J7525
TAGAMET HCL	300 MG	IM, IV	S0023
TALWIN	30 MG	IM, SC, IV	J3070
TAMOXIFEN CITRATE	10 MG	ORAL	S0187
TAXOL	30 MG	IV	J9265
TAXOTERE	20 MG	IV	J9170
TAZICEF	500 MG	IM, IV	J0713
TEBAMIDE	250 MG	ORAL	Q0173
TEBOROXIME TECHNETIUM TC 99	PER STUDY DOSE	IV	A9501
TEBOROXIME, TECHNETIUM	PER STUDY DOSE	IV	A9501
TECHNEPLEX	25 MCI	IV	A9539
TECHNESCAN	UP TO 30 MCI	IV	A9561
TECHNESCAN FANOLESOMAB	STUDY DOSE	IV	A9566
TECHNESCAN MAA	10 MCI	IV	A9540
TECHNESCAN MAG3	STUDY DOSE	IV	A9562
TECHNESCAN PYP	25 MCI	IV	A9538
TECHNESCAN PYP KIT	UP TO 25 MCI	IV	A9538
TECHNETIUM SESTAMBI	40 MCI	IV	A9500
~~TECHNETIUM TC 99M ACRCITUMOMAB~~	~~PER STUDY DOSE~~	~~IV~~	~~A9568~~
TECHNETIUM TC 99M APCITIDE	20 MCI	IV	A9504
TECHNETIUM TC 99M ARCITUMOMAB, DIAGNOSTIC	45 MCI	IV	A9568
TECHNETIUM TC 99M BICISATE	25 MCI	IV	A9557
TECHNETIUM TC 99M DEPREOTIDE	35 MCI	IV	A9536
TECHNETIUM TC 99M EXAMETAZIME	25 MCI	IV	A9521
TECHNETIUM TC 99M FANOLESOMAB	25 MCI	IV	A9566
TECHNETIUM TC 99M LABELED RED BLOOD CELLS	30 MCI	IV	A9560
TECHNETIUM TC 99M MACROAGGREGATED ALBUMIN	10 MCI	IV	A9540
TECHNETIUM TC 99M MDI-MDP	30 MCI	IV	A9503
TECHNETIUM TC 99M MEBROFENIN	15 MCI	IV	A9537
TECHNETIUM TC 99M MEDRONATE	30 MCI	IV	A9503
TECHNETIUM TC 99M MERTIATIDE	15 MCI	IV	A9562
TECHNETIUM TC 99M OXIDRONATE	30 MCI	IV	A9561
TECHNETIUM TC 99M PENTETATE	75 MCI	INH	A9539

Drug Name	*Unit Per*	*Route*	*Code*
TECHNETIUM TC 99M PENTETATE	25 MCI	IV	**A9539**
TECHNETIUM TC 99M PYROPHOSPHATE	25 MCI	IV	**A9538**
TECHNETIUM TC 99M SODIUM GLUCEPATATE	25 MCI	IV	**A9550**
TECHNETIUM TC 99M SUCCIMER	10 MCI	IV	**A9551**
TECHNETIUM TC 99M SULFUR COLLOID	20 MCI	IV	**A9541**
TECHNETIUM TC 99M TETROFOSMIN, DIAGNOSTIC	STUDY DOSE	IV	**A9502**
TECHNETIUM TC-99M EXAMETAZIME LABELED AUTOLOGOUS WHITE BLOOD CELLS	PER STUDY DOSE	IV	**A9569**
TECHNETIUM TC-99M TEBOROXIME	PER STUDY DOSE	IV	**A9501**
TECHNILITE	PER MCI	IV	**A9512**
TEMODAR	100 MG	ORAL	**J8700**
TEMOZOLOMIDE	100 MG	ORAL	**J8700**
TEMSIROLIMUS	1 MG	IV	**J9330**
TENDON, POROUS MATRIX	1 SQ CM	OTH	**C9356**
TENDON, POROUS MATRIX CROSS-LINKED AND GLYCOSAMINOGLYCAN MATRIX	SQ CM	OTH	**C9356**
~~TENECTEPLASE~~	~~50 MG~~	~~IV~~	~~**J3100**~~
TENECTEPLASE	1 MG	IV	**J3101**
TENIPOSIDE	50 MG	IV	**Q2017**
TENOGLIDE TENDON PROTECTOR	1 SQ CM	OTH	**C9356**
TENOGLIDE TENDON PROTECTOR SHEET	SQ CM	OTH	**C9356**
TEQUIN	10 MG	IV	**J1590**
TERBUTALINE SULFATE	1 MG	SC, IV	**J3105**
TERBUTALINE SULFATE, COMPOUNDED, CONCENTRATED	1 MG	INH	**J7680**
TERBUTALINE SULFATE, COMPOUNDED, UNIT DOSE	1 MG	INH	**J7681**
TERIPARATIDE	10 MCG	SC	**J3110**
TERRAMYCIN	50 MG	IM	**J2460**
TESTERONE	50 MG	IM	**J3140**
TESTOSTERONE CYPIONATE	1 CC, 200 MG	IM	**J1080**
TESTOSTERONE CYPIONATE	UP TO 100 MG	IM	**J1070**
TESTOSTERONE CYPIONATE & ESTRADIOL CYPIONATE	1 ML	IM	**J1060**
TESTOSTERONE ENANTHATE	100 MG	IM	**J3120**
TESTOSTERONE ENANTHATE	200 MG	IM	**J3130**
TESTOSTERONE ENANTHATE & ESTRADIOL VALERATE	UP TO 1 CC	IM	**J0900**
TESTOSTERONE PELLET	75 MG	OTH	**S0189**
TESTOSTERONE PROPIONATE	100 MG	IM	**J3150**
TESTOSTERONE SUSPENSION	50 MG	IM	**J3140**
TESTRO AQ	50 MG	IM	**J3140**
TETANUS IMMUNE GLOBULIN	250 U	IM	**J1670**
TETRACYCLINE HCL	250 MG	IV	**J0120**
T-GEN	250 MG	ORAL	**Q0173**
THALLOUS CHLORIDE	1 MCI	IV	**A9505**
THALLOUS CHLORIDE TL-201	1 MCI	IV	**A9505**
THALLOUS CHLORIDE USP	1 MCI	IV	**A9505**
THEELIN AQUEOUS	1 MG	IM, IV	**J1435**
THEOPHYLLINE	40 MG	IV	**J2810**
THERACYS	VIAL	IV	**J9031**
THIAMINE HCL	100 MG	INJ	**J3411**
THIETHYLPERAZINE MALEATE	10 MG	IM	**J3280**
THIETHYLPERAZINE MALEATE	10 MG	ORAL	**Q0174**
THIMAZIDE	250 MG	ORAL	**Q0173**
THIOTEPA	15 MG	IV	**J9340**
THORAZINE	10 MG	ORAL	**Q0171**
THORAZINE	25 MG	ORAL	**Q0172**
THORAZINE	50 MG	IM, IV	**J3230**
THROMBATE III	1 IU	IV	**J7197**
THYMOGLOBULIN	25 MG	OTH	**J7511**
THYROGEN	0.9 MG	IM, SC	**J3240**
THYROTROPIN ALPHA	0.9 MG	IM, SC	**J3240**
TICARCILLIN DISODIUM AND CLAVULANATE	3.1 G	IV	**S0040**
TICE BCG	VIAL	OTH	**J9031**
TICON	250 MG	IM	**Q0173**
TIGAN	200 MG	IM	**J3250**
TIGECYCLINE	1 MG	IV	**J3243**
TIJECT-20	200 MG	IM	**J3250**
TIMENTIN	3.1 G	IV	**S0040**
TINZAPARIN	1,000 IU	SC	**J1655**
TIROFIBAN HCL	0.25 MG	IM, IV	**J3246**
~~TISSUEMEND~~	~~PER SQ. CM.~~	~~OTH~~	~~**J7348**~~
TISSUEMEND	SQ CM	OTH	**Q4109**
~~TNKASE~~	~~50 MG~~	~~IV~~	~~**J3100**~~
TNKASE	1 MG	IV	**J3101**
TOBI	300 MG	INH	**J7682**
TOBRAMYCIN COMPOUNDED, UNIT DOSE	300 MG	INH	**J7685**
TOBRAMYCIN SULFATE	80 MG	IM, IV	**J3260**
TOBRAMYCIN, NONCOMPOUNDED, UNIT DOSE	300 MG	INH	**J7682**
TOLAZOLINE HCL	25 MG	IV	**J2670**
TOPOSAR	10 MG	IV	**J9181**
~~TOPOSAR~~	~~100 MG~~	~~IV~~	~~**J9182**~~
TOPOTECAN	4 MG	IV	**J9350**
TOPOTECAN	0.25 MG	ORAL	**J8705**
TORECAN	10 MG	ORAL	**Q0174**
TORISEL	1 MG	IV	**J9330**
TORISEL	1 MG	IV	**J9330**
TORNALATE	PER MG	INH	**J7629**
TORNALATE CONCENTRATE	PER MG	INH	**J7628**
TORSEMIDE	10 MG	IV	**J3265**
TOSITUMOMAB DIAGNOSTIC	DOSE	IV	**A9544**
TOSITUMOMAB THERAPEUTIC	DOSE	IV	**A9545**
TOTECT	PER 250 MG	IV	**J1190**
~~TRANSCYTE~~	~~PER 247 SQ CM~~	~~OTH~~	~~**J7340**~~
TRASTUZUMAB	10 MG	IV	**J9355**
TRASYLOL	10,000 KIU	IV	**J0365**
~~TREANDA~~	~~1 MG~~	~~IV~~	~~**C9243**~~
TREANDA	1 MG	IV	**J9033**
TRELSTAR DEPOT	3.75 MG	IM	**J3315**
TRELSTAR DEPOT PLUS DEBIOCLIP KIT	3.75 MG	IM	**J3315**
TRELSTAR LA	3.75 MG	IM	**J3315**

Drug Name	Unit Per	Route	Code
TREPROSTINIL	1 MG	SC	J3285
TRETINOIN	5 G	OTH	S0117
TRIAM-A	10 MG	IM	J3301
TRIAMCINOLONE ACETONIDE	10 MG	IM	J3301
TRIAMCINOLONE ACETONIDE, PRESERVATIVE FREE	1 MG	INJ	J3300
TRIAMCINOLONE DIACETATE	5 MG	IM	J3302
TRIAMCINOLONE HEXACETONIDE	5 MG	VAR	J3303
TRIAMCINOLONE, COMPOUNDED, CONCENTRATED	1 MG	INH	J7683
TRIAMCINOLONE, COMPOUNDED, UNIT DOSE	1 MG	INH	J7684
TRIBAN	250 MG	ORAL	Q0173
TRI-KORT	10 MG	IM	J3301
TRILIFON	4 MG	ORAL	Q0175
TRILOG	10 MG	IM	J3301
TRILONE	5 MG	IM	J3302
TRIMETHOBENZAMIDE HCL	200 MG	IM	J3250
TRIMETHOBENZAMIDE HCL	250 MG	ORAL	Q0173
TRIMETREXATE GLUCURONATE	25 MG	IV	J3305
TRIPTORELIN PAMOATE	3.75 MG	IM	J3315
TRISENOX	1 MG	IV	J9017
TRIVARIS	1 MG	VAR	J3300
TROBICIN	2 G	IM	J3320
TRUXADRYL	50 MG	IV, IM	J1200
TYGACIL	1 MG	IV	J3243
TYPE A BOTOX	1 U	OTH	J0585
TYSABRI	1 MG	IV	J2323
ULTRALENTE	5 U	SC	J1815
ULTRATAG	30 MCI	IV	A9560
ULTRA-TECHNEKOW	PER MCI	IV	A9512
~~ULTRAVIST~~	~~1 ML~~	~~IV~~	~~Q9920~~
~~ULTRAVIST 150~~	~~1 ML~~	~~IV~~	~~Q9910~~
~~ULTRAVIST 240~~	~~1 ML~~	~~IV~~	~~Q9915~~
~~ULTRAVIST 370~~	~~1 ML~~	~~IV~~	~~Q9915~~
UNASYN	1.5 G	IM, IV	J0295
UNCLASSIFIED BIOLOGICS			J3590
UREA	40 G	IV	J3350
UROFOLLITROPIN	75 IU	SC, IM	J3355
UROKINASE	250,000 IU	IV	J3365
UROKINASE	5,000 IU	IV	J3364
VALERGEN	10 MG	IM	J1380
VALERGEN	20 MG	IM	J1390
VALIUM	5 MG	IV, IM	J3360
VALRUBICIN INTRAVESICAL	200 MG	OTH	J9357
VALSTAR	200 MG	OTH	J9357
VANCOCIN	500 MG	IM, IV	J3370
VANCOMYCIN HCL	500 MG	IV, IM	J3370
VANTAS	50 MG	OTH	J9225
~~VECTIBIX~~	~~10 MG~~	~~IV~~	~~Q9915~~
VECTIBIX	10 MG	IV	J9303
VELCADE	0.1 MG	IV	J9041
VELOSULIN	5 U	SC	J1815
VELOSULIN BR	5 U	SC	J1815
VENOFER	1 MG	IV	J1756
~~VENOGLOBULIN-S~~	~~1 G~~	~~IV~~	~~Q0945~~
VENTOLIN NONCOMPOUNDED, CONCENTRATED	1 MG	INH	J7611
VENTOLIN NONCOMPOUNDED, UNIT DOSE	1 MG	INH	J7613
VEPESID	10 MG	IV	J9181
~~VEPESID~~	~~100 MG~~	~~IV~~	~~J9182~~
VEPESID	50 MG	ORAL	J8560
VERITAS	SQ CM	OTH	C9354
VERSED	1 MG	IM, IV	J2250
VERTEPORFIN	0.1 MG	IV	J3396
VFEND	200 MG	IV	J3465
VIAGRA	25 MG	ORAL	S0090
VIDAZA	1 MG	SC	J9025
VIDEX	25 MG	ORAL	S0137
VINBLASTINE SULFATE	1 MG	IV	J9360
VINCRISTINE SULFATE	1 MG	IV	J9370
VINCRISTINE SULFATE	2 MG	IV	J9375
VINORELBINE TARTRATE	10 MG	IV	J9390
VIRILON	1 CC, 200 MG	IM	J1080
~~VISIPAQUE 270~~	~~1 ML~~	~~IV~~	~~Q9915~~
~~VISIPAQUE 320~~	~~1 ML~~	~~IV~~	~~Q9920~~
VISTAJECT-25	25 MG	IM	J3410
VISTARIL	25 MG	IM	J3410
VISTARIL	25 MG	ORAL	Q0177
VISTIDE	375 MG	IV	J0740
VISUDYNE	0.1 MG	IV	J3396
VITAMIN B-12 CYANOCOBALAMIN	1,000 MCG	IM, SC	J3420
VITRASE	1 USP	OTH	J3471
VITRASE	1,000 USP	OTH	J3472
VITRASERT	4.5 MG	OTH	J7310
VITRAVENE	1.65 MG	OTH	J1452
VIVITROL	1 MG	IM	J2315
VON WILLEBAND FACTOR VIII COMPLEX, HUMAN	PER FACTOR VIII IU	IV	J7186
VON WILLEBRAND FACTOR COMPLEX, HUMATE-P	IU	IV	J7187
~~VON WILLEBRAND FACTOR COMPLEX, RISTOCETIN COFACTOR~~	~~IU~~	~~IV~~	~~Q4096~~
VORICONAZOLE	200 MG	IV	J3465
VUMON	50 MG	IV	Q2017
WEHAMINE	50 MG	IM, IV	J1240
WEHDRYL	50 MG	IM, IV	J1200
WELBUTRIN SR	150 MG	ORAL	S0106
WINRHO SDF	100 IU	IV	J2792
WYCILLIN	600,000 U	IM, IV	J2510
XELODA	150 MG	ORAL	J8520
XELODA	500 MG	ORAL	J8521
XENON XE-133	10 MCI	OTH	A9558
XOLAIR	5 MG	SC	J2357
XYLOCAINE	10 MG	IV	J2001
YTTRIUM 90 IBRITUMOMAB TIUXETAN	TX DOSE	IV	A9543
~~ZALCITABINE (DDC)~~	~~0.375 MG~~	~~ORAL~~	~~S0141~~
ZANAMIVIR (BRAND NAME)	10 MG	INH	G9034
ZANAMIVIR (GENERIC)	10 MG	INH	G9018

APPENDIX 1 — TABLE OF DRUGS

Drug Name	Unit Per	Route	Code
ZANOSAR	1 GM	IV	J9320
ZANTAC	25 MG	INJ	J2780
ZEMAIRA	10 MG	IV	J0256
ZEMPLAR	1 MCG	IV, IM	J2501
ZENAPAX	25 MG	OTH	J7513
ZEVALIN	UP TO 5 MCI	IV	A9542
ZEVALIN DIAGNOSTIC	TX DOSE	IV	A9542
ZEVALIN THERAPEUTIC	TX DOSE	IV	A9543
ZICONOTIDE	1 MCG	IT	J2278
ZIDOVUDINE	10 MG	IV	J3485
ZIDOVUDINE	100 MG	ORAL	S0104
ZINACEFT	PER 750 MG	IM, IV	J0697
ZINECARD	250 MG	IV	J1190
ZIPRASIDONE MESYLATE	10 MG	IM	J3486
ZITHROMAX	1 G	ORAL	Q0144
ZITHROMAX	500 MG	IV	J0456
ZOFRAN	1 MG	IV	J2405
ZOFRAN	8 MG	ORAL	Q0179
ZOFRAN	4 MG	ORAL	S0181
ZOLADEX	3.6 MG	SC	J9202
ZOLEDRONIC ACID	1 MG	IV	J3487
ZOLEDRONIC ACID (RECLAST)	1 MG	IV	J3488
~~ZOLEDRONIC ACID FOR PAGET'S DISEASE~~	~~1 MG~~	~~IV~~	~~70015~~
ZOMETA	1 MG	IV	J3487
ZORBTIVE	1 MG	SC	J2941
ZOSYN	1 G/1.125 GM	IV	J2543
ZOVIRAX	5 MG	IV	J0133
~~ZOVIRAX~~	~~50 MG~~	~~IV~~	~~70015~~
ZYPREXA	2.5 MG	IM	S0166
ZYVOX	200 MG	IV	J2020

NOT OTHERWISE CLASSIFIED DRUGS

Drug Name	Unit Per	Route	Code
ALFENTANIL	500 MCG	IV	J3490
~~ALGUCOSIDE ALFA~~	~~1 MG~~	~~IV~~	~~J3490~~
ALLOPURINOL SODIUM	500 MG	IV	J3490
AMINOCAPROIC ACID	250 MG	IV	J3490
~~ARFORMOTEROL TATRATE~~	~~15 MCG~~	~~INH~~	~~J3490~~
ARGININE HYDROCHLORIDE	300 ML	IV	J3490
ASCORBIC ACID	250 MG	IV	J3490
ATROPINE SULFATE/EDROPHONIUM CHLORIDE	10 MG	IV	J3490
AZTREONAM	500 MG	IV	J3490
~~BENDAMUSTINE HCL~~	~~1 MG~~	~~IV~~	~~J3490~~
BUMETANIDE	0.25 MG	IM, IV	J3490
BUPIVACAINE, 0.25%	1 ML	OTH	J3490
BUPIVACAINE, 0.50%	1 ML	OTH	J3490
BUPIVACAINE, 0.75%	1 ML	OTH	J3490
CALCIUM CHLORIDE	100 MG	IV	J3490
CIMETIDINE HCL	150 MG	IM, IV	J3490
CLAVULANTE POTASSIUM/TICARCILLIN DISODIUM	0.1-3 GM	IV	J3490
CLINDAMYCIN PHOSPHATE	150 MG	IV	J3490
COPPER SULFATE	0.4 MG	INJ	J3490
DEXTROSE 50%	50 ML	IV	J3490
DILTIAZEM HCL	5 MG	IV	J3490
DILTIAZEM HCL	5 MG	IV	J3490
DOXAPRAM HCL	20 MG	IV	J3490
DOXYCYCLINE HYCLATE	100 MG	INJ	J3490
~~ECULIZUMAB~~	~~1 MG~~	~~IV~~	~~J3490~~
EDROPHONIUM CHLORIDE	10 MG	IM, IV	J3490
ENALAPRILAT	1.25 MG	IV	J3490
ESMOLOL HCL	10 MG	IV	J3490
ESOMEPRAZOLE SODIUM	20 MG	IV	J3490
ETOMIDATE	2 MG	IV	J3490
FAMOTIDINE	10 MG	IV	J3490
FLUMAZENIL	0.1 MG	IV	J3490
FOLIC ACID	5 MG	SC, IM, IV	J3490
GLYCOPYRROLATE	0.2 MG	IM, IV	J3490
~~HEPAGAMB INTRAVENOUS~~	~~0.5 ML~~	~~IV~~	~~J3490~~
~~IDURSULFASE~~	~~1 MG~~	~~IV~~	~~J3490~~
IXABEPILONE	1 MG	IV	J3490
KETAMINE HCL	10 MG	IM, IV	J3490
LABETALOL HCL	5 MG	INJ	J3490
LEVETIRACETAM (KEPPRA INTRAVENOUS)	10 MG	IV	J3490
LIDOCAINE	1 ML	VAR	J3490
METOPROLOL TARTRATE	1 MG	IV	J3490
METRONIDAZOLE INJ	500 MG	IV	J3490
MORRHUATE SODIUM	50 MG	OTH	J3490
NAFCILLIN SODIUM	1 GM	IM, IV	J3490
NALMEFENE HCL	10 MCG	IV	J3490
NITROGLYCERIN	5 MG	IV	J3490
OLANZAPINE	0.5 MG	IM	J3490
~~PANITUMUMAB~~	~~1 MG~~	~~IV~~	~~J3490~~
~~PANITUMUMAB~~	~~1MG~~	~~IV~~	~~J3490~~
~~PEGASYS~~	~~180 MCG~~	~~SC~~	~~J3490~~
~~PEGINTERFERON ALFA-2A~~	~~180 MCG~~	~~SC~~	~~J3490~~
POTASSIUM ACETATE	2 MEQ	IV	J3490
POTASSIUM POSPHATE	3 MMOL	IV	J3490
PROPOFOL	10 MG	IV	J3490
PROTONIX	40 MG	IV	J3490
~~RANIBIZUMAB INJ~~	~~0.5 MG~~	~~OTH~~	~~J3490~~
RIFAMPIN	600 MG	IV	J3490
SARRACENIA PURPURA	1 ML	INJ	J3490
SODIUM ACETATE	2 MEQ		J3490
SODIUM BICARBONATE, 8.4%	50 ML	IV	J3490
SODIUM CHLORIDE, HYPERTONIC	250 CC	IV	J3490
SODIUM THIOSULFATE	100 MG	IV	J3490
SURGIMEND	0.5 SQ CM	OTH	J3490
TEMSIROLIMUS	1 MG	IV	J9330
~~TRIAMCINOLONE ACETONIDE, PRESERVATIVE FREE~~	~~1 MG~~	~~INJ~~	~~J3490~~
VALPROATE SODIUM	100 MG	IV	J3490
~~VASOPRESSIN~~	~~20 UNITS~~	~~SC, IM~~	~~J3490~~
~~VECURONIUM BROMIDE~~	~~1 MG~~	~~IV~~	~~J3490~~
~~VERAPAMIL HCL~~	~~2.5 MG~~	~~IV~~	~~J3490~~

APPENDIX 2 — MODIFIERS

A modifier is a two-position alpha or numeric code that is added to the end of a CPT code to clarify the services being billed. Modifiers provide a means by which a service can be altered without changing the procedure code. They add more information, such as the anatomical site, to the code. In addition, they help to eliminate the appearance of duplicate billing and unbundling. Modifiers are used to increase accuracy in reimbursement, coding consistency, editing, and to capture payment data.

A1 Dressing for one wound

A2 Dressing for 2 wounds

A3 Dressing for 3 wounds

A4 Dressing for 4 wounds

A5 Dressing for 5 wounds

A6 Dressing for 6 wounds

A7 Dressing for 7 wounds

A8 Dressing for 8 wounds

A9 Dressing for 9 or more wounds

AA Anesthesia services performed personally by anesthesiologist

AD Medical supervision by a physician: more than 4 concurrent anesthesia procedures

AE Registered dietician

AF Specialty physician

AG Primary physician

AH Clinical psychologist

AJ Clinical social worker

AK Non participating physician

AM Physician, team member service

AP Determination of refractive state was not performed in the course of diagnostic ophthalmological examination

AQ Physician providing a service in an unlisted health professional shortage area (HPSA)

AR Physician provider services in a physician scarcity area

AS Physician assistant, nurse practitioner, or clinical nurse specialist services for assistant at surgery

AT Acute treatment (this modifier should be used when reporting service 98940, 98941, 98942)

AU Item furnished in conjunction with a urological, ostomy, or tracheostomy supply

AV Item furnished in conjunction with a prosthetic device, prosthetic or orthotic

AW Item furnished in conjunction with a surgical dressing

AX Item furnished in conjunction with dialysis services

BA Item furnished in conjunction with parenteral enteral nutrition (PEN) services

BL Special acquisition of blood and blood products

BO Orally administered nutrition, not by feeding tube

BP The beneficiary has been informed of the purchase and rental options and has elected to purchase the item

BR The beneficiary has been informed of the purchase and rental options and has elected to rent the item

BU The beneficiary has been informed of the purchase and rental options and after 30 days has not informed the supplier of his/her decision

CA Procedure payable only in the inpatient setting when performed emergently on an outpatient who expires prior to admission

CB Service ordered by a renal dialysis facility (RDF) physician as part of the ESRD beneficiary's dialysis benefit, is not part of the composite rate, and is separately reimbursable

CC Procedure code change (use CC when the procedure code submitted was changed either for administrative reasons or because an incorrect code was filed)

CD AMCC test has been ordered by an ESRD facility or MCP physician that is part of the composite rate and is not separately billable

CE AMCC test has been ordered by an ESRD facility or MCP physician that is a composite rate test but is beyond the normal frequency covered under the rate and is separately reimbursable based on medical necessity

CF AMCC test has been ordered by an ESRD facility or MCP physician that is not part of the composite rate and is separately billable

CG Policy criteria applied

CR Catastrophe/Disaster related

E1 Upper left, eyelid

E2 Lower left, eyelid

E3 Upper right, eyelid

E4 Lower right, eyelid

EA Erythropoetic stimulating agent (ESA) administered to treat anemia due to anticancer chemotherapy

EB Erythropoetic stimulating agent (ESA) administered to treat anemia due to anticancer radiotherapy

EC Erythropoetic stimulating agent (ESA) administered to treat anemia not due to anticancer radiotherapy or anticancer chemotherapy

ED Hematocrit level has exceeded 39% (or hemoglobin level has exceeded 13.0 G/dl) for 3 or more consecutive billing cycles immediately prior to and including the current cycle

EE Hematocrit level has not exceeded 39% (or hemoglobin level has not exceeded 13.0 G/dl) for 3 or more consecutive billing cycles immediately prior to and including the current cycle

EJ Subsequent claims for a defined course of therapy, e.g., EPO, sodium hyaluronate, infliximab

EM Emergency reserve supply (for ESRD benefit only)

EP Service provided as part of Medicaid early periodic screening diagnosis and treatment (EPSDT) program

ET Emergency services

EY No physician or other licensed health care provider order for this item or service

F1 Left hand, 2nd digit

F2 Left hand, third digit

F3 Left hand, 4th digit

F4 Left hand, fifth digit

F5 Right hand, thumb

F6 Right hand, 2nd digit

F7 Right hand, third digit

F8 Right hand, 4th digit

F9 Right hand, 5th digit

FA Left hand, thumb

FB Item provided without cost to provider, supplier or practitioner, or full credit received for replaced device (examples, but not limited to, covered under warranty, replaced due to defect, free samples)

FC Partial credit received for replaced device

FP Service provided as part of family planning program

G1 Most recent URR reading of less than 60

G2 Most recent URR reading of 60 to 64.9

G3 Most recent URR reading of 65 to 69.9

G4 Most recent URR reading of 70 to 74.9

G5 Most recent URR reading of 75 or greater

G6 ESRD patient for whom less than 6 dialysis sessions have been provided in a month

G7 Pregnancy resulted from rape or incest or pregnancy certified by physician as life threatening

G8 Monitored anesthesia care (MAC) for deep complex, complicated, or markedly invasive surgical procedure

G9	Monitored anesthesia care for patient who has history of severe cardiopulmonary condition
GA	Waiver of liability statement on file
GB	Claim being resubmitted for payment because it is no longer covered under a global payment demonstration
GC	This service has been performed in part by a resident under the direction of a teaching physician
GD	Units of service exceeds medically unlikely edit value and represents reasonable and necessary services
GE	This service has been performed by a resident without the presence of a teaching physician under the primary care exception
GF	Nonphysician (e.g., nurse practitioner (NP), certified registered nurse anesthetist (CRNA), certified registered nurse (CRN), clinical nurse specialist (CNS), physician assistant (PA)) services in a critical access hospital
GG	Performance and payment of a screening mammogram and diagnostic mammogram on the same patient, same day
GH	Diagnostic mammogram converted from screening mammogram on same day
GJ	Opt out physician or practitioner emergency or urgent service
GK	Reasonable and necessary item/service associated with GA or GZ modifier
GL	Medically unnecessary upgrade provided instead of nonupgraded item, no charge, no advance beneficiary notice (ABN)
GM	Multiple patients on one ambulance trip
GN	Services delivered under an outpatient speech language pathology plan of care
GO	Services delivered under an outpatient occupational therapy plan of care
GP	Services delivered under an outpatient physical therapy plan of care
GQ	Via asynchronous telecommunications system
GR	This service was performed in whole or in part by a resident in a department of veterans affairs medical center or clinic, supervised in accordance with VA policy
GS	Dosage of EPO or darbepoetin alfa has been reduced and maintained in response to hematocrit or hemoglobin level
GT	Via interactive audio and video telecommunication systems
GV	Attending physician not employed or paid under arrangement by the patient's hospice provider
GW	Service not related to the hospice patient's terminal condition
GY	Item or service statutorily excluded, does not meet the definition of any Medicare benefit or for non-Medicare insurers, is not a contract benefit
GZ	Item or service expected to be denied as not reasonable and necessary
H9	Court-ordered
HA	Child/adolescent program
HB	Adult program, nongeriatric
HC	Adult program, geriatric
HD	Pregnant/parenting women's program
HE	Mental health program
HF	Substance abuse program
HG	Opioid addiction treatment program
HH	Integrated mental health/substance abuse program
HI	Integrated mental health and mental retardation/developmental disabilities program
HJ	Employee assistance program
HK	Specialized mental health programs for high-risk populations
HL	Intern
HM	Less than bachelor degree level
HN	Bachelors degree level
HO	Masters degree level
HP	Doctoral level
HQ	Group setting
HR	Family/couple with client present
HS	Family/couple without client present
HT	Multi-disciplinary team
HU	Funded by child welfare agency
HV	Funded state addictions agency
HW	Funded by state mental health agency
HX	Funded by county/local agency
HY	Funded by juvenile justice agency
HZ	Funded by criminal justice agency
J1	Competitive acquisition program no-pay submission for a prescription number
J2	Competitive acquisition program, restocking of emergency drugs after emergency administration
J3	Competitive acquisition program (CAP), drug not available through CAP as written, reimbursed under average sales price methodology
JA	Administered intravenously
JB	Administered subcutaneously
JC	Skin substitute used as a graft
JD	Skin substitute not used as a graft
JW	Drug amount discarded/not administered to any patient
K0	Lower extremity prosthesis functional level 0—does not have the ability or potential to ambulate or transfer safely with or without assistance and a prosthesis does not enhance their quality of life or mobility
K1	Lower extremity prosthesis functional level 1 - has the ability or potential to use a prosthesis for transfers or ambulation on level surfaces at fixed cadence, typical of the limited and unlimited household ambulator.
K2	Lower extremity prosthesis functional level 2 - has the ability or potential for ambulation with the ability to traverse low level environmental barriers such as curbs, stairs or uneven surfaces, typical of the limited community ambulator.
K3	Lower extremity prosthesis functional level 3—has the ability or potential for ambulation with variable cadence, typical of the community ambulator who has the ability to traverse most environmental barriers and may have vocational, therapeutic, or exercise activity that demands prosthetic utilization beyond simple locomotion
K4	Lower extremity prosthesis functional level 4 - has the ability or potential for prosthetic ambulation that exceeds the basic ambulation skills, exhibiting high impact, stress, or energy levels, typical of the prosthetic demands of the child, active adult, or athlete.
KA	Add on option/accessory for wheelchair
KB	Beneficiary requested upgrade for ABN, more than 4 modifiers identified on claim
KC	Replacement of special power wheelchair interface
KD	Drug or biological infused through DME
KE	Bid under round one of the DMEPOS competitive bidding program for use with noncompetitive bid base equipment
KF	Item designated by FDA as class III device
KG	DMEPOS item subject to DMEPOS competitive bidding program number 1
KH	DMEPOS item, initial claim, purchase or first month rental
KI	DMEPOS item, 2nd or 3rd month rental
KJ	DMEPOS item, parenteral enteral nutrition (PEN) pump or capped rental, months 4 to 15
KK	DMEPOS item subject to DMEPOS competitive bidding program number 2
KL	DMEPOS item delivered via mail
KM	Replacement of facial prosthesis including new impression/moulage

KN	Replacement of facial prosthesis using previous master model
KO	Single drug unit dose formulation
KP	First drug of a multiple drug unit dose formulation
KQ	Second or subsequent drug of a multiple drug unit dose formulation
KR	Rental item, billing for partial month
KS	Glucose monitor supply for diabetic beneficiary not treated with insulin
KT	Beneficiary resides in a competitive bidding area and travels outside that competitive bidding area and receives a competitive bid item.
KU	DMEPOS item subject to DMEPOS competitive bidding program number 3
KV	DMEPOS item subject to DMEPOS competitive bidding program that is furnished as part of a professional service
KW	DMEPOS item subject to DMEPOS competitive bidding program number 4
KX	Requirements specified in the medical policy have been met
KY	DMEPOS item subject to DMEPOS competitive bidding program number 5
KZ	New coverage not implemented by managed care
LC	Left circumflex coronary artery
LD	Left anterior descending coronary artery
LL	Lease/rental (use the LL modifier when DME equipment rental is to be applied against the purchase price)
LR	Laboratory round trip
LS	FDA-monitored intraocular lens implant
LT	Left side (used to identify procedures performed on the left side of the body)
M2	Medicare secondary payer (MSP)
MS	Six month maintenance and servicing fee for reasonable and necessary parts and labor which are not covered under any manufacturer or supplier warranty
NR	New when rented (use the NR modifier when DME which was new at the time of rental is subsequently purchased)
NU	New equipment
P1	A normal healthy patient
P2	A patient with mild systemic disease
P3	A patient with severe systemic disease
P4	A patient with severe systemic disease that is a constant threat to life
P5	A moribund patient who is not expected to survive without the operation
P6	A declared brain-dead patient whose organs are being removed for donor purposes
PL	Progressive addition lenses
PR	Ambulance transportation from physician's office (includes HMO non-hospital facility, clinic, etc.)to residence
Q0	Investigational clinical service provided in a clinical research study that is in an approved clinical research study
Q1	Routine clinical service provided in a clinical research study that is in an approved clinical research study
Q2	HCFA/ORD demonstration project procedure/service
Q3	Live kidney donor surgery and related services
Q4	Service for ordering/referring physician qualifies as a service exemption
Q5	Service furnished by a substitute physician under a reciprocal billing arrangement
Q6	Service furnished by a locum tenens physician
Q7	One Class A finding
Q8	Two Class B findings
Q9	One class B and 2 class C findings
QB	Physician providing service in a rural HPSA
QC	Single channel monitoring
QD	Recording and storage in solid state memory by a digital recorder
QE	Prescribed amount of oxygen is less than 1 liter per minute (LPM)
QF	Prescribed amount of oxygen exceeds 4 liters per minute (LPM) and portable oxygen is prescribed
QG	Prescribed amount of oxygen is greater than 4 liters per minute (LPM)
QH	Oxygen conserving device is being used with an oxygen delivery system
QJ	Services/items provided to a prisoner or patient in state or local custody, however the state or local government, as applicable, meets the requirements in 42 CFR 411.4(B)
QK	Medical direction of 2, 3, or 4 concurrent anesthesia procedures involving qualified individuals
QL	Patient pronounced dead after ambulance called
QM	Ambulance service provided under arrangement by a provider of services
QN	Ambulance service furnished directly by a provider of services
QP	Documentation is on file showing that the laboratory test(s) was ordered individually or ordered as a CPT-recognized panel other than automated profile codes 80002-80019, G0058, G0059, and G0060
QQ	Claim submitted with a written statement of intent
QS	Monitored anesthesia care service
QT	Recording and storage on tape by an analog tape recorder
QU	Physician providing service in an urban HPSA
QW	CLIA waived test
QX	CRNA service: with medical direction by a physician
QY	Medical direction of one certified registered nurse anesthetist (CRNA) by an anesthesiologist
QZ	CRNA service: without medical direction by a physician
RA	Replacement of a DME item
RB	Replacement of a part of DME furnished as part of a repair
RC	Right coronary artery
RD	Drug provided to beneficiary, but not administered "incident-to"
RE	Furnished in full compliance with FDA-mandated risk evaluation and mitigation strategy (REMS)
RR	Rental (use the RR modifier when DME is to be rented)
RT	Right side (used to identify procedures performed on the right side of the body)
SA	Nurse practitioner rendering service in collaboration with a physician
SB	Nurse midwife
SC	Medically necessary service or supply
SD	Services provided by registered nurse with specialized, highly technical home infusion training
SE	State and/or federally-funded programs/services
SF	Second opinion ordered by a professional review organization (PRO) per section 9401, p.l. 99-272 (100% reimbursement - no Medicare deductible or coinsurance)
SG	Ambulatory surgical center (ASC) facility service
SH	Second concurrently administered infusion therapy
SJ	Third or more concurrently administered infusion therapy
SK	Member of high risk population (use only with codes for immunization)
SL	State supplied vaccine
SM	Second surgical opinion
SN	Third surgical opinion
SQ	Item ordered by home health
SS	Home infusion services provided in the infusion suite of the IV therapy provider

ST Related to trauma or injury

SU Procedure performed in physician's office (to denote use of facility and equipment)

SV Pharmaceuticals delivered to patient's home but not utilized

SW Services provided by a certified diabetic educator

SY Persons who are in close contact with member of high-risk population (use only with codes for immunization)

T1 Left foot, 2nd digit

T2 Left foot, 3rd digit

T3 Left foot, 4th digit

T4 Left foot, 5th digit

T5 Right foot, great toe

T6 Right foot, 2nd digit

T7 Right foot, 3rd digit

T8 Right foot, 4th digit

T9 Right foot, 5th digit

TA Left foot, great toe

TC Technical component. Under certain circumstances, a charge may be made for the technical component alone. Under those circumstances the technical component charge is identified by adding modifier 'TC' to the usual procedure number. Technical component charges are institutional charges and not billed separately by physicians. However, portable x-ray suppliers only bill for technical component and should utilize modifier TC. The charge data from portable x-ray suppliers will then be used to build customary and prevailing profiles.

TD RN

TE LPN/LVN

TF Intermediate level of care

TG Complex/high tech level of care

TH Obstetrical treatment/services, prenatal or postpartum

TJ Program group, child and/or adolescent

TK Extra patient or passenger, nonambulance

TL Early intervention/individualized family service plan (IFSP)

TM Individualized education program (IEP)

TN Rural/outside providers' customary service area

TP Medical transport, unloaded vehicle

TQ Basic life support (BSL) transport by a volunteer ambulance provider

TR School-based individualized education program (IEP) services provided outside the public school district responsible for the student

TS Follow-up service

TT Individualized service provided to more than one patient in same setting

TU Special payment rate, overtime

TV Special payment rates, holidays/weekends

TW Back-up equipment

U1 Medicaid level of care 1, as defined by each state

U2 Medicaid level of care 2, as defined by each state

U3 Medicaid level of care 3, as defined by each state

U4 Medicaid level of care 4, as defined by each state

U5 Medicaid level of care 5, as defined by each state

U6 Medicaid level of care 6, as defined by each state

U7 Medicaid level of care 7, as defined by each state

U8 Medicaid level of care 8, as defined by each state

U9 Medicaid level of care 9, as defined by each state

UA Medicaid level of care 10, as defined by each state

UB Medicaid level of care 11, as defined by each state

UC Medicaid level of care 12, as defined by each state

UD Medicaid level of care 13, as defined by each state

UE Used durable medical equipment

UF Services provided in the morning

UG Services provided in the afternoon

UH Services provided in the evening

UJ Services provided at night

UK Services provided on behalf of the client to someone other than the client (collateral relationship)

UN Two patients served

UP Three patients served

UQ Four patients served

UR Five patients served

US Six or more patients served

VP Aphakic patient

APPENDIX 3 — ABBREVIATIONS AND ACRONYMS

HCPCS Abbreviations and Acronyms

The following abbreviations and acronyms are used in the HCPCS descriptions:

/	or
<	less than
<=	less than equal to
>	greater than
>=	greater than equal to
AC	alternating current
AFO	ankle-foot orthosis
AICC	anti-inhibitor coagulant complex
AK	above the knee
AKA	above knee amputation
ALS	advanced life support
AMP	ampule
ART	artery
ART	Arterial
ASC	ambulatory surgery center
ATT	attached
A-V	Arteriovenous
AVF	arteriovenous fistula
BICROS	bilateral routing of signals
BK	below the knee
BLS	basic life support
BMI	body mass index
BP	blood pressure
BTE	behind the ear (hearing aid)
CAPD	continuous ambulatory peritoneal dialysis
Carb	carbohydrate
CBC	complete blood count
cc	cubic centimeter
CCPD	continuous cycling peritoneal analysis
CHF	congestive heart failure
CIC	completely in the canal (hearing aid)
CIM	Coverage Issue Manual
Clsd	closed
cm	centimeter
CMN	certificate of medical necessity
CMS	Centers for Medicare and Medicaid Services
CMV	Cytomegalovirus
Conc	concentrate
Conc	concentrated
Cont	continuous
CP	clinical psychologist
CPAP	continuous positive airway pressure
CPT	Current Procedural Terminology
CRF	chronic renal failure
CRNA	certified registered nurse anesthetist
CROS	contralateral routing of signals
CSW	clinical social worker
CT	computed tomography
CTLSO	cervical-thoracic-lumbar-sacral orthosis
cu	cubic
DC	direct current
DI	diurnal rhythm
Dx	diagnosis
DLI	donor leukocyte infusion
DME	durable medical equipment
DME MAC	durable medical equipment Medicare administrative contractor
DMEPOS	Durable Medical Equipment, Prosthestics, Orthotics and Other Supplies
DMERC	durable medical equipment regional carrier
DR	diagnostic radiology
DX	diagnostic
e.g.	for example
Ea	each
ECF	extended care facility
EEG	electroencephalogram
EKG	electrocardiogram
EMG	electromyography
EO	elbow orthosis
EP	electrophysiologic
EPO	epoetin alfa
EPSDT	early periodic screening, diagnosis and treatment
ESRD	end-stage renal disease
Ex	extended
Exper	experimental
Ext	external
F	french
FDA	Food and Drug Administration
FDG-PET	Positron emission with tomography with 18 fluorodeoxyglucose
Fem	female
FO	finger orthosis
FPD	fixed partial denture
Fr	french
ft	foot
G-CSF	filgrastim (granulocyte colony-stimulating factor)
gm	gram (g)
H2O	water
HCl	hydrochloric acid, hydrochloride
HCPCS	Healthcare Common Procedural Coding System
HCT	hematocrit
HFO	hand-finger orthosis
HHA	home health agency
HI	high
HI-LO	high-low
HIT	home infusion therapy
HKAFO	hip-knee-ankle foot orthosis
HLA	human leukocyte antigen
HMES	heat and moisture exchange system
HNPCC	hereditary non-polyposis colorectal cancer
HO	hip orthosis
HPSA	health professional shortage area
HST	home sleep test
IA	intra-arterial administration
ip	interphalangeal
I-131	Iodine 131
ICF	intermediate care facility
ICU	intensive care facility
IM	intramuscular
in	inch
INF	infusion
INH	inhalation solution
INJ	injection
IOL	intraocular lens
IPD	intermittent peritoneal dialysis
IPPB	intermittent positive pressure breathing
IT	intrathecal administration
ITC	in the canal (hearing aid)
ITE	in the ear (hearing aid)

APPENDIX 3 — ABBREVIATIONS AND ACRONYMS

IU	international units
IV	intravenous
IVF	in vitro fertilization
KAFO	knee-ankle-foot orthosis
KO	knee orthosis
KOH	potassium hydroxide
L	left
LASIK	laser in situ keratomileusis
LAUP	laser assisted uvulopalatoplasty
lbs	pounds
LDL	low density lipoprotein
Lo	low
LPM	liters per minute
LPN/LVN	Licensed Practical Nurse/Licensed Vocational Nurse
LSO	lumbar-sacral orthosis
MAC	Medicare administrative contractor
mp	metacarpophalangeal
mcg	microgram
mCi	millicurie
MCM	Medicare Carriers Manual
MCP	metacarparpophalangeal joint
MCP	monthly capitation payment
mEq	milliequivalent
MESA	microsurgical epididymal sperm aspiration
mg	milligram
mgs	milligrams
MHT	megahertz
ml	milliliter
mm	millimeter
mmHg	millimeters of Mercury
MRA	magnetic resonance angiography
MRI	magnetic resonance imaging
NA	sodium
NCI	National Cancer Institute
NEC	not elsewhere classified
NG	nasogastric
NH	nursing home
NMES	neuromuscular electrical stimulation
NOC	not otherwise classified
NOS	not otherwise specified
O2	oxygen
OBRA	Omnibus Budget Reconciliation Act
OMT	osteopathic manipulation therapy
OPPS	outpatient prospective payment system
ORAL	oral administration
OSA	obstructive sleep apnea
Ost	ostomy
OTH	other routes of administration
oz	ounce
PA	physician's assistant
PAR	parenteral
PCA	patient controlled analgesia
PCH	pouch
PEN	parenteral and enteral nutrition
PENS	percutaneous electrical nerve stimulation
PET	positron emission tomography
PHP	pre-paid health plan
PHP	physician hospital plan
PI	paramedic intercept
PICC	peripherally inserted central venous catheter
PKR	photorefractive keratotomy
Pow	powder
PRK	photoreactive keratectomy
PRO	peer review organization
PSA	prostate specific antigen
PTB	patellar tendon bearing
PTK	phototherapeutic keratectomy
PVC	polyvinyl chloride
R	right
Repl	replacc
RN	registered nurse
RP	retrograde pyelogram
Rx	prescription
SACH	solid ankle, cushion heel
SC	subcutaneous
SCT	specialty care transport
SEO	shoulder-elbow orthosis
SEWHO	shoulder-elbow-wrist-hand orthosis
SEXA	single energy x-ray absorptiometry
SGD	speech generating device
SGD	sinus rhythm
SM	samarium
SNCT	sensory nerve conduction test
SNF	skilled nursing facility
SO	sacroilliac othrosis
SO	shoulder orthosis
Sol	solution
SQ	square
SR	screen
ST	standard
ST	sustained release
Syr	syrup
TABS	tablets
Tc	Technetium
Tc 99m	technetium isotope
TENS	transcutaneous electrical nerve stimulator
THKAO	thoracic-hip-knee-ankle orthosis
TLSO	thoracic-lumbar-sacral-orthosis
TM	temporomandibular
TMJ	temporomandibular joint
TPN	total parenteral nutrition
U	unit
uCi	microcurie
VAR	various routes of administration
w	with
w/	with
w/o	with or without
WAK	wearable artificial kidney
wc	wheelchair
WHFO	wrist-hand-finger orthotic
Wk	week
w/o	without
Xe	xenon (isotope mass of xenon 133)

APPENDIX 4 — PUB 100 REFERENCES

The Centers for Medicare and Medicaid Services restructured its paper-based manual system as a web-based system on October 1, 2003. Called the online CMS manual system, it combines all of the various program instructions into internet-only manuals (IOMs), which are used by all CMS programs and contractors. Complete versions of all of the manuals can be found at http://www.cms.hhs.gov/manuals.

Effective September 30, 2003, the former method of publishing program memoranda (PMs) to communicate program instructions was replaced by the following four templates:

- One-time notification
- Manual revisions
- Business requirements
- Confidential requirements

The web-based system has been organized by functional area (e.g., eligibility, entitlement, claims processing, benefit policy, program integrity) in an effort to eliminate redundancy within the manuals, simplify updating, and make CMS program instructions available more quickly. The web-based system contains the functional areas included below:

Pub. 100	Introduction
Pub. 100-1	Medicare General Information, Eligibility, and Entitlement Manual
Pub. 100-2	Medicare Benefit Policy Manual
Pub. 100-3	Medicare National Coverage Determinations Manual
Pub. 100-4	Medicare Claims Processing Manual
Pub. 100-5	Medicare Secondary Payer Manual
Pub. 100-6	Medicare Financial Management Manual
Pub. 100-7	State Operations Manual
Pub. 100-8	Medicare Program Integrity Manual
Pub. 100-9	Medicare Contractor Beneficiary and Provider Communications Manual
Pub. 100-10	Quality Improvement Organization Manual
Pub. 100-11	Reserved
Pub. 100-12	State Medicaid Manual (under development)
Pub. 100-13	Medicaid State Children's Health Insurance Program (under development)
Pub. 100-14	Medicare ESRD Network Organizations Manual
Pub. 100-15	State Buy-In Manual
Pub. 100-16	Medicare Managed Care Manual
Pub. 100-17	CMS/Business Partners Systems Security Manual
Pub. 100-18	Reserved
Pub. 100-19	Demonstrations
Pub. 100-20	One-Time Notification
Pub. 100-21	Recurring Update Notification

A brief description of the Medicare manuals primarily used for *CPC Expert* follows:

The **National Coverage Determinations Manual** (NCD), is organized according to categories such as diagnostic services, supplies, and medical procedures. The table of contents lists each category and subject within that category. Revision transmittals identify any new or background material, recap the changes, and provide an effective date for the change.

When complete, the manual will contain two chapters. Chapter 1 currently includes a description of CMS's national coverage determinations. When available, chapter 2 will contain a list of HCPCS codes related to each coverage determination. The manual is organized in accordance with CPT category sequences.

The **Medicare Benefit Policy Manual** contains Medicare general coverage instructions that are not national coverage determinations. As a general rule, in the past these instructions have been found in chapter II of the **Medicare Carriers Manual**, the **Medicare Intermediary Manual**, other provider manuals, and program memoranda.

The **Medicare Claims Processing Manual** contains instructions for processing claims for contractors and providers.

The **Medicare Program Integrity Manual** communicates the priorities and standards for the Medicare integrity programs.

100-1,1,10.1

Hospital Insurance (Part A) for Inpatient Hospital, Hospice, Home Health and Skilled Nursing Facility (SNF) Services - A Brief Description

Hospital insurance is designed to help patients defray the expenses incurred by hospitalization and related care. In addition to inpatient hospital benefits, hospital insurance covers post hospital extended care in SNFs and post hospital care furnished by a home health agency in the patient's home. Blood clotting factors, for hemophilia patients competent to use such factors to control bleeding without medical or other supervision, and items related to the administration of such factors, are also a Part A benefit for beneficiaries in a covered Part A stay. The purpose of these additional benefits is to provide continued treatment after hospitalization and to encourage the appropriate use of more economical alternatives to inpatient hospital care. Program payments for services rendered to beneficiaries by providers (i.e., hospitals, SNFs, and home health agencies) are generally made to the provider. In each benefit period, payment may be made for up to 90 inpatient hospital days, and 100 days of post hospital extended care services .Hospices also provide Part A hospital insurance services such as short-term inpatient care. In order to be eligible to elect hospice care under Medicare, an individual must be entitled to Part A of Medicare and be certified as being terminally ill. An individual is considered to be terminally ill if the individual has a medical prognosis that his or her life expectancy is 6 months or less if the illness runs its normal course.

100-1,3,20.5

Blood Deductibles (Part A and Part B)

Program payment may not be made for the first 3 pints of whole blood or equivalent units of packed red cells received under Part A and Part B combined in a calendar year. However, blood processing (e.g., administration, storage) is not subject to the deductible.

The blood deductibles are in addition to any other applicable deductible and coinsurance amounts for which the patient is responsible.

The deductible applies only to the first 3 pints of blood furnished in a calendar year, even if more than one provider furnished blood.

100-1,3,20.5.2

Part B Blood Deductible

Blood is furnished on an outpatient basis or is subject to the Part B blood deductible and is counted toward the combined limit. It should be noted that payment for blood may be made to the hospital under Part B only for blood furnished in an outpatient setting. Blood is not covered for inpatient Part B services.

100-1,3,20.5.3

Items Subject to Blood Deductibles

The blood deductibles apply only to whole blood and packed red cells. The term whole blood means human blood from which none of the liquid or cellular components have been removed. Where packed red cells are furnished, a unit of packed red cells is considered equivalent to a pint of whole blood. Other components of blood such as platelets, fibrinogen, plasma, gamma globulin, and serum albumin are not subject to the blood deductible. However, these components of blood are covered as biologicals.

Refer to Pub. 100-04, Medicare Claims Processing Manual, chapter 4, Sec.231 regarding billing for blood and blood products under the Hospital Outpatient Prospective Payment System (OPPS).

100-1,5,90.2

Laboratory Defined

Laboratory means a facility for the biological, microbiological, serological, chemical, immuno-hematological, hematological, biophysical, cytological, pathological, or other examination of materials derived from the human body for the purpose of providing information for the diagnosis, prevention, or treatment of any disease or impairment of, or the assessment of the health of, human beings. These examinations also include procedures to determine, measure, or otherwise describe the presence or absence of various substances or organisms in the body. Facilities only collecting or preparing specimens (or both) or only serving as a mailing service and not performing testing are not considered laboratories.

100-2,1,10

Covered Inpatient Hospital Services Covered Under Part A

A3-3101, HO-210

Patients covered under hospital insurance are entitled to have payment made on their behalf for inpatient hospital services. (Inpatient hospital services do not include extended care services provided by hospitals pursuant to swing bed approvals. See Pub. 100-1, Chapter 8, Sec.10.1, "Hospital Providers of Extended Care Services."). However, both inpatient hospital and inpatient SNF benefits are provided under Part A - Hospital Insurance Benefits for the Aged and Disabled, of Title XVIII).

Additional information concerning the following topics can be found in the following manual chapters:

- Benefit periods is found in Chapter 3, "Duration of Covered Inpatient Services";
- Copayment days is found in Chapter 2, "Duration of Covered Inpatient Services";
- Lifetime reserve days is found in Chapter 5, "Lifetime Reserve Days";
- Related payment information is housed in the Provider Reimbursement Manual.

Blood must be furnished on a day which counts as a day of inpatient hospital services to be covered as a Part A service and to count toward the blood deductible. Thus, blood is not covered under Part A and does not count toward the Part A blood deductible when furnished to an inpatient after the inpatient has exhausted all benefit days in a benefit period, or where the individual has elected not to use lifetime reserve days. However, where the patient is discharged on their first day of entitlement or on the hospital's first day of participation, the hospital is permitted to submit a billing form with no accommodation charge, but with ancillary charges including blood.

The records for all Medicare hospital inpatient discharges are maintained in CMS for statistical analysis and use in determining future PPS DRG classifications and rates.

Non-PPS hospitals do not pay for noncovered services generally excluded from coverage in the Medicare Program. This may result in denial of a part of the billed charges or in denial of the entire admission, depending upon circumstance. In PPS hospitals, the following are also possible:

1. In appropriately admitted cases where a noncovered procedure was performed, denied services may result in payment of a different DRG (i.e., one which excludes payment for the noncovered procedure); or
2. In appropriately admitted cases that become cost outlier cases, denied services may lead to denial of some or all of an outlier payment.

The following examples illustrate this principle. If care is noncovered because a patient does not need to be hospitalized, the intermediary denies the admission and makes no Part A (i.e., PPS) payment unless paid under limitation on liability. Under limitation on liability, Medicare payment may be made when the provider and the beneficiary were not aware the services were not necessary and could not reasonably be expected to know that he services were not necessary. For detailed instructions, see the Medicare Claims Processing Manual, Chapter 30,"Limitation on Liability." If a patient is appropriately hospitalized but receives (beyond routine services) only noncovered care, the admission is denied.

NOTE: The intermediary does not deny an admission that includes covered care, even if noncovered care was also rendered. Under PPS, Medicare assumes that it is paying for only the covered care rendered whenever covered services needed to treat and/or diagnose the illness were in fact provided.

If a noncovered procedure is provided along with covered nonroutine care, a DRG change rather than an admission denial might occur. If noncovered procedures are elevating costs into the cost outlier category, outlier payment is denied in whole or in part.

When the hospital is included in PPS, most of the subsequent discussion regarding coverage of inpatient hospital services is relevant only in the context of determining the appropriateness of admissions, which DRG, if any, to pay, and the appropriateness of payment for any outlier cases.

If a patient receives items or services in excess of, or more expensive than, those for which payment can be made, payment is made only for the covered items or services or for only the appropriate prospective payment amount. This provision applies not only to inpatient services, but also to all hospital services under Parts A and B of the program. If the items or services were requested by the patient, the hospital may charge him the difference between the amount customarily charged for the services requested and the amount customarily charged for covered services.

An inpatient is a person who has been admitted to a hospital for bed occupancy for purposes of receiving inpatient hospital services. Generally, a patient is considered an inpatient if formally admitted as inpatient with the expectation that he or she will remain at least overnight and occupy a bed even though it later develops that the patient can be discharged or transferred to another hospital and not actually use a hospital bed overnight.

The physician or other practitioner responsible for a patient's care at the hospital is also responsible for deciding whether the patient should be admitted as an inpatient. Physicians should use a 24-hour period as a benchmark, i.e., they should order admission for patients who are expected to need hospital care for 24 hours or more, and treat other patients on an outpatient basis. However, the decision to admit a patient is a complex medical judgment which can be made only after the physician has considered a number of factors, including the patient's medical history and current medical needs, the types of facilities available to inpatients and to outpatients, the hospital's by-laws and admissions policies, and the relative appropriateness of treatment in each setting. Factors to be considered when making the decision to admit include such things as:

The severity of the signs and symptoms exhibited by the patient;

The medical predictability of something adverse happening to the patient;

The need for diagnostic studies that appropriately are outpatient services (i.e., their performance does not ordinarily require the patient to remain at the hospital for 24 hours or more) to assist in assessing whether the patient should be admitted; and

The availability of diagnostic procedures at the time when and at the location where the patient presents.

Admissions of particular patients are not covered or noncovered solely on the basis of the length of time the patient actually spends in the hospital. In certain specific situations coverage of services on an inpatient or outpatient basis is determined by the following rules:

Minor Surgery or Other Treatment - When patients with known diagnoses enter a hospital for a specific minor surgical procedure or other treatment that is expected to keep them in the hospital for only a few hours (less than 24), they are considered outpatients for coverage purposes regardless of: the hour they came to the hospital, whether they used a bed, and whether they remained in the hospital past midnight.

Renal Dialysis - Renal dialysis treatments are usually covered only as outpatient services but may under certain circumstances be covered as inpatient services depending on the patient's condition. Patients staying at home, who are ambulatory, whose conditions are stable and who come to the hospital for routine chronic dialysis treatments, and not for a diagnostic workup or a change in therapy, are considered outpatients. On the other hand, patients undergoing short-term dialysis until their kidneys recover from an acute illness (acute dialysis), or persons with borderline renal failure who develop acute renal failure every time they have an illness and require dialysis (episodic dialysis) are usually inpatients. A patient may begin dialysis as an inpatient and then progress to an outpatient status.

Under original Medicare, the Quality Improvement Organization (QIO), for each hospital is responsible for deciding, during review of inpatient admissions on a case-by-case basis, whether the admission was medically necessary. Medicare law authorizes the QIO to make these judgments, and the judgments are binding for purposes of Medicare coverage. In making these judgments, however, QIOs consider only the medical evidence which was available to the physician at the time an admission decision had to be made. They do not take into account other information (e.g., test results) which became available only after admission, except in cases where considering the post-admission information would support a finding that an admission was medically necessary.

Refer to Parts 4 and 7 of the QIO Manual with regard to initial determinations for these services. The QIO will review the swing bed services in these PPS hospitals as well.

NOTE: When patients requiring extended care services are admitted to beds in a hospital, they are considered inpatients of the hospital. In such cases, the services furnished in the hospital will not be considered extended care services, and payment may not be made under the program for such services unless the services are extended care services furnished pursuant to a swing bed agreement granted to the hospital by the Secretary of Health and Human Services.

100-2,1,10.1.4

Charges for Deluxe Private Room

A3-3101.1.D, HO-210.1.D

Beneficiaries found to need a private room (either because they need isolation for medical reasons or because they need immediate admission when no other accommodations are available) may be assigned to any of the provider's private rooms. They do not have the right to insist on the private room of their choice, but their preferences should be given the same consideration as if they were paying all provider charges themselves. The program does not, under any circumstances, pay for personal comfort items. Thus, the program does not pay for deluxe accommodations and/or services. These would include a suite, or a room substantially more spacious than is required for treatment, or specially equipped or decorated, or serviced for the comfort and convenience of persons willing to pay a differential for such amenities. If the beneficiary (or representative) requests such deluxe accommodations, the provider should advise that there will be a charge, not covered by Medicare, of a specified amount per day (not exceeding the differential defined in the next sentence); and may charge the beneficiary that amount for each day he/she occupies the deluxe accommodations. The maximum amount the provider may charge the beneficiary for such accommodations is the differential between the most prevalent private room rate at the time of admission and the customary charge for the room occupied. Beneficiaries may not be charged this differential if they (or their representative) do not request the deluxe accommodations.

The beneficiary may not be charged such a differential in private room rates if that differential is based on factors other than personal comfort items. Such factors might include differences between older and newer wings, proximity to lounge, elevators or nursing stations, desirable view, etc. Such rooms are standard 1-bed units and not deluxe rooms for purposes of these instructions, even though the provider may call them deluxe and have a higher customary charge for them. No additional charge may be imposed upon the beneficiary who is assigned to a room that may be somewhat more desirable because of these factors.

100-2,1,40

Supplies, Appliances, and Equipment

Supplies, appliances, and equipment, which are ordinarily furnished by the hospital for the care and treatment of the beneficiary solely during the inpatient hospital stay, are covered inpatient hospital services.

Under certain circumstances, supplies, appliances, and equipment used during the beneficiary's inpatient stay are covered under Part A even though the supplies, appliances and equipment leave the hospital with the patient upon discharge. These are circumstances in which it would be unreasonable or impossible from a medical standpoint to limit the patient's use of the item to the periods during which the individual is an inpatient. Examples of items covered under this rule are:

- Items permanently installed in or attached to the patient's body while an inpatient, such as cardiac valves, cardiac pacemakers, and artificial limbs; and
- Items which are temporarily installed in or attached to the patient's body while an inpatient, and which are also necessary to permit or facilitate the patient's release from the hospital, such as tracheotomy or drainage tubes.

Hospital "admission packs" containing primarily toilet articles, such as soap, toothbrushes, toothpaste, and combs, are covered under Part A if routinely furnished by the hospital to all its inpatients. If not routinely furnished to all patients, the packs are not covered. In that situation, the hospital may charge beneficiaries for the pack, but only if they request it with knowledge of what they are requesting and what the charge to them will be.

Supplies, appliances, and equipment furnished to an inpatient for use only outside the hospital are not, in general, covered as inpatient hospital services. However, a temporary or disposable item, which is medically necessary to permit or facilitate the patient's departure from the hospital and is required until the patient can obtain a continuing supply, is covered as an inpatient hospital service.

Oxygen furnished to hospital inpatients is covered under Part A as an inpatient supply.

100-2,10,20

Coverage Guidelines for Ambulance Service Claims

B3-2125

Payment may be made for expenses incurred by a patient for ambulance service provided conditions l, 2, and 3 in the left-hand column have been met. The right-hand column indicates the documentation needed to establish that the condition has been met.

Conditions	Review Action
1. Patient was transported by an approved supplier of ambulance services.	1. Ambulance supplier is listed in the table of approved ambulance companies (§10.1.3)
2. The patient was suffering from an illness or injury, which contraindicated transportation by other means. (§10.2)	2. (a) The contractor presumes the requirement was met if the submitted documentation indicates that the patient: • Was transported in an emergency situation, e.g., as a result of an accident, injury or acute illness, or • Needed to be restrained to prevent injury to the beneficiary or others; or • Was unconscious or in shock; or • Required oxygen or other emergency treatment during transport to the nearest appropriate facility; or • Exhibits signs and symptoms of acute respiratory distress or cardiac distress such as shortness of breath or chest pain; or • Exhibits signs and symptoms that indicate the possibility of acute stroke; or • Had to remain immobile because of a fracture that had not been set or the possibility of a fracture; or • Was experiencing severe hemorrhage; or • Could be moved only by stretcher; or • Was bed-confined before and after the ambulance trip. (b) In the absence of any of the conditions listed in (a)above additional documentation should be obtained to establish medical need where the evidence indicates the existence of the circumstances listed below: (i) Patient's condition would not ordinarily require movement by stretcher, or (ii) The individual was not admitted as a hospital inpatient (except in accident cases), or (iii) The ambulance was used solely because other means of transportation were unavailable, or (iv) The individual merely needed assistance in getting from his room or home to a vehicle. (c) Where the information indicates a situation not listed in 2(a) or 2(b) above, refer the case to your supervisor.
3. The patient was transported from and to points listed below.	3. Claims should show the ZIP code of the point of pickup
(a) From patient's residence (or other place where need arose) to hospital or skilled nursing facility.	(a) i. Condition met if trip began within the institution's service area as shown in the carrier's locality guide ii. Condition met where the trip began outside the institution's service area if the institution was the nearest one with appropriate facilities.

NOTE: A patient's residence is the place where he or she makes his/her home and dwells permanently, or for an extended period of time. A skilled nursing facility is one, which is listed in the Directory of Medical Facilities as a participating SNF or as an institution which meets §1861(j)(1) of the Act.

NOTE: A claim for ambulance service to a participating hospital or skilled nursing facility should not be denied on the grounds that there is a nearer nonparticipating institution having appropriate facilities.

Conditions	Review Action
(b) Skilled nursing facility to a hospital or hospital to a skilled nursing facility.	(b) (i) Condition met if the ZIP code of the pickup point is within the service area of the destination as shown in the carrier's locality guide. (ii) Condition met where the ZIP code of the pickup point is outside the service area of the destination if the destination institution was the nearest appropriate facility.
(c) Hospital to hospital or skilled nursing facility to skilled nursing facility.	(c) Condition met if the discharging institution was not an appropriate facility and the admitting institution was the nearest appropriate facility.
(d) From a hospital or skilled nursing facility to patient's residence.	(d) (i) Condition met if patient's residence is within the institution's service area as shown in the carrier's locality guide. (ii) Condition met where the patient's residence is outside the institution's service area if the institution was the nearest appropriate facility.
(e) Round trip for hospital or participating skilled nursing facility inpatients to the nearest hospital or nonhospital treatment facility.	(e) Condition met if the reasonable and necessary diagnostic or therapeutic service required by patient's condition is not available at the institution where the beneficiary is an inpatient.

NOTE: Ambulance service to a physician's office or a physician-directed clinic is not covered. See §10.3.7 above, where a stop is made at a physician's office en route to a hospital and §10.3.3 for additional exceptions.)

4. Ambulance services involving hospital admissions in Canada or Mexico are covered (Medicare Claims Processing Manual, Chapter 1, "General Billing Requirements, " §§10.1.3.) if the following conditions are met:	(a) The foreign hospitalization has been determined to be covered; and (b) The ambulance service meets the coverage requirements set forth in §§10-10.3. If the foreign hospitalization has been determined to be covered on the basis of emergency services (See the Medicare Claims Processing Manual, Chapter 1, "General Billing Requirements," §10.1.3), the necessity requirement (§10.2) and the destination requirement (§10.3) are considered met.
5. The carrier will make partial payment for otherwise covered ambulance service, which exceeded limits defined in item	(a) From the pickup point to the nearest appropriate facility, or (b) From the nearest appropriate facility to the beneficiary's residence where he or she is being returned home from a distant institution.
6. The carrier will base the payment on the amount payable had the patient been transported:	

100-2,13,30

Rural Health Clinic and Federally Qualified Health Center Service Defined

Payments for covered RHC/FQHC services furnished to Medicare beneficiaries are made on the basis of an all-inclusive rate per covered visit (except for pneumococcal and influenza vaccines and their administration, which is paid at 100 percent of reasonable cost). The term "visit" is defined as a face-to-face encounter between the patient and a physician, physician assistant, nurse practitioner, certified nurse midwife, visiting nurse, clinical psychologist, or clinical social worker during which an RHC/FQHC service is rendered. As a result of section 5114 of the Deficit Reduction Act of 2005 (DRA), the FQHC definition of a face-to-face encounter is expanded to include encounters with qualified practitioners of Outpatient Diabetes Self-Management Training Services (DSMT) and medical nutrition therapy (MNT) services when the FQHC meets all relevant program requirements for the provision of such services.

Encounters with (1) more than one health professional; and (2) multiple encounters with the same health professional which take place on the same day and at a single location, constitute a single visit. An exception occurs in cases in which the patient, subsequent to the first encounter, suffers an illness or injury requiring additional diagnosis or treatment.

100-2,15,100

Surgical Dressings, Splints, Casts, and Other Devices Used for Reductions of Fractures and Dislocations

B3-2079, A3-3110.3, HO-228.3

Surgical dressings are limited to primary and secondary dressings required for the treatment of a wound caused by, or treated by, a surgical procedure that has been performed by a physician or other health care professional to the extent permissible under State law. In addition, surgical dressings required after debridement of a wound are also covered, irrespective of the type of debridement, as long as the debridement was reasonable and necessary and was performed by a health care professional acting within the scope of his/her legal authority when performing this function. Surgical dressings are covered for as long as they are medically necessary. Primary dressings are therapeutic or protective coverings applied directly to wounds or lesions either on the skin or caused by an opening to the skin. Secondary dressing materials that serve a therapeutic or protective function and that are needed to secure a primary dressing are also covered. Items such as adhesive tape, roll gauze, bandages, and disposable compression material are examples of secondary dressings. Elastic stockings, support hose, foot coverings, leotards, knee supports, surgical leggings, gauntlets, and pressure garments for the arms and hands are examples of items that are not ordinarily covered as surgical dressings. Some items, such as transparent film, may be used as a primary or secondary dressing. If a physician, certified nurse midwife, physician assistant, nurse practitioner, or clinical nurse specialist applies surgical dressings as part of a professional service that is billed to Medicare, the surgical dressings are considered incident to the professional services of the health care practitioner. (See Sec. 60.1, 180, 190, 200, and 210.) When surgical dressings are not covered incident to the services of a health care practitioner and are obtained by the patient from a supplier (e.g., a drugstore, physician, or other health care practitioner that qualifies as a supplier) on an order from a physician or other health care professional authorized under State law or regulation to make such an order, the surgical dressings are covered separately under Part B. Splints and casts, and other devices used for reductions of fractures and dislocations are covered under Part B of Medicare. This includes dental splints.

100-2,15,110

Durable Medical Equipment - General

B3-2100, A3-3113, HO-235, HHA-220

Expenses incurred by a beneficiary for the rental or purchases of durable medical equipment (DME) are reimbursable if the following three requirements are met:

- The equipment meets the definition of DME (Sec.110.1);
- The equipment is necessary and reasonable for the treatment of the patient's illness or injury or to improve the functioning of his or her malformed body member (Sec.110.1); and
- The equipment is used in the patient's home. The decision whether to rent or purchase an item of equipment generally resides with the beneficiary, but the decision on how to pay rests with CMS. For some DME, program payment policy calls for lump sum payments and in others for periodic payment. Where covered DME is furnished to a beneficiary by a supplier of services other than a provider of services, the DMERC makes the reimbursement. If a provider of services furnishes the equipment, the intermediary makes the reimbursement. The payment method is identified in the annual fee schedule update furnished by CMS. The CMS issues quarterly updates to a fee schedule file that contains rates by HCPCS code and also identifies the classification of the HCPCS code within the following categories. Category Code Definition IN Inexpensive and Other Routinely Purchased Items FS Frequently Serviced Items CR Capped Rental Items OX Oxygen and Oxygen Equipment OS Ostomy, Tracheostomy & Urological Items SD Surgical Dressings PO Prosthetics & Orthotics SU Supplies TE Transcutaneous Electrical Nerve Stimulators The DMERCs, carriers, and intermediaries, where appropriate, use the CMS files to determine payment rules. See the Medicare Claims Processing Manual, Chapter 20, "Durable Medical Equipment, Surgical Dressings and Casts, Orthotics and Artificial Limbs, and Prosthetic Devices," for a detailed description of payment rules for each classification. Payment may also be made for repairs, maintenance, and delivery of equipment and for expendable and nonreusable items essential to the effective use of the equipment subject to the conditions in Sec.110.2. See the Medicare Benefit Policy Manual, Chapter 11, "End Stage Renal Disease," for hemodialysis equipment and supplies.

100-2,15,110.1

Definition of Durable Medical Equipment

B3-2100.1, A3-3113.1, HO-235.1, HHA-220.1, B3-2100.2, A3-3113.2, HO-235.2, HHA-220.2

- Durable medical equipment is equipment which:
- Can withstand repeated use;
- Is primarily and customarily used to serve a medical purpose;
- Generally is not useful to a person in the absence of an illness or injury; and

- Is appropriate for use in the home.

All requirements of the definition must be met before an item can be considered to be durable medical equipment. The following describes the underlying policies for determining whether an item meets the definition of DME and may be covered.

A. Durability

An item is considered durable if it can withstand repeated use, i.e., the type of item that could normally be rented. Medical supplies of an expendable nature, such as incontinent pads, lambs wool pads, catheters, ace bandages, elastic stockings, surgical facemasks, irrigating kits, sheets, and bags are not considered "durable" within the meaning of the definition. There are other items that, although durable in nature, may fall into other coverage categories such as supplies, braces, prosthetic devices, artificial arms, legs, and eyes.

B. Medical Equipment

Medical equipment is equipment primarily and customarily used for medical purposes and is not generally useful in the absence of illness or injury. In most instances, no development will be needed to determine whether a specific item of equipment is medical in nature. However, some cases will require development to determine whether the item constitutes medical equipment. This development would include the advice of local medical organizations (hospitals, medical schools, medical societies) and specialists in the field of physical medicine and rehabilitation. If the equipment is new on the market, it may be necessary, prior to seeking professional advice, to obtain information from the supplier or manufacturer explaining the design, purpose, effectiveness and method of using the equipment in the home as well as the results of any tests or clinical studies that have been conducted.

1. Equipment Presumptively
   MedicalItems such as hospital beds, wheelchairs, hemodialysis equipment, iron lungs, respirators, intermittent positive pressure breathing machines, medical regulators, oxygen tents, crutches, canes, trapeze bars, walkers, inhalators, nebulizers, commodes, suction machines, and traction equipment presumptively constitute medical equipment. (Although hemodialysis equipment is covered as a prosthetic device (Sec.120), it also meets the definition of DME, and reimbursement for the rental or purchase of such equipment for use in the beneficiary's home will be made only under the provisions for payment applicable to DME. See the Medicare Benefit Policy Manual, Chapter 11, "End Stage Renal Disease," Sec.30.1, for coverage of home use of hemodialysis.) NOTE: There is a wide variety in types of respirators and suction machines. The DMERC's medical staff should determine whether the apparatus specified in the claim is appropriate for home use.

2. Equipment Presumptively Nonmedical
   Equipment which is primarily and customarily used for a nonmedical purpose may not be considered "medical" equipment for which payment can be made under the medical insurance program. This is true even though the item has some remote medically related use. For example, in the case of a cardiac patient, an air conditioner might possibly be used to lower room temperature to reduce fluid loss in the patient and to restore an environment conducive to maintenance of the proper fluid balance. Nevertheless, because the primary and customary use of an air conditioner is a nonmedical one, the air conditioner cannot be deemed to be medical equipment for which payment can be made. Other devices and equipment used for environmental control or to enhance the environmental setting in which the beneficiary is placed are not considered covered DME. These include, for example, room heaters, humidifiers, dehumidifiers, and electric air cleaners. Equipment which basically serves comfort or convenience functions or is primarily for the convenience of a person caring for the patient, such as elevators, stairway elevators, and posture chairs, do not constitute medical equipment. Similarly, physical fitness equipment (such as an exercycle), first-aid or precautionary-type equipment (such as preset portable oxygen units), self-help devices (such as safety grab bars), and training equipment (such as Braille training texts) are considered nonmedical in nature.

3. Special Exception Items
   Specified items of equipment may be covered under certain conditions even though they do not meet the definition of DME because they are not primarily and customarily used to serve a medical purpose and/or are generally useful in the absence of illness or injury. These items would be covered when it is clearly established that they serve a therapeutic purpose in an individual case and would include:

a. Gel pads and pressure and water mattresses (which generally serve a preventive purpose) when prescribed for a patient who had bed sores or there is medical evidence indicating that they are highly susceptible to such ulceration; and

b. Heat lamps for a medical rather than a soothing or cosmetic purpose, e.g., where the need for heat therapy has been established.

In establishing medical necessity for the above items, the evidence must show that the item is included in the physician's course of treatment and a physician is supervising its use.

NOTE: The above items represent special exceptions and no extension of coverage to other items should be inferred

C. Necessary and Reasonable

Although an item may be classified as DME, it may not be covered in every instance. Coverage in a particular case is subject to the requirement that the equipment be necessary and reasonable for treatment of an illness or injury, or to improve the functioning of a malformed body member. These considerations will bar payment for equipment which cannot reasonably be expected to perform a therapeutic function in an individual case or will permit only partial therapeutic function in an individual case or will permit only partial payment when the type of equipment furnished substantially exceeds that required for the treatment of the illness or injury involved. See the Medicare Claims Processing Manual, Chapter 1, "General Billing Requirements;" Sec.60, regarding the rules for providing advance beneficiary notices (ABNs) that advise beneficiaries, before items or services actually are furnished, when Medicare is likely to deny payment for them. ABNs allow beneficiaries to make an informed consumer decision about receiving items or services for which they may have to pay out-of-pocket and to be more active participants in their own health care treatment decisions.

1. Necessity for the Equipment
   Equipment is necessary when it can be expected to make a meaningful contribution to the treatment of the patient's illness or injury or to the improvement of his or her malformed body member. In most cases the physician's prescription for the equipment and other medical information available to the DMERC will be sufficient to establish that the equipment serves this purpose.

2. Reasonableness of the Equipment
   Even though an item of DME may serve a useful medical purpose, the DMERC or intermediary must also consider to what extent, if any, it would be reasonable for the Medicare program to pay for the item prescribed. The following considerations should enter into the determination of reasonableness:

1. Would the expense of the item to the program be clearly disproportionate to the therapeutic benefits which could ordinarily be derived from use of the equipment?

2. Is the item substantially more costly than a medically appropriate and realistically feasible alternative pattern of care?

3. Does the item serve essentially the same purpose as equipment already available to the beneficiary?

3. Payment Consistent With What is Necessary and Reasonable
   Where a claim is filed for equipment containing features of an aesthetic nature or features of a medical nature which are not required by the patient's condition or where there exists a reasonably feasible and medically appropriate alternative pattern of care which is less costly than the equipment furnished, the amount payable is based on the rate for the equipment or alternative treatment which meets the patient's medical needs. The acceptance of an assignment binds the supplier-assignee to accept the payment for the medically required equipment or service as the full charge and the supplier-assignee cannot charge the beneficiary the differential attributable to the equipment actually furnished.

4. Establishing the Period of Medical Necessity
   Generally, the period of time an item of durable medical equipment will be considered to be medically necessary is based on the physician's estimate of the time that his or her patient will need the equipment. See the Medicare Program Integrity Manual, Chapters 5 and 6, for medical review guideline

D. Definition of a Beneficiary's Home

For purposes of rental and purchase of DME a beneficiary's home may be his/her own dwelling, an apartment, a relative's home, a home for the aged, or some other type of institution. However, an institution may not be considered a beneficiary's home if it:

- Meets at least the basic requirement in the definition of a hospital, i.e., it is primarily engaged in providing by or under the supervision of physicians, to inpatients, diagnostic and therapeutic services for medical diagnosis, treatment, and care of injured, disabled, and sick persons, or rehabilitation services for the rehabilitation of injured, disabled, or sick persons; or
- Meets at least the basic requirement in the definition of a skilled nursing facility, i.e., it is primarily engaged in providing to inpatients skilled nursing care and related services for patients who require medical or nursing care, or rehabilitation services for the rehabilitation of injured, disabled, or sick persons.

Thus, if an individual is a patient in an institution or distinct part of an institution which provides the services described in the bullets above, the individual is not entitled to have separate Part B payment made for rental or purchase of DME. This is because such an institution may not be considered the individual's home. The same concept applies even if the patient resides in a bed or portion of the institution not certified for Medicare.

If the patient is at home for part of a month and, for part of the same month is in an institution that cannot qualify as his or her home, or is outside the U.S., monthly payments may be made for the entire month. Similarly, if DME is returned to the provider before the end of a payment month because the beneficiary died in that month or because the equipment became unnecessary in that month, payment may be made for the entire month.

100-2,15,110.2

Repairs, Maintenance, Replacement, and Delivery

Under the circumstances specified below, payment may be made for repair, maintenance, and replacement of medically required DME, including equipment which had been in use before the user enrolled in Part B of the program. However, do not pay for repair, maintenance, or replacement of equipment in the frequent and substantial servicing or oxygen equipment payment categories. In addition, payments for repair and maintenance may not include payment for parts and labor covered under a manufacturer's or supplier's warranty.

A. Repairs

To repair means to fix or mend and to put the equipment back in good condition after damage or wear. Repairs to equipment which a beneficiary owns are covered when necessary to make the equipment serviceable. However, do not pay for repair of previously denied equipment or equipment in the frequent and substantial servicing or oxygen equipment payment categories. If the expense for repairs exceeds the estimated expense of purchasing or renting another item of equipment for the remaining period of medical need, no payment can be made for the amount of the excess. (See subsection C where claims for repairs suggest malicious damage or culpable neglect.) Since renters of equipment recover from the rental charge the expenses they incur in maintaining in working order the equipment they rent out, separately itemized charges for repair of rented equipment are not covered. This includes items in the frequent and substantial servicing, oxygen equipment, capped rental, and inexpensive or routinely purchased payment categories which are being rented. A new Certificate of Medical Necessity (CMN) and/or physician's order is not needed for repairs. For replacement items, see Subsection C below.

B. Maintenance

Routine periodic servicing, such as testing, cleaning, regulating, and checking of the beneficiary's equipment, is not covered. The owner is expected to perform such routine maintenance rather than a retailer or some other person who charges the beneficiary. Normally, purchasers of DME are given operating manuals which describe the type of servicing an owner may perform to properly maintain the equipment. It is reasonable to expect that beneficiaries will perform this maintenance. Thus, hiring a third party to do such work is for the convenience of the beneficiary and is not covered. However, more extensive maintenance which, based on the manufacturers' recommendations, is to be performed by authorized technicians, is covered as repairs for medically necessary equipment which a beneficiary owns. This might include, for example, breaking down sealed components and performing tests which require specialized testing equipment not available to the beneficiary. Do not pay for maintenance of purchased items that require frequent and substantial servicing or oxygen equipment. Since renters of equipment recover from the rental charge the expenses they incur in maintaining in working order the equipment they rent out, separately itemized charges for maintenance of rented equipment are generally not covered. Payment may not be made for maintenance of rented equipment other than the maintenance and servicing fee established for capped rental items. For capped rental items which have reached the 15-month rental cap, contractors pay claims for maintenance and servicing fees after 6 months have passed from the end of the final paid rental month or from the end of the period the item is no longer covered under the supplier's or manufacturer's warranty, whichever is later. See the Medicare Claims Processing Manual, Chapter 20, "Durable Medical Equipment, Prosthetics and Orthotics, and Supplies (DMEPOS)," for additional instruction and an example. A new CMN and/or physician's order is not needed for covered maintenance.

C. Replacement

Replacement refers to the provision of an identical or nearly identical item. Situations involving the provision of a different item because of a change in medical condition are not addressed in this section.

Equipment which the beneficiary owns or is a capped rental item may be replaced in cases of loss or irreparable damage. Irreparable damage refers to a specific accident or to a natural disaster (e.g., fire, flood). A physician's order and/or new Certificate of Medical Necessity (CMN), when required, is needed to reaffirm the medical necessity of the item.

Irreparable wear refers to deterioration sustained from day-to-day usage over time and a specific event cannot be identified. Replacement of equipment due to irreparable wear takes into consideration the reasonable useful lifetime of the equipment. If the item of equipment has been in continuous use by the patient on either a rental or purchase basis for the equipment's useful lifetime, the beneficiary may elect to obtain a new piece of equipment. Replacement may be reimbursed when a new physician order and/or new CMN, when required, is needed to reaffirm the medical necessity of the item.

The reasonable useful lifetime of durable medical equipment is determined through program instructions. In the absence of program instructions, carriers may determine the reasonable useful lifetime of equipment, but in no case can it be less than 5 years. Computation of the useful lifetime is based on when the equipment is delivered to the beneficiary, not the age of the equipment. Replacement due to wear is not covered during the reasonable useful lifetime of the equipment. During the reasonable useful lifetime, Medicare does cover repair up to the cost of replacement (but not actual replacement) for medically necessary equipment owned by the beneficiary. (See subsection A.)

Charges for the replacement of oxygen equipment, items that require frequent and substantial servicing or inexpensive or routinely purchased items which are being rented are not covered. Cases suggesting malicious damage, culpable neglect, or wrongful disposition of equipment should be investigated and denied where the DMERC determines that it is unreasonable to make program payment under the circumstances. DMERCs refer such cases to the program integrity specialist in the RO.

D. Delivery

Payment for delivery of DME whether rented or purchased is generally included in the fee schedule allowance for the item. See Pub. 100-04, Medicare Claims Processing Manual, Chapter 20, "Durable Medical Equipment, Prosthetics and Orthotics, and Supplies (DMEPOS)," for the rules that apply to making reimbursement for exceptional cases.

100-2,15,110.3

Coverage of Supplies and Accessories

B3-2100.5, A3-3113.4, HO-235.4, HHA-220.5 B3-2100.5, A3-3113.4, HO-235.4, HHA-220.5

Payment may be made for supplies, e.g., oxygen, that are necessary for the effective use of durable medical equipment. Such supplies include those drugs and biologicals which must be put directly into the equipment in order to achieve the therapeutic benefit of the durable medical equipment or to assure the proper functioning of the equipment, e.g., tumor chemotherapy agents used with an infusion pump or heparin used with a home dialysis system. However, the coverage of such drugs or biologicals does not preclude the need for a determination that the drug or biological itself is reasonable and necessary for treatment of the illness or injury or to improve the functioning of a malformed body member. In the case of prescription drugs, other than oxygen, used in conjunction with durable medical equipment, prosthetic, orthotics, and supplies (DMEPOS) or prosthetic devices, the entity that dispenses the drug must furnish it directly to the patient for whom a prescription is written. The entity that dispenses the drugs must have a Medicare supplier number, must possess a current license to dispense prescription drugs in the State in which the drug is dispensed, and must bill and receive payment in its own name. A supplier that is not the entity that dispenses the drugs cannot purchase the drugs used in conjunction with DME for resale to the beneficiary. Reimbursement may be made for replacement of essential accessories such as hoses, tubes, mouthpieces, etc., for necessary DME, only if the beneficiary owns or is purchasing the equipment.Payment may be made for supplies, e.g., oxygen, that are necessary for the effective use of durable medical equipment. Such supplies include those drugs and biologicals which must be put directly into the equipment in order to achieve the therapeutic benefit of the durable medical equipment or to assure the proper functioning of the equipment, e.g., tumor chemotherapy agents used with an infusion pump or heparin used with a home dialysis system. However, the coverage of such drugs or biologicals does not preclude the need for a determination that the drug or biological itself is reasonable and necessary for treatment of the illness or injury or to improve the functioning of a malformed body member. In the case of prescription drugs, other than oxygen, used in conjunction with durable medical equipment, prosthetic, orthotics, and supplies (DMEPOS) or prosthetic devices, the entity that dispenses the drug must furnish it directly to the patient for whom a prescription is written. The entity that dispenses the drugs must have a Medicare supplier number, must possess a current license to dispense prescription drugs in the State in which the drug is dispensed, and must bill and receive payment in its own name. A supplier that is not the entity that dispenses the drugs cannot purchase the drugs used in conjunction with DME for resale to the beneficiary. Reimbursement may be made for replacement of essential accessories such as hoses, tubes, mouthpieces, etc., for necessary DME, only if the beneficiary owns or is purchasing the equipment.

100-2,15,120

Prosthetic Devices

B3-2130, A3-3110.4, HO-228.4, A3-3111, HO-229

A. General

Prosthetic devices (other than dental) which replace all or part of an internal body organ (including contiguous tissue), or replace all or part of the function of a permanently inoperative or malfunctioning internal body organ are covered when furnished on a physician's order. This does not require a determination that there is no possibility that the patient's condition may improve sometime in the future. If the medical record, including the judgment of the attending physician, indicates the condition is of long and indefinite duration, the test of permanence is considered met. (Such a device may also be covered under Sec.60.I as a supply when furnished incident to a physician's service.)

Examples of prosthetic devices include artificial limbs, parenteral and enteral (PEN) nutrition, cardiac pacemakers, prosthetic lenses (see subsection B), breast prostheses (including a surgical brassiere) for postmastectomy patients, maxillofacial devices, and devices which replace all or part of the ear or nose. A urinary collection and retention system with or without a tube is a prosthetic device replacing bladder function in case of permanent urinary incontinence. The foley catheter is also considered a prosthetic device when ordered for a patient with permanent urinary incontinence. However, chucks, diapers, rubber sheets, etc., are supplies that are not covered under this provision. Although hemodialysis equipment is a prosthetic device, payment for the rental or purchase of such equipment in the home is made only for use under the provisions for payment applicable to durable medical equipment.

An exception is that if payment cannot be made on an inpatient's behalf under Part A, hemodialysis equipment, supplies, and services required by such patient could be covered under Part B as a prosthetic device, which replaces the function of a kidney. See the Medicare Benefit Policy Manual, Chapter 11, "End Stage Renal Disease," for payment for hemodialysis equipment used in the home. See the Medicare Benefit Policy Manual, Chapter 1, "Inpatient Hospital Services," Sec.10, for additional instructions on hospitalization for renal dialysis.

NOTE: Medicare does not cover a prosthetic device dispensed to a patient prior to the time at which the patient undergoes the procedure that makes necessary the use of the device. For example, the carrier does not make a separate Part B payment for an intraocular lens (IOL) or pacemaker that a physician, during an office visit prior to the actual surgery, dispenses to the patient for his or her use. Dispensing a prosthetic device in this manner raises health and safety issues. Moreover, the need for the device cannot be clearly established until the procedure that makes its use possible is successfully performed. Therefore, dispensing a prosthetic device in this manner is not considered reasonable and necessary for the treatment of the patient's condition.

Colostomy (and other ostomy) bags and necessary accouterments required for attachment are covered as prosthetic devices. This coverage also includes irrigation and flushing equipment and other items and supplies directly related to ostomy care, whether the attachment of a bag is required.

Accessories and/or supplies which are used directly with an enteral or parenteral device to achieve the therapeutic benefit of the prosthesis or to assure the proper functioning of the device may also be covered under the prosthetic device benefit subject to the additional guidelines in the Medicare National Coverage Determinations Manual.

Covered items include catheters, filters, extension tubing, infusion bottles, pumps (either food or infusion), intravenous (I.V.) pole, needles, syringes, dressings, tape, Heparin Sodium (parenteral only), volumetric monitors (parenteral only), and parenteral and enteral nutrient solutions. Baby food and other regular grocery products that can be blenderized and used with the enteral system are not covered. Note that some of these items, e.g., a food pump and an I.V. pole, qualify as DME. Although coverage of the enteral and parenteral nutritional therapy systems is provided on the basis of the prosthetic device benefit, the payment rules relating to lump sum or monthly payment for DME apply to such items.

The coverage of prosthetic devices includes replacement of and repairs to such devices as explained in subsection D.

Finally, the Benefits Improvement and Protection Act of 2000 amended Sec.1834(h)(1) of the Act by adding a provision (1834 (h)(1)(G)(i)) that requires Medicare payment to be made for the replacement of prosthetic devices which are artificial limbs, or for the replacement of any part of such devices, without regard to continuous use or useful lifetime restrictions if an ordering physician determines that the replacement device, or replacement part of such a device, is necessary.

Payment may be made for the replacement of a prosthetic device that is an artificial limb, or replacement part of a device if the ordering physician determines that the replacement device or part is necessary because of any of the following:

1. A change in the physiological condition of the patient;
2. An irreparable change in the condition of the device, or in a part of the device; or
3. The condition of the device, or the part of the device, requires repairs and the cost of such repairs would be more than 60 percent of the cost of a replacement device, or, as the case may be, of the part being replaced.

This provision is effective for items replaced on or after April 1, 2001. It supersedes any rule that that provided a 5-year or other replacement rule with regard to prosthetic devices.

B. Prosthetic Lenses

The term "internal body organ" includes the lens of an eye. Prostheses replacing the lens of an eye include post-surgical lenses customarily used during convalescence from eye surgery in which the lens of the eye was removed. In addition, permanent lenses are also covered when required by an individual lacking the organic lens of the eye because of surgical removal or congenital absence. Prosthetic lenses obtained on or after the beneficiary's date of entitlement to supplementary medical insurance benefits may be covered even though the surgical removal of the crystalline lens occurred before entitlement.

1. Prosthetic Cataract Lenses
   One of the following prosthetic lenses or combinations of prosthetic lenses furnished by a physician (see Sec.30.4 for coverage of prosthetic lenses prescribed by a doctor of optometry) may be covered when determined to be reasonable and necessary to restore essentially the vision provided by the crystalline lens of the eye:

- Prosthetic bifocal lenses in frames;
- Prosthetic lenses in frames for far vision, and prosthetic lenses in frames for near vision; or
- When a prosthetic contact lens(es) for far vision is prescribed (including cases of binocular and monocular aphakia), make payment for the contact lens(es) and prosthetic lenses in frames for near vision to be worn at the same time as the contact lens(es), and prosthetic lenses in frames to be worn when the contacts have been removed.

Lenses which have ultraviolet absorbing or reflecting properties may be covered, in lieu of payment for regular (untinted) lenses, if it has been determined that such lenses are medically reasonable and necessary for the individual patient. Medicare does not cover cataract sunglasses obtained in addition to the regular (untinted) prosthetic lenses since the sunglasses duplicate the restoration of vision function performed by the regular prosthetic lenses.

2. Payment for Intraocular Lenses (IOLs) Furnished in Ambulatory Surgical Centers (ASCs)
   Effective for services furnished on or after March 12, 1990, payment for intraocular lenses (IOLs) inserted during or subsequent to cataract surgery in a Medicare certified ASC is included with the payment for facility services that are furnished in connection with the covered surgery. Refer to the Medicare Claims Processing Manual, Chapter 14, "Ambulatory Surgical Centers," for more information.
3. Limitation on Coverage of Conventional Lenses One pair of conventional eyeglasses or conventional contact lenses furnished after each cataract surgery with insertion of an IOL is covered.

C. Dentures

Dentures are excluded from coverage. However, when a denture or a portion of the denture is an integral part (built-in) of a covered prosthesis (e.g., an obturator to fill an opening in the palate), it is covered as part of that prosthesis.

D. Supplies, Repairs, Adjustments, and Replacement

Supplies are covered that are necessary for the effective use of a prosthetic device (e.g., the batteries needed to operate an artificial larynx). Adjustment of prosthetic devices required by wear or by a change in the patient's condition is covered when ordered by a physician. General provisions relating to the repair and replacement of durable medical equipment in Sec.110.2 for the repair and replacement of prosthetic devices are applicable. (See the Medicare Benefit Policy Manual, Chapter 16, "General Exclusions from Coverage," Sec.40.4, for payment for devices replaced under a warranty.) Replacement of conventional eyeglasses or contact lenses furnished in accordance with Sec.120.B.3 is not covered. Necessary supplies, adjustments, repairs, and replacements are covered even when the device had been in use before the user enrolled in Part B of the program, so long as the device continues to be medically required.

100-2,15,130

Leg, Arm, Back, and Neck Braces, Trusses, and Artificial Legs, Arms, and Eyes

B3-2133, A3-3110.5, HO-228.5, AB-01-06 dated 1/18/01

These appliances are covered under Part B when furnished incident to physicians' services or on a physician's order. A brace includes rigid and semi-rigid devices which are used for the purpose of supporting a weak or deformed body member or restricting or eliminating motion in a diseased or injured part of the body. Elastic stockings, garter belts, and similar devices do not come within the scope of the definition of a brace. Back braces include, but are not limited to, special corsets, e.g., sacroiliac, sacrolumbar, dorsolumbar corsets, and belts. A terminal device (e.g., hand or hook) is covered under this provision whether an artificial limb is required by the patient. Stump stockings and harnesses (including replacements) are also covered when these appliances are essential to the effective use of the artificial limb.

Adjustments to an artificial limb or other appliance required by wear or by a change in the patient's condition are covered when ordered by a physician.

Adjustments, repairs and replacements are covered even when the item had been in use before the user enrolled in Part B of the program so long as the device continues to be medically required.

100-2,15,140

Therapeutic Shoes for Individuals with Diabetes

B3-2134

Coverage of therapeutic shoes (depth or custom-molded) along with inserts for individuals with diabetes is available as of May 1, 1993. These diabetic shoes are covered if the requirements as specified in this section concerning certification and prescription are fulfilled. In addition, this benefit provides for a pair of diabetic shoes even if only one foot suffers from diabetic foot disease. Each shoe is equally equipped so that the affected limb, as well as the remaining limb, is protected. Claims for therapeutic shoes for diabetics are processed by the Durable Medical Equipment Regional Carriers (DMERCs). Therapeutic shoes for diabetics are not DME and are not considered DME nor orthotics, but a separate category of coverage under Medicare Part B. (See Sec.1861(s)(12) and Sec.1833(o) of the Act.)

A. Definitions

The following items may be covered under the diabetic shoe benefit:

1. Custom-Molded ShoesCustom-molded shoes are shoes that:

- Are constructed over a positive model of the patient's foot;
- Are made from leather or other suitable material of equal quality;
- Have removable inserts that can be altered or replaced as the patient's condition warrants; and
- Have some form of shoe closure.

2. Depth Shoes

   Depth shoes are shoes that:

- Have a full length, heel-to-toe filler that, when removed, provides a minimum of 3/16 inch of additional depth used to accommodate custom-molded or customized inserts;
- Are made from leather or other suitable material of equal quality;
- Have some form of shoe closure; and
- Are available in full and half sizes with a minimum of three widths so that the sole is graded to the size and width of the upper portions of the shoes according to the American standard last sizing schedule or its equivalent. (The American standard last sizing schedule is the numerical shoe sizing system used for shoes sold in the United States.)

3. Inserts

   Inserts are total contact, multiple density, removable inlays that are directly molded to the patient's foot or a model of the patient's foot and that are made of a suitable material with regard to the patient's condition.

B. Coverage

1. Limitations

   For each individual, coverage of the footwear and inserts is limited to one of the following within one calendar year:

- No more than one pair of custom-molded shoes (including inserts provided with such shoes) and two additional pairs of inserts; or
- No more than one pair of depth shoes and three pairs of inserts (not including the noncustomized removable inserts provided with such shoes).

2. Coverage of Diabetic Shoes and Brace

   Orthopedic shoes, as stated in the Medicare Claims Processing Manual, Chapter 20, "Durable Medical Equipment, Surgical Dressings and Casts, Orthotics and Artificial Limbs, and Prosthetic Devices," generally are not covered. This exclusion does not apply to orthopedic shoes that are an integral part of a leg brace. In situations in which an individual qualifies for both diabetic shoes and a leg brace, these items are covered separately. Thus, the diabetic shoes may be covered if the requirements for this section are met, while the brace may be covered if the requirements of Sec.130 are met.

3. Substitution of Modifications for Inserts

   An individual may substitute modification(s) of custom-molded or depth shoes instead of obtaining a pair(s) of inserts in any combination. Payment for the modification(s) may not exceed the limit set for the inserts for which the individual is entitled. The following is a list of the most common shoe modifications available, but it is not meant as an exhaustive list of the modifications available for diabetic shoes:

Rigid Rocker Bottoms - These are exterior elevations with apex positions for 51 percent to 75 percent distance measured from the back end of the heel. The apex is a narrowed or pointed end of an anatomical structure. The apex must be positioned behind the metatarsal heads and tapered off sharply to the front tip of the sole. Apex height helps to eliminate pressure at the metatarsal heads. Rigidity is ensured by the steel in the shoe. The heel of the shoe tapers off in the back in order to cause the heel to strike in the middle of the heel;

- Roller Bottoms (Sole or Bar) - These are the same as rocker bottoms, but the heel is tapered from the apex to the front tip of the sole;
- Metatarsal Bars- An exterior bar is placed behind the metatarsal heads in order to remove pressure from the metatarsal heads. The bars are of various shapes, heights, and construction depending on the exact purpose;
- Wedges (Posting) - Wedges are either of hind foot, fore foot, or both and may be in the middle or to the side. The function is to shift or transfer weight bearing upon standing or during ambulation to the opposite side for added support, stabilization, equalized weight distribution, or balance; and
- Offset Heels- This is a heel flanged at its base either in the middle, to the side, or a combination, that is then extended upward to the shoe in order to stabilize extreme positions of the hind foot. Other modifications to diabetic shoes include, but are not limited to flared heels, Velcro closures, and inserts for missing toes.

4. Separate Inserts Inserts may be covered and dispensed independently of diabetic shoes if the supplier of the shoes verifies in writing that the patient has appropriate footwear into which the insert can be placed. This footwear must meet the definitions found above for depth shoes and custom-molded shoes.

C. Certification

The need for diabetic shoes must be certified by a physician who is a doctor of medicine or a doctor of osteopathy and who is responsible for diagnosing and treating the patient's diabetic systemic condition through a comprehensive plan of care. This managing physician must:

- Document in the patient's medical record that the patient has diabetes;
- Certify that the patient is being treated under a comprehensive plan of care for diabetes, and that the patient needs diabetic shoes; and
- Document in the patient's record that the patient has one or more of the following conditions:
- Peripheral neuropathy with evidence of callus formation;
  - History of pre-ulcerative calluses;
  - History of previous ulceration;
  - Foot deformity;
  - Previous amputation of the foot or part of the foot; or
  - Poor circulation.

D. Prescription

Following certification by the physician managing the patient's systemic diabetic condition, a podiatrist or other qualified physician who is knowledgeable in the fitting of diabetic shoes and inserts may prescribe the particular type of footwear necessary.

E. Furnishing

Footwear The footwear must be fitted and furnished by a podiatrist or other qualified individual such as a pedorthist, an orthotist, or a prosthetist. The certifying physician may not furnish the diabetic shoes unless the certifying physician is the only qualified individual in the area. It is left to the discretion of each carrier to determine the meaning of "in the area."

100-2,15,150

Dental Services

B3-2136

As indicated under the general exclusions from coverage, items and services in connection with the care, treatment, filling, removal, or replacement of teeth or structures directly supporting the teeth are not covered. "Structures directly supporting the teeth" means the periodontium, which includes the gingivae, dentogingival junction, periodontal membrane, cementum of the teeth, and alveolar process.

In addition to the following, see Pub 100-01, the Medicare General Information, Eligibility, and Entitlement Manual, Chapter 5, Definitions and Pub 3, the Medicare National Coverage Determinations Manual for specific services which may be covered when furnished by a dentist. If an otherwise noncovered procedure or service is performed by a dentist as incident to and as an integral part of a covered procedure or service performed by the dentist, the total service performed by the dentist on such an occasion is covered.

EXAMPLE 1: The reconstruction of a ridge performed primarily to prepare the mouth for dentures is a noncovered procedure. However, when the reconstruction of a ridge is performed as a result of and at the same time as the surgical removal of a tumor (for other than dental purposes), the totality of surgical procedures is a covered service.

EXAMPLE 2: Medicare makes payment for the wiring of teeth when this is done in connection with the reduction of a jaw fracture.

The extraction of teeth to prepare the jaw for radiation treatment of neoplastic disease is also covered. This is an exception to the requirement that to be covered, a noncovered procedure or service performed by a dentist must be an incident to and an integral part of a covered procedure or service performed by the dentist. Ordinarily, the dentist extracts the patient's teeth, but another physician, e.g., a radiologist, administers the radiation treatments.

When an excluded service is the primary procedure involved, it is not covered, regardless of its complexity or difficulty. For example, the extraction of an impacted tooth is not covered. Similarly, an alveoplasty (the surgical improvement of the shape and condition of the alveolar process) and a frenectomy are excluded from coverage when either of these procedures is performed in connection with an excluded service, e.g., the preparation of the mouth for dentures. In a like manner, the removal of a torus palatinus (a bony protuberance of the hard palate) may be a covered service. However, with rare exception, this surgery is performed in connection with an excluded service, i.e., the preparation of the mouth for dentures. Under such circumstances, Medicare does not pay for this procedure.

Dental splints used to treat a dental condition are excluded from coverage under 1862(a)(12) of the Act. On the other hand, if the treatment is determined to be a covered medical condition (i.e., dislocated upper/lower jaw joints), then the splint can be covered.

Whether such services as the administration of anesthesia, diagnostic x-rays, and other related procedures are covered depends upon whether the primary procedure being performed by the dentist is itself covered. Thus, an x-ray taken in connection with the reduction of a fracture of the jaw or facial bone is covered. However, a single x-ray or x-ray survey taken in connection with the care or treatment of teeth or the periodontium is not covered.

Medicare makes payment for a covered dental procedure no matter where the service is performed. The hospitalization or nonhospitalization of a patient has no direct bearing on the coverage or exclusion of a given dental procedure.

Payment may also be made for services and supplies furnished incident to covered dental services. For example, the services of a dental technician or nurse who is under the direct supervision of the dentist or physician are covered if the services are included in the dentist's or physician's bill.

100-2,15,230

Practice of Physical Therapy, Occupational Therapy, and Speech-Language Pathology

A. Group Therapy Services.

Contractors pay for outpatient physical therapy services (which includes outpatient speech-language pathology services) and outpatient occupational therapy services provided simultaneously to two or more individuals by a practitioner as group therapy services (97150). The individuals can be, but need not be performing the same activity. The physician or therapist involved in group therapy services must be in constant attendance, but one-on-one patient contact is not required.

B. Therapy Students

1. General
   Only the services of the therapist can be billed and paid under Medicare Part B. The services performed by a student are not reimbursed even if provided under "line of sight" supervision of the therapist; however, the presence of the student "in the room" does not make the service unbillable. Pay for the direct (one-to-one) patient contact services of the physician or therapist provided to Medicare Part B patients. Group therapy services performed by a therapist or physician may be billed when a student is also present "in the room".

EXAMPLES:

Therapists may bill and be paid for the provision of services in the following scenarios:

- The qualified practitioner is present and in the room for the entire session. The student participates in the delivery of services when the qualified practitioner is directing the service, making the skilled judgment, and is responsible for the assessment and treatment.
- The qualified practitioner is present in the room guiding the student in service delivery when the therapy student and the therapy assistant student are participating in the provision of services, and the practitioner is not engaged in treating another patient or doing other tasks at the same time
- The qualified practitioner is responsible for the services and as such, signs all documentation. (A student may, of course, also sign but it is not necessary since the Part B payment is for the clinician's service, not for the student's services).

2. Therapy Assistants as Clinical Instructors
   Physical therapist assistants and occupational therapy assistants are not precluded from serving as clinical instructors for therapy students, while providing services within their scope of work and performed under the direction and supervision of a licensed physical or occupational therapist to a Medicare beneficiary.
3. Services Provided Under Part A and Part B
   The payment methodologies for Part A and B therapy services rendered by a student are different. Under the MPFS (Medicare Part B), Medicare pays for services provided by physicians and practitioners that are specifically authorized by statute. Students do not meet the definition of practitioners under Medicare Part B. Under SNF PPS, payments are based upon the case mix or Resource Utilization Group (RUG) category that describes the patient. In the rehabilitation groups, the number of therapy minutes delivered to the patient determines the RUG category. Payment levels for each category are based upon the costs of caring for patients in each group rather than providing pecific payment for each therapy service as is done in Medicare Part B.

100-2,15,280.1

Glaucoma Screening

A. Conditions of Coverage

The regulations implementing the Benefits Improvements and Protection Act of 2000, Sec.102, provide for annual coverage for glaucoma screening for beneficiaries in the following high risk categories:

- Individuals with diabetes mellitus;
- Individuals with a family history of glaucoma; or
- African-Americans age 50 and over. In addition, beginning with dates of service on or after January 1, 2006, 42 CFR 410.23(a)(2), revised, the definition of an eligible beneficiary in a high-risk category is expanded to include:
- Hispanic-Americans age 65 and over.

Medicare will pay for glaucoma screening examinations where they are furnished by or under the direct supervision in the office setting of an ophthalmologist or optometrist, who is legally authorized to perform the services under State law. Screening for glaucoma is defined to include:

- A dilated eye examination with an intraocular pressure measurement; and
- A direct ophthalmoscopy examination, or a slit-lamp biomicroscopic examination.

Payment may be made for a glaucoma screening examination that is performed on an eligible beneficiary after at least 11 months have passed following the month in which the last covered glaucoma screening examination was performed.

The following HCPCS codes apply for glaucoma screening:

G0117 Glaucoma screening for high-risk patients furnished by an optometrist or ophthalmologist; and

G0118 Glaucoma screening for high-risk patients furnished under the direct supervision of an optometrist or ophthalmologist.

The type of service for the above G codes is: TOS Q.

For providers who bill intermediaries, applicable types of bill for screening glaucoma services are 13X, 22X, 23X, 71X, 73X, 75X, and 85X. The following revenue codes should be reported when billing for screening glaucoma services:

- Comprehensive outpatient rehabilitation facilities (CORFs), critical access hospitals (CAHs), skilled nursing facilities (SNFs), independent and provider-based RHCs and free standing and provider-based FQHCs bill for this service under revenue code 770. CAHs electing the optional method of payment for outpatient services report this service under revenue codes 96X, 97X, or 98X.
- Hospital outpatient departments bill for this service under any valid/appropriate revenue code. They are not required to report revenue code 770.

B. Calculating the Frequency

Once a beneficiary has received a covered glaucoma screening procedure, the beneficiary may receive another procedure after 11 full months have passed. To determine the 11-month period, start the count beginning with the month after the month in which the previous covered screening procedure was performed.

C. Diagnosis Coding Requirements

Providers bill glaucoma screening using screening ("V") code V80.1 (Special Screening for Neurological, Eye, and Ear Diseases, Glaucoma). Claims submitted without a screening diagnosis code may be returned to the provider as unprocessable.

D. Payment Methodology

1. Carriers
Contractors pay for glaucoma screening based on the Medicare physician fee schedule. Deductible and coinsurance apply. Claims from physicians or other providers where assignment was not taken are subject to the Medicare limiting charge (refer to the Medicare Claims Processing Manual, Chapter 12, "Physician/Non-physician Practitioners," for more information about the Medicare limiting charge).

2. Intermediaries
Payment is made for the facility expense as follows:

- Independent and provider-based RHC/free standing and provider-based FQHC - payment is made under the all inclusive rate for the screening glaucoma service based on the visit furnished to the RHC/FQHC patient;
- CAH - payment is made on a reasonable cost basis unless the CAH has elected the optional method of payment for outpatient services in which case, procedures outlined in the Medicare Claims Processing Manual, Chapter 3, Sec.30.1.1, should be followed;
- CORF - payment is made under the Medicare physician fee schedule;
- Hospital outpatient department - payment is made under outpatient prospective payment system (OPPS);
- Hospital inpatient Part B - payment is made under OPPS;
- SNF outpatient - payment is made under the Medicare physician fee schedule (MPFS); and
- SNF inpatient Part B - payment is made under MPFS. Deductible and coinsurance apply.

E. Special Billing Instructions for RHCs and FQHCs

Screening glaucoma services are considered RHC/FQHC services. RHCs and FQHCs bill the contractor under bill type 71X or 73X along with revenue code 770 and HCPCS codes G0117 or G0118 and RHC/FQHC revenue code 520 or 521 to report the related visit. Reporting of revenue code 770 and HCPCS codes G0117 and G0118 in addition to revenue code 520 or 521 is required for this service in order for CWF to perform frequency editing.

Payment should not be made for a screening glaucoma service unless the claim also contains a visit code for the service. Therefore, the contractor installs an edit in its system to assure payment is not made for revenue code 770 unless the claim also contains a visit revenue code (520 or 521).

100-2,15,290

Foot Care

A. Treatment of Subluxation of Foot

Subluxations of the foot are defined as partial dislocations or displacements of joint surfaces, tendons ligaments, or muscles of the foot. Surgical or nonsurgical treatments undertaken for the sole purpose of correcting a subluxated structure in the foot as an isolated entity are not covered.

However, medical or surgical treatment of subluxation of the ankle joint (talo-crural joint) is covered. In addition, reasonable and necessary medical or surgical services, diagnosis, or treatment for medical conditions that have resulted from or are associated with partial displacement of structures is covered. For example, if a patient has osteoarthritis that has resulted in a partial displacement of joints in the foot, and the primary treatment is for the osteoarthritis, coverage is provided.

B. Exclusions from Coverage

The following foot care services are generally excluded from coverage under both Part A and Part B. (See Sec.290.F and Sec.290.G for instructions on applying foot care exclusions.)

1. Treatment of Flat Foot
The term "flat foot" is defined as a condition in which one or more arches of the foot have flattened out. Services or devices directed toward the care or correction of such conditions, including the prescription of supportive devices, are not covered.

2. Routine Foot Care
Except as provided above, routine foot care is excluded from coverage. Services that normally are considered routine and not covered by Medicare include the following:

- The cutting or removal of corns and calluses;
- The trimming, cutting, clipping, or debriding of nails; and
- Other hygienic and preventive maintenance care, such as cleaning and soaking the feet, the use of skin creams to maintain skin tone of either ambulatory or bedfast patients, and any other service performed in the absence of localized illness, injury, or symptoms involving the foot.

3. Supportive Devices for Feet
Orthopedic shoes and other supportive devices for the feet generally are not covered. However, this exclusion does not apply to such a shoe if it is an integral part of a leg brace, and its expense is included as part of the cost of the brace. Also, this exclusion does not apply to therapeutic shoes furnished to diabetics.

C. Exceptions to Routine Foot Care Exclusion

1. Necessary and Integral Part of Otherwise Covered Services
In certain circumstances, services ordinarily considered to be routine may be covered if they are performed as a necessary and integral part of otherwise covered services, such as diagnosis and treatment of ulcers, wounds, or infections.

2. Treatment of Warts on Foot
The treatment of warts (including plantar warts) on the foot is covered to the same extent as services provided for the treatment of warts located elsewhere on the body.

3. Presence of Systemic Condition
The presence of a systemic condition such as metabolic, neurologic, or peripheral vascular disease may require scrupulous foot care by a professional that in the absence of such condition(s) would be considered routine (and, therefore, excluded from coverage). Accordingly, foot care that would otherwise be considered routine may be covered when systemic condition(s) result in severe circulatory embarrassment or areas of diminished sensation in the individual's legs or feet. (See subsection A.)

In these instances, certain foot care procedures that otherwise are considered routine (e.g., cutting or removing corns and calluses, or trimming, cutting, clipping, or debriding nails) may pose a hazard when performed by a nonprofessional person on patients with such systemic conditions. (See Sec.290.G for procedural instructions.)

4. Mycotic Nails
In the absence of a systemic condition, treatment of mycotic nails may be covered. The treatment of mycotic nails for an ambulatory patient is covered only when the physician attending the patient's mycotic condition documents that (1) there is clinical evidence of mycosis of the toenail, and (2) the patient has marked limitation of ambulation, pain, or secondary infection resulting from the thickening and dystrophy of the infected toenail plate.

The treatment of mycotic nails for a nonambulatory patient is covered only when the physician attending the patient's mycotic condition documents that (1) there is clinical evidence of mycosis of the toenail, and (2) the patient suffers from pain or secondary infection resulting from the thickening and dystrophy of the infected toenail plate.

For the purpose of these requirements, documentation means any written information that is required by the carrier in order for services to be covered. Thus, the information submitted with claims must be substantiated by information found in the patient's medical record. Any information, including that contained in a form letter, used for documentation purposes is subject to carrier verification in order to ensure that the information adequately justifies coverage of the treatment of mycotic nails.

D. Systemic Conditions That Might Justify Coverage

Although not intended as a comprehensive list, the following metabolic, neurologic, and peripheral vascular diseases (with synonyms in parentheses) most commonly represent the underlying conditions that might justify coverage for routine foot care.

- Diabetes mellitus *
- Arteriosclerosis obliterans (A.S.O., arteriosclerosis of the extremities, occlusive peripheral arteriosclerosis)
- Buerger's disease (thromboangiitis obliterans)
- Chronic thrombophlebitis *
- Peripheral neuropathies involving the feet -
- Associated with malnutrition and vitamin deficiency *
  - Malnutrition (general, pellagra)
  - Alcoholism
  - Malabsorption (celiac disease, tropical sprue)
  - Pernicious anemia
- Associated with carcinoma *
- Associated with diabetes mellitus *
- Associated with drugs and toxins *
- Associated with multiple sclerosis *
- Associated with uremia (chronic renal disease) *
- Associated with traumatic injury
- Associated with leprosy or neurosyphilis

- Associated with hereditary disorders
- Hereditary sensory radicular neuropathy
- Angiokeratoma corporis diffusum (Fabry's)
- Amyloid neuropathy

When the patient's condition is one of those designated by an asterisk (*), routine procedures are covered only if the patient is under the active care of a doctor of medicine or osteopathy who documents the condition.

E. Supportive Devices for Feet

Orthopedic shoes and other supportive devices for the feet generally are not covered. However, this exclusion does not apply to such a shoe if it is an integral part of a leg brace, and its expense is included as part of the cost of the brace. Also, this exclusion does not apply to therapeutic shoes furnished to diabetics.

F. Presumption of Coverage

In evaluating whether the routine services can be reimbursed, a presumption of coverage may be made where the evidence available discloses certain physical and/or clinical findings consistent with the diagnosis and indicative of severe peripheral involvement. For purposes of applying this presumption the following findings are pertinent:

Class A Findings
Nontraumatic amputation of foot or integral skeletal portion thereof.

Class B Findings
Absent posterior tibial pulse;

Advanced trophic changes as: hair growth (decrease or absence) nail changes (thickening) pigmentary changes (discoloration) skin texture (thin, shiny) skin color (rubor or redness) (Three required); and

Absent dorsalis pedis pulse.

Class C Findings
Claudication;

Temperature changes (e.g., cold feet);

Edema;

Paresthesias (abnormal spontaneous sensations in the feet); and

Burning.

The presumption of coverage may be applied when the physician rendering the routine foot care has identified:

1. A Class A finding;
2. Two of the Class B findings; or
3. One Class B and two Class C findings.

Cases evidencing findings falling short of these alternatives may involve podiatric treatment that may constitute covered care and should be reviewed by the intermediary's medical staff and developed as necessary.

For purposes of applying the coverage presumption where the routine services have been rendered by a podiatrist, the contractor may deem the active care requirement met if the claim or other evidence available discloses that the patient has seen an M.D. or D.O. for treatment and/or evaluation of the complicating disease process during the 6-month period prior to the rendition of the routine-type services. The intermediary may also accept the podiatrist's statement that the diagnosing and treating M.D. or D.O. also concurs with the podiatrist's findings as to the severity of the peripheral involvement indicated.

Services ordinarily considered routine might also be covered if they are performed as a necessary and integral part of otherwise covered services, such as diagnosis and treatment of diabetic ulcers, wounds, and infections.

G. Application of Foot Care Exclusions to Physician's Services

The exclusion of foot care is determined by the nature of the service. Thus, payment for an excluded service should be denied whether performed by a podiatrist, osteopath, or a doctor of medicine, and without regard to the difficulty or complexity of the procedure.

When an itemized bill shows both covered services and noncovered services not integrally related to the covered service, the portion of charges attributable to the noncovered services should be denied. (For example, if an itemized bill shows surgery for an ingrown toenail and also removal of calluses not necessary for the performance of toe surgery, any additional charge attributable to removal of the calluses should be denied.)

In reviewing claims involving foot care, the carrier should be alert to the following exceptional situations:

1. Payment may be made for incidental noncovered services performed as a necessary and integral part of, and secondary to, a covered procedure. For example, if trimming of toenails is required for application of a cast to a fractured foot, the carrier need not allocate and deny a portion of the charge for the trimming of the nails. However, a separately itemized charge for such excluded service should be disallowed. When the primary procedure is covered the administration of anesthesia necessary for the performance of such procedure is also covered.
2. Payment may be made for initial diagnostic services performed in connection with a specific symptom or complaint if it seems likely that its treatment would be covered even though the resulting diagnosis may be one requiring only noncovered care.

The name of the M.D. or D.O. who diagnosed the complicating condition must be submitted with the claim. In those cases, where active care is required, the approximate date the beneficiary was last seen by such physician must also be indicated.

NOTE: Section 939 of P.L. 96-499 removed "warts" from the routine foot care exclusion effective July 1, 1981.

Relatively few claims for routine-type care are anticipated considering the severity of conditions contemplated as the basis for this exception. Claims for this type of foot care should not be paid in the absence of convincing evidence that nonprofessional performance of the service would have been hazardous for the beneficiary because of an underlying systemic disease. The mere statement of a diagnosis such as those mentioned in Sec.D above does not of itself indicate the severity of the condition. Where development is indicated to verify diagnosis and/or severity the carrier should follow existing claims processing practices which may include review of carrier's history and medical consultation as well as physician contacts.

The rules in Sec.290.F concerning presumption of coverage also apply.

Codes and policies for routine foot care and supportive devices for the feet are not exclusively for the use of podiatrists. These codes must be used to report foot care services regardless of the specialty of the physician who furnishes the services. Carriers must instruct physicians to use the most appropriate code available when billing for routine foot care.

100-2,15,290

Foot Care

Subluxations of the foot are defined as partial dislocations or displacements of joint surfaces, tendons ligaments, or muscles of the foot. Surgical or nonsurgical treatments undertaken for the sole purpose of correcting a subluxated structure in the foot as an isolated entity are not covered.

However, medical or surgical treatment of subluxation of the ankle joint (talo-crural joint) is covered. In addition, reasonable and necessary medical or surgical services, diagnosis, or treatment for medical conditions that have resulted from or are associated with partial displacement of structures is covered. For example, if a patient has osteoarthritis that has resulted in a partial displacement of joints in the foot, and the primary treatment is for the osteoarthritis, coverage is provided.

B. Exclusions from Coverage

The following foot care services are generally excluded from coverage under both Part A and Part B. (See Sec.290.F and Sec.290.G for instructions on applying foot care exclusions.)

1. Treatment of Flat Foot The term "flat foot" is defined as a condition in which one or more arches of the foot have flattened out. Services or devices directed toward the care or correction of such conditions, including the prescription of supportive devices, are not covered.
2. Routine Foot Care Except as provided above, routine foot care is excluded from coverage. Services that normally are considered routine and not covered by Medicare include the following: The cutting or removal of corns and calluses; The trimming, cutting, clipping, or debriding of nails; and Other hygienic and preventive maintenance care, such as cleaning and soaking the feet, the use of skin creams to maintain skin tone of either ambulatory or bedfast patients, and any other service performed in the absence of localized illness, injury, or symptoms involving the foot.
3. Supportive Devices for Feet Orthopedic shoes and other supportive devices for the feet generally are not covered.

However, this exclusion does not apply to such a shoe if it is an integral part of a leg brace, and its expense is included as part of the cost of the brace. Also, this exclusion does not apply to therapeutic shoes furnished to diabetics.

C. Exceptions to Routine Foot Care Exclusion

1. Necessary and Integral Part of Otherwise Covered Services In certain circumstances, services ordinarily considered to be routine may be covered if they are performed as a

necessary and integral part of otherwise covered services, such as diagnosis and treatment of ulcers, wounds, or infections.

2. Treatment of Warts on Foot The treatment of warts (including plantar warts) on the foot is covered to the same extent as services provided for the treatment of warts located elsewhere on the body.

3. Presence of Systemic Condition The presence of a systemic condition such as metabolic, neurologic, or peripheral vascular disease may require scrupulous foot care by a professional that in the absence of such condition(s) would be considered routine (and, therefore, excluded from coverage).

Accordingly, foot care that would otherwise be considered routine may be covered when systemic condition(s) result in severe circulatory embarrassment or areas of diminished sensation in the individual's legs or feet. (See subsection A.) In these instances, certain foot care procedures that otherwise are considered routine (e.g., cutting or removing corns and calluses, or trimming, cutting, clipping, or debriding nails) may pose a hazard when performed by a nonprofessional person on patients with such systemic conditions. (See Sec.290.G for procedural instructions.) 4. Mycotic Nails In the absence of a systemic condition, treatment of mycotic nails may be covered.

The treatment of mycotic nails for an ambulatory patient is covered only when the physician attending the patient's mycotic condition documents that (1) there is clinical evidence of mycosis of the toenail, and (2) the patient has marked limitation of ambulation, pain, or secondary infection resulting from the thickening and dystrophy of the infected toenail plate.

The treatment of mycotic nails for a nonambulatory patient is covered only when the physician attending the patient's mycotic condition documents that (1) there is clinical evidence of mycosis of the toenail, and (2) the patient suffers from pain or secondary infection resulting from the thickening and dystrophy of the infected toenail plate.

For the purpose of these requirements, documentation means any written information that is required by the carrier in order for services to be covered. Thus, the information submitted with claims must be substantiated by information found in the patient's medical record. Any information, including that contained in a form letter, used for documentation purposes is subject to carrier verification in order to ensure that the information adequately justifies coverage of the treatment of mycotic nails.

D. Systemic Conditions That Might Justify Coverage

Although not intended as a comprehensive list, the following metabolic, neurologic, and peripheral vascular diseases (with synonyms in parentheses) most commonly represent the underlying conditions that might justify coverage for routine foot care.

Diabetes mellitus * Arteriosclerosis obliterans (A.S.O., arteriosclerosis of the extremities, occlusive peripheral arteriosclerosis) Buerger's disease (thromboangiitis obliterans) Chronic thrombophlebitis * Peripheral neuropathies involving the feet - Associated with malnutrition and vitamin deficiency * Malnutrition (general, pellagra) Alcoholism Malabsorption (celiac disease, tropical sprue) Pernicious anemia Associated with carcinoma * Associated with diabetes mellitus * Associated with drugs and toxins * Associated with multiple sclerosis * Associated with uremia (chronic renal disease) * Associated with traumatic injury Associated with leprosy or neurosyphilis Associated with hereditary disorders Hereditary sensory radicular neuropathy Angiokeratoma corporis diffusum (Fabry's) Amyloid neuropathy When the patient's condition is one of those designated by an asterisk (*), routine procedures are covered only if the patient is under the active care of a doctor of medicine or osteopathy who documents the condition.

E. Supportive Devices for Feet

Orthopedic shoes and other supportive devices for the feet generally are not covered.However, this exclusion does not apply to such a shoe if it is an integral part of a leg brace, and its expense is included as part of the cost of the brace. Also, this exclusion does not apply to therapeutic shoes furnished to diabetics.

F. Presumption of Coverage

In evaluating whether the routine services can be reimbursed, a presumption of coverage may be made where the evidence available discloses certain physical and/or clinical findings consistent with the diagnosis and indicative of severe peripheral involvement. For purposes of applying this presumption the following findings are pertinent:

Class A Findings

Nontraumatic amputation of foot or integral skeletal portion thereof.

Class B Findings

Absent posterior tibial pulse; Advanced trophic changes as: hair growth (decrease or absence) nail changes (thickening) pigmentary changes (discoloration) skin texture (thin, shiny) skin color (rubor or redness) (Three required);

and Absent dorsalis pedis pulse.

Class C Findings

Claudication;

Temperature changes (e.g., cold feet);

Edema;

Paresthesias (abnormal spontaneous sensations in the feet); and

Burning.

The presumption of coverage may be applied when the physician rendering the routine foot care has identified:

1. A Class A finding;
2. Two of the Class B findings; or
3. One Class B and two Class C findings.

Cases evidencing findings falling short of these alternatives may involve podiatric treatment that may constitute covered care and should be reviewed by the intermediary's medical staff and developed as necessary.

For purposes of applying the coverage presumption where the routine services have been rendered by a podiatrist, the contractor may deem the active care requirement met if the claim or other evidence available discloses that the patient has seen an M.D. or D.O. for treatment and/or evaluation of the complicating disease process during the 6-month period prior to the rendition of the routine-type services. The intermediary may also accept the podiatrist's statement that the diagnosing and treating M.D. or D.O. also concurs with the podiatrist's findings as to the severity of the peripheral involvement indicated.

Services ordinarily considered routine might also be covered if they are performed as a necessary and integral part of otherwise covered services, such as diagnosis and treatment of diabetic ulcers, wounds, and infections.

G. Application of Foot Care Exclusions to Physician's Services

The exclusion of foot care is determined by the nature of the service. Thus, payment for an excluded service should be denied whether performed by a podiatrist, osteopath, or a doctor of medicine, and without regard to the difficulty or complexity of the procedure.

When an itemized bill shows both covered services and noncovered services not integrally related to the covered service, the portion of charges attributable to the noncovered services should be denied. (For example, if an itemized bill shows surgery for an ingrown toenail and also removal of calluses not necessary for the performance of toe surgery, any additional charge attributable to removal of the calluses should be denied.) In reviewing claims involving foot care, the carrier should be alert to the following exceptional situations:

1. Payment may be made for incidental noncovered services performed as a necessary and integral part of, and secondary to, a covered procedure. For example, if trimming of toenails is required for application of a cast to a fractured foot, the carrier need not allocate and deny a portion of the charge for the trimming of the nails. However, a separately itemized charge for such excluded service should be disallowed. When the primary procedure is covered the administration of anesthesia necessary for the performance of such procedure is also covered.
2. Payment may be made for initial diagnostic services performed in connection with a specific symptom or complaint if it seems likely that its treatment would be covered even though the resulting diagnosis may be one requiring only noncovered care.

The name of the M.D. or D.O. who diagnosed the complicating condition must be submitted with the claim. In those cases, where active care is required, the approximate date the beneficiary was last seen by such physician must also be indicated.

NOTE: Section 939 of P.L. 96-499 removed "warts" from the routine foot care exclusion effective July 1, 1981.

Relatively few claims for routine-type care are anticipated considering the severity of conditions contemplated as the basis for this exception. Claims for this type of foot care should not be paid in the absence of convincing evidence that nonprofessional performance of the service would have been hazardous for the beneficiary because of an underlying systemic disease. The mere statement of a diagnosis such as those mentioned in Sec.D above does not of itself indicate the severity of the condition. Where development is indicated to verify diagnosis and/or severity the carrier should follow existing claims processing practices, which may include review of carrier's history and medical consultation as well as physician contacts.

The rules in Sec.290.F concerning presumption of coverage also apply.

Codes and policies for routine foot care and supportive devices for the feet are not exclusively for the use of podiatrists. These codes must be used to report foot care services regardless of the specialty of the physician who furnishes the services. Carriers must instruct physicians to use the most appropriate code available when billing for routine foot care.

100-2,15,300

Diabetes Self-Management Training Services

Section 4105 of the Balanced Budget Act of 1997 permits Medicare coverage of diabetes self-management training (DSMT) services when these services are furnished by a certified provider who meets certain quality standards. This program is intended to educate beneficiaries in the successful self-management of diabetes. The program includes instructions in self-monitoring of blood glucose; education about diet and exercise; an insulin treatment plan developed specifically for the patient who is insulin-dependent; and motivation for patients to use the skills for self-management.

Diabetes self-management training services may be covered by Medicare only if the treating physician or treating qualified non-physician practitioner who is managing the beneficiary's diabetic condition certifies that such services are needed. The referring physician or qualified non-physician practitioner must maintain the plan of care in the beneficiary's medical record and documentation substantiating the need for training on an individual basis when group training is typically covered, if so ordered. The order must also include a statement signed by the physician that the service is needed as well as the following:

- The number of initial or follow-up hours ordered (the physician can order less than 10 hours of training);
- The topics to be covered in training (initial training hours can be used for the full initial training program or specific areas such as nutrition or insulin training); and
- A determination that the beneficiary should receive individual or group training.

The provider of the service must maintain documentation in a file that includes the original order from the physician and any special conditions noted by the physician.

When the training under the order is changed, the training order/referral must be signed by the physician or qualified non-physician practitioner treating the beneficiary and maintained in the beneficiary's file in the DSMT's program records.

NOTE: All entities billing for DSMT under the fee-for-service payment system or other payment systems must meet all national coverage requirements.

100-2,15,300.2

Certified Providers

A designated certified provider bills for DSMT provided by an accredited DSMT program. Certified providers must submit a copy of their accreditation certificate to the contractor. The statute states that a "certified provider" is a physician or other individual or entity designated by the Secretary that, in addition to providing outpatient self-management training services, provides other items and services for which payment may be made under title XVIII, and meets certain quality standards. The CMS is designating all providers and suppliers that bill Medicare for other individual services such as hospital outpatient departments, renal dialysis facilities, physicians and durable medical equipment suppliers as certified. All suppliers/providers who may bill for other Medicare services or items and who represent a DSMT program that is accredited as meeting quality standards can bill and receive payment for the entire DSMT program. Registered dietitians are eligible to bill on behalf of an entire DSMT program on or after January 1, 2002, as long as the provider has obtained a Medicare provider number. A dietitian may not be the sole provider of the DSMT service.

The CMS will not reimburse services on a fee-for-service basis rendered to a beneficiary under Part A.

NOTE: While separate payment is not made for this service to Rural Health Clinics (RHCs), the service is covered but is considered included in the all-inclusive encounter rate. Effective January 1, 2006, payment for DSMT provided in a Federally Qualified Health Clinic (FQHC) that meets all of the requirements identified in Pub. 100-04, chapter 18, section 120 may be made in addition to one other visit the beneficiary had during the same day.

All DSMT programs must be accredited as meeting quality standards by a CMS approved national accreditation organization. Currently, CMS recognizes the American Diabetes Association and the Indian Health Service as approved national accreditation organizations. Programs without accreditation by a CMS-approved national accreditation organization are not covered. Certified providers may be asked to submit updated accreditation documents at any time or to submit outcome data to an organization designated by CMS.

Enrollment of DMEPOS Suppliers The DMEPOS suppliers are reimbursed for diabetes training through local carriers. In order to file claims for DSMT, a DMEPOS supplier must be enrolled in the Medicare program with the National Supplier Clearinghouse (NSC). The supplier must also meet the quality standards of a CMS-approved national accreditation organization as stated above. DMEPOS suppliers must obtain a provider number from the local carrier in order to bill for DSMT.

The carrier requires a completed Form CMS-855, along with an accreditation certificate as part of the provider application process. After it has been determined that the quality standards are met, a billing number is assigned to the supplier. Once a supplier has received a provider identification (PIN) number, the supplier can begin receiving reimbursement for this service.

Carriers should contact the National Supplier Clearinghouse (NSC) according to the instruction in Pub 100-08, the Medicare Program Integrity Manual, Chapter 10, "Healthcare Provider/Supplier Enrollment," to verify an applicant is currently enrolled and eligible to receive direct payment from the Medicare program.

The applicant is assigned specialty 87.

Any DMEPOS supplier that has its billing privileges deactivated or revoked by the NSC will also have the billing number deactivated by the carrier.

100-2,15,300.3

Frequency of Training

A - Initial Training

The initial year for DSMT is the 12 month period following the initial date.

Medicare will cover initial training that meets the following conditions:

- Is furnished to a beneficiary who has not previously received initial or follow-up training under HCPCS codes G0108 or G0109;
- Is furnished within a continuous 12-month period;
- Does not exceed a total of 10 hours* (the 10 hours of training can be done in any combination of 1/2 hour increments);
- With the exception of 1 hour of individual training, training is usually furnished in a group setting, which can contain other patients besides Medicare beneficiaries, and;
- One hour of individual training may be used for any part of the training including insulin training.

* When a claim contains a DSMT HCPCS code and the associated units cause the total time for the DSMT initial year to exceed '10' hours, a CWF error will set.

B - Follow-Up Training

Medicare covers follow-up training under the following conditions:

- No more than 2 hours individual or group training per beneficiary per year;
- Group training consists of 2 to 20 individuals who need not all be Medicare beneficiaries;
- Follow-up training for subsequent years is based on a 12 month calendar after completion of the full 10 hours of initial training;
- Follow-up training is furnished in increments of no less than one-half hour*; and
- The physician (or qualified non-physician practitioner) treating the beneficiary must document in the beneficiary's medical record that the beneficiary is a diabetic.

*When a claim contains a DSMT HCPCS code and the associated units cause the total time for any follow-up year to exceed 2 hours, a CWF error will set.

100-2,15,300.4

Coverage Requirements for Individual Training

Medicare covers training on an individual basis for a Medicare beneficiary under any of the following conditions:

- No group session is available within 2 months of the date the training is ordered;
- The beneficiary's physician (or qualified non-physician practitioner) documents in the beneficiary's medical record that the beneficiary has special needs resulting from conditions, such as severe vision, hearing or language limitations or other such special conditions as identified by the treating physician or non-physician practitioner, that will hinder effective participation in a group training session; or
- The physician orders additional insulin training.

The need for individual training must be identified by the physician or non-physician practitioner in the referral.

NOTE: If individual training has been provided to a Medicare beneficiary and subsequently the carrier or intermediary determines that training should have been provided in a group, carriers and intermediaries down-code the reimbursement from individual to the group level and provider education would be the appropriate actions instead of denying the service as billed.

100-2,15,50

Drugs and Biologicals

B3-2049, A3-3112.4.B, HO-230.4.B

The Medicare program provides limited benefits for outpatient drugs. The program covers drugs that are furnished "incident to" a physician's service provided that the drugs are not usually self-administered by the patients who take them.

Generally, drugs and biologicals are covered only if all of the following requirements are met:

- They meet the definition of drugs or biologicals (see Sec.50.1);
- They are of the type that are not usually self-administered. (see Sec.50.2);
- They meet all the general requirements for coverage of items as incident to a physician's services (see Sec.Sec.50.1 and 50.3);
- They are reasonable and necessary for the diagnosis or treatment of the illness or injury for which they are administered according to accepted standards of medical practice (see Sec.50.4);
- They are not excluded as noncovered immunizations (see Sec.50.4.4.2); and
- They have not been determined by the FDA to be less than effective. (See Sec.Sec.50.4.4).

Medicare Part B does generally not cover drugs that can be self-administered, such as those in pill form, or are used for self-injection. However, the statute provides for the coverage of some self-administered drugs. Examples of self-administered drugs that are covered include blood-clotting factors, drugs used in immunosuppressive therapy, erythropoietin for dialysis patients, osteoporosis drugs for certain homebound patients, and certain oral cancer drugs. (See Sec.110.3 for coverage of drugs, which are necessary to the effective use of Durable Medical Equipment (DME) or prosthetic devices.)

100-2,15,50.2

Determining Self-Administration of Drug or Biological

AB-02-072, AB-02-139, B3-2049.2

The Medicare program provides limited benefits for outpatient prescription drugs. The program covers drugs that are furnished "incident to" a physician's service provided that the drugs are not usually self-administered by the patients who take them. Section 112 of the Benefits, Improvements & Protection Act of 2000 (BIPA) amended sections 1861(s)(2)(A) and 1861(s)(2)(B) of the Act to redefine this exclusion. The prior statutory language referred to those drugs "which cannot be self-administered." Implementation of the BIPA provision requires interpretation of the phrase "not usually self-administered by the patient".

A. Policy

Fiscal intermediaries and carriers are instructed to follow the instructions below when applying the exclusion for drugs that are usually self-administered by the patient. Each individual contractor must make its own individual determination on each drug. Contractors must continue to apply the policy that not only the drug is medically reasonable and necessary for any individual claim, but also that the route of administration is medically reasonable and necessary. That is, if a drug is available in both oral and injectable forms, the injectable form of the drug must be medically reasonable and necessary as compared to using the oral form.

For certain injectable drugs, it will be apparent due to the nature of the condition(s) for which they are administered or the usual course of treatment for those conditions, they are, or are not, usually self-administered. For example, an injectable drug used to treat migraine headaches is usually self-administered. On the other hand, an injectable drug, administered at the same time as chemotherapy, used to treat anemia secondary to chemotherapy is not usually self-administered.

B. Administered

The term "administered" refers only to the physical process by which the drug enters the patient's body. It does not refer to whether the process is supervised by a medical professional (for example, to observe proper technique or side-effects of the drug). Only injectable (including intravenous) drugs are eligible for inclusion under the "incident to" benefit. Other routes of administration including, but not limited to, oral drugs, suppositories, topical medications are all considered to be usually self-administered by the patient.

C. Usually

For the purposes of applying this exclusion, the term "usually" means more than 50 percent of the time for all Medicare beneficiaries who use the drug. Therefore, if a drug is self-administered by more than 50 percent of Medicare beneficiaries, the drug is excluded from coverage and the contractor may not make any Medicare payment for it. In arriving at a single determination as to whether a drug is usually self-administered, contractors should make a separate determination for each indication for a drug as to whether that drug is usually self-administered.

After determining whether a drug is usually self-administered for each indication, contractors should determine the relative contribution of each indication to total use of the drug (i.e., weighted average) in order to make an overall determination as to whether the drug is usually self-administered. For example, if a drug has three indications, is not self-administered for the first indication, but is self administered for the second and third indications, and the first indication makes up 40 percent of total usage, the second indication makes up 30 percent of total usage, and the third indication makes up 30 percent of total usage, then the drug would be considered usually self-administered.

Reliable statistical information on the extent of self-administration by the patient may not always be available. Consequently, CMS offers the following guidance for each contractor's consideration in making this determination in the absence of such data:

1. Absent evidence to the contrary, presume that drugs delivered intravenously are not usually self-administered by the patient.
2. Absent evidence to the contrary, presume that drugs delivered by intramuscular injection are not usually self-administered by the patient. (Avonex, for example, is delivered by intramuscular injection, not usually self-administered by the patient.) The contractor may consider the depth and nature of the particular intramuscular injection in applying this presumption. In applying this presumption, contractors should examine the use of the particular drug and consider the following factors:
3. Absent evidence to the contrary, presume that drugs delivered by subcutaneous injection are self-administered by the patient. However, contractors should examine the use of the particular drug and consider the following factors:

   A. Acute Condition - Is the condition for which the drug is used an acute condition? If so, it is less likely that a patient would self-administer the drug. If the condition were longer term, it would be more likely that the patient would self-administer the drug.

   B. Frequency of Administration - How often is the injection given? For example, if the drug is administered once per month, it is less likely to be self-administered by the patient. However, if it is administered once or more per week, it is likely that the drug is self-administered by the patient. In some instances, carriers may have provided payment for one or perhaps several doses of a drug that would otherwise not be paid for because the drug is usually self-administered. Carriers may have exercised this discretion for limited coverage, for example, during a brief time when the patient is being trained under the supervision of a physician in the proper technique for self-administration. Medicare will no longer pay for such doses. In addition, contractors may no longer pay for any drug when it is administered on an outpatient emergency basis, if the drug is excluded because it is usually self-administered by the patient.

D. Definition of Acute Condition

For the purposes of determining whether a drug is usually self-administered, an acute condition means a condition that begins over a short time period, is likely to be of short duration and/or the expected course of treatment is for a short, finite interval. A course of treatment consisting of scheduled injections lasting less than two weeks, regardless of frequency or route of administration, is considered acute. Evidence to support this may include Food and Drug administration (FDA) approval language, package inserts, drug compendia, and other information.

E. By the Patient

The term "by the patient" means Medicare beneficiaries as a collective whole. The carrier includes only the patients themselves and not other individuals (that is, spouses, friends, or other care-givers are not considered the patient). The determination is based on whether the drug is self-administered by the patient a majority of the time that the drug is used on an outpatient basis by Medicare beneficiaries for medically necessary indications.

The carrier ignores all instances when the drug is administered on an inpatient basis. The carrier makes this determination on a drug-by-drug basis, not on a beneficiary-by-beneficiary basis. In evaluating whether beneficiaries as a collective whole self-administer, individual beneficiaries who do not have the capacity to self-administer any drug due to a condition other than the condition for which they are taking the drug in question are not considered. For example, an individual afflicted with paraplegia or advanced dementia would not have the capacity to self-administer any injectable drug, so such individuals would not be included in the population upon which the determination for self-administration by the patient was based. Note that some individuals afflicted with a less severe stage of an otherwise debilitating condition would be included in the population upon which the determination for "self-administered by the patient" was based; for example, an early onset of dementia.

F. Evidentiary Criteria

Contractors are only required to consider the following types of evidence: peer reviewed medical literature, standards of medical practice, evidence-based practice guidelines, FDA approved label, and package inserts. Contractors may also consider other evidence submitted by interested individuals or groups subject to their judgment.

Contractors should also use these evidentiary criteria when reviewing requests for making a determination as to whether a drug is usually self-administered, and requests for reconsideration of a pending or published determination.

Please note that prior to the August 1, 2002, one of the principal factors used to determine whether a drug was subject to the self-administered exclusion was whether the FDA label contained instructions for self-administration. However, CMS notes that under the new standard, the fact that the FDA label includes instructions for self-administration is not, by itself, a determining factor that a drug is subject to this exclusion.

G. Provider Notice of Noncovered Drugs

Contractors must describe on their Web site the process they will use to determine whether a drug is usually self-administered and thus does not meet the "incident to" benefit category. Contractors must publish a list of the injectable drugs that are subject to the self-administered exclusion on their Web site, including the data and rationale that led to the determination. Contractors will report the workload associated with developing new coverage statements in CAFM 21208.

Contractors must provide notice 45 days prior to the date that these drugs will not be covered. During the 45-day time period, contractors will maintain existing medical review and payment procedures. After the 45-day notice, contractors may deny payment for the drugs subject to the notice.

Contractors must not develop local medical review policies (LMRPs) for this purpose because further elaboration to describe drugs that do not meet the ‚Äòincident to' and the ‚Äònot usually self-administered' provisions of the statute are unnecessary. Current LMRPs based solely on these provisions must be withdrawn. LMRPs that address the self-administered exclusion and other information may be reissued absent the self-administered drug exclusion material. Contractors will report this workload in CAFM 21206. However, contractors may continue to use and write LMRPs to describe reasonable and necessary uses of drugs that are not usually self-administered. H. Conferences Between Contractors Contractors' Medical Directors may meet and discuss whether a drug is usually self-administered without reaching a formal consensus. Each contractor uses its discretion as to whether or not it will participate in such discussions. Each contractor must make its own individual determinations, except that fiscal intermediaries may, at their discretion, follow the determinations of the local carrier with respect to the self-administered exclusion.

I. Beneficiary Appeals

If a beneficiary's claim for a particular drug is denied because the drug is subject to the "self-administered drug" exclusion, the beneficiary may appeal the denial. Because it is a "benefit category" denial and not a denial based on medical necessity, an Advance Beneficiary Notice (ABN) is not required. A "benefit category" denial (i.e., a denial based on the fact that there is no benefit category under which the drug may be covered) does not trigger the financial liability protection provisions of Limitation On Liability (under Sec.1879 of the Act). Therefore, physicians or providers may charge the beneficiary for an excluded drug.

J. Provider and Physician Appeals

A physician accepting assignment may appeal a denial under the provisions found in Chapter 29 of the Medicare Claims Processing Manual.

K. Reasonable and Necessary

Carriers and fiscal intermediaries will make the determination of reasonable and necessary with respect to the medical appropriateness of a drug to treat the patient's condition. Contractors will continue to make the determination of whether the intravenous or injection form of a drug is appropriate as opposed to the oral form. Contractors will also continue to make the determination as to whether a physician's office visit was reasonable and necessary. However, contractors should not make a determination of whether it was reasonable and necessary for the patient to choose to have his or her drug administered in the physician's office or outpatient hospital setting. That is, while a physician's office visit may not be reasonable and necessary in a specific situation, in such a case an injection service would be payable.

L. Reporting Requirements

Each carrier and intermediary must report to CMS, every September 1 and March 1, its complete list of injectable drugs that the contractor has determined are excluded when furnished incident to a physician's service on the basis that the drug is usually self-administered. The CMS anticipates that contractors will review injectable drugs on a rolling basis and publish their list of excluded drugs as it is developed. For example, contractors should not wait to publish this list until every drug has been reviewed.

Contractors must send their exclusion list to the following e-mail address: drugdata@cms.hhs.gov a template that CMS will provide separately, consisting of the following data elements in order:

1. Carrier Name
2. State
3. Carrier ID#
4. HCPCS
5. Descriptor
6. Effective Date of Exclusion
7. End Date of Exclusion
8. Comments

Any exclusion list not provided in the CMS mandated format will be returned for correction. To view the presently mandated CMS format for this report, open the file located at: http://cms.hhs.gov/manuals/pm_trans/AB02_139a

100-2,15,50.4.2

Unlabeled Use of Drug

B3-2049.3

An unlabeled use of a drug is a use that is not included as an indication on the drug's label as approved by the FDA. FDA approved drugs used for indications other than what is indicated on the official label may be covered under Medicare if the carrier determines the use to be medically accepted, taking into consideration the major drug compendia, authoritative medical literature and/or accepted standards of medical practice. In the case of drugs used in an anti-cancer chemotherapeutic regimen, unlabeled uses are covered for a medically accepted indication as defined in Sec.50.5. These decisions are made by the contractor on a case-by-case basis.

100-2,15,50.5

Self-Administered Drugs and Biologicals

B3-2049.5

Medicare Part B does not cover drugs that are usually self-administered by the patient unless the statute provides for such coverage. The statute explicitly provides coverage, for blood clotting factors, drugs used in immunosuppressive therapy, erythropoietin for dialysis patients, certain oral anti-cancer drugs and anti-emetics used in certain situations.

100-2,16,10

General Exclusions From Coverage

A3-3150, HO-260, HHA-232, B3-2300

No payment can be made under either the hospital insurance or supplementary medical insurance program for certain items and services, when the following conditions exist:

- Not reasonable and necessary (Sec.20);
- No legal obligation to pay for or provide (Sec.40);
- Paid for by a governmental entity (Sec.50);
- Not provided within United States (Sec.60);
- Resulting from war (Sec.70);
- Personal comfort (Sec.80);
- Routine services and appliances (Sec.90);
- Custodial care (Sec.110);
- Cosmetic surgery (Sec.120);
- Charges by immediate relatives or members of household (Sec.130);
- Dental services (Sec.140);
- Paid or expected to be paid under workers' compensation (Sec.150);
- Nonphysician services provided to a hospital inpatient that were not provided directly or arranged for by the hospital (Sec.170);
- Services Related to and Required as a Result of Services Which are not Covered Under Medicare (Sec.180);
- Excluded foot care services and supportive devices for feet (Sec.30); or
- Excluded investigational devices (See Chapter 14, Sec.30).

100-2,16,140

Dental Services Exclusion

A3-3162, HO-260.13, B3-2336

Items and services in connection with the care, treatment, filling, removal, or replacement of teeth, or structures directly supporting the teeth are not covered. Structures directly supporting the teeth mean the periodontium, which includes the gingivae, dentogingival junction, periodontal membrane, cementum, and alveolar process. However, payment may be made for certain other services of a dentist. (See the Medicare Benefit Policy Manual, Chapter 15, "Covered Medical and Other Health Services," Sec.150.)

The hospitalization or nonhospitalization of a patient has no direct bearing on the coverage or exclusion of a given dental procedure.

When an excluded service is the primary procedure involved, it is not covered regardless of its complexity or difficulty. For example, the extraction of an impacted tooth is not covered. Similarly, an alveoplasty (the surgical improvement of the shape and condition of the alveolar process) and a frenectomy are excluded from coverage when either of these procedures is performed in connection with an excluded service, e.g., the preparation of the mouth for dentures. In like manner, the removal of the torus palatinus (a bony protuberance of the hard palate) could be a covered service. However, with rare exception, this surgery is performed in connection with an excluded service, i.e., the preparation of the mouth for dentures. Under such circumstances, reimbursement is not made for this purpose.

The extraction of teeth to prepare the jaw for radiation treatments of neoplastic disease is also covered. This is an exception to the requirement that to be covered, a noncovered procedure or service performed by a dentist must be an incident to and an integral part of a covered procedure or service performed by the dentist. Ordinarily, the dentist extracts the patient's teeth, but another physician, e.g., a radiologist, administers the radiation treatments.

Whether such services as the administration of anesthesia, diagnostic x-rays, and other related procedures are covered depends upon whether the primary procedure being performed by the dentist is covered. Thus, an x-ray taken in connection with the reduction of a fracture of the jaw or facial bone is covered. However, a single x-ray or xray survey taken in connection with the care or treatment of teeth or the periodontium is not covered.

See also the Medicare Benefit Policy Manual, Chapter 1, "Inpatient Hospital Services, Sec.70, and Chapter 15, "Covered Medical and Other Health Services," Sec.150 for additional information on dental services.

100-2,16,20

Services Not Reasonable and Necessary

A3-3151, HO-260.1, B3-2303, AB-00-52 - 6/00

Items and services which are not reasonable and necessary for the diagnosis or treatment of illness or injury or to improve the functioning of a malformed body member are not covered, e.g., payment cannot be made for the rental of a special hospital bed to be used by the patient in their home unless it was a reasonable and necessary part of the patient's treatment. See also Sec.80.

A health care item or service for the purpose of causing, or assisting to cause, the death of any individual (assisted suicide) is not covered. This prohibition does not apply to the provision of an item or service for the purpose of alleviating pain or discomfort, even if such use may increase the risk of death, so long as the item or service is not furnished for the specific purpose of causing death.

100-2,16,90

Routine Services and Appliances

A3-3157, HO-260.7, B3-2320, R-1797A3 - 5/00

Routine physical checkups; eyeglasses, contact lenses, and eye examinations for the purpose of prescribing, fitting, or changing eyeglasses; eye refractions by whatever practitioner and for whatever purpose performed; hearing aids and examinations for hearing aids; and immunizations are not covered.

The routine physical checkup exclusion applies to (a) examinations performed without relationship to treatment or diagnosis for a specific illness, symptom, complaint, or injury; and (b) examinations required by third parties such as insurance companies business establishments, or Government agencies.

If the claim is for a diagnostic test or examination performed solely for the purpose of establishing a claim under title IV of Public Law 91-173, "Black Lung Benefits," the service is not covered under Medicare and the claimant should be advised to contact their Social Security office regarding the filing of a claim for reimbursement under the "Black Lung" program.

The exclusions apply to eyeglasses or contact lenses, and eye examinations for the purpose of prescribing, fitting, or changing eyeglasses or contact lenses for refractive errors. The exclusions do not apply to physicians' services (and services incident to a physicians' service) performed in conjunction with an eye disease, as for example, glaucoma or cataracts, or to post-surgical prosthetic lenses which are customarily used during convalescence from eye surgery in which the lens of the eye was removed, or to permanent prosthetic lenses required by an individual lacking the organic lens of the eye whether by surgical removal or congenital disease. Such prosthetic lens is a replacement for an internal body organ - the lens of the eye. (See the Medicare Benefit Policy Manual, Chapter 15, "Covered Medical and Other Health Services," Sec.120). Expenses for all refractive procedures, whether performed by an ophthalmologist (or any other physician) or an optometrist and without regard to the reason for performance of the refraction, are excluded from coverage.

A. Immunizations

Vaccinations or inoculations are excluded as immunizations unless they are either

Directly related to the treatment of an injury or direct exposure to a disease or condition, such as antirabies treatment, tetanus antitoxin or booster vaccine, botulin antitoxin, antivenin sera, or immune globulin. (In the absence of injury or direct exposure, preventive immunization (vaccination or inoculation) against such diseases as smallpox, polio, diphtheria, etc., is not covered.); or

Specifically covered by statute, as described in the Medicare Benefit Policy Manual, Chapter 15, "Covered Medical and Other Health Services," Sec.50.

B. Antigens

Prior to the Omnibus Reconciliation Act of 1980, a physician who prepared an antigen for a patient could not be reimbursed for that service unless the physician also administered the antigen to the patient. Effective January 1, 1981, payment may be made for a reasonable supply of antigens that have been prepared for a particular patient even though they have not been administered to the patient by the same physician who prepared them if:

The antigens are prepared by a physician who is a doctor of medicine or osteopathy, and "The physician who prepared the antigens has examined the patient and has determined a plan of treatment and a dosage regimen.

A reasonable supply of antigens is considered to be not more than a 12-week supply of antigens that has been prepared for a particular patient at any one time. The purpose of the reasonable supply limitation is to assure that the antigens retain their potency and effectiveness over the period in which they are to be administered to the patient. (See the Medicare Benefit Policy Manual, Chapter 15, "Covered Medical and Other Health Services," Sec.50.4.4.2)

100-2,6,10

Medical and Other Health Services Furnished to Inpatients of Participating Hospitals

Payment may be made under Part B for physician services and for the nonphysician medical and other health services listed below when furnished by a participating hospital (either directly or under arrangements) to an inpatient of the hospital, but only if payment for these services cannot be made under Part A.

In PPS hospitals, this means that Part B payment could be made for these services if:

- No Part A prospective payment is made at all for the hospital stay because of patient exhaustion of benefit days before admission;
- The admission was disapproved as not reasonable and necessary (and waiver of liability payment was not made);
- The day or days of the otherwise covered stay during which the services were provided were not reasonable and necessary (and no payment was made under waiver of liability);
- The patient was not otherwise eligible for or entitled to coverage under Part A (See the Medicare Benefit Policy Manual, Chapter 1, Sec.150, for services received as a result of noncovered services); or
- No Part A day outlier payment is made (for discharges before October 1997) for one or more outlier days due to patient exhaustion of benefit days after admission but before the case's arrival at outlier status, or because outlier days are otherwise not covered and waiver of liability payment is not made.

However, if only day outlier payment is denied under Part A (discharges before October 1997), Part B payment may be made for only the services covered under Part B and furnished on the denied outlier days.

In non-PPS hospitals, Part B payment may be made for services on any day for which Part A payment is denied (i.e., benefit days are exhausted; services are not at the hospital level of care; or patient is not otherwise eligible or entitled to payment under Part A).

Services payable are:

- Diagnostic x-ray tests, diagnostic laboratory tests, and other diagnostic tests;
- X-ray, radium, and radioactive isotope therapy, including materials and services of technicians;
- Surgical dressings, and splints, casts, and other devices used for reduction of fractures and dislocations;
- Prosthetic devices (other than dental) which replace all or part of an internal body organ (including contiguous tissue), or all or part of the function of a permanently inoperative or malfunctioning internal body organ, including replacement or repairs of such devices;

- Leg, arm, back, and neck braces, trusses, and artificial legs, arms, and eyes including adjustments, repairs, and replacements required because of breakage, wear, loss, or a change in the patient's physical condition;
- Outpatient physical therapy, outpatient speech-language pathology services, and outpatient occupational therapy (see the Medicare Benefit Policy Manual, Chapter 15, "Covered Medical and Other Health Services," Sec.Sec.220 and 230);
- Screening mammography services;
- Screening pap smears;
- Influenza, pneumococcal pneumonia, and hepatitis B vaccines;
- Colorectal screening;
- Bone mass measurements;
- Diabetes self-management;
- Prostate screening;
- Ambulance services;
- Hemophilia clotting factors for hemophilia patients competent to use these factors without supervision);
- Immunosuppressive drugs;
- Oral anti-cancer drugs;
- Oral drug prescribed for use as an acute anti-emetic used as part of an anti-cancer chemotherapeutic regimen; and
- Epoetin Alfa (EPO).

Coverage rules for these services are described in the Medicare Benefit Policy Manual, Chapters: 11, "End Stage Renal Disease (ESRD);" 14, "Medical Devices;" or 15, "Medical and Other Health Services."

For services to be covered under Part A or Part B, a hospital must furnish nonphysician services to its inpatients directly or under arrangements. A nonphysician service is one which does not meet the criteria defining physicians' services specifically provided for in regulation at 42 CFR 415.102. Services "incident to" physicians' services (except for the services of nurse anesthetists employed by anesthesiologists) are nonphysician services for purposes of this provision. This provision is applicable to all hospitals participating in Medicare, including those paid under alternative arrangements such as State cost control systems, and to emergency hospital services furnished by nonparticipating hospitals.

In all hospitals, every service provided to a hospital inpatient other than those listed in the next paragraph must be treated as an inpatient hospital service to be paid for under Part A, if Part A coverage is available and the beneficiary is entitled to Part A. This is because every hospital must provide directly or arrange for any nonphysician service rendered to its inpatients, and a hospital can be paid under Part B for a service provided in this manner only if Part A coverage does not exist.

These services, when provided to a hospital inpatient, may be covered under Part B, even though the patient has Part A coverage for the hospital stay. This is because these services are covered under Part B and not covered under Part A. They are:

- Physicians' services (including the services of residents and interns in unapproved teaching programs);
- Influenza vaccine;
- Pneumoccocal vaccine and its administration;
- Hepatitis B vaccine and its administration;
- Screening mammography services;
- Screening pap smears and pelvic exams;
- Colorectal screening;
- Bone mass measurements;
- Diabetes self management training services; and
- Prostate screening.

However, note that in order to have any Medicare coverage at all (Part A or Part B), any nonphysician service rendered to a hospital inpatient must be provided directly or arranged for by the hospital.

100-2,6,20.6

Outpatient Observation Services

A. Outpatient Observation Services Defined

Observation care is a well-defined set of specific, clinically appropriate services, which include ongoing short term treatment, assessment, and reassessment before a decision can be made regarding whether patients will require further treatment as hospital inpatients or if they are able to be discharged from the hospital. Observation status is commonly assigned to patients who present to the emergency department and who then require a significant period of treatment or monitoring in order to make a decision concerning their admission or discharge.

Observation services are covered only when provided by the order of a physician or another individual authorized by State licensure law and hospital staff bylaws to admit patients to the hospital or to order outpatient tests. In the majority of cases, the decision whether to discharge a patient from the hospital following resolution of the reason for the observation care or to admit the patient as an inpatient can be made in less than 48 hours, usually in less than 24 hours. In only rare and exceptional cases do reasonable and necessary outpatient observation services span more than 48 hours.

Hospitals may bill for patients who are directly admitted to the hospital for outpatient observation services. A "direct admission" occurs when a physician in the community refers a patient to the hospital for observation, bypassing the clinic or emergency department (ED). Effective for services furnished on or after January 1, 2003, hospitals may bill for patients directly admitted for observation services.

See, the Medicare Claims Processing Manual, Pub. 100-04, chapter 4, section 290, at http://www.cms.hhs.gov/manuals/downloads/clm104c04.pdf for billing and payment instructions for outpatient observation services.

B. Coverage of Outpatient Observation Services

When a physician orders that a patient be placed under observation care, the patient's status is that of an outpatient. The purpose of observation is to determine the need for further treatment or for inpatient admission. Thus, a patient receiving observation services may improve and be released, or be admitted as an inpatient (see Pub. 100-02, Medicare Benefit Policy Manual, Chapter 1, Section 10 "Covered Inpatient Hospital Services Covered Under Part A" at http://www.cms.hhs.gov/manuals/Downloads/bp102c01.pdf). For more information on correct reporting of observation services, see the Medicare Claims Processing Manual, Pub. 100-04, chapter 4, section 290.2.2.)

All hospital observation services, regardless of the duration of the observation care, that are medically reasonable and necessary are covered by Medicare. Observation services are reported using HCPCS code G0378 (Hospital observation service, per hour). Beginning January 1, 2008, HCPCS code G0378 for hourly observation services is assigned status indicator N, signifying that its payment is always packaged. No separate payment is made for observation services reported with HCPCS code G0378. In most circumstances, observation services are supportive and ancillary to the other separately payable services provided to a patient. In certain circumstances when observation care is billed in conjunction with a high level clinic visit (Level 5), high level emergency department visit (Level 4 or 5), critical care services, or direct admission to observation as an integral part of a patient's extended encounter of care, payment may be made for the entire extended care encounter through one of two composite APCs when certain criteria are met. For information about billing and payment methodology for observation services in years prior to CY 2008, see the Medicare Claims Processing Manual, Pub. 100-04, chapter 4, sections 290.3-290.4. For information about payment for extended assessment and management under composite APCs, see section 290.5.

Payment for all reasonable and necessary observation services is packaged into the payments for other separately payable services provided to the patient in the same encounter. Observation services that are packaged through assignment of status indicator N are covered OPPS services. Since the payment for these services is included in the APC payment for other separately payable services on the claim, hospitals must not bill Medicare beneficiaries directly for the packaged services.

C. Services Not Covered by Medicare and Notification to the Beneficiary

In making the determination whether an ABN can be used to shift liability to a beneficiary for the cost of non-covered items or services related to an encounter that includes observation care, the provider should follow a two step process. First, the provider must decide whether the item or service meets either the definition of observation care or would be otherwise covered. If the item or service does not meet the definitional requirements of any Medicare-covered benefit under Part B, then the item or service is not covered by Medicare and an ABN is not required to shift the liability to the beneficiary. However, the provider may choose to provide voluntary notification for these items or services.

Second, if the item or service meets the definition of observation services or would be otherwise covered, then the provider must decide whether the item or service is "reasonable and necessary" for the beneficiary on the occasion in question, or if the item or service exceeds any frequency limitation for the particular benefit or falls outside of a timeframe for receipt of a particular benefit. In these cases, the ABN would be used to shift the liability to the beneficiary (see the Medicare Claims Processing Manual; Pub. 100-04, Chapter 30, "Financial Liability Protections,"

Section 20, at http://www.cms.hhs.gov/manuals/downloads/clm104c30.pdf for information regarding Limitation On Liability (LOL) Under Sec.1879 Where Medicare Claims Are Disallowed).

If an ABN is not issued to the beneficiary, the provider may be held liable for the cost of the item or service unless the provider/supplier is able to demonstrate that they did not know and could not have reasonably been expected to know that Medicare would not pay for the item or service.

100-3,240.4

NCD for Continuous Positive Airway Pressure (CPAP) Therapy For Obstructive Sleep Apnea (OSA) (240.4)

B. Nationally Covered Indications

Effective for claims with dates of service on and after March 13, 2008, the Centers for Medicare & Medicaid Services (CMS) determines that CPAP therapy when used in adult patients with OSA is considered reasonable and necessary under the following situations:

1. The use of CPAP is covered under Medicare when used in adult patients with OSA. Coverage of CPAP is initially limited to a 12-week period to identify beneficiaries diagnosed with OSA as subsequently described who benefit from CPAP. CPAP is subsequently covered only for those beneficiaries diagnosed with OSA who benefit from CPAP during this 12-week period.
2. The provider of CPAP must conduct education of the beneficiary prior to the use of the CPAP device to ensure that the beneficiary has been educated in the proper use of the device. A caregiver, for example a family member, may be compensatory, if consistently available in the beneficiary's home and willing and able to safely operate the CPAP device.
3. A positive diagnosis of OSA for the coverage of CPAP must include a clinical evaluation and a positive:
   a. attended PSG performed in a sleep laboratory; or
   b. unattended HST with a Type II home sleep monitoring device; or
   c. unattended HST with a Type III home sleep monitoring device; or
   d. unattended HST with a Type IV home sleep monitoring device that measures at least 3 channels.
4. The sleep test must have been previously ordered by the beneficiaryÔø¾s treating physician and furnished under appropriate physician supervision.
5. An initial 12-week period of CPAP is covered in adult patients with OSA if either of the following criterion using the AHI or RDI are met:
   a. AHI or RDI greater than or equal to 15 events per hour, or
   b. AHI or RDI greater than or equal to 5 events and less than or equal to 14 events per hour with documented symptoms of excessive daytime sleepiness, impaired cognition, mood disorders or insomnia, or documented hypertension, ischemic heart disease, or history of stroke.
6. The AHI or RDI is calculated on the average number of events of per hour. If the AHI or RDI is calculated based on less than 2 hours of continuous recorded sleep, the total number of recorded events to calculate the AHI or RDI during sleep testing must be at a minimum the number of events that would have been required in a 2-hour period.
7. Apnea is defined as a cessation of airflow for at least 10 seconds. Hypopnea is defined as an abnormal respiratory event lasting at least 10 seconds with at least a 30% reduction in thoracoabdominal movement or airflow as compared to baseline, and with at least a 4% oxygen desaturation.
8. Coverage with Evidence Development (CED): Medicare provides the following limited coverage for CPAP in adult beneficiaries who do not qualify for CPAP coverage based on criteria 1-7 above. A clinical study seeking Medicare payment for CPAP provided to a beneficiary who is an enrolled subject in that study must address one or more of the following questions
   a. In Medicare-aged subjects with clinically identified risk factors for OSA, how does the diagnostic accuracy of a clinical trial of CPAP compare with PSG and Type II, III & IV HST in identifying subjects with OSA who will respond to CPAP?
   b. In Medicare-aged subjects with clinically identified risk factors for OSA who have not undergone confirmatory testing with PSG or Type II, III & IV HST, does CPAP cause clinically meaningful harm?

The study must meet the following additional standards:

c. The principal purpose of the research study is to test whether a particular intervention potentially improves the participantsÔø¾ health outcomes.

d. The research study is well-supported by available scientific and medical information or it is intended to clarify or establish the health outcomes of interventions already in common clinical use.

e. The research study does not unjustifiably duplicate existing studies.

f. The research study design is appropriate to answer the research question being asked in the study.

g. The research study is sponsored by an organization or individual capable of executing the proposed study successfully.

h. The research study is in compliance with all applicable Federal regulations concerning the protection of human subjects found at 45 CFR Part 46. If a study is Food and Drug Administration-regulated, it also must be in compliance with 21 CFR Parts 50 and 56.

i. All aspects of the research study are conducted according to the appropriate standards of scientific integrity.

j. The research study has a written protocol that clearly addresses, or incorporates by reference, the Medicare standards.

k. The clinical research study is not designed to exclusively test toxicity or disease pathophysiology in healthy individuals. Trials of all medical technologies measuring therapeutic outcomes as one of the objectives meet this standard only if the disease or condition being studied is life-threatening as defined in 21 CFR Ôø¾ 312.81(a) and the patient has no other viable treatment options.

l. The clinical research study is registered on the ClinicalTrials.gov Web site by the principal sponsor/investigator prior to the enrollment of the first study subject.

m. The research study protocol specifies the method and timing of public release of all pre-specified outcomes to be measured, including release of outcomes if outcomes are negative or study is terminated early. The results must be made public within 24 months of the end of data collection. If a report is planned for publication in a peer-reviewed journal, then that initial release may be an abstract that meets the requirements of the International Committee of Medical Journal Editors. However, a full report of the outcomes must be made public no later than 3 years after the end of data collection.

n. The research study protocol must explicitly discuss subpopulations affected by the treatment under investigation, particularly traditionally underrepresented groups in clinical studies, how the inclusion and exclusion criteria affect enrollment of these populations, and a plan for the retention and reporting of said populations in the trial. If the inclusion and exclusion criteria are expected to have a negative effect on the recruitment or retention of underrepresented populations, the protocol must discuss why these criteria are necessary.

o. The research study protocol explicitly discusses how the results are or are not expected to be generalizable to the Medicare population to infer whether Medicare patients may benefit from the intervention. Separate discussions in the protocol may be necessary for populations eligible for Medicare due to age, disability, or Medicaid eligibility.

C. Nationally Non-covered Indications

Effective for claims with dates of services on and after March 13, 2008, other diagnostic tests for the diagnosis of OSA, other than those noted above for prescribing CPAP, are not sufficient for the coverage of CPAP.

D. Other

N/A

(This NCD last reviewed March

100-4,1,10.1.4.1

Physician and Ambulance Services Furnished in Connection With Covered Foreign Inpatient Hospital Services

Payment is made for necessary physician and ambulance services that meet the other coverage requirements of the Medicare program, and are furnished in connection with and during a period of covered foreign hospitalization.

A. Coverage of Physician and Ambulance Services Furnished Outside the U.S.

Where inpatient services in a foreign hospital are covered, payment may also be made for

- Physicians' services furnished to the beneficiary while he/she is an inpatient,
- Physicians' services furnished to the beneficiary outside the hospital on the day of his/her admission as an inpatient, provided the services were for the same condition for which the beneficiary was hospitalized (including the services of a Canadian ship,Äôs physician who furnishes emergency services in Canadian waters on the day the patient is admitted to a Canadian hospital for a covered emergency stay and,
- Ambulance services, where necessary, for the trip to the hospital in conjunction with the beneficiary's admission as an inpatient. Return trips from a foreign hospital are not covered.

In cases involving foreign ambulance services, the general requirements in Chapter 15 are also applicable, subject to the following special rules:

- If the foreign hospitalization was determined to be covered on the basis of emergency services, the medical necessity requirements outlined in Chapter 15 are considered met.
- The definition of:
  - physician
  - for purposes of coverage of services furnished outside the U.S., is expanded to include a foreign practitioner, provided the practitioner is legally licensed to practice in the country in which the services are furnished.
- Only the enrollee can file for Part B benefits; the assignment method may not be used.
- Where the enrollee is deceased, the rules for settling Part B underpayments are applicable. Payment is made to the foreign physician or foreign ambulance company on an unpaid bill provided the physician or ambulance company accepts the payment as the full charge for the service, or payment an be made to a person who has agreed to assume legal liability to pay the physician or supplier. Where the bill is paid, payment may be made in accordance with Medicare regulations. The regular deductible and coinsurance requirements apply to physicians' and ambulance service

100-4,1,30.3.5

Effect of Assignment Upon Purchase of Cataract Glasses FromParticipating Physician or Supplier on Claims Submitted to Carriers

B3-3045.4

A pair of cataract glasses is comprised of two distinct products: a professional product (the prescribed lenses) and a retail commercial product (the frames). The frames serve not only as a holder of lenses but also as an article of personal apparel. As such, they are usually selected on the basis of personal taste and style. Although Medicare will pay only for standard frames, most patients want deluxe frames. Participating physicians and suppliers cannot profitably furnish such deluxe frames unless they can make an extra (noncovered) charge for the frames even though they accept assignment.

Therefore, a participating physician or supplier (whether an ophthalmologist, optometrist, or optician) who accepts assignment on cataract glasses with deluxe frames may charge the Medicare patient the difference between his/her usual charge to private pay patients for glasses with standard frames and his/her usual charge to such patients for glasses with deluxe frames, in addition to the applicable deductible and coinsurance on glasses with standard frames, if all of the following requirements are met:

A. The participating physician or supplier has standard frames available, offers them for saleto the patient, and issues and ABN to the patient that explains the price and other differences between standard and deluxe frames. Refer to Chapter 30.

B. The participating physician or supplier obtains from the patient (or his/her representative) and keeps on file the following signed and dated statement:

____

Name of Patient Medicare Claim Number

Having been informed that an extra charge is being made by the physician or supplier for deluxe frames, that this extra charge is not covered by Medicare, and that standard frames are available for purchase from the physician or supplier at no extra charge, I have chosen to purchase deluxe frames. ____________

Signature Date

C. The participating physician or supplier itemizes on his/her claim his/her actual charge for the lenses, his/her actual charge for the standard frames, and his/her actual extra charge for the deluxe frames (charge differential). Once the assigned claim for deluxe frames has been processed, the carrier will follow the ABN instructions as described in Sec.60.

100-4,11,30.3

Data Required on Claim to FI

See Pub. 100-02, Chapter 9, Secs.10 & 20.2 for coverage requirements for Hospice benefits. This section addresses only the submittal of claims. See section 20, of this chapter for information on Notice of Election (NOE) transaction types (81A,C,E and 82A,C,E).

Before billing, the hospice must submit an admission notice to the FI (see section 20). The Social Security Act at Sec.1862 (a)(22) requires that all claims for Medicare payment must be submitted in an electronic form specified by the Secretary of Health and Human Services, unless an exception described at Sec.1862 (h) applies. The electronic form required for billing hospice services is the ANSI X12N 837 Institutional claim transaction. Since the data structure of the 837 transaction is difficult to express in narrative form and to provide assistance to small providers excepted from the electronic claim requirement, the instructions below are given relative to the data element names on the UB-04 (Form CMS-1450) hardcopy form. Each data element name is shown in bold type. Information regarding the form locator numbers that correspond to these data element names and a table to crosswalk UB-04 form locators to the 837 transaction is found in Chapter 25.

Because claim formats serve the needs of many payers, some data elements may not be needed by a particular payer. Detailed information is given only for items required for Medicare hospice claims. Items not listed need not be completed although hospices may complete them when billing multiple payers.

Provider Name, Address, and Telephone Number The hospice enters this information for their agency.

Type of Bill This three-digit alphanumeric code gives three specific pieces of information. The first digit identifies the type of facility. The second classifies the type of care. The third indicates the sequence of this bill in this particular benefit period. It is referred to as a "frequency" code.

Code Structure

1st Digit - Type of Facility
8 - Special facility (Hospice)

2nd Digit - Classification (Special Facility Only)
1 - Hospice (Nonhospital based)
2 - Hospice (Hospital based)

3rd Digit Frequency	Definition
0 - Nonpayment/Zero Claims	Used when no payment from Medicare is anticipated.
I - Admit Through Discharge Claim	This code is used for a bill encompassing an entire course of hospice treatment for which the provider expects payment from the payer, i.e., no further bills will be submitted for this patient.
2 - Interim - First Claim	This code is used for the first of an expected series of payment bills for a hospice course of treatment.
3 - Interim - Continuing Claim	This code is used when a payment bill for a hospice course of treatment has already been submitted and further bills are expected to be submitted.
4 - Interim - Last Claim	This code is used for a payment bill that is the last of a series for a hospice course of treatment. The "Through" date of this bill (FL 6) is the discharge date, transfer date, or date of death.
5 - Late Charges	Use this code for late charges that need to be billed. Late charges can be submitted only for revenue codes not on the original bill. For additional information on late charge bills see Chapter 3.
7 - Replacement of Prior Claim	This code is used by the provider when it wants to correct (other than late charges) a previously submitted bill. This is the code used on the corrected or "new" bill. For additional information on replacement bills see Chapter 3.
8 - Void/Cancel of a Prior Claim	This code is used to cancel a previously processed claim. For additional information on void/cancel bills see Chapter 3.

Statement Covers Period (From-Through)

The hospice shows the beginning and ending dates of the period covered by this bill in numeric fields (MM-DD-YY). The hospice does not show days before the patient's entitlement began. Since the 12-month hospice "cap period" (see Sec.80.2) ends each year on October 31, hospices must submit separate bills for October and November.

Patient Name/Identifier

The hospice enters the beneficiary's name exactly as it appears on the Medicare card.

Patient Address

Patient Birth date

Patient Sex

The hospice enters the appropriate address, date of birth and gender information describing the beneficiary.

Admission/Start of Care Date

The hospice enters the admission date, which must be the same date as the effective date of the hospice election or change of election. The date of admission may not precede the physician's certification by more than 2 calendar days.

The admission date stays the same on all continuing claims for the same hospice election.

The hospice enters the month, day, and year numerically as MM-DD-YY.

Patient Discharge Status

This code indicates the patient's status as of the "Through" date (FL 6) of the billing period. The hospice enters the most appropriate NUBC approved code.

The codes most commonly used on hospice claims include:

01 Discharged to home or self care

30 Still patient 40 Expired at home

41 Expired in a medical facility, such as a hospital, SNF, ICF or freestanding hospice

42 Expired - place unknown

50 Discharged/Transferred to Hospice - home

51 Discharged/Transferred to Hospice - medical facility

Condition Codes

The hospice enters any appropriate NUBC approved code(s) identifying conditions related to this bill that may affect processing.

Codes listed below are only those most frequently applicable to hospice claims. For a complete list of codes, see Chapter 25.

07	Treatment of Non-terminal Condition for Hospice	Code indicates the patient has elected hospice care but the provider is not treating the terminal condition, and is, therefore, requesting regular Medicare payment.
20	Beneficiary Requested Billing	Code indicates the provider realizes the services on this bill are at a noncovered level of care or otherwise excluded from coverage, but the beneficiary has requested a formal determination.
21	Billing for Denial Notice	Code indicates the provider realizes services are at a noncovered level of care or excluded, but requests a denial notice from Medicare in order to bill Medicaid or other insurers.

Occurrence Codes and Dates

The hospice enters any appropriate NUBC approved code(s) and associated date(s) defining specific event(s) relating to this billing period. Event codes are two numeric digits, and dates are six numeric digits (MM-DD-YY). If there are more occurrences than there are spaces on the form, use FL 36 (occurrence span) to record additional occurrences and dates.

Codes listed below are only those most frequently applicable to hospice claims. For a complete list of codes, see Chapter 25.

Code	Title	Definition
23	Cancellation of Hospice Election Period (FI USE Only)	Code indicates date on which a hospice period of election is cancelled by an FI as opposed to revocation by the beneficiary.
24	Date Insurance Denied	Code indicates the date of receipt of a denial of coverage by a higher priority payer.
27	Date of Hospice Certification or Re-Certification	Code indicates the date of certification or re-certification of the hospice benefit period, beginning with the first 2 initial benefit periods of 90 days each and the subsequent 60-day benefit periods. Note regarding transfers from one hospice to another hospice: If a patient is in the first certification period when they transfer to another hospice, the receiving hospice would use the same certification date as the previous hospice until the next certification period. However, if they were in the next certification at the time of transfer, then they would enter that date in the Occurrence Code 27 and date.
42	Date of Termination of Hospice Benefit	Enter code to indicate the date on which beneficiary terminated his/her election to receive hospice benefits. This code can be used only when the beneficiary has revoked the benefit, has been decertified or discharged. It cannot be used in transfer situations.

Occurrence Span Code and Dates

The hospice enters any appropriate NUBC approved code(s) and associated beginning and ending date(s) defining a specific event relating to this billing period are shown. Event codes are two alphanumeric digits and dates are shown numerically as MM-DD-YY.

Codes listed below are only those most frequently applicable to hospice claims. For a complete list of codes, see Chapter 25.

Code	Title	Definition
M2	Dates of Inpatient Respite Care	Code indicates From/Through dates of a period of inpatient respite care for hospice patients to differentiate separate respite periods of less than 5 days each. M2 is used when respite care is provided more than once during a benefit period.
77	Provider Liability -Utilization Charged	Code indicates From/Through dates for a period of non-covered hospice care for which the provider accepts payment liability (other than for medical necessity or custodial care).

Hospices must use occurrence span code 77 to identify days of care that are not covered by Medicare due to untimely physician recertification. This is particularly important when the non-covered days fall at the beginning of a billing period.

Value Codes and Amounts

The hospice enters any appropriate NUBC approved code(s) and the associated value amounts identifying numeric information related to this bill that may affect processing.

The most commonly used value codes on hospice claims are value codes 61 and G8, which are used to report the location of the site of hospice services. Otherwise, value codes are commonly used only to indicate Medicare is secondary to another payer. For detailed information on reporting Medicare secondary payer information, see the Medicare Secondary Payer Manual.

Code	Title	Definition
61	Place of Residence where Service is Furnished (Routine Home Care and Continuous Home Care)	MSA or Core-Based Statistical Area (CBSA) number (or rural State code) of the location where the hospice service is delivered. A residence can be an inpatient facility if an individual uses that facility as a place of residence. It is the level of care that is required and not the location where hospice services are provided that determines payment. In other words, if an individual resides in a freestanding hospice facility and requires routine home care, then claims are submitted for routine home care. Hospices must report value code 61 when billing revenue codes 0651 and 0652.

Code	Title	Definition
G8	Facility where Inpatient Hospice Service is Delivered (General Inpatient and Inpatient Respite Care).	MSA or Core Based Statistical Area (CBSA) number (or rural State code) of the facility where inpatient hospice services are delivered. Hospices must report value code G8 when billing revenue codes 0655 and 0656.

If hospice services are provided to the beneficiary in more than one CBSA area during the billing period, the hospice reports the CBSA that applies at the end of the billing period. This applies for either routine home care and continuous home care (e.g., the beneficiary's residence changes between locations in different CBSAs) or for general inpatient and inpatient respite care (e.g., the beneficiary is served in inpatient facilities in different CBSAs).

Revenue Codes

The hospice assigns a revenue code for each type of service provided and enter the appropriate four-digit numeric revenue code to explain each charge.

For claims with dates of service before July 1, 2008, hospices only reported the revenue codes in the table below. Effective on claims with dates of service on or after January 1, 2008, additional revenue codes will be reported describing the visits provided under each level of care. However, Medicare payment will continue to be reflected only on claim lines with the revenue codes in this table.

Code	Description	Standard Abbreviation
0651*	Routine Home Care	RTN Home
0652*	Continuous Home Care	CTNS Home A minimum of 8 hours of primarily nursing care within a 24-hour period. The 8-hours of care does not need to be continuous within the 24-hour period, but a need for an aggregate of 8 hours of primarily nursing care is required. Nursing care must be provided by a registered nurse or a licensed practical nurse. If skilled intervention is required for less than 8 aggregate hours (or less than 32 units) within a 24 hour period, then the care rendered would be covered as a routine home care day. Services provided by a nurse practitioner as the attending physician are not included in the CHC computation nor is care that is not directly related to the crisis included in the computation. CHC billing should reflect direct patient care during a period of crisis and should not reflect time related to staff working hours, time taken for meal breaks, time used for educating staff, time used to report etc.
0655***	Inpatient Respite Care	IP Respite
0656***	General Inpatient Care	GNL IP
0657**	Physician Services	PHY SER (must be accompanied by a physician procedure code)

* Reporting of value code 61 is required with these revenue codes.

**Reporting of modifier GV is required with

this revenue code when billing physician services performed by a nurse practitioner.

***Reporting of value code G8 is required with these revenue codes.

NOTE: Hospices use revenue code 0657 to identify hospice charges for services furnished to patients by physician or nurse practitioner employees, or physicians or nurse practitioners receiving compensation from the hospice. Physician services performed by a nurse practitioner require the addition of the modifier GV in conjunction with revenue code 0657. Procedure codes are required in order for the FI to determine the reimbursement rate for the physician services. Appropriate procedure codes are available from the FI.

Effective on claims with dates of service on or after July 1, 2008, hospices must report the number of visits that were provided to the beneficiary in the course of delivering the hospice levels of care billed with the codes above. Charges for these codes will be reported on the appropriate level of care line. Total number of patient care visits is to be reported by the discipline (registered nurse, nurse practitioner, licensed nurse, home health aide (also known as a hospice aide), social worker, physician or nurse practitioner serving as the beneficiary's attending physician) for each week at each location of service. If visits are provided in multiple sites, a separate line for each site and for each discipline will be required. The total number of visits does not imply the total number of activities or interventions provided. If patient care visits in a particular discipline are not provided under a given level of care or service location, do not report a line for the corresponding revenue code.

To constitute a visit, the discipline, (as defined above) must have provided care to the beneficiary. Services provided by a social worker to the beneficiary's family also constitute a visit. For example, phone calls, documentation in the medical/clinical record, interdisciplinary group meetings, obtaining physician orders, rounds in a facility or any other activity that is not related to the provision of items or services to a beneficiary, do not count towards a visit to be placed on the claim. In addition, the visit must be reasonable and necessary for the palliation and management of the terminal illness and related conditions as described in the patient's plan of care.

Example 1: Week 1: A visit by the RN was made to the beneficiary's home on Monday and Wednesday where the nurse assessed the patient, verified effect of pain medications, provided patient teaching, obtained vital signs and documented in the medical record. A

home health aide assisted the patient with a bath on Tuesday and Thursday. There were no social work or physician visits. Thus for that week there were 2 visits provided by the nurse and 2 by the home health aide. Since there were no visits by the social worker or by the physician, there would not be any line items for each of those disciplines.

Example 2: If a hospice patient is receiving routine home care while residing in a nursing home, the hospice would record visits for all of its physicians, nurses, social workers, and home health aides who visit the patient to provide care for the palliation and management of the terminal illness and related conditions, as described in the patient's plan of care. In this example the nursing home is acting as the patient's home. Only the patient care provided by the hospice staff constitutes a visit.

Hospices must enter the following revenue codes, when applicable: 055X Skilled Nursing

Required detail: The earliest date of service this discipline was provided during the delivery of each level of care in each service location, service units which represent the number of visits provided in that location, and a charge amount.

- 056X Medical Social Services

Required detail: The earliest date of service this discipline was provided during the delivery of each level of care in each service location, service units which represent the number of visits provided in that location, and a charge amount.

- 057X Home Health Aide

Required detail: The earliest date of service this discipline was provided during the delivery of each level of care in each service location, service units which represent the number of visits provided in that location, and a charge amount.

Hospices should follow NUBC coding guidelines for the use of the appropriate fourth position (the "X") when reporting these revenue codes.

Visits by registered nurses, licensed vocational nurses and nurse practitioners (unless the nurse practitioner is acting as the beneficiary's attending physician) are reported under revenue code 055X.

All visits to provide care related to the palliation and management of the terminal illness or related conditions, whether provided by hospice employees or provided under arrangement, must be reported. The one exception is related to General Inpatient Care. CMS is not requiring hospices to report visit data at this time for visits made by non-hospice staff providing General Inpatient Care in contract facilities. However, General Inpatient Care visits related to the palliation and management of the terminal illness or related conditions provided by hospice staff in contract facilities must be reported , and all General Inpatient Care visits related to the palliation and management of the terminal illness or related conditions provided in hospice-owned facilities must be reported.

HCPCS/Accommodation Rates/HIPPS Rate Codes

For services provided on or before December 31, 2006, HCPCS codes are required only to report procedures on service lines for attending physician services (revenue 657). Level of care revenue codes (651, 652, 655 or 656) do not require HCPCS coding.

For services provided on or after January 1, 2007, hospices must also report a HCPCS code along with each level of care revenue code (651, 652, 655 and 656) to identify the type of service location where that level of care was provided.

The following HCPCS codes will be used to report the type of service location for hospice services:

HCPCS Code	Definition
Q5001	HOSPICE CARE PROVIDED IN PATIENT'S HOME/RESIDENCE
Q5002	HOSPICE CARE PROVIDED IN ASSISTED LIVING FACILITY
Q5003	HOSPICE CARE PROVIDED IN NURSING LONG TERM CARE FACILITY (LTC) OR NON-SKILLED NURSING FACILITY (NF)
Q5004	HOSPICE CARE PROVIDED IN SKILLED NURSING FACILITY (SNF)
Q5005	HOSPICE CARE PROVIDED IN INPATIENT HOSPITAL
Q5006	HOSPICE CARE PROVIDED IN INPATIENT HOSPICE FACILITY
Q5007	HOSPICE CARE PROVIDED IN LONG TERM CARE HOSPITAL (LTCH)
Q5008	HOSPICE CARE PROVIDED IN INPATIENT PSYCHIATRIC FACILITY
Q5009	HOSPICE CARE PROVIDED IN PLACE NOT OTHERWISE SPECIFIED (NOS)

If care is rendered at multiple locations, each location is to be identified on the claim with a corresponding HCPCS code. For example, routine home care may be provided for a portion of the billing period in the patient's residence and another portion in an assisted living facility. In this case, report one revenue code 651 line with HCPCS code Q5001 and the number of days of routine home care provided in the residence and another revenue code 651 line with HCPCS code Q5002 and the number of days of routine home care provided in the assisted living facility.

- Q5003 is to be used for skilled nursing facility residents in a non Medicare covered stay and nursing facility residents.
- Q5004 is to be used for skilled nursing facility residents in a Medicare covered stay.

These service location HCPCS codes are not required on revenue code lines describing the visits provided under each level of care (e.g. 055X, 056X, 057X).

Service Date The HIPAA standard 837 Institutional claim format requires line item dates of service for all outpatient claims. Medicare classifies hospice claims as outpatient claims (see Chapter 1, Sec.60.4). For services provided on or before December 31, 2006, CMS allows hospices to satisfy the line item date of service requirement by placing any valid date within the FL 6 Statement Covers Period dates on line items on hospice claims.

For services provided on or after January 1, 2007, service date reporting requirements will vary between continuous home care lines (revenue code 652) and other revenue code lines.

Revenue code 652 - report a separately dated line item for each day that continuous home care is provided, reporting the number of hours, or parts of hours rounded to 15-minute increments, of continuous home care that was provided on that date.

Other payment revenue codes - report a separate line for each level of care provided at each service location type, as described in the instructions for HCPCS coding reported above. Hospices report the earliest date that each level of care was provided at each service location. Attending physician services should be individually dated, reporting the date that each HCPCS code billed was delivered.

Non-payment service revenue codes - report dates as described in the table above under Revenue Codes.

Service Units
The hospice enters the number of units for each type of service. Units are measured in days for revenue codes 651, 655, and 656, in hours for revenue code 652, and in procedures for revenue code 657. For services provided on or after January 1, 2007, hours for revenue code 652 are reported in 15-minute increments. For services provided on or after January 1, 2008, units for visit discipline revenue codes are measured by the number of visits.

Total Charges
The hospice enters the total charge for the service described on each revenue code line. This information is being collected for purposes of research and will not affect the amount of reimbursement.

Payer Name
The hospice identifies the appropriate payer(s) for the claim.

National Provider Identifier - Billing Provider

The hospice enters its own National Provider Identifier (NPI).

Principal Diagnosis Code
The hospice enters diagnosis coding as required by ICD-9-CM Coding Guidelines. Hospices may not report V-codes as the primary diagnosis on hospice claims. The principal diagnosis code describes the terminal illness of the hospice patient and V-codes do not describe terminal conditions.

Other Diagnosis Codes
The hospice enters diagnosis coding as required by ICD-9-CM Coding Guidelines.

Attending Provider Name and Identifiers
The hospice enters the National Provider Identifier (NPI) and name of the physician currently responsible for certifying the terminal illness, and signing the individual's plan of care for medical care and treatment.

Other Provider Name and Identifiers
If the attending physician is a nurse practitioner, the hospice enters the NPI and name of the nurse practitioner.

100-4,11,40.1.3.1

Care Plan Oversight

Care plan oversight (CPO) exists where there is physician supervision of patients under care of hospices that require complex and multidisciplinary care modalities involving regular physician development and/or revision of care plans. Implicit in the concept of CPO is the expectation that the physician has coordinated an aspect of the patient's care with the hospice during the month for which CPO services were billed.

For a physician or NP employed by or under arrangement with a hospice agency, CPO functions are incorporated and are part of the hospice per diem payment and as such may not be separately billed.

For information on separately billable CPO services by the attending physician or nurse practitioner see Chapter 12, 180 of this manual.

100-4,12,180

Care Plan Oversight Services

The Medicare Benefit Policy Manual, Chapter 15, contains requirements for coverage for medical and other health services including those of physicians and non-physician practitioners.

Care plan oversight (CPO) is the physician supervision of a patient receiving complex and/or multidisciplinary care as part of Medicare-covered services provided by a participating home health agency or Medicare approved hospice.

CPO services require complex or multidisciplinary care modalities involving: Regular physician development and/or revision of care plans; Review of subsequent reports of patient status; Review of related laboratory and other studies; Communication with other health professionals not employed in the same practice who are involved in the patient's care; Integration of new information into the medical treatment plan; and/or Adjustment of medical therapy.

The CPO services require recurrent physician supervision of a patient involving 30 or more minutes of the physician's time per month. Services not countable toward the 30 minutes threshold that must be provided in order to bill for CPO include, but are not limited to: Time associated with discussions with the patient, his or her family or friends to adjust medication or treatment; Time spent by staff getting or filing charts; Travel time; and/or Physician's time spent telephoning prescriptions into the pharmacist unless the telephone conversation involves discussions of pharmaceutical therapies.

Implicit in the concept of CPO is the expectation that the physician has coordinated an aspect of the patient's care with the home health agency or hospice during the month for which CPO services were billed. The physician who bills for CPO must be the same physician who signs the plan of care.

Nurse practitioners, physician assistants, and clinical nurse specialists, practicing within the scope of State law, may bill for care plan oversight. These non-physician practitioners must have been providing ongoing care for the beneficiary through evaluation and management services. These non-physician practitioners may not bill for CPO if they have been involved only with the delivery of the Medicare-covered home health or hospice service.

A. Home Health CPO

Non-physician practitioners can perform CPO only if the physician signing the plan of care provides regular ongoing care under the same plan of care as does the NPP billing for CPO and either: The physician and NPP are part of the same group practice; or If the NPP is a nurse practitioner or clinical nurse specialist, the physician signing the plan of care also has a collaborative agreement with the NPP; or If the NPP is a physician assistant, the physician signing the plan of care is also the physician who provides general supervision of physician assistant services for the practice.

Billing may be made for care plan oversight services furnished by an NPP when: The NPP providing the care plan oversight has seen and examined the patient; The NPP providing care plan oversight is not functioning as a consultant whose participation is limited to a single medical condition rather than multidisciplinary coordination of care; and The NPP providing care plan oversight integrates his or her care with that of the physician who signed the plan of care.

NPPs may not certify the beneficiary for home health care.

B. Hospice CPO

The attending physician or nurse practitioner (who has been designated as the attending physician) may bill for hospice CPO when they are acting as an "attending physician".

An "attending physician" is one who has been identified by the individual, at the time he/she elects hospice coverage, as having the most significant role in the determination and delivery of their medical care. They are not employed nor paid by the hospice. The care plan oversight services are billed using Form CMS-1500 or electronic equivalent.

For additional information on hospice CPO, see Chapter 11, 40.1.3.1 of this manual.

100-4,12,180.1

Care Plan Oversight Billing Requirements

A. Codes for Which Separate Payment May Be Made

Effective January 1, 1995, separate payment may be made for CPO oversight services for 30 minutes or more if the requirements specified in the Medicare Benefits Policy Manual, Chapter 15 are met.

Providers billing for CPO must submit the claim with no other services billed on that claim and may bill only after the end of the month in which the CPO services were rendered. CPO services may not be billed across calendar months and should be submitted (and paid) only for one unit of service.

Physicians may bill and be paid separately for CPO services only if all the criteria in the Medicare Benefit Policy Manual, Chapter 15 are met.

B. Physician Certification and Recertification of Home Health Plans of Care

Effective 2001, two new HCPCS codes for the certification and recertification and development of plans of care for Medicare-covered home health services were created.

See the Medicare General Information, Eligibility, and Entitlement Manual, Pub. 100-01, Chapter 4, "Physician Certification and Recertification of Services," 10-60, and the Medicare Benefit Policy Manual, Pub. 100-02, Chapter 7, "Home Health Services", 30.

The home health agency certification code can be billed only when the patient has not received Medicare-covered home health services for at least 60 days. The home health agency recertification code is used after a patient has received services for at least 60 days (or one certification period) when the physician signs the certification after the initial certification period. The home health agency recertification code will be reported only once every 60 days, except in the rare situation when the patient starts a new episode before 60 days elapses and requires a new plan of care to start a new episode.

C. Provider Number of Home Health Agency (HHA) or Hospice

For claims for CPO submitted on or after January 1, 1997, physicians must enter on the Medicare claim form the 6-character Medicare provider number of the HHA or hospice providing Medicare-covered services to the beneficiary for the period during which CPO services was furnished and for which the physician signed the plan of care. Physicians are responsible for obtaining the HHA or hospice Medicare provider numbers.

Additionally, physicians should provide their UPIN to the HHA or hospice furnishing services to their patient.

NOTE: There is currently no place on the HIPAA standard ASC X12N 837 professional format to specifically include the HHA or hospice provider number required for a care plan oversight claim. For this reason, the requirement to include the HHA or hospice provider number on a care plan oversight claim is temporarily waived until a new version of this electronic standard format is adopted under HIPAA and includes a place to provide the HHA and hospice provider numbers for care plan oversight claims.

100-4,12,190.3

List of Medicare Telehealth Services

The use of a telecommunications system may substitute for a face-to-face, "hands on" encounter for consultation, office visits, individual psychotherapy, pharmacologic management, psychiatric diagnostic interview examination, end stage renal disease related services, and individual medical nutrition therapy. These services and corresponding current procedure terminology (CPT) or Healthcare Common Procedure Coding System (HCPCS) codes are listed below.

Consultations (CPT codes 99241 - 99275) - Effective October 1, 2001 - December 31, 2005; Consultations (CPT codes 99241 - 99255) - Effective January 1, 2006; Office or other outpatient visits (CPT codes 99201 - 99215); Individual psychotherapy (CPT codes 90804 - 90809); Pharmacologic management (CPT code 90862); and Psychiatric diagnostic interview examination (CPT code 90801) - Effective March 1, 2003.

End Stage Renal Disease (ESRD) related services (HCPCS codes G0308, G0309, G0311, G0312, G0314, G0315, G0317, and G0318) - Effective January 1, 2005.

Individual Medical Nutrition Therapy (HCPCS codes G0270, 97802, and 97803) (Effective January 1, 2006).

Neurobehavioral status exam (CPT code 96116) (Effective January 1, 2008).

100-4,12,190.7

Contractor Editing of Telehealth Claims

Medicare telehealth services (as listed in section 190.3) are billed with either the "GT" or "GQ" modifier. The contractor shall approve covered telehealth services if the physician or practitioner is licensed under State law to provide the service. Contractors must familiarize themselves with licensure provisions of States for which they process claims and disallow telehealth services furnished by physicians or practitioners who are not authorized to furnish the applicable telehealth service under State law. For example, if a nurse practitioner is not licensed to provide individual psychotherapy under State law, he or she would not be permitted to receive payment for individual psychotherapy under Medicare. The contractor shall install edits to ensure that only properly licensed physicians and practitioners are paid for covered telehealth services.

If a contractor receives claims for professional telehealth services coded with the "GQ" modifier (representing "via asynchronous telecommunications system"), it shall approve/pay for these services only if the physician or practitioner is affiliated with a Federal telemedicine demonstration conducted in Alaska or Hawaii. The contractor may require the physician or practitioner at the distant site to document his or her participation in a Federal telemedicine demonstration program conducted in Alaska or Hawaii prior to paying for telehealth services provided via asynchronous, store and forward technologies.

If a contractor denies telehealth services because the physician or practitioner may not bill for them, the contractor uses MSN message 21.18: "This item or service is not covered when performed or ordered by this practitioner." The contractor uses remittance advice message 52 when denying the claim based upon MSN message 21.18.

If a service is billed with one of the telehealth modifiers and the procedure code is not designated as a covered telehealth service, the contractor denies the service using MSN message 9.4: "This item or service was denied because information required to make payment was incorrect." The remittance advice message depends on what is incorrect, e.g., B18 if procedure code or modifier is incorrect, 125 for submission billing errors, 4-12 for difference inconsistencies. The contractor uses B18 as the explanation for the denial of the claim.

The only claims from institutional facilities that FIs shall pay for telehealth services at the distant site, except for MNT services, are for physician or practitioner services when the distant site is located in a CAH that has elected Method II, and the physician or practitioner has reassigned his/her benefits to the CAH. The CAH bills its regular FI for the professional services provided at the distant site via a telecommunications system, in any of the revenue codes 096x, 097x or 098x. All requirements for billing distant site telehealth services apply.

Claims from hospitals or CAHs for MNT services are submitted to the hospital's or CAH's regular FI. Payment is based on the non-facility amount on the Medicare Physician Fee Schedule for the particular HCPCS codes.

100-4,12,210.1

Application of Limitation

B3-2472 - 2472.5

A. Status of Patient

The limitation is applicable to expenses incurred in connection with the treatment of an individual who is not an inpatient of a hospital. Thus, the limitation applies to mental health services furnished to a person in a physician's office, in the patient's home, in a skilled nursing facility, as an outpatient, and so forth. The term "hospital" in this context means an institution, which is primarily engaged in providing to inpatients, by or under the supervision of physician(s): Diagnostic and therapeutic services for medical diagnosis, treatment and care of injured, disabled, or sick persons; Rehabilitation services for injured, disabled, or sick persons; or Psychiatric services for the diagnosis and treatment of mentally ill patients.

B. Disorders Subject to Limitation

The term "mental, psychoneurotic, and personality disorders" is defined as the specific psychiatric conditions described in the American Psychiatric Association's (APA) "Diagnostic and Statistical Manual of Mental Disorders, Third Edition - Revised (DSMIII- R)." When the treatment services rendered are both for a psychiatric condition as defined in the DSM-III-R and one or more nonpsychiatric conditions, separate the expenses for the psychiatric aspects of treatment from the expenses for the nonpsychiatric aspects of treatment. However, in any case in which the psychiatric treatment component is not readily distinguishable from the nonpsychiatric treatment component, all of the expenses are allocated to whichever component constitutes the primary diagnosis.

1. Diagnosis Clearly Meets Definition - If the primary diagnosis reported for a particular service is the same as or equivalent to a condition described in the APA's DSM-III-R, the expense for the service is subject to the limitation except as described in subsection D.
2. Diagnosis Does Not Clearly Meet Definition - When it is not clear whether the primary diagnosis reported meets the definition of mental, psychoneurotic, and personality disorders, it may be necessary to contact the practitioner to clarify the diagnosis. In deciding whether contact is necessary in a given case, give consideration to such factors as the type of services rendered, the diagnosis, and the individual's previous utilization history.

C. Services Subject to Limitation

Carriers apply the limitation to claims for professional services that represent mental health treatment furnished to individuals who are not hospital inpatients by physicians, clinical psychologists, clinical social workers, and other allied health professionals.

Items and supplies furnished by physicians or other mental health practitioners in connection with treatment are also subject to the limitation. (The limitation also applies to CORF claims processed by intermediaries.) Carriers apply the limitation only to treatment services. It does not apply to diagnostic services as described in subsection D. Testing services performed to evaluate a patient's progress during treatment are considered part of treatment and are subject to the limitation.

D. Services Not Subject to Limitation

1. Diagnosis of Alzheimer's Disease or Related Disorder - When the primary diagnosis reported for a particular service is Alzheimer's Disease (coded 331.0 in the "International Classification of Diseases, 9th Revision") or Alzheimer's or other disorders coded 290.XX in the APA's DSM-III-R, carriers look to the nature of the service that has been rendered in determining whether it is subject to the limitation. Typically, treatment provided to a patient with a diagnosis of Alzheimer's Disease or a related disorder represents medical management of the patient's condition (rather than psychiatric treatment) and is not subject to the limitation. However, when the primary treatment rendered to a patient with such a diagnosis is psychotherapy, it is subject to the limitation.
2. Brief Office Visits for Monitoring or Changing Drug Prescriptions - Brief office visits for the sole purpose of monitoring or changing drug prescriptions used in the treatment of mental, psychoneurotic and personality disorders are not subject to the limitation. These visits are reported using HCPCS code M0064 (brief office visit for the sole purpose of monitoring or changing drug prescriptions used in the treatment of mental, psychoneurotic, and personality disorders). Claims where the diagnosis reported is a mental, psychoneurotic, or personality disorder (other than a diagnosis specified in subsection A) are subject to the limitation except for the procedure identified by HCPCS code M0064.
3. Diagnostic Services - Carriers do not apply the limitation to tests and evaluations performed to establish or confirm the patient's diagnosis. Diagnostic services include psychiatric or psychological tests and interpretations, diagnostic consultations, and initial evaluations.

   An initial visit to a practitioner for professional services often combines diagnostic evaluation and the start of therapy. Such a visit is neither solely diagnostic nor solely therapeutic. Therefore, carriers deem the initial visit to be diagnostic so that the limitation does not apply. Separating diagnostic and therapeutic components of a visit is not administratively feasible, unless the practitioner already has separately identified them on the bill. Determining the entire visit to be therapeutic is not justifiable since some diagnostic work must be done before even a tentative diagnosis can be made and certainly before therapy can be instituted. Moreover, the patient should not be disadvantaged because therapeutic as well as diagnostic services were provided in the initial visit. In the rare cases where a practitioner's diagnostic services take more than one visit, carriers do not apply the limitation to the additional visits. However, it is expected such cases are few. Therefore, when a practitioner bills for more than one visit for professional diagnostic services, carriers request documentation to justify the reason for more than one diagnostic visit.
4. Partial Hospitalization Services Not Directly Provided by Physician - The limitation does not apply to partial hospitalization services that are not directly provided by a physician. These services are billed by hospitals and community mental health centers (CMHCs) to intermediaries.

E. Computation of Limitation

Carriers determine the Medicare allowed payment amount for services subject to the limitation.

They:

- Multiply this amount by 0.625;
- Subtract any unsatisfied deductible; and,
- Multiply the remainder by 0.8 to obtain the amount of Medicare payment.

The beneficiary is responsible for the difference between the amount paid by Medicare and the full allowed amount.

EXAMPLE A:

A beneficiary is referred to a Medicare participating psychiatrist who performs a diagnostic evaluation that costs $350. Those services are not subject to the limitation, and they satisfy the deductible. The psychiatrist then conducts 10 weekly therapy sessions for which he/she charges $125 each. The Medicare allowed amount is $90 each, for a total of $900.

Apply the limitation by multiplying 0.625 times $900, which equals $562.50.

Apply regular 20 percent coinsurance by multiplying 0.8 times $562.50, which equals $450 (the amount of Medicare payment).

The beneficiary is responsible for $450 (the difference between Medicare payment and the allowed amount).

EXAMPLE B:

A beneficiary was an inpatient of a psychiatric hospital and was discharged on January 1, 1992. During his/her inpatient stay he/she was diagnosed and therapy was begun under a treatment team that included a clinical psychologist. He/she received post-discharge therapy from the psychologist for 12 sessions, at which point the psychologist administered testing that showed the patient had recovered sufficiently to warrant termination of therapy. The allowed amount for the therapy sessions was $80 each, and the amount for the testing was $125, for a total of $1085. All services in 1992 were subject to the limitation, since the diagnosis had been completed in the hospital and the subsequent testing was a part of therapy.

Apply the limitation by multiplying 0.625 times $1085, which gives $678.13.

Since the deductible must be met for 1992, subtract $100 from $678.13, for a remainder of $578.13.

Determine Medicare payment by multiplying the remainder by 0.8, which equals $462.50.

The beneficiary is responsible for $622.50.

100-4,12,30.4

Cardiovascular System (Codes 92950-93799)

A. Echocardiography Contrast Agents

Effective October 1, 2000, physicians may separately bill for contrast agents used in echocardiography. Physicians should use HCPCS Code A9700 (Supply of Injectable Contrast Material for Use in Echocardiography, per study). The type of service code is 9. This code will be carrier-priced.

B. Electronic Analyses of Implantable Cardioverter-defibrillators and Pacemakers

The CPT codes 93731, 93734, 93741 and 93743 are used to report electronic analyses of single or dual chamber pacemakers and single or dual chamber implantable cardioverterdefibrillators. In the office, a physician uses a device called a programmer to obtain information about the status and performance of the device and to evaluate the patient's cardiac rhythm and response to the implanted device. Advances in information technology now enable physicians to evaluate patients with implanted cardiac devices without requiring the patient to be present in the physician's office. Using a manufacturer's specific monitor/transmitter, a patient can send complete device data and specific cardiac data to a distant receiving station or secure Internet server. The electronic analysis of cardiac device data that is remotely obtained provides immediate and long-term data on the device and clinical data on the patient's cardiac functioning equivalent to that obtained during an in-office evaluation. Physicians should report the electronic analysis of an implanted cardiac device using remotely obtained data as described above with CPT code 93731, 93734, 93741 or 93743, depending on the type of cardiac device implanted in the patient.

100-4,12,60

Payment for Pathology Services

B3-15020, AB-01-47 (CR1499)

A. General Payment Rule

Payment may be made under the fee schedule for the professional component of physician laboratory or physician pathology services furnished to hospital inpatients or outpatients by hospital physicians or by independent laboratories, if they qualify as the reassignee for the physician service.. Payment may be made under the fee schedule, as noted below, for the technical component (TC) of pathology services furnished by an independent laboratory to hospital inpatients or outpatients. Payment may be made under the fee schedule for the technical component of physician pathology services furnished by an independent laboratory, or a hospital if it is acting as an independent laboratory, to non-hospital patients. The Medicare physician fee schedule identifies those physician laboratory or physician pathology services that have a technical component service.

CMS published a final regulation in 1999 that would no longer allow independent laboratories to bill under the physician fee schedule for the TC of physician pathology services. The implementation of this regulation was delayed by Section 542 of the Benefits and Improvement and Protection Act of 2000 (BIPA). Section 542 allows the Medicare carrier to continue to pay for the TC of physician pathology services when an independent laboratory furnishes this service to an inpatient or outpatient of a covered hospital. This provision is applicable to TC services furnished in 2001, 2002, 2003, 2004, 2005 or 2006.

For this provision, a covered hospital is a hospital that had an arrangement with an independent laboratory that was in effect as of July 22, 1999, under which a laboratory furnished the TC of physician pathology services to fee-for-service Medicare beneficiaries who were hospital inpatients or outpatients, and submitted claims for payment for the TC to a carrier. The TC could have been submitted separately or combined with the professional component and reported as a combined service.

The term, fee-for-service Medicare beneficiary, means an individual who:

- Is entitled to benefits under Part A or enrolled under Part B of title XVIII or both; and
- Is not enrolled in any of the following: A Medicare + Choice plan under Part C of such title; a plan offered by an eligible organization under 1876 of the Social Security Act; a program of all-inclusive care for the elderly under 1894; or a social health maintenance organization demonstration project established under Section 4108 of the Omnibus Budget Reconciliation Act of 1987.

In implementing Section 542, the carriers should consider as independent laboratories those entities that it has previously recognized as independent laboratories. An independent laboratory that has acquired another independent laboratory that had an arrangement of July 22, 1999, with a covered hospital, can bill the TC of physician pathology services for that hospital's inpatients and outpatients under the physician fee schedule.

An independent laboratory that furnishes the TC of physician pathology services to inpatients or outpatients of a hospital that is not a covered hospital may not bill the carrier for the TC of physician pathology services during the time 542 is in effect.

If the arrangement between the independent laboratory and the covered hospital limited the provision of TC physician pathology services to certain situations or at particular times, then the independent laboratory can bill the carrier only for these limited services.

The carrier shall require independent laboratories that had an arrangement, on or prior to July 22, 1999 with a covered hospital, to bill for the technical component of physician pathology services to provide a copy of this agreement, or other documentation substantiating that an arrangement was in effect between the hospital and the independent laboratory as of this date. The independent laboratory must submit this documentation for each covered hospital that the independent laboratory services.

See Chapter 16 for additional instruction on laboratory services including clinical diagnostic laboratory services.

Physician laboratory and pathology services are limited to:

- Surgical pathology services;
- Specific cytopathology, hematology and blood banking services that have been identified to require performance by a physician and are listed below;
- Clinical consultation services that meet the requirements in subsection D below; and
- Clinical laboratory interpretation services that meet the requirements and which are specifically listed in subsection E below.

B. Surgical Pathology Services

Surgical pathology services include the gross and microscopic examination of organ tissue performed by a physician, except for autopsies, which are not covered by Medicare. Surgical pathology services paid under the physician fee schedule are reported under the following CPT codes:

88300, 88302, 88304, 88305, 88307, 88309, 88311, 88312, 88313, 88314, 88318, 88319, 88321, 88323, 88325, 88329, 88331, 88332, 88342, 88346, 88347, 88348, 88349, 88355, 88356, 88358, 88361, 88362, 88365, 88380.

Depending upon circumstances and the billing entity, the carriers may pay professional component, technical component or both.

C. Specific Hematology, Cytopathology and Blood Banking Services

Cytopathology services include the examination of cells from fluids, washings, brushings or smears, but generally excluding hematology. Examining cervical and vaginal smears are the most common service in cytopathology. Cervical and vaginal smears do not require interpretation by a physician unless the results are or appear to be abnormal. In such cases, a physician personally conducts a separate microscopic evaluation to determine the nature of an abnormality. This microscopic evaluation ordinarily does require performance by a physician. When medically necessary and when furnished by a physician, it is paid under the fee schedule.

These codes include 88104, 88106, 88107, 88108, 88112, 88125, 88141, 88160, 88161, 88162, 88172, 88173, 88180, 88182.

For services furnished prior to January 1, 1999, carriers pay separately under the physician fee schedule for the interpretation of an abnormal pap smear furnished to a hospital inpatient by a physician. They must pay under the clinical laboratory fee schedule for pap smears furnished in all other situations. This policy also applies to screening pap smears requiring a physician interpretation. For services furnished on or after January 1, 1999, carriers allow separate payment for a physician's interpretation of a pap smear to any patient (i.e., hospital or non-hospital) as long as: (1) the laboratory's screening personnel suspect an abnormality; and (2) the physician reviews and interprets the pap smear.

This policy also applies to screening pap smears requiring a physician interpretation and described in the National Coverage Determination Manual and Chapter 18. These services are reported under codes P3000 or P3001.

Physician hematology services include microscopic evaluation of bone marrow aspirations and biopsies. It also includes those limited number of peripheral blood smears which need to be referred to a physician to evaluate the nature of an apparent abnormality identified by the technologist. These codes include 85060, 38220, 85097, and 38221.

Carriers pay the professional component for the interpretation of an abnormal blood smear (code 85060) furnished to a hospital inpatient by a hospital physician or an independent laboratory.

For the other listed hematology codes, payment may be made for the professional component if the service is furnished to a patient by a hospital physician or independent laboratory. In addition, payment may be made for these services furnished to patients by an independent laboratory.

Codes 38220 and 85097 represent professional-only component services and have no technical component values.

Blood banking services of hematologists and pathologists are paid under the physician fee schedule when analyses are performed on donor and/or patient blood to determine compatible donor units for transfusion where cross matching is difficult or where contamination with transmissible disease of donor is suspected.

The blood banking codes are 86077, 86078, and 86079 and represent professional component only services. These codes do not have a technical component.

D. Clinical Consultation Services

- Clinical consultations are paid under the physician fee schedule only if they:
- Are requested by the patient's attending physician;
- Relate to a test result that lies outside the clinically significant normal or expected range in view of the condition of the patient;
- Result in a written narrative report included in the patient's medical record; and
- Require the exercise of medical judgment by the consultant physician.

Clinical consultations are professional component services only. There is no technical component. The clinical consultation codes are 80500 and 80502.

Routine conversations held between a laboratory director and an attending physician about test orders or results do not qualify as consultations unless all four requirements are met. Laboratory personnel, including the director, may from time to time contact attending physicians to report test results or to suggest additional testing or be contacted by attending physicians on similar matters. These contacts do not constitute clinical consultations. However, if in the course of such a contact, the attending physician requests a consultation from the pathologist, and if that consultation meets the other criteria and is properly documented, it is paid under the fee schedule.

EXAMPLE: A pathologist telephones a surgeon about a patient's suitability for surgery based on the results of clinical laboratory test results. During the course of their conversation, the surgeon ask the pathologist whether, based on test results, patient history and medical records, the patient is a candidate for surgery. The surgeon's request requires the pathologist to render a medical judgment and provide a consultation. The athologist follows up his/her oral advice with a written report and the surgeon notes in the patient's medical record that he/she requested a consultation. This consultation is paid under the fee schedule.

In any case, if the information could ordinarily be furnished by a nonphysician laboratory specialist, the service of the physician is not a consultation payable under the fee schedule.

See the Program Integrity Manual for guidelines for related data analysis to identify inappropriate patterns of billing for consultations.

E. Clinical Laboratory Interpretation Services

Only clinical laboratory interpretation services listed below and which meet the criteria in subsections D.1, D.3, and D.4 for clinical consultations and, as a result, are billable under the fee schedule. These services are reported under the clinical laboratory code with modifier 26. These services can be paid under the physician fee schedule if they are furnished to a patient by a hospital pathologist or an independent laboratory. Note that a hospital's standing order policy can be used as a substitute for the individual request by the patient's attending physician. Carriers are not allowed to revise CMS's list to accommodate local medical practice. The CMS periodically reviews this list and adds or deletes clinical laboratory codes as warranted.

Clinical Laboratory Interpretation Services

Code	Definition
83020	Hemoglobin; electrophoresis
83912	Nucleic acid probe, with electrophoresis, with examination and report
84165	Protein, total, serum; electrophoretic fractionation and quantitation
84181	Protein; Western Blot with interpretation and report, blood or other body fluid
84182	Protein; Western Blot, with interpretation and report, blood or other body fluid, immunological probe for band identification; each
85390	Fibrinolysin; screening
85576	Platelet; aggregation (in vitro), any agent
86255	Fluorescent antibody; screen
86256	Fluorescent antibody; titer
86320	Immunoelectrophoresis; serum, each specimen
86325	Immunoelectrophoresis; other fluids (e.g.urine) with concentration, each specimen
86327	Immunoelectrophoresis; crossed (2 dimensional assay)
86334	Immunofixation electrophoresis
87164	Dark field examination, any source (e.g. penile, vaginal, oral, skin); includes specimen collection
87207	Smear, primary source, with interpretation; special stain for inclusion bodies or intracellular parasites (e.g. malaria, kala azar, herpes)
88371	Protein analysis of tissue by Western Blot, with interpretation and report.
88372	Protein analysis of tissue by Western Blot, immunological probe for band identification, each
89060	Crystal identification by light microscopy with or without polarizing lens analysis, any body fluid (except urine)

100-4,13,140

Bone Mass Measurements (BMMs)

Sections H1861(s)(15)H and H(rr)(1)H of the Social Security Act (the Act) (as added by 4106 of the Balanced Budget Act (BBA) of 1997) standardize Medicare coverage of medically necessary bone mass measurements by providing for uniform coverage under Medicare Part B. This coverage is effective for claims with dates of service furnished on or after July 1, 1998.

Effective for dates of service on and after January 1, 2007, the CY 2007 Physician Fee Schedule final rule expanded the number of beneficiaries qualifying for BMM by reducing the dosage requirement for glucocorticoid (steroid) therapy from 7.5 mg of prednisone per day to 5.0 mg. It also changed the definition of BMM by removing coverage for a single-photon absorptiometry as it is not considered reasonable and necessary under section 1862 (a)(1)(A) of the Act. Finally, it required that in the case of monitoring and confirmatory baseline BMMs, they be performed with a dual-energy xray absorptiometry (axial) test.

Conditions of Coverage for BMMs are located in Pub.100-02, Medicare Benefit Policy Manual, chapter 15.

100-4,13,40.1.2

HCPCS Coding Requirements

Providers must report HCPCS codes when submitting claims for MRA of the chest, abdomen, head, neck or peripheral vessels of lower extremities. The following HCPCS codes should be used to report these services:

MRA of head	70544, 70544-26, 70544-TC
MRA of head	70545, 70545-26, 70545-TC
MRA of head	70546, 70546-26, 70546-TC
MRA of neck	70547, 70547-26, 70547-TC
MRA of neck	70548, 70548-26, 70548-TC
MRA of neck	70549, 70549-26, 70549-TC
MRA of chest	71555, 71555-26, 71555-TC
MRA of pelvis	72198, 72198-26, 72198-TC
MRA of abdomen (dates of service on or after July 1, 2003) - see below.	74185, 74185-26, 74185-TC
MRA of peripheral vessels of lower extremities	73725, 73725-26, 73725-TC

Hospitals subject to OPPS should report the following C codes in place of the above HCPCS codes as follows:

- MRA of chest 71555: C8909 - C8911
- MRA of abdomen 74185: C8900 - C8902
- MRA of peripheral vessels of lower extremities 73725: C8912 - C8914

For claims with dates of service on or after July 1, 2003, coverage under this benefit has been expanded for the use of MRA for diagnosing pathology in the renal or aortoiliac arteries. The following HCPCS code should be used to report this expanded coverage of MRA:

- MRA, pelvis, with or without contrast material(s) 72198, 72198-26, 72198-TC

Hospitals subject to OPPS report the following C codes in place of HCPCS code 72198:

- MRA, pelvis, with or without contrast material(s) 72198: C8918 - C8920

Providers utilizing the UB-92 flat file, use record type 61, HCPCS code (Field No. 6) to report HCPCS/CPT code. Providers utilizing the hard copy UB-92, report the HCPCS/CPT code in FL 44 "HCPCS/Rates." Providers utilizing the Medicare A 837 Health Care Claim version 3051 implementations 3A.01 and 1A.C1, report the HCPCS/CPT in 2-395-SV202-02.

100-4,13,60.14

Billing Requirements for PET Scans for Non-Covered Indications

For services performed on or after January 28, 2005, contractors shall accept claims with the following HCPCS code for non-covered PET indications:

- - G0235: PET imaging, any site not otherwise specified

Short Descriptor: PET not otherwise specified

Type of Service: 4

NOTE:This code is for a non-covered service.

100-4,13,60.3

PET Scan Qualifying Conditions and HCPCS Code Chart

Below is a summary of all covered PET scan conditions, with effective dates.

NOTE: The G codes below except those a # can be used to bill for PET Scan services through January 27, 2005. Effective for dates of service on or after January 28, 2005, providers must bill for PET Scan services using the appropriate CPT codes. See section 60.3.1. The G codes with a # can continue to be used for billing after January 28, 2005 and these remain non-covered by Medicare. (NOTE: PET Scanners must be FDA-approved.)

Conditions	Coverage Effective Date	****HCPCS/CPT
*Myocardial perfusion imaging (following previous PET G0030-G0047) single study, rest or stress (exercise and/or pharmacologic)	3/14/95	G0030
*Myocardial perfusion imaging (following previous PET G0030-G0047) multiple studies, rest or stress (exercise and/or pharmacologic)	3/14/95	G0031
*Myocardial perfusion imaging (following rest SPECT, 78464); single study, rest or stress (exercise and/or pharmacologic)	3/14/95	G0032
*Myocardial perfusion imaging (following rest SPECT 78464); multiple studies, rest or stress (exercise and/or pharmacologic)	3/14/95	G0033
*Myocardial perfusion (following stress SPECT 78465); single study, rest or stress (exercise and/or pharmacologic)	3/14/95	G0034
*Myocardial Perfusion Imaging (following stress SPECT 78465); multiple studies, rest or stress (exercise and/or pharmacologic)	3/14/95	G0035

Conditions	Coverage Effective Date	****HCPCS/CPT
*Myocardial Perfusion Imaging (following coronary angiography 93510-93529); single study, rest or stress (exercise and/or pharmacologic)	3/14/95	G0036
*Myocardial Perfusion Imaging, (following coronary angiography), 93510-93529); multiple studies, rest or stress (exercise and/or pharmacologic)	3/14/95	G0037
*Myocardial Perfusion Imaging (following stress planar myocardial perfusion, 78460); single study, rest or stress (exercise and/or pharmacologic).	3/14/95	G0038
*Myocardial Perfusion Imaging (following stress planar myocardial perfusion, 78460); multiple studies, rest or stress (exercise and/or pharmacologic)	3/14/95	G0039
*Myocardial Perfusion Imaging (following stress echocardiogram 93350); single study, rest or stress (exercise and/or pharmacologic)	3/14/95	G0040
*Myocardial Perfusion Imaging (following stress echocardiogram, 93350); multiple studies, rest or stress (exercise and/or pharmacologic)	3/14/95	G0041
*Myocardial Perfusion Imaging (following stress nuclear ventriculogram 78481 or 78483); single study, rest or stress (exercise and/or pharmacologic)	3/14/95	G0042
*Myocardial Perfusion Imaging (following stress nuclear ventriculogram 78481 or 78483); multiple studies, rest or stress (exercise and/or pharmacologic)	3/14/95	G0043
*Myocardial Perfusion Imaging (following stress ECG, 93000); single study, rest or stress (exercise and/or pharmacologic)	3/14/95	G0044
*Myocardial perfusion (following stress ECG, 93000), multiple studies; rest or stress (exercise and/or pharmacologic)	3/14/95	G0045
*Myocardial perfusion (following stress ECG, 93015), single study; rest or stress (exercise and/or pharmacologic)	3/14/95	G0046
*Myocardial perfusion (following stress ECG, 93015); multiple studies, rest or stress (exercise and/or pharmacologic)	3/14/95	G0047
PET imaging regional or whole body; single pulmonary nodule	1/1/98	G0125
Lung cancer, non-small cell (PET imaging whole body) Diagnosis, Initial Staging, Restaging	7/1/01	G0210 G0211 G0212
Colorectal cancer (PET imaging whole body) Diagnosis, Initial Staging, Restaging	7/1/01	G0213 G0214 G0215
Melanoma (PET imaging whole body) Diagnosis, Initial Staging, Restaging	7/1/01	G0216 G0217 G0218
Melanoma for non-covered indications Lymphoma (PET imaging whole body)	7/1/01	#G0219
Diagnosis, Initial Staging, Restaging	7/1/01	G0220 G0221 G0222
Head and neck cancer; excluding thyroid and CNS cancers (PET imaging whole body or regional) Diagnosis, Initial Staging, Restaging	7/1/01	G0223 G0224 G0225

100-4,13,60.3.1

Appropriate CPT Codes Effective for PET Scans for Services Performed on or After January 28, 2005

NOTE: All PET scan services require the use of a radiopharmaceutical diagnostic imaging agent (tracer). The applicable tracer code should be billed when billing for a PET scan service. See section 60.3.2 below for applicable tracer codes.

CPT Code	Description
78459	Myocardial imaging, positron emission tomography (PET), metabolic evaluation
78491	Myocardial imaging, positron emission tomography (PET), perfusion, single study at rest or stress
78492	Myocardial imaging, positron emission tomography (PET), perfusion, multiple studies at rest and/or stress
78608	Brain imaging, positron emission tomography (PET); metabolic evaluation
78811	Tumor imaging, positron emission tomography (PET); limited area (eg, chest, head/neck)
78812	Tumor imaging, positron emission tomography (PET); skull base to mid-thigh
78813	Tumor imaging, positron emission tomography (PET); whole body
78814	Tumor imaging, positron emission tomography (PET) with concurrently acquired computed tomography (CT) for attenuation correction and anatomical localization; limited area (eg, chest, head/neck)
78815	Tumor imaging, positron emission tomography (PET) with concurrently acquired computed tomography (CT) for attenuation correction and anatomical localization; skull base to mid-thigh
78816	Tumor imaging, positron emission tomography (PET) with concurrently acquired computed tomography (CT) for attenuation correction and anatomical localization; whole body

100-4,13,60.3.2

Tracer Codes Required for PET Scans

The following tracer codes are applicable only to CPT 78491 and 78492. They can not be reported with any other code.

Institutional providers billing the fiscal intermediary.

HCPCS	Description
*A9555	Rubidium Rb-82, Diagnostic, Per study dose, Up To 60 Millicuries
* Q3000 (Deleted effective 12/31/05)	Supply of Radiopharmaceutical Diagnostic Imaging Agent, Rubidium Rb-82, per dose
A9526	Nitrogen N-13 Ammonia, Diagnostic, Per study dose, Up To 40 Millicuries

NOTE: For claims with dates of service prior to 1/01/06, providers report Q3000 for supply of radiopharmaceutical diagnostic imaging agent, Rubidium Rb-82. For claims with dates of service 1/01/06 and later, providers report A9555 for radiopharmaceutical diagnostic imaging agent, Rubidium Rb-82 in place of Q3000.

Physicians / practitioners billing the carrier:

HCPCS	Description
*A4641	Supply of Radiopharmaceutical Diagnostic Imaging Agent, Not Otherwise Classified
A9526	Nitrogen N-13 Ammonia, Diagnostic, Per study dose, Up To 40 Millicuries
A9555	Rubidium Rb-82, Diagnostic, Per study dose, Up To 60 Millicuries

*NOTE: Effective January 1, 2008, tracer code A4641 is not applicable for PET Scans.

The following tracer codes are applicable only to CPT 78459, 78608, 78811-78816. They can not be reported with any other code:

Institutional providers billing the fiscal intermediary:

HCPCS	Description
* A9552	Fluorodeoxyglucose F18, FDG, Diagnostic, Per study dose, Up to 45 Millicuries

* C1775 (Deleted effective 12/31/05)	Supply of Radiopharmaceutical Diagnostic Imaging Agent, Fluorodeoxyglucose F18, (2-Deoxy-2-18F Fluoro-D-Glucose), Per dose (4-40 Mci/Ml)
**A4641	Supply of Radiopharmaceutical Diagnostic Imaging Agent, Not Otherwise Classified

* NOTE: For claims with dates of service prior to 1/01/06, OPPS hospitals report C1775 for supply of radiopharmaceutical diagnostic imaging agent, Fluorodeoxyglucose F18. For claims with dates of service 1/01/06 and later, providers report A9552 for radiopharmaceutical diagnostic imaging agent, Fluorodeoxyglucose F18 in place of C1775.

** NOTE: Effective January 1, 2008, tracer code A4641 is not applicable for PET Scans.

Physicians / practitioners billing the carrier:

HCPCS	Description
A9552	Fluorodeoxyglucose F18, FDG, Diagnostic, Per study dose, Up to 45 Millicuries
*A4641	Supply of Radiopharmaceutical Diagnostic Imaging Agent, Not Otherwise Classified

*NOTE: Effective January 1, 2008, tracer code A4641 is not applicable for PET Scans.

100-4,13,60.7.1

Darbepoetin Alfa (Aranesp) Facility Billing Requirements

Revenue code 0636 is used to report Aranesp.

The HCPCS code for aranesp must be included: HCPCS HCPCS Description Dates of Service Q4054 Injection, darbepoetin alfa, 1mcg (for ESRD on Dialysis) 1/1/2004 through 12/31/2005 J0882 Injection, darbepoetin alfa, 1mcg (for ESRD on Dialysis) 1/1/2006 to present The hematocrit reading taken prior to the last administration of Aranesp during the billing period must also be reported on the UB-92/Form CMS-1450 with value code 49. For claims with dates of service on or after April 1, 2006, a hemoglobin reading may be reported on Aranesp claims using value code 48.

Effective January 1, 2006 the definition of value code 48 and 49 used to report the hemoglobin and hematocrit readings are changed to indicate the patient's most recent reading taken before the start of the billing period.

To report a hematocrit or hemoglobin reading for a new patient on or after January 1, 2006, the provider should report the reading that prompted the treatment of darbepoetin alfa. The provider may use results documented on form CMS 2728 or the patient's medical records from a transferring facility.

The payment allowance for Aranesp is the only allowance for the drug and its administration when used for ESRD patients. Effective January 1, 2005, the cost of supplies to administer Aranesp may be billed to the FI. HCPCS A4657 and Revenue Code 270 should be used to capture the charges for syringes used in the administration of Aranesp. The maximum number of administrations of Aranesp for a billing cycle is 5 times in 30/ 31days.

100-4,16,10

Background

B3-2070, B3-2070.1, B3-4110.3, B3-5114

Diagnostic X-ray, laboratory, and other diagnostic tests, including materials and the services of technicians, are covered under the Medicare program. Some clinical laboratory procedures or tests require Food and Drug Administration (FDA) approval before coverage is provided.

A diagnostic laboratory test is considered a laboratory service for billing purposes, regardless of whether it is performed in:

- A physician's office, by an independent laboratory;
- By a hospital laboratory for its outpatients or nonpatients;
- In a rural health clinic; or
- In an HMO or Health Care Prepayment Plan (HCPP) for a patient who is not a member.

When a hospital laboratory performs laboratory tests for nonhospital patients, the laboratory is functioning as an independent laboratory, and still bills the fiscal intermediary (FI). Also, when physicians and laboratories perform the same test, whether manually or with automated equipment, the services are deemed similar. Laboratory services furnished by an independent laboratory are covered under SMI if the laboratory is an approved Independent Clinical Laboratory. However, as is the case of all diagnostic services, in order to be covered these services must be related to a patient's illness or injury (or symptom or complaint) and ordered by a physician. A small number of laboratory tests can be covered as a preventive screening service.

See the Medicare Benefit Policy Manual, Chapter 15, for detailed coverage requirements.

See the Medicare Program Integrity Manual, Chapter 10, for laboratory/supplier enrollment guidelines.

See the Medicare State Operations Manual for laboratory/supplier certification requirements.

100-4,16,60.2

Travel Allowance

In addition to a specimen collection fee allowed under Sec.60.1, Medicare, under Part B, covers a specimen collection fee and travel allowance for a laboratory technician to draw a specimen from either a nursing home patient or homebound patient under Sec.1833(h)(3) of the Act and payment is made based on the clinical laboratory fee schedule. The travel allowance is intended to cover the estimated travel costs of collecting a specimen and to reflect the technician's salary and travel costs.

The additional allowance can be made only where a specimen collection fee is also payable, i.e., no travel allowance is made where the technician merely performs a messenger service to pick up a specimen drawn by a physician or nursing home personnel. The travel allowance may not be paid to a physician unless the trip to the home, or to the nursing home was solely for the purpose of drawing a specimen. Otherwise travel costs are considered to be associated with the other purposes of the trip. The travel allowance is not distributed by CMS. Instead, the carrier must calculate the travel allowance for each claim using the following rules for the particular Code. The following HCPCS codes are used for travel allowances:

- Per Mile Travel Allowance (P9603)
- The minimum "per mile travel allowance" is $1.035. The per mile travel allowance is to be used in situations where the average trip to patients' homes is longer than 20 miles round trip, and is to be pro-rated in situations where specimens are drawn or picked up from non-Medicare patients in the same trip. - one way, in connection with medically necessary laboratory specimen collection drawn from homebound or nursing home bound patient; prorated miles actually traveled (carrier allowance on per mile basis); or
- The per mile allowance was computed using the Federal mileage rate plus an additional 45 cents a mile to cover the technician's time and travel costs. Contractors have the option of establishing a higher per mile rate in excess of the minimum (1.035 cents a mile in CY 2008) if local conditions warrant it. The minimum mileage rate will be reviewed and updated in conjunction with the clinical lab fee schedule as needed. At no time will the laboratory be allowed to bill for more miles than are reasonable or for miles not actually traveled by the laboratory technician.

Example 1: In CY 2008, a laboratory technician travels 60 miles round trip from a lab in a city to a remote rural location, and back to the lab to draw a single Medicare patient's blood. The total reimbursement would be $62.10 (60 miles x 1.035 cents a mile), plus the specimen collection fee.

Example 2: In CY 2008, a laboratory technician travels 40 miles from the lab to a

Medicare patient's home to draw blood, and then travels an additional 10 miles to a non-Medicare patient's home and then travels 30 miles to return to the lab. The total miles traveled would be 80 miles. The claim submitted would be for one half of the miles traveled or $41.40 (40 x 1.035), plus the specimen collection fee.

Flat Rate (P9604)

The CMS will pay a minimum of $9.55 one way flat rate travel allowance. The flat rate travel allowance is to be used in areas where average trips are less than 20 miles round trip. The flat rate travel fee is to be pro-rated for more than one blood drawn at the same address, and for stops at the homes of Medicare and non-Medicare patients. The laboratory does the pro-ration when the claim is submitted based on the number of patients seen on that trip. The specimen collection fee will be paid for each patient encounter.

This rate is based on an assumption that a trip is an average of 15 minutes and up to 10 miles one way. It uses the Federal mileage rate and a laboratory technician's time of $17.66 an hour, including overhead. Contractors have the option of establishing a flat rate in excess of the minimum of $9.55, if local conditions warrant it. The minimum national flat rate will be reviewed and updated in conjunction with the clinical laboratory fee schedule, as necessitated by adjustments in the Federal travel allowance and salaries.

The claimant identifies round trip travel by use of the LR modifier

Example 3: A laboratory technician travels from the laboratory to a single Medicare patient's home and returns to the laboratory without making any other stops. The flat rate would be calculated as follows: 2 x $9.55 for a total trip reimbursement of $19.10, plus the specimen collection fee.

Example 4: A laboratory technician travels from the laboratory to the homes of five patients to draw blood, four of the patients are Medicare patients and one is not. An additional flat rate would be charged to cover the 5 stops and the return trip to the lab (6 x $9.55 = $57.30). Each of the claims submitted would be for $11.46 ($57.30 /5 = $11.46). Since one of the patients is non-

Medicare, four claims would be submitted for $11.46 each, plus the specimen collection fee for each.

Example 5: A laboratory technician travels from a laboratory to a nursing home and draws blood from 5 patients and returns to the laboratory. Four of the patients are on Medicare and one is not. The $9.55 flat rate is multiplied by two to cover the return trip to the laboratory (2 x $9.55 = $19.10) and then divided by five (1/5 of $19.10 = $3.82).

Since one of the patients is non-Medicare, four claims would be submitted for $3.82 each, plus the specimen collection fee.

If a carrier determines that it results in equitable payment, the carrier may extend the former payment allowances for additional travel (such as to a distant rural nursing home) to all circumstances where travel is required. This might be appropriate, for example, if the carrier's former payment allowance was on a per mile basis. Otherwise, it should establish an appropriate allowance and inform the suppliers in its service area. If a carrier decides to establish a new allowance, one method is to consider developing a travel allowance consisting of:

- The current Federal mileage allowance for operating personal automobiles, plus a personnel allowance per mile to cover personnel costs based upon an estimate of average hourly wages and average driving speed.

Carriers must prorate travel allowance amounts claimed by suppliers by the number of patients (including Medicare and non-Medicare patients) from whom specimens were drawn on a given trip.

The carrier may determine that payment in addition to the routine travel allowance determined under this section is appropriate if:

- The patient from whom the specimen must be collected is in a nursing home or is homebound; and
- The clinical laboratory tests are needed on an emergency basis outside the general business hours of the laboratory making the collection.

Subsequent updated travel allowance amounts will be issued by CMS via Recurring Update Notification (RUN) on an annual basis.

100-4,18,10.2.1

Healthcare Common Procedure Coding System (HCPCS) andDiagnosis Codes

Vaccines and their administration are reported using separate codes. The following codes are for reporting the vaccines only.

HCPCS	Definition
90655	Influenza virus vaccine, split virus, preservative free, for children 6-35 months of age, for intramuscular use;
90656	Influenza virus vaccine, split virus, preservative free, for use in individuals 3 years and above, for intramuscular use;
90657	Influenza virus vaccine, split virus, for children 6-35 months of age, for intramuscular use;
90658	Influenza virus vaccine, split virus, for use in individuals 3 years of age and above, for intramuscular use;
90659	Influenza virus vaccine, whole virus, for intramuscular or jet injection use (Discontinued December 31, 2003);
90660	Influenza virus vaccine, live, for intranasal use;
90669	Pneumococcal conjugate vaccine, polyvalent, for children under 5 years, for intramuscular use
90732	Pneumococcal polysaccharide vaccine, 23-valent, adult or immunosuppressed patient dosage, for use in individuals 2 years or older, for subcutaneous or intramuscular use;
90740	Hepatitis B vaccine, dialysis or immunosuppressed patient dosage (3 dose schedule), for intramuscular use;
90743	Hepatitis B vaccine, adolescent (2 dose schedule), for intramuscular use;
90744	Hepatitis B vaccine, pediatric/adolescent dosage (3 dose schedule), for intramuscular use;
90746	Hepatitis B vaccine, adult dosage, for intramuscular use; and
90747	Hepatitis B vaccine, dialysis or immunosuppressed patient dosage (4 dose schedule), for intramuscular use.

The following codes are for reporting administration of the vaccines only. The administration of the vaccines is billed using:

HCPCS	Defintion
G0008	Administration of influenza virus vaccine;
G0009	Administration of pneumococcal vaccine; and
*G0010	Administration of hepatitis B vaccine.
*90471	Immunization administration. (For OPPS hospitals billing for the hepatitis B vaccine administration)
*90472	Each additional vaccine. (For OPPS hospitals billing for the hepatitis B vaccine administration)

* NOTE: For claims with dates of service prior to January 1, 2006, OPPS and non-OPPS hospitals report G0010 for Hepatitis B vaccine administration. For claims with dates of service January 1, 2006 and later, OPPS hospitals report 90471 or 90472 for hepatitis B vaccine administration as appropriate in place of G0010.

One of the following diagnosis codes must be reported as appropriate. If the sole purpose for the visit is to receive a vaccine or if a vaccine is the only service billed on a claim the applicable following diagnosis code may be used.

Diagnosis Code	Description
V03.82	Pneumococcus
V04.81**	Influenza
V06.6***	Pneumococcus and Influenza
V05.3	Hepatitis B

**Effective for influenza virus claims with dates of service October 1, 2003 and later.

***Effective October 1, 2006, providers may report diagnosis code V06.6 on claims for pneumococcus and/or influenza virus vaccines when the purpose of the visit was to receive both vaccines.

If a diagnosis code for pneumococcus, hepatitis B, or influenza virus vaccination is not reported on a claim, contractors may not enter the diagnosis on the claim. Contractors must follow current resolution processes for claims with missing diagnosis codes.

If the diagnosis code and the narrative description are correct, but the HCPCS code is incorrect, the carrier or intermediary may correct the HCPCS code and pay the claim. For example, if the reported diagnosis code is V04.81 and the narrative description (if annotated on the claim) says "flu shot" but the HCPCS code is incorrect, contractors may change the HCPCS code and pay for the flu vaccine. Effective October 1, 2006, carriers/AB MACs should follow the instructions in Pub. 100-04, Chapter 1, Section 80.3.2.1.1 (Carrier Data Element Requirements) for claims submitted without a HCPCS code.

Claims for Hepatitis B vaccinations must report the I.D. Number of referring physician. In addition, if a doctor of medicine or osteopathy does not order the influenza virus vaccine, the intermediary claims require:

UPIN code SLF000 to be reported on claims submitted prior to the date when Medicare will no longer accept identifiers other than NPIs, or

The provider's own NPI to be reported in the NPI field for the attending physician on claims submitted when NPI requirements are implemented.

100-4,18,10.2.2.1

FI Payment for Pneumococcal Pneumonia Virus, InfluenzaVirus, and Hepatitis B Virus Vaccines and Their Administration

Payment for Vaccines

Payment for all of these vaccines is on a reasonable cost basis for hospitals, home health agencies (HHAs), skilled nursing facilities (SNFs), critical access hospitals (CAHs), and hospital-based renal dialysis facilities (RDFs). Payment for comprehensive outpatient rehabilitation facilities (CORFs), Indian Health Service hospitals (IHS), IHS CAHs and independent RDFs is based on 95 percent of the average wholesale price (AWP). Section 10.2.4 of this chapter contains information on payment of these vaccines when provided by RDFs or hospices. See Sec.10.2.2.2 for payment to independent and provider- based Rural Health Centers and Federally Qualified Health Clinics.

Payment for these vaccines is as follows:

Facility	Type of Bill	Payment
Hospitals, other than Indian Health Service (IHS) Hospitals and Critical Access Hospitals (CAHs)	12x, 13x	Reasonable cost
IHS Hospitals	12x, 13x, 83x	95% of AWP
IHS CAHs	85x	95% of AWP
CAHs	85x	Reasonable cost
Method I and Method II		
Skilled Nursing Facilities	22x, 23x	Reasonable cost
Home Health Agencies	34x	Reasonable cost
Comprehensive Outpatient Rehabilitation Facilities	75x	95% of the AWP
Independent Renal Dialysis Facilities	72x	95% of the AWP
Hospital-based Renal Dialysis Facilities	72x	Reasonable cost

Payment for Vaccine Administration

Payment for the administration of Influenza Virus and PPV vaccines is as follows:

Facility	Type of Bill	Payment
Hospitals, other than IHS Hospitals and CAHs	12x, 13x	Outpatient Prospective Payment System (OPPS) for hospitals subject to OPPS Reasonable cost for hospitals not subject to OPPS
IHS Hospitals	12x, 13x, 83x	MPFS as indicated in guidelines below.
IHS CAHs	85x	MPFS as indicated in guidelines below.
CAHs	85x	Reasonable cost
Method I and II		
Skilled Nursing Facilities	22x, 23x	MPFS as indicated in the guidelines below
Home Health Agencies	34x	OPPS
Comprehensive Outpatient Rehabilitation Facilities	75x	MPFS as indicated in the guidelines below
Independent RDFs	72x	MPFS as indicated in the guidelines below
Hospital-based RDFs	72x	Reasonable cost

Guidelines for pricing PPV and Influenza vaccine administration under the MPFS.

Make reimbursement based on the rate in the MPFS associated with the CPT code 90782 or 90471 as follows:

HCPCS code	Effective prior to March 1, 2003	Effective on and after March 1, 2003
G0008	90782	90471
G0009	90782	90471

See Sec.10.2.2.2 for payment to independent and provider based Rural Health Centers and Federally Qualified Health Clinics.

Payment for the administration of Hepatitis B vaccine is as follows:

Facility	Type of Bill	Payment
Hospitals other than IHS hospitals and CAHs	12x, 13x	Outpatient Prospective Payment System (OPPS) for hospitals subject to OPPS Reasonable cost for hospitals not subject to OPPS
IHS Hospitals	12x, 13x, 83x	MPFS as indicated in the guidelines below
CAHs	85x	Reasonable cost
Method I and II		
IHS CAHs	85x	MPFS as indicated in guidelines below.
Skilled Nursing Facilities	22x, 23x	MPFS as indicated in the chart below
Home Health Agencies	34x	OPPS
Comprehensive Outpatient Rehabilitation Facilities	75x	MPFS as indicated in the guidelines below
Independent RDFs	72x	MPFS as indicated in the chart below
Hospital-based RDFs	72x	Reasonable cost

Guidelines for pricing Hepatitis B vaccine administration under the MPFS.

Make reimbursement based on the rate in the MPFS associated with the CPT code 90782 or 90471 as follows:

HCPCS code	Effective prior to March 1, 2003	Effective on and after March 1, 2003
G0010	90782	90471

See Sec.10.2.2.2 for payment to independent and provider based Rural Health Centers and Federally Qualified Health Clinics.

100-4,18,10.2.2.1

FI/AB MAC Payment for Pneumococcal Pneumonia Virus, Influenza Virus, and Hepatitis B Virus Vaccines and Their Administration

Payment for Vaccines

Payment for all of these vaccines is on a reasonable cost basis for hospitals, home health agencies (HHAs), skilled nursing facilities (SNFs), critical access hospitals (CAHs), and hospital-based renal dialysis facilities (RDFs). Payment for comprehensive outpatient rehabilitation facilities (CORFs), Indian Health Service hospitals (IHS), IHS CAHs and independent RDFs is based on 95 percent of the average wholesale price (AWP). Section 10.2.4 of this chapter contains information on payment of these vaccines when provided by RDFs or hospices. See Sec.10.2.2.2 for payment to independent and provider- based Rural Health Centers and Federally Qualified Health Clinics.

Payment for these vaccines is as follows:

Facility	Type of Bill	Payment
Hospitals, other than Indian Health Service (IHS) Hospitals and Critical Access Hospitals (CAHs)	12x, 13x	Reasonable cost
IHS Hospitals	12x, 13x, 83x	95% of AWP
IHS CAHs	85x	95% of AWP
CAHs	85x	Reasonable cost
Method I and Method II		
Skilled Nursing Facilities	22x, 23x	Reasonable cost
Home Health Agencies	34x	Reasonable cost
Comprehensive Outpatient Rehabilitation Facilities	75x	95% of the AWP
Independent Renal Dialysis Facilities	72x	95% of the AWP
Hospital-based Renal Dialysis	72x	Reasonable cost

Facilities

Payment for Vaccine Administration

Payment for the administration of influenza virus and pneumococcal vaccines is as follows:

Facility	Type of Bill	Payment
Hospitals, other than IHS Hospitals and CAHs	12x, 13x	Outpatient Prospective Payment System (OPPS) for hospitals subject to OPPS
Reasonable cost for hospitals not subject to OPPS IHS Hospitals	12x, 13x, 83x	MPFS as indicated in guidelines below.
IHS CAHs	85x	MPFS as indicated in guidelines below.
CAHs Method I and II	85x	Reasonable cost
Skilled Nursing Facilities	22x, 23x	MPFS as indicated in the guidelines below

Facility	Type of Bill	Payment
Home Health Agencies	34x	OPPS
Comprehensive Outpatient Rehabilitation Facilities	75x	MPFS as indicated in the guidelines below
Independent RDFs	72x	MPFS as indicated in the guidelines below
Hospital-based RDFs	72x	Reasonable cost

Guidelines for pricing pneumococcal and influenza virus vaccine administration under the MPFS.

Make reimbursement based on the rate in the MPFS associated with the CPT code 90782 or 90471 as follows:

HCPCS code	Effective prior to March 1, 2003	Effective on and after March 1, 2003
G0008	90782	90471
G0009	90782	90471

See Sec.10.2.2.2 for payment to independent and provider based Rural Health Centers and Federally Qualified Health Clinics.

Payment for the administration of hepatitis B vaccine is as follows:

Facility	Type of Bill	Payment
Hospitals other than IHS hospitals and CAHs	12x, 13x	Outpatient Prospective Payment System (OPPS) for hospitals subject to OPPS
Reasonable cost for hospitals not subject to OPPS IHS Hospitals	12x, 13x, 83x	MPFS as indicated in the guidelines below
CAHs	85x	Reasonable cost
Method I and II		
IHS CAHs	85x	MPFS as indicated in guidelines below.
Skilled Nursing Facilities	22x, 23x	MPFS as indicated in the chart below
Home Health Agencies	34x	OPPS
Comprehensive Outpatient Rehabilitation Facilities	75x	MPFS as indicated in the guidelines below
Independent RDFs	72x	MPFS as indicated in the chart below
Hospital-based RDFs	72x	Reasonable cost

Guidelines for pricing hepatitis B vaccine administration under the MPFS.

Make reimbursement based on the rate in the MPFS associated with the CPT code 90782 or 90471 as follows:

HCPCS code	Effective prior to March 1, 2003	Effective on and after March 1, 2003
G0010	90782	90471

See Sec.10.2.2.2 for payment to independent and provider based Rural Health Centers and Federally Qualified Health Clinics.

100-4,18,10.2.5.2

Carrier/AB MAC Payment Requirements

Payment for pneumococcal, influenza virus, and hepatitis B vaccines follows the same standard rules that are applicable to any injectable drug or biological. (See chapter 17 for procedures for determining the payment rates for pneumococcal and influenza virus vaccines.) Effective for claims with dates of service on or after February 1, 2001, Sec.114, of the Benefits Improvement and Protection Act of 2000 mandated that all drugs and biologicals be paid based on mandatory assignment. Therefore, all providers of influenza virus and pneumococcal vaccines must accept assignment for the vaccine.

Prior to March 1, 2003, the administration of pneumococcal, influenza virus, and hepatitis B vaccines, (HCPCS codes G0008, G0009, and G0010), though not reimbursed directly through the MPFS, were reimbursed at the same rate as HCPCS code 90782 on the MPFS for the year that corresponded to the date of service of the claim.

Prior to March 1, 2003, HCPCS codes G0008, G0009, and G0010 are reimbursed at the same rate as HCPCS code 90471. Assignment for the administration is not mandatory, but is applicable should the provider be enrolled as a provider type "Mass Immunization Roster Biller," submits roster bills, or participates in the centralized billing program.

Carriers/AB MACs may not apply the limiting charge provision for pneumococcal, influenza virus vaccine, or hepatitis B vaccine and their administration in accordance with Secs.1833(a)(1) and 1833(a)(10)(A) of the Social Security Act (the Act.) The administration of the influenza virus vaccine is covered in the influenza virus vaccine benefit under Sec.1861(s)(10)(A) of the Act, rather than under the physicians' services benefit. Therefore, it is not eligible for the 10 percent Health Professional Shortage Area (HPSA) incentive payment or the 5 percent Physician Scarcity Area (PSA) incentive payment.

No Legal Obligation to Pay Nongovernmental entities that provide immunizations free of charge to all patients, regardless of their ability to pay, must provide the immunizations free of charge to Medicare beneficiaries and may not bill Medicare. (See Pub. 100-02, Medicare Benefit Policy Manual, chapter 16.) Thus, for example, Medicare may not pay for influenza virus vaccinations administered to Medicare beneficiaries if a physician provides free vaccinations to all non-Medicare patients or where an employer offers free vaccinations to its employees. Physicians also may not charge Medicare beneficiaries more for a vaccine than they would charge non-Medicare patients. (See Sec.1128(b)(6)(A) of the Act.)

When an employer offers free vaccinations to its employees, it must also offer the free vaccination to an employee who is also a Medicare beneficiary. It does not have to offer free vaccinations to its non-Medicare employees.

Nongovernmental entities that do not charge patients who are unable to pay or reduce their charges for patients of limited means, yet expect to be paid if the patient has health insurance coverage for the services provided, may bill Medicare and expect payment.

Governmental entities (such as PHCs) may bill Medicare for pneumococcal, hepatitis B, and influenza virus vaccines administered to Medicare beneficiaries when services are rendered free of charge to non-Medicare beneficiaries.

100-4,18,10.3.1.1

Centralized Billing for Influenza Virus and Pneumococcal Vaccines to Medicare Carriers/AB MACs

The CMS currently authorizes a limited number of providers to centrally bill for influenza virus and pneumococcal immunization claims. Centralized billing is an optional program available to providers who qualify to enroll with Medicare as the

provider type "Mass Immunization Roster Biller," as well as to other individuals and entities that qualify to enroll as regular Medicare providers. Centralized billers must roster bill, must accept assignment, and must bill electronically.

To qualify for centralized billing, a mass immunizer must be operating in at least three payment localities for which there are three different contractors processing claims. Individuals and entities providing the vaccine and administration must be properly licensed in the State in which the immunizations are given and the contractor must verify this through the enrollment process.

Centralized billers must send all claims for influenza virus and pneumococcal immunizations to a single contractor for payment, regardless of the jurisdiction in which the vaccination was administered. (This does not include claims for the Railroad Retirement Board, United Mine Workers or Indian Health Services. These claims must continue to go to the appropriate processing entity.) Payment is made based on the payment locality where the service was provided. This process is only available for claims for the influenza virus and pneumococcal vaccines and their administration. The general coverage and coding rules still apply to these claims.

This section applies only to those individuals and entities that provide mass immunization services for influenza virus and pneumococcal vaccinations and that have been authorized by CMS to centrally bill. All other providers, including those individuals and entities that provide mass immunization services that are not authorized to centrally bill, must continue to bill for these claims to their regular carrier/AB MAC per the instructions in Sec.10.3.1 of this chapter.

The claims processing instructions in this section apply only to the designated processing contractor. However, all carriers/AB MACs must follow the instructions in Sec.10.3.1.1.J, below, "Provider Education Instructions for All Carriers/AB MACs." A. Processing Contractor Trailblazers Health Enterprises is designated as the sole contractor for the payment of influenza virus and pneumococcal claims for centralized billers from October 1, 2000, through the length of the contract. The CMS central office will notify centralized billers of the appropriate contractor to bill when they receive their notification of acceptance into the centralized billing program.

B. Request for Approval

Approval to participate in the CMS centralized billing program is a two part approval process. Individuals and corporations who wish to enroll as a CMS mass immunizer centralized biller must send their request in writing. CMS will complete Part 1 of the approval process by reviewing preliminary demographic information included in the request for participation letter. Completion of Part 1 is not approval to set up vaccination clinics, vaccinate beneficiaries, and bill Medicare for reimbursement. All new participants must complete Part 2 of the approval process (Form CMS-855 Application) before they may set up vaccination clinics, vaccinate Medicare beneficiaries, and bill Medicare for reimbursement. If an individual or entity's request is approved for centralized billing, the approval is limited to 12 months from September to August 31 of the next year. It is the responsibility of the centralized biller to reapply for approval each year. The designated contractor shall provide in writing to CMS and approved centralized billers notification of completion and approval of Part 2 of the approval process. The designated contractor may not process claims for any centralized biller who has not completed Parts 1 and 2 of the approval process. If claims are submitted by a provider who has not received approval of Parts 1 and 2 of the approval process to participate as a centralized biller, the contractor must return the claims to the provider to submit to the local carrier/AB MAC for payment.

C. Notification of Provider Participation to the Processing Contractor

Before September 1 of every year, CMS will provide the designated contractor with the names of the entities that are authorized to participate in centralized billing for the 12 month period beginning September 1 and ending August 31 of the next year.

D. Enrollment

Though centralized billers may already have a Medicare provider number, for purposes of centralized billing, they must also obtain a provider number from the processing contractor for centralized billing through completion of the Form CMS-855 (Provider Enrollment Application). Providers/suppliers are encouraged to apply to enroll as a centralized biller early as possible. Applicants who have not completed the entire enrollment process and received approval from CMS and the designated contractor to participate as a Medicare mass immunizer centralized biller will not be allowed to submit claims to Medicare for reimbursement.

Whether an entity enrolls as a provider type "Mass Immunization Roster Biller" or some other type of provider, all normal enrollment processes and procedures must be followed. Authorization from CMS to participate in centralized billing is dependent upon the entity's ability to qualify as some type of Medicare provider. In addition, as under normal enrollment procedures, the contractor must verify that the entity is fully qualified and certified per State requirements in each State in which they plan to operate.

The contractor will activate the provider number for the 12-month period from September 1 through August 31 of the following year. If the provider is authorized to participate in the centralized billing program the next year, the contractor will extend the activation of the provider number for another year. The entity need not re-enroll with the contractor every year. However, should there be changes in the States in which the entity plans to operate, the contractor will need to verify that the entity meets all State certification and licensure requirements in those new States.

E. Electronic Submission of Claims on Roster Bills

Centralized billers must agree to submit their claims on roster bills in an Electronic Media Claims standard format using the appropriate version of American National Standards Institute (ANSI) format. Contractors should refer to the appropriate ANSI Implementation Guide to determine the correct location for this information on electronic claims. The processing contractor must provide instructions on acceptable roster billing formats to the approved centralized billers. Paper claims will not be accepted.

F. Required Information on Roster Bills for Centralized Billing

In addition to the roster billing instructions found in Sec.10.3.1 of this chapter, centralized billers must complete on the electronic format the area that corresponds to Item 32 and 33 on Form CMS 1500 (08-05). The contractor must use the ZIP Code in Item 32 to determine the payment locality for the claim. Item 33 must be completed to report the provider of service/supplier's billing name, address, ZIP Code, and telephone number. In addition, the NPI of the billing provider or group must be appropriately reported.

For electronic claims, the name, address, and ZIP Code of the facility are reported in:

- The HIPAA compliant ANSI X12N 837: Claim level loop 2310D NM101=FA. When implemented, the facility (e.g., hospitals) NPI will be captured in the loop 2310D NM109 (NM108=XX) if one is available. Prior to NPI, enter the tax information in loop 2310D NM109 (NM108=24 or 34) and enter the Medicare legacy facility identifier in loop 2310D REF02 (REF01=1C). Report the address, city, state, and ZIP Code in loop 2310D N301 and N401, N402, and N403. Facility data is not required to be reported at the line level for centralized billing.

G. Payment Rates and Mandatory Assignment

The payment rates for the administration of the vaccinations are based on the Medicare Physician Fee Schedule (MPFS) for the appropriate year. Payment made through the MPFS is based on geographic locality. Therefore, payments vary based on the geographic locality where the service was performed.

The HCPCS codes G0008 and G0009 for the administration of the vaccines are not paid on the MPFS. However, prior to March 1, 2003, they must be paid at the same rate as HCPCS code 90782, which is on the MPFS. The designated contractor must pay per the correct MPFS file for each calendar year based on the date of service of the claim. Beginning March 1, 2003, HCPCS codes G0008, G0009, and G0010 are to be reimbursed at the same rate as HCPCS code 90471.

In order to pay claims correctly for centralized billers, the designated contractor must have the correct name and address, including ZIP Code, of the entity where the service was provided.

The following remittance advice and Medicare Summary Notice (MSN) messages apply:

- Claim adjustment reason code 16, "Claim/service lacks information which is needed for adjudication. At least one Remark Code must be provided (may be comprised of either the Remittance Advice Remark Code or NCPDP Reject Reason Code.)" and Remittance advice remark code MA114, "Missing/incomplete/invalid information on where the services were furnished." and MSN 9.4 - "This item or service was denied because information required to make payment was incorrect." The payment rates for the vaccines must be determined by the standard method used by Medicare for reimbursement of drugs and biologicals. (See chapter 17 for procedures for determining the payment rates for vaccines.) Effective for claims with dates of service on or after February 1, 2001, Sec.114, of the Benefits Improvement and Protection Act of 2000 mandated that all drugs and biologicals be paid based on mandatory assignment. Therefore, all providers of influenza virus and pneumococcal vaccines must accept assignment for the vaccine. In addition, as a requirement for both centralized billing and roster billing, providers must agree to accept assignment for the administration of the vaccines as well. This means that they must agree to accept the amount that Medicare pays for the vaccine and the administration. Also, since there is no coinsurance or deductible for the influenza virus and pneumococcal benefit, accepting assignment means that Medicare beneficiaries cannot be charged for the vaccination.

H. Common Working File Information

To identify these claims and to enable central office data collection on the project, special processing number 39 has been assigned. The number should be entered on the HUBC claim record to CWF in the field titled Demonstration Number.

I. Provider Education Instructions for the Processing Contractor

The processing contractor must fully educate the centralized billers on the processes for centralized billing as well as for roster billing. General information on influenza virus and pneumococcal coverage and billing instructions is available on the CMS Web site for providers.

J. Provider Education Instructions for All Carriers/AB MACs

By April 1 of every year, all carriers/AB MACs must publish in their bulletins and put on their Web sites the following notification to providers. Questions from interested providers should be forwarded to the central office address below. Carriers/AB MACs must enter the name of the assigned processing contractor where noted before sending.

NOTIFICATION TO PROVIDERS

Centralized billing is a process in which a provider, who provides mass immunization services for influenza virus and pneumococcal pneumonia virus (PPV) immunizations, can send all claims to a single contractor for payment regardless of the geographic locality in which the vaccination was administered. (This does not include claims for the Railroad Retirement Board, United Mine Workers or Indian Health Services. These claims must continue to go to the appropriate processing entity.) This process is only available for claims for the influenza virus and pneumococcal vaccines and their administration. The administration of the vaccinations is reimbursed at the assigned rate based on the Medicare physician fee schedule for the appropriate locality. The vaccines are reimbursed at the assigned rate using the Medicare standard method for reimbursement of drugs and biologicals.

Individuals and entities interested in centralized billing must contact CMS central office, in writing, at the following address by June 1 of the year they wish to begin centrally billing.

Center for Medicare & Medicaid Services Division of Practitioner Claims Processing Provider Billing and Education Group 7500 Security Boulevard Mail Stop C4-10-07 Baltimore, Maryland 21244 By agreeing to participate in the centralized billing program, providers agree to abide by the following criteria.

CRITERIA FOR CENTRALIZED BILLING

To qualify for centralized billing, an individual or entity providing mass immunization services for influenza virus and pneumococcal vaccinations must provide these services in at least three payment localities for which there are at least three different contractors processing claims.

Individuals and entities providing the vaccine and administration must be properly licensed in the State in which the immunizations are given.

Centralized billers must agree to accept assignment (i.e., they must agree to accept the amount that Medicare pays for the vaccine and the administration).

NOTE: The practice of requiring a beneficiary to pay for the vaccination upfront and to file their own claim for reimbursement is inappropriate. All Medicare providers are required to file claims on behalf of the beneficiary per Sec.1848(g)(4)(A) of the Social Security Act and centralized billers may not collect any payment.

The contractor assigned to process the claims for centralized billing is chosen at the discretion of CMS based on such considerations as workload, user-friendly software developed by the contractor for billing claims, and overall performance. The assigned contractor for this year is [Fill in name of contractor.]

The payment rates for the administration of the vaccinations are based on the Medicare physician fee schedule (MPFS) for the appropriate year. Payment made through the MPFS is based on geographic locality. Therefore, payments received may vary based on the geographic locality where the service was performed. Payment is made at the assigned rate.

The payment rates for the vaccines are determined by the standard method used by Medicare for reimbursement of drugs and biologicals. Payment is made at the assigned rate.

Centralized billers must submit their claims on roster bills in an approved Electronic Media Claims standard format. Paper claims will not be accepted.

Centralized billers must obtain certain information for each beneficiary including name, health insurance number, date of birth, sex, and signature. [Fill in name of contractor] must be contacted prior to the season for exact requirements. The responsibility lies with the centralized biller to submit correct beneficiary Medicare information (including the beneficiary's Medicare Health Insurance Claim Number) as the contractor will not be able to process incomplete or incorrect claims.

Centralized billers must obtain an address for each beneficiary so that a Medicare Summary Notice (MSN) can be sent to the beneficiary by the contractor. Beneficiaries are sometimes confused when they receive an MSN from a contractor other than the contractor that normally processes their claims which results in unnecessary beneficiary inquiries to the Medicare contractor. Therefore, centralized billers must provide every beneficiary receiving an influenza virus or pneumococcal vaccination with the name of the processing contractor. This notification must be in writing, in the form of a brochure or handout, and must be provided to each beneficiary at the time he or she receives the vaccination.

Centralized billers must retain roster bills with beneficiary signatures at their permanent location for a time period consistent with Medicare regulations. [Fill in name of contractor] can provide this information.

Though centralized billers may already have a Medicare provider number, for purposes of centralized billing, they must also obtain a provider number from [Fill in name of contractor]. This can be done by completing the Form CMS-855 (Provider Enrollment Application), which can be obtained from [Fill in name of contractor].

If an individual or entity's request for centralized billing is approved, the approval is limited to the 12 month period from September 1 through August 31 of the following year. It is the responsibility of the centralized biller to reapply to CMS CO for approval each year by June 1. Claims will not be processed for any centralized biller without permission from CMS.

Each year the centralized biller must contact [Fill in name of contractor] to verify understanding of the coverage policy for the administration of the pneumococcal vaccine, and for a copy of the warning language that is required on the roster bill.

The centralized biller is responsible for providing the beneficiary with a record of the pneumococcal vaccination.

The information in items 1 through 8 below must be included with the individual or entity's annual request to participate in centralized billing:

1. Estimates for the number of beneficiaries who will receive influenza virus vaccinations;
2. Estimates for the number of beneficiaries who will receive pneumococcal vaccinations;
3. The approximate dates for when the vaccinations will be given;
4. A list of the States in which influenza virus and pneumococcal clinics will be held;
5. The type of services generally provided by the corporation (e.g., ambulance, home health, or visiting nurse);
6. Whether the nurses who will administer the influenza virus and pneumococcal vaccinations are employees of the corporation or will be hired by the corporation specifically for the purpose of administering influenza virus and pneumococcal vaccinations;
7. Names and addresses of all entities operating under the corporation's application;
8. Contact information for designated contact person for centralized billing program.

100-4,18,10.4.1

In order to prevent duplicate payment by the same FI/AB MAC, CWF edits by line item on the FI/AB MAC number, the beneficiary Health Insurance Claim (HIC) number, and the date of service, the influenza virus procedure codes 90657, 90658, or 90659, the pneumonia procedure code 90732, and the administration codes G0008 or G0009.

If CWF receives a claim with either HCPCS codes 90657, 90658 or 90659, and it already has on record a claim with the same HIC number, same FI/AB MAC number, same date of service, and any one of those HCPCS codes, the second claim submitted to CWF rejects.

If CWF receives a claim with HCPCS code 90732 and it already has on record a claim with the same HIC number, same FI/AB MAC number, same date of service, and the same HCPCS code, the second claim submitted to CWF rejects when all four items match.

If CWF receives a claim with HCPCS administration codes G0008 or G0009 and it already has on record a claim with the same HIC number, same FI/AB MAC number, same date of service, and same procedure code, CWF rejects the second claim submitted when all four items match.

CWF returns to the FI/AB MAC a reject code "7262" for this edit. FIs/AB MACs must deny the second claim and use the same messages they currently use for the denial of duplicate claims.

100-4,18,120.1

Coding and Payment of DSMT Services

The following HCPCS codes are used to report DSMT: G0108 - Diabetes outpatient self-management training services, individual, per 30 minutes.

G0109 - Diabetes outpatient self-management training services, group session (2 or more), per 30 minutes.

The type of service for these codes is 1.

Type of Facility	Payment Method	Type of Bill
Physician (billed to the carrier)	MPFS	NA
Hospitals subject to OPPS	MPFS	12X, 13X
Method I and Method II Critical Access Hospitals (CAHs) (technical services)	101% of reasonable cost	12X and 85X
Indian Health Service (IHS) providers billing hospital outpatient Part B	OMB-approved outpatient per visit all inclusive rate (AIR)	13X
IHS providers billing inpatient Part B	All-inclusive inpatient ancillary per diem rate	12X
IHS CAHs billing outpatient Part B	101% of the all-inclusive facility specific per visit rate	85X
IHS CAHs billing inpatient Part B	101% of the all-inclusive facility specific per diem rate	12X
FQHCs*	All-inclusive encounter rate with other qualified services. Separate visit payment available with HCPCS.	73X
Skilled Nursing Facilities **	MPFS non-facility rate	22X, 23X
Maryland Hospitals under jurisdiction of the Health Services Cost Review Commission (HSCRC)	94% of provider submitted charges in accordance with the terms of the Maryland Waiver	12X, 13X
Home Health Agencies (can be billed only if the service is provided outside of the treatment plan)	MPFS non-facility rate	34X

* Effective January 1, 2006, payment for DSMT provided in an FQHC that meets all of the requirements as above, may be made in addition to one other visit the beneficiary had during the same day, if this qualifying visit is billed on TOB 73X, with HCPCS G0108 or G0109, and revenue codes 0520, 0521, 0522, 0524, 0525, 0527, 0528, or 0900.

** The SNF consolidated billing provision allows separate part B payment for training services for beneficiaries that are in skilled Part A SNF stays, however, the SNF must submit these services on a 22 bill type. Training services provided by other provider types must be reimbursed by X the SNF.

NOTE: An ESRD facility is a reasonable site for this service, however, because it is required to provide dietician and nutritional services as part of the care covered in the composite rate, ESRD facilities are not allowed to bill for it separately and do not receive separate reimbursement. Likewise, an RHC is a reasonable site for this service, however it must be provided in an RHC with other qualifying services and paid at the all-inclusive encounter rate.

Deductible and co-insurance apply.

100-4,18,20.4

Billing Requirements - FI/A/B MAC Claims

Contractors use the weekly-updated MQSA file to verify that the billing facility is certified by the FDA to perform mammography services, and has the appropriate certification to perform the type of mammogram billed (film and/or digital). (See Sec.20.1.) FIs/A/B MACs use the provider number submitted on the claim to identify the facility and use the MQSA data file to verify the facility's certification(s). FIs/A/B MACs complete the following activities in processing mammography claims:

If the provider number on the claim does not correspond with a certified mammography facility on the MQSA file, then intermediaries/A/B MACs deny the claim.

When a film mammography HCPCS code is on a claim, the claim is checked for a "1" film indicator.

If a film mammography HCPCS code comes in on a claim and the facility is certified for film mammography, the claim is paid if all other relevant Medicare criteria are met.

If a film mammography HCPCS code is on a claim and the facility is certified for digital mammography only, the claim is denied.

When a digital mammography HCPCS code is on a claim, the claim is checked for "2" digital indicator.

If a digital mammography HCPCS code is on a claim and the facility is certified for digital mammography, the claim is paid if all other relevant Medicare criteria are met.

If a digital mammography HCPCS code is on a claim and the facility is certified for film mammography only, the claim is denied.

NOTE: The Common Working File (CWF) no longer receives the mammography file for editing purposes.

Except as provided in the following sections for RHCs and FQHCs, the following procedures apply to billing for screening mammographies: The technical component portion of the screening mammography is billed on Form CMS-1450 under bill type 12X, 13X, 14X**, 22X, 23X or 85X using revenue code 0403 and HCPCS code 77057* (76092*).

The technical component portion of the diagnostic mammography is billed on Form CMS-1450 under bill type 12X, 13X, 14X**, 22X, 23X or 85X using revenue code 0401 and HCPCS code 77055* (76090*), 77056* (76091*), G0204 and G0206.

Separate bills are required for claims for screening mammographies with dates of service prior to January 1, 2002. Providers include on the bill only charges for the screening mammography. Separate bills are not required for claims for screening mammographies with dates of service on or after January 1, 2002.

See separate instructions below for rural health clinics (RHCs) and federally qualified health centers (FQHCs).

* For claims with dates of service prior to January 1, 2007, providers report CPT codes 76090, 76091, and 76092. For claims with dates of service January 1, 2007 and later, providers report CPT codes 77055, 77056, and 77057 respectively.

** For claims with dates of service April 1, 2005 and later, hospitals bill for all mammography services under the 13X type of bill or for dates of service April 1, 2007 and later, 12X or 13X as appropriate. The 14X type of bill is no longer applicable. Appropriate bill types for providers other than hospitals are 22X, 23X, and 85X.

In cases where screening mammography services are self-referred and as a result an attending physician NPI is not available, the provider shall duplicate their facility NPI in the attending physician identifier field on the claim.

100-4,18,60.1

Payment

Payment (contractor) is under the MPFS except as follows:

- Fecal occult blood tests (82270* (G0107*) and G0328) are paid under the clinical diagnostic lab fee schedule except reasonable cost is paid to all non-OPPS hospitals, including CAHs, but not IHS hospitals billing on TOB 83x. IHS hospitals billing on TOB 83x are paid the ASC payment amount. Other IHS hospitals (billing on TOB 13x) are paid the OMB approved AIR, or the facility specific per visit amount as applicable. Deductible and coinsurance do not apply for these tests. See section A below for payment to Maryland waiver on TOB 13X. Payment from all hospitals for non-patient laboratory specimens on TOB 14X will be based on the clinical diagnostic fee schedule, including CAHs and Maryland waiver hospitals

Flexible sigmoidoscopy (code G0104) is paid under OPPS for hospital outpatient departments and on a reasonable cost basis for CAHs; or current payment methodologies for hospitals not subject to OPPS.

Colonoscopies (G0105 and G0121) and barium enemas (G0106 and G0120) are paid under OPPS for hospital outpatient departments and on a reasonable costs basis for CAHs or current payment methodologies for hospitals not subject to OPPS. Also colonoscopies may be done in an Ambulatory Surgical Center (ASC) and when done in an ASC the ASC rate applies. The ASC rate is the same for diagnostic and screening colonoscopies. The ASC rate is paid to IHS hospitals when the service is billed on TOB 83x.

Prior to January 1, 2007, deductible and coinsurance apply to HCPCS codes G0104, G0105, G0106, G0120, and G0121. Beginning with services provided on or after January 1, 2007, Section 5113 of the Deficit Reduction Act of 2005 waives the requirement of the annual Part B deductible for these screening services. Coinsurance still applies. Coinsurance and deductible applies to the diagnostic colorectal service codes listed below.

The following screening codes must be paid at rates consistent with the diagnostic codes indicated.

Screening Code	Diagnostic Code
G0104	45330
G0105 and G0121	45378
G0106 and G0120	74280

A. Special Payment Instructions for TOB 13X Maryland Waiver Hospitals

For hospitals in Maryland under the jurisdiction of the Health Services Cost Review Commission, screening colorectal services HCPCS codes G0104, G0105, G0106, 82270* (G0107*), G0120, G0121 and G0328 are paid according to the terms of the waiver, that is 94% of submitted charges minus any unmet existing deductible, co-insurance and non-covered charges. Maryland Hospitals bill TOB 13X for outpatient colorectal cancer screenings.

B. Special Payment Instructions for Non-Patient Laboratory Specimen (TOB 14X) for all hospitals

Payment for colorectal cancer screenings (82270* (G0107*) and G0328) to a hospital for a non-patient laboratory specimen (TOB 14X), is the lesser of the actual charge, the fee schedule amount, or the National Limitation Amount (NLA), (including CAHs and Maryland Waiver hospitals). Part B deductible and coinsurance do not apply.

*NOTE: For claims with dates of service prior to January 1, 2007, physicians, suppliers, and providers report HCPCS code G0107. Effective January 1, 2007, code G0107 is discontinued and replaced with CPT code 82270.

100-4,18,60.2

HCPCS Codes, Frequency Requirements, and Age Requirements (If Applicable)

Effective for services furnished on or after January 1, 1998, the following codes are used for colorectal cancer screening services:

- 82270* (G0107*) - Colorectal cancer screening; fecal-occult blood tests, 1-3 simultaneous determinations;
- G0104 - Colorectal cancer screening; flexible sigmoidoscopy;
- G0105 - Colorectal cancer screening; colonoscopy on individual at high risk;
- G0106 - Colorectal cancer screening; barium enema; as an alternative to G0104, screening sigmoidoscopy;
- G0120 - Colorectal cancer screening; barium enema; as an alternative to G0105, screening colonoscopy.

Effective for services furnished on or after July 1, 2001, the following codes are used for colorectal cancer screening services:

- G0121 - Colorectal cancer screening; colonoscopy on individual not meeting criteria for high risk. Note that the description for this code has been revised to remove the term "noncovered."
- G0122 - Colorectal cancer screening; barium enema (noncovered).

Effective for services furnished on or after January 1, 2004, the following code is used for colorectal cancer screening services as an alternative to 82270* (G0107*):

- G0328 - Colorectal cancer screening; immunoassay, fecal-occult blood test, 1-3 simultaneous determinations

*NOTE: For claims with dates of service prior to January 1, 2007, physicians, suppliers, and providers report HCPCS code G0107. Effective January 1, 2007, code G0107 is discontinued and replaced with CPT code 82270.

- G0104 - Colorectal Cancer Screening; Flexible Sigmoidoscopy

Screening flexible sigmoidoscopies (code G0104) may be paid for beneficiaries who have attained age 50, when performed by a doctor of medicine or osteopathy at the frequencies noted below.

For claims with dates of service on or after January 1, 2002, contractors pay for screening flexible sigmoidoscopies (code G0104) for beneficiaries who have attained age 50 when these services were performed by a doctor of medicine or osteopathy, or by a physician assistant, nurse practitioner, or clinical nurse specialist (as defined in Sec.1861(aa)(5) of the Act and in the Code of Federal Regulations at42 CFR 410.74,410.75, and410.76) at the frequencies noted above. For claims with dates of service prior to January 1, 2002, contractors pay for these services under the conditions noted only when a doctor of medicine or osteopathy performs them.

For services furnished from January 1, 1998, through June 30, 2001, inclusive:

- Once every 48 months (i.e., at least 47 months have passed following the month in which the last covered screening flexible sigmoidoscopy was done).
- For services furnished on or after July 1, 2001:
- Once every 48 months as calculated above unless the beneficiary does not meet the criteria for high risk of developing colorectal cancer (refer to Sec.60.3 of this chapter) and he/she has had a screening colonoscopy (code G0121) within the preceding 10 years. If such a beneficiary has had a screening colonoscopy within the preceding 10 years, then he or she can have covered a screening flexible sigmoidoscopy only after at least 119 months have passed following the month that he/she received the screening colonoscopy (code G0121).

NOTE:If during the course of a screening flexible sigmoidoscopy a lesion or growth is detected which results in a biopsy or removal of the growth; the appropriate diagnostic procedure classified as a flexible sigmoidoscopy with biopsy or removal should be billed and paid rather than code G0104.

G0105 - Colorectal Cancer Screening; Colonoscopy on Individual at High Risk

Screening colonoscopies (code G0105) may be paid when performed by a doctor of medicine or osteopathy at a frequency of once every 24 months for beneficiaries at high risk for developing colorectal cancer (i.e., at least 23 months have passed following the month in which the last covered G0105 screening colonoscopy was performed). Refer to Sec.60.3of this chapter for the criteria to use in determining whether or not an individual is at high risk for developing colorectal cancer.

NOTE:If during the course of the screening colonoscopy, a lesion or growth is detected which results in a biopsy or removal of the growth, the appropriate diagnostic procedure classified as a colonoscopy with biopsy or removal should be billed and paid rather than code G0105.

A. Colonoscopy Cannot be Completed Because of Extenuating Circumstances

1. FIs

   When a covered colonoscopy is attempted but cannot be completed because of extenuating circumstances, Medicare will pay for the interrupted colonoscopy as long as the coverage conditions are met for the incomplete procedure. However, the frequency standards associated with screening colonoscopies will not be applied by CWF. When a covered colonoscopy is next attempted and completed, Medicare will pay for that colonoscopy according to its payment methodology for this procedure as long as coverage conditions are met, and the frequency standards will be applied by CWF. This policy is applied to both screening and diagnostic colonoscopies.

   When submitting a facility claim for the interrupted colonoscopy, providers are to suffix the colonoscopy HCPCS codes with a modifier of "-73" or" -74" as appropriate to indicate that the procedure was interrupted. Payment for covered incomplete screening colonoscopies shall be consistent with payment methodologies currently in place for complete screening colonoscopies, including those contained in42 CFR 419.44(b). In situations where a critical access hospital (CAH) has elected payment Method II for CAH patients, payment shall be consistent with payment methodologies currently in place as outlined in Chapter 3. As such, instruct CAHs that elect Method II payment to use modifier "-53" to identify an incomplete screening colonoscopy (physician professional service(s) billed in revenue code 096X, 097X, and/or 098X). Such CAHs will also bill the technical or facility component of the interrupted colonoscopy in revenue code 075X (or other appropriate revenue code) using the "-73" or "-74" modifier as appropriate.

Note that Medicare would expect the provider to maintain adequate information in the patient's medical record in case it is needed by the contractor to document the incomplete procedure.

2. Carriers

   When a covered colonoscopy is attempted but cannot be completed because of extenuating circumstances (see Chapter 12), Medicare will pay for the interrupted colonoscopy at a rate consistent with that of a flexible sigmoidoscopy as long as coverage conditions are met for the incomplete procedure. When a covered colonoscopy is next attempted and completed, Medicare will pay for that colonoscopy according to its payment methodology for this procedure as long as coverage conditions are met. This policy is applied to both screening and diagnostic colonoscopies.

   When submitting a claim for the interrupted colonoscopy, professional providers are to suffix the colonoscopy code with a modifier of "-53" to indicate that the procedure was interrupted. When submitting a claim for the facility fee associated with this procedure, Ambulatory Surgical Centers (ASCs) are to suffix the colonoscopy code with "-73" or "-74" as appropriate. Payment for covered screening colonoscopies, including that for the associated ASC facility fee when applicable, shall be consistent with payment for diagnostic colonoscopies, whether the procedure is complete or incomplete.

Note that Medicare would expect the provider to maintain adequate information in the patient's medical record in case it is needed by the contractor to document the incomplete procedure.

- G0106 - Colorectal Cancer Screening; Barium Enema; as an Alternative to G0104, Screening Sigmoidoscopy

Screening barium enema examinations may be paid as an alternative to a screening sigmoidoscopy (code G0104). The same frequency parameters for screening sigmoidoscopies (see those codes above) apply. In the case of an individual aged 50 or over, payment may be made for a screening barium enema examination (code G0106) performed after at least 47 months have passed following the month in which the last screening barium enema or screening flexible sigmoidoscopy was performed. For example, the beneficiary received a screening barium enema examination as an alternative to a screening flexible sigmoidoscopy in January 1999. Start counts beginning February 1999. The beneficiary is eligible for another screening barium enema in January 2003. The screening barium enema must be ordered in writing after a determination that the test is the appropriate screening test. Generally, it is expected that this will be a screening double contrast enema unless the individual is unable to withstand such an exam. This means that in the case of a particular individual, the attending physician must determine that the estimated screening potential for the barium enema is equal to or greater than the screening potential that has been estimated for a screening flexible sigmoidoscopy for the same individual. The screening single contrast barium enema also requires a written order from the beneficiary's attending physician in the same manner as described above for the screening double contrast barium enema examination.

- 82270* (G0107*) - Colorectal Cancer Screening; Fecal-Occult Blood Test, 1-3 Simultaneous Determinations

Effective for services furnished on or after January 1, 1998, screening FOBT (code 82270* (G0107*) may be paid for beneficiaries who have attained age 50, and at a frequency of once every 12 months (i.e., at least 11 months have passed following the month in which the last covered screening FOBT was performed). This screening FOBT means a guaiac-based test for peroxidase activity, in which the beneficiary completes it by taking samples from two different sites of three consecutive stools. This screening requires a written order from the beneficiary's attending physician. (The term "attending physician" is defined to mean a doctor of medicine or osteopathy (as defined in Sec.1861(r)(1)of the Act) who is fully knowledgeable about the beneficiary's medical condition, and who would be responsible for using the results of any examination performed in the overall management of the beneficiary's specific medical problem.)

Effective for services furnished on or after January 1, 2004, payment may be made for a immunoassay-based FOBT (G0328, described below) as an alternative to the guaiacbased FOBT, 82270* (G0107*). Medicare will pay for only one covered FOBT per year, either 82270* (G0107*) or G0328, but not both.

*NOTE: For claims with dates of service prior to January 1, 2007, physicians, suppliers, and providers report HCPCS code G0107. Effective January 1, 2007, code G0107 is discontinued and replaced with CPT code 82270.

- G0328 - Colorectal Cancer Screening; Immunoassay, Fecal-Occult Blood Test, 1-3 Simultaneous Determinations

Effective for services furnished on or after January 1, 2004, screening FOBT, (code G0328) may be paid as an alternative to 82270* (G0107*) for beneficiaries who have attained age 50. Medicare will pay for a covered FOBT (either 82270* (G0107*) or G0328, but not both) at a frequency of once every 12 months (i.e., at least 11 months have passed following the month in which the last covered screening FOBT was performed). Screening FOBT, immunoassay, includes the use of a spatula to collect the appropriate number of samples or the use of a special brush for the collection of samples, as determined by the individual manufacturer's instructions. This screening requires a written order from the beneficiary's attending physician. (The term "attending physician" is defined to mean a doctor of medicine or osteopathy (as defined in Sec.1861(r)(1) of the Act) who is fully knowledgeable about the beneficiary's medical condition, and who would be responsible for using the results of any examination performed in the overall management of the beneficiary's specific medical problem.)

- G0120 - Colorectal Cancer Screening; Barium Enema; as an Alternative to or G0105, Screening Colonoscopy

Screening barium enema examinations may be paid as an alternative to a screening colonoscopy (code G0105) examination. The same frequency parameters for screening colonoscopies (see those codes above) apply. In the case of an individual who is at high risk for colorectal cancer, payment may be made for a screening barium enema examination (code G0120) performed after at least 23 months have passed following the month in which the last screening barium enema or the last screening colonoscopy was performed. For example, a beneficiary at high risk for developing colorectal cancer received a screening barium enema examination (code G0120) as an alternative to a screening colonoscopy (code G0105) in January 2000. Start counts beginning February 2000. The beneficiary is eligible for another screening barium enema examination (code G0120) in January 2002. The screening barium enema must be ordered in writing after a determination that the test is the appropriate screening test. Generally, it is expected that this will be a screening double contrast enema unless the individual is unable to withstand such an exam. This means that in the case of a particular individual, the attending physician must determine that the estimated screening potential for the barium enema is equal to or greater than the screening potential that has been estimated for a screening colonoscopy, for the same individual. The screening single contrast barium enema also requires a written order from the beneficiary's attending physician in the same manner as described above for the screening double contrast barium enema examination.

- G0121 - Colorectal Screening; Colonoscopy on Individual Not Meeting Criteria for High Risk - Applicable On and After July 1, 2001

Effective for services furnished on or after July 1, 2001, screening colonoscopies (code G0121) performed on individuals not meeting the criteria for being at high risk for developing colorectal cancer (refer to Sec.60.3 of this chapter) may be paid under the following conditions:

- At a frequency of once every 10 years (i.e., at least 119 months have passed following the month in which the last covered G0121 screening colonoscopy was performed.)

If the individual would otherwise qualify to have covered a G0121 screening colonoscopy based on the above but has had a covered screening flexible sigmoidoscopy (code G0104), then he or she may have covered a G0121 screening colonoscopy only after at least 47 months have passed following the month in which the last covered G0104 flexible sigmoidoscopy was performed.

NOTE:If during the course of the screening colonoscopy, a lesion or growth is detected which results in a biopsy or removal of the growth, the appropriate diagnostic procedure classified as a colonoscopy with biopsy or removal should be billed and paid rather than code G0121.

- G0122 - Colorectal Cancer Screening; Barium Enema

The code is not covered by Medicare.

100-4,18,60.6

Billing Requirements for Claims Submitted to FIs

Follow the general bill review instructions in Chapter 25. Hospitals use the ANSI X12N 837I to bill the FI or on the hardcopy Form CMS-1450. Hospitals bill revenue codes and HCPCS codes as follows:

Screening Test/Procedure	Revenue Code	HCPCS Code	TOB
Fecal Occult blood test	030X	82270*** (G0107***), G0328	13X, 14X**, 22X, 23X, 83X, 85X
Barium enema	032X	G0106, G0120, G0122	13X, 22X, 23X, 85X****
Flexible Sigmoidoscopy	*	G0104	13X, 22X, 23X, 83X, 85X****
Colonoscopy-high risk	*	G0105, G0121	13X, 22X, 23X, 83X, 85X****

* The appropriate revenue code when reporting any other surgical procedure.

** 14X is only applicable for non-patient laboratory specimens.

*** For claims with dates of service prior to January 1, 2007, physicians, suppliers, and providers report HCPCS code G0107. Effective January 1, 2007, code G0107, is discontinued and replaced with CPT code 82270.

**** CAHs that elect Method II bill revenue code 096X, 097X, and/or 098X for professional services and 075X (or other appropriate revenue code) for the technical or facility component.

A Special Billing Instructions for Hospital Inpatients

When these tests/procedures are provided to inpatients of a hospital, they are covered under this benefit. However, the provider bills on bill type 13X using the discharge date of the hospital stay to avoid editing in the Common Working File (CWF) as a result of the hospital bundling rules.

100-4,20,100.2.2

Evidence of Medical Necessity for Parenteral and Enteral Nutrition (PEN) Therapy

The PEN coverage is determined by information provided by the treating physician and the PEN supplier. A completed certification of medical necessity (CMN) must accompany and support initial claims for PEN to establish whether coverage criteria are met and to ensure that the PEN therapy provided is consistent with the attending or ordering physician's prescription.

Contractors ensure that the CMN contains pertinent information from the treating physician. Uniform specific medical data facilitate the review and promote consistency in coverage determinations and timelier claims processing.The medical and prescription information on a PEN CMN can be most appropriatelycompleted by the treating physician or from information in the patient's records by an employee of the physician for the physician's review and signature.

Although PEN suppliers sometimes may assist in providing the PEN services, they cannot complete the CMN since they do not have the same access to patient information needed to properly enter medical or prescription information. Contractors use appropriate professional relations issuances, training sessions, and meetings to ensure that all persons and PEN suppliers are aware of this limitation of their role. When properly completed, the PEN CMN includes the elements of a prescription as well as other data needed to determine whether Medicare coverage is possible. This practice will facilitate prompt delivery of PEN services and timely submittal of the related claim.

100-4,20,160.1

Billing for Total Parenteral Nutrition and Enteral NutritionFurnished to Part B Inpatients

A3-3660.6, SNF-544, SNF-559, SNF-260.4, SNF-261, HHA-403, HO-438, HO-229

Inpatient Part A hospital or SNF care includes total parenteral nutrition (TPN) systems and enteral nutrition (EN).

For inpatients for whom Part A benefits are not payable (e.g., benefits are exhausted or the beneficiary is entitled to Part B only), total parenteral nutrition (TPN) systems and enteral nutrition (EN) delivery systems are covered by Medicare as prosthetic devices when the coverage criteria are met. When these criteria are met, the medical equipment and medical supplies (together with nutrients) being used comprise covered prosthetic devices for coverage purposes rather than durable medical equipment. However, reimbursement rules relating to DME continue to apply to such items.

When a facility supplies TPN or EN systems that meet the criteria for coverage as a prosthetic device to an inpatient whose care is not covered under Part A, the facility must bill one of the DMERCs. Additionally, HHAs, SNFs, and hospitals that provide PEN supplies, equipment and nutrients as a prosthetic device under Part B must use the CMS-1500 or the related NSF or ANSI ASC X12N 837 format to bill the appropriate DMERC. The DMERC is determined according to the residence of the beneficiary. Refer to Sec.10 for jurisdiction descriptions.

FIs return claims containing PEN charges for Part B services where the bill type is 12x,

13x, 22x, 23x, 32x, 33x, or 34x with instructions to the provider to bill the DMERC.

100-4,3,10.4

Payment of Nonphysician Services for Inpatients

All items and nonphysician services furnished to inpatients must be furnished directly by the hospital or billed through the hospital under arrangements. This provision applies to all hospitals, regardless of whether they are subject to PPS.

Other Medical Items, Supplies, and Services the following medical items, supplies, and services furnished to inpatients are covered under Part A. Consequently, they are covered by the prospective payment rate or reimbursed as reasonable costs under Part A to hospitals excluded from PPS.

- Laboratory services (excluding anatomic pathology services and certain clinical pathology services);

- Pacemakers and other prosthetic devices including lenses, and artificial limbs, knees, and hips;
- Radiology services including computed tomography (CT) scans furnished to inpatients by a physician's office, other hospital, or radiology clinic;
- Total parenteral nutrition (TPN) services; and
- Transportation, including transportation by ambulance, to and from another hospital or freestanding facility to receive specialized diagnostic or therapeutic services not available at the facility where the patient is an inpatient.

The hospital must include the cost of these services in the appropriate ancillary service cost center, i.e., in the cost of the diagnostic or therapeutic service. It must not show them separately under revenue code 0540.

EXCEPTIONS

Pneumococcal Vaccine -is payable under Part B only and is billed by the hospital on the Form CMS-1450.

Ambulance Service For purposes of this section "hospital inpatient" means beneficiary who has been formally admitted it does not include a beneficiary who is in the process of being transferred from one hospital to another. Where the patient is transferred from one hospital to another, and is admitted as an inpatient to the second, the ambulance service is payable under only Part B. If transportation is by a hospital owned and operated ambulance, the hospital bills separately on Form CMS-1450 as appropriate. Similarly, if the hospital arranges for the ambulance transportation with an ambulance operator, including paying the ambulance operator, it bills separately. However, if the hospital does not assume any financial responsibility, the billing is to the carrier by the ambulance operator or beneficiary, as appropriate, if an ambulance is used for the transportation of a hospital inpatient to another facility for diagnostic tests or special treatment the ambulance trip is considered part of the DRG, and not separately billable, if the resident hospital is under PPS.

Part B Inpatient Services Where Part A benefits are not payable, payment maybe made to the hospital under Part B for certain medical and other health services. See Chapter 4 for a description of Part B inpatient services.

Anesthetist Services "Incident to" Physician Services

If a physician's practice was to employ anesthetists and to bill on a reasonable charge basis for these services and that practice was in effect as of the last day of the hospital's most recent 12-month cost reporting period ending before September 30, 1983, the physician may continue that practice through cost reporting periods beginning October 1, 1984. However, if the physician chooses to continue this practice, the hospital may not add costs of the anesthetist's service to its base period costs for purposes of its transition payment rates. If it is the existing or new practice of the physician to employ certified registered nurse anesthetists (CRNAs) and other qualified anesthetists and include charges for their services in the physician bills for anesthesiology services for the hospital's cost report periods beginning on or after October 1, 1984, and before October 1, 1987, the physician may continue to do so.

B. Exceptions/Waivers

These provisions were waived before cost reporting periods beginning on or after October1, 1986, under certain circumstances. The basic criteria for waiver was that services furnished by outside suppliers are so extensive that a sudden change in billing practices would threaten the stability of patient care. Specific criteria for waiver and processing procedures are in Sec.2804 of the Provider Reimbursement Manual (CMS Pub. 15-1).

100-4,3,20.7.3

Payment for Blood Clotting Factor Administered to Hemophilia Patients

Section 6011 of Public Law (P.L.) 101-239 amended Sec.1886(a)(4) of the Social Security Act (the Act) to provide that prospective payment system (PPS) hospitals receive anadditional payment for the costs of administering blood clotting factor to Medicare hemophiliacs who are hospital inpatients. Section 6011(b) of P.L. 101.239 specified that the payment be based on a predetermined price per unit of clotting factor multiplied by the number of units provided. This add-on payment originally was effective for blood clotting factors furnished on or after June 19, 1990, and before December 19, 1991. Section 13505 of P. L. 103-66 amended Sec.6011 (d) of P.L. 101-239 to extend the period covered by the add-on payment for blood clotting factors administered to Medicare inpatients with hemophilia through September 30, 1994. Section 4452 of P.L. 105-33 amended Sec.6011(d) of P.L. 101-239 to reinstate the add-on payment for the costs of administering blood clotting factor to Medicare beneficiaries who have hemophilia and who are hospital inpatients for discharges occurring on or after October 1, 1998.

Local carriers shall process non-institutional blood clotting factor claims.

The FIs shall process institutional blood clotting factor claims payable under either Part A or Part B.

A. Inpatient Bills

Under the Inpatient Prospective Payment System (PPS), hospitals receive a special add-on payment for the costs of furnishing blood clotting factors to Medicare beneficiaries with hemophilia, admitted as inpatients of PPS hospitals. The clotting factor add-on payment is calculated using the number of units (as defined in the HCPCS code long descriptor) billed by the provider under special instructions for units of service.

The PPS Pricer software does not calculate the payment amount. The Fiscal Intermediary Standard System (FISS) calculates the payment amount and subtracts the charges from those submitted to Pricer so that the clotting factor charges are not included in cost outlier computations.

Blood clotting factors not paid on a cost or PPS basis are priced as a drug/biological under the Medicare Part B Drug Pricing File effective for the specific date of service. As of January 1, 2005, the average sales price (ASP) plus 6 percent shall be used.

If a beneficiary is in a covered Part A stay in a PPS hospital, the clotting factors are paid in addition to the DRG/HIPPS payment (For FY 2004, this payment is based on 95 percent of average wholesale price.) For a SNF subject to SNF/PPS, the payment is bundled into the SNF/PPS rate.

For SNF inpatient Part A, there is no add-on payment for blood clotting factors.

The codes for blood-clotting factors are found on the Medicare Part B Drug Pricing File. This file is distributed on a quarterly basis.

For discharges occurring on or after October 1, 2000, and before December 31, 2005, report HCPCS Q0187 based on 1 billing unit per 1.2 mg. Effective January 1, 2006, HCPCS code J7189 replaces Q0187 and is defined as 1 billing unit per 1 microgram (mcg).

The examples below include the HCPCS code and indicate the dosage amount specified in the descriptor of that code. Facilities use the units field as a multiplier to arrive at the dosage amount.

EXAMPLE 1

HCPCS Drug Dosage

J7189 Factor VIIa 1 mcg

Actual dosage: 13,365 mcg

On the bill, the facility shows J7189 and 13,365 in the units field (13,365 mcg divided by 1 mcg = 13,365 units).

NOTE:The process for dealing with one international unit (IU) is the same as the process of dealing with one microgram.

EXAMPLE 2

HCPCS Drug Dosage

J9355 Trastuzumab 10 mg

Actual dosage: 140 mg

On the bill, the facility shows J9355 and 14 in the units field (140 mg divided by 10mg = 14 units). When the dosage amount is greater than the amount indicated for the HCPCS code, the facility rounds up to determine units. When the dosage amount is less than the amount indicated for the HCPCS code, use 1 as the unit of measure.

EXAMPLE 3

HCPCS Drug Dosage

J3100 Tenecteplase 50 mg

Actual Dosage: 40 mg

The provider would bill for 1 unit, even though less than 1 full unit was furnished.

At times, the facility provides less than the amount provided in a single use vial and there is waste, i.e.; some drugs may be available only in packaged amounts that exceed the needs of an individual patient. Once the drug is reconstituted in the hospital's pharmacy, it may have a limited shelf life. Since an individual patient may receive less than the fully reconstituted amount, we encourage hospitals to schedule patients in such a way that the hospital can use the drug most efficiently. However, if the hospital must discard the remainder of a vial after administering part of it to a Medicare patient, the provider may bill for the amount of drug discarded plus the amount administered.

Example 1:

Drug X is available only in a 100-unit size. A hospital schedules three Medicare patients to receive drug X on the same day within the designated shelf life of the product. An appropriate hospital staff member administers 30 units to each patient. The remaining 10 units are billed to Medicare on the account of the last patient. Therefore, 30 units are billed on behalf of the first patient seen and 30 units are billed on behalf of the second patient seen. Forty units are billed on behalf of the last patient seen because the hospital had to discard 10 units at that point.

Example 2:

An appropriate hospital staff member must administer 30 units of drug X to a Medicare patient, and it is not practical to schedule another patient who requires the same drug. For example, the hospital has only one patient who requires drug X, or the hospital sees the patient for the first time and did not know the patient's condition. The hospital bills for 100 units on behalf of the patient, and Medicare pays for 100 units.

When the number of units of blood clotting factor administered to hemophiliac inpatients exceeds 99,999, the hospital reports the excess as a second line for revenue code 0636 and repeats the HCPCS code. One hundred thousand fifty (100,050) units are reported on one line as 99,999, and another line shows 1,051.

Revenue Code 0636 is used. It requires HCPCS. Some other inpatient drugs continue to be billed without HCPCS codes under pharmacy.

No changes in beneficiary notices are required. Coverage is applicable to hospital Part A claims only. Coverage is also applicable to inpatient Part B services in SNFs and all types of hospitals, including CAHs. Separate payment is not made to SNFs for beneficiaries in an inpatient Part A stay.

B. FI Action

The FI is responsible for the following:

- It accepts HCPCS codes for inpatient services;
- It edits to require HCPCS codes with Revenue Code 0636. Multiple iterations of the revenue code are possible with the same or different HCPCS codes. It does not edit units except to ensure a numeric value;
- It reduces charges forwarded to Pricer by the charges for hemophilia clotting factors in revenue code 0636. It retains the charges and revenue and HCPCS codes for CWF; and
- It modifies data entry screens to accept HCPCS codes for hospital (including CAH) swing bed, and SNF inpatient claims (bill types 11X, 12X, 18x, 21x and, 22x).

The September 1, 1993, IPPS final rule (58 FR 46304) states that payment will be made for the blood clotting factor only if an ICD-9-CM diagnosis code for hemophilia is included on the bill.

Since inpatient blood-clotting factors are covered only for beneficiaries with hemophilia, the FI must ensure that one of the following hemophilia diagnosis codes is listed on the bill before payment is made:

- 286.0 Congenital factor VIII disorder
- 286.1 Congenital factor IX disorder
- 286.2 Congenital factor IX disorder
- 286.3 Congenital deficiency of other clotting factor
- 286.4 von Willebrands' disease

Effective for discharges on or after August 1, 2001, payment may also be made if one of the following diagnosis codes is reported:

- 286.5 Hemorrhagic disorder due to circulating anticoagulants
- 286.7 Acquired coagulation factor deficiency

C. Part A Remittance Advice

1. X12.835 Ver. 003030M

   For remittance reporting PIP and/or non-PIP payments, the Hemophilia Add on will be reported in a claims level 2-090-CAS segment (CAS is the element identifier) exhibiting an "OA" Group Code and adjustment reason code "97" (payment is included in the allowance for the basic service/ procedure) followed by the associated dollar amount (POSITIVE) and units of service. For this version of the 835, "OA" group coded line level CAS segments are informational and are not included in the balancing routine. The Hemophilia Add On amount will always be included in the 2-010-CLP04 Claim Payment Amount.

   For remittance reporting PIP payments, the Hemophilia Add On will also be reported in the provider level adjustment (element identifier PLB) segment with the provider level adjustment reason code "CA" (Manual claims adjustment) followed by the associated dollar amount (NEGATIVE).

NOTE: A data maintenance request will be submitted to ANSI ASC X12 for a new PLB adjustment reason code specifically for PIP payment Hemophilia Add On situations for future use. However, continue to use adjustment reason code "CA" until further notice.

The FIs enter MA103 (Hemophilia Add On) in an open MIA (element identifier) remark code data element. This will alert the provider that the reason code 97 and PLB code "CA" adjustments are related to the Hemophilia Add On.

2. X12.835 Ver. 003051

   For remittances reporting PIP and/or non-PIP payments, Hemophilia Add On information will be reported in the claim level 2-062-AMT and 2-064-QTY segments. The 2-062-AMT01 element will carry a "ZK" (Federal Medicare claim MANDATE - Category 1) qualifier code followed by the total claim level Hemophilia Add On amount (POSITIVE). The 2-064QTY01 element will carry a "FL" (Units) qualifier code followed by the number of units approved for the Hemophilia Add On for the claim. The Hemophilia Add On amount will always be included in the 2-010-CLP04 Claim Payment Amount.

NOTE: A data maintenance request will be submitted to ANSI ASC X12 for a new AMT qualifier code specifically for the Hemophilia Add On for future use. However, continue to use adjustment reason code "ZK" until further notice.

For remittances reporting PIP payments, the Hemophilia Add On will be reported in the provider level adjustment PLB segment with the provider level adjustment reason "ZZ" followed by the associated dollar amount (NEGATIVE).

NOTE: A data maintenance request will be submitted to ANSI ASC X12 for a new PLB, adjustment reason code specifically for the Hemophilia Add On for future use. However, continue to use PLB adjustment reason code "ZZ" until further notice. The FIs enter MA103 (Hemophilia Add On) in an open MIA remark code data element. This will alert the provider that the ZK, FL and ZZ entries are related to the Hemophilia Add On. (Effective with version 4010 of the 835, report ZK in lieu of FL in the QTY segment.)

3. Standard Hard Copy Remittance Advice

   For paper remittances reporting non-PIP payments involving Hemophilia Add On, add a "Hemophilia Add On" category to the end of the "Pass Thru Amounts" listings in the "Summary" section of the paper remittance. Enter the total of the Hemophilia Add On amounts due for the claims covered by this remittance next to the Hemophilia Add On heading.

   The FIs add the Remark Code "MA103" (Hemophilia Add On) to the remittance advice under the REM column for those claims that qualify for Hemophilia Add On payments.

   This will be the full extent of Hemophilia Add On reporting on paper remittance notices; providers wishing more detailed information must subscribe to the Medicare Part A specifications for the ANSI ASC X12N 835, where additional information is available.

See chapter 22, for detailed instructions and definitions.

100-4,3,40.2.2

Charges to Beneficiaries for Part A Services

The hospital submits a bill even where the patient is responsible for a deductible which covers the entire amount of the charges for non-PPS hospitals, or in PPS hospitals, where the DRG payment amount will be less than the deductible.

A hospital receiving payment for a covered hospital stay (or PPS hospital that includes at least one covered day, or one treated as covered under guarantee of payment or limitation on liability) may charge the beneficiary, or other person, for items and services furnished during the stay only as described in subsections A through H. If limitation of liability applies, a beneficiary's liability for payment is governed by the limitation on liability notification rules in Chapter 30 of this manual. For related notices for inpatient hospitals, see CMS Transmittal 594, Change Request3903, dated June 24, 2005.

A. Deductible and Coinsurance

The hospital may charge the beneficiary or other person for applicable deductible and coinsurance amounts. The deductible is satisfied only by charges for covered services. The FI deducts the deductible and coinsurance first from the PPS payment. Where the deductible exceeds the PPS amount, the excess will be applied to a subsequent payment to the hospital. (See Chapter 3 of the Medicare General Information, Eligibility, and Entitlement Manual for specific policies.)

B. Blood Deductible

The Part A blood deductible provision applies to whole blood and red blood cells, and reporting of the number of pints is applicable to both PPS and non-PPS hospitals. (See Chapter 3 of the Medicare General Information, Eligibility, and Entitlement Manual for specific policies.) Hospitals shall report charges for red blood cells using revenue code 381, and charges for whole blood using revenue code 382.

C. Inpatient Care No Longer Required

The hospital may charge for services that are not reasonable and necessary or that constitute custodial care. Notification may be required under limitation of liability. See CMS Transmittal 594,

Change Request3903, dated June 24, 2005, section V. of the attachment, for specific notification requirements. Note this transmittal will be placed in Chapter 30 of this manual at a future point. Chapter 1, section 150 of this manual also contains related billing information in addition to that provided below.

In general, after proper notification has occurred, and assuming an expedited decision is received from a Quality Improvement Organization (QIO), the following entries are required on the bill the hospital prepares:

- Occurrence code 3l (and date) to indicate the date the hospital notified the patient in accordance with the first bullet above;
- Occurrence span code 76 (and dates) to indicate the period of noncovered care for which it is charging the beneficiary;
- Occurrence span code 77 (and dates) to indicate the period of noncovered care for which the provider is liable, when it is aware of this prior to billing; and
- Value code 3l (and amount) to indicate the amount of charges it may bill the beneficiary for days for which inpatient care was no longer required. They are included as noncovered charges on the bill.

D. Change in the Beneficiary's Condition

If the beneficiary remains in the hospital after receiving notice as described in subsection C, and the hospital, the physician who concurred in the hospital's determination, or the QIO, subsequently determines that the beneficiary again requires inpatient hospital care, the hospital may not charge the beneficiary or other person for services furnished after the beneficiary again required inpatient hospital care until proper notification occurs (see subsection C).

If a patient who needs only a SNF level of care remains in the hospital after the SNF bed becomes available, and the bed ceases to be available, the hospital may continue to charge the beneficiary. It need not provide the beneficiary with another notice when the patient chose not to be discharged to the SNF bed.

E. Admission Denied

If the entire hospital admission is determined to be not reasonable or necessary, limitation of liability may apply. See 2005 CMS transmittal 594, section V. of the attachment, for specific notification requirements.

NOTE: This transmittal will be placed in Chapter 30 of this manual at a future point.

In such cases the following entries are required on the bill:

- Occurrence code 3l (and date) to indicate the date the hospital notified the beneficiary.
- Occurrence span code 76 (and dates) to indicate the period of noncovered care for which the hospital is charging the beneficiary.
- Occurrence span code 77 (and dates) to indicate any period of noncovered care for which the provider is liable (e.g., the period between issuing the notice and the time it may charge the beneficiary) when the provider is aware of this prior to billing.
- Value code 3l (and amount) to indicate the amount of charges the hospital may bill the beneficiary for hospitalization that was not necessary or reasonable. They are included as noncovered charges on the bill.

F. Procedures, Studies and Courses of Treatment That Are Not Reasonable or Necessary

If diagnostic procedures, studies, therapeutic studies and courses of treatment are excluded from coverage as not reasonable and necessary (even though the beneficiary requires inpatient hospital care) the hospital may charge the beneficiary or other person for the services or care according the procedures given in CMS Transmittal 594, Change Request3903, dated June 24, 2005.

The following bill entries apply to these circumstances:

- Occurrence code 32 (and date) to indicate the date the hospital provided the notice to the beneficiary.
- Value code 3l (and amount) to indicate the amount of such charges to be billed to the beneficiary. They are included as noncovered charges on the bill.

G. Nonentitlement Days and Days after Benefits Exhausted

If a hospital stay exceeds the day outlier threshold, the hospital may charge for some, or all, of the days on which the patient is not entitled to Medicare Part A, or after the Part A benefits are exhausted (i.e., the hospital may charge its customary charges for services furnished on those days). It may charge the beneficiary for the lesser of:

- The number of days on which the patient was not entitled to benefits or after the benefits were exhausted; or
- The number of outlier days. (Day outliers were discontinued at the end of FY 1997.)

If the number of outlier days exceeds the number of days on which the patient was not entitled to benefits, or after benefits were exhausted, the hospital may charge for all days on which the patient was not entitled to benefits or after benefits were exhausted. If the number of days on which the beneficiary was not entitled to benefits, or after benefits were exhausted, exceeds the number of outlier days, the hospital determines the days for which it may charge by starting with the last day of the stay (i.e., the day before the day of discharge) and identifying and counting off in reverse order, days on which the patient was not entitled to benefits or after the benefits were exhausted, until the number of days counted off equals the number of outlier days. The days counted off are the days for which the hospital may charge.

H. Contractual Exclusions

In addition to receiving the basic prospective payment, the hospital may charge the beneficiary for any services that are excluded from coverage for reasons other than, or in addition to, absence of medical necessity, provision of custodial care, non-entitlement to Part A, or exhaustion of benefits. For example, it may charge for most cosmetic and dental surgery.

I. Private Room Care

Payment for medically necessary private room care is included in the prospective payment. Where the beneficiary requests private room accommodations, the hospital must inform the beneficiary of the additional charge. (See the Medicare Benefit Policy Manual, Chapter 1.) When the beneficiary accepts the liability, the hospital will supply the service, and bill the beneficiary directly. If the beneficiary believes the private room was medically necessary, the beneficiary has a right to a determination and may initiate a Part A appeal.

J. Deluxe Item or Service

Where a beneficiary requests a deluxe item or service, i.e., an item or service which is more expensive than is medically required for the beneficiary's condition, the hospital may collect the additional charge if it informs the beneficiary of the additional charge. That charge is the difference between the customary charge for the item or service most commonly furnished by the hospital to private pay patients with the beneficiary's condition, and the charge for the more expensive item or service requested. If the beneficiary believes that the more expensive item or service was medically necessary, the beneficiary has a right to a determination and may initiate a Part A appeal.

K - Inpatient Acute Care Hospital Admission Followed By a Death or Discharge Prior To Room Assignment

A patient of an acute care hospital is considered an inpatient upon issuance of written doctor's orders to that effect. If a patient either dies or is discharged prior to being assigned and/or occupying a room, a hospital may enter an appropriate room and board charge on the claim. If a patient leaves of their own volition prior to being assigned and/or occupying a room, a hospital may enter an appropriate room and board charge on the claim as well as a patient status code 07 which indicates they left against medical advice. A hospital is not required to enter a room and board charge, but failure to do so may have a minimal impact on future DRG weight calculations.

100-4,3,40.3

Outpatient Services Treated as Inpatient Services

A3-3610.3, HO-415.6, HO-400D, A-03-008, A-03-013, A-03-054

A. Outpatient Services Followed by Admission Before Midnight of the Following Day (Effective For Services Furnished Before October 1, 1991)

When a beneficiary receives outpatient hospital services during the day immediately preceding the hospital admission, the outpatient hospital services are treated as inpatient services if the beneficiary has Part A coverage. Hospitals and FIs apply this provision only when the beneficiary is admitted to the hospital before midnight of the day following receipt of outpatient services. The day on which the patient is formally admitted as an inpatient is counted as the first inpatient day.

When this provision applies, services are included in the applicable PPS payment and not billed separately. When this provision applies to hospitals and units excluded from the hospital PPS, services are shown on the bill and included in the Part A payment. See Chapter 1 for FI requirements for detecting duplicate claims in such cases.

B. Preadmission Diagnostic Services (Effective for Services Furnished On or After January 1, 1991)

Diagnostic services (including clinical diagnostic laboratory tests) provided to a beneficiary by the admitting hospital, or by an entity wholly owned or wholly operated by the admitting hospital (or by another entity under arrangements with the admitting hospital), within 3 days prior to and including the date of the beneficiary's admission are deemed to be inpatient services and included in the inpatient payment, unless there is no Part A coverage. For example, if a patient is admitted on a Wednesday, outpatient services provided by the hospital on Sunday, Monday, Tuesday, or Wednesday are included in the inpatient Part A payment.

This provision does not apply to ambulance services and maintenance renal dialysis services (see the Medicare Benefit Policy Manual, Chapters 10 and 11, respectively). Additionally, Part A services furnished by skilled nursing facilities, home health agencies, and hospices are excluded from the payment window provisions.

For services provided before October 31, 1994, this provision applies to both hospitals subject to the hospital inpatient prospective payment system (IPPS) as well as those hospitals and units excluded from IPPS.

For services provided on or after October 31, 1994, for hospitals and units excluded from IPPS, this provision applies only to services furnished within one day prior to and including the date of the beneficiary's admission. The hospitals and units that are excluded from IPPS are: psychiatric hospitals and units; inpatient rehabilitation facilities (IRF) and units; long-term care hospitals (LTCH); children's hospitals; and cancer hospitals.

Critical access hospitals (CAHs) are not subject to the 3-day (nor 1-day) DRG payment window.

An entity is considered to be "wholly owned or operated" by the hospital if the hospital is the sole owner or operator. A hospital need not exercise administrative control over a facility in order to operate it. A hospital is considered the sole operator of the facility if the hospital has exclusive responsibility for implementing facility policies (i.e., conducting or overseeing the facility's routine operations), regardless of whether it also has the authority to make the policies.

For this provision, diagnostic services are defined by the presence on the bill of the following revenue and/or CPT codes:

- 0254 - Drugs incident to other diagnostic services
- 0255 - Drugs incident to radiology
- 030X - Laboratory
- 031X - Laboratory pathological
- 032X - Radiology diagnostic
- 0341, 0343 - Nuclear medicine, diagnostic/Diagnostic Radiopharmaceuticals
- 035X - CT scan
- 0371 - Anesthesia incident to Radiology
- 0372 - Anesthesia incident to other diagnostic services
- 040X - Other imaging services
- 046X - Pulmonary function
- 0471 - Audiology diagnostic
- 0481, 0489- Cardiology, Cardiac Catheter Lab/Other Cardiology with CPT codes 93501, 93503, 93505, 93508, 93510, 93526, 93541, 93542, 93543, 93544, 93556, 93561, or 93562 diagnostic
- 0482- Cardiology, Stress Test
- 0483- Cardiology, Echocardiology
- 053X - Osteopathic services
- 061X - MRT
- 062X - Medical/surgical supplies, incident to radiology or other diagnostic services
- 073X - EKG/ECG
- 074X - EEG
- 0918- Testing- Behavioral Health
- 092X - Other diagnostic services

The CWF rejects services furnished January 1, 1991, or later when outpatient bills for diagnostic services with through dates or last date of service (occurrence span code 72) fall on the day of admission or any of the 3 days immediately prior to admission to an IPPS or IPPS-excluded hospital. This reject applies to the bill in process, regardless of whether the outpatient or inpatient bill is processed first. Hospitals must analyze the two bills and report appropriate corrections. For services on or after October 31, 1994, for hospitals and units excluded from IPPS, CWF will reject outpatient diagnostic bills that occur on the day of or one day before admission. For IPPS hospitals, CWF will continue to reject outpatient diagnostic bills for services that occur on the day of or any of the 3 days prior to admission. Effective for dates of service on or after July 1, 2008, CWF will reject diagnostic services when the line item date of service (LIDOS) falls on the day of admission or any of the 3 days immediately prior to an admission to an IPPS hospital or on the day of admission or one day prior to admission for hospitals excluded from IPPS.

Hospitals in Maryland that are under the jurisdiction of the Health Services Cost Review Commission are subject to the 3-day payment window.

C. Other Preadmission Services (Effective for Services Furnished On or After October 1, 1991)

Nondiagnostic outpatient services that are related to a patient's hospital admission and that are provided by the hospital, or by an entity wholly owned or wholly operated by the admitting hospital (or by another entity under arrangements with the admitting hospital), to the patient during the 3 days immediately preceding and including the date of the patient's admission are deemed to be inpatient services and are included in the inpatient payment. Effective March 13, 1998, we defined nondiagnostic preadmission services as being related to the admission only when there is an exact match (for all digits) between the ICD-9-CM principal diagnosis code assigned for both the preadmission services and the inpatient stay. Thus, whenever Part A covers an admission, the hospital may bill nondiagnostic preadmission services to Part B as outpatient services only if they are not related to the admission. The FI shall assume, in the absence of evidence to the contrary, that such bills are not admission related and, therefore, are not deemed to be inpatient (Part A) services. If there are both diagnostic and nondiagnostic preadmission services and the nondiagnostic services are unrelated to the admission, the hospital may separately bill the nondiagnostic preadmission services to Part B. This provision applies only when the patient has Part A coverage. This provision does not apply to ambulance services and maintenance renal dialysis. Additionally, Part A services furnished by skilled nursing facilities, home health agencies, and hospices are excluded from the payment window provisions.

For services provided before October 31, 1994, this provision applies to both hospitals subject to IPPS as well as those hospitals and units excluded from IPPS (see section B above).

For services provided on or after October 31, 1994, for hospitals and units excluded from IPPS, this provision applies only to services furnished within one day prior to and including the date of the beneficiary's admission.

Critical access hospitals (CAHs) are not subject to the 3-day (nor 1-day) DRG payment window.

Hospitals in Maryland that are under the jurisdiction of the Health Services Cost Review Commission are subject to the 3-day payment window.

Effective for dates of service on or after July 1, 2008, CWF will reject therapeutic services when the line item date of service (LIDOS) falls on the day of admission or any of the 3 days immediately prior to an admission to an IPPS hospital or on the day of admission or one day prior to admission for hospitals excluded from IPPS.

100-4,32,100

Billing Requirements for Expanded Coverage of Cochlear Implantation

Effective for dates of services on and after April 4, 2005, the Centers for Medicare & Medicaid Services (CMS) has expanded the coverage for cochlear implantation to cover moderate-to-profound hearing loss in individuals with hearing test scores equal to or less than 40% correct in the best aided listening condition on tape-recorded tests of open-set sentence recognition and who demonstrate limited benefit from amplification. (See Publication 100-03, chapter 1, section 50.3, for specific coverage criteria).

In addition CMS is covering cochlear implantation for individuals with open-set sentence recognition test scores of greater than 40% to less than or equal to 60% correct but only when the provider is participating in, and patients are enrolled in, either:

- A Food and Drug Administration (FDA)-approved category B investigational device exemption (IDE) clinical trial; or
- A trial under the CMS clinical trial policy (see Pub. 100-03, section 310.1); or
- A prospective, controlled comparative trial approved by CMS as consistent with the evidentiary requirements for national coverage analyses and meeting specific quality standards.

100-4,32,50

Deep Brain Stimulation for Essential Tremor and Parkinson,Äôs Disease

Deep brain stimulation (DBS) refers to high-frequency electrical stimulation of anatomic regions deep within the brain utilizing neurosurgically implanted electrodes. These DBS electrodes are stereotactically placed within targeted nuclei on one (unilateral) or both (bilateral) sides of the brain. There are currently three targets for DBS -- the thalamic ventralis intermedius nucleus (VIM), subthalamic nucleus (STN) and globus pallidus interna (GPi).

Essential tremor (ET) is a progressive, disabling tremor most often affecting the hands. ET may also affect the head, voice and legs. The precise pathogenesis of ET is unknown. While it may start at any age, ET usually peaks within the second and sixth decades. Beta-adrenergic blockers and anticonvulsant medications are usually the first line treatments for reducing the severity of tremor. Many patients, however, do not adequately respond or cannot tolerate these medications. In these medically refractory ET patients, thalamic VIM DBS may be helpful for symptomatic relief of tremor.

Parkinson's disease (PD) is an age-related progressive neurodegenerative disorder involving the loss of dopaminergic cells in the substantia nigra of the midbrain. The disease is characterized by tremor, rigidity, bradykinesia and progressive postural instability. Dopaminergic medication is typically used as a first line treatment for reducing the primary symptoms of PD. However, after prolonged use, medication can become less effective and can produce significant adverse events such as dyskinesias and other motor function complications. For patients who become unresponsive to medical treatments and/or have intolerable side effects from medications, DBS for symptom relief may be considere

100-4,4,160

Clinic and Emergency Visits

CMS has acknowledged from the beginning of the OPPS that CMS believes that CPT Evaluation and Management (E/M) codes were designed to reflect the activities of physicians and do not describe well the range and mix of services provided by hospitals during visits of clinic and emergency department patients. While awaiting the development of a national set of facility-specific codes and guidelines, providers should continue to apply their current internal guidelines to the existing CPT codes. Each hospital's internal guidelines should follow the intent of the CPT code descriptors, in that the guidelines should be designed to reasonably relate the intensity of hospital resources to the different levels of effort represented by the codes. Hospitals should ensure that their guidelines accurately reflect resource distinctions between the five levels of codes.

Effective January 1, 2007, CMS is distinguishing between two types of emergency departments: Type A emergency departments and Type B emergency departments.

A Type A emergency department is defined as an emergency department that is available 24 hours a day, 7 days a week and is either licensed by the State in which it is located under applicable State law as an emergency room or emergency department or it is held out to the public (by name, posted signs, advertising, or other means) as a place that provides care for emergency medical conditions on an urgent basis without requiring a previously scheduled appointment.

A Type B emergency department is defined as an emergency department that meets the definition of a "dedicated emergency department" as defined in 42 CFR 489.24 under the EMTALA regulations. It must meet at least one of the following requirements: (1) It is licensed by the State in which it is located under applicable State law as an emergency room or emergency department; (2) It is held out to the public (by name, posted signs, advertising, or other means) as a place that provides care for emergency medical conditions on an urgent basis without requiring a previously scheduled appointment; or (3) During the calendar year immediately preceding the calendar year in which a determination under 42 CFR 489.24 is being made, based on a representative sample of patient visits that occurred during that calendar year, it provides at least one-third of all of its outpatient visits for the treatment of emergency medical conditions on an urgent basis without requiring a previously scheduled appointment.

Hospitals must bill for visits provided in Type A emergency departments using CPT emergency department E/M codes. Hospitals must bill for visits provided in Type B emergency departments using the G-codes that describe visits provided in Type B emergency departments.

Hospitals that will be billing the new Type B ED visit codes may need to update their internal guidelines to report these codes.

Emergency department and clinic visits are paid in some cases separately and in other cases as part of a composite APC payment. See section 10.2.1 of this chapter for further details.

100-4,4,160.1

Critical Care Services

Beginning January 1, 2007, critical care services will be paid at two levels, depending on the presence or absence of trauma activation. Providers will receive one payment rate for critical care without trauma activation and will receive additional payment when critical care is associated with trauma activation.

To determine whether trauma activation occurs, follow the National Uniform Billing Committee (NUBC) guidelines in the Claims Processing Manual, Pub 100-04, Chapter 25, Sec.75.4 related to the reporting of the trauma revenue codes in the 68x series. The revenue code series 68x can be used only by trauma centers/hospitals as licensed or designated by the state or local government authority authorized to do so, or as verified by the American College of Surgeons. Different subcategory revenue codes are reported by designated Level 1-4 hospital trauma centers. Only patients for whom there has been prehospital notification based on triage information from prehospital caregivers, who meet either local, state or American College of Surgeons field triage criteria, or are delivered by inter-hospital transfers, and are given the appropriate team response can be billed a trauma activation charge.

When critical care services are provided without trauma activation, the hospital may bill CPT code 99291, Critical care, evaluation and management of the critically ill or critically injured patient; first 30-74 minutes (and 99292, if appropriate). If trauma activation occurs under the circumstances described by the NUBC guidelines that would permit reporting a charge under 68x, the hospital may also bill one unit of code G0390, which describes trauma activation associated with hospital critical care services. Revenue code 68x must be reported on the same date of service. The OCE will edit to ensure that G0390 appears with revenue code 68x on the same date of service and that only one unit of G0390 is billed. CMS believes that trauma activation is a one-time occurrence in association with critical care services, and therefore, CMS will only pay for one unit of G0390 per day.

The CPT code 99291 is defined by CPT as the first 30-74 minutes of critical care. This 30 minute minimum has always applied under the OPPS. The CPT code 99292, Critical care, evaluation and management of the critically ill or critically injured patient; each additional 30 minutes, remains a packaged service under the OPPS, so that hospitals do not have the ongoing administrative burden of reporting precisely the time for each critical service provided. As the CPT guidelines indicate, hospitals that provide less than 30 minutes of critical care should bill for a visit, typically an emergency department visit, at a level consistent with their own internal guidelines.

Under the OPPS, the time that can be reported as critical care is the time spent by a physician and/or hospital staff engaged in active face-to-face critical care of a critically ill or critically injured patient. If the physician and hospital staff or multiple hospital staff members are simultaneously engaged in this active face-to-face care, the time involved can only be counted once.

In CY 2007 hospitals may continue to report a charge with RC 68x without any HCPCS code when trauma team activation occurs. In order to receive additional payment when critical care services are associated with trauma activation, the hospital must report G0390 on the same date of service as RC 68x, in addition to CPT code 99291 (or 99292, if appropriate.)

In CY 2007 hospitals should continue to report 99291 (and 99292 as appropriate) for critical care services furnished without trauma team activation. CPT 99291 maps to APC 0617 (Critical Care). (CPT 99292 is packaged and not paid separately, but should be reported if provided.)

Critical care services are paid in some cases separately and in other cases as part of a composite APC payment. See Section 10.2.1 of this chapter for further details.

100-4,4,200.1

Billing for Corneal Tissue

Corneal tissue will be paid on a cost basis, not under OPPS. To receive cost based reimbursement hospitals must bill charges for corneal tissue using HCPCS code V2785.

100-4,4,200.3.4

Billing for Linear Accelerator (Robotic Image-Guided and Non-Robotic Image-Guided) SRS Planning and Delivery

Effective for services furnished on or after January 1, 2006, hospitals must bill using existing CPT codes that most accurately describe the service furnished for both robotic and non-robotic image-guided SRS planning. For robotic image-guided SRS delivery, hospitals must bill using HCPCS code G0039 for the first session and HCPCS code G0340 for the second through the fifth sessions. For non-robotic image-guided SRS delivery, hospitals must bill G0173 for delivery if the delivery occurs in one session, and G0251 for delivery per session (not to exceed five sessions) if delivery occurs during multiple sessions.

Linear Accelerator-Based Robotic Image-Guided SRS Planning Use existing CPT codes Delivery G0339 (complete, 1P st P session) G0340 (2P nd P - 5P th P session) Linear Accelerator-Based Non-Robotic Image-Guided SRS Planning Use existing CPT codes Delivery G0173 (single session) G0251 (multiple) G0173 Linear accelerator based stereotactic radiosurgery, delivery including collimator changes and custom plugging, complete course of treatment in one session, all lesions.

- G0251 Linear accelerator based stereotactic radiosurgery, delivery including collimator changes and custom plugging, fractionated treatment, all lesions, per session, maximum 5 sessions per course of treatment.
- G0339 Image-guided robotic linear accelerator-based stereotactic radiosurgery, complete course of therapy in one session or first session of fractionated treatment.
- G0340 Image-guided robotic linear accelerator-based stereotactic radiosurgery, delivery including collimator changes and custom plugging, fractionated treatment, all lesions, per session, second through fifth sessions, maximum five sessions per course of treatment.

100-4,4,200.4

Billing for Amniotic Membrane

Hospitals should report HCPCS code V2790 (Amniotic membrane for surgical reconstruction, per procedure) to report amniotic membrane tissue when the tissue is used. A specific procedure code associated with use of amniotic membrane tissue is CPT code 65780 (Ocular surface reconstruction; amniotic membrane transplantation).

Payment for the amniotic membrane tissue is packaged into payment for CPT code 65780 or other procedures with which the amniotic membrane is used.

100-4,4,200.6

Billing and Payment for Alcohol and/or Substance Abuse Assessment and Intervention Services

For CY 2008, the CPT Editorial Panel has created two new Category I CPT codes for reporting alcohol and/or substance abuse screening and intervention services. They are CPT code 99408 (Alcohol and/or substance (other than tobacco) abuse structured screening (e.g., AUDIT, DAST), and brief intervention (SBI) services; 15 to 30 minutes); and CPT code 99409 (Alcohol and/or substance (other than tobacco) abuse structured screening (e.g., AUDIT, DAST), and brief intervention (SBI) services; greater than 30 minutes). However, screening services are not covered by Medicare without specific statutory authority, such as has been provided for mammography, diabetes, and colorectal cancer screening. Therefore, beginning January 1, 2008, the OPPS recognizes two parallel G-codes (HCPCS codes G0396 and G0397) to allow for appropriate reporting and payment of alcohol and substance abuse structured assessment and intervention services that are not provided as screening services, but that are performed in the context of the diagnosis or treatment of illness or injury.

Contractors shall make payment under the OPPS for HCPCS code G0396 (Alcohol and/or substance (other than tobacco) abuse structured assessment (e.g., AUDIT, DAST) and brief intervention, 15 to 30 minutes) and HCPCS code G0397, (Alcohol and/or substance(other than tobacco) abuse structured assessment (e.g., AUDIT, DAST) and intervention greater than 30 minutes), only when reasonable and necessary (i.e., when the service is provided to evaluate patients with signs/symptoms of illness or injury) as per section 1862(a)(1)(A) of the Act.

HCPCS codes G0396 and G0397 are to be used for structured alcohol and/or substance (other than tobacco) abuse assessment and intervention services that are distinct from other clinic and emergency department visit services performed during the same encounter. Hospital resources expended performing services described by HCPCS codes G0396 and G0397 may not be counted as resources for determining the level of a visit service and vice versa (i.e., hospitals may not double count the same facility resources in order to reach a higher level clinic or emergency department visit). However, alcohol and/or substance structured assessment or intervention services lasting less than 15 minutes should not be reported using these HCPCS codes, but the hospital resources expended should be included in determining the level of the visit service reported.

100-4,4,200.7.2

Cardiac Echocardiography With Contrast

Hospitals are instructed to bill for echocardiograms with contrast using the applicable HCPCS code(s) included in Table 200.7.2 below. Hospitals should also report the appropriate units of the HCPCS codes for the contrast agents used in the performance of the echocardiograms.

Table 200.7.2 - HCPCS Codes For Echocardiograms With Contrast HCPCS Long Descriptor C8921 Transthoracic echocardiography with contrast for congenital cardiac anomalies; complete C8922 Transthoracic echocardiography with contrast for congenital cardiac anomalies; follow-up or limited study C8923 Transthoracic echocardiography with contrast, realtime with image documentation (2D) with or without HCPCS Long Descriptor M-mode recording; complete C8924 Transthoracic echocardiography with contrast, realtime with image documentation (2D) with or without M-mode recording; follow-up or limited study C8925 Transesophageal echocardiography (TEE) with contrast, real time with image documentation (2D) (with or without M-mode recording); including probe placement, image acquisition, interpretation and report C8926 Transesophageal echocardiography (TEE) with contrast for congenital cardiac anomalies; including probe placement, image acquisition, interpretation and report C8927 Transesophageal echocardiography (TEE) with contrast for monitoring purposes, including probe placement, real time 2-dimensional image acquisition and interpretation leading to ongoing (continuous) assessment of (dynamically changing) cardiac pumping function and to therapeutic measures on an immediate time basis C8928 Transthoracic echocardiography with contrast, realtime with image documentation (2D), with or without M-mode recording, during rest and cardiovascular stress test using treadmill, bicycle exercise and/or pharmacologically induced stress, with interpretation and report

100-4,4,230.2.1

Administration of Drugs Via Implantable or Portable Pumps

for Implantable or Portable Pumps 2005 CPT Final CY 2006 OPPS 2005 CPT 2005 Description Code Description SI APC n/a n/a C8957 Intravenous infusion for therapy/diagnosis; initiation of prolonged infusion (more than 8 hours), requiring use of portable or implantable pump S 0120 96414 Chemotherapy administration, intravenous; infusion technique, initiation of prolonged infusion (more than 8 hours), requiring the use of a portable or implantable pump 96416 Chemotherapy administration, intravenous infusion technique; initiation of prolonged chemotherapy infusion (more than 8 hours), requiring use of portable or implantable pump S 0117 96425 Chemotherapy administration, infusion technique, initiation of prolonged infusion (more than 8 hours), requiring the use of a portable or implantable pump) 96425 Chemotherapy administration, intra-arterial; infusion technique, initiation of prolonged infusion (more than 8 hours), requiring the use of a portable or implantable pump S 0117 96520 Refilling and maintenance of portable pump 96521 Refilling and maintenance of portable pump T 0125 2005 CPT Final CY 2006 OPPS 2005 CPT 2005 Description Code Description SI APC 96530 Refilling and maintenance of implantable pump or reservoir for drug delivery, systemic [e.g. Intravenous, intra-arterial] 96522 Refilling and maintenance of implantable pump or reservoir for drug delivery, systemic (e.g., intravenous, intra-arterial) T 0125 n/a n/a 96523 Irrigation of implanted venous access device for drug delivery systems N - Hospitals are to report HCPCS code C8957 and CPT codes 96416 and 96425 to indicate the initiation of a prolonged infusion that requires the use of an implantable or portable pump. CPT codes 96521, 92522, and 96523 should be used by hospitals to indicate refilling and maintenance of drug delivery systems or irrigation of implanted venous access devices for such systems, and may be reported for the servicing of devices used for therapeutic drugs other than chemotherapy.

100-4,4,230.2.3

Non-Chemotherapy Drug Administration

Table 5: CY 2006 OPPS Non-Chemotherapy Drug Administration -Intravenous Infusion Technique

2005 CPT	Final CY 2006 OPPS	2005 CPT	2005 Description	Code	Description	SI	APC
90780	Intravenous infusion for therapy/diagnosis, administered by physician or under direct supervision of physician; up to one hour\	C8950	Intravenous infusion for therapy/diagnosis; up to 1 hour	S	0120		
90781	Intravenous infusion for therapy/diagnosis, administered by physician or under direct supervision of physician; each additional hour, up to eight (8) hours (List separately in addition to code for primary procedure)	C8951	Intravenous infusion for therapy/diagnosis; each additional hour (List separately in addition to C8950)	N	-	n/a	n/a
		C8957	Intravenous infusion for therapy/diagnosis; initiation of prolonged infusion (more than 8 hours), requiring use of portable or implantable pump	S	120		

Hospitals are to report HCPCS code C8950 to indicate an infusion of drugs other than anti-neoplastic drugs furnished on or after January 1, 2006 (except as noted at 230.2.2(A) above). HCPCS code C8951 should be used to report all additional infusion hours, with no limit on the number of hours billed per line. Medically necessary separate therapeutic or diagnostic hydration services should be reported with C8950 and C8951, as these are considered intravenous infusions for therapy/diagnosis.

HCPCS codes C8950 and C8951 should not be reported when the infusion is a necessary and integral part of a separately payable OPPS procedure.

When more than one nonchemotherapy drug is infused, hospitals are to code HCPCS codes C8950 and C8951 (if necessary) to report the total duration of an infusion, regardless of the number of substances or drugs infused. Hospitals are reminded to bill separately for each drug infused, in addition to the drug administration services.

The OCE pays one APC for each encounter reported by HCPCS code C8950, and only pays one APC for C8950 per day (unless Modifier 59 is used). Payment for additional hours of infusion reported by HCPCS code C8951 is packaged into the payment for the initial infusion. While no separate payment will be made for units of HCPCS code C8951, hospitals are instructed to report all codes that appropriately describe the services provided and the corresponding charges so that CMS may capture specific historical hospital cost data for future payment rate setting activities.

OCE logic assumes that all services for non-chemotherapy infusions billed on the same date of service were provided during the same encounter. Where a beneficiary makes two separate visits to the hospital for non-chemotherapy infusions in the same day, hospitals are to report modifier 59 for non-chemotherapy infusion codes during the second encounter that were also furnished in the first encounter. The OCE identifies modifier 59 and pays up to a maximum number of units per day, as listed in Table 1.

EXAMPLE 1

A beneficiary receives infused drugs that are not anti-neoplastic drugs (including hydrating solutions) for 2 hours. The hospital reports one unit of HCPCS code C8950 and one unit of HCPCS code C8951. The OCE will pay one unit of APC 0120. Payment for the unit of HCPCS code C8951 is packaged into the payment for one unit of APC 0120. (NOTE: See 230.1 for drug billing instructions.)

EXAMPLE 2

A beneficiary receives infused drugs that are not anti-neoplastic drugs (including hydrating solutions) for 12 hours. The hospital reports one unit of HCPCS code C8950 and eleven units of HCPCS code C8951. The OCE will pay one unit of APC 0120. Payment for the 11 units of HCPCS code C8951 is packaged into the payment for one unit of APC 0120. (NOTE: See 230.1 for drug billing instructions.)

EXAMPLE 3

A beneficiary experiences multiple attempts to initiate an intravenous infusion before a successful infusion is started 20 minutes after the first attempt. Once started, the infusion lasts one hour. The hospital reports one unit of HCPCS code C8950 to identify the 1 hour of infusion time. The 20 minutes spent prior to the infusion attempting to establish an IV line are not separately billable in the OPPS. The OCE pays one unit of APC 0120. (NOTE: See 230.1 for drug billing instructions.)

B. Administration of Non-Chemotherapy Drugs by a Route Other Than Intravenous Infusion

Table 6: CY 2006 OPPS Non-Chemotherapy Drug Administration -Route Other Than Intravenous Infusion

2005 CPT	Final CY 2006 OPPS	2005 CPT	2005 Description	Code	Description	SI	APC
90784	Therapeutic, prophylactic or diagnostic injection (specify material injected); intravenous	C8952	Therapeutic, prophylactic or diagnostic injection; intravenous push	X	0359		
90782	Therapeutic, prophylactic or diagnostic injection (specify material injected); subcutaneous or intramuscular	90772	Therapeutic, prophylactic or diagnostic injection (specify substance or drug); subcutaneous or intramuscular	X	0353		
90783	Therapeutic, prophylactic or diagnostic injection (specify material injected); intra-arterial	90773	Therapeutic, prophylactic or diagnostic injection (specify substance or drug); intra-arterial	X	0359		
90779	Unlisted therapeutic, prophylactic or diagnostic intravenous or intra-arterial, injection or infusion	90779	Unlisted therapeutic, prophylactic or diagnostic intravenous or intra-arterial injection or infusion	X	0352		

100-4,4,231.4

Billing for Split Unit of Blood

HCPCS code P9011 was created to identify situations where one unit of blood or a blood product is split and some portion of the unit is transfused to one patient and the other portions are transfused to other patients or to the same patient at other times. When a patient receives a transfusion of a split unit of blood or blood product, OPPS providers should bill P9011 for the blood product transfused, as well as CPT 86985 (Splitting, blood products) for each splitting procedure performed to prepare the blood product for a specific patient.

Providers should bill split units of packed red cells and whole blood using Revenue Code 389 (Other blood), and should not use Revenue Codes 381 (Packed red cells) or 382 (Whole blood). Providers should bill split units of other blood products using the applicable revenue codes for the blood product type, such as 383 (Plasma) or 384 (Platelets), rather than 389. Reporting revenue codes according to these specifications will ensure the Medicare beneficiary's blood deductible is applied correctly.

EXAMPLE: OPPS provider splits off a 100cc aliquot from a 250 cc unit of leukocytereduced red blood cells for a transfusion to Patient X. The hospital then splits off an 80cc aliquot of the remaining unit for a transfusion to Patient Y. At a later time, the remaining 70cc from the unit is transfused to Patient Z.

In billing for the services for Patient X and Patient Y, the OPPS provider should report the charges by billing P9011 and 86985 in addition to the CPT code for the transfusion service, because a specific splitting service was required to prepare a split unit for transfusion to each of those patients. However, the OPPS provider should report only P9011 and the CPT code for the transfusion service for Patient Z because no additional splitting was necessary to prepare the split unit for transfusion to Patient Z. The OPPS provider should bill Revenue Code 0389 for each split unit of the leukocyte-reduced red blood cells that was transfused.

100-4,4,240

Inpatient Part B Hospital Services

Inpatient Part B services which are paid under OPPS include:

- Diagnostic x-ray tests, and other diagnostic tests (excluding clinical diagnostic laboratory tests);
- X-ray, radium, and radioactive isotope therapy, including materials and services of technicians;
- Surgical dressings applied during an encounter at the hospital and splints, casts, and other devices used for reduction of fractures and dislocations (splints and casts, etc., include dental splints);
- Implantable prosthetic devices;
- Hepatitis B vaccine and its administration, and certain preventive screening services (pelvic exams, screening sigmoidoscopies, screening colonoscopies, bone mass measurements, and prostate screening.)
  - Bone Mass measurements;
  - Prostate screening;
  - Immunosuppressive drugs;
  - Oral anti-cancer drugs;
  - Oral drug prescribed for use as an acute anti-emetic used as part of an anti-cancer chemotherapeutic regimen; and
  - Epoetin Alfa (EPO)

NOTE: Payment for some of these services is packaged into the payment rate of other separately payable services.

Inpatient Part B services paid under other payment methods include:

- Clinical diagnostic laboratory tests, prosthetic devices other than implantable ones and other than dental which replace all or part of an internal body organ (including contiguous tissue), or all or part of the function of a permanently inoperative or malfunctioning internal body organ, including replacement or repairs of such devices;
- Leg, arm, back and neck braces; trusses and artificial legs; arms and eyes including adjustments, repairs, and replacements required because of breakage, wear, loss, or a change in the patient's physical condition; take home surgical dressings; outpatient physical therapy; outpatient occupational therapy; and outpatient speech-language pathology services;
- Ambulance services;
- Screening pap smears, screening colorectal tests, and screening mammography;
- Influenza virus vaccine and its administration, pneumococcal vaccine and its administration;
- Diabetes self-management;
- Hemophilia clotting factors for hemophilia patients competent to use these factors without supervision).

See Chapter 6 of the Medicare Benefit Policy Manual for a discussion of the circumstances under which the above services may be covered as Part B Inpatient services.

100-4,4,290.1

Observation Services Overview

Observation care is a well-defined set of specific, clinically appropriate services, which include ongoing short term treatment, assessment, and reassessment, that are furnished while a decision is being made regarding whether patients will require further treatment as hospital inpatients or if they are able to be discharged from the hospital. Observation status is commonly assigned to patients who present to the emergency department and who then require a significant period of treatment or monitoring in order to make a decision concerning their admission or discharge. Observation services are covered only when provided by the order of a physician or another individual authorized by State licensure law and hospital staff bylaws to admit patients to the hospital or to order outpatient services.

Observation services must also be reasonable and necessary to be covered by Medicare. In only rare and exceptional cases do reasonable and necessary outpatient observation services span more than 48 hours. In the majority of cases, the decision whether to discharge a patient from the hospital following resolution of the reason for the observation care or to admit the patient as an inpatient can be made in less than 48 hours, usually in less than 24 hours.

100-4,4,290.2.2

Reporting Hours of Observation

Observation time begins at the clock time documented in the patient's medical record, which coincides with the time the patient is placed in a bed for the purpose of initiating observation care in accordance with a physician's order. Hospitals should round to the nearest hour. For example, a patient who was placed in an observation bed at 3:03 p.m. according to the nurses' notes and discharged to home at 9:45 p.m. should have a "7" placed in the units field of the reported observation HCPCS code.

General standing orders for observation services following all outpatient surgery are not recognized. Hospitals should not report as observation care, services that are part of another Part B service, such as postoperative monitoring during a standard recovery period (e.g., 4-6 hours), which should be billed as recovery room services. Similarly, in the case of patients who undergo diagnostic testing in a hospital outpatient department, routine preparation services furnished prior to the testing and recovery afterwards are included in the payments for those diagnostic services. Observation services should not be billed concurrently with diagnostic or therapeutic services for which active monitoring is a part of the procedure (e.g., colonoscopy, chemotherapy). In situations where such a procedure interrupts observation services, hospitals would record for each period of observation services the beginning and ending times during the hospital outpatient encounter and add the length of time for the periods of observation services together to reach the total number of units reported on the claim for the hourly observation services HCPCS code G0378 (Hospital observation service, per hour).

Observation time ends when all medically necessary services related to observation care are completed. For example, this could be before discharge when the need for observation has ended, but other medically necessary services not meeting the definition of observation care are provided (in which case, the additional medically necessary services would be billed separately or included as part of the emergency department or clinic visit). Alternatively, the end time of observation services may coincide with the time the patient is actually discharged from the hospital or admitted as an inpatient.

Observation time may include medically necessary services and follow-up care provided after the time that the physician writes the discharge order, but before the patient is discharged. However, reported observation time would not include the time patients remain in the observation area after treatment is finished for reasons such as waiting for transportation home.

If a period of observation spans more than 1 calendar day, all of the hours for the entire period of observation must be included on a single line and the date of service for that line is the date that observation care begins.

100-4,4,290.5.1

Billing and Payment for Observation Services Beginning January 1, 2008

Observation services are reported using HCPCS code G0378 (Hospital observation service, per hour). Beginning January 1, 2008, HCPCS code G0378 for hourly observation services is assigned status indicator N, signifying that its payment is always packaged. No separate payment is made for observation services reported with HCPCS code G0378, and APC 0339 is deleted as of January 1, 2008. In most circumstances, observation services are supportive and ancillary to the other services provided to a patient. In certain circumstances when observation care is billed in conjunction with a high level clinic visit (Level 5), high level emergency department visit (Level 4 or 5), critical care services, or direct admission as an integral part of a patient's extended encounter of care, payment may be made for the entire extended care encounter through one of two composite APCs when certain criteria are met. For information about payment for extended assessment and management composite APCs, see Sec.10.2.1 (Composite APCs) of this chapter.

APC 8002 (Level I Extended Assessment and Management Composite) describes an encounter for care provided to a patient that includes a high level (Level 5) clinic visit or direct admission to observation in conjunction with observation services of substantial duration (8 or more hours). APC 8003 (Level II Extended Assessment and Management Composite) describes an encounter for care provided to a patient that includes a high level (Level 4 or 5) emergency department visit or critical care services in conjunction with observation services of substantial duration. There is no limitation on diagnosis for payment of these composite APCs; however, composite APC payment will not be made when observation services are reported in association with a surgical procedure (T status procedure) or the hours of observation care reported are less than 8. The I/OCE evaluates every claim received to determine if payment through a composite APC is appropriate. If payment through a composite APC is inappropriate, the I/OCE, in conjunction with the Pricer, determines the appropriate status indicator, APC, and payment for every code on a claim.

All of the following requirements must be met in order for a hospital to receive an APC payment for an extended assessment and management composite APC:

1. Observation Time
   a. Observation time must be documented in the medical record.
   b. A beneficiary's time in observation (and hospital billing) begins with the beneficiary's admission to an observation bed.
   c. A beneficiary's time in observation (and hospital billing) ends when all clinical or medical interventions have been completed, including follow-up care furnished by hospital staff and physicians that may take place after a physician has ordered the patient be released or admitted as an inpatient.
   d. The number of units reported with HCPCS code G0378 must equal or exceed 8 hours.
2. Additional Hospital Services
   a. The claim for observation services must include one of the following services in addition to the reported observation services. The additional services listed below must have a line item date of service on the same day or the day before the date reported for observation: An emergency department visit (CPT code 99284 or 99285) or A clinic visit (CPT code 99205 or 99215); or Critical care (CPT code 99291); or Direct admission to observation reported with HCPCS code G0379 (APC 0604) must be reported on the same date of service as the date reported for observation services.
   b. No procedure with a T status indicator can be reported on the same day or day before observation care is provided.
3. Physician Evaluation
   a. The beneficiary must be in the care of a physician during the period of observation, as documented in the medical record by admission, discharge, and other appropriate progress notes that are timed, written, and signed by the physician.
   b. The medical record must include documentation that the physician explicitly assessed patient risk to determine that the beneficiary would benefit from observation care.

Criteria 1 and 3 related to observation care beginning and ending time and physician evaluation apply regardless of whether the hospital believes that observation services will be packaged or will meet the criteria for extended assessment and management composite payment.

Only observation services that are billed on a 13X bill type may be considered for a composite APC payment.

Non-repetitive services provided on the same day as either direct admission to observation care or observation services must be reported on the same claim because the OCE claim-by-claim logic cannot function properly unless all services related to the episode of observation care, including hospital clinic visits, emergency department visits, critical care services, and T status procedures, are reported on the same claim.

Additional guidance can be found in Change Request 4047, Transmittal 763, issued on November 25, 2005.

If a claim for services providing during an extended assessment and management encounter including observation care does not meet all of the requirements listed above, then the usual APC logic will apply to separately payable items and services on the claim; the special logic for direct admission will apply, and payment for the observation care will be packaged into payments for other separately payable services provided to the beneficiary in the same encounter.

100-4,5,10.2

A. Financial Limitation Prior to the Balanced Budget Refinement Act (BBRA)

Section 4541(a)(2) of the Balanced Budget Act (BBA) (P.L. 105-33) of 1997, which added ¬ß1834(k)(5) to the Act, required payment under a prospective payment system for outpatient rehabilitation services (except those furnished by or under arrangements with a hospital). Outpatient rehabilitation services include the following services:

- Physical therapy (which includes outpatient speech-language pathology); and
- Occupational therapy.

Section 4541(c) of the BBA required application of a financial limitation to all outpatient rehabilitation services (except those furnished by or under arrangements with a hospital). In 1999, an annual per beneficiary limit of $1,500 applied to all outpatient physical therapy services (including speech-language pathology services). A separate limit applied to all occupational therapy services. The limit is based on incurred expenses and includes applicable deductible and coinsurance. The BBA provided that the limits be indexed by the Medicare Economic Index (MEI) each year beginning in 2002.

The limitation is based on therapy services the Medicare beneficiary receives, not the type of practitioner who provides the service. Physical therapists, speech-language pathologists, occupational therapists as well as physicians and certain nonphysician practitioners could render a therapy service.

As a transitional measure, effective in 1999, providers/suppliers were instructed to keep track of the allowed incurred expenses. This process was put in place to assure providers/suppliers did not bill Medicare for patients who exceeded the annual limitations for physical therapy, and for occupational therapy services rendered by individual providers/suppliers. In 2003 and later, the limitation was applied through CMS systems.

B. Moratoria and Exceptions for Therapy Claims

Section 221 of the BBRA of 1999 placed a 2-year moratorium on the application of the financial limitation for claims for therapy services with dates of service January 1, 2000, through December 31, 2001.

Section 421 of the Medicare, Medicaid, and SCHIP Benefits Improvement and Protection Act (BIPA) of 2000, extended the moratorium on application of the financial limitation to claims for outpatient rehabilitation services with dates of service January 1, 2002, through December 31, 2002. Therefore, the moratorium was for a 3-year period and applied to outpatient rehabilitation claims with dates of service January 1, 2000, through December 31, 2002.

In 2003, there was not a moratorium on therapy caps. Implementation was delayed until September 1, 2003. Therapy caps were in effect for services rendered on September 1, 2003 through December 7, 2003.

Congress re-enacted a moratorium on financial limitations on outpatient therapy services on December 8, 2003 that extended through December 31, 2005. Caps were implemented again on January 1, 2006 and policies were modified to allow exceptions as directed by the Deficit Reduction Act of 2005 only for calendar year 2006. The Tax Relief and Health Care Act of 2006 extended the cap exceptions process through calendar year 2007. The Medicare, Medicaid, and SCHIP Extension Act of 2007 extended the cap exceptions process for services furnished through June 30, 2008.

Future exceptions. The cap exception for therapy services billed by outpatient hospitals was part of the original legislation and applies as long as caps are in effect. Exceptions to caps based on the medical necessity of the service are in effect only when Congress legislates the exceptions, as they did for 2007. References to the exceptions process in subsection C of this section apply only when the exceptions are in effect.

C. Application of Financial Limitations

Financial limitations on outpatient therapy services, as described above, began for therapy services rendered on or after on January 1, 2006. See C 1 to C 7 of this section when exceptions to therapy caps apply. The limits were $1740 in 2006 and $1780 in 2007. For 2008, the annual limit on the allowed amount for outpatient physical therapy and speech-language pathology combined is $1810; the limit for occupational therapy is $1810. Limits apply to outpatient Part B therapy services from all settings except outpatient hospital (place of service code 22 on carrier claims) and hospital emergency room (place of service code 23 on carrier claims). These excluded hospital services are reported on types of bill 12x or 13x on intermediary claims.

Contractors apply the financial limitations to the Medicare Physician Fee Schedule (MPFS) amount (or the amount charged if it is smaller) for therapy services for each beneficiary.

As with any Medicare payment, beneficiaries pay the coinsurance (20 percent) and any deductible that may apply. Medicare will pay the remaining 80 percent of the limit after the deductible is met. These amounts will change each calendar year. Medicare Contractors shall publish the financial limitation amount in educational articles. It is also available at 1-800-Medicare.

Medicare shall apply these financial limitations in order, according to the dates when the claims were received. When limitations apply, the Common Working File (CWF) tracks the limits. Shared System Maintainers are not responsible for tracking the dollar amounts of incurred expenses of rehabilitation services for each therapy limit.

In processing claims where Medicare is the secondary payer, the shared system takes the lowest secondary payment amount from MSPPAY and sends this amount on to CWF as the amount applied to therapy limits.

1. Exceptions to Therapy Caps - General

   The Tax Relief and Health Care Act of 2006 directed CMS to extend a process to allow for exceptions to the caps for services received in CY2007 in cases where continued therapy services are medically necessary. The following policies concerning exceptions to caps due to medical necessity apply only when the exceptions process is in effect. With the exception of the use of the KX modifier, the guidance in this section concerning medical necessity applies as well to services provided before caps are reached.

   Instructions for contractors to manage automatic process for exceptions will be found in the Program Integrity Manual, chapter 3, section 3.4.1.2. Provider and supplier information concerning exceptions is in this manual and in IOM Pub. 100-02, chapter 15, section 220.3. Exceptions shall be identified by a modifier on the claim and supported by documentation.

   Since the providers and suppliers will take an active role in obtaining an exception for a beneficiary, this manual section is written to address them as well as Medicare contractors.

   The beneficiary may qualify for use of the cap exceptions at any time during the episode when documented medically necessary services exceed caps. All covered and medically necessary services qualify for exceptions to caps.

   In 2006, the Exception Processes fell into two categories, Automatic Process Exceptions, and Manual Process Exceptions. Beginning January 1, 2007, there is no manual process for exceptions. All services that require exceptions to caps shall be processed using the automatic process. All requests for exception are in the form of a KX modifier added to claim lines. (See subsection C6 for use of the KX modifier.)

   Use of the automatic process for exceptions increases the responsibility of the provider/supplier for determining and documenting that services are appropriate.

   Also, use of the automatic process for exception does not exempt services from manual or other medical review processes as described in 100-08, Chapter 3, Section 3.4.1.1.1. Rather, atypical use of the automatic exception process may invite contractor scrutiny. Particular care should be taken to document improvement and avoid billing for services that do not meet the requirements for skilled services, or for services which are maintenance rather than rehabilitative treatment (See Pub. 100-02, chapter 15, sections 220.2, 220.3, and 230).

   The KX modifier, described in subsection C6, is added to claim lines to indicate that the clinician attests that services are medically necessary and justification is documented in the medical record.

2. Automatic Process Exceptions

   The term "automatic process exceptions" indicates that the claims processing for the exception is automatic, and not that the exception is automatic. An exception may be made when the patient‚Äôs condition is justified by documentation indicating that the beneficiary requires continued skilled therapy, i.e., therapy beyond the amount payable under the therapy cap, to achieve their prior functional status or maximum expected functional status within a reasonable amount of time.

   No special documentation is submitted to the contractor for automatic process exceptions. The clinician is responsible for consulting guidance in the Medicare manuals and in the professional literature to determine if the beneficiary may qualify for the automatic process exception when documentation justifies medically necessary services above the caps. The clinician's opinion is not binding on the Medicare contractor who makes the final determination concerning whether the claim is payable.

   Documentation justifying the services shall be submitted in response to any Additional Documentation Request (ADR) for claims that are selected for medical review. Follow the documentation requirements in Pub. 100-02, chapter 15, section 220.3. If medical records are requested for review, clinicians may include, at their discretion, a summary that specifically addresses the justification for therapy cap exception.

   In making a decision about whether to utilize the automatic process exception, clinicians shall consider, for example, whether services are appropriate to--

- The patient's condition including the diagnosis, complexities and severity (A list of the excepted evaluation codes are in C.2.a. A list of the ICD-9 codes for conditions and complexities that might qualify a beneficiary for exception to caps is in 10.2 C3. The list is a guideline and neither assures that services on the list will be excepted nor limits provision of covered and medically necessary services for conditions not on the list);
- The services provided including their type, frequency and duration;

- The interaction of current active conditions and complexities that directly and significantly influence the treatment such that it causes services to exceed caps.

In addition, the following should be considered before using the automatic exception process:

a. Exceptions for Services

Evaluation. The CMS will except therapy evaluations from caps after the therapy caps are reached when evaluation is necessary, e.g., to determine if the current status of the beneficiary requires therapy services. For example, the following evaluation procedures may be appropriate:

92506, 92597, 92607, 92608, 92610, 92611, 92612, 92614, 92616, 96105, 97001, 97002, 97003, 97004.

These codes will continue to be reported as outpatient therapy procedures as described in the Claims Processing Manual, Chapter 5, Section 20(B) "Applicable Outpatient Rehabilitation HCPCS Codes." They are not diagnostic tests. Definition of evaluations and documentation is found in Pub 100-02, sections 220 and 230.

Other Services. There are a number of sources that suggest the amount of certain services that may be typical, either per service, per episode, per condition, or per discipline. For example, see the CSC- Utilization and Edit Report, 2006, Appendices at www.cms.hhs.gov/TherapyServices (Studies and Reports). Professional literature and guidelines from professional associations also provide a basis on which to estimate whether the type, frequency and intensity of services are appropriate to an individual. Clinicians and contractors should utilize available evidence related to the patient's condition to justify provision of medically necessary services to individual beneficiaries, especially when they exceed caps. Contractors shall not limit medically necessary services that are justified by scientific research applicable to the beneficiary. Neither contractors nor clinicians shall utilize professional literature and scientific reports to justify payment for continued services after an individual's goals have been met earlier than is typical. Conversely, professional literature and scientific reports shall not be used as justification to deny payment to patients whose needs are greater than is typical or when the patient‚Äôs condition is not represented by the literature.

b. Exceptions for Conditions or Complexities Identified by ICD-9 codes.

Clinicians may utilize the automatic process for exception for any diagnosis for which they can justify services exceeding the cap. Based upon analysis of claims data, research and evidence based practice guidelines, CMS has identified conditions and complexities represented by ICD-9 codes that may be more likely than others to require therapy services that exceed therapy caps. This list appears in 10.2 C3. Clinicians may use the automatic process of exception for beneficiaries who do not have a condition or complexity on this list when they justify the provision of therapy services that exceed caps for that patient's condition.

NOT ALL patients who have a condition or complexity on the list are "automatically" excepted from therapy caps. See Pub. 100-02, chapter 15, section 230.3 for documenting the patient's condition and complexities. Contractors may scrutinize claims from providers whose services exceed caps more frequently than is typical.

Regardless of the condition, the patient must also meet other requirements for coverage. For example, the patient must require skilled treatment for a covered, medically necessary service; the services must be appropriate in type, frequency and duration for the patient's condition and service must be documented appropriately. Guidelines for utilization of therapy services may be found in Medicare manuals, Local Coverage Determinations of Medicare contractors, and professional guidelines issued by associations and states.

Bill the most relevant diagnosis. As always, when billing for therapy services, the ICD-9 code that best relates to the reason for the treatment shall be on the claim, unless there is a compelling reason. For example, when a patient with diabetes is being treated for gait training due to amputation, the preferred diagnosis is abnormality of gait (which characterizes the treatment). Where it is possible in accordance with State and local laws and the contractors Local Coverage Determinations, avoid using vague or general diagnoses. When a claim includes several types of services, or where the physician/NPP must supply the diagnosis, it may not be possible to use the most relevant therapy code in the primary position. In that case, the relevant code should, if possible, be on the claim in another position.

Codes representing the medical condition that caused the treatment are used when there is no code representing the treatment. Complicating conditions are preferably used in non-primary positions on the claim and are billed in the primary position only in the rare circumstance that there is no more relevant code.

The condition or complexity that caused treatment to exceed caps must be related to the therapy goals and must either be the condition that is being treated or a complexity that directly and significantly impacts the rate of recovery of the condition being treated such that it is appropriate to exceed the caps. Codes marked as complexities represented by ICD-9 codes on the list below are unlikely to require therapy services that would exceed the caps unless they occur in a patient who also has another condition (either listed or not listed). Therefore, documentation for an exception should indicate how the complexity (or combination of complexities) directly and significantly affects treatment for a therapy condition. For example, if the condition underlying the reason for therapy is V43.64, hip replacement, the treatment may have a goal to ambulate 60' with stand-by assistance and a KX modifier may be appropriate for gait training (assuming the severity of the patient is such that the services exceed the cap). Alternatively, it would not be appropriate to use the KX modifier for a patient who recovered from hip replacement last year and is being treated this year for a sprain of a severity which does not justify extensive therapy exceeding caps.

3. ICD-9 Codes That are Likely to Qualify for the Automatic Process Therapy Cap Exception Based Upon Clinical Condition or Complexity

When using this table, refer to the ICD-9 code book for coding instructions. Some contractors' Local Coverage Determinations do not allow the use of some of the codes on this list in the primary diagnosis position on a claim. If the contractor has determined that these codes do not characterize patients who require medically necessary services, providers/suppliers may not use these codes, but must utilize a billable diagnosis code allowed by their contractor to describe the patient's condition. Contractors shall not apply therapy caps to services based on the patient's condition, but only on the medical necessity of the service for the condition. If a service would be payable before the cap is reached and is still medically necessary after the cap is reached, that service is excepted. Providers/suppliers may use the automatic process for exception for medically necessary services when the patient has a billable condition that is not on the list below. The diagnosis on the list below may be put in a secondary position on the claim and/or in the medical records, as the contractor directs.

When two codes are listed in the left cell in a row, all the codes between them are also eligible for exception. If one code is in the cell, only that one code is likely to qualify for exception. The descriptions in the table are not always identical to those in the ICD-9 code book, but may be summaries. Contact your contractor for interpretation if you are not sure that a condition or complexity is applicable for automatic process exception.

It is very important to recognize that most of the conditions on this list would not ordinarily result in services exceeding the cap. Use the KX modifier only in cases where the condition of the individual patient is such that services are APPROPRIATELY provided in an episode that exceeds the cap. In most cases, the severity of the condition, comorbidities, or complexities will contribute to the necessity of services exceeding the cap, and these should be documented. Routine use of the KX modifier for all patients with these conditions will likely show up on data analysis as aberrant and invite inquiry. Be sure that documentation is sufficiently detailed to support the use of the modifier.

The following ICD-9 codes describe the conditions (etiology or underlying medical conditions) that may result in excepted conditions (marked X) and complexities (marked *) that MIGHT cause medically necessary therapy services to qualify for the automatic process exception for each discipline separately. When the field corresponding to the therapy discipline treating and the diagnosis code is marked with a dash (‚Äì) services by that discipline are not appropriate for that diagnosis and, therefore, services do not qualify for exception to caps.

These codes are grouped only to facilitate reference to them. The codes may be used only when the code is applicable to the condition being actively treated. For example, an exception should not be claimed for a diagnosis of hip replacement when the service provided is for an unrelated dysphagia.

ICD-9 Cluster	ICD-9 (Cluster) Description	PT	OT	SLP
V43.61-V43.69	Joint Replacement	X	X	--
V45.4	Arthrodesis Status	*	*	--
V45.81-V45.82 and V45.89	Other Postprocedural Status	*	*	--
V49-61-V49.67	Upper Limb Amputation Status	X	X	--
V49.71-V49.77	Lower Limb Amputation Status	X	X	--
V54.10-V54.29	Aftercare for Healing Traumatic or Pathologic Fracture	X	X	--
V58.71-V58.78	Aftercare Following Surgery to Specified Body Systems, Not Elsewhere Classified	*	*	*
244.0-244.9	Acquired Hypothyroidism	*	*	*

X Automatic (only ICD-9 needed on claim)

* Complexity (requires another ICD-9 on claim)

-- Does not serve as qualifying ICD-9 on claim

ICD-9 Cluster	ICD-9 (Cluster) Description	PT	OT	SLP
250.00-251.9	Diabetes Mellitus and Other Disorders of Pancreatic Internal Secretion	*	*	*
276.0-276.9	Disorders of Fluid, Electrolyte, and Acid-Base Balance	*	*	*
278.00-278.01	Obesity and Morbid Obesity	*	*	*
280.0-289.9	Diseases of the blood and blood-forming organs	*	*	*
290.0-290.43	Dementias	*	*	*
294.0-294.9	Persistent Mental Disorders due to Conditions Classified Elsewhere	*	*	*
295.00-299.91	Other Psychoses	*	*	*
300.00-300.9	Anxiety, Disassociative and Somatoform Disorders	*	*	*
310.0-310.9	Specific Nonpsychotic Mental Disorders due to Brain Damage	*	*	*
311	Depressive Disorder, Not Elsewhere Classified	*	*	*
315.00-315.9	Specific delays in Development	*	*	*
317	Mild Mental Retardation	*	*	*
320.0-326	Inflammatory Diseases of the Central Nervous System	*	*	*
330.0-337.9	Hereditary and Degenerative Diseases of the Central Nervous System	X	X	X
340-345.91 and 348.0-349.9	Other Disorders of the Central Nervous System	X	X	X
353.0-359.9	Disorders of the Peripheral Nervous system	X	X	--
365.00-365.9	Glaucoma	*	*	*
369.00-369.9	Blindness and Low Vision	*	*	*
386.00-386.9	Vertiginous Syndromes and Other Disorders of Vestibular System	*	*	*
389.00-389.9	Hearing Loss	*	*	*
401.0-405.99	Hypertensive Disease	*	*	*
410.00-414.9	Ischemic Heart Disease	*	*	*
415.0-417.9	Diseases of Pulmonary Circulation	*	*	*
420.0-429.9	Other Forms of Heart Disease	*	*	*
430-438.9	Cerebrovascular Disease	X	X	X
440.0-448.9	Diseases of Arteries, Arterioles, and Capillaries	*	*	*
451.0-453.9 and 456.0-459.9	Diseases of Veins and Lymphatics, and Other Diseases of Circulatory System	*	*	*
465.0-466.19	Acute Respiratory Infections	*	*	*
478.30-478.5	Paralysis, Polyps, or Other Diseases of Vocal Cords	*	*	*
480.0-486	Pneumonia	*	*	*
490-496	Chronic Obstructive Pulmonary Disease and Allied Conditions	*	*	*
507.0-507.8	Pneumonitis due to solids and liquids	*	*	*
510.0-519.9	Other Diseases of Respiratory System	*	*	*
560.0-560.9	Intestinal Obstruction Without Mention of Hernia	*	*	*
578.0-578.9	Gastrointestinal Hemorrhage	*	*	*
584.5-586	Renal Failure and Chronic Kidney Disease	*	*	*
590.00-599.9	Other Diseases of Urinary System	*	*	*
682.0-682.8	Other Cellulitis and Abscess	*	*	--
707.00-707.9	Chronic Ulcer of Skin	*	*	--
710.0-710.9	Diffuse Diseases of Connective Tissue	*	*	*

X Automatic (only ICD-9 needed on claim)

* Complexity (requires another ICD-9 on claim)

-- Does not serve as qualifying ICD-9 on claim

ICD-9 Cluster	ICD-9 (Cluster) Description	PT	OT	SLP
711.00-711.99	Arthropathy Associated with Infections	*	*	--
712.10-713.8	Crystal Arthropathies and Arthropathy Associated with Other Disorders Classified Elsewhere	*	*	--
714.0-714.9	Rheumatoid Arthritis and Other Inflammatory Polyarthropathies	*	*	--
715.00-715.98	Osteoarthrosis and Allied Disorders (Complexity except as listed below)	*	*	--
715.09	Osteoarthritis and allied disorders, multiple sites	X	X	--
715.11	Osteoarthritis, localized, primary, shoulder region	X	X	--
715.15	Osteoarthritis, localized, primary, pelvic region and thigh	X	X	--
715.16	Osteoarthritis, localized, primary, lower leg	X	X	--
715.91	Osteoarthritis, unspecified id gen. or local, shoulder	X	X	--
715.96	Osteoarthritis, unspecified if gen. or local, lower leg	X	X	--
716.00-716.99	Other and Unspecified Arthropathies	*	*	--
717.0-717.9	Internal Derangement of Knee	*	*	--
718.00-718.99	Other Derangement of Joint (Complexity except as listed below)	*	*	--
718.49	Contracture of Joint, Multiple Sites	X	X	--
719.00-719.99	Other and Unspecified Disorders of Joint (Complexity except as listed below)	*	*	--
719.7	Difficulty Walking	X	X	--
720.0-724.9	Dorsopathies	*	*	--
725-729.9	Rheumatism, Excluding Back (Complexity except as listed below)	*	*	--
726.10-726.19	Rotator Cuff Disorder and Allied Syndromes	X	X	--
727.61-727.62	Rupture of Tendon, Nontraumatic	X	X	--
730.00-739.9	Osteopathies, Chondropathies, and Acquired Musculoskeletal Deformities (Complexity except as listed below)	*	*	--
733.00	Osteoporosis	X	X	--
741.00-742.9 and 745.0-748.9 and 754.0-756.9	Congenital Anomalies	*	*	*
780.31-780.39	Convulsions	*	*	*
780.71-780.79	Malaise and Fatigue	*	*	*
780.93	Memory Loss	*	*	*
781.0-781.99	Symptoms Involving Nervous and Musculoskeletal System (Complexity except as listed below)	*	*	*
781.2	Abnormality of Gait	X	X	--
781.3	Lack of Coordination	X	X	--
783.0-783.9	Symptoms Concerning Nutrition, Metabolism, and Development	*	*	*
784.3-784.69	Aphasia, Voice and Other Speech Disturbance, Other Symbolic Dysfunction	*	*	X
785.4	Gangrene	*	*	--
786.00-786.9	Symptoms involving Respiratory System and Other Chest Symptoms	*	*	*
787.2	Dysphagia	*	*	X
800.00-828.1	Fractures (Complexity except as listed below)	*	*	--

X Automatic (only ICD-9 needed on claim)

* Complexity (requires another ICD-9 on claim)

-- Does not serve as qualifying ICD-9 on claim

ICD-9 Cluster	ICD-9 (Cluster) Description	PT	OT	SLP
806.00-806.9	Fracture of Vertebral Column With Spinal Cord Injury	X	X	--
810.11-810.13	Fracture of Clavicle	X	X	--
811.00-811.19	Fracture of Scapula	X	X	--
812.00-812.59	Fracture of Humerus	X	X	--
813.00-813.93	Fracture of Radius and Ulna	X	X	--
820.00-820.9	Fracture of Neck of Femue	X	X	--
821.00-821.39	Fracture of Other and Unspecified Parts of Femur	X	X	--
828.0-828.1	Multiple Fractures Involving Both Lower Limbs, Lower with Upper Limb, and Lower Limb(s) with Rib(s) and Sternum	X	X	--
830.0-839.9	Dislocations	X	X	--
840.0-848.8	Sprains and Strains of Joints and Adjacent Muscles	*	*	--
851.00-854.19	Intracranial Injury, excluding those with Skull Fracture	X	X	X
888.00-884.2	Open Wound of Upper Limb	*	*	--
885.0-887.7	Traumatic Amputation, Thumb(s), Finger(s), Arm and Hand (complete)(partial)	X	X	--
890.0-894.2	Open Wound Lower Limb	*	*	--
895.0-897.7	Traumatic Amputation, Toe(s), Foot/Feet, Leg(s) (complete) (partial)			
905.0-905.9	Late Effects of Musculoskeletal and Connective Tissue Injuries	*	*	*
907.0-907.9	Late Effect of Injuries to the Nervous System	*	*	*
941.00-949.5	Burns	*	*	*
952.00-952.9	Spinal Cord Injury Without Evidence of Spinal Bone Injury	X	X	X
953.0-953.8	Injury to Nerve Roots and Spinal Plexus	X	X*	
959.01	Head Injury, Unspecified	X	X	X

X Automatic (only ICD-9 needed on claim)

* Complexity (requires another ICD-9 on claim)

-- Does not serve as qualifying ICD-9 on claim

100-4,8,60.4.1

Epoetin Alfa (EPO) Facility Billing Requirements

Revenue codes required for reporting EPO:

Revenue Codes Dates of Service	Bill Type 72x	Bill Type 12x	Bill type 13x	Bill type 85x
0634 - administrations under 10,000 units	1/1/04 - present	4/1/06 - present	1/1/04 - present	1/1/04 - present
0635 - administrations of 10,000 units or more	1/1/04 - present	4/1/06 - present	1/1/04 - present	1/1/04 - present
0636 - detailed drug coding	N/A	1/1/04 - 3/31/06	N/A	

N/A For additional hospital billing instructions related to bill types 12x, 13x and 85x see also sections 60.4.3.1 and 60.4.3.2 of this chapter.

The HCPCS code for EPO must be included:

HCPCS	HCPCS Description	Dates of Service
Q4055	Injection, Epoetin alfa, 1,000 units (for ESRD on Dialysis)	1/1/2004 through 12/31/2005
J0886	Injection, Epoetin alfa, 1,000 units (for ESRD on Dialysis)	1/1/2006 through 12/31/2006
Q4081	1 Injection, Epoetin alfa, 100	1/1/2007 to present

The number of units of EPO administered during the billing period is reported with value code 68. Medicare no longer requires value code 68 for claims with dates of service on or after January 1, 2008. Each administration of epoetin alfa (EPO) is reported on a separate line item with the units reported used as a multiplier by the dosage description in the HCPCS to arrive at the dosage per administration.

Append the GS modifier to report a line item that represents an administration of EPO at the reduced dosage following existing instructions in section 60.4 of this chapter. The hematocrit reading taken prior to the last administration of EPO during the billing period must also be reported on the UB-92/Form CMS-1450 with value code 49. Effective January 1, 2006 the definition of value code 49 used to report the hematocrit reading is changed to indicate the patient's most recent hematocrit reading taken before the start of the billing period.

The hemoglobin reading taken during the billing period must be reported on the UB- 92/Form CMS-1450 with value code 48. Effective January 1, 2006 the definition of value code 48 used for the hemoglobin reading is changed to indicate the patient's most recent hemoglobin reading taken before the start of the billing period.

To report a hemoglobin or hematocrit reading for a new patient on or after January 1, 2006, the provider should report the reading that prompted the treatment of epoetin alfa. The provider may use results documented on form CMS 2728 or the patient's medical records from a transferring facility.

The maximum number of administrations of EPO for a billing cycle is 13 times in 30 days and 14 times in 31 days.

APPENDIX 5 — NEW, CHANGED, DELETED, AND REINSTATED HCPCS CODES FOR 2009

New Codes

A6545 Gradient compression wrap, nonelastic, below knee, 30-50 mm Hg, each

A9284 Spirometer, nonelectronic, includes all accessories

A9580 Sodium fluoride F-18, diagnostic, per study dose, up to 30 millicuries

C8929 Transthoracic echocardiography with contrast, or without contrast followed by with contrast, real-time with image documentation (2D), includes M-mode recording, when performed, complete, with spectral doppler echocardiography, and with color flow doppler echocardiography

C8930 Transthoracic echocardiography, with contrast, or without contrast followed by with contrast, real-time with image documentation (2D), includes M-mode recording, when performed, during rest and cardiovascular stress test using treadmill, bicycle exercise and/or pharmacologically induced stress, with interpretation and report; including performance of continuous electrocardiographic monitoring, with physician supervision

C9245 Injection, romiplostim, 10 mcg

C9246 Injection, gadoxetate disodium, per ml

C9247 Iobenguane, I-123, diagnostic, per study dose, up to 10 millicuries

C9248 Injection, clevidipine butyrate, 1 mg

C9356 Tendon, porous matrix of cross-linked collagen and glycosaminoglycan matrix (TenoGlide Tendon Protector Sheet), per square centimeter

C9358 Dermal substitute, native, non-denatured collagen (SurgiMend Collagen Matrix), per 0.5 square centimeters

C9359 Porous purified collagen matrix bone void filler (Integra Mozaik Osteoconductive Scaffold Putty, Integra OS Osteoconductive Scaffold Putty), per 0.5 cc

C9898 Radiolabeled product provided during a hospital inpatient stay

C9899 Implanted prosthetic device, payable only for inpatients who do not have inpatient coverage

D0417 Collection and preparation of saliva sample for laboratory diagnostic testing

D0418 Analysis of saliva sample

D3222 Partial pulpotomy for apexogenesis, permanent tooth with incomplete root development

D5991 Topical medicament carrier

E0487 Spirometer, electronic, includes all accessories

E0656 Segmental pneumatic appliance for use with pneumatic compressor, trunk

E0657 Segmental pneumatic appliance for use with pneumatic compressor, chest

E0770 Functional electrical stimulator, transcutaneous stimulation of nerve and/or muscle groups, any type, complete system, not otherwise specified

E1354 Oxygen accessory, wheeled cart for portable cylinder or portable concentrator, any type, replacement only, each

E1356 Oxygen accessory, battery pack/cartridge for portable concentrator, any type, replacement only, each

E1357 Oxygen accessory, battery charger for portable concentrator, any type, replacement only, each

E1358 Oxygen accessory, DC power adapter for portable concentrator, any type, replacement only, each

E2230 Manual wheelchair accessory, manual standing system

E2231 Manual wheelchair accessory, solid seat support base (replaces sling seat), includes any type mounting hardware

E2295 Manual wheelchair accessory, for pediatric size wheelchair, dynamic seating frame, allows coordinated movement of multiple positioning features

G0398 Home sleep study test (HST) with type II portable monitor, unattended; minimum of 7 channels: EEG, EOG, EMG, ECG/heart rate, airflow, respiratory effort and oxygen saturation

G0399 Home sleep test (HST) with type III portable monitor, unattended; minimum of 4 channels: 2 respiratory movement/airflow, 1 ECG/heart rate and 1 oxygen saturation

G0400 Home sleep test (HST) with type IV portable monitor, unattended; minimum of 3 channels

G0402 Initial preventive physical examination; face-to-face visit, services limited to new beneficiary during the first 12 months of Medicare enrollment

G0403 Electrocardiogram, routine ECG with 12 leads; performed as a screening for the initial preventive physical examination with interpretation and report

G0404 Electrocardiogram, routine ECG with 12 leads; tracing only, without interpretation and report, performed as a screening for the initial preventive physical examination

G0405 Electrocardiogram, routine ECG with 12 leads; interpretation and report only, performed as a screening for the initial preventive physical examination

G0406 Follow-up inpatient telehealth consultation, limited, physicians typically spend 15 minutes communicating with the patient via telehealth

G0407 Follow-up inpatient telehealth consultation, intermediate, physicians typically spend 25 minutes communicating with the patient via telehealth

G0408 Follow-up inpatient telehealth consultation, complex, physicians typically spend 35 minutes or more communicating with the patient via telehealth

G0409 Social work and psychological services, directly relating to and/or furthering the patient's rehabilitation goals, each 15 minutes, face-to-face; individual (services provided by a CORF qualified social worker or psychologist in a CORF)

G0410 Group psychotherapy other than of a multiple family group, in a partial hospitalization setting, approximately 45 to 50 minutes

G0411 Interactive group psychotherapy, in a partial hospitalization setting, approximately 45 to 50 minutes

G0412 Open treatment of iliac spine(s), tuberosity avulsion, or iliac wing fracture(s), unilateral or bilateral for pelvic bone fracture patterns which do not disrupt the pelvic ring, includes internal fixation, when performed

G0413 Percutaneous skeletal fixation of posterior pelvic bone fracture and/or dislocation, for fracture patterns which disrupt the pelvic ring, unilateral or bilateral, (includes ilium, sacroiliac joint and/or sacrum)

G0414 Open treatment of anterior pelvic bone fracture and/or dislocation for fracture patterns which disrupt the pelvic ring, unilateral or bilateral, includes internal fixation when performed (includes pubic symphysis and/or superior/inferior rami)

G0415 Open treatment of posterior pelvic bone fracture and/or dislocation, for fracture patterns which disrupt the pelvic ring, unilateral or bilateral, includes internal fixation, when performed (includes ilium, sacroiliac joint and/or sacrum)

G0416 Surgical pathology, gross and microscopic examination for prostate needle saturation biopsy sampling, 1-20 specimens

G0417 Surgical pathology, gross and microscopic examination for prostate needle saturation biopsy sampling, 21-40 specimens

G0418 Surgical pathology, gross and microscopic examination for prostate needle saturation biopsy sampling, 41-60 specimens

G0419 Surgical pathology, gross and microscopic examination for prostate needle saturation biopsy sampling, greater than 60 specimens

G8485 Clinician intends to report the diabetes measure group

G8486 Clinician intends to report the preventive care measure group

G8487 Clinician intends to report the chronic kidney disease (CKD) measure group

New Codes (continued)

G8488	Clinician intends to report the end stage renal disease (ESRD) measure group
G8489	I intend to report the coronary artery disease (CAD) measures group
G8490	I intend to report the rheumatoid arthritis measures group
G8491	I intend to report the HIV/AIDS measures group
G8492	I intend to report the perioperative care measures group
G8493	I intend to report the back pain measures group
G8494	All quality actions for the applicable measures in the diabetes mellitus measures group have been performed for this patient
G8495	All quality actions for the applicable measures in the CKD measures group have been performed for this patient
G8496	All quality actions for the applicable measures in the preventive care measures group have been performed for this patient
G8497	All quality actions for the applicable measures in the coronary artery bypass graft (CABG) measures group have been performed for this patient
G8498	All quality actions for the applicable measures in the coronary artery disease (CAD) measures group have been performed for this patient
G8499	All quality actions for the applicable measures in the rheumatoid arthritis measures group have been performed for this patient
G8500	All quality actions for the applicable measures in the HIV/AIDS measures group have been performed for this patient
G8501	All quality actions for the applicable measures in the perioperative care measures group have been performed for this patient
G8502	All quality actions for the applicable measures in the back pain measures group have been performed for this patient
G8503	Documentation that prophylactic antibiotic was given within one hour (if fluoroquinolone or vancomycin, two hours) prior to surgical incision (or start of procedure when no incision is required)
G8504	Documentation of order for prophylactic antibiotics to be given within one hour (if fluoroquinolone or vancomycin, two hours) prior to surgical incision (or start of procedure when no incision is required)
G8505	Documentation that prophylactic antibiotic was not given within one hour (if fluoroquinolone or vancomycin, two hours) prior to surgical incision (or start of procedure when no incision is required), reason not specified
G8506	Patient receiving angiotensin converting enzyme (ACE) inhibitor or angiotensin receptor blocker (ARB) therapy
G8507	Provider documentation that patient is not eligible for patient verification of current medications
G8508	Documentation of pain assessment (including location, intensity and description) prior to initiation of treatment or documentation of the absence of pain as a result of assessment through discussion with the patient including the use of a standardized tool; no documentation of a follow-up plan, patient not eligible
G8509	Documentation of pain assessment (including location, intensity and description) prior to initiation of treatment or documentation of the absence of pain as a result of assessment through discussion with the patient including the use of a standardized tool; no documentation of a follow-up plan, reason not specified
G8510	Negative screen for clinical depression using a standardized tool, patient not eligible/appropriate for follow-up plan documented
G8511	Screen for clinical depression using a standardized tool documented, follow up plan not documented, reason not specified
G8512	Pain severity quantified; pain present
G8513	ABI measured and documented
G8514	Clinician documented that patient was not an eligible candidate for ABI measurement measure
G8515	ABI measurement was not obtained
G8516	Patient screened for future falls risk; documentation of two or more falls in the past year or any fall with injury in the past year
G8517	Patient screened for future fall risk; documentation of no falls in the past year or only one fall without injury in the past year
G8518	Clinical stage prior to surgery for lung cancer and esophageal cancer resection was recorded
G8519	Clinician documented that patient was not eligible for clinical stage prior to surgery for lung cancer and esophageal cancer resection measure
G8520	Clinician stage prior to surgery for lung cancer and esophageal cancer resection was not recorded, reason not specified
G8521	Antiplatelet therapy received (ASA [81-325 mg/day] and/or clopidogrel [75 mg/day]) within 48 hours of the initiation of surgery and at discharge
G8522	Clinician documented that patient was not an eligible candidate for antiplatelet therapy
G8523	Antiplatelet therapy not received 48 hours prior to CEA and at discharge, reason not specified
G8524	Patch closure used for patient undergoing conventional CEA
G8525	Clinician documented that patient did not receive conventional CEA
G8526	Patch closure not used for patient undergoing conventional CEA, reason not specified
G8527	Documentation of order for cefazolin or cefuroxime for antimicrobial prophylaxis
G8528	Clinician documented that patient was ineligible for prophylactic antibiotic selection measure
G8529	Order for cefazolin or cefuroxime for antimicrobial prophylaxis not documented, reason not specified
G8530	Autogenous AV fistula received
G8531	Clinician documented that patient was not an eligible candidate for autogenous AV fistula
G8532	Clinician documented that patient received vascular access other than autogenous AV fistula, reason not specified
G8533	Participation by a physician or other clinician in systematic clinical database registry that includes consensus-endorsed quality measures
G8534	Documentation of an elder maltreatment screen and follow-up plan
G8535	No documentation of an elder maltreatment screen, patient not eligible
G8536	No documentation of an elder maltreatment screen, reason not specified
G8537	Elder maltreatment screen documented, follow-up plan not documented, patient not eligible
G8538	Elder maltreatment screen documented, follow-up plan not documented, reason not specified
G8539	Documentation of a current functional outcome assessment using a standardized tool and care plan based on identified deficiencies
G8540	Documentation that the patient is not eligible for a functional outcome assessment using a standardized tool
G8541	No documentation of a current functional outcome assessment using a standardized tool, reason not specified
G8542	Documentation of a current functional outcome assessment using a standardized tool; no documentation of a care plan, patient not eligible
G8543	Documentation of a current functional outcome assessment using a standardized tool; no documentation of a care plan, reason not specified
G8544	I intend to report the coronary artery bypass graft (CABG) measures group
J0641	Injection, levoleucovorin calcium, 0.5 mg
J1267	Injection, doripenem, 10 mg
J1453	Injection, fosaprepitant, 1 mg
J1459	Injection, immune globulin (Privigen), intravenous, nonlyophilized (e.g., liquid), 500 mg

New Codes (continued)

Code	Description
J1930	Injection, lanreotide, 1 mg
J1953	Injection, levetiracetam, 10 mg
J2785	Injection, regadenoson, 0.1 mg
J3101	Injection, tenecteplase, 1 mg
J3300	Injection, triamcinolone acetonide, preservative free, 1 mg
J7186	Injection, antihemophilic factor VIII/von Willebrand factor complex (human), per factor VIII i.u.
J7606	Formoterol fumarate, inhalation solution, FDA approved final product, noncompounded, administered through DME, unit dose form, 20 mcg
J8705	Topotecan, oral, 0.25 mg
J9033	Injection, bendamustine HCl, 1 mg
J9207	Injection, ixabepilone, 1 mg
J9330	Injection, temsirolimus, 1 mg
K0672	Addition to lower extremity orthosis, removable soft interface, all components, replacement only, each
L0113	Cranial cervical orthotic, torticollis type, with or without joint, with or without soft interface material, prefabricated, includes fitting and adjustment
L6711	Terminal device, hook, mechanical, voluntary opening, any material, any size, lined or unlined, pediatric
L6712	Terminal device, hook, mechanical, voluntary closing, any material, any size, lined or unlined, pediatric
L6713	Terminal device, hand, mechanical, voluntary opening, any material, any size, pediatric
L6714	Terminal device, hand, mechanical, voluntary closing, any material, any size, pediatric
L6721	Terminal device, hook or hand, heavy-duty, mechanical, voluntary opening, any material, any size, lined or unlined
L6722	Terminal device, hook or hand, heavy-duty, mechanical, voluntary closing, any material, any size, lined or unlined
L8604	Injectable bulking agent, dextranomer/hyaluronic acid copolymer implant, urinary tract, 1 ml, includes shipping and necessary supplies
Q4100	Skin substitute, not otherwise specified
Q4101	Skin substitute, Apligraf, per sq cm
Q4102	Skin substitute, Oasis wound matrix, per sq cm
Q4103	Skin substitute, Oasis burn matrix, per sq cm
Q4104	Skin substitute, Integra bilayer matrix wound dressing (BMWD), per sq cm
Q4105	Skin substitute, Integra dermal regeneration template (DRT), per sq cm
Q4106	Skin substitute, Dermagraft, per sq cm
Q4107	Skin substitute, GRAFTJACKET, per sq cm
Q4108	Skin substitute, Integra matrix, per sq cm
Q4109	Skin substitute, TissueMend, per sq cm
Q4110	Skin substitute, PriMatrix, per sq cm
Q4111	Skin substitute, GammaGraft, per sq cm
Q4112	Allograft, Cymetra, injectable, 1 cc
Q4113	Allograft, GRAFTJACKET express, injectable, 1cc
Q4114	Integra flowable wound matrix, injectable, 1 cc
S2118	Metal-on-metal total hip resurfacing, including acetabular and femoral components
S2270	Insertion of vaginal cylinder for application of radiation source or clinical brachytherapy (report separately in addition to radiation source delivery)
S3628	Placement alpha microglobulin-1 rapid immunoassay for detection of rupture of fetal membranes
S3711	Circulating tumor cell test
S3860	Genetic testing, comprehensive cardiac ion channel analysis, for variants in 5 major cardiac ion channel genes for individuals with high index of suspicion for familial long QT syndrome (LQTS) or related syndromes
S3861	Genetic testing, sodium channel, voltage-gated, type V, alpha subunit (SCN5A) and variants for suspected Brugada Syndrome
S3862	Genetic testing, family-specific ion channel analysis, for blood-relatives of individuals (index case) who have previously tested positive for a genetic variant of a cardiac ion channel syndrome using either one of the above test configurations or confirmed results from another laboratory
S9433	Medical food nutritionally complete, administered orally, providing 100% of nutritional intake

Changed Codes

Code	Description
A6010	Collagen based wound filler, dry form, sterile, per gram of collagen
A6011	Collagen based wound filler, gel/paste, sterile, per gram of collagen
A6021	Collagen dressing, sterile, pad size 16 sq in or less, each
A6022	Collagen dressing, sterile, pad size more than 16 sq in but less than or equal to 48 sq in, each
A6023	Collagen dressing, sterile, pad size more than 48 sq in, each
A6024	Collagen dressing wound filler, sterile, per 6 in
A6196	Alginate or other fiber gelling dressing, wound cover, sterile, pad size 16 sq in or less, each dressing
A6197	Alginate or other fiber gelling dressing, wound cover, sterile, pad size more than 16 sq in but less than or equal to 48 sq in, each dressing
A6198	Alginate or other fiber gelling dressing, wound cover, sterile, pad size more than 48 sq in, each dressing
A6199	Alginate or other fiber gelling dressing, wound filler, sterile, per 6 in
A6203	Composite dressing, sterile, pad size 16 sq in or less, with any size adhesive border, each dressing
A6204	Composite dressing, sterile, pad size more than 16 sq in, but less than or equal to 48 sq in, with any size adhesive border, each dressing
A6205	Composite dressing, sterile, pad size more than 48 sq in, with any size adhesive border, each dressing
A6206	Contact layer, sterile, 16 sq in or less, each dressing
A6207	Contact layer, sterile, more than 16 sq in but less than or equal to 48 sq in, each dressing
A6208	Contact layer, sterile, more than 48 sq in, each dressing
A6209	Foam dressing, wound cover, sterile, pad size 16 sq in or less, without adhesive border, each dressing
A6210	Foam dressing, wound cover, sterile, pad size more than 16 sq in but less than or equal to 48 sq in, without adhesive border, each dressing
A6211	Foam dressing, wound cover, sterile, pad size more than 48 sq in, without adhesive border, each dressing
A6212	Foam dressing, wound cover, sterile, pad size 16 sq in or less, with any size adhesive border, each dressing
A6213	Foam dressing, wound cover, sterile, pad size more than 16 sq in but less than or equal to 48 sq in, with any size adhesive border, each dressing
A6214	Foam dressing, wound cover, sterile, pad size more than 48 sq in, with any size adhesive border, each dressing
A6215	Foam dressing, wound filler, sterile, per gram
A6219	Gauze, nonimpregnated, sterile, pad size 16 sq in or less, with any size adhesive border, each dressing
A6220	Gauze, nonimpregnated, sterile, pad size more than 16 sq in but less than or equal to 48 sq in, with any size adhesive border, each dressing

Changed Codes (continued)

A6221 Gauze, nonimpregnated, sterile, pad size more than 48 sq in, with any size adhesive border, each dressing

A6222 Gauze, impregnated with other than water, normal saline, or hydrogel, sterile, pad size 16 sq in or less, without adhesive border, each dressing

A6223 Gauze, impregnated with other than water, normal saline, or hydrogel, sterile, pad size more than 16 sq in, but less than or equal to 48 sq in, without adhesive border, each dressing

A6224 Gauze, impregnated with other than water, normal saline, or hydrogel, sterile, pad size more than 48 sq in, without adhesive border, each dressing

A6228 Gauze, impregnated, water or normal saline, sterile, pad size 16 sq in or less, without adhesive border, each dressing

A6229 Gauze, impregnated, water or normal saline, sterile, pad size more than 16 sq in but less than or equal to 48 sq in, without adhesive border, each dressing

A6230 Gauze, impregnated, water or normal saline, sterile, pad size more than 48 sq in, without adhesive border, each dressing

A6231 Gauze, impregnated, hydrogel, for direct wound contact, sterile, pad size 16 sq in or less, each dressing

A6232 Gauze, impregnated, hydrogel, for direct wound contact, sterile, pad size greater than 16 sq in, but less than or equal to 48 sq in, each dressing

A6233 Gauze, impregnated, hydrogel, for direct wound contact, sterile, pad size more than 48 sq in, each dressing

A6234 Hydrocolloid dressing, wound cover, sterile, pad size 16 sq in or less, without adhesive border, each dressing

A6235 Hydrocolloid dressing, wound cover, sterile, pad size more than 16 sq in but less than or equal to 48 sq in, without adhesive border, each dressing

A6236 Hydrocolloid dressing, wound cover, sterile, pad size more than 48 sq in, without adhesive border, each dressing

A6237 Hydrocolloid dressing, wound cover, sterile, pad size 16 sq in or less, with any size adhesive border, each dressing

A6238 Hydrocolloid dressing, wound cover, sterile, pad size more than 16 sq in but less than or equal to 48 sq in, with any size adhesive border, each dressing

A6239 Hydrocolloid dressing, wound cover, sterile, pad size more than 48 sq in, with any size adhesive border, each dressing

A6240 Hydrocolloid dressing, wound filler, paste, sterile, per oz

A6241 Hydrocolloid dressing, wound filler, dry form, sterile, per gram

A6242 Hydrogel dressing, wound cover, sterile, pad size 16 sq in or less, without adhesive border, each dressing

A6243 Hydrogel dressing, wound cover, sterile, pad size more than 16 sq in but less than or equal to 48 sq in, without adhesive border, each dressing

A6244 Hydrogel dressing, wound cover, sterile, pad size more than 48 sq in, without adhesive border, each dressing

A6245 Hydrogel dressing, wound cover, sterile, pad size 16 sq in or less, with any size adhesive border, each dressing

A6246 Hydrogel dressing, wound cover, sterile, pad size more than 16 sq in but less than or equal to 48 sq in, with any size adhesive border, each dressing

A6247 Hydrogel dressing, wound cover, sterile, pad size more than 48 sq in, with any size adhesive border, each dressing

A6248 Hydrogel dressing, wound filler, gel, sterile, per fl oz

A6251 Specialty absorptive dressing, wound cover, sterile, pad size 16 sq in or less, without adhesive border, each dressing

A6252 Specialty absorptive dressing, wound cover, sterile, pad size more than 16 sq in but less than or equal to 48 sq in, without adhesive border, each dressing

A6253 Specialty absorptive dressing, wound cover, sterile, pad size more than 48 sq in, without adhesive border, each dressing

A6254 Specialty absorptive dressing, wound cover, sterile, pad size 16 sq in or less, with any size adhesive border, each dressing

A6255 Specialty absorptive dressing, wound cover, sterile, pad size more than 16 sq in but less than or equal to 48 sq in, with any size adhesive border, each dressing

A6256 Specialty absorptive dressing, wound cover, sterile, pad size more than 48 sq in, with any size adhesive border, each dressing

A6257 Transparent film, sterile, 16 sq in or less, each dressing

A6258 Transparent film, sterile, more than 16 sq in but less than or equal to 48 sq in, each dressing

A6259 Transparent film, sterile, more than 48 sq in, each dressing

A6260 Wound cleansers, sterile, any type, any size

A6261 Wound filler, gel/paste, sterile, per fl oz, not otherwise specified

A6262 Wound filler, dry form, sterile, per gram, not otherwise specified

A6266 Gauze, impregnated, other than water, normal saline, or zinc paste, sterile, any width, per linear yd

A6407 Packing strips, nonimpregnated; sterile, up to 2 in in width, per linear yd

A9502 Technetium Tc-99m tetrofosmin, diagnostic, per study dose

C8921 Transthoracic echocardiography with contrast, or without contrast followed by with contrast, for congenital cardiac anomalies; complete

C8922 Transthoracic echocardiography with contrast, or without contrast followed by with contrast, for congenital cardiac anomalies; follow-up or limited study

C8923 Transthoracic echocardiography with contrast, or without contrast followed by with contrast, real-time with image documentation (2D) with or without M-mode recording; complete

C8924 Transthoracic echocardiography with contrast, or without contrast followed by with contrast, real-time with image documentation (2D) with or without M-mode recording; follow-up or limited study

C8925 Transesophageal echocardiography (TEE) with contrast, or without contrast followed by with contrast, real time with image documentation (2D) (with or without M-mode recording); including probe placement, image acquisition, interpretation and report

C8926 Transesophageal echocardiography (TEE) with contrast, or without contrast followed by with contrast, for congenital cardiac anomalies; including probe placement, image acquisition, interpretation and report

C8927 Transesophageal echocardiography (TEE) with contrast, or without contrast followed by with contrast, for monitoring purposes, including probe placement, real time 2-dimensional image acquisition and interpretation leading to ongoing (continuous) assessment of (dynamically changing) cardiac pumping function and to therapeutic measures on an immediate time basis

C8928 Transthoracic echocardiography with contrast, or without contrast followed by with contrast, real-time with image documentation (2D), with or without M-mode recording, during rest and cardiovascular stress test using treadmill, bicycle exercise and/or pharmacologically induced stress, with interpretation and report

D0486 Laboratory accession of brush biopsy sample, microscopic examination, preparation and transmission of written report

D1203 Topical application of fluoride, child

D1204 Topical application of fluoride, adult

D3310 Endodontic therapy, anterior tooth (excluding final restoration)

D3320 Endodontic therapy, bicuspid tooth (excluding final restoration)

D3330 Endodontic therapy, molar (excluding final restoration)

D4210 Gingivectomy or gingivoplasty, 4 or more contiguous teeth or tooth bounded spaces per quadrant

D4211 Gingivectomy or gingivoplasty, 1 to 3 contiguous teeth or tooth bounded spaces per quadrant

D4240 Gingival flap procedure, including root planing, 4 or more contiguous teeth or tooth bounded spaces per quadrant

D4241 Gingival flap procedure, including root planing, 1 to 3 contiguous teeth or tooth bounded spaces per quadrant

Changed Codes (continued)

D4260 Osseous surgery (including flap entry and closure), 4 or more contiguous teeth or tooth bounded spaces per quadrant

D4261 Osseous surgery (including flap entry and closure), 1 to 3 contiguous teeth or tooth bounded spaces per quadrant

D5211 Upper partial denture - resin base (including any conventional clasps, rests and teeth)

D5212 Lower partial denture - resin base (including any conventional clasps, rests and teeth)

E0764 Functional neuromuscular stimulation, transcutaneous stimulation of sequential muscle groups of ambulation with computer control, used for walking by spinal cord injured, entire system, after completion of training program

G0129 Occupational therapy services requiring the skills of a qualified occupational therapist, furnished as a component of a partial hospitalization treatment program, per session (45 minutes or more)

G0248 Demonstration, prior to initial use, of home INR monitoring for patient with either mechanical heart valve(s), chronic atrial fibrillation, or venous thromboembolism who meets Medicare coverage criteria, under the direction of a physician; includes: face-to-face demonstration of use and care of the INR monitor, obtaining at least one blood sample, provision of instructions for reporting home INR test results, and documentation of patient ability to perform testing prior to its use

G0250 Physician review, interpretation, and patient management of home INR testing for a patient with either mechanical heart valve(s), chronic atrial fibrillation, or venous thromboembolism who meets Medicare coverage criteria; includes face-to-face verification by the physician that the patient uses the device in the context of the management of the anticoagulation therapy following initiation of the home INR monitoring; not occurring more frequently than once a week

G0275 Renal angiography, nonselective, one or both kidneys, performed at the same time as cardiac catheterization and/or coronary angiography, includes positioning or placement of any catheter in the abdominal aorta at or near the origins (ostia) of the renal arteries, injection of dye, flush aortogram, production of permanent images, and radiologic supervision and interpretation (List separately in addition to primary procedure).

G8417 Calculated BMI above the upper parameter and a follow-up plan was documented in the medical record

G8418 Calculated BMI below the lower parameter and a follow-up plan was documented in the medical record

G8419 Calculated BMI outside normal parameters, no follow-up plan was documented in the medical record

G8420 Calculated BMI within normal parameters and documented

G8427 List of current medications with dosages (includes prescription, over-the-counter, herbals, vitamin/mineral/dietary nutritional supplements) and verification with the patient or authorized representative documented by the provider

G8428 Provider documentation of current medications with dosages (includes prescription, over-the-counter, herbals, vitamin/mineral/dietary nutritional supplements) without documented patient verification

G8429 Incomplete or no provider documentation that patient's current medications with dosages (includes prescription, over-the-counter, herbals, vitamin/mineral/dietary nutritional supplements were assessed

G8430 Provider documentation that patient is not eligible for medication assessment

G8431 Positive screen for clinical depression using a standardized tool and a follow-up plan documented

G8433 Screening for clinical depression using a standardized tool not documented, patient not eligible/appropriate

G8437 Documentation of clinician and patient involvement with the development of a plan of care including signature by the practitioner/therapist and either a co-signature by the patient or documented verbal agreement obtained from the patient or, when necessary, an authorized representative

G8438 No documentation of clinician and patient involvement with the development of a plan of care including signature by the practitioner/therapist and either a co-signature by the patient or documented verbal agreement obtained from the patient or, when necessary, an authorized representative

G8439 Documentation that patient is not eligible for co-developing a plan of care including signature by the practitioner/therapist and either a co-signature by the patient or documented verbal agreement obtained from the patient or, when necessary, an authorized representative

G8440 Documentation of pain assessment (including location, intensity and description) prior to initiation of treatment or documentation of the absence of pain as a result of assessment through discussion with the patient including the use of a standardized tool and a follow-up plan is documented

G8446 Provider does have access to a qualified e-prescribing system and some or all of the prescriptions generated during the encounter were printed or phoned in as required by state or Federal law or regulations, patient request or pharmacy system being unable to receive electronic transmission; or because they were for narcotics or other controlled substances

G8447 Patient encounter was documented using a CCHIT certified EHR

G8448 Patient encounter was documented using a qualified (non-CCHIT certified) EHR

G8457 Current tobacco nonuser

G8485 I intend to report the diabetes mellitus measures group

G8486 I intend to report the preventive care measures group

G8487 I intend to report the chronic kidney disease (CKD) measures group

J0270 Injection, alprostadil, 1.25 mcg (code may be used for Medicare when drug administered under the direct supervision of a physician, not for use when drug is self-administered)

J0348 Injection, anidulafungin, 1 mg

J1572 Injection, immune globulin, (Flebogamma/Flebogamma Dif), intravenous, nonlyophilized (e.g., liquid), 500 mg

J2788 Injection, Rho D immune globulin, human, minidose, 50 mcg (250 i.u.)

J2790 Injection, Rho D immune globulin, human, full dose, 300 mcg (1500 i.u.)

J3301 Injection, triamcinolone acetonide, not otherwise specified, 10 mg

J7639 Dornase alfa, inhalation solution, FDA-approved final product, noncompounded, administered through DME, unit dose form, per mg

J9000 Injection, doxorubicin HCl, 10 mg

J9001 Injection, doxorubicin HCl, all lipid formulations, 10 mg

J9010 Injection, alemtuzumab, 10 mg

J9015 Injection, aldesleukin, per single use vial

J9017 Injection, arsenic trioxide, 1 mg

J9020 Injection, asparaginase, 10,000 units

J9040 Injection, bleomycin sulfate, 15 units

J9045 Injection, carboplatin, 50 mg

J9050 Injection, carmustine, 100 mg

J9098 Injection, cytarabine liposome, 10 mg

J9100 Injection, cytarabine, 100 mg

J9110 Injection cytarabine 500 mg

J9120 Injection, dactinomycin, 0.5 mg

J9150 Injection, daunorubicin, 10 mg

J9151 Injection, daunorubicin citrate, liposomal formulation, 10 mg

J9160 Injection, denileukin diftitox, 300 mcg

J9165 Injection, diethylstilbestrol diphosphate, 250 mg

J9170 Injection, docetaxel, 20 mg

J9181 Injection, etoposide, 10 mg

Changed Codes (continued)

J9185	Injection, fludarabine phosphate, 50 mg
J9190	Injection, fluorouracil, 500 mg
J9200	Injection, floxuridine, 500 mg
J9201	Injection, gemcitabine HCl, 200 mg
J9206	Injection, irinotecan, 20 mg
J9208	Injection, ifosfamide, 1 g
J9209	Injection, mesna, 200 mg
J9211	Injection, idarubicin HCl, 5 mg
J9213	Injection, interferon, alfa-2a, recombinant, 3 million units
J9214	Injection, interferon, alfa-2b, recombinant, 1 million units
J9215	Injection, interferon, alfa-N3, (human leukocyte derived), 250,000 IU
J9216	Injection, interferon, gamma-1B, 3 million units
J9230	Injection, mechlorethamine HCl, (nitrogen mustard), 10 mg
J9265	Injection, paclitaxel, 30 mg
J9266	Injection, pegaspargase, per single dose vial
J9268	Injection, pentostatin, 10 mg
J9270	Injection, plicamycin, 2.5 mg
J9300	Injection, gemtuzumab ozogamicin, 5 mg
J9310	Injection, rituximab, 100 mg
J9320	Injection, streptozocin, 1 g
J9340	Injection, thiotepa, 15 mg
J9350	Injection, topotecan, 4 mg
J9355	Injection, trastuzumab, 10 mg
J9357	Injection, valrubicin, intravesical, 200 mg
J9360	Injection, vinblastine sulfate, 1 mg
J9390	Injection, vinorelbine tartrate, 10 mg
J9600	Injection, porfimer sodium, 75 mg
K0669	Wheelchair accessory, wheelchair seat or back cushion, does not meet specific code criteria or no written coding verification from DME PDAC
K0899	Power mobility device, not coded by DME PDAC or does not meet criteria
L3905	Wrist-hand orthotic (WHO), includes one or more nontorsion joints, elastic bands, turnbuckles, may include soft interface, straps, custom fabricated, includes fitting and adjustment
L4360	Walking boot, pneumatic and/or vacuum, with or without joints, with or without interface material, prefabricated, includes fitting and adjustment
L8681	Patient programmer (external) for use with implantable programmable neurostimulator pulse generator, replacement only
L8689	External recharging system for battery (internal) for use with implantable neurostimulator, replacement only
L8695	External recharging system for battery (external) for use with implantable neurostimulator, replacement only

Deleted Codes

C9003	C9237	C9238	C9239	C9240	C9723	G0297
G0300	G0308	G0309	G0310	G0311	G0312	G0313
G0314	G0315	G0316	G0317	G0318	G0319	G0320
G0321	G0322	G0323	G0324	G0325	G0326	G0327
G0332	G0344	G0366	G0367	G0368	G0377	G0394
J1751	J1752	J3100	J7340	J7341	J7342	J7343
J7344	J7346	J7347	J7348	J7349	J7602	J7603
J9182	L2860	L3890	L5993	L5994	L5995	L7611
L7612	L7613	L7614	L7621	L7622	S0141	S0143
S2075	S2076	S2077	S2135	S9092		

Reinstated Codes

J7611	Albuterol, inhalation solution, FDA-approved final product, noncompounded, administered through DME, concentrated form, 1 mg
J7612	Levalbuterol, inhalation solution, FDA-approved final product, noncompounded, administered through DME, concentrated form, 0.5 mg
J7613	Albuterol, inhalation solution, FDA-approved final product, noncompounded, administered through DME, unit dose, 1 mg
J7614	Levalbuterol, inhalation solution, FDA-approved final product, noncompounded, administered through DME, unit dose, 0.5 mg

APPENDIX 6 — PLACE OF SERVICE AND TYPE OF SERVICE

Place-of-Service Codes for Professional Claims

Database (last updated September 25, 2007)

Listed below are place of service codes and descriptions. These codes should be used on professional claims to specify the entity where service(s) were rendered. Check with individual payers (e.g., Medicare, Medicaid, other private insurance) for reimbursement policies regarding these codes. If you would like to comment on a code(s) or description(s), please send your request to posinfo@cms.hhs.gov.

01	Pharmacy	A facility or location where drugs and other medically related items and services are sold, dispensed, or otherwise provided directly to patients.
02	Unassigned	N/A
03	School	A facility whose primary purpose is education.
04	Homeless shelter	A facility or location whose primary purpose is to provide temporary housing to homeless individuals (e.g., emergency shelters, individual or family shelters).
05	Indian Health Service freestanding facility	A facility or location, owned and operated by the Indian Health Service, which provides diagnostic, therapeutic (surgical and non-surgical), and rehabilitation services to American Indians and Alaska natives who do not require hospitalization.
06	Indian Health Service provider-based facility	A facility or location, owned and operated by the Indian Health Service, which provides diagnostic, therapeutic (surgical and nonsurgical), and rehabilitation services rendered by, or under the supervision of, physicians to American Indians and Alaska natives admitted as inpatients or outpatients.
07	Tribal 638 freestanding facility	A facility or location owned and operated by a federally recognized American Indian or Alaska native tribe or tribal organization under a 638 agreement, which provides diagnostic, therapeutic (surgical and nonsurgical), and rehabilitation services to tribal members who do not require hospitalization.
08	Tribal 638 Provider-based Facility	A facility or location owned and operated by a federally recognized American Indian or Alaska native tribe or tribal organization under a 638 agreement, which provides diagnostic, therapeutic (surgical and nonsurgical), and rehabilitation services to tribal members admitted as inpatients or outpatients.
09	Prison/correctional facility	A prison, jail, reformatory, work farm, detention center, or any other similar facility maintained by either federal, state or local authorities for the purpose of confinement or rehabilitation of adult or juvenile criminal offenders.
10	Unassigned	N/A
11	Office	Location, other than a hospital, skilled nursing facility (SNF), military treatment facility, community health center, State or local public health clinic, or intermediate care facility (ICF), where the health professional routinely provides health examinations, diagnosis, and treatment of illness or injury on an ambulatory basis.
12	Home	Location, other than a hospital or other facility, where the patient receives care in a private residence.
13	Assisted living facility	Congregate residential facility with self-contained living units providing assessment of each resident's needs and on-site support 24 hours a day, 7 days a week, with the capacity to deliver or arrange for services including some health care and other services.
14	Group home	A residence, with shared living areas, where clients receive supervision and other services such as social and/or behavioral services, custodial service, and minimal services (e.g., medication administration).
15	Mobile unit	A facility/unit that moves from place-to-place equipped to provide preventive, screening, diagnostic, and/or treatment services.
16	Temporary lodging	A short-term accommodation such as a hotel, campground, hostel, cruise ship or resort where the patient receives care, and which is not identified by any other POS code.
17-19	Unassigned	N/A
20	Urgent care facility	Location, distinct from a hospital emergency room, an office, or a clinic, whose purpose is to diagnose and treat illness or injury for unscheduled, ambulatory patients seeking immediate medical attention.
21	Inpatient hospital	A facility, other than psychiatric, which primarily provides diagnostic, therapeutic (both surgical and nonsurgical), and rehabilitation services by, or under, the supervision of physicians to patients admitted for a variety of medical conditions.
22	Outpatient hospital	A portion of a hospital which provides diagnostic, therapeutic (both surgical and nonsurgical), and rehabilitation services to sick or injured persons who do not require hospitalization or institutionalization.
23	Emergency room—hospital	A portion of a hospital where emergency diagnosis and treatment of illness or injury is provided.
24	Ambulatory surgical center	A freestanding facility, other than a physician's office, where surgical and diagnostic services are provided on an ambulatory basis.
25	Birthing center	A facility, other than a hospital's maternity facilities or a physician's office, which provides a setting for labor, delivery, and immediate post-partum care as well as immediate care of new born infants.
26	Military treatment facility	A medical facility operated by one or more of the uniformed services. Military treatment facility (MTF) also refers to certain former U.S. Public Health Service (USPHS) facilities now designated as uniformed service treatment facilities (USTF).
27-30	Unassigned	N/A
31	Skilled nursing facility	A facility which primarily provides inpatient skilled nursing care and related services to patients who require medical, nursing, or rehabilitative services but does not provide the level of care or treatment available in a hospital.
32	Nursing facility	A facility which primarily provides to residents skilled nursing care and related services for the rehabilitation of injured, disabled, or sick persons, or, on a regular basis, health-related care services above the level of custodial care to other than mentally retarded individuals.
33	Custodial care facility	A facility which provides room, board, and other personal assistance services, generally on a long-term basis, and which does not include a medical component.

34	Hospice	A facility, other than a patient's home, in which palliative and supportive care for terminally ill patients and their families are provided.
35-40	Unassigned	N/A
41	Ambulance—land	A land vehicle specifically designed, equipped and staffed for lifesaving and transporting the sick or injured.
42	Ambulance—air or water	An air or water vehicle specifically designed, equipped and staffed for lifesaving and transporting the sick or injured.
43-48	Unassigned	N/A
49	Independent clinic	A location, not part of a hospital and not described by any other place-of-service code, that is organized and operated to provide preventive, diagnostic, therapeutic, rehabilitative, or palliative services to outpatients only.
50	Federally qualified health center	A facility located in a medically underserved area that provides Medicare beneficiaries preventive primary medical care under the general direction of a physician.
51	Inpatient psychiatric facility	A facility that provides inpatient psychiatric services for the diagnosis and treatment of mental illness on a 24-hour basis, by or under the supervision of a physician.
52	Psychiatric facility-partial hospitalization	A facility for the diagnosis and treatment of mental illness that provides a planned therapeutic program for patients who do not require full time hospitalization, but who need broader programs than are possible from outpatient visits to a hospital-based or hospital-affiliated facility.
53	Community mental health center	A facility that provides the following services: outpatient services, including specialized outpatient services for children, the elderly, individuals who are chronically ill, and residents of the CMHC's mental health services area who have been discharged from inpatient treatment at a mental health facility; 24 hour a day emergency care services; day treatment, other partial hospitalization services, or psychosocial rehabilitation services; screening for patients being considered for admission to state mental health facilities to determine the appropriateness of such admission; and consultation and education services.
54	Intermediate care facility/mentally retarded	A facility which primarily provides health-related care and services above the level of custodial care to mentally retarded individuals but does not provide the level of care or treatment available in a hospital or SNF.
55	Residential substance abuse treatment facility	A facility which provides treatment for substance (alcohol and drug) abuse to live-in residents who do not require acute medical care. Services include individual and group therapy and counseling, family counseling, laboratory tests, drugs and supplies, psychological testing, and room and board.
56	Psychiatric residential treatment center	A facility or distinct part of a facility for psychiatric care which provides a total 24-hour therapeutically planned and professionally staffed group living and learning environment.
57	Non-residential substance abuse treatment facility	A location which provides treatment for substance (alcohol and drug) abuse on an ambulatory basis. Services include individual and group therapy and counseling, family counseling, laboratory tests, drugs and supplies, and psychological testing.
58-59	Unassigned	N/A
60	Mass immunization center	A location where providers administer pneumococcal pneumonia and influenza virus vaccinations and submit these services as electronic media claims, paper claims, or using the roster billing method. This generally takes place in a mass immunization setting, such as, a public health center, pharmacy, or mall but may include a physician office setting.
61	Comprehensive inpatient rehabilitation facility	A facility that provides comprehensive rehabilitation services under the supervision of a physician to inpatients with physical disabilities. Services include physical therapy, occupational therapy, speech pathology, social or psychological services, and orthotics and prosthetics services.
62	Comprehensive outpatient rehabilitation facility	A facility that provides comprehensive rehabilitation services under the supervision of a physician to outpatients with physical disabilities. Services include physical therapy, occupational therapy, and speech pathology services.
63-64	Unassigned	N/A
65	End-stage renal disease treatment facility	A facility other than a hospital, which provides dialysis treatment, maintenance, and/or training to patients or caregivers on an ambulatory or home-care basis.
66-70	Unassigned	N/A
71	Public health clinic	A facility maintained by either state or local health departments that provides ambulatory primary medical care under the general direction of a physician.
72	Rural health clinic	A certified facility which is located in a rural medically underserved area that provides ambulatory primary medical care under the general direction of a physician.
73-80	Unassigned	N/A
81	Independent laboratory	A laboratory certified to perform diagnostic and/or clinical tests independent of an institution or a physician's office.
82-98	Unassigned	N/A
99	Other place of service	Other place of service not identified above.

Type of Service

Common Working File Type of Service (TOS) Indicators

For submitting a claim to the Common Working File (CWF), use the following table to assign the proper TOS. Some procedures may have more than one applicable TOS. CWF will reject alerts on codes with incorrect TOS designations. CWF is rejecting codes with incorrect TOS designations.

The only exceptions to this table are:

- Surgical services billed for dates of service through December 31, 2007, containing the ASC facility service modifier SG must be reported as TOS F. Effective for services on or after January 1, 2008, the SG modifier is no longer applicable for Medicare services. ASC providers should discontinue applying the SG modifier on ASC facility claims. The indicator F does not appear in the TOS table because its use depends upon claims submitted with POS 24 (ASC facility) from an ASC (specialty 49). This became effective for dates of service January 1, 2008, or after.
- Surgical services billed with an assistant-at-surgery modifier (80-82, AS,) must be reported with TOS 8. The 8 indicator does not appear on the TOS table because its use is dependent upon the use of the appropriate modifier. (See Pub. 100-4 *Medicare Claims Processing Manual,* chapter 12, "Physician/Practitioner Billing," for instructions on when assistant-at-surgery is allowable.)
- Psychiatric treatment services that are subject to the outpatient mental health treatment limitation should be reported with TOS T.
- TOS H appears in the list of descriptors. However, it does not appear in the table. In CWF, "H" is used only as an indicator for hospice. The carrier should not submit TOS H to CWF at this time.
- For outpatient services, when a transfusion medicine code appears on a claim that also contains a blood product, the service is paid under reasonable charge at 80 percent; coinsurance and deductible apply. When

transfusion medicine codes are paid under the clinical laboratory fee schedule they are paid at 100 percent; coinsurance and deductible do not apply.

Note: For injection codes with more than one possible TOS designation, use the following guidelines when assigning the TOS:

When the choice is L or 1:

- Use TOS L when the drug is used related to ESRD; or
- Use TOS 1 when the drug is not related to ESRD and is administered in the office.

When the choice is G or 1:

- Use TOS G when the drug is an immunosuppressive drug; or
- Use TOS 1 when the drug is used for other than immunosuppression.

When the choice is P or 1:

- Use TOS P if the drug is administered through durable medical equipment (DME); or
- Use TOS 1 if the drug is administered in the office.

The place of service or diagnosis may be considered when determining the appropriate TOS. The descriptors for each of the TOS codes listed in the following table are:

0	Whole blood
1	Medical care
2	Surgery
3	Consultation
4	Diagnostic radiology
5	Diagnostic laboratory
6	Therapeutic radiology
7	Anesthesia
8	Assistant at surgery
9	Other medical items or services
A	Used DME
B	High risk screening mammography
C	Low risk screening mammography
D	Ambulance
E	Enteral/parenteral nutrients/supplies
F	Ambulatory surgical center (facility usage for surgical services)
G	Immunosuppressive drugs
H	Hospice
J	Diabetic shoes
K	Hearing items and services
L	ESRD supplies
M	Monthly capitation payment for dialysis
N	Kidney donor
P	Lump sum purchase of DME, prosthetics, orthotics
Q	Vision items or services
R	Rental of DME
S	Surgical dressings or other medical supplies
T	Outpatient mental health treatment limitation
U	Occupational therapy
V	Pneumococcal/flu vaccine
W	Physical therapy

Berenson-Eggers Type of Service (BETOS) Codes

The BETOS coding system was developed primarily for analyzing the growth in Medicare expenditures. The coding system covers all HCPCS codes; assigns a HCPCS code to only one BETOS code; consists of readily understood clinical categories (as opposed to statistical or financial categories); consists of categories that permit objective assignment; is stable over time; and is relatively immune to minor changes in technology or practice patterns.

BETOS Codes and Descriptions:

1. Evaluation and Management

1. M1A Office visits—new
2. M1B Office visits—established
3. M2A Hospital visit—initial
4. M2B Hospital visit—subsequent
5. M2C Hospital visit—critical care
6. M3 Emergency room visit
7. M4A Home visit
8. M4B Nursing home visit
9. M5A Specialist—pathology
10. M5B Specialist—psychiatry
11. M5C Specialist—ophthalmology
12. M5D Specialist—other
13. M6 Consultations

2. Procedures

1. P0 Anesthesia
2. P1A Major procedure—breast
3. P1B Major procedure—colectomy
4. P1C Major procedure—cholecystectomy
5. P1D Major procedure—TURP
6. P1E Major procedure—hysterectomy
7. P1F Major procedure—explor/decompr/excis disc
8. P1G Major procedure—other
9. P2A Major procedure, cardiovascular—CABG
10. P2B Major procedure, cardiovascular—aneurysm repair
11. P2C Major procedure, cardiovascular—thromboendarterectomy
12. P2D Major procedure, cardiovascular—coronary angioplasty (PTCA)
13. P2E Major procedure, cardiovascular—pacemaker insertion
14. P2F Major procedure, cardiovascular—other
15. P3A Major procedure, orthopedic—hip fracture repair
16. P3B Major procedure, orthopedic—hip replacement
17. P3C Major procedure, orthopedic—knee replacement
18. P3D Major procedure, orthopedic—other
19. P4A Eye procedure—corneal transplant
20. P4B Eye procedure—cataract removal/lens insertion
21. P4C Eye procedure—retinal detachment
22. P4D Eye procedure—treatment of retinal lesions
23. P4E Eye procedure—other
24. P5A Ambulatory procedures—skin
25. P5B Ambulatory procedures—musculoskeletal
26. P5C Ambulatory procedures—groin hernia repair
27. P5D Ambulatory procedures—lithotripsy
28. P5E Ambulatory procedures—other
29. P6A Minor procedures—skin
30. P6B Minor procedures—musculoskeletal

31. P6C Minor procedures—other (Medicare fee schedule)
32. P6D Minor procedures—other (non-Medicare fee schedule)
33. P7A Oncology—radiation therapy
34. P7B Oncology—other
35. P8A Endoscopy—arthroscopy
36. P8B Endoscopy—upper gastrointestinal
37. P8C Endoscopy—sigmoidoscopy
38. P8D Endoscopy—colonoscopy
39. P8E Endoscopy—cystoscopy
40. P8F Endoscopy—bronchoscopy
41. P8G Endoscopy—laparoscopic cholecystectomy
42. P8H Endoscopy—laryngoscopy
43. P8I Endoscopy—other
44. P9A Dialysis services (Medicare fee schedule)
45. P9B Dialysis services (non-Medicare fee schedule)

3. **Imaging**

1. I1A Standard imaging—chest
2. I1B Standard imaging—musculoskeletal
3. I1C Standard imaging—breast
4. I1D Standard imaging—contrast gastrointestinal
5. I1E Standard imaging—nuclear medicine
6. I1F Standard imaging—other
7. I2A Advanced imaging—CAT/CT/CTA; brain/head/neck
8. I2B Advanced imaging—CAT/CT/CTA; other
9. I2C Advanced imaging—MRI/MRA; brain/head/neck
10. I2D Advanced imaging—MRI/MRA; other
11. I3A Echography—eye
12. I3B Echography—abdomen/pelvis
13. I3C Echography—heart
14. I3D Echography—carotid arteries
15. I3E Echography—prostate, transrectal
16. I3F Echography—other
17. I4A Imaging/procedure—heart, including cardiac catheterization
18. I4B Imaging/procedure—other

4. **Tests**

1. T1A Lab tests—routine venipuncture (non-Medicare fee schedule)
2. T1B Lab tests—automated general profiles
3. T1C Lab tests—urinalysis
4. T1D Lab tests—blood counts
5. T1E Lab tests—glucose
6. T1F Lab tests—bacterial cultures
7. T1G Lab tests—other (Medicare fee schedule)
8. T1H Lab tests—other (non-Medicare fee schedule)
9. T2A Other tests—electrocardiograms
10. T2B Other tests—cardiovascular stress tests
11. T2C Other tests—EKG monitoring
12. T2D Other tests—other

5. **Durable Medical Equipment**

1. D1A Medical/surgical supplies
2. D1B Hospital beds
3. D1C Oxygen and supplies
4. D1D Wheelchairs
5. D1E Other DME
6. D1F Prosthetic/orthotic devices
7. D1G Drugs administered through DME

6. **Other**

1. O1A Ambulance
2. O1B Chiropractic
3. O1C Enteral and parenteral
4. O1D Chemotherapy
5. O1E Other drugs
6. O1F Hearing and speech services
7. O1G Immunizations/vaccinations

7. **Exceptions/Unclassified**

1. Y1 Other—Medicare fee schedule
2. Y2 Other—Non-Medicare fee schedule
3. Z1 Local codes
4. Z2 Undefined codes